CHARLESTON'S
COOPER RIVER BRIDGE RUN

A Complete History In Words And Photos

By Cedric Jaggers

www.EveningPostBooks.com

Published by
Evening Post Books
Charleston, South Carolina
www.EveningPostBooks.com

Copyright © 2011 by Cedric Jaggers
All rights reserved.
First edition

Editors: John M. Burbage, Jason Lesley
Design: Gill Guerry
Cover photo by: Mic Smith

No part of this book may be reproduced or transmitted in any form or by any means, electronic or mechanical, including photocopying, recording or by information storage and retrieval system – except by a reviewer who may quote brief passages in a review to be printed in a magazine, newspaper, or on the Web – without permission in writing from the publisher. For information, please contact the publisher.

First printing 2011
Printed in the United States of America

A CIP catalog record for this book has been applied
for from the Library of Congress.

ISBN: 978-0-9825154-9-5

Table of Contents

Introduction 7
1978: The Beginning Of The Legend 10
1979: One Lane On The Bridge For The Last Time 20
1980: The First Time Over The 'Old Bridge' And The Only Tie Race 24
1981: Marc Embler The First Local Overall Winner 28
1982: An Unexpected Winner 34
1983: David Branch Takes Course Record Under 30 Minutes 44
1984: David Branch Becomes First Two Time Winner, Prize Money Added 50
1985: First Certified Course Used, Third Hottest Race Ever 58
1986: The Fog, The Wreck, The Delay, The Second Hottest Race Ever 70
1987: The Coldest, Windiest Race Ever 80
1988: Professional Timing Used For The First Time 86
1989: Grete Waitz Female Winner Despite Mixup At Start 94
1990: Unlucky 13? No Way, Rain Stops Before Race And Number 13 Wins 102
1991: Carolina Runners Surprise Favorites 110
1992: The Kenyans Begin A Long Winning Streak 114
1993: Kenyans Take Top Three Spots 120
1994: It Was Oprah's Race 128
1995: Back On The 'New' Pearman Bridge, First Time Over 10,000 Finishers 136
1996: Liz McColgan Of Scotland Takes Female Crown 144
1997: Elana Meyer Sets Female Course Record 154
1998: Elana Meyer First Two Time Female Winner Despite Windiest Race 162
1999: Eunice Sagero First Female Kenyan Winner 172
2000: James Koskei Wins In Course Record 27:40 178
2001: Warm Weather Slows All The Runners 186
2002: Twenty-Fifth Anniversary Race Medallions To All Finishers 194
2003: Heat Sends Record 200 To Medical Treatment 202
2004: Sallie Barsosio Female Winner After Four Second Place Finishes 210
2005: Last Bridge Run On The Pearman Bridge 216
2006: First Race On New Ravenel Bridge 226
2007: All Finishers Of 30th Annual Race Get Gold Medallions 236
2008: Kenyans Take First Nine Places 246
2009: Ethiopian Tilahun Regassa Ends Kenyan Winning Streak 254
2010: Near Perfect Conditions And Timing Chips Please Second Largest Crowd Ever 266
Appendix 276

Introduction

By Julian E. Smith III, race director

    As historian for the Cooper River Bridge Run, Cedric Jaggers has documented many important statistics, facts and stories. And in true Charleston style, there are many secrets that have yet to be told - until now.

    This book paints a picture of the race from 1978 to 2010, highlighting in detail the event's mission and vision. As race director, I enjoyed reading this book and learning about things that happened before my reign began 19 years ago. Cedric Jaggers' passion is evident not only for running but for the Cooper River Bridge Run.

Introduction and Explanation
By Cedric Jaggers

Kathy and Cedric Jaggers ran the Bridge Run together after her MS diagnosis.

Write what you know. That's what people who decide to write a book are told. So why would I write about the Cooper River Bridge Run? I first thought about it in 1984 when I was editing the *Low Country Runner*, newsletter of the Charleston Running Club. There had been six Bridge Runs - I had run five of them - and it seemed like nobody had much information on past races.

I decided to put together what I called the newsletter's Bridge Run Edition. I had newspaper clippings from the races, results of the second through sixth races - that race was one of the first to mail out complete results to finishers every year - and, of course, past newsletters. I interviewed people from the first race. I wrote a brief history of the race, basically with a paragraph or two on each race, and if you compared, you would notice some of the verbage from that first history has made it into this book.

History, like life, is what happens while you are busy making other plans. In my second Bridge Run in 1980, I was proud to break the 40-minute barrier for the first time. And 18 years later I was ecstatic when my wife, Kathy, won third place Grand Master division prize money the first year it was offered. I never thought of myself as an historian, only as a runner. My highest overall finish in any Bridge Run was 60th and my highest age group placement was third. But I kept up with the race every year and added another paragraph or two summarizing each race. I also began covering the race each year for *Running Journal* magazine.

In 1988 there was an unusually long delay for the awards ceremony at the Maritime Center. Since a lot of folks were standing around waiting and I had my clipboard and pen, I decided to ask people about their Bridge Run. It seemed like something fun to do for the newsletter. It was well received, and with only a few exceptions I've done it every year. It is really interesting to read what people said about the races.

In 1993 Benita Schlau was race director. She called and asked if I would write a history of the race for the Bridge Run Committee. I was glad to do it and sent it to her along with photocopies of the 1978-1987 race results (which the committee did not have and which I felt they should have and display).

In 2002 I was surprised and immensely honored to be inducted into the Cooper River Bridge Run Hall of Fame. When I consider the great runners and contributors to the race, I feel inadequate and unworthy of the honor, but it is one I really appreciate.

Time flies when you are having fun. The years were slipping by and I kept running the race (yes, more slowly every year) and people, including staff from the *Post and Courier,* started calling me the race historian. Until 2005, Kathy and I used to answer a lot of long distance phone calls - we had moved to Rock Hill, S.C., in 1991 - asking us to look up their times in the race results. It seemed we were the only ones with results for every year.

I kept the results for every race in a binder, one-inch for the early years, two-inches as the race grew larger. We would look them up for folks who could give us the year and a reasonable estimate of their time. For people who said something like, "I ran one of the early years. Can you find my time for me?" The answer was no. Since the first year was the only year the race did not have at least 1,000 finishers and has grown exponentially, it would have been nearly impossible.

In 2005 one of the running magazines mentioned that the New York City Marathon had results of all its races online. It was obvious to me that the Bridge Run should do the same, so I offered to lend the Bridge Run Committee my results. Assistant Race Director Michael Desrosiers made the 200-mile drive up from Charleston to our house in the northern part of the state and picked up all the results to scan or retype. You can find those results on the Bridge Run website www.BridgeRun.com. Now they post the results almost as soon as the race is over.

So here it is 2011 and I've run 32 of the 33 Bridge Runs. I regret not getting to run the first one. Someone in the office where I worked had told me about it since they knew I ran regularly. Unfortunately I broke my leg playing City League soccer shortly before the race. There are fewer than a half-dozen runners who hold the distinction of having run all 33 races. But I'm proud to have run as many as I have, so when I express an opinion about one of the Bridge Runs, the odds are pretty good that I ran the race.

Here is the concept of this book: One chapter for each of the 33 races. The first part will, of course, be a recitation of the facts of the race, and something that I had to recreate for about two-thirds of the years from the results. The complete list of award winners for every race will close each chapter. I think a complete record of everyone who has ever won an award in the race is very important, as are interviews, articles, etc. about that particular race to give others a chance to have their say are included. Then at the end of the book are some appendixes of facts and figures.

I really love the Bridge Run. I am glad the Bridge Run, while not perfect, tries to do the right thing.

• The BR was early on in timing every runner and mailing the race results.

• The BR was early on in using a certified course to ensure an accurate race distance for runners.

• The BR was a leader in presenting Masters Division and then Grand Masters Division awards.

• The BR was early on in presenting proportionately deeper age group awards in the larger age groups.

A race that grows from 766 finishers in 1978 to 33,057 finishers in 2010 is obviously doing a lot of things right. And good races do not happen by accident but due to the hard work of a lot of people, and I wish I could thank them all. I love the Expo. I love the race. I love the post race crowd in Marion Square waiting for or ignoring the awards ceremony. I love it all.

If not for the Bridge Run, Kathy and I would probably never have talked to Olympians Jim Ryun, Craig Virgin and Grete Waitz as well as other great runners. And I know for sure that we would never have had breakfast with Catherine Ndereba the morning after she won the Bridge Run and just one week before she won the Boston Marathon. I also know I would never have talked to and bought a beer for Frank Shorter. So now here is my chance to tell you, not about my Bridge Run but about everybody's Cooper River Bridge Run.

766 entrants, 653 male and 113 female, participated in the first Cooper River Bridge Run in 1978. News and Courier photo by Bill Jordan

Chapter 1
1978
The Beginning Of The Legend

At 10 a.m. on Sunday morning April 2, 1978, the starting gun was fired for the first Cooper River Bridge Run. Even at that time it was successful beyond organizers' wildest expectations. Or was it? The first race entry form had this prophetic line just under the race name: "destined to become a legend."

Race director Keith Hamilton said the best part of the day for him was standing in the parking lot at Patriots Point after the race started and seeing the bridge covered with humanity. He had expected 500 runners and 340 had pre-registered. The $3 entry fee included a T-shirt that Hamilton had designed. There were only four awards categories in the first race, with merchandise awards three deep in each. The categories were: open male, open female, Masters male and Masters female.

Race day morning was sweltering: 82 degrees. Despite the heat, another 600 or 700 runners registered. Olympian (1952 marathon) Ted Corbitt was one of the runners. Many fell out from the heat and some had to be hospitalized. In the early days of road racing there was a lot of debate about providing water to runners on race courses since the AAU (later replaced by the TAC and now USATF) did not allow it. The committee voted not to provided water for the first Bridge Run. Terry Hamlin, president of the Charleston Running Club, told the committee that despite AAU rules he was putting out a water stop. He said he rented two buffet tables and had two volunteers man the station located just as the course turned onto Meeting Street. It wasn't enough, he said, but it was all he could do.

The race began at Patriots Point in Mount Pleasant, went across the reversible lane of the new bridge (use of the bridge had required legislation sponsored by State Senator Dewey Wise), went down Meeting Street to finish at White Point Gardens on the Battery. After the race began, police made race officials move the finish line about 150 yards, which made the course short.

Monday's *News and Courier* headline read "Atlantan Wins 1st Bridge Run" with the subtitle "More than 1,000 Join in 10,000-Meter Race". Benji Durden of Atlanta, who later made the 1980 U.S. Olympic marathon team, ran away from the field and won easily in 30:22.

"Durden, who got to the finish line ahead of everyone else and before most spectators who watched the start of the run at Patriots Point could drive to the finish line in their cars, hardly looked tired," the newspaper said. But Durden confessed to feeling low on energy because he had run Saturday in a 15 kilometer (9.3 mile) race in Jacksonville, Fla. "I ran fast," Durden said, "and no one ran with me."

Gary Wilson of The Citadel was lead bicyclist for the race, and he said Benji was going so fast he had trouble keeping up with him going up the bridge and had to work to catch him going down. Two of Baptist College's (now Charleston Southern University) track team members, both from Kenya, were next: Francis Mwobobia Ruchugo in 31:34 and Anderson Obare in 31:44. Russ Pate from Columbia was the first South Carolina finisher, placing fourth in 31:54.

Bob Schlau of Charleston remembers an interesting development in the race. He said he was running just behind the two Kenyans, and he knew that Francis was a steeplechase runner. As the runners approached the barrier blocking the reversible lane, the only lane open for the runners, he could see that the bar was down instead of up as it was supposed to be. Francis didn't go around the barrier - he hurdled it just as he would in a steeplechase.

Lisa Lorrain of Atlanta, who was traveling with Benji and his wife, was an easy winner and the only female under 40 minutes as she ran 39:39. Marty Long of Summerville, S.C., was second in 43:53 while Julie Embler of Greenville, S.C., was third in 45:01.

Male Masters award winners were Bill Wooley, 36:44, Rudy Nimmons, 39:29 and Alan Miles, 39:45. Women Masters winners were A. Lipowski, 46:12, Eileen Hallman, 59:00, and Diana Osbertson, 59:15. Complete results were mailed to all pre-registered runners, establishing a tradition. Results have been mailed for all but one Bridge Run and the available results for that year were published in the Charleston Running Club newsletter. The results show 766 runners (653 male and 113 female) crossing the finish line. A total of 66 runners ran faster than 40 minutes. There were 425 runners, 55 percent of the finishers, who crossed the finish line in less than 50 minutes. A total of 638, 83 percent of the runners, finished the race in under an hour.

The idea of a race across the Cooper River Bridge originated from a remark Dr. Norman Walsh, a surgeon, made to Dr. Marcus Newberry of MUSC. They were running together and Dr. Newberry was talking about putting on a race. Dr Walsh said, "If you're going to have a run in Charleston, you ought to do it on the only mountain in town, the bridge." Dr. Newberry took the idea and ran with it, so to speak. Dr. Newberry had been impressed on a visit to his Ohio home by the track constructed by Bonne Bell Cosmetics to encourage employees to run and stay fit. He wanted to get the Charleston community involved in running and fitness and decided a run across the bridge would do it.

Dr. Newberry got together with Terry Hamlin, then president of the Charleston Running Club. They set up a committee comprised of representatives from the Charleston Running Club, The Citadel, the Medical University and the College of Charleston. They worked out the details, overcame numerous obstacles and started the Cooper River Bridge Run. State Senator Dewey Wise intervened with the S.C. Department of Transportation to allow use of the bridge. He met with the highway commissioner and said he remembered him saying, "We don't close bridges for people. Bridges are for vehicles." The Bridge Run would prove that at least one day a year, bridges were for people as well.

Other Voices
An Interview With Dr. Marcus Newberry Founder Of The Cooper River Bridge Run

Telephone interview with Cedric Jaggers on July 31, 2010

CJ - Will you tell us how the Bridge Run came about?

Marc - During medical school, residency and a faculty position in Dallas, I had gained weight. After moving to Charleston for a faculty position at the Medical University of South Carolina (MUSC), I wanted to get fit and was impressed by Dr. Brian Smith, who lived on the Isle of Palms and ran to work every day at MUSC. That was considered pretty strange back then. In 1974 I ran the bicentennial run at Charles Towne Landing where Keith Hamilton was race director. I talked to him and got some tips on running. Terry Hamlin also worked at MUSC and he was the president of the Charleston Running Club. He gave me some advice on running. I ran with Dewey Wise (a state senator) and Dr. Norman Walsh, a surgeon. I talked about the idea of putting on a race in Charleston and Norm said, "If you are going to do a run in Charleston, you ought to do it on the only mountain in town, the bridge." And I remember we all looked at the bridge.

From that point forward the idea to stage a race over the Cooper River Bridge and to promote it as something for fitness and health for the entire community really took hold in my mind. I started talking to people. Keith Hamilton agreed to help and then we brought in The Citadel since Gary Wilson worked there. Terry Hamlin was there to represent the Charleston Running Club.

I went to the board of trustees at MUSC. At the time I was Dean of the College of Medicine and presented the idea. Back in the '70s it seemed like MUSC was always getting bad publicity so I presented it as an idea for good publicity. I promised them the front page of the newspaper every year forever and it would always be good publicity. That promise has never been broken.

The police chief at the time was John Conroy, and he was a runner, so when I approached him, I didn't have to convince him. He knew what I wanted to do and he was all in favor of it - a run over the bridge. So he and I visited Mayor Joe Riley and that brought in the City of Charleston.

Then I went to visit the Highway Department. They were polite but didn't want to set a precedent. They were afraid if they let us put on a race over the bridge, they'd have to let everyone do a race every weekend over it and that would cause a lot of disruption.

Fortunately I had some connections and talked to Dewey Wise about it. He got the Legislature to pass a state law allowing the use of the bridge one day per year for a race.

He and Ted Stern, president of the College of Charleston, arranged for the College of Charleston to come in on the race. Then we got the Town of Mount Pleasant and Parks, Recreation and Tourism to join in. And all those organizations and institutions became the Bridge Run Committee and set about making the race happen.

We didn't have any money, so we depended on a lot of in-kind help, personnel time, and people donating their own time. So the board was institutions, not individuals and I think that turned out to be important. We all wanted the race to be something for the community, not just for our benefit.

CJ - Keith Hamilton told me it was a committee decision to have invited runners the first year. "Marc Newberry knew somebody in the Atlanta Track Club and he contacted them and made arrangements for Benji Durden and Lisa Lorrain to come." Were you satisfied with how that came about and how it worked out?

Marc - I knew some people involved with the Peachtree race in Atlanta and got in touch with them. Benji Durden was very gracious to come. He was getting to be well known, and it put us on the map. He came with Lisa Lorrain and I wanted Gayle Barron, who was a well known runner. I hoped she would come because she was a nurse and there was the medical connection. (Note: Gayle was not able to come to the race. CJ) At the time we weren't looking for national recognition - we just wanted it to be a good local event for the community.

I did talk to some people outside the community including Russ Pate at the University of South Carolina, well known then for being a good runner and now for his work on fitness at USC. (Note: Russ finished fourth overall and was the first South Carolina finisher in the first Bridge Run. CJ) I knew Dr. George Sheehan and asked him to come, but he couldn't come. Later, it worked out that he could and he ran the race several years in a row and wrote about it in Runner's World and gave the race national recognition.

CJ - Keith also said he didn't enjoy being race director that first year and wouldn't do it again. How did you decide on a replacement?

Marc - Keith had had heart disease; in fact, he was interested in fitness probably because of that. But after the first race he came in and said he wouldn't do it again because of the pressure and the complaints. I know we had scheduled it on a Sunday morning and after the race I must have gotten a call or letter from every preacher in town and we hurried to change the race to Saturday.

CJ - Were you ever asked or did you ever want to be the race director?

Marc - No. It never came up. Most people probably assumed I didn't want to be director because I was busy and didn't have the experience or time to do it. I was more a person who could see problems and help solve them since I had some connections.

As time went on the committee kept hearing from sponsors and people who wanted to make the race a national thing. I had misgivings about prize money and world class runners. I was an obstacle. I woke up one day thinking, "It's time for me to go." I told them and that is when we formalized the committee. I remember thinking of George Washington's example: If you get out of the way before they throw you out, you become a hero. I decided to take his advice. Without me knowing it, they created and named the award for the first local male and female runner after me. I was honored and I will always appreciate it. It helps keep up local interest and is something for the community.

CJ - I know you ran the Bridge Run when you lived in Charleston. Do you still enjoy running it?

Marc - I don't run now. I try to walk it every year. I had polio when I was small and it left me with a moderate deformity in the left leg. Running seemed to aggravate it more as I got older. I have respiratory problems if I run. I try to stay in shape by walking and riding a stationary bike and a Concept 2 Rowing Ergometer, as well as some weight training.

CJ - Did you think the Bridge Run would become what it has become?

Marc - No. No, I was basically just looking to develop a local run, something on the order of the Charles Towne Landing race Keith had done. Something to promote health and fitness. My assumption is that crossing the Bridge was what put it on a course to become what it has. The people of Charleston just open up to the race and runners who come in. It is a community race which has grown big and the community owns it.

The Bridge Run Committee is a board not of individuals but of institutions and I think that has served the race well. When someone leaves or retires, the institution appoints a new member, and the board, not individuals, control the race.

Julian Smith is the longest serving race director and has served through all the growth and put the Bridge Run on a sound financial footing. They've added the Children's Run and the charity connection of donating money to the local charities. It is a great thing for the community.

Other Voices
Keith Hamilton, First Bridge Run Race Director

Note: This interview first appeared in the March-April 1984 issue of the Low Country Runner, several years before Keith Hamilton's untimely death. Now I wish I had asked him more questions. CJ

CJ - How did you get to be race director?

Keith - I had honchoed some of the first races in the Low Country in 1974 and '75 along with Quaddy Jones, leading up to the '76 Bicentennial run at Charles Towne Landing. So I was drafted because I at least had some limited experience.

CJ - How was the course selected and who selected it?

Keith - The course was a committee decision. We wanted it to end at the Battery with the bridge as the focal point. For the rest, we were just looking for 10 kilometers.

CJ - By whom and how was the course measured?

Keith - Terry Hamlin measured the course first in his car, and then as close as he could rolling a wheel over it at 2 or 3 a.m.

CJ - How many runners did you expect?

Keith - We expected 500 max. We ran out of numbers and everything trying to meet the rush of late registration.

CJ - Did you compile complete results?

Keith - No. We had the results somewhere in a cardboard box. I'm not exactly sure, but the number 890 or 898 finishers sticks in my mind. We had no numbers and no way of letting the finish line know. We did not have walkie-talkies. We had not considered until 5 minutes before starting the race how to get the timing watch to the finish line. So Gary Wilson of The Citadel rode his bicycle ahead of Benji Durden, carrying the official watch. He had trouble staying with Benji going up the bridge. I think he said he had to get off and push it once, and he somehow got to the finish line maybe 30 seconds ahead of Benji. That seems pretty funny now.

(Note: complete results were compiled, apparently by someone else on the Bridge Run Committee and mailed only to the pre-registered runners. They show a total of 766 finishers and a transcribed version can be seen on the www.BridgeRun.com website. I thought no results existed but was talking to my friends Maurice and Barbara Davidson (who had run the 1978 race) a few years after this interview and they had the results and let me copy them. CJ)

CJ - How did you select the invited runners?

Keith - It was a committee decision to get them. I didn't entirely agree. I thought it should be more of an event for local people. Marc Newberry knew somebody in the Atlanta Track Club and he contacted them and made arrangements for Benji Durden and Lisa Lorrain to come.

CJ - Who designed the T-shirt logo?

Keith - I designed the basic idea and Terry Hamlin added a few artistic touches and took it to Silkworm for printing. I selected the pale blue color because I was Citadel and it was The Citadel color. (Note from the 1984 *Low Country Runner* - That design was used for the first five years, and is in the opinion of most runners whom I've talked to, far superior to any of the designs used since. CJ)

CJ - Did you think it would become what it has become?

Keith - Yes I really did. I felt it would become something given its uniqueness and the large numbers we got the initial year. I felt real good about the future.

CJ - What was the worst thing about being Bridge Run race director?

Keith - The start was organized and I realized I had not considered how I was going to get myself to the finish to give out awards. I felt I had to have my hand in too many pots. Responsibility needed to be spread. The anxiety of trying to do everything was bad. The race started at 10 a.m. on a Sunday morning. The complaints from people trying to get to church with Meeting Street blocked off were bad. I understand them now, but I did not then. Senator Dewey Wise and a lot of others went down due to the heat which was about 82 degrees when we started. I was checking on them, getting them to the hospital and was very concerned about them. The worst thing was concern for the people who went down from the heat.

CJ - What was the best thing about being Bridge Run race director?

Keith - With the amount of effort everyone puts in, it was seeing it come to fruition. Standing in the parking lot at Patriots Point after the race started and seeing the bridge covered with humanity. Realizing that it had turned into a real experience. Then it was a happening at White Point Gardens (on the Battery). There was a real festive fair like atmosphere after the race. People hung around and talked. The joy of effort. The camaraderie.

CJ - Did you enjoy being the Bridge Run race director?

Keith - No, I really didn't. I withdrew because I didn't.

CJ - Would you do it again?

Keith - It was gratifying, but I really wouldn't want to do it again.

Interview With Benji Durden, Winner Of The First Cooper River Bridge Run

Telephone interview with Cedric Jaggers on May 25, 2010

CJ - You won the first Cooper River Bridge Run 33 years ago. What do you remember about it?

Benji - If my memory is not muddled I had run Jacksonville the day before and they arranged a private plane to pick us up and land somewhere in the Charleston area. They put us up at the beach. I was somewhat dubious and hesitant - two races in two days - but we did that more back then. There were two spans on the bridge and I was pleasantly surprised at how well I felt. It was hot that day if I recall, and heat didn't bother me since I was already sweatsuit training then. I wasn't challenged any time during the race. (Note: Benji became well known for running in layers of full sweatsuits even in the hottest weather to build heat conditioning. Obviously, it worked for him. CJ) Somebody keeps putting the Bridge Run as one of the major events in my life on my Wikipedia page entry. I go in and take it out and they put it back in. You should look at it sometime. (Note, I assured him that I was not the guilty party and that I would look at the page.

CJ - It says in Wikipedia that the course was short, is that true? (I told Benji that it was true, that the police made the race organizers move the finish line after the race had begun. CJ)

CJ - Did you know the lead bicyclist said he had trouble keeping up with you going up the bridge? He was carrying the official timing watch and was worried that you would get to the finish line before he did.

Benji - I know a couple of times I got up close to him but I wasn't worried. He had to carry his weight and the weight of the bike up the bridge. I've carried the timing watch for the Bolder Boulder 10K race in Colorado and know how it feels to rush to get it there before the first runner.

CJ - Since you had run the 15k River Run in Jacksonville the day before, did you expect to win the Bridge Run?

Benji - I knew I was going to the race and anticipated winning, but I wasn't sure how I'd do it. I had done a number of double races on weekends, but never a 15k and a 10k, so it was a new one that day.(When I mentioned that Kenyans attending Baptist College were second and third, he responded by saying the Kenyans were not as tough back then. CJ)

CJ - What is your 10k PR and when and where did you run it?

Benji - In 1981 or 1982 I ran a PR 28:36 and placed sixth at Peachtree in Atlanta.

CJ - Some readers may not know that two years after you won the Bridge Run, you were runner-up in the Olympic Trials Marathon in 2:10:41 and qualified for the U.S. team, and that you ran a PR 2:09:57 at the 1983 Boston Marathon. You didn't get to go to the Olympics in Moscow due to President Carter's boycott in 1980. How did you feel about that then?

Benji - I was conflicted about the whole boycott thing because it was pointless. The Russians would not pull out of Afghanistan because we were not going to the Olympics, but I was against the Russian invasion of Afghanistan. It didn't mean that much because we knew we weren't going before we ran the Trials. At the first of the year a bunch of us, Mary Decker (Slaney), Don Kardong, Ron Tabb and some others were watching cable news at Bob Anderson's (then publisher of Runners World) and when they were talking about the invasion I said we wouldn't go to Moscow for the Olympics and they didn't agree with me. Carter announced the boycott before the Trials so we knew we were not going.

CJ - How do you feel about it now?

Benji - You can't go back. I probably got more publicity from not getting to run, than if we had gotten to go and do it. We got to run the Goodwill Games in Moscow in 1986 and conditions might have been the same in '80 and I didn't run that well at Goodwill. The Soviet Union had third world conditions - it was bad - there was virtually no place that bad off in the Western world. In 1980 the western countries that did go had lots of athletes get sick. There was some speculation that something had been put in the food. The food, even in 1986 was barely edible and I lost 10 pounds while there before we ran the marathon. You don't want to lose 10 pounds and then run a marathon. The temperature was in the upper 80s or 90s. A Russian runner and I were running with a Japanese runner who just collapsed. It was like a death run. So we quit at about 18 or 19 miles. He said, "I know a shortcut back" and we both stopped running and took it.

CJ - You probably don't remember meeting my wife, Kathy, and me after you and she were the winners of the Osteopathic Scholarship 5k in Atlanta in 1980. Kathy asked you why you did not run the Bridge Run again and you said, "I wasn't invited." Did you ever consider running the Bridge Run again after it grew in size and notoriety?

Benji - I vaguely remember that race. I thought about running the 25th anniversary Bridge Run or maybe if they got all the winners to come back. But I was never invited back.

CJ - I know you coach runners and operate a finish line service with your wife now. Do you ever run any races now?

Benji - I run when I'm healthy and don't have any work conflict. The last races I did were a half-marathon in Tallahassee and a marathon in Wyoming. My wife, Amy, and I are trying to do a marathon in every state. I've only done 21 states and do a couple a year so at that rate it will take until I'm in my late 70s to do it.

CJ - You've probably read John Parker's excellent novel *Again To Carthage* and know that you figure prominently in the next to last chapter. Did he talk to you about it and how do you feel about the book?

Benji - John and I met each other in 1970 at the SEC championship mile. He won and I was sixth. In the late '70s he wrote a story about me for *The Runner* magazine and I've kept up with him. He and I have had a long friendship. He called and asked me lots of questions about Marathons and training, and I finally asked him what he was doing. We spent about six hours on the phone talking about things and I was his deep background for the book. There are a few anachronisms in the book, but it was a story that was true to the realities of marathon training. In his first book *Once A Runner* he didn't use the real names of the characters even when they were real people, but in *Carthage* he did. I liked the book a lot. He had the characters right.

CJ - Over the years have you kept up with the Bridge Run at all?

Benji - I've seen results over the years and had to check times. It still pops up in my memory - you remember the races you win.

CJ - Have you thought about running the Bridge Run again?

Benji - It might be fun to run it again in 2012 when I'll be 60.

The First Bridge Run

By Terry Hamlin, Originally appeared in the March-April 1984 Low Country Runner

The first Cooper River Bridge Run came about as a result originally of a collaboration between Dr. Marc Newberry and me. One day he came to my lab and said, "I have an idea about a race, a race over the bridge." He came to me because he knew I was a runner and I was president of the Charleston Running Club at the time. I was working in clinical chemistry at the Medical University.

Marc wanted to have MUSC and the CRC tie together the community fitness concept, so to speak, and thought a run across the bridge was a good way to publicize the concept. I said, "Great, I've thought about that too, but there are a lot of problems." We hashed the ideas and problems out.

We decided more people needed to be involved, so we formed a committee which included Roy Hill, Keith Hamilton, Brian Smith and others. We decided on a date, the first week in April, and met every week at the Medical University for about two and a half months before the race.

We found out one thing that might put a damper on the race. We'd made contact with a Mr. Cobb in the Highway Department. Permission to use the bridge had been denied, on his own authority, I think. He said, "You can't do that." My reaction was my usual calm demeanor: Feed Cobb to the sharks.

Marc had an ace in the hole. He knew State Senator Dewey Wise. They decided to go through legal channels to get it done. A resolution was passed in the South Carolina Legislature allowing us the use of the reversible lane of the new bridge one day per year for one hour. That took care of the Highway Department. The battle would be fought again two years later for use of the old bridge.

The actual course was a result of a discussion between Keith Hamilton and me. He had an idea of what might work, and we knew where we wanted it to finish - at the Battery. Keith and I got into my old Chevrolet Vega and went to Patriots Point where the race would start. We wanted the course to have as many straight lines as possible. So we went over the new bridge, down Meeting Street to the Battery, up to Fort Sumter house and turned left up Murray Boulevard. We didn't know how far we'd have to go. It ended up being just before where Murray makes the hard left and becomes East Bay Street.

Later, Walter Pringle, who measured the race courses for the CRC a lot in the early years, measured the Bridge Run course with a calibrated wheel and that's how it got to be reasonably accurate. Then the morning of the race the city police decided to move the finish line south several hundred feet to near King Street. We had a big finish banner, and I've still got pictures of the finish. It was too late for us to change the start, so the course was short.

We wanted to bring in a good runner to give the race some international flair. We were tossing around names of runners to get. Bill Rodgers and Frank Shorter came up, but when we contacted them, they wanted five or six thousand dollars and we didn't have that kind of money.

We got a recommendation, I think, from Jeff Galloway in Atlanta, saying that Benji Durden - he made the U.S. Olympic Marathon team two years later - was an up-and-coming runner. So we called and asked and he said he would come. Benji, his wife and a running friend named Lisa Lorrain, who had run a 2:51 marathon, which was pretty good then, flew in from Jacksonville on Saturday. Benji had placed third there that day at the River Run 15k. He was edged by Bill Rodgers and I forget who else. Benji and his wife stayed at my house and we had a little party the night before the race. I knew he was serious when he turned down a Budweiser.

We'd tried to project how many runners we'd have. We figured we'd get at most five or six hundred. We had 340 pre-registered. I went to the start area to handle late registration with a couple of girls, a couple of hundred applications and a few pencils.

All of a sudden all these people showed up and I was running around trying to get tables and everything set up. I was in a near panic. I thought, "My name is mud." We ran out of everything. We didn't have enough numbers or entry forms or anything. I wrote on a piece of paper "I Will Not Sue, etc. . . ." and had people sign it and pay the $3 entry fee.

We had seven or eight hundred people sign up race morning. I remember hoping that somebody without a number wouldn't win because then what would we do?

Race day was a Sunday. It dawned hot and still. The committee had voted not to have water on the course. I voted in favor of it, but the others thought it wasn't needed. It was. We nearly lost a few that year and I still get upset over that decision. I kept saying to myself, "It's 80 degrees, we're going to kill some people it's so hot." I could see the headlines "Running Club President Terry Hamlin Kills 36 People In Road Race". Instead of DNF we would have DNL - Did Not Live - listed on the results. I was worried.

I registered people right up till time to start the race. At the last minute, virtually the last second, I left the registration table and handed Keith Hamilton the starting gun and lined up. I ran the race worried and looking around. I saw some people dropping and got more worried, but I kept going; I had to help at the finish. I think I finished in about 38 minutes - I remember I was 36th place. (Note - per the official results 36th place was racer #120 - most names were not listed, time was 37:20 - an excellent time considering the heat. CJ)

At the finish line we ran out of everything: patience first. We had one 5 gallon cooler of water. We had too few finish place cards. We had T-shirt distribution set up at a booth and we had about 500 T-shirts and 900 or so runners finished the race and we had all these irate runners screaming at us.

We ran out of ambulances to carry runners who'd passed out from the heat to the hospital. We had to take them in station wagons. Sen. Wise collapsed after he finished and he had to be taken to the hospital. I think 30 some people had to go to the emergency room. Keith Hamilton and his crew did a fantastic job working the finish considering the number of runners and our shortage of help.

Benji and Lisa both won handily. It was a mad dash after the awards ceremony to get them to the airport in time for their flight. I don't think they even got a shower - just, "Here's your new running suit (award), here's your trophy, put on your sweats and let's go."

Complete results were supposed to be mailed. I don't know what happened there. Marc was supposed to take care of that, but it never got done. We were all probably so relieved that we didn't get sued we just forgot about it. (Note: The results were mailed only to pre-registered runners. The Bridge Run Committee borrowed them and all the other pre-computerized results from me in 2005 and scanned or transcribed them and posted them on the BridgeRun.Com website. CJ)

The Cooper River Bridge Run survived despite the heat and other problems. I'm proud to have had a hand in its formation, and I respect the work that putting on the race involves. So if you are not going to run it, think about giving this year's organizers a hand. Believe me, they will appreciate it.

Leading The First Bridge Run

By Gary Wilson, Originally appeared in the March-April 1984 Low Country Runner

I got involved in the first Bridge Run because I was at The Citadel, in the Department of Physical Education. All of us in the department: Keith Hamilton, me and a lot of cadets helped put it on.

Keith was the race director and he knew I rode bicycles, so he asked me if I'd be interested in leading the runners so they wouldn't get lost. There had never been a race like that before, so we wanted to be sure that didn't happen.

It was hot that day. The race didn't begin until 10 a.m. and that was too late in the day. You could feel the heat going over the spans. Even the breeze was a warm breeze, not cool at all. It was hot and muggy, really rough.

We timed the race with watches. Keith fired the starting gun, started a couple of watches and handed them to me to take to the finish line. As a matter of fact, I think we did it that way for two or three years. Little did we know all we needed was a radio.

Anyway, they fired the gun at Patriots Point and by the time I got the watches the lead guys were long gone and runners were everywhere. I wasn't all the way at the back of the crowd, but I was having to thread my way through lots of runners to try and catch the leaders.

By the time I cleared the crowd, the leader was going up the first span. I was on a three-speed bicycle and he was going up it about as fast as I could. For a while I wondered if he was going to get to the finish line before I did. But I caught him near the top of the first span and realized I wouldn't have any trouble the rest of the way. I didn't know who he was. I learned later that he was Benji Durden from Atlanta.

When we got to the finish area at the Battery it was just incredible. That was a great place to finish with all that space, we thought. As more and more people finished, it turned into a party. It was unbelievable. It was so successful people were crowded around everywhere. It was too successful; it killed using that area as the finish again. People were everywhere and the residents couldn't get in and out of their houses. That first Bridge Run was something.

The First Bridge Run Was My First Race

By Margaret Wright, Originally appeared in the March-April 1984 Low Country Runner

I started running in January of 1978 at the age of 57. I was so dumb about running that I wore tennis shoes. I'd never heard of running shoes. I thought the word Adidas was the name of a town in Greece. I ran at night in dark clothes so no one could see me.

Terry Hamlin and I worked in the labs at MUSC. He set me straight about shoes and I bought my first pair of running shoes, Etonics. I was amazed at how much easier it was to run. I could really fly - if you can call 13 minutes per mile flying!

I joined the Charleston Running Club which met upstairs over the Charleston County Library; Terry was the president. I heard them talking about the first Bridge Run, to be held on Sunday, April 2, and toyed with the idea, then asked for options. Terry wasn't too optimistic since I'd never run more than two miles at a time. Brian Smith said to try it and walk if I had to.

I submitted my application and the $3 entry fee a week before the race. I ran from my house on Folly Beach to the Loran Coast Guard Station and back - my first six miles. The next day I stepped in a pothole on the way home from evening Mass and sprained my ankle. Bridge Run hopes seemed dashed, but the Lord had pity on me (because I hurt myself going to church?) and the sprain healed quickly.

Race day dawned sunny and beautiful. I was uptight and out early and jogged in circles on the beach, announcing to all who passed by that I was getting ready for the Bridge Run.

I'd never been to a race and didn't know that people wore shorts and singlets or T's. I donned an old pair of corduroy slacks and a beat-up polo shirt and headed for Patriots Point (where the race started then) and the 10 o'clock start.

I was overwhelmed by the crowd and was nervous and scared about being totally last and being abandoned on the bridge long after the race was over.

A small group of Furman students gathered in one corner of the parking lot for a little religious service - hymns and a prayer for the runners. I needed all the help I could get so I joined them.

Then we were off, and I ran to the foot of the first span and walked up it. Then I ran to the second hill and walked again. There was a fresh breeze blowing and Charleston looked so beautiful shimmering in the sunlight. I thought, "Hey, piece of cake!" Then we hit Meeting Street and the heat overwhelmed us. I had never run in the heat before and was totally unnerved. I didn't see any water stops but a group of us found a service station hose where we drank and squirted ourselves. This freshened us enough to make it to the Battery and the finish line.

I was so ecstatic at finishing that I hugged everyone, strangers and all. I had completed the course in 71 minutes. My son was working the finish line and had saved me a T-shirt - my very first. I treated it like it was made of gold, carrying it all over the Medical University the next day for everyone to admire.

Running The FirstBridge Run

By Doug Williams, Originally appeared in the March-April 1984 Low Country Runner

The reason I ran the first Bridge Run was because I was in a running class at the College of Charleston which was being taught by Jean Hamilton, wife of Keith Hamilton, the Bridge Run race director that year. She was encouraging everybody in the class to go out and run the race. I spoke at her class this January (1984) and she still has it. They call it aerobics now, but the main thrust of the class is running. It is still based on Ken Cooper's books now as it was then. It was my first race.

It was really hot that Sunday morning. I had gotten there an hour early and didn't know what to do. I must have tied my shoes 100 times. I still have those shoes; a pair of old original Converse World Class Trainers, maybe the first running shoes Converse made - the ones with stars on the bottom. I found the race T-shirt the other day too.

The parking lot at Patriots Point was a madhouse. People were parking everywhere not realizing that was where the runners would have to run. When they started the race, people ran around cars and I remember one guy jumped over a car.

I think it was *Runner's World* magazine that had just done a piece on Ted Corbitt, who ran in the 1952 Olympic Marathon, and I knew he was going to be there because Mrs. Hamilton had mentioned it. I saw him and noticed the size of his shoes. There were at least an inch and a half, maybe two inches longer than his feet and a good inch too wide. They were New Balance 320s.

I couldn't believe his shoes fit so badly, so when I was talking to him I asked him to let me measure the extra space with my thumb, so I remember how much space there was real clearly. I said, "Do you always wear them so big?" And he replied, "They'll fit better at the end of the race." I saw him after the race and they had filled out a lot, not the length so much as the width.

They ran out of numbers for runners because so many more people late registered than they had expected. I had a number, but I can't remember what they did for the folks who didn't.

We started and I went out way too fast, I didn't know it, because I started out with Ted Corbitt. We got to the start of the first span, the race went up the reversible lane of the new bridge, and I was convulsing or whatever, and he said, "See you later." Maybe it was a combination of him speeding up and me dying, but he moved away unbelievably fast. It seemed like he moved like a gazelle up the bridge, and he didn't sweat. He was so smooth it looked like he was out for a Sunday stroll.

As we were going up the second span it was so hot that some woman who was running in a T-shirt whipped off the shirt and ran in her bra. I don't know who she was or who else ran the first year, but she was in a pretty good group of guys and I'll bet they remember her.

We came off the bridge and everybody wanted water but there wasn't any even though the race application said there would be. I saw some people running over to the service station just after you got off the bridge on Meeting Street using the hose to get water, but I didn't stop. The station is still in business - the owner now charges people a quarter to use the bathroom.

When we got to the White Horse Inn, Dewey Wise was right in front of me. All of a sudden he dropped like a stone. He just fell right on his face. It was just the heat. Three or four people standing outside the White Horse grabbed him and took him inside so I kept on going. I think he made it to the finish line later on. It wasn't anything serious.

All I wanted to do was finish. I wasn't worried about time: 6.2 miles was like a Marathon, we had only been running two or three miles a day. When I got to the Battery there was some kind of banner and a bunch of people standing by it yelling and I thought it was the finish so I sprinted like crazy. I got there and found out we had to go around a half block or more to the finish line.

I was beat. I walked and got up to a jog in time to cross the finish line. I don't know what my time or finish place was, the race application said results would be mailed but they never were, and I didn't care, I was just happy to be there.

So we finished up and looked for water and there wasn't any. Somebody was selling Cokes for about three times what they usually sold for, but like most of the runners I didn't have any money on me. He was doing good business, mainly with the families who had come to watch.

I remember Keith Hamilton was on the electric megaphone saying something like: "This is the biggest race in South Carolina, look around. I can't believe how many runners there are. Look how many people there are."

As they were getting ready for the awards ceremony somebody pointed out the winner, Benji Durden. He was being interviewed over by the side of the bandstand at White Point Gardens. He had on a white singlet and he was just dripping sweat. I remember thinking, "That sure is a skinny guy."

The scene at the finish was like a battlefield - like Peachtree (in Atlanta) is now. All those runners lying around and walking around and all the people packed into that little area on the Battery. Everybody was milling around looking for each other.

A lot of people didn't have any way to get back to their cars parked at the start. So they asked folks who needed a ride to line up on one side of the bandstand and people with cars to line up on the other. Then the ones who needed rides just sort of grabbed the ones with cars. I rode in a little foreign car with six people. I didn't know any of them and some girl sat on my lap. I thought this running thing was pretty fun so I ran a race the next weekend.

The Bridge Run is the only race I've run every year. There were a couple of years I almost didn't get to. In fact, one year I wasn't registered and ended up running on Bob Priest's number, but somehow I've run it every year. I'm glad I ran the first Bridge Run and I'm looking forward to running the next Bridge Run.

1978 Awards

Merchandise was awarded to the top 3 males and females overall and masters only.

Overall Male
1. Benji Durden .... Atlanta, GA 30:22
2. Francis Mwobobia Ruchugo   Kenya 31:34
3. Anderson Obare .... Kenya 31:44

Overall Female
1. Lisa Lorrain .... Atlanta, GA 39:39
2. Marty Long .... Summerville, SC 43:53
3. Julie Embler .... Greenville, SC 45:01

Masters Male
1. Bill Wooley .... Unknown 36:44
2. Rudy Nimmons .... Unknown 39:29
3. Alan Miles .... Unknown 39:45

Masters Female
1. A. Lipowski .... Unknown 46:12
2. Eileen Hallman .... Columbia, SC 59:00
3. Diana Osbertson .... Unknown 59:15

This awards list compiled by Cedric Jaggers from original 1978 paper race results and from the April 3, 1978, *News and Courier*.

Runners shared the bridge with vehicular traffic in this year's event. News and Courier photo

Chapter 2
1979
One Lane On The Bridge For The Last Time

The second Bridge Run, March 31, 1979, was moved back a day, from Sunday to Saturday, due to complaints from churches. The entry fee was raised to $4 with T-shirt and $2 without. The time was moved back an hour to 9 a.m. to try to avoid the heat of the previous year. The date change worked as it was just under 60 degrees when the race began. Water was also provided for runners as they came off the bridge.

The course was changed. It began in Mount Pleasant at Patriots Point in front of the aircraft carrier *Yorktown*, ran into a bottleneck as runners took the parking lot road out to Coleman Boulevard, went across the reversible lane (one of the three lanes) of the Silas Pearman "New" Bridge, as runners called it at the time, down East Bay Street to Market Street, then across Market and up Meeting Street to George Street to finish at the College of Charleston near the cistern.

When the race began, Avery Goode from Clover, S.C., took the lead and was never challenged as he won in 32:55. "I've never run in Charleston before, and I thought I could do pretty well," Goode told the *News and Courier*.

The battle for second place was exciting as Bob Schlau of Charleston overtook Silky Sillivan, a Navy man from California who was stationed in Charleston, and edged him by 6 seconds in 33:33. Schlau, a local favorite, said he was training for the Boston Marathon which would be held the next week. He said he almost didn't run the Bridge Run but decided to use it as a training run so he started out at a conservative pace. When he came off the bridge and was told he was in third place, he said he realized he might have been able to win the race and decided to go after the leaders, but it was too late.

In the female division, Marty Long, a student at the College of Charleston who had run track at Summerville High School, moved up from her runner-up spot in the Bridge Run, to the winner's spot in 40:10. Susan Jones of Charleston was second in 40:42 and Michelle Moore of Atlanta, Ga., was third in 41:40. "These races are fun," Long told the newspaper. "There isn't the pressure like in high school."

As runners approached the finish near the cistern at the College of Charleston, the narrow streets led to a stack of runners trying to cross the finish line designated for males. The delay lasted from about 44 minutes until the crowd had thinned 5 or 6 minutes later. At one point the crowd was so thick that men stood for 30 seconds to a minute before being allowed to cross the finish line and have a time recorded.

The first three Masters were Jones (first name not shown on mailed results) 38:35, John Dunkleberg of the Isle of Palms, S.C., 38:46, and Charles Duell of Charleston third, 41:20. Female Masters winners were: Glassman, 52:04, Margaret Wright of Folly Beach, S.C., 56:51, and Pat Rhode of Walterboro, S.C., 57:22.

"I know running isn't for everybody," Dr. Brian Smith told the newspaper, "but there are so many possible physical and mental rewards that it would be worthwhile for anyone to give it a chance." He also wrote out the complete results showing last name only which were mailed to the finishers; male results to all the men and female results to all the women. There were 1,350 entrants and 1,050 official finishers, 778 male and 237 female with 47 runners breaking the 40-minute barrier, 423 runners broke the 50-minute barrier and 821 runners finished under 60 minutes.

The Cooper River Bridge Run almost ended right there. The Highway Department had made the reversible lane on the Silas Pearman Bridge one-way when heavy trucks were banned from the old Grace Memorial Bridge for safety reasons. The reversible lane was no longer available for the race as it had been in 1978 and 1979, and the Highway Department denied a request for use of the old bridge for the run. Fortunately, Sen. Wise came to the rescue again. He pushed through legislation allowing the Bridge Run to continue by using the old bridge one morning per year. A special award was created and named to honor the senator. The Dewey Wise Trophy is awarded each year to the oldest runner who runs a time faster than his or her age in minutes.

Other Voices
An Interview With Avery Goode, Winner Of The 1979 Cooper River Bridge Run

Telephone interview with Cedric Jaggers on June 26, 2010

CJ - Did you run the first Bridge Run?

Avery -No, I didn't run the first one.

CJ - You won the 1979 (second) Bridge Run in 32:55, 38 seconds, or about a tenth of a mile ahead of second place. Going into the race, did you expect to win it?

Avery - I had no idea what I was going to do. I had gotten invited down by some people I met at another race. You lived in Charleston then, did you know Carl Jenkins Jr. and Elaine and their friend Moe whose last name I can't recall? (I told him I did, and that Moe was Moe Glunt and that Carl Sr. was a good runner then too - which he recalled. CJ) They were from Charleston and said it was a fun race and they would love to have me come down. I stayed with Moe that year and the next year with Carl and Elaine. I had no idea what to expect in the race.

CJ - What do you remember about the race? First mile split? Lead all the way? Did you feel challenged at any point?

Avery - I don't remember my first split. I started out hard. I realized as soon as the race got started I was on my own and couldn't feel anybody behind me. We came off the bridge and made a series of right-hand turns to get onto East Bay Street and I was almost hit by a police car turning the corner. It was nobody's fault, just one of those things. I don't know if he thought he had enough time to get by me or if I thought I did, but it brought me back to reality. It made me think, "Hey you'd better concentrate and think about what you are doing."

I never felt challenged at any point. I took out at the pace I wanted to run and held it. I always ran that way. I never ran my best time when I wasn't pressed.

We finished the race close to the cistern at the College of Charleston. Some radio station had a gorilla as a mascot and that station interviewed me a bit.

CJ - What did you get for winning the race?

Avery - A handshake, a "Please come back." They presented a trophy they said would have the winners' names on it and be shared around. I don't know what happened to that trophy. So I did not get one single thing. I wish maybe they would share some of that prize money from later on with me.

CJ - You ran the race again in 1980 and finished third in 32:10, 54 seconds, behind two Alleghany Track Club runners who tied. Coming into that race, did you think you might win for the second year in a row?

Avery -In 1980 I felt like I should go after it, being the winner of the second year. I remember going out hard and taking the lead. I remember those two guys passed me at the peak of the bridge and I chased after them the rest of the way.

Once they passed me nobody else came up and I realized I couldn't catch them. I remember making the attempt to chase them, but they were too fast for me. Nobody came up on me so I ran alone again to the finish like the previous year.

CJ - What is your 10k P.R. and where did you run it?

Avery - My fastest time at 10k was 30:16, but that was before certified courses. Whether it was a legit course of 6.2 miles I don't know. It was at the Greenwood Tech 10k in the fall of '78 before I ran the Bridge Run for the first time.

The 10k was not my best race. I had more success at the 10 mile and in the half Marathon.

CJ - How many Bridge Runs have you run?

Avery - I ran those two, then I ran the Bridge Run one more time with my sister.

CJ - Why did you stop?

Avery - I had a lot of biomechanical problems and I would break down. I had a leg length difference which I could never overcome. I wanted to run a 1:05 half marathon to feel I could run a marathon and ran a 1:07 and got injured. I got distraught over getting injured all the time. I got injured, disillusioned and just got out of it. I quit racing for about 20 years.

CJ - You got into really good shape and ran some fantastic times at large and small races when you became a Masters Division runner. Did you consider running the B.R. then?

Avery - I was running well and had the opportunity to run the Bridge Run or the Carlsbad 5k which I had never run. That's the year I probably should have gone to the Bridge Run and might have had some success, but I went to Carlsbad. (Note: he had success at that race, running 16:47 at age 48 in 2002. CJ)

CJ - Do you think you will run the Bridge Run again?

Avery - No. Once again biomechanical problems came in and I got so many injuries I just can't keep doing it. My knee got so bad it hurt to walk, so I had to quit running. It hurts now even when I ride a bike. I can walk now without pain, but I can't run.

CJ - Anything you would like to add?

Avery - I remember it being a great time and I met a lot of great people. You could meet so many great people, not just at that race but at all of them: people from all different walks of life. It didn't matter where they were from or what they did, we just all had great camaraderie.

Bridge Run '79

By Brian Smith, Originally Appeared In The May 1979 Charleston Running Club Newsletter

Fifteen hundred runners, a two-mile, two-humped bridge, sparkling water, a strong headwind, a mass start, cloudy sky, and 10,000 meters were the main ingredients for the largest participant sporting event ever held in the Lowcountry. For most it was a beautiful experience, if taken as a whole. Similarly, for most, there were agonizing spots when the miles seemed to stretch to infinity, when the air ran out of oxygen and legs turned to concrete.

Avery Goode, a teacher from Clover, S.C., won the male division in 32 minutes 55 seconds. Bob Schlau was second and Silky Sillivan third. The first woman was Marty Long, a student at the College of Charleston, in 40 minutes 20 seconds. Susan Jones was second, and Michele Moore third. There were 11 age group divisions for males and six for females. Club runners featured prominently among the winners.

Floating trophies were initiated this year for the first male and first female. They were donated by J.C. Long and the Athlete's Foot, respectively. A thousand dollars in gift certificates were divided up among 105 of the age group award winners.

The bottled water people, Carolina Mountain Water and Mountain Valley Water, did a super job in providing fluids at the start, mid-point and finish.

It appeared that virtually every member available was in the Bridge Run. We've had many new members join following the event.

1979 Awards

According to the race entry form, merchandise awards went to the first three male and female finishers. However, according to Dr. Brian Smith, who hand wrote the results, there were actually 11 male age groups and six female age groups which I have reconstructed from the original results which show last name only. First names have been added only when I am relatively sure of correctness. CJ

Overall Winners Male
1 Avery Goode.............Clover, SC............32:55
2 Bob Schlau ....Charleston, SC 33:33
3 Silky Sillivan ....Charleston, SC 33:39

Overall Winners Female
1 Marty Long..............Summerville, SC.......40:10
2 Susan Jones ....Charleston, SC 40:42
3 Michelle Moore ....Atlanta, GA 41:40

Masters winners Male
1 Jones ....hometown?............38:35
2 John Dunkleberg...........Isle of Palms, SC 38:46
3 Charles Duell ....Charleston, SC 41:20

Masters winners Female
1 Glassman ....hometown?............52:04
2 Margaret Wright...........Folly Beach, SC 56:51
3 Pat Rhode ....Walterboro, SC 57:22

Age Groups
(Note overall and masters winners included in age group awards)

Male 7-10
1 Linning...................55:18
2 Thompson 58:15
3 Hamrick 60:00
4 Matthews 61:11
5 Heath 61:46

Female 10-14
1 Hancock..................56:59
2 Currey 57:30
3 Woodward 57:59
4 Rogers 60:48
5 Davis 62:14

Male 11-14
1 Ward.....................35:44
2 Sample...................41:40
3 Johnson 42:38
4 Owens 45:31
5 Doscher 45:54

Male 15-19
1 Green 37:59
2 Wetherall................38:25
3 Stetts 38:39
4 Allen 38:49
5 Braswell.................39:00

Female 15-19
1 Moore, Michelle 41:40
2 Johnson 48:59
3 Rogers 50:54
4 Shaw 51:34
5 McGee 53:48

Male 20-24
1 Sillivan, Silky...........33:39
2 McManus 35:12
3 Armour...................36:15
4 Bridgman.................36:18
5 Herman 37:22

Female 20-29
1 Long, Marty..............40:10
2 Jones, Susan.............40:42
3 Van Dyke 44:47
4 Cline 45:05
5 Hoover 45:58

Male 25-29
1 Goode, Avery.............32:55
2 McCann 35:41
3 Shipley..................36:14
4 Bickerton................37:06
5 Hamlin, Terry 37:14

Male 30-34
1 Schlau, Bob 33:33
2 O'Neill..................38:16
3 Cody, Roland Butch 38:28
4 Barnwell 38:38
5 Nottingham 38:47

Female 30-39
1 Bailey, Gail.............45:25
2 Reed, Anne Boone 45:45
3 Tarleau 47:22
4 Bishop 48:51
5 Ross.....................48:57

Male 35-39
1 Comer, Steve 37:41
2 Glunt, Moe 38:32
3 McClary, Clebe 38:47
4 Johnson 38:51
5 Owens 38:53

Male 40-44
1 Jones....................38:35
2 Dunkleburg, John 38:46
3 Duell, Charles 41:20
4 Hallman 41:43
5 Blagg 42:00

Female 40-49
1 Glassman.................52:04
2 Rhode, Pat 57:22
3 McKenzie 57:36
4 Hopkins, Lynn 58:21
5 Smith 65:42

Male 45-49
1 Lesto, Ken 42:02
2 Ezell 50:17
3 Hay 54:09
4 Morgan 54:32
5 Middleton 54:33

Male 50-59
1 Smith, Brian 42:26
2 Woodward 42:54
3 Mellard, David 43:21
4 Kirk, Robert.............44:17
5 Moore, Laurence 45:41

Female 50 - Over
1 Wright, Margaret.........55:51
2 Farrara 77:11

Male 60 - Over
1 McRoy....................43:38
2 Baskett, Tom.............50:10

Compiled by Cedric Jaggers from original paper results.

Headed for the finish line.
News and Courier photo by Stephanie Harvin

Chapter 3
1980
The First Time Over The 'Old Bridge' And The Only Tie Race

The third Bridge Run, held March 29, 1980, produced the race's only tie. Alleghany Nike Track Club teammates Kim Burke and Steve Littleton from Pittsburgh, Pa., who had just run in the Florida Relays in Gainesville and were driving home, crossed the line together in 31:26. "This was a last-minute thing for us, we were heading back (from the Relays) and decided to run it," Littleton told the Sunday *News and Courier*. "The course was easy. When you run hills all the time like the ones in Pittsburgh, you become used to them. But the traveling definitely got to us."

Burke said, "We just sat back and took it easy. After the third mile, we felt comfortable and went ahead. We met a lot of nice people." We just sat back and took it easy."

Defending champion Avery Goode of Clover, was never able to challenge them and finished third in 32:10. "If I could do it all over again," he said, "I wouldn't let the two guys surge right before the third mile started. That's where I lost it. I let them go ahead. I always like to win. I didn't expect to win it last year. This year I didn't know what to expect. You win a few and lose a lot."

Michelle Moore from Atlanta, Ga., moved up from third place in the previous race to win in 41:29. "I feel good," she said. "I did a lot better than I did last year." Two Charleston runners provided excitement as Gail Bailey outkicked Anne Boone Reed for second place by one second in 42:43. "The bridge was a bearcat," Bailey said. "It was a much harder race than last year's."

Reed said, "I'm real pleased. I keep coming home with trophies and my daughter (Christine, age 6) will do some more bragging to her friends."

The top Masters finishers were Ed Ledford of Charleston in 37:08, Bernie Sher, second in 37:42 and Maynard Ealing, third in 38:02. Pat Rhode of Walterboro was female Masters winner in 49:53, followed by Jackie Krawcheck of Charleston in 50:06 and Patricia Goodwin in 51:27. The newly created Dewey Wise Trophy for the oldest runner with a time under his or her age in minutes, was awarded to Tom Baskett, 66, of Charleston, who ran 47:18.

For the second year in a row, the temperature was just under 60 degrees for the 9 a.m. start. Runners had to fight a strong 10 mile per hour headwind going up the bridge. There were 1,500 entrants and the complete results list showed 1,330 official finishers, 1,063 male and 267 female, with 115 runners faster than 40 minutes, 750 runners under 50 minutes and 1,185 under 60 minutes.

The race used its third new course in its three-year history as the "new" Silas Pearman Bridge could no longer be used since the reversible lane had been converted to a third southbound lane, and it was decided all traffic could not be stopped for the race. Legislation sponsored by Sen. Wise allowed use of the "old"

Grace Memorial Bridge. The race crossed the older and steeper bridge but gained from the use of both lanes (the entire bridge) instead of just one lane as in the previous two races. It started again at Patriots Point in Mount Pleasant, came on to Coleman Boulevard, (again with a bottleneck of runners coming out of the parking lot), crossed over the old bridge, went down East Bay Street, across Queen Street to Logan, up Coming Street to finish at George Street beside the College of Charleston near the cistern.

The entry fee remained $4 with T-shirt, $2 without.

Other Voices
The 3rd Annual Cooper River Bridge Run
By Brian Smith, Originally appeared in the May 1980 Charleston Running Club Newsletter

Marathon running surgeon Norm Walsh was the loudest of the early voices wanting a race over the Cooper River Bridge. Mark Newberry made it a reality in 1978. The race has grown in size each year. The bridges are a magnet to runners with 1,400 registering for this year's run and 1,330 crossing the finish line. There is no way to know how many started. Scores of individuals ran unofficially and did not, as instructed, cross the finish line.

The start went flawlessly despite the failure of the police to aid with parking. Dave Mellard organized the split times. They were transmitted from the finish line by the Charleston Amateur Radio Society and were amplified by mini-P.A. systems at each mile, a tough piece of management that worked flawlessly.

We ran into a 15-knot headwind over the bridges, cooling but slowing. That was my first shot at the old bridge. The uphills didn't seem any worse than those of the new bridge.

We came to the first water station shortly after passing under the bridges. There was plenty of water when I went by, but I heard they ran out for one brief period. I came off the bridge feeling good, but the long plug down East Bay seemed like 1,000 miles. (Note: Brian finished in 42:30 taking second place in his age division. CJ)

Two EMS units were on station. Neither had a call. The monitors and police provided excellent traffic control. Two cyclists from Coastal Cyclists Club led the race. The male race was won in a dead heat by two runners from Pittsburgh, Pa., Kim Burke and Steve Lyttleton, in 31:26. Avery Goode, who won last year, followed 44 seconds behind the winners. The female race was won by Michelle Moore, 18, from Atlanta in 41:29. Club members Anne Reed and Gail Bailey ran shoulder to shoulder for second with Gail crossing the finish line 1 second ahead of Anne. The Senator Dewey Wise Trophy was added to this year's race for the oldest person to finish with a time in minutes less than their age. Tom Baskett 66, won this in 47 minutes, qualifying by almost 20 minutes. Many club members showed remarkable improvement, like Ed Ledford, Nita Jacques, Bert Glassman and Bob Kirk. Scores of others set PR's.

In keeping with the previous two races, the finish organization was unable to absorb the mainstream of male runners around the 50-minute mark. Two Chronomix times and printers did not arrive from DHEC, Columba, as promised, and we were unable to post times immediately after the race as we had promised. The Athlete's Foot supported the event generously, providing $1,000 in gift certificates to almost 100 age group placers. Gold, silver and bronze medals, 94 in all, were also distributed.

Dannon Yogurt was available at the finish. I was dismayed to see the masses of yogurt containers discarded on George Street. Runners have acted more thoughtfully in the past. Club members led by Reid Wiseman worked hard to leave the area as we had found it. Next year we'll do better in many ways.

1980 Awards

Overall Winners Male
1. Kim Burke .... Pittsburg, PA 31:26
1. Steve Littleton .... Pittsburg, PA 31:26
3. Avery Goode .... Clover, SC 32:10

Overall Winners Female
1. Michelle Moore .... Atlanta, GA 41:29
2. Gail Bailey .... Charleston, SC 42:43
3. Anne Boone Reed .... Charleston, SC 42:44

Masters Male
1. Ed Ledford .... Charleston, SC 37:08
2. Bernie Sher .... Charleston, SC 37:42
3. Maynard Ealing .... hometown ? 38:02

Masters Female
1. Pat Rhode .... Walterboro, SC 49:53
2. Jackie Krawcheck .... Charleston, SC 50:06
3. Patricia Goodwin .... hometown ? 51:27

First time Special award:
Dewey Wise Trophy for oldest finisher with time faster than their age in minutes:
1. Tom Baskett, 66 .... Charleston, SC 47:18

Age Groups
(Note overall winners included in age group awards)

Male 7-10
1. Luke Lucas 52:38
2. Matt Stanley 55:40
3. Andy Rogers 56:53
4. Joshua Campbell 62:03
5. Michael Cone 67:40

Female 10-14
1. Katherine Purcell 50:07
2. Kathy Hart 50:46
3. Kathleen Currey 51:06
4. June Duell 52:17
5. Charity Johnston 60:42

Male 11-14
1. Chad Davis 38:19
2. Bobby Slotkin 39:01
3. Darby Marshall 41:17
4. Chip Owen 41:47
5. Fredrick Anderson 42:35

Male 15-19
1. Teever Handal 36:08
2. Mark Shuford 36:22
3. Bryan Blalock 36:42
4. Bernard Brown 36:58
5. Shayne Merritt 37:36

Female 15-19
1. Michelle Moore 41:29
2. Rhonda Morris 43:53
3. Cathy Breland 47:34
4. Leigh Johnson 47:41
5. Jennifer Johnson 47:42

Male 20-24
1. Kim Burke 31:26
1. Steve Littleton 31:26
3. Marc Embler 32:18 .... 32:18
4. David Luhrs 32:48
5. Randy McManus 33:46

Female 20-29
1. Susan Riser 43:29
2. Gearin Broderick 43:34
3. Marty Long 43:41
4. Laura Harrington 43:46
5. Sallie Driggers 43:50

Male 25-29
1. Avery Goode 32:10
2. Bill Marable 33:00
3. Mical Embler 33:28
4. Joe Debs 33:50
5. Lou Rice 36:09

Male 30-34
1. Paul Rogers 33:15
2. Bob Schlau 35:22
3. Howard Grubs 35:45
4. Jim O'Neill 36:49
5. Brian Double 37:12

Female 30-39
1. Gail Bailey 42:43
2. Anne Reed (Boone) 42:44
3. Eileen McGrath 44:10
4. Barbara Paulsen 46:36
5. Teresa Bishop 47:22

Male 35-39
1. David McCann 34:57
2. Maurice Glunt 36:42
3. Clebe McClary 37:00
4. Louis Tisdale 37:48
5. Robin Heath 37:52

Male 40-44
1. Ed Ledford 35:08
2. Bernard Sher 37:42
3. Maynard Ealing 38:02
4. Don Austell 39:42
5. Walter Lancaster 39:50

Female 40-49
1. Pat Rhode 49:53
2. Jackie Krawcheck 50:06
3. Patricia Goodwin 51:27
4. Lynn Hopkins 51:31
5. Nancy Newberry 52:09

Male 45-49
1. Tony Foster 40:41
2. Ken Lesto 41:33
3. Timothy Twomey 42:08
4. Teddy Weeks 42:16
5. Bill McCrary 42:36

Male 50-59
1. Robert Kirk 41:57
2. Brian Smith 42:06
3. Lawrence Moore 42:30
4. David Mellard 42:39
5. John Moore 44:14

Female 50 - Over
1. Betty Sawyer 57:11
2. Wyndall Henderson 63:37
3. Shirley Schade 68:07
4. Sally Kirk 71:03

Male 60 - Over
1. Tom Baskett 47:18
2. Carl Jenkins 48:30

This awards list, except for the Dewey Wise Award, was included in the official race results which were mailed to all finishers.

Climbing the second span of the Grace Bridge. News and Courier photo by Stephanie Harvin

Chapter 4

1981
Marc Embler The First Local Overall Winner

The fourth Bridge Run was held March 28, 1981. It was again about 60 degrees for the 9 a.m. start and very windy. For the first time, runners enjoyed a tailwind going up the bridge. The course and entry fee were unchanged from 1980. Marc Embler, who had just moved to the Charleston area two weeks before the race to accept a coaching position at Baptist College (now Charleston Southern University) while completing his master's degree at the University of South Carolina in Columbia, and Bicky Timms from Anderson, S.C., battled all the way over the bridge. Marc took the lead and pulled away slowly to win 30:54 to 31:19. Marc is the only local resident to ever win the overall male title. Kevin McDonald was third in 31:38.

"I wanted to win. I thought this might be the year," Marc told the *News and Courier*, which pointed out he had finished fourth the previous year. A picture in the *Moultrie News* shows Embler and Timms at the 3-mile mark, with the pack in the distance.

"Once everybody got to the foot of the bridge, they slowed down and we kept the same pace," Marc told the *News and Courier*. "The two hills made it kind of tough. Me and Bicky just ran together and tried to pace ourselves. We didn't really surge."

Marc began to pull away at the end of the bridge. "I didn't want to make a move until the last mile," he said, "but Bicky slipped a little. I made my move then."

Timms said. "I was running as hard as I could. He (Embler) is always tough. I really went out to run my own race, but I figured if I could keep him within seeing distance and he got tired, I would still be within striking distance." But Embler never faded, and Timms had to settle for a personal best time and second place.

Kiki Sweigart of Darien, Conn., rated one of the country's top 10 marathoners that year, ran away from the women's field, setting a course record 35:10 which stood until 1984. She was pleased with her race as she had been suffering from sciatica. "I was happy just to be able to run and not have pain," she said. "I felt very good until about 4 miles, then I got tired. The leg didn't bother me. I had a real good run across the bridge. I was a little skeptical of what I'd do on the hills, but I had a good run." Michelle Moore of Atlanta, Ga., caught Sallie Driggers of Hanahan, S.C., going down the second span of the bridge and pulled slowly away to take second 38:36 to 38:52.

The top Masters were Ed Ledford of Charleston, 36:36, E. Crum, 37:25, Bernie Sher, 37:54. Female Masters winners were Suzanne Foster, 44:49, and Pat Rhode, 45:54, both from Walterboro and Barbara Rolfs, 47:35, from Charleston. Carl Jenkins Sr., 65, from North Charleston, won the Dewey Wise Trophy for the oldest runner who runs a time faster than his age.

There were 1,650 entrants and the results showing runners' first initial and last name, list 1,338 official finishers: 1,046 male and 292 female. A total of 138 runners finished under the 40-minute barrier, 135 male, three female, and 697 males and 67 females ran faster than 50 minutes. There were a total of 1,211 runners who completed the race in less than an hour, which means 90 percent; a record which appears unlikely to be broken. The Sunday *News and Courier* listed overall winners only first place in each age division.

The race used the same course as in 1980. It started at Patriots Point, came out to Coleman Boulevard (again with the bottleneck coming out of the parking lot), crossed over the old Grace Memorial Bridge, headed down East Bay Street towards town, then cut across Queen Street to Logan, up Coming Street to finish at George Street beside the College of Charleston.

Other Voices
Interview With Marc Embler, 1981 Winner
Telephone interview with Cedric Jaggers on July 23, 2010

CJ - The results of the first Bridge Run in 1978, which have last name only, show an Embler finishing fifth in 33:04 and another Embler eleventh in 33:54. Was one of them you and the other your brother?

Marc - I was fifth. I'm sure the other one was my older brother Mical.

CJ - There are a couple of conflicting bits of information about where you were living when you won the 1981 Bridge Run. One said you were attending Baptist College (now Charleston Southern), and the other said you were living in Columbia going to the University of South Carolina.

Marc - I had moved to Charleston a few weeks before the race and was living here (in Charleston) and commuting to USC to finish my graduate degree. I had gotten a job as a coach at Baptist College to start in the fall.

CJ - So you had finished fifth in the first Bridge Run in 33:04, didn't run the second Bridge Run, and then finished fourth in the third Bridge Run in 1980 in 32:18. Did you expect to win the 1981 Bridge Run?

Marc - Yeah, I did. I say expect, I kind of looked around at the field - 1980 and 1981 were kind of my breakthrough years. I had run three times under 30 minutes. The Thursday before the race I had gone to the track and done a workout: 800 meters four times in 2:10, then a 440 in 80 seconds. A total track workout of 2 miles in 9:07. Race morning, I looked around and saw the competition. I felt I should win IF I ran up to my capability.

CJ - Do you remember your first mile split in the 1981 race?

Marc - My split? I have no idea. I only remember the first mile split from one race, the Governor's Cup 5 mile in ?? (year). There were three of us running together and they were really hammering each other and I stayed with them. It was 4:16 and I said to myself, "OH NO!" and I didn't have a good race the rest of the way. They did OK, but I didn't.

CJ - Were you ever challenged during the '81 Bridge Run?

Marc - Yeah by Bicky Timms. I knew him and we were friends, we had a good running rivalry. I remember thinking we were together near the top of the Bridge. I said to myself, right before we get to the top, I'm going to go. I did and put a gap on him. I had enough that he wasn't going to catch me, but it wasn't a cakewalk.

CJ - How did you feel about winning?

Marc - After any win you feel great, and I felt great about it. I don't think I felt the magnitude of winning the Bridge Run until afterwards when I went to a party at Terry Hamlin's that evening and everybody was going on about it.

Years afterward it seems even bigger. After all the races I ran and won all over the South, I was doing the *Racing South* Grand Prix, the Bridge Run is the one people recognize and it is my claim to fame. To win a race like the Bridge Run was really good.

CJ - Were you satisfied with your time?

Marc - Yeah, I think that's a good way to put it. Satisfied. I was hoping to get a little closer to 30 minutes. But once I got the lead, I was racing to try to protect the lead and that was more important than the time. So I was satisfied with the time because I won.

CJ - What did you get for winning?

Marc - A trophy, which I don't know where it is. The "floating trophy" for the winners. So I don't have anything to show for it. When people ask me what I got I say a trophy. They didn't have prize money back then.

CJ - I recall you finished second the next year, 1982 behind the 'Unknown Officer' as the *News and Courier* described him? Did you think you might win the Bridge Run again?

Marc - You've brought up a devastating memory in my racing career. In 1982 I knew I was going to win. I was fit and more than confident. I looked around at the starting line and didn't see anybody I thought could beat me. The race started and a crewcut guy took off. If you remember then, nobody but Citadel cadets had crewcuts, so I figured he was a cadet and he'd be back to me after the first mile. After two miles I said to myself, "Let's go get him." The whole race I tried to reel him in. I made gains but I couldn't get him, he had too much of a lead. If I had known I would have gone out with him.

Would I have won? Yeah, probably. I'd have had a good shot at it because of the shape I was in, but I had started out too conservatively.

I was really depressed because at that point I knew how important the Bridge Run was. My parents were waiting at the finish line and this guy comes up first, and they are saying, "Something is wrong." Twenty or thirty seconds later I came in. I still hear about it.

Until about four and a half miles in the race I still thought he would crack. I thought he would come back to me, but he didn't. I learned a lesson that day.

CJ - Do you know how many Bridge Runs you have run? Or is it easier to say which ones you did not run (and why)?

Marc - I've run about all of them except 1979. I couldn't run due to coaching track. Then I ran every one until my son was playing baseball and was inducted. I've missed four or five total, probably including 1993 or 1995. I've never missed one due to an injury.

CJ - Do you have a favorite Bridge Run besides the one you won?

Marc - There's always the last one. This past year was fun. You win them at the bottom of the bridge. I had told Rives Poe she would never beat me. So I'm coming down the bridge and I see her about 300 yards ahead of me. I was hauling it and I caught her at the bottom, turned around and ran backwards and yelled out at her, "You'll never beat me." Some guy heard me and looked at me like I was crazy and I had to explain what was going on. Then I ran with Rives for about a mile or so, then ran off and left her. (Note: In the 2010 race, Rives ran a Personal Best 37:04 to take the female division of the Marcus Newberry Award, Marc ran 36:49 to take 3rd in the 50-54 age division. CJ) She may beat me someday when I get older, since she's 20 years younger, but not yet. I wasn't toying with her, I had to work hard to beat her.

CJ - What is your 10k PR and where and when did you run it?

Marc - 29:38 at the Hilton Head Hyatt 10k.

CJ - You were inducted into the Cooper River Bridge Run Hall of Fame in 2006. How did you feel about that?

Marc - It was certainly a great honor, humbling. I look at other people in it and look at myself and feel unworthy.

CJ - Do you plan to continue running the Bridge Run, and if yes, do you have any goals for it (such as winning Grand Masters etc.)?

Marc - I will always run the Bridge Run as long as I'm physically able. My mother did it this year at age 80. There are two races I'll always do: the Bridge Run and Turkey Day (in Charleston). I had a goal to always break 40 on the Bridge Run and a couple of years ago I didn't do it so that goal is gone. As you get older your goals change. About the Bridge Run I feel like "Been there done that, can't do better." I did a 50-mile endurance run recently and want to get into endurance running and do the 100 Mile Western States run.

I don't have specific goals for the Bridge Run. I set my Bridge Run time goals two months before the race and decide what I'm trying for. I always want to break 40.

CJ - Anything you would like to add?

Marc - It's amazing how the race has turned into the event it has. Not too many

Competitors make their way across the bridge to Charleston.
News and Courier photo by Stephanie Harvin

South Carolinians or Americans can say, "I'm going to go there and win that race." It's really an event. I'm glad I can still be there.

Fourth Bridge Run A Success

Originally appeared in the May-June 1981 issue of *The Lowcountry Runner (No author listed)*

This year's event had organizational problems. The club's participation in this event was uncertain until the last few weeks before the race. A disproportionately small group of club members worked extremely hard to stage as good a race as possible in the brief time available.

It is usually unwise to attempt to rank the contributions of individuals, but Nancy Turner probably warrants the number one slot, with Rob Johnson a close second. They worked long hours and drove many miles for the Bridge Run. The following were also key helpers: Sam Query, T-shirts; Beth Bennett, finish; Harry Holden, fluids; Dave Mellard, split times; Tom Baskett, trophies; Walter Pringle, course marking and measuring; Joe Hurst, cups. Some of the above had as many as 10 club members working for them.

Both female and male records were broken this year, Kiki Sweigart 35:10 and Marc Embler 30:54. The following wind over the bridge also proved advantageous to most runners. Carl Jenkins won the third largest trophy; the Dewey Wise Award, for oldest finisher. Carl's time, 44:17; his age: 65.

Times in general were much faster this year. The running potential of our young people was apparent in the finish of 15-year-old C. Copeland. Tom Cronan of The Citadel got together a team of 45 people to attempt to gain complete control of the male finish line. Maximum density of about 90 finishers per second was reached about the 52:00 mark. The chutes were unable to absorb the mass, and congestion resulted. The finish line organization was able to post "Chronomix" times at once, and were able to call the 63 age group winners from that melee without an error. Results were mailed to all entrants.

1981 Awards

Note the overall winners were included in the Age Groups

Overall Male
1. Marc Embler .... Charleston, SC 30:54
2. Bicky Timms .... Anderson, SC 31:09
3. Kevin McDonald .... hometown? 31:38

Overall Female
1. Kiki Sweigart .... Darien, CT 35:10
2. Michelle Moore .... Atlanta, GA 38:26
3. Sallie Driggers .... Hanahan, SC 38:52

Masters Male
1. Ed Ledford .... Charleston, SC 36:36
2. E. Crum .... hometown ? 37:25
3. Bernie Sher .... hometown ? 37:54

Masters Female
1. Suzanne Foster .... Walterboro, SC 44:49
2. Pat Rhode .... Walterboro, SC 45:54
3. Barbara Rolfs .... Charleston, SC 47:35

Special award:
Dewey Wise Trophy for oldest finisher who runs a time faster than his or her age:
Carl Jenkins, 65 .... N. Charleston, SC 44:15

Age Groups

Note the different age groups and depth of awards based on the number of entrants for males and females.
(Note - Results show only the last name and first initial, I have added first names only when I am fairly sure of them)

12 & under Male
1. B. Martin 43:43
2. G. Sproule 44:00
3. M. Purcell 45:58

12 & under Female
1. M. Jacobi 50:16
2. S. Martin 56:23
3. H. Maher 56:26

13 - 15 Male
1. C. Copeland 35:19
2. C. Davis 36:31
3. B. Slotkin 38:33
4. J. Horry 39:13

13- 15 Female
1. Kathy Hart 44:04
2. F. Chase 48:17
3. J. Head 49:20
4. K. Purcell 49:24

16-18 Male
1. J. Madden 35:51
2. Paul Laymon 36:01
3. B. Blalock 37:06
4. B. Miller 37:46
5. Mical Embler 37:53
6. Edward Moore 38:06

16-19 Female
1. Michelle Moore 38:26
2. A. Goode 42:50
3. A. Jones 43:13
4. R. Morris 44:37

19-22 Male
1. Bicky Timms 31:29
2. E. Pennebaker 32:35
3. M. Shier 33:04
4. R. Folts 34:31
5. M. Reay 34:38
6. D. Shelly 34:57
7. R. Daniels 35:09
8. S. Shiers 35:18

23-26 Male
1. Marc Embler 30:54
2. Bill Marable 32:25
3. J. Debs 32:48
4. R. Thompson 33:21
5. Chuck Magera 33:47
6. S. Juteler 34:10
7. M. Tyner 34:20
8. David Bourgeois 35:13

20-29 Female
1. Kiki Sweigart 35:10
2. Marty Long 40:26
3. S.J. Riser 41:07
4. M.B. Van Pelt 43:21
5. N. Osborne 43:37
6. C.C. Turner 44:53

27-29 Male
1. R. Dalton 32:19
2. D. Brown 32:28
3. D. Bayne 33:01
4. Lou Rice 34:13
5. Tommy Bolus 34:49
6. Terry Hamlin 35:41
7. L. Gammons 35:42
8. V. Englebert 36:22

30-34 Male
1. K. McDonald 31:38
2. K. Layne 32:32
3. P. Rogers 32:45
4. Bob Schlau 33:07
5. Robert Priest 34:00
6. Bruce Tate 35:05

30-39 Female
1. Sallie Driggers 38:52
2. Anne Boone Reed 41:41
3. Gail Bailey 42:02
4. Barbara Moore 43:39
5. Mary Thompson 43:58
6. N.L Ayers 48:59

35-39 Male
1. D. McCann 34:44
2. Dupree Elvington 36:38
3. H. Grubbs 36:40
4. S. Gary 37:44
5. D. Giorgio 37:52
6. Chuck Greer 38:02

40-44 Male
1. Ed Ledford 36:36
2. Bernie Sher 37:54
3. Larry Millhouse 38:16
4. H. Schwartz 39:20
5. Don Austell 39:31
6. J. Reavis 40:11

40-49 Female
1. Suzanne Foster 44:49
2. Pat Rhode 45:54
3. Barbara Rolfs 47:35
4. C. Johnson 49:10

45-49 Male
1. E. Crum 37:25
2. J. Gilmore 38:15
3. Ken Kurts 38:30
4. Bob Walton 39:22

50-59 Male
1. Avery Goode Sr. 40:04
2. Charles Moore 40:06
3. Robert Kirk 41:22
4. David Mellard 41:35

50 & Over Female
1. Garthedon Embler 50:13
2. Margaret Wright 53:19

60 & Over Male
1. M. Hanagriff 42:58
2. Carl Jenkins 44:15

This age group awards list was included with the official race results which were mailed to all finishers.

Runners sprint for the finish line.
News and Courier photo by Wade Spees

Chapter 5
1982
An Unexpected Winner

It was a crisp 45 degrees with a strong headwind waiting for the runners as they headed up the bridge for the fifth Bridge Run. It started at 9 a.m. on March 27, 1982. The course was the same as the previous year. It started in Mount Pleasant at Patriots Point, came out to Coleman Boulevard, once again there was a bottleneck as runners came out of the parking lot. They crossed the old Grace Memorial Bridge, headed down East Bay Street towards town, then cut across Queen Street to Logan, up Coming Street to finish at George Street beside the College of Charleston.

The Sunday *News and Courier*'s headline said, " 'Unknown' Officer King of the Span." Mark Donahue, a U.S. Navy officer from Fairfax, Va., on six weeks temporary duty in Charleston, surprised everyone when he took the lead early and increased it going over the bridge. He pulled away on the downhills and was never challenged, winning in 30:28. Defending champion Marc Embler of Charleston was second in 31:12. "I'd say I was 20 seconds behind when we got off the bridge," Embler said. "He really moved out on the downhills."

Donahue told the *News and Courier*, "I guess nobody in Charleston knew about me. I didn't know myself how I would compare to others, but I was ready for a good run." Robbie Devlin of Summerville, S.C., was third in 32:09 with Ken Wilson of Manning, S.C., fourth in 32:26 and Michael Reed of Charleston fifth in 32:59.

In the women's division, Sallie Driggers of Hanahan, S.C., went to the front quickly and won easily in 37:21. She continued her streak of having won every race she entered in 1982. "I certainly felt the pressure from all the media coverage," she told the *News and Courier*. "I knew what I could do, but I was worried about that Miss X (unknown runner) showing up and beating me. I was told I was ahead of the next female by 45 seconds after we got off the bridge. I really pushed the last two miles. I don't care if those are males or females ahead of me, I want to pass people until the very end." Jane Lesesne from North Carolina was second in 38:53 while Anne Boone Reed of Charleston ran her best Bridge Run to take third in 38:59. Gail Bailey of Sullivan's Island was fourth in 39:43 while Eileen McGrath of Charleston was fifth in 39:59.

The top Masters were Ed Ledford of Charleston in 36:05, Clebe McClary of Florence, S.C., second in 37:11 and Steve Comer of Charleston third in 37:39. Peggy Ledford of Charleston was female Masters winner in 42:46 with Lynn Hopkins of Charleston second in 47:17 and J. Blair third in 47:21. Edward Lancaster, 70, of Lumber City, Ga., finished in 53:05 to win the Dewey Wise Trophy.

Guest speaker at the free pre-race symposium was author Dr. George Sheehan. The race entry form called him "probably the best known of the nation's running gurus." In the race, he ran under 40 minutes (39:10 for 105th place overall) and was so pleased that he wrote about it in *Runners World* magazine, giving the Bridge Run its first major national publicity. In the article he referred to the woman whom he battled virtually the entire race and gave her credit for helping him break the 40-minute barrier for the first time in years. The woman was well-known Charleston area runner Anne Reed Boone, who had finished as the third place woman in her personal best time of 38:59.

Dr. Brian Smith was race director. Race entry fee was raised to $5 with T-shirt, $2 without. There were 2,100 entrants and the complete results showed 1,734 official finishers, 1,348 male and 386 female. The 40-minute time barrier was broken by 146 runners, five of them female. For the first time over a thousand runners, 1,007, finished the race in less than 50 minutes, a record 58 percent. A total of 1,525 crossed the finish in less than an hour. The Sunday *News and Courier* listed the top five males' and top five females' names, hometowns and times, and first place winner in each age division.

Other Voices
Interview with Dr. Brian Smith, 1982 Race Director

By Cedric Jaggers

CJ - You were race director for the second through fifth Bridge Runs. Did you run the first Bridge Run?

Brian - I was race director for only one: 1982 since it was a rotating position and it was my turn as the Executive Committee Chairperson.

CJ - So who was the race director for 1979, 1980 and 1981 races?

Brian - I'm hazy but we were poorly structured as a committee. Marc organized all the meetings at his office and presided and the chores were allocated to those who volunteered. I suppose we considered him race director for 1979 and 1980. Either in 1980 or 1981, my wife, Mildred, Marc, his secretary, Georgette Hollroyd, and I worked in Marc's office stuffing envelopes with shirts, pins, numbers, etc. most of Saturday night. At 2 a.m. Mildred and I had to leave, but I believe Marc and Georgette worked through the night. After that, the committee began to meet at restaurants but still in rather an unstructured way and I can't recall if or who were the definite race directors.

CJ - If yes, how did you do?

Brian - Yes - It was a short course since the finish line was moved during the race and I ran just over 40 minutes.

CJ - You were probably more involved in helping put on the first Bridge Run than a lot of people know. How deep was your involvement - will you tell us about it and tell us what all you did?

Brian - Marc Newberry or I came up with the idea of having a scientific symposium on the Saturday before the race. He gave me a free hand and provided academic funds for travel, honoraria, etc. I invited the most reputable exercise physiologists and the like but chose the keynote speaker, Ted Corbitt. He is a black native South Carolinian who represented the USA in the marathon at the Helsinki Olympics 1952. He was our house guest for three days and we spoke at great length. He was a raw food vegan who brought much of his own food with him. He was also the founder of the movement to measure race courses in the USA with the greatest available accuracy - which got me hooked.

CJ - You hand wrote the race results in 1979. How did you decide to do that and how long did it take you to do it?

Brian - Early transmission of complete results to all participants was my priority - once I got my hands on the chute cards it didn't take long, and Marc provided funds to mail them.

CJ - The race had to move from the one lane on the Silas Pearman Bridge to the two lanes of the Grace Memorial Bridge. A lot of readers may not know how close the race came to being cancelled when the DOT said the race could not happen after the third race. Dewey Wise had to sponsor legislation to allow use of the "new" bridge. How involved in this were you?

Brian - My involvement was only a few phone calls to Dewey Wise to try to impress him with the potential of the Bridge Run. And to tell him how events like the Boston Marathon were soon accepted by residents, politicians and the business community.

CJ - Some runners might be surprised to know that you ran the Bridge Run when you were the race director. How many Bridge Runs have you run?

Brian - I ran 1978 - 1985 and about four events after that with poorly trained family members with time around 60 minutes.

CJ - What is your best Bridge Run time?

Brian - 1978 on the short course; just over 40 minutes, but a think I ran a few of the early ones in under 42 minutes.

CJ - You were well known for running barefooted. Did your run the Bridge Run barefooted?

Brian - No. I ran the Island Marathon barefooted on the Isle of Palms, but my feet gave out on the fourth lap (Note - it was a 4 loop course on the street. CJ) and I finished in 4:05. When I was running with 5-ounce shoes I ran around 4:15.

CJ - Do you have a favorite Bridge Run of the ones you directed?

Brian - I only directed 1982 and that one had chute back up and other problems.

CJ - Do you have a favorite of the ones you didn't direct?

Brian - The 1986 race because the results were good and I provided performance indices for all the runners (see the first page of the results for an explanation) (Note: I looked at the original paper results and here is the explanation exactly as it appeared - 'A Performance Index, on a scale of 1 to 1,000 has been calculated for each runner age 14 or older. This yields a crude measure of aerobic ability regardless of age or sex. A P.I. of 500 for a man age 43 denotes that this man ran 50 percent as fast as the current 10km world record for men age 43. Similarly, a P.I. of 750 for a woman age 22 means that she ran 75 percent as fast as the current 10km world record for her age and sex. World records for the very young are not well established. Brian Smith.' CJ) I believed a performance index to be of great significance but only a minute percentage of other runners thought likewise.

CJ - You were always a big proponent of fairness in age groups, and very early into computerizing race results. Was it your idea to use the unusual one year age groups in the 1982 Bridge Run? If yes, how do you think that worked out?

Brian - Yes, I thought it a good idea, but it was not the norm and most active runners wanted the customary age groups.

CJ - After the fifth Bridge Run in 1982, newsletter editor Christine Randall quoted you in the *Low Country Runner* as saying it was the "Worst race I've ever been involved with." What did you mean, and is that why you decided not to be the race director again?

Brian - The finish line problems were what I was talking about. We had wrongly decided to keep using single chutes, despite some calls for going to multiple chutes. There was a huge stack up in the chutes including one understandable one caused by Dr. George Shcchan at the end of the line shaking everyone's hands and causing a terrible bottleneck and major crunch at the finish line. Ben Peeples and his team salvaged the situation by frantically recording finish times and race numbers. I was replaced as race director because it was a rotating position among Executive Committee members and I was no longer the Charleston Running Club committee member.

CJ - What do you think of the growth of the race, and how large do you think it can get or should get?

Brian - The race grew faster than I predicted. Modern hard and software can handle a race of almost any size and the event is a minor but important factor in prodding more to become active, lose weight etc.

CJ - You were inducted into the Cooper River Bridge Run Hall of Fame in 2003. How did you feel about that?

Brian - I'm not into honors as they are all too often unfair.

CJ - A lot of runners may not know that the code at the end of almost all the full USATF certification numbers for South Carolina i.e. SC09028BS stands for Brian Smith since you are the USATF official who checks the paperwork and then certifies and signs the certificate that courses have been accurately measured. How do you come into that position?

Brian - As I said earlier, I organized a scientific symposium on the Saturday before the 1978 Bridge Run and invited Ted Corbitt as the keynote speaker. He was the sole founder of the organization that formulated methods to measure courses with the greatest available accuracy. He was our house guest for three days. We spoke at great length and he readily convinced me of the importance of accurate courses. This led me to get involved in ensuring that courses are measured accurately.

CJ - Anything you would like to add or say about the Bridge Run?

Brian - I had a passion for the Bridge Run and don't regret the time spent. If you are interested in my opinion of Marc Newberry, I knew him well as medical school dean and race founder. He is an unusually capable man of great integrity - keeps his hand close to his vest and never pointed out blame when much might have been. He was on no ego trip and a champ at steering a majority into an agreeable consensus. After starting MUSC onto a climb from a 5th rate school to its present elevated position, he left to work at a less elevated position in North Carolina.

Interview: Sallie Driggers, 82 Female Winner
By Cedric Jaggers

CJ - Did you run the First Bridge Run? If not, which was the first one you ran?

Sallie - No, I didn't run the first one, I had just had a baby. My first Bridge Run was in 1980. I remember thinking, "I have no idea what I'm doing." But then, of course, you get hooked, and I wanted to get better, I got on a waiting list for Jim Fixx's book about running, and I bought some Brooks shoes.

CJ - When you ran your first Bridge Run did you think you would win it one day?

Sallie - Yes, but there was nothing printed at the time on how to do it. I had run track in high school and the longest distance girls were allowed to run was 440 yards, once around the track. Things were different back then. I remember watching a guy I was dating run the mile and thinking, "I can do that," so I asked the coach and was told the longest women can run is 440, they just aren't built to run long distances. So I said 'OK' and that was it.

I knew I was fast, I had a lot of energy, I was just getting going when the 440 would be over. I never won the 440. I just ran. Nobody told me it was a sport.

My first road race was the Epilepsy 5k in Charleston, I think in the spring of 1978. I got such a high, I wanted to figure out how to do this and win. So I wanted to win races, but had no knowledge of how to get fast. We just sat down back then and tried to figure out what to do. We learned that putting in the miles helped make you faster.

CJ - I recall you had run a 35:41 10k before the Bridge Run. Is that your 10k PR when and where was it?

Downhill after the second span of the Grace Bridge, one more overpass ahead, then flat land to the finish. News and Courier photo by Stephanie Harvin

Sallie - Yes. I have it as 35:44 at the Charleston Air Base 10k in January 1982.

CJ - Do you have a race that you feel was your best race ever at any distance?

Sallie - Best at any distance? My specialty was 10k so guess the Air Base race would be it. Also the Half Marathon at Savannah when I ran 1:18 was special.

CJ - In 1982 you were the female winner of the B.R. in 37:21, a minute and a half ahead of the next female. You had finished third in 1981. Going into the '82 race did you expect to win it?

Sallie - I knew what I could do with the amount of running I was doing: 90 miles a week running like crazy, but I had no idea how much the other women were running. I thought Michelle Moore, who had won the race before would be back and better, (Note: Michelle had run 41:40 to finish third in 1979, won the 1980 race in 41:29, and in 1981 finished second in 38:36 just 16 seconds ahead of Sallie. CJ) so I kept thinking of what I could do to prepare.

I trained on the bridge at 4 in the morning when there wasn't any traffic. During the race I had my husband, Larry, give me a split time when I came off the bridge because I had learned at other races that split times were often given at the wrong place.

Because of Rosie Ruiz cheating at the Boston Marathon, the Bridge Run had a bicyclist with a flag to stay with the lead male and female runner. The bicyclist kept getting in my way; he was in front of me and going too slow. I remember telling him, "You've got to get out of my way, go with me." I felt I could do more if I needed to. I didn't know where the other girl was. I wanted to win.

CJ - Do you remember your first mile split?

Sallie - No, I did 5 something. It didn't bother me to go out fast. We started at the *Yorktown* (Aircraft Carrier anchored in Patriots Point). Coming out on the access road to Coleman Boulevard I remember all the people lined up beside the road and a lot of them were runners who jumped into the race when we went by. They would try to keep up with us, and then drop off. There were twenty or thirty of them.

CJ - What else do you remember about the race?

Sallie - It was very cold that day. My husband, Larry, was taking care of our kids so my dad drove me to the *Yorktown*. I was warming up and stretching and my dad, who was a Golden Gloves boxer and knew something about competition, asked me if I felt I had prepared adequately. I remember telling him I feel like I could do this with two broken legs. I've prepared and prepared; if the gun doesn't go off I'll jump straight up.

CJ - Were you ever challenged during the race?

Sallie - No, not at that race. I was running against time. I didn't care about them, just about time.

CJ - How did you feel?

Sallie - I was so excited with the speed.

CJ - What did you receive for winning?

Sallie - A big trophy that was tremendous. Brian Smith handed it to me. The awards ceremony was at the cistern (at the College of Charleston).

After the awards ceremony my husband said, "OK, we have to go over and cut the yard at the beach house." They were giving out yogurt, but we had to leave and I didn't get any. I also got a certificate for a free pair of New Balance $100 shoes. I had never seen a pair of New Balance shoes and no shoes that ever cost $100. The certificate was a piece of paper to fill out and send in. We sent it in and when they were delivered I opened them and they were size 11. I said, "They've made a terrible mistake, I can't wear these." Larry reminded me I had plenty of running shoes since T&T Sports was sponsoring me and gave me shoes, so he had ordered his size.

I saw the Cooper River Bridge Run trophy in 1992. All the winners' names were supposed to be engraved on it. It was the year the Wellness Center was being completed. The race packets were being picked up in a large window room upstairs overlooking Courtney Street. When I asked several people where the trophy was, I was directed downstairs to the old part of the building. The trophy was in a glass cabinet. The cabinet was covered with dust from construction and the room was torn apart as the room was being relocated.

My name and 1982 were engraved on the side of the trophy. The updated years had not been added. When I was presented the trophy I was told it would be kept on the *Yorktown* at Patriots Point, for viewing. I don't know where the trophy is now, but I would like to know.

CJ - After your B.R. win you seemed to back off from racing for a while? Why?

Sallie - After the Bridge Run win I had to back off due to pain in my heels. It took about five years for the pain to subside. I got back into running when somebody asked me to help train them to break 40 in the Bridge Run. I thought I could do it without running, but then started doing some running.

CJ - In 2001 you ran 46:09 to win third place Grand Masters prize money. How did you feel about that?

Sallie - That was so neat. I took the money and used it to buy a dress for my daughters wedding; it was just the right amount. I got a very restful feeling just knowing I could still do it.

CJ - In 2002 you were inducted into the inaugural group of the Bridge Run Hall of Fame. How did you feel about that?

Sallie - I was so humbled. It was so kind. I felt so privileged. It was a nice feeling to fall back on. There was still that group of people who created and personalized it. Another part was that I got to eat lunch with the Kenyans and talk to them up close and personal. I learned they frequently run 17 miles, get a massage and later that day run another 17 miles; it's like a full time job. I said to myself I wouldn't want to do that. They ate everything and they were so proud of their Adidas tracksuits.

CJ - Do you plan to continue running the Bridge Run?

Sallie - I do. My son Jacob is now married and is a big triathlon runner. Growing up he always thought running was stupid, and we got up and went to races almost every Saturday morning. He said, "Why can't we stay home on Saturday and watch cartoons like a normal family?" In high school his goal was to beat me. In college, when he hadn't, he asked me about it. I told him he couldn't let me out of his sight if he wanted to beat me. At the Connector Run he and a friend did just that, they kept up, and then he outkicked me. Now he trains for and does triathlons. And now I enjoy running the Bridge to see people and run with my son. We enjoy the atmosphere and camaraderie.

CJ - Anything you would like to add?

Sallie - I'm sure you feel the same way I do: I'm so proud of the people who have taken the responsibility and created such a spectacular race for everybody. The selflessness of the people, and I don't know any of them anymore. It makes me want to do something to help, but I have five grandchildren and get up early every day just to get everything done.

How To Run The Bridge: Top Runners Speak Out

Originally appeared in the March-April 1982 Low Country Runner

Some of the area's best runners agreed to answer questions about the upcoming Bridge Run. They have won and placed well in too many races to list. Cedric Jaggers interviewed them separately: Gail Bailey, Sallie Driggers, Marc Embler, Chuck Magera, Anne Reed and Bob Schlau.

CJ - Is there a best way to run the Bridge Run?

Anne - Just run the bridge. Get used to the incline so it doesn't hurt you.

Bob - Try to do some running on the bridge three to five weeks before the race. Also, do a fair amount of speedwork.

Chuck - No special training. People should run the bridge once beforehand to see what it's like, but don't overtrain on it. Do some speedwork if you can.

Gail - Actually run the bridge and do some quality distance before the race.

Marc - Don't change anything. Try to train on the bridge or on the hills in the area. Especially try to get some hills in.

Sallie - Try to run more hills to build your legs.

CJ - Do you train in any special way for the Bridge Run?

Bob - I try to do some running on the Bridge and a fair amount of speedwork.

Chuck - I do speedwork, but I do that anyway.

Gail - Not in the past. This year I'm trying to do two days of speedwork, fartlek or intervals on the flats one day per week. One day a week I actually run the bridge and plan to do some quality distance. This is the first time I've really trained for a race.

Marc - I try to run the bridge once a week and do some running into the wind.

Sallie - I try to run more hills to build my leg muscles. Try to do quality mileage to get the most out of my training.

Anne - I try to run the bridge as much as possible.

CJ - With two or three weeks left before the run when this newsletter reaches most readers, is there anything you can do to get ready for it?

Chuck - Plan some runs into the wind, maybe some runs on the beach as the wind can be a factor on the bridge.

Gail - Don't be psychologically defeated by the bridge. It's not as hard as some people think. Run it two or three times before the race. You do recover after you make the hills. You can coast going downhill. If you wait till the day of the race you can panic.

Marc - Hopefully everybody has prepared before that, especially if they are going to run it for time. If they are going to race it: three weeks before, nothing special. Two weeks before it reduce mileage about 10 miles and do some faster work to sharpen. The week before, cut back mileage almost in half if you are really aiming for this race.

Sallie - Increase mileage somewhat. Build muscles in legs by swimming or lifting weights or bicycle riding without damaging yourself. What people do is increase mileage too much and hurt themselves.

Anne - Strengthen your quadriceps muscles. Do leg lifts using a small suitcase or purse suspended from your ankles. Run the bridge a couple of times. Run up and down stairs three weeks before the race.

Bob - Not any more than any other race. The first of the two weeks before, get more rest and some fast running. Make your easy days easier than normal. Speedwork, some mild fartlek is good. The last week before the race there is nothing you can do to improve your condition.

CJ - Do you try to run an even pace during the Bridge Run?

Gail - I've never run it smart. I hope to run it smart this year, hold back the first mile; use the same effort up the hills. I hope to run the second half faster than the first.

Sallie - I try to excel uphill and hold my own coming down.

Anne - No. I run a fast first mile, catch my breath before the incline, grind up the hills and go fast downhill.

Bob - I've tried different methods. If running for a good time, I try to run an even pace, but I expect the second mile to be the slowest because of the uphill.

Chuck - Not really. I run conservative but not slow the first mile, try to push uphill since I'm a better hill runner than a lot of people. Get position where I want to be coming off the bridge and hold it coming in to the finish.

CJ - Is there a best way to run the Bridge Run?

Marc - First mile don't push. Then push but don't strain on the bridge. Make a move coming off the bridge because it's so steep coming down that it almost feels uphill on the flats. Don't relax too much on the flats.

Sallie - Have a plan. Run the course with your mind before you run it with your feet. Think when to move to which side of which street. Read the pre-race instructions.

Bob - It depends on the wind. If there's a tailwind: lay behind people going out of the *Yorktown*. Don't hit the first mile too hard. If there is a headwind, stay behind someone until you get on Coleman Boulevard and run an even pace on the bridge by maintaining the same effort.

Chuck - Unless you're shooting for a time or place, just run it to have a good fun time.

Gail - Depends on the shape you are in. If tiptop, run your usual speed. If not in shape, don't go too hard.

CJ - Any special advice for first-time bridge runners?

Sallie - Enjoy it, have fun, don't get hurt. Enjoy the fellowship. Take all the advice you can after the race, ignore it before the race.

Anne - Try to relax. Don't worry about it and it won't be so bad. Don't stop.

Bob - Take it easy on the bridge itself. Don't try to charge going up or down as it can beat up your legs. Be cauious on the bridge then run hard the last three miles.

Chuck - Run a smart race. Be aware of conditions. If it is windy or hot, be aware of it and use your head. Don't kill yourself on the hills if you are not used to it. Be prepared to be sore the next day.

Gail - Be conservative the first mile, take the hill when you come to it. Don't panic.

Marc - The hills are in the first part of the race so be a little conservative during the first part of the race. On the down side of the bridge start picking it up.

CJ - Any advice for people who never run except for the Bridge Run?

Anne - When it begins to hurt bad, stop and walk, then run some more. Don't hurt yourself.

Bob - Take it extremely easy, walk the uphills of the bridge so you'll finish feeling good.

Gail - Take it slow and easy and enjoy yourself. Try to keep going but don't hurt yourself.

Marc - Don't do it. Set it as a goal for next year. If you do it anyway, walk a lot.

Sallie - Don't feel bad if you have to walk. If you need to walk the bridge it's okay. Everybody is a winner in the race just by finishing it, especially if they have a good time doing it.

CJ - What is your Bridge Run and 10k PR?

Anne - BR 40:41, 10k 39:53.

Bob - BR 32:50, 10k 31:48

Chuck - BR 33:40, 10k 30:50

Gail - BR 41:28, 10k 39:06

Marc - BR 30:54, 10k 29:38

Sallie - BR 38:52, 10k 35:41

CJ - What do you hope to run at the Bridge Run this year?

Anne - 39:50

Bob - 32:15 or 32:20 unless I run a marathon the week before. I'm considering running the Wilmington or DC marathons.

Chuck - Anything under 32:00.

Gail - About 39:00

Marc - 30:30, if the weather and wind are like last year.

Sallie - 35:45.

So what did they run? I looked their results up for this book. CJ- -

Anne Reed (Boone) - 38:59 PR, third overall female

Bob Schlau - 33:05, sixth overall finisher

Chuck Magera - not in results

Gail Bailey - 39:43, fourth overall female

Marc Embler - 32:12, second overall finisher

Sallie Driggers - 37:21, overall female winner

Looking Back At The Bridge

By Christine Randall, Originally appeared in the May-June 1982 Low Country Runner

The fifth annual Cooper River Bridge Run is history. Here's a look at it in a nutshell.

Saturday, March 27, dawned clear but chilly, as weeks, months and even years of effort by runners and race officials alike came to fruition. Excitement was high as the more than 2,000 runners gathered at Patriots Point to wait for the 9 a.m. start.

And then they were off. As usual, the eventual winners forged ahead. So did some less accomplished runners, only to find themselves falling by the wayside by the time they hit the bridge.

As always, spectators lined the course cheering from beginning to end and even offering a cup of water or two to those in need.

Despite race director Brian Smith's comment that this year's Bridge Run was the "worst race I've ever been involved with," most runners enjoyed themselves and were willing to overlook problems they came across.

As an added attraction, Dr. George Sheehan joined the field (and won his age group) after giving an informative and entertaining talk at The Citadel Friday night before the race.

Mark Donahue (30:28) and Sallie Driggers (37:21) were the top male and female finishers. Marc Embler, last year's winner, came in second at 31:12. Club members Anne Reed (38:59) and Gail Bailey (39:45) and Eileen McGrath (39:57) were the third, fourth and fifth place finishers.

Edward Lancaster, 70, from Georgia, won the Dewey Wise Trophy with a time of 53:05.

Saying Thanks

By Cedric Jaggers, Originally appeared in the May-June 1982 Low Country Runner

It's easy to criticize, much more difficult to praise or say thank you. I think it is time to say thanks to a lot of people who helped make the fifth Bridge Run as successful as it was. Yes, there were problems, but let's not dwell on them now.

First. A lot of people probably do not know how close the third Bridge Run came to being the final one. Last year, the Highway Department decided not to allow use of the bridge. It took an act of the state legislature to open the bridge for the run. One man was primarily responsible for pushing the legislation through which allows use of the bridge the last Saturday of each March. That man is state Senator Dewey Wise. If it weren't for him, there would have been no fifth (or fourth) Cooper River Bridge Run. Every bridge runner owes him a big thank you.

Second. Every race requires a race director. Some good races in this area have ended because no one was willing to put in the long, often thankless hours of work and headaches required. The larger the race, the worse the problems and the Bridge Run is a big race. Every bridge runner owes Brian Smith a word of thanks for being race director.

Third. Volunteers. I can't name them all but here are some key ones: Harry Holden, water stations; Georgette Holroyd, registration; Chris Cobb, female finish line judge; Richard Godsen, computer finish; the Charleston Amateur Radio Society for split times. Also the hundreds who helped with parking, age-group tables, stuffing race packets, monitors, giving out refreshments and fruit at the finish (for which a word of thanks to Piggly Wiggly) and finally to those who compile and mail out the race results.

To everyone involved and anyone I've neglected to mention: thank you all.

1982 Awards

Note the overall winners were included in the Age Groups which were an experiment in using 1 year age groups for the largest age divisions.

Overall Male
    Mark Donahue..............Fairfax, VA..............30:28
Overall Female
    Sallie Driggers..............Hanahan, SC..............37:21
Masters Male
    Ed Ledford................Charleston, SC..........36:05
Masters Female
    Peggy Ledford..............Charleston, SC..........42:46
Special award:
Dewey Wise Trophy for oldest finisher able to run a time of fewer minutes than his age:
    Edward Lancaster, 70........Lumber City, GA..........53:05

Age Groups

Note the different age groups and depth of awards based on the number of entrants for males and females. (Note - Results show only the last name and first initial, I have added first names only when I am fairly sure of them. CJ)

Male 8 & under
1 D. Hutsell.. 48:56
Male 9-10
1 S. Davis... 43:45
Male 11
1 F. Wiggins.. 42:49
Female 11 & under
1 K. Babka.. 63:47
Male 12
1 M. Martin... 40:54
Female 12-13
1 J. Dority.. 63:26
Male 13
1 J. Dennis.. 43:21
Male 14
1 B. Hagan.. 39:57
Female 14-16
1 K. Martin.. 44:18
Male 15
1 E. Mertins... 38:45
Male 16
1 C. Davis... 36:43
Male 17
1 J. Horry... 37:26
Female 17-19
1 M. Jacobs... 43:40
Male 18
1 Rob Devlin.. 32:09
Male 19
1 Paul Laymon.. 34:43
Male 20
1 M. Arant.. 38:32
Female 20-21
1 A. Littlehale.. 42:48
Male 21
1 M. Reed... 32:59
2 C. Hunter... 35:47
Male 22
1 Mark Donahue.. 30:28
2 M. Reay... 34:34

Female 22-23
1 M. Birk.. 40:48
Male 23
1 J Odell.. 33:52
2 D Bolus... 36:57
Male 24
1 Marc Embler.. 31:12
2 S. Lowery... 36:20
Female 24
1 G. Broderick.. 42:59
Male 25
1 M. Tyner.. 33:44
2 Mike Chodnicki... 34:35
3 David Bourgeois.. 35:44
Female 25
1 J. Craig... 42:42
Male 26
1 S. Jutzeler.. 35:14
2 A. Shoultz.. 37:25
3 D. Gaffney.. 37:44
Female 26
1 Jan Derrick... 44:03
Male 27
1 Bill Marable... 35:06
2 A. Marinelli... 35:25
3 R. Floyd.. 36:03
Female 27
1 K. Wagner.. 47:10
Male 28
1 K. Wilson... 32:36
2 J. Holzworth.. 35:45
3 R. Conrad... 37:32
Female 28
1 C. Almers... 40:50
Male 29
1 C. Gibson... 35:42
2 J Puckett.. 38:53
3 Gary Ricker... 39:11
Female 29
1 S. Fitzgerald.. 47:54
Male 30
1 R. Dalton... 33:26
2 Tommy Bolus... 34:52
3 Terry Hamlin... 36:01
Female 30
1 C. Nelson... 42:14
Male 31
1 D. Simpkins.. 37:05
2 D. Hoppmann... 38:19
3 R. Shirley... 38:33
Female 31
1 Sallie Driggers.. 37:21
Male 32
1 Bruce Tate.. 35:51
2 B. Thomas.. 36:58
3 Ray Baumil... 39:06
Female 32
1 C. Roberts.. 52:27
Male 33
1 T. Jones.. 35:02
2 R. Kale... 36:21
3 Steve Kiser... 36:32
Female 33
1 Eileen McGrath... 39:57

Male 34
1 Bob Schlau.. 33:05
2 J. Hadden... 37:18
3 Cedric Jaggers.. 37:52
Female 34
1 R. Wilson... 48:14
Male 35
1 Robert Jeter... 37:51
2 D. Player... 38:07
Female 35-36
1 Jane Lesesne.. 38:53
Male 36
1 J. Taylor.. 34:31
2 J. O'Neill... 36:44
Male 37
1 M. Hazzard... 40:21
2 H. Blair... 40:42
Female 37-39
1 Bettye Foster... 45:51
Male 38
1 N. Lesesne.. 34:54
2 D. McCann.. 35:30
Male 39
1 M. Owens... 36:17
2 Dupree Elvington... 36:38
Male 40
1 Clebe McClary.. 37:11
Female 40-44
1 Peggy Ledford.. 42:52
Male 41
1 Larry Millhouse... 40:03
Male 42-43
1 Don Austell... 37:48
Male 44-45
1 Ed Ledford.. 36:05
Female 45-49
1 Eileen Hallman... 48:52
Male 46-47
1 B. Jones.. 37:59
Male 48-49
1 Ken Kurts... 39:17
Male 50-54
1 H. Elkins.. 40:24
Female 50-59
1 A. Stanton.. 56:53
Male 55-59
1 David Mellard.. 41:56
Male 60 up
1 George Sheehan.. 39:10
Female 60 up
1 Margaret Wright.. 54:06

The Awards list in the official results included only first initial, last name and time in each division.

David Branch races to record time. News and Courier photo by Wade Spees

Chapter 6

1983

David Branch Takes Course Record Under 30 Minutes, Frank Shorter Misses Prediction

The sixth Bridge Run was held on March 26, 1983, and saw several changes. The starting time was moved to 8:30 a.m. and entry fee was raised to $7 with T-shirt, $3 without. The course added a third major upgrade, the Crosstown Overpass. Roy Hills was the new race director. The T-shirt design and color were changed for the first time, disappointing many traditionalists who had wanted the original design retained and only the color changed. The race began at Patriots Point in Mount Pleasant, came onto Coleman Boulevard, went across the old two-span Grace Memorial Bridge, then over the Crosstown Overpass, down King Street, crossed at Queen Street and up Meeting Street to finish in front of the Federal Building next to Marion Square.

It was almost 50 degrees when the race started, and runners had a crosswind on the bridge. David Branch of Traveler's Rest, S.C., and Mark Friedrich of Camden, S.C.,(now a resident of the Isle of Palms), became the first runners to ever break 30 minutes on any of the Bridge Run courses. Branch took the first mile in 4:25 and slowed only to 5:00 for the second mile going up the first span to hit 2 miles in 9:25 on his way to a course record 29:28. He told the *News and Courier* that winning the race was rewarding "because it's the biggest in-state race ever, and there's something quite appealing to running over a river." Friedrich became the second runner to break the 30-minute barrier, finishing second in 29:58. Marc Embler of Summerville, the 1981 winner, took third in 30:57. "With Branch in the race," he said, "it was over about after the first mile, for all practical purposes. When I lose to real good people and run a good time, I've got to be pleased."

Olympic marathon gold medalist Frank Shorter had predicted at his pre-race clinic that he would break 30 minutes. He was seeded first and wore race number 1; however, he never challenged the leaders and finished fifth in 31:10. "I took it relatively easy, because I'm just getting over an ankle injury from a month ago," he told the *News and Courier* after the race.

In the women's division, Mary Copeland, who had moved to Charleston from Baltimore the previous October, (and who later moved to Ohio) led the entire way. She had won five consecutive races since her move, and made the Bridge Run her sixth in a row. She never had a comfortable lead as Nancy Grayson of Columbia, S.C., stayed within 30 yards all the way. Mary was aware of her margin, based on crowd reaction. The crowd roared as each of the first two females passed. They finished first and second in 38:09 and 38:15, respectively. "It was hard because everyone was expecting me to win the race, and that's a scary position," Copeland told the newspaper. "It bothered me some a few days ago, but it's just something you have to deal with. By this morning I just felt like, 'Well, let's go out and run it and have a good time. This is going to be fun.'

"Usually, I judge who is behind me by how hard the feet fall and the pitch of the breathing, but on the bridge I couldn't tell. The last thing I wanted to do was look around and see. Luckily for me, the crowd cheers more for a woman because it is sort of an oddity. When I came off the ramp, everybody cheered for me, and then I heard the cheers for her a few seconds later, so I knew about how close she was.

"It sure felt good to win. The bridge race is such a big deal here. I didn't realize how great it felt to win until I crossed the finish line." She admitted she was a little disappointed with her time as she was hoping to run 37:20. "The pace just sort of slowed down by itself as I went along," she said. If I had been pushed, I could have run harder, but it felt hard enough to me."

Grayson told the newspaper, "From about the two-mile mark on, there was the same gap between us. Unfortunately, she was the one in front." Marty Long of Greenville, S.C., who lived in Summerville when she was female winner in 1979, ran a personal best time 38:58 and finished third.

The winning male and female Masters were repeats: Ed Ledford and Peggy Ledford both of Charleston in 36:43 and 41:44, respectively. Second place male Masters in 36:54 was Jim Adams of North Augusta, S.C., while Tom Woodward of the Isle of Palms was third in 36:55. Pat Rhode of Walterboro was second female Masters in 45:30 and L. Paxton was third in 46:27. The Dewey Wise Trophy went to Rudy Nimmons, 62, of Seneca, S.C., who ran 38:50.

There were 3,115 entrants and the results showed 2,585 official finishers, 2,052 male and 533 female which made this the largest race ever held in the Carolinas. Including the two runners under 30 there were 234 runners under 40 minutes, three of them female. There were 1,313 finishers under 50 minutes, which was the last time in race history that 50 percent or more of the finishers would accomplish that feat. There were 2,216 runners who managed to finish the race in less than an hour. The *News and Courier* listed the top 100 male and the top 25 female finishers and showed the winner of each age division. Roy Hills was race director for the 1983 race only.

Other Voices
David Branch, Winner, 1983 And 1984, First Two-Time Winner.
By Cedric Jaggers

CJ- When you won the Cooper River Bridge Run in 1983, you were the first person to ever break the 30-minute barrier in the race. What do you remember about the race and how did you feel about breaking that barrier?

David - The biggest thing I remember is that Frank Shorter was in the field. I was fortunate to have a good race. I remember being able to pull away. I felt very good about the race. To run against Shorter and win even though he was at the end of his career was great. There were also good regional class runners and I was glad to win it.

CJ- In 1984 you became the first runner to win two consecutive Bridge Runs. You were not favored before the race. Did being the underdog motivate you more or did you expect to win?

David - I thought I had a competitive chance. I knew Tom Wysocki had been brought in and he'd been successful on the West Coast. I decided to go out and run my race. He was coming on at the end, but I held him off. I was racing to win, happy to win, but if I didn't win it was going to be because I lost to a better person.

CJ- After the 1984 race you said you were getting ready for the Olympic Trials. Which events did you participate in?

David - The Olympic Trials marathon in Buffalo, N.Y. I hoped to break 2:20, but it wasn't in the cards. I was seeded 97th and finished 46th (in 2:22:36, CJ), so I managed to cut my seed in half. It was hot that day and I was glad to finish the race. Some of the other competitors had a chance in the 10k trials and they dropped out so they wouldn't ruin their chances there. I did the best I could, but that race was hot and only two or three runners had a personal best.

CJ- If I am correct, you never ran the Bridge Run again. Why?

David - I did run in '85. I struggled and didn't do well - finished back a ways. (Note, David finished 9th in 30:46. CJ)

CJ- What is your 10k PR and when and where did you run it?

David - 29:11 at the Reedy River Run in Greenville, S.C. I think it was '82 or '83.

CJ- What do you think is the best race you ever ran, and why?

David - It's hard to say but I think one of the best was the Kiawah Island 10 mile, the year it rained so hard. I ran 48:20 and that is still my best 10 mile. Also the Vulcan 10k Run in Birmingham, Ala., in '83 or '84. I won in 29:16 against a good and deep field. Those two stick out as two of the best. Any time I ran against Dave Geer was tough.

CJ- Now you are an associate dean at Old Dominion University in Norfolk, Va. Do you still run?

David - Yes, I run about 30 miles a week now, five days a week. I run short on three workdays and then longer on the weekend; about six miles on Saturday and eight and a half on Sunday. I just do it for sanity and to try to keep the weight down. I usually run at an 8- or 9-minute per mile pace.

CJ- Over the years have you kept up with the Bridge Run at all?

David - Yeah, occasionally I'd go online and see who won and what kind of times. Seems there's been a steady diet of Kenyans running 28 minutes.

CJ- You won the Bridge Run two of the three times you ran it. Benji Durden told me he might run it again when he is 60. Have you thought about running the Bridge Run again after all these years?

David - I'm pretty much set in the middle age shuffle. I haven't competed in so many years I wouldn't know what to do. But, never say never. I've wondered about this since I stopped competing. I ran as long as I could as well as I could but I can't see myself competing. My energy these days is directed toward my career.

Down the road, I might, looking to the end of my career, want to go and race some time. I'm not going to say I'll never compete again. A few years back I was invited, along with all the previous winners, to the 100th anniversary Jackson Day Race. It's the second oldest race in the U.S, next after the Boston Marathon, and they invited back all the winners they could get hold of. I ran it, and it wasn't pretty.

The '84 Bridge Run was one of my best experiences. I have good memories of the Cooper River Bridge Run and of Charleston.

CJ- Anything you would like add?

David - Just that I have fond memories. The hospitality always impressed. I always enjoyed competing at the races and loved the seafood and the Battery. Charleston is a great place. I have a lot of fond memories.

6th Cooper River Bridge Run 10K
By Art Liberman, Originally appeared in the May-June 1983 Low Country Runner

Over 3,100 runners, including Frank Shorter, participated in this year's Bridge Run, making it the largest road race ever held in South Carolina. The weather was perfect, a pleasant 40 degrees with winds out of the southeast, making the ascent up the bridge much easier. The addition to this year's course, the Crosstown Overpass, proved to be surprisingly difficult to climb for many participants. And the strong headwind on King Street did not make the second half of the race any easier.

This year's race was well organized, with a smooth start, ample aid stations, many course monitors and accurate split times. Much credit should go to Chuck Magera and his staff at the finish line, utilizing a new system, which kept this year's large field from backing up. Unfortunately, there were some minor computer problems, and as a result all club members' times were not listed.

Winning this year's Bridge Run was David Branch of Travelers Rest, S.C. Opening the race with a 4:25 first mile, Branch led the whole way and established a new course record with a time of 29:28. His only competition came from Camden's Mark Friedrich, who finished second in 29:58. Marc Embler followed in 30:57 for third place, while Columbia's Kevin McDonald's time of 31:04 was good enough for fourth place. Frank Shorter, coming off an ankle injury, had to settle for fifth place, clocking in at 31:10.

Mary Copeland's time of 38:09 was good enough to edge Columbia's Nancy Grayson, who was never more than 30 yards behind, and finished second in 38:15. The 1979 Bridge Run winner, Marty Long, took third place in 38:48, while Marilyn Davey's 40:25 earned her fourth place. Finishing fifth was Columbia's M. Edge in 40:53.

1983 Awards

Note the overall winners were included in the Age Groups.

Overall Male
David Branch .... Travelers Rest, SC 29:28
Overall Female
Mary Copeland .... Charleston, SC 38:09
Masters Male
Ed Ledford .... Charleston, SC 36:43
Masters Female
Peggy Ledford..................... Charleston, SC 41:44
Special award
Dewey Wise Trophy for oldest finisher who runs a time faster than his or her age:
Rudy Nimmons, 62................ Seneca, SC 38:50

Age Group Awards

Note the different age groups and depth of awards based on the number of entrants for males and females.
(Note - Results show only the last name and first and sometimes second initial. I have added first names only when I am fairly sure of them, most came from the *Low Country Runner* where members of the Charleston Running Club's names and times were listed. CJ)

Male 14 and under
1 John Seymour........................... 37:19
2 Chris Venesky 37:57
3 M. Martin............................. 38:22
4 J.B. Dennis 38:58
5 F. Wiggins 39:58
6 H.R. Griffith......................... 41:28
7 J.A. Babka 42:28
8 S.P. Davis 42:46
9 B.W. Mason 42:50

Female 14 and under
1 M.L. Gathings 46:15
2 A.S. Brennan 47:11

Male 15-19
1 Rob Devlin 31:33
2 R.L. Kendrick......................... 33:27
3 Mitchell Embler 33:41
4 J.K. Wilson 34:46
5 J.B. Thompson 34:59
6 B.S. Rapley........................... 35:28
7 C.C. Davis 36:26
8 D.P. Clayton 36:54
9 D.S. Walsh 37:03
10 R.W. Meilish 37:52
11 J.A. Dangerfield 37:52

Female 15-19
1 K.L. Martin........................... 40:59
2 R.R. Morris........................... 42:23
3 Kathy Hart 42:42
4 D.L. Socall 48:44
5 C.E. Myers 49:54
6 B.L. Irby 50:26

Male 20-24
1 K.J. Bowles 32:30
2 Paul Laymon 32:39
3 P.B. Stewart.......................... 33:04
4 M.S. Fronsoe 33:14
5 S.P. Cox 33:18
6 T. Lord 33:20
7 D.J. Dewar 33:49
8 J.J. Odell 34:00
9 D.R. Arant 34:16
9 F.J. McDowell 46:34
10 K.R. Cotner 35:06
11 R.A. Folts 35:17
12 T. Handal 35:19
13 L.N. Burpee 35:51
14 B.J. Kennedy 36:29
15 R.E. Baczkowski 36:57
16 Nick Cimorelli 37:38
17 K.A. McIntyre 37:41
18 B.A. Smith 37:51
19 T.G. Stagner 38:01
20 J.J. Dodds 38:09
21 R.N. Makhuli 38:27

Female 20-24
1 Mary Copeland 38:09
2 Marty Long 38:58
3 C.M. McSwain 41:49
4 J.F. Gunter 41:50
5 M.A. Moore 43:33
6 Z.B. Lucas 45:21
7 C.T. Griffin 45:21
8 A.A. Goode 46:31

Male 25-29
1 David Branch 29:28
2 Mark Friedrich 29:58
3 Marc Embler 30:57
4 K.J. Williams 31:28
5 K.W. Wilson 31:44
6 M.A. Tyner 33:15
7 Frank Lowry 33:34
8 J.H. Pittman 33:51
9 Bill Marable.......................... 33:53
10 Alan Shoultz 34:07
11 M.I. Lambert 34:43
12 T.J. Reagan 34:56
13 John Holzworth 34:56
14 D. Plaspohl 35:02
15 P.E. Smith 35:10
16 J.J. Dorociak 35:24
17 Roland Butch Cody 35:26
18 Mike Chodnicki 35:30
19 R.B. Floyd 35:35
20 S.N. Roark 35:49
21 T. Deming 35:55
22 Joe Eck 35:58
23 S.F. Jutzeler 36:04
24 Mark Spencer 36:10
25 R.A. Teague 36:16
26 R. Howitt 36:30
27 D.G. Brian 36:47
28 R. Josephs 36:48
29 J.L. Fann 37:05
30 D.M. Bourgeois........................ 37:14
31 A.D. Braswell......................... 37:17

Female 25-29
1 M. Edge 40:53
2 Sara Dorociak 40:54
3 K.G. Wagner 41:53
4 A.T. Weston 42:08
5 Jeanie Sink 42:43
6 J.M. Decamilla 42:45
7 Jean Craig 42:47
8 Janet Ballinger 42:50

9	B.A. Weller	42:52
10	Bonnie Poore	43:18
11	Ginger Gregory	44:01
12	Gail Pennington	44:06
13	S.S. Plaspohl	44:55
14	E.S. Pruems	45:11
15	T.A. Sligh	45:24
16	J.E. Buhcanan	45:59

Male 30-34
1	K.R. McDonald	31:04
2	L.W. Cook Jr	34:03
3	J.V. Carrouth	34:32
4	M.F. Phillips	34:37
5	Tom Bolus	34:56
6	Mario Salas	34:57
7	J.D. Cash	35:04
8	J.D. Benton	35:08
9	T.P. Jones	35:11
10	M.J. Gass	35:13
11	B.E. Crouse	35:43
12	Billy Davey	35:45
13	Terry Hamlin	35:48
14	W.A. West	36:17
15	Sam Derrick	36:20
16	A. Gonzales	36:21
17	J.L. Torres	36:35
18	Skip Hewitt	36:40
19	Charlie Post	36:41
20	V.A. Englert	36:47
21	Gary Ricker	36:49
22	S.D. Spencer	36:52
23	W.N. Derrick	36:56
24	Leon Locklear	36:58
25	D.E.L. Bergan	37:06
26	R.S. Cook	37:11
27	C.S. Graham	37:13
28	D. Ferguson	37:29
29	Steve Kiser	37:32
30	S.H. Hopper	37:37
31	R.P. Madill Jr	37:54
32	K.D. Olson	38:10
33	D.A. Nelson	38:49
34	D. Hoover	38:50

Female 30-34
1	Nancy Grayson	38:15
2	Marilyn Davey	40:25
3	R.L. Hoover	41:17
4	C.D. Nelson	41:22
5	Coleen Archambault	43:37
6	Carol Davis	43:53
7	B.M. Nalley	44:08
8	J.T. Cox	46:22
9	Didi Wilder	46:23

Male 35-39
1	Frank Shorter	31:18
2	W Jones	31:38
3	Bob Schlau	31:52
4	Robert Priest	33:19
5	J W Britton	33:49
6	L J Tonzi	35:21
7	J Oneill	35:34
8	D L Whybrew	36:07
9	R M Barnwell	36:09
10	W E Hogg	36:31
11	R A Lewis	36:45
12	D P McCann	37:00
13	D.L. Player	37:13
14	S.R. Figueroa	37:23
15	J.M. Madden	37:26
16	R.E. Enderle	37:34
17	R.L. Hudson	37:50
18	T.M. King	37:53
19	S.J. Davis	37:56
20	Cedric Jaggers	38:02
21	W.B. Keenan	38:21
22	R.D. Bibb	38:36
23	Chuck Greer	38:42
24	M.A. Lake	38:54
25	J.E. Pennington	39:01
26	Vernon Bennett	39:08
27	John Schreiber	39:15
28	W.D. Anderson	39:29

Female 35-39
1	Gail Bailey	41:48
2	Barbara Moore	45:09
3	M.S. Risher	45:44
4	R. Wilson	46:38
5	S.A. Doscher	46:50
6	Kathy Jaggers	47:24

Male 40-44
1	Jim Adams	36:54
2	Tom Woodward	36:55
3	Don Austell	37:21
4	W.J. Hollaway	37:28
5	M.W. Tanner	37:36
6	M.R. Owens	37:40
7	Dupree Elvington	37:48
8	John Dunkelberg	37:53
9	John Sneed	38:04
10	Clebe McClary	38:06
11	Gary Rolfs	38:12
12	Lenny Silverman	38:14
13	Barry Ledford	38:20
14	R.F. Bailey	39:01

Female 40-49
1	Peggy Ledford	41:44
2	Pat Rhode	45:30
3	L.R. Paxton	46:27
4	Lynn Hopkins	46:48

Male 45-49
1	Ed Ledford	36:43
2	S. Yarborough	37:45
3	Ken Kurts	37:52
4	B.P. Jones	38:25
5	J. Gilmore	39:20
6	R.L. Lewis	39:39
7	H.W. McCormick	40:11
8	C. Bauknight	40:11

Male 50-54
| 1 | Bob Walton | 38:51 |
| 2 | Lee Swofford | 39:42 |

Female 50 and over
| 1 | Garthedon Embler | 50:06 |
| 2 | Margaret Wright | 50:55 |

Male 55-59
| 1 | Lawrence Moore | 41:38 |
| 2 | J. Moore | 44:45 |

Male 60 and over
| 1 | Rudy Nimmons | 38:50 |
| 2 | David Mellard | 42:54 |

Reconstructed from the Official Results by Cedric Jaggers

Opposite:
Runners and walkers swarm across the Grace Bridge.
News and Courier photo by Bill Jordan

Runners make their way over the Grace Memorial Bridge. News and Courier photo by Wade Spees

Chapter 7

1984

David Branch Becomes First Two-Time Winner; Prize Money Added

The seventh Bridge Run was held on March 31, 1984. The entry fee remained at $7 with T-shirt, but the no T-shirt option was dropped. For the first time, the race had been named one of the top races in the country in *The Runner* magazine. It was scheduled to start at 8:30 a.m., but two 15-minute delays awaiting overloaded shuttle buses, set the actual start time back to 9 a.m. The weather cooperated with clear skies, low humidity and a temperature of 50 degrees.

For the first time the race did not start at Patriots Point as the increased number of runners had created dangerous congestion on the narrow access road. The race started at the Common (Shopping Mall) just across Shem Creek in Mount Pleasant. The course followed Coleman Boulevard across the old Grace Memorial Bridge, went over the Crosstown Overpass, down King Street across Market Street, then up Meeting Street to finish in front of the Federal Building. Mark Blatchford was the new race director.

For the first time, prize money was awarded. A total of $3,000 was paid: $1,500 to male and $1,500 to female winners. The prize money attracted some fast runners and if you believed the pre-race publicity then you knew that Mathew Motshawarateu or Tom Wysocki was sure to outrun the defending race champion David Branch and take the course record down into the high 28-minute range. Maybe Branch didn't read it or maybe he decided not to believe it or worry about it and he went to the front early with a 4:35 first mile. John Rogers from Raleigh, N.C., took the lead going up the first span, but Branch pulled even and at the 3-mile mark Branch took the lead again. He became the first person to successfully defend a Bridge Run title. Branch also broke his own course record to win in 29:25, establishing his second course record in as many years, one which stood for six years. Pre-race favorite Tom Wysocki from El Toro, Calif., who had run a 28:34 10k on the track and had already qualified for the Olympic trials, came on strong to take second in 29:32, with Rogers holding on for third in 29:45.

"I look forward to the bridge," Branch told the *News and Courier*. "I sure do. I consider the bridge to be an advantage for me. I have respect for the bridge, but I'm not intimidated by it. I don't think people gave me a chance. And there was the pressure of being the defending champion and going against a stacked field. Getting the lead on the bridge was the key. After that, I was in front and able to look over my shoulder. I felt good about being able to come back here and defend it. This is probably equally as important as any race I've won."

After the race he also said he knew he was being reeled in near the finish, but when he saw the finish line he got a new lease on life and hung on to win.

Wysocki said, "David really nailed me on the bridge. I let him get too big a lead there. I charged to catch up, but the finish line came too quickly."

Rogers added, "Wysocki was the class of the field, but he didn't run that well. Dave Branch was so strong and he really wanted to win."

The women's race was never close as Brenda Webb from Knoxville, Tenn., running her last road race before the Olympic Trials, set a course record 34:09. She started the race easily in the lead, running a 5:20 first mile, and was never challenged. "It was fun," Webb told the newspaper. "I thought I would have competition the first 2 miles and then I'd overtake them on the hills. But it was an easy race for me. I'm pleased I could run 34 minutes as easily as I did. When I got here, I got a little nervous about the bridge. Those hills are definitely a challenge since they come at the 2-, 3- and 4-mile marks."

Ruth Wysocki, who later in the year would gain fame in the Olympic Trials by upsetting Mary Decker, was second in 35:04. When asked about the upcoming Trials race against Decker she said, "I think at this point, I'm closer to her than the same time last year, but she's too fast. She's Number One in the world." She also commented on the course and the crowd, saying, "The course was real nice, and that makes it go much easier. And there were more people than I expected cheering along the way. I thought that helped." Nancy Grayson from Columbia, S.C., was third in 36:37.

The top Masters runners were Bill Voight, 35:48, Jim Adams of North Augusta, S.C., 35:57, and Jim Blackwell, 36:00. Nationally ranked Masters runner Cindy Dalrymple was female winner in 36:57. Charlestonians took second and third: Peggy Ledford in 43:12 and Joyce Ploeger in 46:54. The Dewey Wise trophy was awarded to Caldwell Nixon, 75, of Denver, N.C., who ran 60:22.

The pre-race clinic was conducted by author Dr. George Sheehan and Brenda Webb. It was free and open to the public.

For the first time there was live television coverage on Channel 4. It was unannounced and was breakaway from regular coverage to show short, live segments.

There were 4,460 entrants and the results showed 3,784 official finishers, 2,977 male and 807 female. There were four men under 30 minutes, 324 men and 15 women under 40 minutes, with 1,699 finishing under 50 minutes and a total of 2,746 finishing in less than an hour. The Sunday *News and Courier* listed the top 100 males and top 30 females and showed three deep in each group. The inaugural untimed Bridge Walk attracted a field estimated at 1,300 to 1,500 participants.

Other Voices
An Interview With New Bridge Run Director Mark Blatchford
Originally appeared in the March-April 1984 Low Country Runner By Cedric Jaggers

CJ - How did you get to be race director?

Mark - The Bridge Run executive committee members each year elect one person as chairperson. The chairperson is race director unless he or she delegates it to someone else. This year I'm chairperson and race director. My assistant race directors are Bob Priest of the Charleston Running Club and Karl Gueldner of Parks, Recreation & Tourist Committee.

CJ - How was the course selected and who selected it?

Mark - We changed the finish line in '83 and I recommended that we move the start this year from Patriots Point out to Coleman Boulevard to try to avoid the 23-second lag for the last runner to reach the starting line. We wanted the start near Moultrie School for parking purposes with the actual start near the Common. We wanted the course to go down King Street and across Market Street since that will one day be the central part of downtown with a pedestrian mall in that area. I think the third hill, the Crosstown Overpass, surprised a lot of people last year. I don't think there will be any course changes in the future.

CJ - By whom and how was the course measured?

Mark - Bob Priest used a calibrated bicycle. The paperwork for TAC sanction and certification has already been sent in.

CJ - How many runners do you expect this year?

Mark - We expect 4,000 based on growth in the past. We hope to have more spectators this year on King Street and at Marion Square.

CJ - Will you be mailing complete results?

Mark - Complete results will be compiled and mailed, we hope, within two weeks after the race. We plan to give complete results to the *News & Courier* (newspaper) the day of the race and hope they will print the complete results in their next day Sunday edition. We are buying a Colorado Timing Systems Race Clock with a countdown system and built in speakers. We plan to rent it to organizations for their races for $50. It will be available at no charge to the Running Club. This year there will be six separate chutes with a computer to time each chute and a master computer to integrate the results. Brian Smith is in charge of the computerized finish.

CJ - How did you select invited runners?

Mark - The committee got together and voted on the people we wanted. We called around looking for who was available, especially class female runners. Sue King was lined up originally, but her agent never returned her contract so we got Brenda Webb of Knoxville. She may not be as well known, but she has a better 10k time (Note: Her PR of 32:28 should put her among the top 20 finishers, CJ) We hope to attract more female runners this year.

CJ - How was it decided to pay prize money?

Mark - Sponsorship was so strong this year that we had enough money to consider doing it. We wanted to increase our depth of field and we thought the way to do it was to offer prize money?

CJ - Who designed the T-shirt logo?

Mark - We were not comfortable with last year's design. We wanted the Charleston skyline in the logo. The artist who did the actual new design was Lee Helmer.

CJ - What do you see in the future for the bridge run?

Mark - I don't know. We'll have to wait and see. We may have to set a number of entrants limitation someday. Or we may have the top 1,000 runners start 30 seconds ahead of the pack so the faster runners can get clear, rather than just say 5,000 entrants and no more. Since the purpose of the run is to promote health and fitness, we don't want to leave those slower people out. We are trying to hit both ends: elite and casual runners.

CJ - What is the worst thing about being bridge run race director?

Mark - Preparing for the finish line. That's a nightmare. I'm spending eight hours a day and have been for the past month. There are a lot of variables that have to be monitored, but the finish line is where problems can happen. We are using mostly city staff this year so we hope that will help. We've tried to arrange responsibility for the race so that Running Club members will be through with their responsibilities and free to run in the race. We are doing the finish line at the Great Kiawah Island 10 mile & 3 mile race for practice and to give our people a taste of what working a finish line is like.

CJ - What is the best thing about being brigde run race director?

Mark - Dealing with people. It is fun to make these contacts and deal with runners and sponsors. When you can sit back and know you've accomplished so much. The ultimate is to pull off the perfect race. The challenge. I feel I've got to do a tremendous job just to equal Roy Hill's job of last year. Trying to make the quality a little better each year.

CJ - Are you enjoying it?

Mark - I am. I've even been in the last two Sundays working to keep up with it. The key is not to get behind on something. I've got great support from the others on the executive committee. That is what makes a success - the support staff.

CJ - Would you do it again?

Mark - I'll tell you that after the race. If it is not successful, I'll say let somebody else do it next time. If it is successful, I'll be happy to do it again.

1984 Bridge Run Post Race Interviews by Chuck Magera

Chuck Magera videotaped the finish of the 1984 race. Then he conducted some post race interviews in Marion Square, before, during and after the awards ceremony. These interviews are transcribed here by Cedric Jaggers - with the noise level of the post race crowd and the age of the source material, I did the best I could and added official time and place from the race results. I appreciate Chuck letting me use them.

CM - Here I am with Jeff Stone, 2:48 marathoner. How was your race today?

Jeff - Great. I lost my concentration when Frank Lowry had the dry heaves. Couldn't see the guys out front. My splits were pretty good coming down the hill. They were really bad going up.

CM - How was the wind?

Jeff - Pretty good, pretty good. Not bad at all. (Results: 46th male overall, 34:37)

CM - Mario Salas - I want to get your impressions of the Bridge Run. What did you think?

Mario - It was grueling. It was hell. But we ran and we're glad. (Results: 105th male overall, 36:42)

CM - (To Marc Embler) You're on. What are your impressions of the race today?

Marc - (Laughing) I'll never do it again."

CM - What did you think of the times today?

Marc - Great.(6th overall, 30:42)

CM - (To Billy Wieters) What did you think of the race?

Billy - It's the first time I've ever broken 40. I'll take it. It was beautiful.

CM - How was the bridge?

Billy - The bridge was no sweat.

CM - What did you think of the new course?

Billy - I liked it a lot. (Results: 300th male overall, 39:49)

CM - Benita Brooks (Schlau) What did you think of the race?

Benita - I felt fantastic. Downhill was great, I love it. I must have passed 100 people.

CM - Was it a P.R. today?

Benita - Yes, a minute 30 off my best time. My best time was 39:58 and I ran 38:30. Results: 10th female overall, 38:30)

CM - To Bob Schlau What did you think of the race today?

Bob - I thought it was super.

CM - Tell me about your race; how did it go?

Bob - 30:44. 15:05 at 3 miles, 14:30 from 3 to 6.

CM - Strategy today?

Bob - To run faster than I ever have before.

CM - Did you see Marc (Embler)in the race?

Bob - Yeah, I was trying to run down Embler, about made it, but ran out of time.

CM - What did you think about (race winner) Branch today?

Bob - Now that I have contacts (contact lenses) I was able to watch the race and see what was going on.

CM - How was it up there?

Bob - It wasn't as fast as I thought they'd be.

CM - Do you think the wind was a factor today?

Bob - It was a help I think.(Results: 7th overall, 30:47)

CM - The running couple Ginger Gregory and Butch Cody. Can I get your impressions of the run today? You are on:

Butch - No. (Results 62nd male overall, 35:31)

Ginger - Yes. I ran. My race was 44:33. Bad. I didn't feel well for a whole week before today. (Results: 55th female overall, 44:36)

CM - To Gail Bailey How was your race today, your time?

Gail - Great. 39:17

CM - What did you think about the race today?

Gail - I thought it was a super race.

CM - What about the wind?

Gail - It was at my back, where it's supposed to be.

CM - What did you think of the women's race today overall?

Gail - Oh, I thought it was good. I think those top women didn't run as well as they thought they were going to.(Results: 12th female overall, 39:19)

CM - To Judy Melton Oh, the Greenville Track Club (she had on a GTC singlet). Judy, you're on. How did you do?

Judy - not real good 44:30.

CM - Was that not what you thought you'd do?

Judy - Yeah, considering.

CM - What did you think of the Bridge Run today?

Judy - It was the best race I have ever run. It was the most fantastic race I've ever run. Seeing all the people going up the bridge and all the different colored shirts and coming down the bridge.(Results: 57th female overall, 44:43)

CM - To Tanis Manseau Tell me about your race today.

Tanis - Well, it was breezy up on the bridge and I had a great time.

CM - What was your time?

Tanis - It was right at 38. I'll say 38:10, 38:15.

CM - Was that a good time for you?

Tanis - Not too bad. I enjoyed myself, had a good race and I look forward to doing it again next year.(Results: 180th male overall, 38:17)

CM - To Art Liberman How was your race today?

Art - Well, I was pretty happy. It was a good run, my time was 40:36.

CM - Is that good for you?

Women's winner Brenda Webb of Knoxville Tenn. pauses to reflect upon her victory.

News and Courier photo by Stephanie Harvin

Art - No, I ran 40:24 at a race at Hilton Head. I think the overall race today went well. Unfortunately I wasn't up with the leaders, so I couldn't see what they were doing.(Results: 388th male overall, 40:36)

CM - To Gene (no last name spoken), a Charleston Running Club member from Columbia. How was your race today?

Gene - Well, I didn't run the time I wanted to, but I really enjoyed it. This is a great race. I ran pretty good, but it's tough.

CM - How was the wind today?

Gene - I didn't really notice the wind, I didn't even think about the wind.

CM - George Getty, an Anderson Road Runner. George, how'd you do today?

George - Oh, I did good.

CM - What was your time today?

George - 35:16.

CM - Was that a good time for you? George - No.

CM - No? George - No. (Results: 55th male overall, 35:18)

CM - To Mike Chodnicki (who was standing next to George Getty). How about you Mr. Chodnicki?

Mike - Well, I was a little upset with the start, but it was all right and I ran a good time so I'm happy.

CM - What was your time? Mike - 34:20.

CM - Cool. That is a good time. That's what, your second best time ever?

Mike - third fastest.(Results: 41st overall male, 34:25)

CM - To Paul Laymon How'd you do today?

Paul - Well, it was a P.R. for me today.

CM - What was your time? **Paul** - 31, about 31:10.

CM - A good time. What place were you overall? **Paul** - 8th.

CM - Eighth. How was your race?

Paul - It was really good, right from the starting line. (Results: 8th overall, 31:15)

CM - To David Branch (race winner) (Note - I could not make out the question on the video).

David - I had to just go out hard and get it done.

CM - Your first mile? **David** - 4:35.

CM - (Inaudible question) **David** - Near the finish John Rogers was near, I looked back, saw him, saw the finish line and got a new lease on life, so to speak. It was a good effort. I'm pleased with it. There is no question, he was reeling me in.

CM - Plans?

David - To go to the Olympic Trials marathon and maybe the 10k trials. (Results: overall race winner, 29:25.)

Survey: Your Favorite Bridge Run?

By Art Liberman, Originally appeared in the March-April 1984 Low Country Runner

In this, its seventh year, the Cooper River Bridge Run has evolved into one of the Southeast's top races. In fact, those that seldom if ever race during the year are drawn to the Bridge Run. It's hard to believe that what was once a dream of MUSC's Dr. Marcus Newberry in 1977, attracting about 700 runners in its debut, could very well have over 4,000 participants in this year's field.

The Bridge, as it is affectionately referred to by local runners, has a unique appeal and attraction that brings runners back year after year. Just about every Charleston Running Club member has run the Bridge at least once, and posing the question "Which Bridge Run was your favorite and why?" conjures up many interesting race stories. Interviews were conducted in person for the most part, with the following club members. Next to each name are, in parentheses, the number of Bridge Runs participated in; the year that was the most memorable or favorite, and why. Only members who ran at least two Bridge Runs were considered for this survey.

Colleen Archambault (4) 1983 - best Bridge Run time; good weather; both psychologically and physically better prepared.

Jane Bennett (4) none - dislikes all Bridge Runs because they hurt.

Jerry Cavannagh (5) 1983 - best Bridge Run time; favorite course.

Barbara Davidson (3) 1983 - best Bridge Run time; favorite finish area at Marion Square.

Maurice Davidson (6) 1982 - favorite course, with its finish at the College of Charleston.

Mary Helen Gammon (4) 1980 - the special feeling of one's first Bridge Run; remembers the four runners wearing brown leotards dressed as a cockroach running fast in tandem.

Robin Harden (3) 1980 - The unique and thrilling feeling of her first Bridge Run.

Ken Kurts (3) 1982 - Sick all week prior to the race with the flu, Ken remembers his original plan to oversleep the start. But unable to do so, he showed up just minutes before the gun. He ran the race in his warmups and finished in a time slower than any other year. Ken won his age group, something he was never able to do at other races, although he ran faster those previous years. Ken comments: "You can't expect to win if you don't show up."

Barry Ledford (3) 1983 - set a 10k PR by about one and a half minutes.

Ed Ledford (6) 1982 - set a PR at the time; good weather. Favorite finish area at the College of Charleston.

Charlie Post (3) 1983 - while he was running very well at the time, Charlie remembers the Bridge Run he race walked "getting many funny looks."

Anne Boone Reed (4) 1982 - setting a PR in that race, proud of beating George Sheehan, who referred to Anne as "that girl" in an article he wrote.

Barbara Rolfs (4) 1983 - credits her best Bridge Run time to running with Barbara Davidson.

Gary Rolfs (5) 1978 - In just his second race and first 10k, Gary ran the Bridge Run in about 39:00 wearing high top basketball shoes.

Bob Schlau (6) 1983 - best Bridge Run time - 31:50, good race organization, good entry field, enjoyed meeting Frank Shorter.

Lenny Silverman (6) 1978 - favorite finish area at The Battery, was inspired by the special presentation to blind runner George Hallman of Columbia at the awards ceremony.

Anne Sneed (2) 1983 - Best Bridge Run time as a result of being better prepared.

Brian Smith (5) 1978 - The novelty of the first Bridge Run.

Billy Wieters (4) 1983 - set a PR as a result of training well, the bus ride to Patriots Point, the King Street section of the course.

Margaret Wright (4) 1983 - the finish area at Marion Square, as all previous finishes were too congested.

My First Bridge Run - Trish Hale

Originally appeared in the May-June 1984 Low Country Runner

This was a one time race for me. I've been training and entering races since November. At that time the Bridge Run was so far away I had plenty of time to get ready.

As it got closer I became worried. When I first considered running the Bridge, I didn't run at all so I didn't have a clue as to what it would take to get ready. The more I trained, the more I wondered if I really wanted to do this. I listened to less than uplifting stories from past Bridge Runs and I just knew I had taken on more than I was ready for.

However, as my friends and I drove the route on Friday before the race, I decided this was going to be an experience I wouldn't miss for anything. The symposium by Dr. Sheehan and Brenda Webb further heightened the mood.

When the sun came up on "Bridge Day" I was already on my way. I no longer felt it would be impossible. I figured it wasn't asking a lot. I wanted to do it in under 50 minutes without hurting my legs, being knocked down or throwing up.

Everyone I talked to that morning was eager to get going. It was a cheerful joking group on the shuttle bus. When the driver asked if there were any walkers on board, someone said laughingly "I hope not." As we rode over the new Bridge, a lot of us checked out the old Bridge knowing the next time we saw it we'd be on it.

Finally it was time to run. After months of waiting for this moment, it was here. I discovered the Bridge wasn't as difficult as I imagined and the flat part wasn't as easy. But I did it in less than 50, I didn't get hurt or knocked down, nor did I throw up. Mission accomplished!

Once I walked out of the finish chute I felt great. I did it! Then the great let down hit. Is that all? It's over? I felt depressed.

Finally I found a cure for my depression! I'm training for the 1985 Cooper River Bridge Run. I want to do it in under 45 minutes and I don't want to ... well you know the rest. See you next year on the Bridge!

1984 Awards

Prize money winners:

(Prize money awarded for the first time)

Overall Male

1	David Branch	Travelers Rest	29:25	$800
2	Tom Wysocki	El Toro, CA	29:32	$500
3	John Rogers	Raleigh, NC	29:45	$200

Overall Female

1	Brenda Webb	Knoxville, TN	34:09	$800
2	Ruth Wysocki	El Toro, CA	35:04	$500
3	Nancy Grayson	Columbia, SC	36:37	$200

Masters Male

Bill Voight ... 35:48

Masters Female

Cindy Dalrymple ... 36:57

Special award:

Dewey Wise Trophy for oldest finisher with fastest time less than his or her age in minutes:

Caldwell Nixon, 75 ... Denver, NC ... 60:22

Age group award winners

(Given To Top 10% In Each Division).

Male 14 & under (107 finishers, 11 awards)

1 Chris Venesky ... 35:54
2 Jamey Henson ... 37:25
3 Mack Marti ... 37:33
4 Ricky Russell ... 38:30
5 Peter Durst ... 38:33
6 Gregory Burch ... 38:46
7 Jarrett Keim ... 39:21
8 Alston Middleton ... 40:16
9 Eddie Mills ... 40:22
10 Brad McKay ... 40:37

Female 14 & under (29 finishers, 3 awards)

1 Monica Gathings ... 44:13
2 Kelli George ... 44:31
3 Shannon Canter ... 44:37

Male 15-19 (105 finishers, 11 awards)

1 Larry Clark ... 33:56
2 Kenzie Cook ... 36:36
3 Douglas Clayton ... 37:21
4 Reginald Collins ... 38:13
5 Bob Marangelli ... 38:18
6 Randy Elliott ... 38:23
7 James Horry ... 39:03
8 Douglas Warthen ... 39:06
9 Robert Williams ... 39:36
10 John Martin ... 39:48
11 Charles Whisenant ... 39:50

Female 15-19 (38 finishers, 4 awards)

1 Kristie Martin ... 42:15
2 Malena Ahlin ... 47:28
3 Kathy Hart ... 48:15
4 Ann Gibson ... 48:16

Male 20-24 (341 finishers, 34 awards)

1 Paul Laymon ... 31:15
2 Dave Kraus ... 31:16
3 Randall Ward ... 31:48
4 Max Minter ... 32:07
5 Teever Handal ... 33:04
6 David Morris ... 33:07
7 Rob Devlin ... 33:26
8 Mark Johnson ... 33:50
9 Lynwood Barker ... 34:33
10 Daniel Brown ... 34:45
11 Pace Kessenich ... 35:15
12 James Madden ... 35:25
13 Edward Moore ... 35:29
14 Gregory Pizzuti ... 35:36
15 James Mead ... 35:41
16 Luke Barnwell ... 35:45
17 Robert Squires ... 35:46
18 Gene Hallman Jr ... 36:01
19 Joseph Garand ... 36:25
20 Andy Pinson ... 36:29
21 Huey Inman ... 36:33
22 Donnie Holt ... 36:45
23 Tony Sexton ... 36:59
24 Ralph Oliver ... 37:02
25 William Harlan ... 37:03
26 Randall Thompson ... 37:07
27 Brian Kennedy ... 37:08
28 Michael Anderson ... 37:12
29 Mark Adams ... 37:16
30 Andrew Rukstelis ... 37:27
31 Michael Anderson ... 37:42
32 Gary Quinney ... 37:51
33 Steve O'Neill ... 37:53
34 John Massey ... 38:15

Female 20-24 (129 finishers, 13 awards)

1 Marcia McCoy ... 37:35
2 Mary Campbell ... 37:36
3 Mitzi Jacobs ... 42:13
4 Karen Kanes ... 42:33
5 Anne Behan ... 43:55
6 Barbara Atkinson ... 43:59
7 Cathy Myers ... 44:30
8 Karen Rhodes ... 44:56
9 Jean Gunter ... 45:49
10 Liz Holland ... 45:51
11 Valerie Howard ... 45:52
12 Alethea Goode ... 45:54
13 Mary Malony ... 46:41

Male 25-29 (595 finishers, 60 awards)

1 Ray McDaniels ... 29:54
2 Dave Altieri ... 30:28
3 Marc Embler ... 30:42
4 Mathew Motshwarateu ... 31:42
5 Joe Sullivan ... 31:47
6 David Smith ... 32:14
7 Kenneth Bowles ... 32:28
8 Bill Fisher ... 32:33
9 Bill Marable ... 32:43
10 David Luhrs ... 32:48
11 Mark Koenig ... 33:12
12 David Hankins ... 33:35
13 John Zizzi ... 33:43
14 Robert Lowery ... 33:58
15 David Bourgeois ... 34:05
16 Michael McIntyre ... 34:06
17 Mike Lambert ... 34:16
18 Frank Lowry ... 34:17
19 William Burgess ... 34:19
20 Mike Chodnicki ... 34:25
21 Paul Smith ... 34:32
22 Jeff Stone ... 34:37
23 Barry Pinkney ... 35:02
24 Scott Roark ... 35:12
25 Colby Smith ... 35:13
26 Adrian Pellegrini ... 35:25
27 Jim Gummow ... 35:26
28 Roland Butch Cody ... 35:31
29 Ronnie Floyd ... 35:33
30 Chris Alexander ... 35:53
31 David Plaspohl ... 36:03
32 Michael McMillan ... 36:08
33 Thom Gehring ... 36:15
34 Gary Klaben ... 36:17
35 Marc Plantico ... 36:19
36 Tim Hamilton ... 36:21
37 Skip McQuillan ... 36:28
38 Hal Carlson ... 36:42
39 Steve Robb ... 36:43
40 Kenneth Colmer ... 36:54
41 Timi Kennedy ... 36:56
42 James Ambrose ... 36:59
43 Tracy Giles ... 37:05
44 Frank Tucker ... 37:09
45 James Fann ... 37:18
46 Glen Chamberlain ... 37:25
47 D A Vanderboegh ... 37:32
48 Charlie Monroe ... 37:32
49 Steve Staley ... 37:34
50 Chip Long ... 37:43
51 Murdock Taylor ... 37:49
52 David Dalhouse ... 37:50
53 Buell Whitehead ... 38:01
54 Edward Vasques ... 38:07
55 Michael Whiteside ... 38:08
56 Tanis Manseau ... 38:17
57 Russ Dixon ... 38:18
58 Steve Strom ... 38:22
59 Frank Sloan ... 38:22
60 Selby Richardson ... 38:25

Female 25-29 (213 finishers, 22 awards)

1 Janet Ballenger ... 38:08
2 Susan Spence ... 39:30
3 Michele Haskins ... 40:12
4 Kathi Wagner ... 40:53
5 Cheryl McSwain ... 42:02
6 Gearin Daly ... 42:18
7 Jan Derrick ... 42:56
8 Mary Alice Curtiss ... 43:36
9 Becky Weller ... 43:54
10 Robin Stanley ... 44:05
11 Pat Crofton ... 44:07
12 Candace Strobach ... 44:24
13 Cheryl Caldwell ... 44:32
14 Lisa Cox ... 44:32
15 Nancy O'Hara ... 44:53
16 Linda Miyasato ... 44:54
17 Tessa Masters ... 45:10
18 Sara Plaspohl ... 45:32
19 Sara Dorociak ... 45:54
20 Lisa Duffee ... 46:08
21 Julie Waugh ... 46:47
22 Gayle Pennington ... 47:06

Male 30-34 (622 finishers, 62 awards)

1 Gordon English ... 31:48
2 Leon Cook ... 32:15

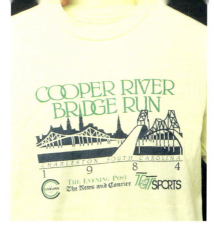

3	Buddy Carrouth	33:47
4	Frankie Phillips	34:23
5	Ravion Cannon	35:07
6	George Getty	35:18
7	Mike Willoughby	35:27
8	Duane Wolff	35:42
9	Victor Englert	35:44
10	Billy Davey	35:53
11	Leon Lockelar	36:02
12	Martin Gazz	36:10
13	Ben Rodriquez	36:20
14	Terry Hamlin	36:34
15	Charles Newman	36:35
16	Rodney Cook	36:36
17	Mario Salas	36:42
18	James White	36:47
19	Steve Spencer	36:48
20	Doug Nelson	36:50
21	James Boyd	36:58
22	William Derrick	37:06
23	Timothy Rhyne	37:18
24	Gary Ricker	37:22
25	John Hammel	37:24
26	Bill Dunleavy	37:35
27	William McKnight	37:40
28	Harold Johnson	37:41
29	Bill Thomas	37:49
30	William Paggi	37:49
31	Ron Lewandowski	37:50
32	Hugh Jacobs	37:51
33	Gunther Traber	37:52
34	Joseph Young	38:17
35	William Driscoll	38:21
36	John Wilson	38:22
37	Phil Mozie	38:25
38	David Russell	38:27
39	Clark Wyly	38:33
40	Austin Hubbard	38:35
41	John Todd	38:39
42	Michael Holmes	38:39
43	Larry D'Ippolito	38:40
44	Jonathan Anderson	38:41
45	Derrick Hoover	38:43
46	Edward Kent	38:45
47	Glenn Dennis	38:48
48	William Hollingsworth	38:59
49	Bobo Brinson	39:01
50	Peter Wertimer	39:01
51	Steve madden	39:04
52	Shawn Nettles	39:05
53	Stephen McClave	39:13
54	Bill Barfield	39:13
55	Trenholm Walker	39:14
56	Robert Brodeur	39:15
57	Michael Waters	39:16
58	Steven Eisner	39:16
59	M G Lancianese	39:18
60	William Taylor	39:24
61	Herbert Grantham	39:30
62	Sam Hopper	39:34

Female 30-34 (184 finishers, 18 awards)

1	Kiki Sweigart	37:13
2	Deb Ethredge	37:32
3	Benita Brooks (Schlau)	38:30
4	Catherine Lempesis	39:19
5	Marilyn Davey	39:49
6	Carol Davis	40:13
7	Carolyn Nelson	40:58
8	Maggie Cable	41:01
9	Rachel Hoover	41:42
10	Deborah Massey	43:30
11	Bonnie Poore Long	44:00
12	Jeanne Sink	44:06
13	Becky Nalley	44:17
14	Carla Linker	44:24
15	Cathy Russell	44:34
16	Terry Rickson	44:35
17	Ginger Gregory	44:36
18	Deborah Estes	45:14

Male 35-39 (521 finishers, 52 awards)

1	Bob Schlau	30:47
2	Wallie Jones	33:55
3	John Peters	34:14
4	Jim O'Neill	34:33
5	Thomas Jones	34:36
6	Michael H Smith	34:47
7	Joe Taylor	35:09
8	Marris Johnson	35:21
9	Robert Wilson	35:52
10	Kenneth Klein	36:06
11	Jay Britton	36:15
12	Don Player	36:16
13	Clayton Krejci	36:18
14	David Reese	36:22
15	Bill Peay	36:29
16	Alfred Cortez	36:32
17	Jimmy Hadden	36:35
18	Tommy Walton	36:45
19	Donald Reynolds	36:51
20	Richard Lewis	37:37
21	Jimmy Bailey	37:45
22	Edwin Bazen	37:49
23	Steven Annan	37:50
24	Michael Keenan	37:52
25	Steve Swan	37:54
26	Cedric Jaggers	37:56
27	Vernon Bennett	38:23
28	G. Starrenburg	38:31
29	James Horne	38:38
30	William Marston	38:41
31	Steven Hoppe	38:42
32	Monty King	39:06
33	Russell Brown	39:07
34	Randy Whitt	39:11
35	Phillip Dickert	39:13
36	John Gurhrie	39:16
37	John Schreiber	39:19
38	Morgan Hewitt	39:24
39	William Anderson	39:26
40	Lonnie Hill	39:30
41	Michael Lake	39:31
42	William Sloan	39:38
43	Paul Davis	39:43
44	James Goodson	39:48
45	Billy Wieters	39:49
46	Gary Pell	39:52
47	Paul King	39:54
48	John Lancaster	39:59
49	Hugh Wilder	40:02
50	Richard Kuhn	40:03
51	James Rivers	40:08
52	Bob Brockhouse	40:10

Female 35-39 (120 finishers, 12 awards)

1	Peggy Schug	39:02
2	Gail Bailey	39:19
3	Anne Boone Reed	40:02
4	Mary Ryan	42:23
5	Brenda Pantoja	42:31
6	Patricia Carter	43:01
7	Barbara Moore	43:20
8	Colleen Archambault	44:16
9	Bonnie Hipkins	44:30
10	Judy Melton	44:43
11	Kathy Jaggers	45:07
12	Mary Gibson	46:27

Male 40-44 (314 finishers, 32 awards)

1	James Adams	35:57
2	Jim Balkwell	36:00
3	Tom Woodward	36:26
4	Dupree Elvington	36:46
5	William Hollaway	36:51
6	Clebe McClary	37:00
7	Matthew Hutmaker	37:23
8	Jim Reavis	37:31
9	William Hogg	37:39
10	Reaves Gasque	37:46
11	J W McClung	38:40
12	Doug Giorgio	38:42
13	John Burden	38:47
14	Clyde Mizell	38:48
15	Carl Jenkins Jr	38:58
16	Marty Cook	39:04
17	Bill Vetsch	39:19
18	Charles Smith	39:26
19	James Keller	39:27
20	Maurice Davidson	39:45
21	Walter Burcham	39:45
22	Bradley Ford	39:46
23	Louis Tisdale	39:49
24	Joe Allen	39:51
25	Gary Rolfs	39:49
26	Joe Alexander	40:02
27	Paul Serridge	40:05
28	Martin Perlmutter	40:21
29	David W Smith	40:32
30	Roy Plunkett	40:58
31	Edward McCameron	41:12
32	Sam Schuman	41:18

Female 40-44 (49 finishers, 5 awards)

1	Cindy Dalrymple	36:57
2	Peggy Ledford	43:12
3	Joyce Ploeger	46:54
4	Kay Hughes	48:47
5	Bettye Foster	49:43

Male 45-49 (152 finishers, 15 awards)

1	Ed Ledford	36:17
2	Sam Yarborough	36:54
3	Don Austell	37:44
4	Jack Gilmore	37:52
5	Chris Brookhouse	38:29
6	Bobby Hollis	40:13
7	Robert Bell	40:13
8	Paul Benz	40:15
9	Charles Duell	40:27
10	James Harrell	40:37
11	Burrell Landes	40:42
12	Bernard Sher	40:43
13	Jerry Kavanagh	41:25
14	George Hallman	41:44
15	Bob Foster	42:01

Female 45-49 (17 finishers, 3 awards)

1	Pat Rhode	47:12
2	Lynn Hopkins	47:38
3	Suzanne Foster	48:05

Male 50-54 (85 finishers, 9 awards

1	Bill Voight	35:48
2	Ken Kurts	37:34
3	Lee Swofford	39:07
4	Bob Walton	39:56
5	Charles Moore	39:56
6	Bill Wooley	40:27
7	Gerald Dorn	40:51
8	Sam Query	41:03
9	Laurence Donoho	41:49

Female 50-54 (8 finishers, 3 awards)

1	Nancy Bell	47:29
2	Eileen Hallman	55:17
3	Ann Stanton	56:26

Male 55-59 (41 finishers, 4 awards)

1	Lawrence Moore	42:26
2	Robert Kirk	43:10
3	Joe Conrad	44:05
4	George Pearson	44:46

Female 55-59 (5 finishers, 3 awards)

1	Frances Conrad	56:46
2	Sally Kirk	1:07:27
3	Wyndall Henderson	1:10:07

Male 60-64 (14 finishers, 3 awards)

1	Rudy Nimmon	40:18
2	David Mellard	42:49
3	Keys Stuart	45:59

Female 60-64 (2 finishers)

| 1 | Margaret Wright | 51:50 |
| 2 | Shirley Schade | 1:05:34 |

Male 65 and over (5 finishers, 3 awards)

1	George Sheehan	40:20
2	Carl Jenkins Sr	46:12
3	Caldwell Nixon	1:00:22

Compiled by Cedric Jaggers from original complete race results.

Mike O'Reilly (No. 3) passes a couple of runners en route to his victory. News and Courier photo by Wade Spees

Chapter 8
1985
First Certified Course, Third Hottest Race Ever

The eighth Bridge Run began on time at 8:30 a.m. on March 30, 1985. It was a hot, sunny morning but fortunately a cloud cover came up about half an hour before the race. This held the temperature down to 70 degrees, making it the second hottest Bridge Run to date. The course was the same as the previous year, beginning on Coleman Boulevard in Mount Pleasant just across Shem Creek, then across the "old" Grace Memorial Bridge and Crosstown Overpass, down King Street to Market, cutting across to Meeting Street and up to the finish in front of the Federal Building.

There was one difference: It was TAC certified (later called USATF certified) (#SC85012WN) for the first time, only the 12th race to be certified in South Carolina that year and among the first courses certified, as no courses had been certified before 1984. The new course led to some mile marker confusion as the markers were set for miles 2 and 3 where the mile marks for the previous race had been. This led to the mile 2 and 3 markers being set long past where they should have actually been.

In 1985, the race joined the *Racing South* (now *Running Journal*) magazine Grand Prix race circuit. Joining the circuit attracted a number of high caliber, though not world class, athletes to the race.

However, there were world class runners on hand, and the course record was widely expected to be shattered, but the heat had something to say about that. In fact, even the elite runners said the heat had added about a minute to their expected times.

Jake Storey and Mark Scrutton of England began forcing the pace right away and pushed through the first mile in 4:25. Three runners caught them on the Crosstown Overpass and slowly pulled away on the flats to take the top three places. Mike O'Reilly of Ireland won in 29:28 followed by Craig Holm of New York in 29:32 and Hans Koeleman of Holland (residing in Clemson, S.C.,) was third in 29:40.

"Going over the last hill, I took it up just to see what it was like," O'Reilly told the *News and Courier*. "You know, to do my share of the work. I had thought I'd better hold back a bit. We were thinking we might wind up running 30 minutes plus last night when we were all talking about it. So 29:20s is all right."

He liked the Bridge Run atmosphere. "You don't get anything like this in England," he said. "There, April is the only road racing season, and people barely stay 20 minutes after the race is over. It's nice to see so many people of different ages, whether they are runners or not."

In the women's race, Christina Boxer of England, who was running only her second 10k race, won in 34:08 a new course record. It was one second faster than the old record and just one second short of her personal best time. She went through the first mile in 5:15. Sue Schneider of Minnesota, who finished second, led most of the way and had the lead with 1,000 yards to go, but could not hold off Boxer and finished in 34:15. Dianne Bussa of Michigan was third in 34:42.

"I wanted to run a fast time," Boxer told the *News and Courier*. "Once I saw the course, with the hills, I knew it wasn't one of the fastest courses. So I concentrated on running and trying to win.

"I thought if I pushed too hard on the hills I would tire myself because there are a lot of strong girls here. I said I would keep relaxed and push hard when I get over the last overpass. I'm quite good running downhill. I catch up quite a bit. When you came off the bridge, you lost the breeze and it got ever so hot. I was glad it was only 6.2 miles."

About the Bridge Run she said, "It's exciting. It was good fun. It's got a lot of atmosphere. I enjoyed being here. It's even nicer now that I've won. There is nothing like winning. It's great."

Don Coffman of Frankfort, Ky., was Masters winner in 32:27, followed by Art Williams in 33:54 and Mike Kelly in 33:59. Female Masters: Peggy Ledford, 44:51, and Joyce Ploeger, 46:14, both of Charleston, and Frankie Crume, 46:53. For the second year in a row, Caldwell Nixon, 76, of Lincolnton, N.C., won the Dewey Wise Trophy for this time of 60:50.

For the first time the race was broadcast live on local television, then presented as delayed coverage. Local Channel 5 carried the broadcast live every year through 1990.

Author Dr. George Sheehan was again speaker at the pre-race seminar, and won the 65 and over age division in a time of 42:26. Entry fee was raised to $8. The race entry form had featured a quote from Dr. Sheehan: "I have run other bridges - The George Washington, The Golden Gate, The Verrazzano. All give the impression of solidity and function. For all their architectural brilliance those bridges are matter of fact, utilitarian structures. They are simply there to carry things to the other side. Not so the Cooper River Bridge. It's a double span that crosses two rivers and goes for some two and a half miles to a destination that must be accepted on faith. This bridge carried us up and over and through to some distant land, to a mythical Charleston. It was not a bridge, it was an adventure."

The Sunday *News and Courier* had two full pages of race coverage and listed the top 150 male and top 50 female finishers, as well as listing three deep in each age group. A total of 5,440 runners registered for the race while the results booklet, mailed to all finishers, showed 4,482 official finishers, 3,483 male and 999 female. There were six men under 30 minutes while 283 men and 16 women bettered 40 minutes. A total of 1,624 runners finished the race in less than 50 minutes, while 3,022 crossed the finish line in less than 60 minutes. An estimated 2,000 to 3,000 untimed participants took part in the second (untimed) Bridge Walk. Mark Blatchford was race director for the second year in a row.

Other Voices
1985 Bridge Run Post Race Interviews

Chuck Magera videotaped the finish of the 1985 race. Then he conducted some post race interviews in Marion Square, before the awards ceremony. These interviews are transcribed here by Cedric Jaggers - with the noise level of the post race crowd and the age of the source material, I did the best I could, and added official time and place from the race results. I appreciate Chuck letting me use them. Chuck did his first interview from the stage (probably with the awards list in his hand).

CM - Here's our 21st place finisher Mark Friedrich. How was your race today?
Mark - Terrible.
CM - What were your splits today?
Mark - Terrible.
CM - Terrible? How bad were they?
Mark - Real bad.
CM - What was your first mile?
Mark - About 4:35.
CM - You know the second and third mile marks were way off.
Mark - That didn't help mentally.
CM - You're out of the awards you know.
Mark - How deep are you going? 20?
CM - 15.
Mark - Yeah, I (inaudible) need something - a little work. (Results: 21st overall, 31:50)
CM - All right, talk to you later.
CM - To female race winner Christina Boxer. Tell me about your race today.
Christina - Well, I decided not to go out too fast today because everybody kept talking about the bridge (made hand motion showing steep up and down).
CM - What was your first mile?
Christina - About 5:15. I thought,'Well, I'd better not go any faster than this.'
CM - Were you aware of any other women in the race?
Christina - There were two other girls ahead of me, and I knew they'd be the two to watch. And then Sue broke away going up the hill and I thought 'It's a long way to go' and I didn't push it. My coach would have said you've got to top the hills. I kept catching people going down. I caught all these men and hoped they'd take me up the next hill and when I got over that one I could see Sue starting to slow up, and I thought if I slowly keep gaining, I can pull her back, so . . .
CM - Are you happy with the race?
Christina - Yeah, I'm real pleased.
CM - How was the wind out there today, did you notice it?
Christina - It wasn't as bad as I expected. There was a little bit of breeze when you came off the bridge. (Results: overall female winner, 34:08)

CM - My annual interview with Bob Schlau. Tell me about your race today.

Bob - Well it wasn't what it was last year.

CM - What do you attribute the difference to?

Bob - Well, I think it was a lot warmer, but I don't know why everybody ran so slow.

CM - I think the heat might have been a factor, don't you agree?

Bob - I guess so. A lot of people were dying - but I beat my seed.

CM - You sure did. Good job old man.

Bob - Next year I'll enter the age group (division).(Results 20th overall, 31:42) (Note - runners had to declare for Open or Age Division and could not win awards in both. CJ)

CM - Here we are with a candid interview with our second place runner-up Sue Schneider, tell us about your race Susan.

Sue - Well I should have kicked a little harder.

CM - When did Diana catch you?

Sue - At five and a half.

CM - Did you know how far it was to the finish?

Sue - Yeah, I wish I hadn't because it might have made a difference.

CM - Yeah, Christina said she kind of let you take it out on the hills.

Sue - I knew if I didn't take it out on the hills, she'd be outkicking me anyway, so I hoped to tire her out a little bit.

CM - Are you happy with your time?

Sue - Ummm . . . . (Results: 2nd overall female, 34:15) tape cuts to next interview

CM - Let's talk to that hundred dollar money winner Jeff 'Scuffy' Scuffins.

Jeff - I'm the fattest guy in the top ten (he is shirtless and pats the small roll of belly fat he has). (Results: 6th overall, 29:55)

CM - There he is, Mr. Hans Koeleman, forcing the pace. Hans, tell me about it. You trying to put a hurting on these guys or what?

Hans - (no words, just grins a big smile). (Results: 3rd overall, 29:40)

CM - Paul Laymon, the Air Force's finest (Note: Paul was serving in the Air Force at the time. CJ) Paul, did you take it today, the Age Group?

Paul - I don't know.

CM - What was your place? **Paul** - 23rd.

CM - You did, you took your age group. The top 20 ahead of you are all Open (division). How was your race today?

Paul - I was really happy with the place, but as far as the time goes, everybody was real slow.

CM - What was your first mile? **Paul** - Right at 4 minutes 40 seconds.

CM - You know (mile marks) 2 and 3 were way off. You did realize that the second and third splits were way off? **Paul** - Really?

CM - So, what did you think about running with the big boys today?

Paul - It was fun. I had a good time. Going out the first mile I was right there with them. (Results: 23rd overall, 1st age group 32:07)

CM - Men's runner-up Craig Holm.

Craig - They were calling me the underdog over there.

CM - OK, we know better than that.

Craig - It was fun. I'm kind of a strength runner (inaudible) and that's why I ended up second.

CM - It looked like you kind of laid back the first two miles then tried to pick them off on the hills.

Craig - No, I was going out hard the whole way. I felt like it was as hard as I could.

CM - Did you think you were going to reel him in? **Craig** - I thought I was going to catch him because going up the hills they weren't pulling away, and going down the hills I started to pull away from them.

CM - On King Street I thought you were struggling a little bit when Koeleman took the lead. **Craig** - That's right.

CM - What was going through your mind then?

Craig - I was thinking 'You know, there's not much further to go.' and what I did was . . . I felt like I was struggling and I'll let those guys come to me.(Results: 2nd overall, 29:32)

Tape cuts to awards presentation as Chuck hands award to Ruth Wysocki, who had finished as 6th overall female in 35:54.

Ruth walks up to the microphone and says, "After racing here last year and having such a great time, my husband and I waited a whole year before coming back and telling you how much we love it here. After the Olympic Trials (Note: where she upset Mary Decker Slaney. CJ) I had a dozen long stem roses from the City of Charleston and a beautiful note and this is my chance to say 'Thank You' and we enjoyed our stay here and we'll be back."

I'll Cross That Bridge When I Come To It

By Bob Coskrey, Originally appeared in the March-April 1985   Low Country Runner

Although I've been running since 1979, I've only run in the Cooper River Bridge Run twice. And one of those times deserves an asterisk. It's not that I haven't tried. I guess it's close to being a jinx. Mary Decker (Slaney) would understand perfectly.

My first attempt was in 1981, and up until about a month before the race, I'd never run more than four miles, so my goal was not a particular time really, but just to finish. It was my first race of any kind in fact and I was quite nervous.

I had a horrible fear of coming in dead last (that's a very strangely ominous phrase which middle-aged people like myself should avoid I guess) of being nipped at the finish line by a 9-year-old or an arthritic grandmother.

Fortuitously, I managed to finish somewhere in the middle of the pack, but there were some disquieting moments: 1) Seeing a couple of guys in the throes of the dry heaves; 2) being passed by a runner who was wearing headphones and running backwards, and most unnerving of all; 3) spotting an old flame (from 24 years ago at that time) among the spectators at the corner of Queen and King streets and thinking to myself, "My God, do you think she recognized me? Did she see the guys with the headphones pass me? Boy, she looks sort of old and frumpy. I think I look better than she does, but in retrospect, perhaps I always did. So maybe it's not a valid comparison."

The resultant lapse in concentration probably cost me 30 seconds or so. But with a time of 48:10, did it really matter?

Then came the 1982 race, and falsely buoyed by increased mileage, better times and a few races under my shorts, I hoped to perform considerably better. A muscle strain about a week before the race dashed my precarious hopes. Just as well, I rationalized, she would probably be there at the corner again. Maybe even causing a scene this time; pushing her now pulpy body through scattering spectators and screaming lustfully after my lithe, whippet-like form, "Oh Bob, I was such a fool. It's never too late - I'll even learn to run! I'll even join the Charleston Running Club."

Despite the avoidance of that possible contretemps, I was still deeply disappointed at missing the race. Especially after training on the bridge for five weeks.

A Saturday morning funeral in 1983 thwarts my plans again. Once more I am totally frustrated and my subsequent efforts in lobbying for a law to prohibit any future funerals on the day of the race prove futile. I do achieve some miniscule measure of accomplishment by changing my will to preclude my burial on that day. My intractable wife would not consent to revising her will in that fashion, but she did concede to the stipulation that if her funeral fell on a Bridge Race Saturday, that the burial site would be Marion Square after 12 p.m.

It's 1984: the asterisked race. I am actually at the starting line. I am so ecstatically grateful for this good fortune that I don't care about the 9-year-old or the grandmother beating me. Or about what kind of humiliating spectacle my old girlfriend makes. I'm a seasoned runner of five years now, and I confidently position myself in the 6-minute-per-mile section along with all the other 7- and 8-minute milers.

It's a cold brisk day and I feel good as I near the bridge. A young female voice shouts from the crowd, "Hi, Mr. Coskrey!" probably my old girlfriend disguising her voice. "Leave me alone, for God's sake! It's all over! I just want to run the damn race!" I roar back in the direction of the voice. I suddenly find I am unable to run without the usual hazard of bumping into others, as runners on all sides give me a wide berth.

Calamity. A few yards past the 3-mile mark, at the top of the second span, I step in one of the bridge's expansion joints and twist my ankle. Since most runners are still keeping their distance from me, I am able to hop - cursing - to the side of the bridge. I stand as close to the railing as possible as thousands of runners pass me by. My ankle hurts like hell and I have already decided to forget about trying to finish the race. I start working my way slowly back across the bridge to Mount Pleasant, limping along and holding on to the side of the bridge.

A platoon of Marines rumbles by, running in step. The bridge seems to be trembling or perhaps it's me. The runners continue to stampede by and I realize I've never been a participant and a spectator in the same race.

After about 15 minutes or so, my ankle no longer hurts, but I maintain my limp. If I don't communicate some indication of bodily injury, they'll think I quit just because it was too much for me. I am aware of the absurdity of my thoughts, not to mention my actions, especially when I momentarily forget which ankle to favor (Did someone notice?), but I continue my performance. I can't bear the thought that someone will think I'm a quitter (as if it really made a difference to anyone).

The walkers are starting to move past me now, and God forbid, my old flame may be among them. Then I'd be faced with the dilemma of choosing a direction to flee in: 1) toward Charleston and a certain last place finish, or 2) continue to fake limp back to Mount Pleasant as fast as possible, hoping to avoid her rapacious tendrils of desire.

As infrequently happens in life, I never had to make that burdensome decision as I was ingloriously rescued by a Mount Pleasant Recreation Department van. It was with several police cars and was following the multitude of walkers across the bridge; clearing the bridge of stragglers and other debris.

It is mid-February as I write this - about six weeks before the 1985 race and I'm starting to feel a little anxious. What's it going to be this time? An injury? A funeral? Or will the bridge collapse under the unison running of four companies of Marines?

Well, it's completely out of my control. I'll have to put all of these negative thoughts out of my mind, just as Mary Decker (Slaney) does. If I am fortunate enough to make it to the start - and the finish - it is going to be a new PR, regardless of the distractful tactics of my ancient paramour. I plan on wearing a mask, though she still may be able to recognize the legs. I feel that if Mary can persist in pursuing her goals in spite of her unceasing setbacks, that I should certainly be able to persevere in pursuing my less than imposing one. Mary however, does have a significant advantage over me and most other runners; her superior skills notwithstanding. One which she acquired by having the foresight to marry someone big enough to pick her up and carry her if she gets injured.

Of course, I do have my old girlfriend who looks as though she would have little difficulty in bench pressing a Volkswagen. Maybe I won't wear the mask after all. The Lord works in mysterious ways.

Note: Despite all obstacles, Bob finished the 1985 race in 47:00. CJ

The Best Way To Run The Bridge Is Blindfolded!

By Kathy Jaggers, Originally appeared in the March-April 1985 Low Country Runner

The other night I overheard my husband interviewing a local favorite in the Bridge Run. "What do you think is the best way to run the Bridge?" he asked. I chuckled to myself, "Fast." (Ha, ha) and folded the laundry knowing I would never be interviewed as a local favorite for any race. The best way for me to run the Bridge Run would be blindfolded, or at least with blinders so all I could see would be the white line down the center lane of that tall, frightful, rickety looking structure. (Note: She was referring to what locals always called 'The Old Bridge", i.e. the two-lane Grace Memorial bridge).

For two months, I've endured chatter about training pace, hill work, getting in shape for the Bridge, dropping a few pounds, etc., etc. Such talk causes me to have nightmares. I always dread February and March for that reason. Let me explain. I suffer from a fear of heights. Oh there is a nice sounding term for it - acrophobia, but the bottom line is, the farther I get from the ground, the worse my problem - the fear response.

My best Bridge Run time happened one windy year when the hat I had pulled down almost over my eyes blew off as I started up the first span. I was so scared that the adrenaline pumped for the entire race. It makes for an excellent race time, but the after effects are not pleasant.

Already, the nightmares have begun, and it is just the first week of February as this is written! Every year, I plan my race strategy - do my mileage, intervals, etc. and plan my splits perfectly for that wonderful race I'm going to run someday. Every year I approach that bridge atremble and toss out all plans as I migrate to the white line and the center of the pack of runners, keeping as many bodies between me and the railing as possible. I just want to survive!

I go slightly crazy until we are off that awful bridge. And as if that weren't enough, some masochist has added another "little" bridge (the overpass), to the event. The adrenalin rush from that little overpass gets me down to Marion Square anyway.

I've considered not running the Bridge and just working the event. Some of my Bridge Run times indicate I should have done this long ago . . . But, I'm not a quitter and I really feel good when it is over and once again I triumph over my fear. It's one of those little self-discipline things we runners do to ourselves all the time.

Yes, I'll be there at the starting line March 30 and you can be sure I'll be gravitating toward the white line as I approach that bridge. I plan to make it to the finish line this year with a Bridge PR (doesn't everyone?). But, if you see me going slightly crazy approaching that bridge, just move over and let me have the white line.

Note: Kathy left her blindfold at home and finished the race in 46:58. CJ

How Not To Run The Bridge Run

By Ed Ledford , Originally appeared in the May-June 1985 Low Country Runner

Next year I'll enter the Bridge Walk, or maybe just enter the Bridge Run for a Fun Run! Those were some of my nicer thoughts as I passed the fist mile mark at 5:30 - much too fast, dammit. The burning lungs and first glimpse of the "monster" bridge was just too much. To add insult to injury, I was out of position for the first water station and could only look longingly, with a parched throat.

As everyone knows, the first uphill is a certified torture chamber. No one should hurt that bad at mile 2, wherever mile 2 was, of a 10k. As I gasped for air going down the first span, Cedric J. passed me going at least 100 mph. I thought, "Obscenity, he'll be finished by the time you get to mile 4."

Speaking of mile 4, whatever strategy I had planned at 3 a.m. Saturday (during my usual sleepless night before the Bridge Run) went out the window. Already a minute behind schedule, my thoughts centered on just finishing. My eyes decided they would be more comfortable rolled into the back of my head, and my skin color took on the look of an old green T-shirt from the Turkey Day Run.

One of the cruelest things about the Bridge Run is that you have to "get your act together" twice. Once for the spectators around mile 5, and again from Calhoun Street to the finish. Speaking of mile 5, the second cruelest thing about the Bridge Run is that you have to run by a logical place to stop - the 5-mile mark at Marion Square (as you pass by it). My body desperately wanted to stop there.

Fortunately, or unfortunately, my mind or whatever was left of it won out, and I kept moving. However, my left leg decided it would start a protest movement, and proceeded with a slow shuffle. I would like to apologize to all those spectators at that point. Their ears are probably still burning from the obscenities, but that was just my last ditch attempt at breathing.

Finally, I would like to thank Dupree Elvington for preventing a sure injury by catching me as I fell in the chute. His kindness, and others, continued with fluid assistance, etc. after the race. Maybe next year I'll walk the bridge!

Note: Ed finished the race in a respectable 37:05 (he passed me, though he was too kind to mention it) when I overheated, blew up and finished in 37:28. CJ

Bridge Run Fever

By Leon Locklear, Originally appeared in the March-April 1986 Low Country Runner

You can tell there is something in the air. The weather is getting prettier, people have returned to walking around Park Circle in the evenings and the sidewalk of the only "hill" in town is becoming more crowded every weekend. Since the Bridge Run is going to be held a week later, in April 1986, it would seem to increase the chances of a warmer, muggier temperature at starting time.

This brings to mind the often written about and well publicized precautions for warm weather running. We are all familiar with them but it seems we sometimes fail to take them to heart.

Maybe that's why Cedric asked me to write a few words about why I didn't finish the 1985 Bridge Run. I said "Cedric, are you crazy? Never mind, I'll do it." The 1985 Bridge Run was the first time I entered a race and failed to complete it. I have entered every Bridge Run except the first one, and set a PR of 36:02 in 1984.

But in 1985 I ran like a rookie. In 1985 I was fired up. I warmed up properly and even did some stretching alongside Ruth Wysocki (one of the female race favorites). The crowds, cameras and excitement all added to my fever.

When the gun went off it released unbridled horsepower. First mile splits 5:06, 5:07, 5:08, oh well, maybe a little too quick. At the top of the first span that unbridled horsepower had turned into Clydesdales and I was carrying them on my back. Feets don't fail me now.

Top of the second span: It was turn out the lights, the party is over. I was hot, definitely overheated and just plain hurting. I said, "Brain, I know what you're thinking." Don't you realize there are friends waiting to see you pass by, take your picture and cheer you on? There are only two miles to go. How can you face yourself if you quit? Brain said, "No problem."

Folks, sometimes the pleasure just "ain't" worth the pain. I walked to the finish line and watched everyone finish. Mario, Mike, Huey, Buzz, wife Barbara and brother Bobby all ran smart races from 35:00 to 52:00. They adjusted to the heat and ran smart races.

Then there were those being attended to by EMS technicians. Let me tell you, it is scary to see someone stumbling and weakened by the effects of heat and exhaustion. It's definitely something to be concerned with.

You can avoid all of this by planning your race and sticking to your plan. First be honest with yourself. Then write down your splits for every mile, making sure they are evenly paced and once again, within your abilities. Memorize your spits and listen for them at the mile markers. The key to running a good 10k is proper pace.

I'll be back in 1986 and I promise myself it'll be a different race. I found out one more thing at the post race party. The Wysockis may be fast runners but they can't drink beer as fast as some of us *Low Country Runner*s. Right, Gordon and Buzz? Talk about a runners' high!

Note: I just had to look up Leon's 1986 time for this book: apparently he took his own advice and ran 37:16 to finish and take home a top 5 percent age group award, despite a Bridge Run that was even hotter than the 1985 race. CJ

Interviews:
Local Favorites For The 1985 Bridge Run

Originally appeared in the March-April 1985 Low Country Runner

It would take more space than we have for this newsletter to list all the races these runners have placed highly in or won. Only one of them has ever won the Bridge Run, and now that the race has gotten so big it gets harder for our locals to win every year. Each of them was interviewed separately and asked the same questions, either in person or by telephone. The local favorites I talked to are: Gail Bailey, Benita Brooks (Schlau) Marilyn Davey, Carol Davis, Marc Embler, Paul Laymon, Frank Lowry, David Luhrs, Anne Boone Reed and Bob Schlau. I did not mean to slight any good local runners whom I did not interview. Cedric Jaggers.

CJ - how many bridge runs have you run?

Gail - All but the first one.

Benita - One.

Marilyn - Four.

Carol - Two.

Marc - All but one.

Paul - Four.

Frank - The last two.

David - All of them.
Anne - Five.
Bob - All of them.
CJ - are you entering the open or the age group division?
(Editor's note- All runners had to declare for either the open or age group competition. Open means you are competing for prize money - if you do not finish as one of the top 6 open division runners you receive nothing, just as runners who finish out of the top 5% of their age group receive nothing.)
Gail - Age group.
Benita - Age group.
Marilyn - Age group.
Marc - Probably the open.
Paul - Age group.
Frank - Age group.
David - Age group.
Anne - Age group.
Bob - Open.
CJ - What is your 10k best time?
Gail - 39:06 in the 1981 big brothers/big sisters.
Benita - 38:30 in last year's bridge run.
Marilyn - 39:11 in the 1984 east cooper kiwanis 10k.
Carol - 39:27 at the 1984 jolly folly run.
Marc - 29:38 at the hyatt hilton head in 1980.
Paul - 31:15 at last year's bridge run.
Frank - 32:00 at the 10k mark of the charlie post 15k in 1984.
David - 31:09 in the 1979 black river run in kingstree.
Anne - 37:58 at the 1982 beaufort run through history.
Bob - 30:47 in last year's bridge run.
CJ - What is your best bridge run time and place?
Gail - 39:17 last year, 2nd place overall female in 1980.
Benita - 38:30 for 10th place female last year.
Marilyn - 39:49 last year, 4th place female in 1983.
Carol - Both were last year; 40:13 for 18th place female.
Marc - Best time was last year's 30:42, best place was 1st in 1981.
Paul - Both were last year; 8th place in 31:15.
Frank - 33:34 for 20th place in 1983.
David - 32:48 in 1980 and 1984, 5th place in 1980.

Anne - 38:58 for 3rd place in 1982.
Bob - 30:47 last year, 2nd place in 1979.
CJ - Do you think there is a best way to run the bridge run?
Gail - Yeah, the best way is conservatively. Actually i don't know. Different people probably need different ways. If you feel strong, charge the hills and really run the downhills. I've found that coasting the downhills hurt me. Then, hang on after the bridges.
Benita - Capitalize on the downhill. Run it as fast as you can because you've got almost a mile of downhill. If you can get up enough speed, it helps you on the overall average.
Marilyn - No. It just depends on how you feel that day. I believe in trying to be consistent - first mile same as the last mile.
Carol - For me it's to go out strong and steady without getting too tired, and then to fly downhill.
Marc - Not really. It is all up to the individual, especially on the bridge. For people who run hills well, they should establish themselves in the first half of the race and then hold on. Others who don't run hills well should probably hold back the first half, then go for it after they get off the hills.
Paul - You've got three hills. You need to run hard the first mile before you hit the hill, easy up the hills, really accelerate downhill. Once you get off the hills try to maintain your pace.
Frank - Run a cautious first mile, don't overextend yourself. Save something for the bridges. After that, go.
David - Go out the first mile like you do in every other 10k. Get with the people you usually hang with, or go with someone a little faster. But don't really push the bridges because there is too much distance left after you get off the bridges. Try to have something left when you get off the bridges.
Anne - Take it easy going up the hills and go like crazy going downhill. Then once the bridge is over, run like crazy.
Bob - Personal success has come running the first 3 miles relatively conservatively, then taking off or trying to go the second downhill.
CJ - With only about 3 weeks left when this newsletter gets into everyone's hands, do you have any advice for runners trying to get ready for the bridge run?
Gail - Don't put on any extra pounds and stay sound physically. You can't improve your running that much. You can sharpen with some short speedwork, but be careful.
Benita - I think racing helps. I plan to race the two weeks before the bridge run

because when i lay off i get stale. So do some sharpening up races at 90% effort.

Marilyn - Stick to your game plan. Do what you've been doing.

Carol - Run the bridge and see what it's like. Go to another 10k race a couple of weeks before the bridge run. Try to be in the best health you can.

Marc - Most of your training should have been put in. The last 3 weeks should be used to sharpen up. Do speedwork faster and cut mileage. If you try to increase mileage it can only hurt you.

Paul - I'm going to hit the bridge every saturday morning before 6. I suggest trying to get down to the bridge at least once, just to get used to it. Early saturday morning is best because traffic is really light. Run across the bridge just to get used to the hills, because there aren't any hills in the charleston area.

Frank - Keep running your normal amounts. I wouldn't recommend training on the bridge, it is too dangerous because there is too much traffic and the concrete is too hard.

David - Stay off the bridge. Instead run lots of short high hills; there are a few around. Mentally, any bridge is good, but physically the big bridge is hard on you.

Anne - Do speedwork, lose weight.

Bob - You're not going to get in shape in 3 weeks. Just use the time if you are taking the race seriously, for rest and speedwork. If you are just surviving the race, do 2 more weeks of what you've been doing and the last week take it easy.

CJ - Any advice for first time bridge runners?

Gail - Keep picking them up and putting them down.

Benita - Run your heart out and enjoy.

Marilyn - Enjoy it. It's got to be one of the most thrilling races to run. Watch the people, and have a good time; it's such an accomplishment just to do it.

Carol - Don't ask too much of yourself. Don't hurt yourself on the bridge, it's just not worth it. Go fast after the bridge.

Marc - Have a good time, enjoy it. Be a little cautious going over the bridge, and be sure you have enough left to make the last half of the race.

Paul - It depends on whether it's your first 10k. Just try to take it easy going uphill. You'll want to push yourself because everybody else is going fast and the hills will wipe you out. Try to run faster the second half than the first half of the race. Try to find somebody you know you can run with and try to hold onto them for the whole race.

Frank - If you haven't started training, get started. Pace yourself during the race. It's a long way and there are two spans.

David - Go out and relax. Don't let the bridge scare you.

Anne - Don't start out too fast and don't run too hard going up the hills.

Bob - Be conservative the first mile. The temptation is to take off fast with the more experienced runners. If you do you really will pay for it.

CJ - What do you hope to run this year: your best time and your worst case time.

Gail - Best - break 39. Worst - 40 minutes.

Benita - Best - 38:15. Worst - 39:30.

Marilyn - Best - break 39. Worst - i'd feel like my training had fallen apart if i wasn't just right under 42 minutes.

Carol - Best - i'd like to get in the 39's. Worst - around 41.

Marc - Best - a pr for the bridge, under 30:30. Worst - just to finish. My wife Mary Jo is expecting march 19 and the baby could come late causing real running problems.

Paul - Best - 30:30. Worst - 31:30.

Frank - Best - under 31:30. Worst - can't give a time, anything could happen.

David - Best - under 32:00. Worst - 34:00.

Anne - Best - hope to run in the 38's. Worst - about 40 minutes.

Bob - Best - my dream is to break 30 minutes, but probably 30:25 is my realistic top time. Worst - 31:30.

Aftermath - The Local Favorites' Bridge Runs

Originally appeared in the May-June 1985 Low Country Runner

The fates were cruel: heat and humidity on Bridge Run day this year. These are the same runners who were interviewed in the March-April *Low Country Runner*. All were interviewed separately by telephone by Cedric Jaggers, except for David Luhrs who could not be reached. You can re-read that previous interview to see that their times, like all the other runners, suffered the ravages of the weather.

Gail Bailey: 39:30, 16th female, 1st 35-39

Benita Brooks (Schlau) - 40:14, 19th female

Marilyn Davey: 39:22, 15th female, 1st 30-34

Carol Davis: 41:18, 26th female, 3rd 30-34

Marc Embler: 31:29, 20th overall

Paul Laymon: 32:07, 23rd overall, 1st 20-24

Frank Lowry: 34:34, 44th male, 3rd 25-29

David Luhrs: 35:12, 53rd male, 7th 25-29

Anne Boone Reed: 40:02, 18th female, 3rd 35-39

Bob Schlau: 31:42, 20th overall

CJ - How Was Your Bridge Run?

Gail - When I started going over the hills my legs were burning. I didn't notice I had injured my left knee until two days later. I put on my shoes not expecting it would still hurt and it did. I may have torn the pleca in my knee joint per Dr. Rick Reed. I had no kick at all. Usually I have a good kick. I was zapped. I had no get up and go left at the end.

Benita - Terrible. I thought I was going faster than I was. The effort was more than last year. I'm 10 pounds heavier and doing less mileage and I guess it hurt me.

Marilyn - Fantastic. It was great. It's over. I had trained hard for it. I thought at the top of the second span "This isn't as bad as one of (husband) Billy's workouts that he made me do."

Carol - My Bridge Run was not that good. It was mediocre; the first 2 miles were good, the 2 in the middle were okay, the last 2 miles were lousy. I ran too hard. I just wasn't used to the hills and pushed too hard. When I got on King Street I didn't have anything left.

Marc - Initially I was very disappointed. After looking at everybody else's times, they were slow too and I can't think of an excuse. Even with everybody else running slow, I felt I wasn't where I should have finished. I kept thinking "How did they lengthen the course, they had to stretch the bridge."

Paul - was about a minute and a half off what I expected and I think everybody was. I was pretty pleased with where I was because I was seeded 73rd and finished 23rd. I have to delete the time and accept the place. It was a tough course. I was real happy with the run. I feel like it was a sub 31 minute effort. All in all I feel like my race was a success.

Frank - Not very good. I don't know what more to say. I had trouble on the Crosstown and had to stop a while.

Anne - Bad. My problem began the minute I started going down the first span. I got Charlie horses in my quads. I think I may have over carbo loaded and I went out so fast, 5:50 first mile, and ran up the first span so hard I had cramps in my quads the whole way after that. I'm surprised I ran as fast as I did. I was in good shape for it. I wouldn't have set a PR, but I would have been close to 39 minutes. I couldn't walk up or down stairs for 3 days afterwards.

Bob - So so. I didn't enjoy it nearly as much as last year.

CJ - Did the heat bother you?

Gail - It must have. I didn't feel good. I've felt worst at other races, but not a whole lot. The heat affected me: the week before I had been running well and had a lot of confidence. I feel on a cool clear day I would have run a better time. The humidity was worse than the heat and it really bothered me.

Benita - Heat doesn't seem to bother me, but I was heavier this year so it may have.

Marilyn - No, the heat didn't bother me. I was concentrating so hard I never thought about it. I did notice we lost that breeze when we turned off the King Street extension (Crosstown overpass), but I wasn't thinking about the heat during the race.

Carol - Yes, to a degree. It's not the entire reason nor the only reason I didn't do as well as I hoped to. I remember being hot, but I don't remember it bothering me.

Marc - To be very honest I really don't think it did. I don't have too much trouble in the heat.

Paul - t didn't seem to, but I'm sure it did. I didn't get hot, but I did have to take water and I wasn't expecting to. I went into the race on a real high - went through the fist mile in 4:38 and thought it was going to be my day. But then the bridge fell on me.

Frank - The heat didn't bother me that much. I was just physically tired and wasn't going fast enough for it to bother me.

Anne - No I don't think it affected my race. It didn't help, but I was so loaded with water, but heat usually doesn't bother me.

Bob - I think the heat bothered me. The only thing I can figure out, so many people ran slow, it was just warm and humid enough and windy enough that you didn't notice it.

CJ - Were you satisfied with your time and place?

Gail - Yes I was. I tried as hard as I could and I beat some people I wasn't supposed to beat.

Benita - No. I was very disappointed. I was really upset after the race.

Marilyn - Yes, yes, yes. It was my best Bridge Run ever.

Carol - No. I dropped from 18th to 26th place this year from last. So I wasn't satisfied. I should have been about where I was last year. I did beat my seed however.

Marc - No to both. I was real disappointed with my time. Place wise, I look at the people ahead of me and I felt that even having a bad day, I should have been close to 31 minutes, but time more than place was off. At the top of the second span I gave up a little bit. I didn't start running again until Bob Schlau passed me. I felt like there was nobody ahead of me then that I could catch.

Paul - was not satisfied with the time, but I was real satisfied with the place. Last year I ran 31:15 and I'm in better shape this year but the time was slower. But when I consider who I finished near, I'm pleased with my race.

Frank - No. I was counting on running 31:30 and was a little disappointed. But on that day I was counting myself out of the race from the first mile, so I knew I

Runners swarm like ants over the first span of the Grace Bridge. News and Courier photo by Wade Spees

wasn't going to set any personal records.

Anne - No, definitely not. I'm mad 'cause Gail beat me. I was hurting so bad I felt like I was running 8 minute miles.

Bob - Satisfied with the place. There wasn't anybody ahead of me I thought shouldn't be. I wasn't satisfied with the time. Sometimes on a day like that you have to run for place, not time. The bridge seemed a lot harder than last year though I finished strong. I ran the last 2 miles under 10 minutes, but I didn't run the bridge as fast.

1985 Awards

Note; the race used an Open Division - elite runners contesting for prize money were not eligible for age group awards.

Open Div. money winners:
Overall Male
1 Mike O'Reilly . . . . Ireland . . . . 29:28 . . . $1,000
2 Craig Holm . . . . Victor, NY . . . . 29:32 . . . . $500
3 Hans Koeleman . . . . Holland . . . . 29:40 . . . . $400
4 Mark Scrutton . . . . England . . . . 29:50 . . . . $300
5 Brendan Quinn . . . . Ireland . . . . 29:52 . . . . $200
6 Jeff Scuffins . . . . Clemson, SC . . . . 29:55 . . . . $100

Overall Female . . . . .
1 Christina Boxer . . . . England . . . . 34:08 . . . $1,000
2 Sue Schneider . . . . Minneapolis, MN . . . . . .34:15 . . . . $500
3 Diane Bussa . . . . East Lansing, MI. . . . . . . 34:42 . . . . $400
4 Jan Ettle . . . . St Cloud, MN . . . . 35:35 . . . . $300
5 Candice Strobach . . . . . Charlotte, NC . . . . .35:41 . . . . $200
6 Ruth Wysocki. . . . . Canyon Lake, CA . . . . . . 37:20 . . . . $100

Special award:
Dewey Wise Trophy for oldest finisher who runs a time faster than his or her age in minutes:
Caldwell Nixon, 76 . . . . Lincolnton, NC 60:50

Masters Male
1 Art Williams . . . . Frankfort, KY 33:54

Masters Female
1 Peggy Ledford . . . . Charleston, SC 44:51

Age Group Award Winners
(Ceramic pitchers for the top 3 with additional mugs to the top 5% up to a maximum of 25 in each age group).

Male 14 & under (119 finishers, 6 awards)
1 Mike Strohm 38:18
2 Gregory Burch. 39:05
3 Kevin West. 40:12
4 Kevin Kelley. 40:33
5 Donald Lavigne 41:22
6 Gerrick Mundz 41:55

Female 14 & under (26 fin., 3 awards)
1 Monica Steffes 48:07
2 Stacey Clark. 49:18
3 Danielle DeCandia 54:19

Male 15-19 (152 finishers, 8 awards)
1 Chris LeGourd 34:30
2 E. Linjustiniano. 34:39
3 Richard Golden 35:10
4 Brian Payne 35:51
5 Mark Newnham 36:03

6 Jeff Szcaepanik...... 36:26
7 Alvin Chester...... 36:33
8 David Prockop...... 36:34

Female 15-19 (55 finishers, 3 awards)
1 Rebecca Conklin...... 42:15
2 Sally Christian...... 43:31
3 Fredee Chase...... 44:21

Male 20-24 (367 finishers, 19 awards)
1 Paul Laymon...... 32:07
2 Scott Kidd...... 33:21
3 Daniel Brown...... 33:53
4 Keith Wilson...... 34:26
5 Huey Inman...... 35:11
6 Gary Quinney...... 35:24
7 Owen Woolever...... 35:58
8 Andy Pinson...... 35:59
9 Joseph Garand...... 36:13
10 Edward Moore...... 36:15
11 Thomas Lydon...... 36:19
12 Ian Brzezinski...... 36:20
13 Eddie Parsley...... 36:39
14 John Diggs...... 36:49
15 Skip Miller...... 36:54
16 Scott Murr...... 37:19
17 Ralph Oliver...... 37:29
18 Alex Gordeuk...... 37:40
19 James Koterba...... 37:52

Female 20-24 (160 finishers, 8 awards)
1 Pam Fulk...... 40:42
2 Betsy Veronee...... 42:55
3 Linda Fleming...... 43:14
4 Rhonda Freeman...... 45:25
5 Stacie Lee Novak...... 46:12
6 Denise Holliday...... 46:22
7 Karen Rhodes...... 46:40
8 Louise Small...... 46:42

Male 25-29 (685 finishers, 25 awards)
1 Rex Wiggins...... 32:44
2 Ed Pennebaker...... 33:34
3 Frank Lowry...... 34:34
4 Mike Chodnicki...... 34:57
5 Marc Plantico...... 35:02
6 Skeet Keyes...... 35:11
7 David Luhrs...... 35:12
8 George Howe...... 35:14
9 Randy Carmichael...... 35:15
10 Michael Fronsoe...... 35:28
11 Mike Hart...... 36:00
12 Tim Hamilton...... 36:01
13 Jeff Stone...... 36:04
14 Glen Chamberlain...... 36:05
15 Charles Jones...... 36:21
16 Bill Bauknight...... 36:31
17 Jarvie Young...... 36:54
18 Gene Hallman...... 37:03
19 Brian Mervak...... 37:04
20 Edwin Griggs...... 37:07
21 Timi Kennedy...... 37:18
22 Richard Teague...... 37:20
23 David Bourgeois...... 37:21
24 Gary Eaton...... 37:28
25 Johnny Witt...... 37:29

Female 25-29 (244 finishers, 13 awards)
1 Michele Haskins...... 40:45
2 Gale Courtney...... 40:51
3 Janet Ballenger...... 41:02
4 Cheryl McSwain...... 41:17
5 Nina Parks...... 43:35
6 Jan Derrick...... 43:45
7 Laura Christensen...... 43:53
8 Camille Baldwin...... 43:59
9 Lucy Foxworth...... 44:20
10 Deborah Marion...... 44:22
11 Linda Momeier...... 44:36
12 Lesa Bethea...... 44:54
13 Caroline Scott...... 44:54

Male 30-34 (758 finishers, 25 awards)
1 Kenneth Wilson...... 32:16
2 Mac Coile...... 32:20
3 Jack Dove...... 34:02
4 Frank Kohlenstein...... 34:18
5 Mario Salas...... 35:29
6 Martin Gass...... 35:35
7 J.D. Cash...... 35:48
8 Leon McCray...... 35:50
9 Thomas Nickols...... 36:18
10 Scott Roark...... 36:22
11 Norman Nickel...... 36:38
12 Rick Corbin...... 36:50
13 Tracy Giles...... 35:56
14 Rusty Doyle...... 37:01
15 Fred Mullen...... 37:13
16 Steve Smeal...... 37:19
17 Ricky Vaughn...... 37:20
18 Keith Sanders...... 37:30
19 Larry D'Ippolito...... 37:37
20 Timothy Rhyne...... 37:46
21 David Dawes...... 37:49
22 David Freeze...... 37:57
23 Gary Ricker...... 38:04
24 Michael Holmes...... 38:12
25 William Hollingsworth...... 38:19

Female 30-34 (223 finishers, 12 awards)
1 Marilyn Davey...... 39:22
2 Cindy Kline...... 41:39
3 Carol Davis...... 41:48
4 Bonnie Poore Long...... 41:59
5 Carolyn Nelson...... 42:23
6 Deborah Massey...... 42:28
7 Deborah Himelein...... 42:56
8 Susanne Rhodes...... 43:03
9 Salley Redfearn...... 44:23
10 Peggy Brinson...... 44:48
11 Sissy Claxton...... 44:57
12 Sally Mincher...... 44:59

Male 35-39 (640 finishers, 25 awards)
1 Reed Watson...... 35:06
2 Steve Wesley...... 35:12
3 Thomas Jones...... 35:26
4 Marcus Phillips...... 35:47
5 J Richard Marion...... 35:55
6 Bob Wilson...... 35:56
7 Bill Peay...... 36:07
8 Glenn Dennis...... 36:12

9 Jimmy Hadden...... 36:44
10 Sandy Weatherford...... 36:51
11 Don Player...... 36:55
12 Billy Davey...... 36:59
13 Douglas Gentry...... 37:00
14 Edward Kromka...... 37:11
15 Cedric Jaggers...... 37:28
16 Thomas King...... 37:36
17 Donald Reynolds...... 37:51
18 Tom Blankenship...... 37:53
19 Bill Sloan...... 37:48
20 Richard Barnwell...... 38:13
21 James Horne...... 38:15
22 Skipper Hewitt...... 38:19
23 Larry Standlee...... 38:27
24 Melvin Newton...... 38:29
25 David Kirk...... 38:30

Female 35-39 (146 finishers, 8 awards)
1 Gail Bailey...... 39:30
2 Peggy Schug...... 40:00
3 Anne Boone Reed...... 40:02
4 Gail Sharber...... 42:27
5 Barbara Moore...... 42:58
6 Barbara Paulsen...... 43:05
7 Connie Gruver...... 43:32
8 Lynda Holdridge...... 43:53

Male 40-44 (389 finishers, 20 awards)
1 Don Coffman...... 32:27
2 Art Williams...... 33:54
3 Mike Kelly...... 33:59
4 Morgan Looney...... 34:06
5 Stan Arthur...... 34:58
6 Ken Finney...... 35:49
7 Chris Pappas...... 36:26
8 Clayton Krejci...... 37:02
9 Dupree Elvington...... 37:06
10 Alan Rose...... 37:40
11 William Hollaway...... 37:56
12 James Keller...... 38:15
13 David Miller...... 38:17
14 Matthew Hutmaker...... 38:39
15 Neil Jacobs...... 38:41
16 Tom Morrow...... 38:57
17 Reaves Gasque...... 39:01
18 Douglas Young...... 39:30
19 Ray Fulmer...... 39:32
20 Jon Houser...... 39:36

Female 40-44 (72 finishers, 4 awards)
1 Peggy Ledford...... 44:51
2 Joyce Ploeger...... 46:14
3 Diane Deecheandia...... 48:43
4 Bettye Foster...... 49:19

Male 45-49 (170 finishers, 9 awards)
1 Adrian Craven...... 35:22
2 Ed Ledford...... 37:05
3 James Adams...... 37:27
4 Dean Godwin...... 38:03
5 Don Austell...... 39:42
6 Robert Howell...... 40:01
7 Joe Page...... 40:34
8 Jim Harrell...... 40:51
9 Bruce Morrison...... 40:54

Female 45-49 (31 finishers, 3 awards)
1 Frankie Crume...... 46:53
2 Suzanne Foster...... 49:11
3 Sheila Elmore...... 50:35

Male 50-54 (104 finishers, 6 awards)
1 Gerald Koch...... 36:30
2 Sammie Yarborough...... 38:25
3 Robert Bell...... 38:30
4 Ken Kurts...... 38:31
5 Jack Gilmore...... 38:45
6 Bobby Hollis...... 39:29

Female 50-54 (14 finishers, 3 awards)
1 Wendy Williams...... 48:59
2 Mary Purvis...... 53:58
3 Ann Stanton...... 57:35

Male 55-59 (44 finishers, 3 awards)
1 Gordon English Sr...... 41:32
2 Charles Moore...... 42:11
3 Marvin Mollnow...... 43:48

Female 55-59 (8 finishers, 3 awards)
1 Garthedon Embler...... 49:22
2 Nancy Bell...... 49:55
3 Lois Joop...... 1:00:08

Male 60-64 (18 finishers, 3 awards)
1 David Mellard...... 44:07
2 Waymon Stuart...... 46:30
3 Lawrence Moore...... 46:33

Female 60 & over (4 finishers, 3 awards)
1 Margarete Wright...... 54:37
2 Frances Harvey...... 1:03:15
3 Shirley Shade...... 1:07:33

Male 65 and over (5 finishers, 3 awards)
1 George Sheehan...... 42:26
2 Ed Shaffer...... 43:58
3 Carl Jenkins...... 50:39

Compiled by Cedric Jaggers from original complete race results.

The 1986 race was delayed 30 minutes because of the traffic snarls caused by the fog. News and Courier photo by Wade Spees

CHAPTER 9
1986
The Fog, The Wreck, The Delay, The Second Hottest Race

The ninth Bridge Run will never be forgotten due to fog, delays and heat. The date was moved back into April and the start was scheduled for 8:30 a.m. on April 5, 1986. At 7:20 a.m. misfortune struck. Incredibly dense fog had reduced visibility to about 10 feet, causing a bus to ram into a car and block the "new" Silas Pearman Bridge. That was the only access to the start as the other bridge, the Grace Memorial, was one-way out of Mount Pleasant. At almost the same time, another accident alongside the buses blocked the bridge's remaining lanes.

The fog burned off by the scheduled 8:30 start, but so many cars and buses were still on the bridge that the race didn't begin until 9 a.m. The temperature rose during that time to 72 degrees, making the ninth run second only to the first one for hot weather conditions. After the race, an estimated two dozen runners were treated for heat exhaustion and dehydration.

Ironically, this was the second time that *The Runner* magazine had named the Bridge Run to its best races list and the second time the start was delayed causing the race to lose that ranking. The Sunday *News and Courier* had a superb picture of the fog-covered bridge with the title "The Problem". An estimated 300 to 500 runners were still on the new bridge when the race started. Some of them just jumped out of their cars and joined the race in progress.

The race entry fee was raised to $9 for the 1986 race. For the second year in a row, the race was broadcast live on local TV Channel 5.

Hans Koeleman of Holland had learned from the previous year when he had charged hard and led up the spans of the "old" Grace Memorial Bridge only to fade to third place. This year he stayed with the lead pack, which reached the first mile mark in 4:25, until he got off the bridges. Then he began to pull away on the flats downtown, though he was never comfortable and kept looking over his shoulder as he neared the finish to win in 29:29.

"I felt very good and very relaxed coming off the bridge this time," he told The *News and Courier*. "I really worked toward that. Last year, I didn't feel good coming off the bridge. I was tired. If you come off that bridge tired, it's going to be tough. I felt very, very smooth and rested coming off the bridge. If anybody was going to go, I was going to be able to go with them at any pace. This is only the second road race I've won in my life. I've run so many of them and never really won. I forget what it feels like."

Mark Scrutton of Boulder, Colo., was second in 29:34. "Hans ran a real good race," he said. "He was definitely running well today and put the boot in where it counted." Jim Haughey of Clemson was third in 29:40.

Twin sisters from Newton, Mass., took first and third in the female division as Lesley Welch took the lead going up the first span of the bridge and set a course record 33:37 to win. "I planned on going out slow," she told the newspaper. "The mistake I usually make is I go out too hard and the heat really gets to me. I held back and I felt I had more spunk on the hills. You can't run fast on those hills. But sometimes it's more fun to have a challenging course. You finish a race like this and you feel like you've accomplished a lot more.

"It was really fun, different and challenging, and the people were great. I never expected so many people out watching. I've never run over a bridge in a race like this."

Kathy Pfiefer of Albuquerque, N.M., was second in 34:03 and Lisa Welch was third in 34:20. "Lesley ran by very strongly and kept that up the remainder of the race," Pfiefer said.

Masters winners were: Tom Dooley 33:19, Alan Pilling 33:55 and Mike Kelly 35:14. The female Masters winners were Gail Bailey of Charleston in 39:21, Mary Anne Wehrum of Memphis, Tenn., 40:32 and Natalie Spalding 41:05.

A new award, the Dr. Marcus Newberry trophy, was presented to the first male and female finisher from the Tri-County. Bob Schlau of Charleston was 12th overall in 31:26 and Benita Brooks (Schlau) of Charleston was 15th female in 38:36 to claim these prizes. The Dewey Wise Trophy went to Clayton Brelsford of Wilmington, N.C., 71, who finished in a time of 54:37.

Olympian Jim Ryun was guest speaker at the pre-race symposium and the famed miler, 38 years old on race day, finished the race in 34:11. The race course was changed, and re-TAC certified (#SC86008WN), due to construction downtown. The start was moved over half-a-mile further back on Coleman Boulevard to Moultrie High School, which made the cut-through street Wentworth instead of Market to cross over from King to Meeting streets.

There were 6,684 entrants, and 5,318 official finishers were listed in the results booklet. The results, compiled using a computer program written by Paul Smith of Island Runners, were taken to the printer the Thursday after the race and mailed to all finishers; 4,116 male and 1,202 female. This marked the first time over 1,000 women completed any race in South Carolina. A total of five men broke the 30-minute barrier, while 251 men and 17 women broke 40 minutes. There were 1,872 runners who completed the race in less than 50 minutes while a total of 3,182 managed to cross the line in less than an hour.

The Sunday *News and Courier* had two half-pages of coverage of the race and listed only the top 75 male finishers and the top 30 female finishers of the race, with age group results listed three deep. There were an estimated 3,000 participants in the third untimed Bridge Walk.

Karl Gueldner was the new race director in 1986 and served as director for the ninth through the 12th Bridge Runs, during which time, he became the first paid race director. In 1986 the readers of *Carolina Runner* magazine (now *Running Journal*), voted the Bridge Run "favorite race".

Other Voices
An Interview With Karl Gueldner, 1986 Bridge Run Director
By Cedric Jaggers, Originally appeared in the March-Aril 1986 Low Country Runner

The race director for the Cooper River Bridge Run has a massive task. After all, the race is one of the 100 largest in the nation (51st for 1984, the latest year for which figures are available, according to the National Running Data Center). The Bridge Run was named by *The Runner* magazine, February 1986, as one of the 40 best races in the country, regional division. Karl Gueldner is the new race director. He was interviewed on the telephone by Cedric Jaggers on Feb. 12, 1986.

CJ - How many runners do you expect or hope to have for this year's Bridge Run?

Karl - A shade over 6,000 if everything goes like it has the past few years.

CJ - Why is there a new course this year?

Karl - Because they are building on Beaufain and Hazel and those streets will be torn up. The construction won't be completed in time for the race.

CJ - Will the course be changed next year?

Karl - It should go back to the same course used last year. What we are hoping is to get the people who are building the convention hotel to be a sponsor next year. We could have the symposium, pre-race events and everything centralized. The race would go right by their front door. But nothing is definite for next year right now.

CJ - Almost every runner I've talked to is unhappy with the date change. They feel if it was moved it should have gone earlier in March so it wouldn't be so hot. Why April?

Karl - The rationale was to get away from the NCAA basketball tournament so the race could get more coverage. We also wanted to get away from the Crescent City and Cherry Blossom races which were held the same weekend and competed for the elite runners. But then they both changed dates also due to Easter falling the last weekend in March this year. Since it is March 19th next year, they will probably change back. We figured that one week's difference won't make much difference in the weather. We intend to use the first Saturday in April from now on.

CJ - Will complete results be compiled and mailed out again this year? If yes, by whom?

Karl - Yes. We are going to try to do something different with the results to make them nicer. We plan to put photos in it and make them like a brochure. Dr. Brian Smith will compile results by computer and I guess I'll send them out.

CJ - Have you secured any invited runners yet?

Karl - No. Nobody is definite yet.

CJ - What T-shirt design and color will you use this year?

Karl - We'll use the same logo design as last year for the final time. We plan to change it next year. We haven't decided on the color yet. We'll decide that at the next Bridge Run Committee meeting.

CJ - What is the best thing about being Bridge Run director?

Karl - There isn't any. I've been wondering that myself. The thing I've enjoyed most is organizing it from the start and talking with and meeting so many people. Plus, you can put in your own ideas. You have a little more input as director.

CJ - What is the worst thing about being Bridge Run director?

Karl - I was overwhelmed by the number of overall responsibilities: meeting printing deadlines; taking care of and finding sponsors; just the initial work to get everything going. It's all downhill from there.

CJ - Are you enjoying being Bridge Run director?

Karl - Yes I am. It's been challenging to say the least, and it has increased my respect for running in general and for runners. I don't think you could do it more than a couple of years in a row; you'd get burned out. None of us do it as a job. We are all volunteers trying to do the Bridge Run and keep our work up and maintain the high Bridge Run standards has been the hardest thing.

CJ - Who will be Bridge Run director next year?

Karl - We don't know yet. That comes up after the race is over. The committee will meet and vote on who it will be. (Editor's note from original interview: The BR Committee, each with one vote as to what goes on with the race: City of Charleston - Mark Blatchford, College of Charleston - Roy Hills, Town of Mt Pleasant - Jimmy Seignious, Charleston Running Club - Chuck Magera, Medical University of South Carolina - Bob Kirk, Charleston County Parks and Recreation Commission - Karl Gueldner.)

CJ - Anything you want to add or say to the runners about the Bridge Run?

Karl - We would like to have input from the runners as far as what they feel should be changed. We need positive or negative input. People can write anyone on the committee. We have six members and six viewpoints, so we'd like to hear from runners. Especially the average runner. Drop me a line: Karl Gueldner P.O. Box (address deleted as it is no longer a valid one. CJ)

My 1986 Cooper River Bridge Run

By Susan Kerr, Originally appeared in the May-June 1986 Low Country Runner

I woke up the morning of April 5 with equal feelings of excitement and apprehension. This would be my first Cooper River Bridge Run. In preparation for the race I had been running 20 miles a week and had completed several 10k races. I had tried to run over the bridge only twice and was still very intimidated by it. My goal was to finish in less than an hour and hopefully, to run the whole way.

My running partner, Glenda McCrory, and I planned to leave about 7 a.m. to get to the starting line in time to look for friends and warm up before the race. We left one car downtown with supplies for after the race and headed for Mount Pleasant.

We drove onto the Cooper River Bridge and we were immediately stopped by a long line of traffic. We still had an hour until the start of the race, so we were talking and waving at other runners we recognized. As we crept over the bridge we watched the fog lift until we could see the bridge we would soon be running across.

As it got closer to the 8:30 start time, other runners began leaving their cars and jogging over the bridge. I also was concerned that we would miss the start.

We finally got to Mount Pleasant, parked the car and began jogging to the starting line. We were about a mile away and had only 10 minutes to reach it. This was not much slower than our normal running pace, so we decided to walk as far as we could. We were about two tenths of a mile from the start when we heard the gun go off. We stopped and stretched a little as we waited for the first runners to come by. We started jogging along the side of the road and gradually moved in until we were running in the crowd.

Because we started near the front of the runners, the pace was a little faster than we had planned, but it was difficult to slow down. I was beginning to feel tired as we approached the bridge and my legs had not loosened up any. I also was not prepared for the crowd as we were all compressed onto the narrow lanes of the bridge.

There was little room to pass anyone and looking ahead there was a solid mass of runners. I tried to maintain my pace going up the fist hill, but about three-fourths of the way to the top I gave in and walked to the crest of the hill. When I started running downhill again I was feeling better, but it was difficult to make up lost ground due to the crowd.

I started up the second hill determined to run all the way. The hill seemed to go on forever. I tried not to think about how far it was to the top. I wished for some of the music that had been advertised for the bridge and along King Street to keep my mind off how bad I was feeling.

I had not seen anyone I knew since Glenda left me on the first hill, so I did not have anyone to talk to. Again I found myself walking up the last portion of the hill. As I started running down the hill I knew the worst part of the day was over.

I fought my way to the water stand at the bottom of the hill, then started up the third hill. I had been warned not to take the King Street (Cross Town) overpass too lightly, but it seemed so much smaller than the other hills that I ran up without much difficulty.

I was looking forward to the flat run on King Street. It was hot and there still was no music, but there was a little more room to run. Even though I had walked part of the race, my pace was fast enough that I could still finish in under an hour if I just maintained my speed.

Running by Marion Square where some runners had already finished was very difficult, but the spectators there were encouraging everyone. I kept running down King Street trying not to anticipate the turn to Meeting Street. I did not want to run by the street I thought we would be turning on. I finally made the turn onto Meeting Street and started back towards Marion Square and I knew I would finish the race. I even felt a little energy returning. I crossed the finish line under 59 minutes and headed for the refreshments.

The walk to the water was more difficult than the race. There was no water available when I passed the last two water stops on the course so I was very dry. I got a couple of glasses of water and started looking for friends. I wandered around for about 20 minutes before I saw anyone I knew. Finally, I saw Glenda and we headed for the awards ceremony and then to the celebrations we had been waiting all morning for.

Three Questions About The Bridge Run

Originally appeared in the March-April 1986 Low Country Runner

Bridge Run Director Karl Gueldner said he would like to hear from runners with positive or negative input. I know how hard it is to get people to respond and put pen to paper (sort of like pulling teeth), so I got the running club directory and started to phone people and ended up with a couple dozen. Everyone was asked the same three questions with no warning or setup. I did not tell anyone my opinion until after I'd written down their answers. Responses are alphabetical by last name.

CJ - What do you like best about the bridge run?
Don Austell - The uniqueness of it, going over the bridge into the old historic city.
Marie Borchlewicz - All the people and excitement of it.
Benita Brooks - The size and excitement that it stirs.
Gary Butts - Nothing. That thing has destroyed me.
Tom Davis - The course. It's a little bit of everything; hilly, flat and scenic. It's challenging.
Barry DeCarli - I like the atmosphere.
Sam Derrick - The crowd
Terry Gibson - I like the people, the crowds, the enthusiasm.
Dupree Elvington - I like the fact that it's a tough 10k course.
Linda Frolich - I just like the crowds and the atmosphere. I'm a jogger, there's camaraderie and it's a real fun day. I like the challenge of the bridge.
Dennis Hiott - The best is that it is just a lot of people and it's a lot of fun to have so many people in it.
Ed Hogan - The challenge of running over the bridge. The camaraderie at the after race party.
Madeline Kornahrens - The challenge.
Ed Ledford - It brings so many runners in. The excitement about it: it keeps you on edge for weeks.
Art Liberman - Probably the challenge of the race course, the challenge of the hills.
Barbara Locklear - The finish.
Tommy Mullins - The finish line.
Carolyn Nelson - I like every part of it. Running with everybody. The excitement of running the bridge itself.
Connie Owens - A feeling of accomplishment to get over those bridges.
Frank Palazzolla - The bridge itself and the camaraderie after the run. Also it's well organized.
Joyce Ploeger - The finish. I like racing with the crowds, the fact that it's such a big event here.
Lenny Silverman - The crowd and the excitement.
Peggy Ward - The bridge.
Pana Wilder - The location of the run.
CJ - What Do You Like Least About The Bridge Run?
Don - Gnats at the start and the mental aspect of the viaduct (Crosstown Overpass)
Marie - It takes me too long to run it. Last year it was too hot.
Benita - The pressure of trying to do my best, to do a PR.
Gary - Coming off that third hump on King Street. It seems like a hellhole - it gets hot quick. There is no air, nothing. I hate that part of the race.
Tom - Being Point to point. It makes for logistic and transportation problems. I'd prefer a circular course.
Barry - The bridge.
Sam - The restroom facilities - lack of them - and standing in the lines.
Terry - The incline.
Dupree - The hordes of people and the long wait afterwards for the awards ceremony.

Linda - King Street definitely. That long stretch seems like it never ends.
Dennis - The third bridge (the Crosstown Overpass).
Ed H. - Running on a hot day which has melted me. The 1985 run in the heat when 400 runners, most of whom knew me, passed me on King Street.
Madeline - I was one of the last runners coming in and a lot of people were in the road and I couldn't see the finish or tell where to go. I don't know how that problem could be alleviated.
Ed L. - Last year the heat, but every year the first hill.
Art - I like seeing the Bridge Run grow, but I've been avoiding mega-races if you know what I mean.
Barbara - The bridge, the up part.
Tommy - The first hill. That first span.
Carolyn - Training for it. Trying to get in shape.
Connie - Hot weather.
Frank - They run out of fruit at the finish line by the time I get there since I'm not fast.
Joyce - The unpredictable temperature.
Lenny - The long wait at the awards ceremony.
Peggy - The last mile. It's just not pretty, it looks dirty.
Pana - The slow start, waiting so long to get over the starting line.
CJ - What do you think about the date change from the last weekend in march to the first weekend in april?
Don - I do not like it. There are people who know it has always been the last weekend in March and plan that weekend for the race every year. It's going to make some dedicated runners miss out.
Marie - I wish they would have kept it in March, it'll be hotter. I wish they'd have it earlier so it would be cooler.
Benita - It will probably be hotter so I don't know why they did it.
Gary - I'm skeptical because I think it's going to get hot. I would have gone up a week earlier rather than back a week.
Tom - If I was going to change it, I'd have moved it to March 22 because there's a chance of it being hotter on April 5
Barry - It doesn't bother me too much. I'd like it to be cooler, other than that, it doesn't matter.
Sam - I'm not for it. I thought the last weekend in March was set. I've come to know the last weekend in March as the Bridge Run weekend.
Terry - It will probably be warmer and the worst part about it is if it is warmer.
Dupree - That doesn't affect me. The only kicker is, it could be hotter.
Linda - It doesn't affect me one way or the other. No opinion. One week doesn't matter.
Dennis - I don't like it because it'll be even warmer than it has been in the past, and sometimes it's been too warm.
Ed H. - Being a New Englander, I prefer the cooler weather.
Madeline - I liked it in March as it was.
Ed L. - I don't like that so much. I'd rather it stayed where it was. If it's going to be one of the top 40 races, it should stand alone. It should keep its date.
Art - I like it since I'm involved as publicity director, I think it will get better race coverage.
Barbara - I wish it was the last part of March because it would be cooler.
Tommy - I don't like it. I'd rather it be run in cooler weather. For it to be a race, it should be cooler: the cooler the better.
Carolyn - I like the change. It gives the individual runner longer to train before the race. Spring is in the air.
Connie - I'd rather have it earlier because of the weather; there's more chance of it being hot.
Frank - I don't like it. I prefer to race in the cooler weather. I'd have preferred to move it earlier rather than later.
Joyce - I do not like it. Last year was so hot and this year could be even hotter.
Lenny - I hate it. I don't think it's too good due to the heat. I hate this year particularly because I won't be able to run it as I would have if it had been in March. I had my heart set on running the first 25 Bridge Runs and now I can't.
Peggy - I like that. I like April, it's my best month.
Pana - It's OK. I hadn't really thought about it.

Follow-up: Three Questions After The 1986 Bridge Run

Originally appeared in the May-June 1986 Low Country Runner

Yes, these are the same people who answered questions in the last LCR. All were interviewed by telephone by Cedric Jaggers. It is interesting that all but one of the runners who actually ran the race this year would prefer to see it moved back to March - including the ones who had previously said they preferred April.

CJ - What did you like best about this year's bridge run?
Don Austell - Splitting the chutes and the way the finish line worked.
Marie Borchlewicz - I did the walk this year. The walk wasn't as exciting, but it was better because of the heat.

Benita Brooks - That my time was faster than last year.
Gary Butts - I was totally injury free and got to run it.
Tom Davis - The post race festivities. There was plenty to do and people to talk to.
Barry DeCarli - The finish.
Sam Derrick - The organization. It seemed like it was well organized.
Terry Gibson - The camaraderie. The people that were running the race with us were all talking and helping each other over the rough spots. I liked the split finish line, it helped with the congestion.
Dupree Elvington - The finish when I got across the line.
Linda Frolich - The super amount of fluids and fruits and water that was at the finish.
I started 10 minutes after everyone else due to getting caught on the bridge. When I finished I found I got fruit and cold orange juice. There was plenty of medical attention and enthusiasm. I'm a nurse, and I appreciated the high quality medical care.
Dennis Hiott - The chance to have a good time and see a lot of people you don't usually see at races.
Ed Hogan - Finishing feeling relatively comfortable because I didn't push too hard.
Madeline Kornahrens - I didn't get to run this year.
Ed Ledford - The size and excitement of the crowd.
Art Liberman - I didn't run this year because I did the commentary on WCSC radio. I liked the fact that we had a quality field without household names, but the men's and women's fields were both very talented and deep.
Barbara Locklear - I had bronchitis and didn't get to run. I was real disappointed.
Tommy Mullins - The people who were the actual runners in the race.
Carolyn Nelson - The finish.
Connie Owen - Just such a sense of accomplishment to be at the finish line and not in an ambulance due to the heat. I had to run a mile to get to the start. The mayor was caught in the traffic jam on the bridge in the next car and the police were giving him more detailed reports on what was happening than we heard on the radio. So we knew just what was happening.
Frank Palazzolla - There was enough refreshment and fruit to go around.
Joyce Ploeger - I love everything about it - the big party type atmosphere at Marion Square after the race.
Peggy Ward - The guy I was standing by in the line. He was a friendly guy. But it was a bad experience for me.
Pana Wilder - It still was a nice amiable crowd. There were a lot of nice people there.

CJ - What did you like least about this year's bridge run?
Don - Heat and humidity. I'd like to suggest that they start it at an earlier hour or an earlier date.
Marie - We were still sitting on the bridge at 20 after 8: the traffic problem.
Gary - The date that it was put on because due to that date the temperature and humidity were just horrible.
Benita - The delayed start and the heat.
Tom - The weather.
Barry - The delay, but I understood it. The heat was a close second.
Sam - The traffic.
Terry - The heat. It was really hot and I was trying to keep a 9 minute pace, but when I got to the first span it really beat me down. I was hoping it would be cooler
Dupree - What hurt me the most were those delays; all my adrenalin and emotion was gone. I just went through the motions. Even though it affected everybody, it bothered me a lot.
Linda - Least? They had to worry about people getting there on time. When a race is set they should go ahead and do it at 8:30 (the set time) and not delay it. I'm not a fast runner, but I still don't think it should have been delayed as hot as it was. I missed the start because I didn't leave my house until 7:20. It's my fault I couldn't get to the start on time.
Dennis - The delayed start, but I realize why it happened and I realize it was under no one's control.
Ed H. - I got stuck on the bridge in the car on the way over. I almost didn't get to the start. So the traffic jam was what I liked least.
Ed L. - The delay of the start time, plus setting it up into April. I think that was a disaster. The heat and anxiety raises everybody's body temperature. If you have a delay when it's cool, it's not a disaster, but it is in the heat.
Art - The fact that an act of God kept some people from getting to the start. It was out of their control. It was unfortunate, just because of the traffic accident.
Tommy - The heat factor along with the delay. If they are going to have it in April when they had it, they should consider starting the race at 7 a.m.
Carolyn - The start. I'm a jackrabbit at heart and start out so fast I end up punishing myself the rest of the race.

Connie - Getting to the starting line. It took us an hour and a quarter from downtown.

Frank - The heat. It was just unbearable for me.

Joyce - The delayed start. But there was no way it could have been avoided with the accident.

Peggy - I tripped and fell during the first mile and hurt my knee. But as far as the race it was the heat. It was warm last year, but this year it was really hot. The heat really got me.

Pana - The problem with the starting and some people not being able to start on time.

CJ - Now that it is over, how do you feel about the date change from March to April?

Don - I did not like it at all.

Marie - I think they should keep back in the cooler weather, it's just too hot in April

Benita - I'd rather see it in March because we have a better chance of it not being so hot.

Gary - Disastrous. It makes absolutely no sense in Charleston, South Carolina to run a race at this time of year. They need to move it back to March and move the starting time back.

Tom - Me being a cool weather runner, I'd prefer moving it back to March

Barry - I wish they'd have it at the end of February.

Sam - It was real hot and it hurt a lot of people. It was just too hot.

Terry - Really I think the Saturday in March would have been a nice day to run. I wish it was back in March.

Dupree - Bad mistake. If they are going to change, it should be earlier.

Linda - Hindsight is a marvelous thing. I would state that probably they changed it for Easter. So maybe they should have made it the week before, that is the next to last week in March.

Dennis - I still don't like the date change because it was hotter than the previous week. I'd like it to be moved a month earlier.

Ed H. - It's a matter of chance. I would prefer to move it back a week earlier to have less chance of it being hot.

Ed L. - I still think it's the most abominable thing in the world. If they are going to move it should be to the middle of March.

Art - I personally would like to see it remain the first week in April. The fact that it was hot was just a coincidence. I don't believe that one week makes that much difference in the temperature.

Tommy - I do not like it. I don't care why they changed it. I don't think the Bridge Run should worry about competing with other races. It's big enough now so let those other races worry about the Bridge Run.

Carolyn - I've changed my mind. I totally disagree with them moving it forward. Most people are against the change in date due to the temperature. Most people looking back will say "Why did they do this?" They are going to have to do something, like start the race at 7:30 or even 8 o'clock in case something goes wrong and the start is delayed.

Connie - Keep it in March. Somebody who read the article last time told me I gave such boring answers, but the hotter it is the less happy I am.

Frank - I still don't like it. I feel they changed the date to get rid of a conflict with other races. They care too much about top ranked runners and not enough about the Tri-County runners who support the race.

Joyce - I didn't think a week would really make that much difference.

Peggy - I'd rather the race be in February, but it doesn't really matter. (Laughs) I like it in April so I can use the excuse it was just too hot. If it was cool I couldn't use that excuse.

Pana - Now I feel it's too hot. I wasn't thinking that through before. It was real hot on King Street.

Addition for this book: we just had to know how they did in the race, right? CJ

    Don Austell 39:26
    Marie Borchlewicz untimed walk
    Benita Brooks (Schlau) 38:36
    Gary Butts 41:42
    Tom Davis 39:56
    Barry DeCarli 41:00
    Sam Derrick 49:40
    Ed Hogan 45:44
    Ed Ledford 38:59
    Tommy Mullins 41:08
    Carolyn Nelson 44:11
    Connie Owens unable to find in results
    Frank Palazzolla 58:18
    Joyce Ploeger 43:16
    Lenny Silverman unable to find in results
    Peggy Ward 58:53
    Pana Wilder 56:15

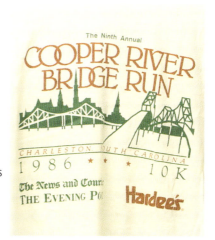

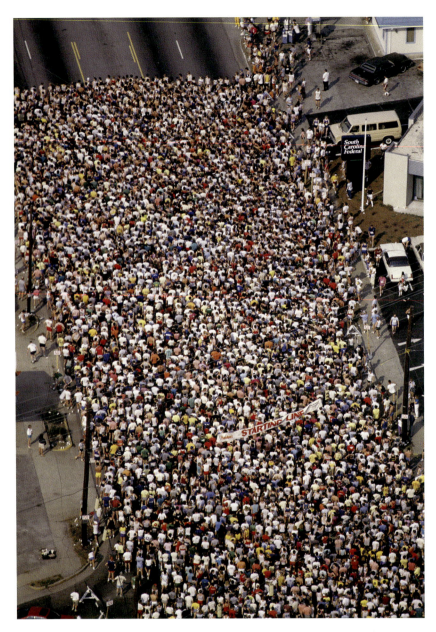

Runners are poised at the starting line on Coleman Boulevard in Mount Pleasant moments before the start of the ninth annual race.

News and Courier photo by Wade Spees

1986 Awards

Note: the race used an 'Invitational Division' - Elite Runners contesting for prize money - not eligible for age group awards.

Prize money winners:
Overall Male
1 Hans Koeleman .... Holland .... 29:29 .. $2,000
2 Matt Scrutton .... Boulder, CO .... 29:34 ...$1,000
3 Jim Haughey .... Clemson, SC .... 29:40 .... $500

Overall Female
1 Lesley Welch .... Newton, MA .... 33:37 .. $2,000
2 Kathy Pfiefer .... Albuquerque NM ..... 34:03 ...$1,000
3 Lisa Welch .... Newton, MA .... 34:20 .... $500

Special award:
Dr Marcus Newberry Award for first local Charleston Tri-County area finisher:
Male
Bob Schlau .... Charleston, SC 31:26
Female
Benita Brooks (Schlau)...... Charleston, SC 38:36

Special award:
Dewey Wise Trophy for oldest finisher with time faster in minutes than his or her age:
Clayton Brelsford, 71 .... Wilmington, NC 54:37

Age Group Award Winners
Ceramic pitchers for the top 3 with additional mugs to the top 5% up to a maximum of 25 in each age group.

Male 14 & under (162 finishers, 8 awards)
1 Mike Strohm 38:00
2 Thomas Cason 38:21
3 Oliver Moore 39:52
4 Reuben Potter 41:38
5 Timothy Nettles 41:52
6 Doug Dennis 42:53
7 Sonny Smith 42:55
8 Biemann Othersen 43:03

Female 14 & under (56 finishers, 3 awards)
1 Katie Stamps..41:10
2 Regan Carr... 47:14
3 Jennifer Lavigne.................................... 49:38

Male 15-19 (204 finishers, 10 awards)
1 David Honea 33:54
2 John Inman 33:56
3 Richard Golden.....................................35:13
4 David Stultz....................................... 35:56
5 Gil McCabe 36:26
6 Gerald Ellis....................................... 36:44
7 Brian Kelbaugh..................................... 37:04
8 Danny Ledford 37:31
9 William Feard...................................... 37:33
10 Trey Knott 38:35

Female 15-19 (56 finishers, 3 awards)
1 S. M. Crawford 40:31
2 Sarah Hams.. 45:12
3 Joan Von Thron.................................... 45:38

Male 20-24 (346 finishers, 17 awards)
1 Paul Laymon..32:14
2 Steven Stebbins 32:28
3 Daniel Clay.. 32:43
4 Robert Wilder..................................... 32:55
5 Tim Blackstone.................................... 33:25
6 Jay Gottesman 33:26
7 John Borsos....................................... 33:57
8 Daniel Brown 35:05
9 Steven Leopard 35:12
10 Delroy Whittaker 35:15
11 Owen Woolever 35:23
12 David Grossman 35:42
13 Andy Pinson 35:58
14 James Koterba 36:03
15 Skip Hagan 36:34
16 Randy Thompson 36:52
17 Scott Murr 37:00

Female 20-24 (165 finishers, 8 awards)
1 Pam Fulk 38:07
2 Megan Othersen 40:17
3 Rhonda Morris 42:36
4 Mari Barrett 44:41
5 Elizabeth Walker 45:22
6 Hamer Salmons 46:43
7 Lynn Foster 46:47
8 Dorothy Case..................................... 47:08

Male 25-29 (834 finishers, 25 awards)
1 Robert Brooks.................................... 32:27
2 Roger Cottrell 33:10
3 Eddie Pennebaker 33:17
4 Gary Gayman 33:32
5 Scott Kidd 33:55
6 Huey Inman....................................... 35:01
7 Paul Burke 35:09
8 Randy Carmichael 35:30
9 Robert Lowery 35:31
10 Jeffrey Stone..................................... 35:37
11 Mark Stultz 35:47
12 Pender Murphy.................................. 36:06
13 Sam Swofford 36:18
14 Gary Quinney 36:21
15 David Luhrs 36:21
16 David Bourgeois................................. 36:22
17 Frank Sloan 36:24
18 Mike Chodnicki................................. 36:47
19 John Breen 36:48
20 Johnny Witt..................................... 36:49
21 Ray Lewis....................................... 36:53
22 Len Astrauskas 37:07
23 Robert Erwin.................................... 37:09
24 Peter Orzech....................................37:10
25 Glenn Hair.......................................37:14

Female 25-29 (318 finishers, 16 awards)
1 Debbie Davis..................................... 37:55
2 Jean Chodnicki...................................38:17
3 Pam Drafts 40:42
4 Debra Gawrych....................................41:42
5 Beth Vukich 42:01
6 Ann Elish 42:02
7 Michele Haskins 42:15
8 Janet Ballenger 42:18
9 Mollie Maready 42:48
10 Missy Astrauskas 42:54
11 Libby Smith..................................... 43:22
12 Pamela Brooks 43:30
13 Gale Courtney................................... 43:57
14 Rebecca Brelsford 44:13
15 Lucy Barr 44:26
16 Stacie Novak 44:27

Male 30-34 (833 finishers, 25 awards)
1. Mac Coile 32:07
2. Skip Frye 33:51
3. Mike Hart 34:27
4. Robbie McLendon 34:55
5. Glen Chamberlain 34:58
6. Richard Teague 35:24
7. Leon McCray 35:55
8. Ravion Cannon 35:56
9. Steven Pavik 36:00
10. Tommy Bolus 36:28
11. Gregory Jones 36:32
12. Doc D Bayne 36:42
13. Steve Smeal 36:50
14. Roland Butch Cody 36:53
15. Michael Wise 36:55
16. David Dawes 37:02
17. Duane Wolff 37:05
18. Leon Locklear 37:16
19. Steve Caskie 37:18
20. David Freeze 37:23
21. Andy Taylor 37:27
22. Gordon English Jr. 37:30
23. Marc Plantico 37:30
24. Charles Kellner 37:31
25. Rusty Doyle 37:51

Female 30-34 (163 finishers, 8 awards)
1. Barbara Balzer 38:34
2. Benita Brooks (Schlau) 38:36
3. Bonnie Poore Long 41:20
4. Carol Davis 41:25
5. Marilyn Davey 42:12
6. Cindy Kline 42:18
7. Ginger Gregory 42:25
8. Candace Almers 43:29

Male 35-39 (771 finishers, 25 awards)
1. Bob Schlau 31:26
2. Jim Ryun 34:11
3. Marcus Phillips 35:16
4. Thomas Jones 35:20
5. William Pierce 35:25
6. Lee Boggs 35:29
7. Lansing Brewer 35:42
8. Larry D'Ippolito 36:42
9. Larry Reece 37:10
10. Bill Driscoll 37:19
11. Robert Potter 37:25
12. Billy Davey 37:26
13. Gregg Byrd 37:29
14. Monty King 37:42
15. Bob Wilson 37:44
16. Bill Sloan 37:54
17. Jimmy Hadden 37:57
18. Don Reynolds 37:58
19. Tom Blankenship 38:01
20. Skipper Hewitt 38:03
21. Cedric Jaggers 38:11
22. Bill Barfield 38:22
23. David Lee 38:22
24. Fred Corder 38:28
25. Bruce Taylor 38:29

Female 35-39 (163 finishers, 8 awards)
1. Nancy Grayson 37:53
2. Anne Boone Reed 40:05
3. Peggy Schug 41:36
4. Sue Norwood 42:36
5. Janet Earhart 42:42
6. Connie Gruver 42:54
7. Debby Sullivan 43:02
8. A. Marcinkowski 44:39

Male 40-44 (483 finishers, 25 awards)
1. Tom Dooley 33:19
2. Alan Pilling 33:55
3. Mike Kelly 35:14
4. Jim O'Neill 36:34
5. Fred Levee 36:57
6. Gary Holdgrafer 37:18
7. Tony Presley 37:23
8. Dupree Elvington 37:41
9. John Bryant 37:46
10. Heinz Maurer 37:52
11. Jim Pennington 37:56
12. Ken Finney 38:49
13. Buddy Price 39:16
14. Donnie Putnam 39:20
15. Bill Seigler 39:33
16. William Anderson 39:49
17. Robert Stump 39:56
18. Rod Lapin 40:03
19. Chuck Greer 40:16
20. Bill Vetsch 40:18
21. Jennings Neely 40:20
22. Reaves Gasque 40:22
23. John Stephens 40:32
24. William Hollaway 40:35
25. Raymond Schroeder 40:42

Female 40-44 (102 finishers, 5 awards)
1. Gail Bailey 39:21
2. Natalie Spalding 41:05
3. Joyce Ploeger 43:16
4. Gail Sharber 43:30
5. Donna Presley 43:31

Male 45-49 (255 finishers, 13 awards)
1. William Burnside 37:04
2. James Keller 38:01
3. James Adams 38:37
4. Olin Hammond 38:43
5. Bob Wood 38:49
6. Ed Ledford 38:59
7. Dean Godwin 39:04
8. David Shaw 39:21
9. Joe Allen 39:22
10. James Don Austell 39:26
11. Joe Page 39:27
12. Bob Gooden 39:37
13. Ed Guettler 40:14

Female 45-49 (45 finishers, 3 awards)
1. Mary Anne Wehrum 40:32
2. Avis Allen 50:24
3. Linda Hendrix 50:47

Male 50-54 (123 finishers, 6 awards)
1. Gerald Koch 36:27
2. Malcolm Gillis 37:01
3. Ken Kurts 38:34
4. Sammie Yarborough 39:14
5. Charles Rose 39:58
6. Don Lins 40:01

Runners head across the John P. Grace Bridge.
News and Courier photo by Wade Spees

Female 50-54 (20 finishers, 3 awards)
1. Wendy Williams 48:00
2. Suzanne Foster 51:13
3. Terryl Woods 54:55

Male 55-59 (56 finishers, 3 awards)
1. Lee Swofford 41:16
2. Neil Wilson 41:20
3. Charles Moore 42:41

Female 55-59 (7 finishers, 3 awards)
1. Nancy Bell 54:03
2. Faye Motley 58:25
3. Jackie McGehee 1:03:45

Male 60-64 (22 finishers, 3 awards)
1. David Mellard 42:57
2. Lawrence Moore 44:24
3. Franklin Mason 47:18

Female 60 & over (4 finishers, 3 awards)
1. Margaret Wright 57:03
2. Ola Moody 1:05:32
3. Jeanette Rowell 1:08:34

Male 65 & over (6 finishers, 3 awards)
1. George Sheehan 47:48
2. Waymon Stuart 48:49
3. Clayton Brelsford 54:37

Compiled by Cedric Jaggers from complete race results.

Race winner Paul Cummings (No. 4), of Orem Utah, heads the leaders of the pack. News and Courier photo by Wade Spees

Chapter 10
1987
The Coldest, Windiest Race Ever

On April 4, 1987, the 10th Bridge Run became the second in a row made unforgettable by the weather. It was the coldest and windiest to date. At the 8 a.m. start, (the time had been set earlier due to the heat of the previous two races) the temperature was only 39 degrees. Not too bad unless you know that there was a steady 20 mile per hour wind gusting to 35 mph on the bridge. To make matters worse, it was a headwind.

Most people expected it to be a fast race as Paul Cummings of Orem, Utah, who was winner of the 1984 Olympic Trials 10,000 meter, was entered. His Personal Best time of 27:43 raised expectations. He predicted that he would run the Bridge Run in 28:20, but conditions definitely intervened.

The race returned to the 1985 certified course; SC85012WN. The race began on Coleman Boulevard in Mount Pleasant just across Shem Creek, then crossed the "old" Grace Memorial bridge and the Crosstown Overpass, down King Street to Market, cutting across to Meeting Street and up to the finish in front of the Federal Building. The entry fee was raised to $10.

The elite runners ran slower than usual due to the wind. When the starting cannon was fired, the lead pack took a very conservative start as it appeared no one wanted to take the lead against the fierce headwind. They ran the first mile in a slow pace (for them) with a pack of 20 runners getting to the first mile mark in 4:55 (as compared to 4:25 first mile in the 1986 race).

Charleston area runner Bob Schlau, runner-up in the 1979 race, said he felt obliged to lead for a while. He would finish 16th overall in 32:23. Local runner David Luhrs was also in the pack at the 1-mile mark and decided to take the lead, "to be on TV." He said he was the first runner onto the bridge and led until the 2-mile mark when "those guys blew by me. When they pass you they don't fool around, they really go fast." He finished the race 28th overall in 34:20.

It continued to be a tactical race for the elite runners during the first 4 miles when a record 10 runners crested the Crosstown Overpass, the third and last hill in the race. Defending champion Hans Koeleman of Holland (by way of Clemson) surged to the lead but was quickly caught by Jeff Smith of Boulder, Colo., and Paul Cummings. From then on it was a three-man race until the 6-mile mark where Cummings surged and pulled away. Then he made a mistake which could have been costly. He followed the Channel 5 television truck (which was broadcasting the race live for the third year in a row) as it turned off the race course onto Calhoun Street which was shortly before the finish line. He was waved back on course and had enough speed to win the closest Bridge Run ever: 30:19.23 to Smith's 30:19.92, with Koeleman third in 30:21.

"I knew I had a bit of a lead, but I got a little disoriented, and fortunately it didn't affect the outcome," Cummings told the *News and Courier*. "We were running a lot harder than the time would indicate. It seemed like the wind was in our face the whole way. It was probably a 29-minute effort."

Smith explained the finish this way, "I was slowing down a bit myself to make the corner. I was going to follow him (Cummings, off the course) until I realized what was happening. Defending champion Koeleman said, "I knew it would be difficult to win this race coming off the bridge. The start was too slow. Some guys took it out, but nobody took a fast pace. Someone was going to have to put on a tremendous surge, especially with Cummings in there. He used to be a (3:54) miler and he won the U.S. Olympic 10,000 meter trials in 1984. He's a very good runner."

The women's race was never in doubt as Mary Ellen McGowan of Gainesville, Fla., won in 34:31. After the race she said she used a pack of men to block the wind and kept an eye out for other women. She never saw any. "When we got to the hill, I started taking it out. There was a bunch of guys there, and I tried to stay with them to block the wind. I thought I'd run 33-something today, but because of the wind and the hills, it wasn't that fast, she told the newspaper.

Sue Schneider of Minneapolis, Minn., making her second Bridge Run appearance, finished second again in 35:10. Afterward she said she was going to have to try something different. "I just kind of let her (McGowan) go on the bridge," she told the newspaper. "I figured I'd make it up later, and I never did. She kept contact with a group, which I think would have made it easier. It sure was cold and windy on the bridge. I ran a lot faster two years ago." Kim Bird of Austell, Ga., was third in 35:48.

Prize money was awarded to the top two Masters males and females for the first time. Richard Weeks of Nashville, Tenn., was Masters winner in 34:43, with Morgan Looney of Birmingham, Ala., next in 34:56 and Don Wright of Mobile, Ala., just out of the money in third at 35:05. Charlestonians Gail Bailey in a time of 38:42, and Anne Boone Reed in 39:59 took home the money with June Hartley of Columbia, S.C., third in 42:33.

The Dr. Marcus Newberry award for first Tri-County finisher went to Tom Mather of Mount Pleasant, 12th overall in 32:04.51 and Megan Othersen (Gorman) of Charleston, sixth female in 37:19.28. The Dewey Wise Trophy went to Clayton Brelsford, 72, of Wilmington, N.C., for the second year in a row. He finished the race in 51:38.

No runners broke the 30-minute barrier; 301 men and 21 women finished under 40 minutes. There were 2,054 runners who crossed the finish line in less than 50 minutes.

Weather conditions played a factor in several ways. There were two water stations on the course, but not too many takers. Almost all the runners were saying they ran a minute or two slower than they had expected due to the wind. A large number of casual runners never took off their sweats or running jackets due to the cold and had their race numbers pinned onto their shirts inside the jackets, creating problems for finish line workers.

A total of 6,997 runners registered for the race: 6,976 crossed the finish line and had times recorded on the (nine lane) Chronomix timer tapes; 5,588 through the male chutes, 1,388 through the female chutes. According to finish line director Chuck Magera, the cold caused tremendous problems. He estimated that about 10 percent or more of those crossing the finish line were unregistered "bandit" runner. Runners without numbers were usually escorted from the race course at George Street prior to reaching the finish line. However, since so many runners had kept their warm-ups on for the race due to the extreme cold, it was impossible to tell if they had a number. Thus the bandits could not be distinguished from the registered runners so all runners were allowed to cross the finish line.

Due to the cold, the awards ceremony was moved to the nearby College of Charleston gymnasium. The race was only the second race in South Carolina to be chosen for TAC (later re-named USATF) drug testing of the winners. The top three males and females and two other runners selected out of the top 25 finishers were tested. The awards ceremony had to be delayed as it took one of the lucky selected winners over two hours to submit the required sample.

The Sunday *News and Courier* estimated that between 5,600 and 5,900 finished the race and listed the top 100 male finishers and the top 50 female finishers, and showed three deep in each age group. For the first and only time, results were not compiled and mailed out to all finishers. All available partial results (the first 1899 male and 468 female names and times) were compiled in early 1988 and published in the March-April 1988 edition of the *Low Country Runner*, newsletter of the Charleston Running Club, which was mailed only to running club members. The newspaper also stated that about 3,500 people registered for the untimed Bridge Walk.

Karl Gueldner was race director for the second year in a row. The January 1987 issue of *Runner's World* magazine had listed the Bridge run as one of the top 25 races in the country.

Other Voices
What About Your Bridge Run? As Told To Cedric Jaggers

Originally appeared in the March-April 1987 Low Country Runner

A cross section of Charleston Running Club members agreed to answer a few questions about the Cooper River Bridge Run before the tenth race in 1987. They were interviewed via telephone by Cedric Jaggers. Responses are listed alphabetically by the respondents' last name.

How many of the nine previous bridge runs have you run?
Don Austell - I've run seven of them.
Jimmy Bailey - All but two, so seven of them.
Doug Bunch - Five of them.

Butch Cody - All except the first one.
Steve Comer - Two or three of them. It's at a bad time of year for me. I always have meetings then.
Barbara Davidson - About five.
Ginger Gregory - All of them, one unofficially.
Nina Parks Herndon - Three.
Peggy Ledford - All but the first few and last year.
Tommy Mullins - Five.
Carol Oates - None. I was out of town last year and had a hurt knee the year before.
Geary Serpas - Six of them.
Sandra Suit - None. I've helped with several of them.
Clark Wyly - All of them; nine.

Did you run the first one? If no, why not? If yes, what do you remember about it?
Don - No. I wasn't running at the time.
Jimmy - No. The first one was on Palm Sunday, I watched it.
Doug - No. I wasn't in Charleston then.
Butch - No. I ran the bridge run (River Run 15k) in Jacksonville and the Bridge Run was the next day. I watched it. Before the race I didn't even know they were having it. I walked out and saw all these crazy people running in the heat. I used to live in the Fort Sumter house (on the Battery where the race finished) and just happened to be walking out and saw the race.
Steve - No Because I was in Hawaii
Barbara - Yes. It was my first race. It was very hot and I walked part of it, in fact, most of it.
Ginger - Yes. That was a great race. My girl friend from New York came down and during the race we met this guy running the same pace and the three of us ran together and became good friends. She had to stop but I finished and met new running friends. I ran it in about 61 minutes. It was hot that day.
Nina - No, I wasn't running back then.
Peggy - No, I wasn't running then.
Tommy - No, but the first Bridge Run was an inspiration and started me running.
Geary - No. I wasn't running back then.
Sandra - No. I wasn't living in Charleston then.
Clark - Yes. I remember the number of local people in the running club who were participating.

Which bridge run was your favorite and why?
Don - The third (1980) Bridge Run. I was 30 flat at 5 miles but it took me 9 minutes and 34 seconds to make the last 1.2 miles. I'll always remember that feeling of having all my mental capacities, but no muscle control. To this day I don't know what happened. I had a good run going that day.
Jimmy - They all hurt so I guess probably the fourth (1981) year when it finished on Cummings. No, it was probably the first year of the Bridge Walk when I walked and jogged with my son.
Doug - It would be hard to pin them down – none is outstanding in my mind.
Butch - I wouldn't be able to tell you which year. Probably one of the ones that started at Patriots Point and finished at the college. I always liked those courses.
Steve - The third (1980) one, when I passed you going down East Bay Street. (Note: I can't complain because I ran a PR and broke 40 minutes for the first time ever at that race, CJ)
Barbara - Three years ago because my goal was to run it in less than 48 minutes, and I did.
Ginger - They kind of all run together. Probably the last one (ninth) because I did a PR.
Nina - 1985 because I ran a good time. Plus it was my husband-to-be's first race even though I didn't know he was to be at that time.
Peggy - The years 82 and 83 when we had a post race party at Anne Boone Reed's house. They seemed friendlier then.
Tommy - My favorite one was in 1985. Reason: It was cooler, I was in better shape and ran a PR.
Geary - I can't answer it. They get bigger every year, but lose some of its camaraderie.
Clark - 1984 and the reason is because I had a good time and I also beat Benita Brooks (Schlau) who tried to beat me. I was going down the second span and she said "I'm going to beat you." I said, "Oh God, I'll never hear the end of it." I held her off and beat her by one second.

What is your best Bridge Run time?
Don: 37:20 something.
Jimmy: 40:15 or so.
Doug: 42 and some change.

Butch: No idea.
Steve: Someplace around 38 min.
Barbara: 47:38.
Ginger: 42:24.
Nina: 43:30.
Peggy: 41:44.
Tommy: 38:44 or 38:45
Geary: 38:20 something.
Clark: 38:12.

What time do you hope to run this year (1987)?

Don: If I break 40 minutes I'll be happy since I'm so fat and out of shape.
Jimmy: 42 or so depending on how much I drink the night before.
Doug: I want to break 40. I've been training real hard for it.
Butch: I'd be real happy to break 35 minutes there. It's a tough course, worth a minute. I don't run hills well
Steve: I probably won't run it this year. I haven't been training to race. I've irritated a hamstring.
Barbara: I'm hoping to do 44 minutes.
Ginger: I want to break 40, but I don't think the bridge is the place to do it, so maybe the low 40's.
Nina: Better than 43:30 if I can get back in shape.
Peggy: I'm going to run it, but I haven't been training for races so I don't know what to predict. It's like starting all over again.
Tommy: I hope to run about a 38. I'm running for a top 5% award cup. I really want one of them and it looks like a 38 or less is what it'll take to get one. I've never gotten one.
Carol: 48 minutes.
Geary: At my current rate of deterioration . . . 40 give or take plus one.
Sandra: Probably about 50 minutes.
Clark: This year I won't be able to run it because of my ruptured Achilles tendon on the bridge last year April 4, 1986. I'll be doing the bridge walk this year.

OK, admit it, you want to know how they did in the cold, windy 1987 race, right? I went through all the existing results and here is what I found:

Don: 41:40
Jimmy: 43:17
Doug: unavailable
Butch: 35:52
Barbara: 45:34
Ginger: 41:24
Nina: 42:17
Peggy: 46:53 (note; not in online results – I checked and found her in my original paper results which were borrowed by the Bridge Run Committee, scanned and used to create the online results file – apparently the female results from places 106-160, times 46:50 to 49:09 were accidentally omitted. CJ)
Tommy: 39:08
Carol: unavailable
Geary: unavailable
Sandra: 54:41

1987 Awards

Awards: Note, the race used an 'Invitational Division' – Elite Runners contesting for prize money – not eligible for age group awards.

Prize money winners:
Overall Male
1 Paul Cummings........ Orem, UT .... 30:19.23 .. $2,000
2 Jeff Smith............. Boulder, CO .... 30:19.92 .. $1,000
3 Hans Koeleman .... Holland .... 30:22 .... $700
4 Martyn Brewer .... Louisville, KY ..... 30:41 .... $500
5 Marty Flynn .... Clemson, SC ...... 30:46 .... $400
6 Jeff Scuffins .... Carrboro, NC ..... 30:51 .... $325
7 Ron Boreham .... Jenkintown, PA ... 30:59 .... $300
8 Steve Venable .... Roswell, GA....... 31:10 .... $225
9 Glen Banker .... Stone Mtn. GA .... 31:36 .... $200
10 Craig Thompson ..... Knoxville, TN ..... 31:45 .... $150
11 John Barbour .... Atlanta, GA .... 31:49 .... $100

Overall Female
1 Mary E. McGowan ..... Gainesville FL ...... 34:32 .. $2,000
2 S Schneider .... Minn., MN .... 35:11 .. $1,000
3 Kim Bird .... Austell, GA .... 35:49 .... $500
4 Laura Caldwell....... Stone Mtn GA .... 36:17 .... $300
5 Ann Wehner......... Martinez GA ..... 37:13 .... $200
6 Megan Othersen ..... Charleston SC .... 37:20 .... $100

Masters Division:
(prize money added for the first time)
Masters Male
1 Richard Weeks........ Nashville, TN ...... 34:43 .... $200
2 Morgan Looney ...... Birmingham AL .... 34:56 .... $100

Masters Female
1 Gail Bailey........... Charleston, SC ..... 38:42 .... $200
2 Anne Boone Reed..... Charleston, SC .... 39:59 .... $100

Dr Marcus Newberry Award:
For first local Charleston Tri-County area finisher:
Male
  Tom Mather .... Mt Pleasant, SC 32:04.51
Female
  Megan Othersen .... Charleston, SC 37:19.28

Special award:
Dewey Wise Trophy for oldest finisher with time faster than his or her age in minutes:
Clayton Brelsford, 72............. Wilmington, NC......... 51:38

Age group award winners
(Ceramic pitchers for the top 3 with additional mugs to the top 5% up to a maximum of 25 in each age group – note the number of awards shown is the number on the awards list I was given after the race; there is no age group list that would enable me to list the number of finishers per age group. CJ):
  *indicates name and time appear on the original awards list used at the awards ceremony on April 4, 1987, but not in the final results provided to me in early 1988. CJ

Male 12 & under (5 awards)
1 Matthew Johnson 41:49
2 Chris Jones.. 44:06
3 Richard Wilson*... 45:30
4 Michael Gambrell 46:35
5 Brian Bauer 46:35

Female 12 & under (3 awards)
1 Lisa Hoskins... 52:02
2 Leslie Wade... 54:06
3 Deborah Saylor*.....................................1:02:28

Male 13-17 (12 awards)
1 Mike Strohm 37:42
2 Tripp Caton 37:51
3 Rodney Westbury 38:06
4 Robert LaFrance...................................... 39:29
5 Chance Regina 39:30
6 Oliver Moore 39:45
7 Greg Willis*.. 39:56
8 Robie Strohm 40:24
9 Jack Murphy 40:31
10 Kevin Cutler... 40:42
11 Alston Middleton 41:20
12 Tim Nettles 41:27

Female 13-17 (4 awards)
1 Katie Stamps... 43:19
2 Mary McEachern 45:03
3 Christy McKay 46:27
4 Monica Steffes 46:32

Male 18-21 (11 awards)
1 Jay Curwen 34:23
2 Gilbert McCabe 35:06
3 Adam Williams 35:16
4 Greg Whitmire 35:17
5 Dale Hoover.. 35:42
6 David Prockop 35:48
7 James Page 35:50
8 Clay Boswell 36:11
9 David Tewksbury 37:13
10 Bobby Marangelli 37:25
11 Gerald Ellis.. 37:28

Female 18-21 (5 awards)
1 Sarah Hams 42:12
2 Michelle Dreon 42:14
3 Ann Gibson 44:54
4 Lynn Sudduth 48:01
5 Lauren Wilkens....................................... 49:22

Male 22-25 (25 awards)
1 Rob Wilder.. 32:16
2 Jim Davis 33:37
3 Jay Gottesman 34:38
4 Ronald Chisolm 35:04
5 Edward Moore 35:26
6 Alexander Gordeuk 35:35
7 Angus McBride 35:59
8 Harold Brown 36:11
9 Andy Pinson 36:21
10 Tom McLean 36:29
11 Paul Davis 36:37
12 Roger Yongue 36:48
13 Joe Myers... 36:53
14 Anthony Horton 36:54
15 Daniel Brown 37:04
16 Keith Batten 37:09
17 Scott Murr 37:30
18 William Whitmire 37:31
19 Martin Troiani*.. 37:32
20 Richard Stephens 37:43
21 John Noricia 37:44
22 Willes Gorthy 37:54
23 Lawrence Persick.................................... 38:01

24 Ross Welch 38:03
25 Steven Hammond 38:04

Female 22-25 (12 awards)

1 Megan Othersen (Gorman) 37:20
2 Pam Witt 37:59.5
3 Yoli Casas 38:57
4 Sally Campbell 39:58
5 Laura Hinkley 40:55
6 Kim Ivey 41:14
7 Jane Belisle 41:47
8 Meredith Thompson 42:28
9 Rhonda Morris 42:46
10 Karen Caines 42:50
11 Lisa Russell 43:33
12 Mari Barrett 43:58

Male 26-29 (25 awards)

1 Tom Mather 32:05
2 David Caborn 34:03
3 Marc Embler 34:14
4 Michael Zengal 34:18
5 David Luhrs 34:20
6 Danny White 34:21
7 Bobby Woods 34:25
8 Jeff Milliman 34:28
9 Eddie Pennebaker 34:55
10 Terry Campbell 34:59
11 Peter Heidbreder 35:09
12 Scott Hirst 35:11
13 John Wehner 35:13
14 Butch Griggs 35:18
15 Richard Keating 35:36
16 Bob Kent 35:38
17 Hadley Ivey 35:56
18 Gary Smith 36:15
19 Jeff Stone 36:17
20 Tim Hamilton 36:19
21 Max Mintor 36:23
22 Johnny Witt 36:30
23 Dean Barten 36:42
24 Jeffrey Lessie 36:44
25 Jarvey Young 36:55

Female 26-29 (16 awards)

1 Debbie Davis 37:55
2 Janet Ballenger 39:56
3 Kelly Bussarow 40:39
4 Deborah Allen 41:21
5 Terry Dillon 41:24
6 Deborah Barlass 41:38
7 Nina Parks Herndon 42:17
8 Weezie Smalls 43:09
9 Terri Blankenship 43:14
10 Tami Thompson 43:44
11 Cheryl Caskie 43:49
12 Celia Cart 43:59.7
13 Ane Geddes 44:09
14 Karen Berry 44:14
15 Michele Stutts 44:17
16 Melissa Himelein 44:49

Male 30-34 (25 awards)

1 Dean Behrmann 34:16
2 Mike Hart 34:35
3 Mac Coile 34:52
4 Michael Dayton 34:53
5 Mike Ward 35:03
6 Steven Pavik 35:07
7 Gary Eaton 35:15
8 Peter Quilty 35:45
9 Roland Butch Cody 35:52
10 Ray Lewis 35:54
11 John Holzworth 36:03
12 Ned Hettinger 36:24
13 Dennis Funk 36:28
14 Gary Ricker 36:30
15 Mike Pate 36:33
16 Ronnie Floyd 36:38
17 Steve Caskie 37:06
18 Daniel Twineham 37:07
19 Ken Tuck 37:08
20 Richard Teague 37:10
21 David Culp 37:34.28
22 Herman Gaviria 37:34.97
23 Monty Coggins 37:41
24 Charles Kellner 37:51.66
25 Anthony Pizutti 37:51.86

Female 30-34 (18 awards)

1 Pam Drafts 38:48
2 Joanne Cox 40:21
3 Lyndell Weeks 40:50
4 Ginger Gregory 41:24
5 Anne Weston 41:43
6 Candace Almers 43:45
7 Donna Starling 44:05
8 Nancy Osborne 44:14
9 Kimberly Rogers 44:30
10 Jean Craig 44:34
11 Susan Query 45:26
12 LInda Olinger 45:28
13 Judy Rasnake 45:49
14 Karla Reichert 46:05
15 Debbie Garland 46:31
16 Maria Griffith 46:33
17 Jane Moore 46:37
18 Beverly Abbott 46:41

Male 35-39 (25 awards)

1 Gordon English 34:07
2 Peter Farwell 35:24
3 Glenn Dennis 35:41
4 Lucky Voiselle 35:53
5 David Mauterer 36:38
6 Norman Nickel 36:39
7 George Getty 36:46
8 Larry D'Ippolito 37:01
9 Michael Julian 37:04
10 Donnie Todd 37:05
11 Marcus Phillips 37:12
12 Duanne Wolf 37:15
13 Samuel Barnett 37:17
14 Tommy Bolus 37:19
15 Jack Todd 37:20
16 Ricky Vaughn 37:22
17 Richard Koenders 37:32
18 Bill Barfield 37:44
19 Franklin Dillman 37:46
20 Steven Lawrence 37:48
21 Paul King 37:49
22 Skipper Hewitt 37:59
23 Bill Harker 38:03
24 Keith Sanders 38:04
25 Billy Davey 38:11

Female 35-39 (12 awards)

1 Nancy Grayson 37:21
2 Peggy Schug 40:41
3 Marilyn Davey 41:22
4 Connie Gruver 41:27
5 Debby Sullivan 42:28
6 Judy Melton 43:30
7 Carol Davis 44:35
8 Cheryl Goodman 45:22
9 Deborah Estes 46:01
10 Bonnie Hipkins 46:39
11 Harriette Gause 46:51
12 Colleen Archambault 47:17

Male 40-44 (25 awards)

1 Richard Weeks 34:44
2 Don Wright 35:06
3 Bob Priest 35:39
4 Terry Van Natta 35:41
5 Art Williams 35:55
6 Dane Freeman 35:58
7 Jim Ellis 35:59.4
8 Morris Williams 36:01
9 Monty King 39:24
10 Reed Watson 36:25
11 Earl Jackson 36:39
12 Bill Peay 36:41
13 Mike McGuinness 37:26
14 Bruce Taylor 37:52
15 George Vosburgh 38:37
16 Dupree Elvington 38:38
17 Phillip Dickert 38:59
18 Bill Seigler 39:10
19 Charles Stoyle 39:25
20 Gary Butts 39:26
21 Bill Mayer 39:36
22 Don Reynolds 39:38
23 Michael Sealy 39:41
24 Russell Brown 39:46
25 Larry Decker 39:57

Female 40-44 (9 awards)

1 Gail Bailey 38:43
2 Anne Boone Reed 39:59.24
3 June Hartley 42:34
4 Gail Sharber* 43:18
5 Bambi Caruthers 43:37
6 Barbara Moore 44:42
7 Barbara Davidson 45:34
8 Sue Jacobs 45:43
9 Kathy Jaggers 45:49

Male 45-49 (16 awards)

1 Morgan Looney 34:57
2 James Adams 37:41
3 Dean Godwin 38:24
4 Buddy Keller 39:37
5 Olin Hammond 39:44
6 John Nutt* 40:00
7 Doyle Martin* 40:02
8 Jimmy Bagwell 40:05
9 Joe Allen 40:29
10 Bill Vetsch 40:34
11 Maurice Davidson 41:29
12 James Don Austell 41:40
13 Jerry Lyles 41:47

14 Theron Cochran 41:48
15 Terry Williams 41:51
16 Joseph Brown 41:52

Female 45-49 (3 awards)

1 Lorraine Evans 44:36
2 Peggy Ledford 46:53
3 Jane Elderkin 48:25

Male 50-54 (7 awards)

1 Ed Ledford 36:32
2 Adrian Craven 36:53
3 Jim Larson 36:56
4 Gerald Koch 38:04
5 Sammie Yarborough 39:28
6 Ed Guettler 40:12
7 Jack Gilmore 40:49

Female 50-54 (3 awards)

1 Susie Kluttz 44:46
2 Marcia Herbst 44:51
3 Jane McBryde 51:28

Male 55-59 (4 awards)

1 Lee Swofford 40:51
2 Stan Chodnicki 41:12
3 Sam Query 43:01
4 Cliff Thomas 45:39

Female 55-59 (3 awards)

1 Garthedon Embler 51:37
2 Ann Stanton* 56:49
3 Faye Motley* 1:04:41
4 Sally Kirk* 1:06:14
5 Wyndall Henderson* 1:10:00

Male 60-64 (3 awards)

1 Gordon English Sr. 41:30
2 David Mellard 44:47
3 Lawrence Moore 46:59

Female 60-64 (3 awards)

1 Shirley Schade* 1:04:51
2 Evelyn Smith* 1:04:53
3 Lucy Jones* 1:13:42

Male 65 & over (3 awards)

1 Roy Dawson 42:27
2 Ed Shaffer 46:49
3 Clayton Brelsford 51:38

Female 65 & over

1 Margaret Wright 53:18

Compiled by Cedric Jaggers from results provided by finish line director Chuck Magera.

The starter's gun goes off and the run begins. News and Courier photo by Tom Spain

Chapter 11
1988
Professional Timing Used For The First Time

Rain was forecast for the 11th Bridge Run, March 26, 1988. Fortunately, the showers held off, but it was overcast, about 65 degrees, and extremely humid and windy. Headwinds gusting from 20 to 25 mph on the bridge seemed mild after the winds of the previous year's race but definitely slowed all the runners.

The lead pack went through the first mile in 4:39 and hit the 2-mile mark in 9:26; then Ashley Johnson of Bowling Green, Ky., broke away and ran alone over the bridge and to the finish line to win in 29:56. Johnson said he felt really strong going up the second span (of the two-span Grace Memorial Bridge) and just pulled away from everyone. He said he was surprised no one went with him.

"Frankly, I came back after my 1985 race (where he finished 11th in 30:11) and wanted a better showing this year. But I didn't think it would go quite that way," he told the *News and Courier*. "I had been prepared for somebody to go with me."

Don Janicki of Tucson, Ariz., was second in 30:20. He told the newspaper, "Ashley was very impressive. After he got ahead on that first hill, I came back a little on the downhills, but I was never really in it after Ashley got the lead." Jim Haughey of Clemson, S.C., was third in 30:30.

Carla Borovicka of Tallahassee, Fla., was female winner in 34:38 as she overtook early leader Joan Nesbit of Durham, N.C., who finished second in 34:56, after they came off the bridges. Defending champion Mary Ellen McGowan of Gainesville, Fla., was third in 35:21. Borovicka said she was more of a track runner and was just getting used to running road races. She told the newspaper, "It was on the downhills that I was able to open up. I'm a pretty big runner (5 feet 9), and I can absorb the shock better than the shorter runners. I didn't know how fast the course was going to be, but this was the sort of race where I wasn't really concerned with my time." Defending champion McGowan told the newspaper, "I'm disappointed I didn't win again. The times weren't really fast today, because it was so humid. I think I'd rather run in the cold like I did here last year."

Mike Hurd from England, was Masters winner in 31:32 while Charleston's Bob Schlau was second in 32:19, just two weeks after qualifying for the U.S. Olympic trials marathon by running 2:19:26 at the Los Angeles Marathon, and Jim Lester of Magna, Utah, was third in 32:47. Gail Bailey of Charleston took her third Masters female crown in a row (taking the title every year since she turned 40) this time winning in 39:12, while Pat Sher of Jacksonville, Fla., was second in 40:22 and Judy Melton of Greenville, S.C., was third in 42:18.

The Dr. Marcus Newberry Award for first Tri-County male and female was a family affair as Bob Schlau won it for his 18th place overall finish, while Benita Schlau was the female recipient for her ninth overall female finish 38:11. For the third year in a row, winner of the Dewey Wise Trophy was Clayton Brelsford, 73, of Wilmington, N.C., with a time of 55:20.

Some of the older runners grumbled because the start area upfront was not roped off for the faster runners and monitored as in the past. As a result, a number of children and casual runners were near the front. This caused congestion as the faster runners had to try to get past them. One well-known local runner, Mark Friedrich, (who ran 29:58 to place as runner-up in the 1983 race) was knocked down at the start but was able to get up after being stepped on by several people and complete the race in 33:45.

Karl Gueldner was race director for the third year in a row. The entry fee was raised to $11. For the first time a professional finish line service, Burns Computer Services, was used and results were compiled using pull tabs from runners' race numbers which were bar-coded and scanned after the runner finished the race. There were 6,904 entrants and the results booklet, which was mailed to all finishers, listed 5,465 official finishers, 4105 male and 1360 female. Only the race winner broke 30 minutes while 268 males and 16 females finished under 40 minutes. A total of 1,768 runners crossed the finish line in less than 50 minutes while 3,451 completed the race in less than an hour.

The race was broadcast live on Channel 5 television for the fourth year in a row. The Sunday *News and Courier* listed the top 97 male finishers and the top 47 female finishers, and listed the top five in each age group, though it improperly included the invitational division prize money winners in the age division award list.

Other voices
Cooper River Bridge Run
By Dr. Robert 'Bob' Kirk, Originally appeared in the March-April 1988 Low Country Runner

This is not meant to be an accurate history, rather an impression based upon my viewpoints both as a mid-pack competitor for all 10 races and for insight gained from being a part of the planning, the creating part of most races.

That 1978 race was my first road race, my first 10K, and opened my brain to USA road racing, and paved the way to the finish line of that very first Island Marathon, (same year) the four loop course that went up and down even more streets than in December '87. Suddenly I became aware that there was a "scientific" method by which to train; that a wonderful periodical, known as Runner's World, existed, and that there was a local runners club led by the lean and the fit: (Bob Schlau, Terry Hamlin and Brian Smith.)

Back in Race 1, we were much more casual and unsophisticated. The weather was suddenly warm and humid, and no one had yet adapted to heat, and the start was late, no water on the course, and despite significant heat injuries, there was no official first aid station. A prominent state legislator-lawyer-runner had a grand mal seizure in White Point Gardens, the finish area that initial year.

No one died and no one sued, though about that vintage a seriously heat damaged runner did sue the Peachtree Race, on the grounds that no one informed him it would be hot in downtown Atlanta on July 4! The suit was thrown out, but led to numerous water stations and insurance. Early on in this racing business the attitude was you were supposed to be fit, sensible, and responsible for yourself — bring your own water to the start if you wanted some. As Dave Scott has said about the original Iron Man Triathlon with no boats for the open-water swim: "If you drowned, you just drowned." But we were lucky back then too.

I remember vividly the very long-range view of Benji Durden as he vanished over the top of hill #1, reversible lane, New Bridge. I was awed that he could be almost a mile in front as I was still a quarter mile from the bridge. Getting over the bridge was easier than expected, though I'd never run it before. It was at least cooler up there and the multiple gnat bites had almost ceased itching.

Going down the final hill I noticed ahead a man/woman combo running hand-in-hand and clearly recall thinking: Yeah, it's a beautiful spring Sunday in a beautiful southern city, and LOVE is wonderful, but running this race holding hands is absurd! I sprinted to see and realized my mistake — it was that gritty blind runner George Hallman running with his wife for guidance. As she grew tired he switched to a male friend who then tangled legs and tripped George about where water was supposed to be in front of the Piggly Wiggly on Meeting Street. He was up as fast as he went down, knees bleeding, exhorting his partner: "Let's go, let's go!"

I ran all the way down to the Battery just behind George. When we reached Broad Street, and boy did it feel hot under the sun on that pavement, someone mentioned the closeness of the finish and once more George urged his partner onward, faster. But like me, the nameless partner could do no better and poor Hallman finished handicapped both by lack of vision and slow partners.

Other moments in other races also stand out; like the year I passed and left my 28-year-old son sweating and fading in the dust of East Bay Street. There were years I even beat both sons, but then, stung and perhaps humiliated, they trained and came back to soundly whip the old man. It's hard to keep youth down (permanently).

This race originated with twice the expected turnout, has grown steadily yearly, has outgrown several courses and their starts and finishes and added on the entire fitness festival week and its culminating walk, and has endured some controversy too — I wonder exactly how or why. It's unique to have a race run by committee, a committee that represents major area educational institutions, and two cities, Parks Recreation Tourism and the running club.

The latter is a natural because of expertise need and much is owed to them (to us) for this, Terry Hamlin being the original expertise guru. Dr. Marc Newberry is the originator of the idea for such a race, maybe with a little help from that local surgeon Norm Walsh (hey Norm, you used to be a helluva competitor. Do you still even run?). Originally it was the late Keith Hamilton at The Citadel and now Gary Wilson continues, even though The Citadel as an institution has dropped out. Roy Hills was until this year the College of Charleston's main man, with some help from Richard Godsen, their administration offering more tolerance than enthusiastic support. It's the two cities that have the most to gain and whose cooperation we need most if this now huge event continues and grows even more.

We've been most fortunate to have two athlete-mayors who are extremely supportive: Joe Riley and Dick Jones are invaluable, know the race, love the race and see that their respective merchants, council, police etc. are with us. Without wide community support there would be no race. Literally none.

Charleston has supplied many volunteers too, and has encouraged and supported Mark Blatchford in being the race director - leader he is. Ah the race director! What a job that one! One that I've consistently dodged.

It's not really so bad until race day when the nightmares begin to actually come true, except the realities seem even worse. In a point-to-point race of this magnitude with a large bottleneck in the middle, something unforeseen, unpredictable and uncontrollable seems inevitable. Mile marker banners are misplaced, the clock operator can't make it and sent his wife who arrives late and in a huff and also doesn't know how to make it work, or there is a beaut of a fog. Maybe a bunch of people somehow manage to miss the well advertised shuttle bus.

Then we used to have some really jam-up races that finished in that beautiful, but narrow Coming Street and George Street corner, by the cistern. Oh there's the usual sudden change in the weather from hot to cold or vice versa. We've burned out a few race directors and consumed innumerable volunteers. Volunteers as a group are incredibly nice, resilient, dedicated, altruistic, lovable and necessary. No vital. And remember the year of that unregistered loonie-in-the-wheelchair, how she flew down those hills. If you don't remember, ask Chuck Magera, the hardest working man I ever saw.

With growth and success the CRBR has met some crossroads. We've chosen commercial sponsors, invited celebrities, flirted with and successfully married the local media, and given prize money for elite Olympians, thus attracting more attention, gaining bigger sponsorship so we can give more awards and prizes. You have to spin some wheels to get to the top (it seems).

We insist on a time and a place for everyone, mailed out promptly – well-l-l-l most years anyway. I'm not so sure why since we all wear those beautifully inexpensive, light, durable and extremely accurate and reliable Japanese watches - don't we know our times? Don't we know if we finished before Joe or behind Alice? There's even a big clock at the finish and the club always has a video to see you and your friends finish again and again if you like that sort of entertainment. Anyway, given the mass start and the crowded bridge and other hazards, no one ever does a PR (Personal Record time) in the CRBR. (Editor's note: I remember how surprised I was at this comment when Dr. Kirk submitted this article for publication in the Low Country Runner. I had previously mentioned in some of my editorials that in 1980 the Cooper River Bridge Run was the first 10K race where I ever broke the 40-minute barrier, an unforgettable PR; a few years later my wife Kathy ran a PR – her first sub 45 minute 10K in the Bridge Run; and I was amazed every year by the large number of PRs run on the Bridge. CJ). My nephew from Atlanta is the only human I know whose 10K PR is at the Bridge—and he's unique anyway. So why do we want this time/place stuff, tell me?

Finally, my crystal ball says the race must take new and bolder turns. We need desperately financial security, in the long-range sense. If Boston can get a million dollars a year for ten years from John Hancock, then surely the CRBR should get much more than the current hand-to-mouth fiscal scene. Sure Boston has 10 times more history and more runners, but somewhere out there is a sponsor just waiting to allow us the use of say 50 thousand a year for 3 years. We need professional top quality finish-line teams, a year round paid race director with a permanent real office, secretary, phone, address, and we deserve cable or national TV coverage. Even though it's not in our by-laws, the committee could put some money back into the community in the form of a scholarship or charity, and our credo of exercise for fitness and health would get more PR and so would those loyal backing institutions (like MUSC for example) who've kept a patient low profile.

After all, is there a more beautiful city in the spring? Who else has a fitness Spoleto? Where else is there a race over a bridge closed by an act of the state General Assembly? It's not only the biggest but best race in the Southeast (excepting Peachtree) and getting bigger/better.

No Place To Hide On The Bridge

By Art Liberman, Originally appeared in the May June 1988 Low Country Runner

Almost everyone who competes in the Bridge Run has a special story to tell regarding his personal experience running South Carolina's largest road race. Realizing the difficulty of the course, along with the usually humid conditions, my goal this year was to run a "creditable" race.

My training was going well and early race performances indicated that I was steadily improving. My plan for the spring racing season was to "peak" for events in April and early May. Yet for the first time in a few years, I was fairly fit for the Bridge Run – no pre-race illnesses, injuries or stress to deal with. With no self-imposed pressure to do well, I was prepared to gracefully accept the time that was displayed on the clock at the finish line.

Although I consider myself a fairly experienced runner, I broke a cardinal rule the afternoon before the race: never experiment with anything new. My error in good judgment revolved around receiving a vigorous leg massage by someone I had never used before so close to a race. The result was extremely relaxed muscles - but too loose for the tremendous shock they would encounter on the downhill sections of the Bridge Run.

My race went well through two miles. My legs felt springy and efficient, my mental perspective was "race ready", and pace was on target. Like just about everyone else, I lost a few seconds on the first incline but maintained a steady effort over the top of the span. But as I began my descent picking up the pace, my left quadriceps began transmitting a danger signal that something was seriously wrong.

Continuing down the span, the pain became so intense that soon, running was impossible. Slowing to a walk, I knew my race was over. Hobbling along the right guardrail near the emergency lane, my mind entertained many thoughts. "Why didn't I get the massage on Thursday as I usually had? Will I be thought of as a quitter by those who pass me?" I had run over 100 races and eight marathons, yet never did I have to walk or drop out of any up to now. Comments from other runners ranged from "Art, are you OK?" by those near the front of the pack to "Come on, you can do it. Don't quit!" from those at the rear, including walkers who were now overtaking me.

Even though I appreciated their encouragement/sympathy/support, I really wasn't in the mood to respond. I only wanted to vanish from the race but the nearest exit was over a mile and a half away. I kept hearing a voice in my mind telling me, "There was no place to hide on the bridge."

Relief was in sight as I finally made it to Saint Phillip Street. At long last I was off the course! There, a resident of the neighborhood riding a bike asked me if I was all right or if there was anything he could do to help. He walked with me for the next mile towards my car, and I told him about my leg cramp. He then asked me if I was angry about DNFing and my response became philosophical. I told him about Charlie Post's accident and how I never take life or good health for granted.

As we introduced ourselves, I told Ronald that I was happy to be able to walk, let alone run and compete in the Bridge Run. Ronald then offered a story about his days at Burke High School and classmates who told him that he couldn't do something. I learned that Ronald enjoyed proving he could accomplish "the impossible". I said that it must be satisfying showing others that he could succeed. Ronald said, "No, I only enjoy showing myself." Hearing that erased all the negative feelings I experienced earlier that morning.

That mile walk along Saint Phillip Street passed very quickly and as we approached my car, I knew it was highly unlikely that I would bump into Ronald any time soon. As we were about to go our separate ways, I thanked Ronald for his companionship and added that it meant a great deal to me. I also told him why the Bridge Run was first established: To promote health and fitness in the community. I thought to myself that he was in pretty good shape – he regularly cycled and played basketball. And since he had served in the Marines, Ronald had determination. I said, "Wouldn't it be great if we bumped into each other one year from now in Marion Square? You'd say, "Remember me from last year? Guess what? I ran the Bridge!" Knowing Ronald only so briefly, I would be willing to bet that he will do it.

Tell Me About Your Bridge Run 1988

By Cedric Jaggers, Originally appeared in the May/June 1988 Low Country Runner

(Bridge Run info for 1988 – 5,465 largest number of official finishers, 6,904 second largest number of entrants to date. Start time temperature 65 degrees.)

At the Bridge Run awards ceremony held at the State Ports Authority Building, (during the long wait for it – as it began at 11:30 rather than the announced 10 A.M.) I had my clipboard and pen in hand and got the idea to ask Charleston Running Club members this question. The responses are in the order I happened to run across the people. CJ

Mark Friedrich: I got knocked down at the start and trampled by about 5 people. There were a lot of people up front who shouldn't have been there. If I had to pick a year for it to happen I'm glad it was this year when I wasn't in top shape. I knew there were potential problems when I saw a kid in a walkman on the front line. I ran about 33:45 – hoping for 33. I might have been there if I hadn't got knocked down. Results time 33:45, 29th male.

Bob Reynolds: Don't ask me about my race. I walked about halfway. I had trouble with the heat after about 3 miles. Results time 51:56, 2,164th male.

Gordon Graham: It was a good run. Those hills were tough on me. It was my first Bridge Run and I felt pretty good at the finish. Results time 46:34, 1,128th male.

Bill Vetsch: I was looking for sub 40 and 40:25. It was hotter than I expected. The breeze was nice, but I'd have liked it if it was about 15 degrees cooler. Results time 40:26, 299th male.

Barbara Davidson: My race was terrible, it really was. Some guy pushed me going up the bridge. Results time 47:11, 98th female.

Mike Chodnicki: Put me down for a PW (Personal Worst). My last 3 miles were 6:20s. The bridges just killed me, I was exhausted. Results time 37:06 110th male.

Doug Williams: Sixty flat. My goal this time was to beat everybody in high tops and I didn't accomplish it. Some guy in full backpack, combat boots and pants beat me. Results time 61:23, 3,609th male.

Bruce Taylor: It was good through the first mile. I went up the first hill and just died. I've run too many long races this year. If it hadn't been for the hills I'd have run OK. It was a little warm out there. I did about what I expected. Results time 38:43, 186th male.

Charles Kellner: I had a pretty good day: my best Bridge Run. I owe it to training with 'Ledford's Loafers'. I've never trained this hard before. I ran about 36:20. Results time 36:27, 84th male.

Nina Parks Herndon: My Bridge Run was what I thought I'd do: about 44:39, realistic for me with my current training. I was proud of myself. I did okay. Results time 44:38, 59th female.

Pat Rhode: I'm not complaining. I did the schedule (in the Jan-Feb LCR) and doing those 20 quarters was something in itself. Results time 49:43, 18th female.

Benita Schlau: I was pleased; it was my best Bridge Run. The first span just took it out of me. We had a headwind but it felt good. So it was a good race for me. Results time 38:11, 9th female, Marcus Newberry award winner, first local female.

David Reese: I ran better at age 40 than I did at 35. This is my best Bridge Run. Results time 36:25, 82nd male.

Dupree Elvington: I ran like a dog. If I'd run any worse I'd have had to practice. But you haven't seen the last of me. I will be back – with a vengeance! Results time 41:01, 344th male.

Bob Walton: It was OK. I got boxed in at the start, but otherwise it was fine. Results time 43:35, 671st male.

Billy Leopard: It was tough, my second Bridge Run. I did manage to run the whole bridge and not walk any. That was my major accomplishment. I was four and a half minutes ahead of last year's time. Unable to find in results.

Dan Sharrard: I carbo loaded all week, trained hard early, took a couple of days off, then had a terrible run. My quads hurt. I ran 37:47 shooting for 37. Results time 37:51, 147th male.

Patrick Connors: PR 48:17. The beginning was crowded. After a while I got used to it. It took forever to go uphill. Downhill it felt like I was being dragged down. It felt like the finish was never coming. Results time 48:17, 1,443rd male.

Larry D'Ippolitto: It was fine until the bottom span of the second hill when I caught a side stitch and stayed in second gear the rest of the way. I got tripped and almost fell down at the finish. I ran about 36:33. Results time 36:36, 91st male.

Mike Strohm: It was all right. I've been running tired. I had 3 track meets this week. I ran 38:07 and I'm surprised I ran that well. I started out too fast. It would have been better if I'd run it more even. Results time 38:10, 159th male.

Leon Locklear: It was an enjoyable little jaunt at 40:02. No pressure, no hype. Results time 40:17, 289th male.

Mike Hart: It hurt. I PR'd, my fourth P.R. this year. About 34:16. Results time 34:17, 33rd male.

Elaine Francis: It was only the second Bridge Run I've done. I wanted to do it in under an hour and I did it in 56 minutes. I was pleased, it was good for me. Results time 57:12, 529th female.

Andrea Berendt: It was a good race but I don't think it's a true indication of what you can do in a 10k. I felt good but I got nauseated on the first span. I didn't feel the third span (the Crosstown overpass). What bothers me is to turn down Market and then Meeting. It's difficult to pick up speed. Unable to find in results.

Alex Morton: It was a PR 43:28, 4 minutes better than last year. That second hill did me in, it was real slow. I had to get it back after that third hill. Results time 43:02, 589th male.

Jim Strohm: It was disgusting; 41:33. I wasn't in shape. I'm glad it's over. Results time 41:40, 395th male.

Dave Carney: Not enough hill training. There are no hills in Lumberton where I live now. The wind on the first span got me. I ran about 38:57, last year I ran 43 minutes. It was fun but I wish I could have run better. That's the way it goes. Results time 38:58, 202nd male.

Andy Taylor: Injuries have been killing me. This is the first race of the year for me. Unable to find in results.

Michael Golemis: 39:50. I was real happy. I haven't even run the bridge in training this year. We live on Folly now and I need some hill work. Results time 39:55, 261st male.

Connie Gruver: My best Bridge Run, about 40:45. I ran the first mile in 5:55 – too fast. I didn't want to do that. I did the Bridge and felt hot. I got on King Street and it got really warm. It was humid. Results time 40:46, 20th female.

Susie Golemis: It was OK. I thought after mile 4 it was pretty hot. I think I ran about 44:30. This was my first race back since having the baby. Results time

44:43, 63rd female.

Dan Clapper: It was wonderful. I followed the Pritikin diet to the best of my ability. I cheated with Granola Bars and oatmeal cookies. I felt I had plenty of energy and I was passing people I usually don't pass so there must be something to it. I ran about 36:30. Results time 36:30, 87th male.

Colleen Archambault: I've been in a slump for about 6 months, so my goal for this was to run it and feel good and I did, but my time was slow. About 48:53. Results time 49:19, 169th female.

Ginger Gregory: P.R. 40:02. Coming up to the finish I was going 'Break it, Break it', I was sprinting. I should have started sooner but I couldn't see the clock. Results time 40:03, 17th female.

Joe Mattingly: I ran 38:03. The only thing I can say is I'm pleased with what I did since I didn't know if I'd get to run and I didn't prepare for it. Results time 38:07, 156th male.

Kelly Busarow: I had an awful race. I went out too fast: 5:40. I walked up the first span, ran down, walked up the second span, ran down and didn't walk anymore. About 41:04. Results time 41:09, 24th female.

Huey Inma: I finished. I ran 35:08. The hills and the humidity got me. It was my second best Bridge Run, but I wanted to be under 35. Results time 35:09, 46th male.

Lucky Voiselle: I ran in a Charleston Running Club singlet for the first time and I did a 35:52. I feel good about it even though I didn't taper for the race since I'm training for the state championship half marathon. I came down to run hard and I did. Results time 35:54, 67th male.

Gail Bailey: About 39:08. The first two miles were smooth. I thought, "This is it!" but the hills – they've never affected me so badly before. I don't think I went out too fast. My legs got heavy and my breathing got heavy going up the first span and I never recovered. I was real tight, my legs, shoulders and arms. I felt heavy and awful and started to see spots. I could feel the lactic acid building up. I wanted to quit so bad. The only thing that kept me going was the people on the side of the street. I couldn't quit in front of them. Results time 39:12, 12th female.

Don Austell: I started out about 10 seconds too quick. I felt OK up the 2 spans but on the viaduct my legs turned to water. It seemed to get hot and humid on King Street. Overall I felt good about the race, but the awards ceremony was delayed too long. I ran about 41:19. Results time 41:19, 368th male.

Dennis Hiott: I don't even want to talk about it. It was hot. Results time 43:18, 636th male.

Beverly Hiott: I'm also speechless. I felt strange. I felt my balance was off. It was fun as usual. Results time 52:49, 299th female.

Martha Luckey: It was my first 10k. I ran it with my brother from Beaufort. Our goal was to finish it in about an hour, but I got real tired with about a mile to go and hot on King Street and had to slow down. I finished it just over an hour and I'm real proud of myself for finishing the race. Results time 63:17, 902nd female.

Kathy Jaggers: I thought I would be in the 45s. But it was too hot and humid for my asthma and I didn't make it. Results time 46:14, 84th female.

Cedric Jaggers: I thought since I was in a new age group (40 now) and in great shape I'd run in the 36s like I did at the Flowertown 10k a few weeks ago. Instead it got hot and I was disappointed when the clock and my watch said 37:33 as I crossed the finish line. Results time 37:40, 137th male.

1988 Awards

Awards: Note, the race used an 'Invitational Division' – Elite Runners contesting for prize money – not eligible for age group awards.

Prize money winners:
Overall Male
1 Ashley Johnson .... Bowling Grn KY ...... 29:56 .. $2,000
2 Don Janicki .... Tucson, AZ .... 30:20 .. $1,000
3 Jim Haughey .... Clemson, SC .... 30:30 .... $700
4 David Krafsur .... Knoxville, TN .... 30:31 .... $500
5 Rickey Pittman .... Knoxville, TN .... 30:46 .... $400
6 Marty Flynn .... Clemson, SC .... 30:51 .... $350
7 Kevin Ruch .... Camp Hill, PA .... 30:59 .... $300
8 David Geer .... Clemson, SC .... 31:35 .... $250
9 Craig Thompson ..... Knoxville, TN .... 31:40 .... $200
10 Rob Wilder .... Summerville, SC ...... 31:42 .... $150

Overall Female
1 Carla Borovicka ..... Tallahase, FL .... 34:38 .. $2,000
2 Joan Nesbit .... Durham, NC .... 34:56 .. $1,000
3 Mary Ellen McGowan .. Gainville FL .... 35:21 .... $700
4 K. Champagne .... Pittsburg, NY .... 36:08 .... $300
5 Kathy Hadler .... Ann Arbor, MI .... 36:15 .... $200
6 Laura Caldwell ...... Stone Mtn, GA .... 36:48 .... $150

Masters Division Male
1 Mike Hurd .... England .... 31:32 .... $300
2 Bob Schlau .... Charleston, SC .... 32:19 .... $200
3 Jim Lester .... Magna, UT .... 32:47 .... $100

Masters Division Female
1 Gail Bailey .... Charleston, SC .... 39:12 .... $300
2 Patt Sher .... Jacksonville, FL ...... 40:22 .... $200
3 Judy Melton .... Greenville, SC .... 42:18 .... $100

Special award:
Dr Marcus Newberry Award for first local Charleston Tri-County area finisher:
Male
  Bob Schlau .... Charleston, SC 32:19
Female
  Benita Schlau .... Charleston, SC 38:11

Special award:
Dewey Wise Trophy for oldest finisher with time faster than his or her age in minutes:
Clayton Brelsford, 73 .... Wilmington, NC 55:20

Age group award winners
(Top 25 or 5%, whichever is less in each age group):

Male 12 & under (68 finishers, 4 awards)
1 Michael Gamrell 42:32
2 Michael Driggers 43:12
3 Thomas Lovingood 44:55
4 Richard Watson 46:15

Female 12 & under (17 fin., 3 awards)
1 Meghan Dunn 50:31
2 Regan Carr 54:58
3 Deborah Saylor 55:49

Male 13-17 (166 finishers, 9 awards)
1 Lawrence Carrigan 36:44
2 Greg Whipple 37:08
3 Mike Strohm 38:10
4 Thomas Stewart 39:37
5 David Glover 39:39
6 Rodney Westbury 40:08
7 Daniel Schuh 40:11
8 Brian White 40:29

Female 13-17 (54 finishers, 3 awards)
1 Mary McEachern 43:51
2 Billie Veber 46:45
3 Melissa Runey 46:57

Male 18-21 (184 finishers, 10 awards)
1 Greg Whitmire 34:31
2 Dylan Cooper 35:13
3 Dale Johnson 35:28
4 William Fearn 35:57
5 Mark Barton 36:22
6 Frederick Whitney 36:22
7 Gerald Ellis 36:27
8 Dale Hoover 36:45
9 Stephen Brody 36:50
10 David Barry 37:17

Female 18-21 (83 finishers, 4 awards)
1 Kappa Peddy 44:41
2 Debbie Niles 44:41
3 Susie Golemis 44:43
4 Kay Breininger 45:32

Male 22-25 (361 finishers, 18 awards)
1 Bjorn Holleland 31:45
2 James Perry 32:47
3 Rob Devlin 32:55
4 Mikal Peveto 33:10
5 Paul Laymon 34:19
6 Paul Kammerer 34:38
7 Steven Leopard 35:39

8 Tom McLean ... 35:46
9 Mitch Embler ... 35:54
10 Edward Moore ... 36:29
11 Jeffrey Woods ... 36:35
12 Andrew Teeuwen ... 36:48
13 William Whitmire ... 37:07
14 Lawrence Trace ... 37:14
15 Gilbert Girbes ... 37:20
16 Steven Mendelson ... 37:49
17 Dan Sharrard ... 37:51
18 Steven Boudreaux ... 37:52

Female 22-25 (157 finishers, 8 awards)
1 Terri Smith ... 39:51
2 Deretsa Vaughn ... 41:05
3 Jane Belisle ... 41:26
4 Annie Broe ... 41:30
5 Tracie Armold ... 42:37
6 Laura Fannin ... 43:03
7 Elizabeth Graham ... 43:45
8 Rhonda Morris ... 44:21

Male 26-29 (608 finishers, 25 awards)
1 Selwyn Blake ... 31:48
2 Steven Stebbins ... 32:25
3 Danny White ... 33:26
4 Larry Brock ... 33:35
5 Eddie Pennebaker ... 34:09
6 Max Minter ... 34:14
7 Philip Cohen ... 34:36
8 Gary Smith ... 34:49
9 Huey Inman ... 35:09
10 Terry Campbell ... 35:16
11 Hadley Ivey ... 35:17
12 Dave Gibson ... 35:29
13 Dave Ansell ... 35:34
14 John Kester ... 35:45
15 John Wehner ... 35:49
16 Scott Murr ... 35:51
17 Richard Norris ... 35:53
18 Scott Hirst ... 36:04
19 Steven Santos ... 36:15
20 David Marshall ... 36:40
21 Bruce Balmer ... 36:42
22 John Grmbach ... 36:45
23 Mikey Fronsoe ... 36:47
24 Gregory McFayden ... 37:25
25 Jack Alexander ... 37:48

Female 26-29 (256 finishers, 13 awards)
1 Cheryl Boessow ... 37:44
2 Kim Ivey ... 39:48
3 Susan Foster ... 40:51
4 Kelly Busarow ... 41:09
5 Karen Caines ... 41:50
6 Susan Burditt ... 42:05
7 Courtney Moore ... 42:10
8 Terry Dillon ... 42:12
9 Patricia Clark ... 43:29
10 Weezi Small ... 44:36
11 Nina Parks Herndon ... 44:38
12 Lynne Burdette ... 44:58
13 Darlene Moes ... 45:33

Male 30-34 (801 finishers, 25 awards)
1 Marc Embler ... 33:08
2 Mark Friedrich ... 33:45
3 Mike Hart ... 34:17

4 David Caborn ... 34:22
5 Keith Johnson ... 35:04
6 Jerry Sanders ... 35:15
7 Paul Bertsch ... 35:25
8 Gary Eaton ... 35:28
9 Michael Fitzgerald ... 35:29
10 Tom Wild ... 35:36
11 Randy Carmichael ... 35:56
12 Ray Lewis ... 36:04
13 John Holzworth ... 36:11
14 Gary Stegall ... 36:14
15 David Bourgeois ... 36:21
16 Richard Teague ... 36:28
17 Dan Clapper ... 36:30
18 Harry Ash ... 36:32
19 Jarvie Young ... 36:51
20 Greg Sveska ... 36:57
21 Bruce Hancock ... 37:05
22 Mike Chodnicki ... 37:06
23 Jay McIntosh ... 37:10
24 Brian Waldrep ... 37:22
25 Ronnie Floyd ... 37:27

Female 30-34 (320 finishers, 16 awards)
1 Pam Drafts ... 38:55
2 Linda Fox ... 39:27
3 Ginger Gregory ... 40:03
4 Anne Weston ... 40:37
5 Janet Thiel ... 41:43
6 Patricia Bushway ... 42:56
7 Patti Patterson ... 43:04
8 Marcia Kennedy ... 43:16
9 Sara Dorociak ... 43:21
10 Michele Stutts ... 43:37
11 Sandy Reid ... 43:44
12 Judy Rasnake ... 44:11
13 Kim Rogers ... 44:18
14 Elizabeth Boineau ... 44:57
15 Maria Griffith ... 45:10
16 Joan Garrison ... 45:26

Male 35-39 (751 finishers, 25 awards)
1 Gordon English ... 33:15
2 Steven Pavik ... 34:52
3 Jim Westmoreland ... 35:18
4 Joseph Denneny ... 35:27
5 David Mauterer ... 35:45
6 Richard Kidd ... 36:13
7 Gary Ricker ... 36:24
8 Charles Kellner ... 36:27
9 Tommy Seymore ... 36:35
10 Larry D'Ippolito ... 36:36
11 John Bernhardt ... 36:44
12 Doc Bayne ... 36:44
13 Glenn Dennis ... 36:51
14 Daniel Williams ... 37:09
15 Paul King ... 37:11
16 Donnie Todd ... 37:19
17 Franklin Dillman ... 37:21
18 Ned Hettinger ... 37:26
19 Rusty Doyle ... 37:26
20 Bill Barfield ... 37:29
21 David Lee ... 37:29
22 Ronald Gillespie ... 37:34
23 Larry Berglind ... 37:37
24 Leon McCray ... 37:46

25 Samuel Barnett ... 37:48

Female 35-39 (233 finishers, 12 awards)
1 Connie Gruver ... 40:46
2 Peggy Schug ... 40:51
3 Ann Allison ... 41:35
4 Marilyn Davey ... 43:28
5 Deborah Estes ... 43:39
6 Susan Query ... 43:50
7 Sallie Driggers ... 44:04
8 Sue Whelan ... 44:40
9 Becky Parris ... 44:49
10 Sally Mincher ... 45:35
11 Elizabeth Crowley ... 45:36
12 Jeanette Houck ... 47:10

Male 40-44 (590 finishers, 25 awards)
1 Michael Hurd ... 31:32
2 Bob Schlau ... 32:19
3 Carl Nicholson ... 33:04
4 Tom Dooley ... 34:10
5 Lawrence Watson ... 34:44
6 Lansing Brewer ... 34:55
7 Don Wright ... 35:05
8 Lucky Voiselle ... 35:54
9 George David Reese ... 36:25
10 Gerry Carner ... 36:36
11 Chuck Barton ... 36:46
12 Chuck Greer ... 37:35
13 Cedric Jaggers ... 37:40
14 Bill Peay ... 37:47
15 Mickey Lackey ... 37:49
16 Phillip Dickert ... 38:25
17 Bill Siegler ... 38:38
18 Bruce Taylor ... 38:43
19 John Douglas ... 39:27
20 Herbert Smith ... 39:43
21 Jimmy Hadden ... 39:50
22 Randy Whitt ... 39:53
23 Ken Lewis ... 40:05
24 Jim Goodman ... 40:17
25 Ronald Jolley ... 40:19

Female 40-44 (131 finishers, 7 awards)
1 Gail Bailey ... 39:12
2 Patt Sher ... 40:21
3 Judy Melton ... 42:18
4 Ellie Smith ... 43:20
5 June Hartley ... 43:27
6 Betty Ryberg ... 43:29
7 Libby Neely ... 43:53

Male 45-49 (309 finishers, 16 awards)
1 Jim Lester ... 32:47
2 Don Coffman ... 33:09
3 Charles Tesenair ... 36:56
4 Art Williams ... 37:26
5 Reginald Smith ... 38:03
6 Philip Gibbs ... 38:27
7 Dean Godwin ... 38:29
8 Boyce Brawley ... 38:41
9 Jimmy Bagwell ... 39:26
10 Wendel Cribb ... 39:29
11 Arnold Eversole ... 39:57
12 Chuck Mammay ... 40:03
13 Bill Vetsch ... 40:26
14 William Hollaway ... 40:31
15 Theron Cochran ... 40:34

16 Olin Hammond ... 40:41

Female 45-49 (64 finishers, 4 awards)
1 Linda Hendrix ... 48:24
2 Avis Allen ... 48:45
3 Sallie Sinkler ... 49:30
4 Pat Rhode ... 49:43

Male 50-54 (141 finishers, 7 awards)
1 Adrian Craven ... 36:17
2 Jim Larson ... 36:37
3 Ed Ledford ... 37:18
4 Gerald Koch ... 37:48
5 Sammie Yarborough ... 39:40
6 James Allen ... 40:18
7 Charlie Harris ... 40:18

Female 50-54 (21 finishers, 3 awards)
1 Susie Kluttz ... 43:44
2 Joyce Hodges ... 48:24
3 Jane McBryde ... 53:44

Male 55-59 (65 finishers, 4 awards)
1 Charles Rose ... 40:23
2 Stan Chodnicki ... 41:17
3 Neil Wilson ... 42:11
4 Bob Walton ... 43:35

Female 55-59 (7 finishers, 3 awards)
1 Mary Anne Woodring ... 43:10
2 Garthedon Embler ... 50:17
3 Mary Trammell ... 1:03:53

Male 60-64 (34 finishers, 3 awards)
1 Richard Johnson ... 43:34
2 Lawrence Moore ... 46:09
3 Franklin Mason ... 46:58

Female 60-64 (7 finishers, 3 awards)
1 Mary Hirl ... 1:02:30
2 Faye Motley ... 1:06:43
3 Ann Adams ... 1:12:00

Male 65-98 (13 finishers, 3 awards)
1 David Mellard ... 43:37
2 Eldridge Lloyd ... 52:01
3 Arnold Hecht ... 55:07

Female 65-98 (3 finishers, 3 awards)
1 Margaret Wright ... 57:15
2 Evelyn Smith ... 1:09:48
3 Shirley Schade ... 1:16:42

Compiled by Cedric Jaggers from complete race results

The leaders near the second crest of the Grace Bridge. News and Courier photo by Stephanie Harvin

CHAPTER 12

1989

Grete Waitz Female Winner Despite Mixup At Start

The 12th Bridge Run was held April 1, 1989, with crisp, clear, 55-degree weather conditions at the 8 a.m. start. The runners had a headwind gusting to 20 mph on the bridge.

When you have one of the biggest names in running, you expect everything to work perfectly. Unfortunately, confusion reigned at the start as an estimated 50 to 100 runners were warming up in front of the starting line when the starting cannon was fired. One of them was the pre-race symposium speaker and favored female, Grete Waitz of Norway. Waitz, nine-time winner of the New York City Marathon and the 1984 Olympic marathon silver medalist, had been lured to the race through the efforts of the Bridge Run Committee and a private sponsor who had put up a $3,000 appearance fee. She waited for defending champion Carla Borovicka of Tallahassee, Fla., to pull even with her, then ran with her over the bridges before pulling steadily away to win by 31 seconds in 33:29. Joan Nesbitt of Durham, N.C., runner-up in 1988, finished third in 34:17.

Waitz's time would have been a course record had she started on the right side of the starting line. After the race she said it was the toughest 10k race she had run. With a 10k personal best of 30:59, she said the bridge incline and the wind added about a minute to the time she might have run on a flat course. "I like that too, because this course has a personality," she said. "It's a challenge, and I enjoyed it." She said she felt good about her chances of breaking the course record, then added, "I first saw the record before I saw the course. It's much more difficult than I thought."

The men's race was closer. Defending champion Ashley Johnson of Bowling Green, Ky., had hoped for a course record. Unfortunately he was tying his shoe when the starting gun fired. He caught and ran in a pack of about 10 runners until they got over the bridges. Then he slowly pulled away to become only the second runner to successfully defend a Bridge Run title. His winning time was 29:48, and he said he thought he might have gotten the record except for the wind. "I wasn't prepared at all when the gun went off," he told the *News and Courier*. "All of a sudden, I looked up and saw 7,000 people coming at me. It was incredible."

On winning two in a row, he said, "This feels really good. You don't do this very often. This race doesn't get any easier just because you've won it before. I thought I might try breaking free early again, but this time they all came with me."

Mike O'Reilly of Boulder, Colo., '85 winner, was second in 29:52 while Erik Hansen of Gainesville, Fla., was third in 29:53. The race was a battle with the lead changing hands through 5 and a half miles before Johnson pushed ahead to win. "Once he (Johnson) went, I think I conceded the victory to him," runner-up O'Reilly told the newspaper. "He had more leg speed than I did."

Johnson never felt comfortable. "I looked behind me near the finish line," he said, "and they weren't as far back as I thought they were."

Charleston's Bob Schlau improved his second place Masters finish from the previous year to become Masters winner in 32:20 with Wes Wessely of Lilburn, Ga., second in 33:04 and Don Coffman of Frankfort, Ky., third in 33:15. Judy Greer of Orlando, Fla., was female Masters winner in 37:38 with Claudia Ciaveralla of Cary, N.C., second in 37:52 and local favorite and defending Masters champion Gail Bailey of Charleston third in 39:20.

The Dr. Marcus Newberry Award for first Tri-County finisher went to Tom Mather of Mount Pleasant, who finished 20th overall in 32:02, and to Megan Othersen (Gorman) of Charleston, ninth female overall in 36:06. The Dewey Wise Award went James Sullivan, 82, of Mount Pleasant, who finished the race in 79 minutes and 36 seconds.

Karl Gueldner was race director for the fourth year in a row. The entry fee was raised to $12. The race was broadcast live on Channel 5 for the fourth year in a row. It attracted 7,510 entrants, and the results booklet listed 5,885 official finishers, 4,433 male and 1,449 female. A total of four men broke the 30-minute barrier. The 40-minute barrier fell to a record 393 runners, a record 364 males (both of which still stand after 33 races) and a then record 29 females. There were 2,159 runners who crossed the finish line in less than 50 minutes and a total of 4,632 runners who completed the race in less than 60 minutes. The Sunday *News and Courier* newspaper listed the top 100 male finishers and the top 50 female finishers, and listed the top five in each age group, though it incorrectly included the invitational division prize money winners in the age division award list. The paper estimated that 5,000 took part in the untimed Bridge Walk.

Other voices
Running With Two-Time Bridge Run Winner Ashley Johnson
By Dennis Hiott, Originally appeared in the May-June 1989 Low Country Runner

On Sunday mornings, I go run with a group, mostly faster than me. Sometimes we meet downtown and run the bridge, sometimes we meet at Patriots Point. The day after the Bridge Run nobody especially wanted to run the bridge, so Barbara and Maurice Davidson, Connie Gruver, Leon Locklear and Tommy Mullins and I met at the *Yorktown* at Patriots Point. I was surprised to see 25 or 30 people there at 7 a.m. including some really fast runners, namely Ashley Johnson, Carla Borovicka, David Reese, Ric Banning, Megan Othersen (Gorman) and Steve Caskie to mention a few.

The whole group started together, with everybody going out the Patriots Point Road. Everybody usually stays together at a slow pace to warm up and then when we get out to Coleman Boulevard, the faster runners usually go ahead and it gets spread out.

That morning Ric Banning, Chris Fleming and David Reese started going fast when we got onto Coleman, but Ashley Johnson and Carla Borovicka (who won the Bridge Run in 1988 and was runnerup in 1989) stayed with the slower groups.

Carla and Ashley were both real friendly. She was running behind the group I was in for a while and talking to Steve Caskie. They were still talking when they speeded up and passed Leon, Jeff Herndon, Stacie Novak, Tanis Manseau; and me.

Ashley stayed with us for about 3 miles up Coleman Boulevard, then turned around and headed back to the *Yorktown*. While he was running with us Connie said something to him about running the slow pace with us. He said the slow pace was fine, that he was only going to run 5 or 6 miles and he'd be running longer the next day. He said he was surprised that nobody has broken the course record over the past few years, but that the wind always seems to be a factor. He said they predicted the wind would be at our backs but that "I never felt it at my back."

Ashley was running easily, but I was running hard. I felt like I was running almost race pace, at least it felt like it the day after the Bridge Run. We were probably running about 6:45 pace. It looked like he picked up the pace when he turned around and headed back.

Nobody asked him too many questions because everybody was running hard except him. It was interesting to run with him. By the time we got back to the *Yorktown* he was gone, but he will be back to defend his title.

I think of those elite runners as being like some other athletes who think they are too good to associate with lesser athletes. But he was a friendly down to earth person.

Grete Waitz Live 5 Television Interview
Transcribed by Cedric Jaggers

Unless you videotaped the live television coverage shown on Charleston's local Channel 5 you probably didn't hear the interview Mark Morgan conducted with Grete Waitz shortly after she won the 1989 Cooper River Bridge Run's female crown. So here is as close a transcription as I can make. CJ

MM: All right, standing here with the women's champion of the 1989 Cooper River Bridge Run, Grete Waitz. Grete, outstanding performance as advertised. Was it as easy as it looked?

Grete: No. It was pretty tough out there, especially on the bridge where it was windy, very windy. We had a lot of headwind, so it was not so easy as it looked.

MM: You told me last night you had driven over the bridge and you had some impressions of it then, and what people had told you before. Did it live up to its billing?

Grete: Definitely, yes. It was just as hard as I thought it was.

MM: How would you compare this race to some of the other ones you've run? You've traveled all over the world, competed everywhere. It's a relatively flat course, except for the bridge.

Grete: Well, that's the toughest 10k I've been running because of the bridge and the conditions on the bridge. But I think that's okay. . . I like that too, because this course has a personality. It's a challenge and I enjoyed it. It was tough, but that's what you are training for.

MM: OK, we're looking at a replay of your finish. Did you have any certain strategy coming in or did you just want to pull away from the rest of the women right off the bat?

Grete: No. I ran with the girl who came in second for the first couple of miles and when we were on the bridges, I left her behind me and I ran by myself from there. Coming down to the last mile I didn't know exactly how far I had to go to the finish line, and suddenly I saw the banner and I was very happy about that.

MM: One final question. I know a lot of folks wonder, having won the New York City Marathon nine times and raced all over the word, how do you get up for a race like this to come to Charleston, South Carolina?

Grete: Well, I was planning on running a marathon in March, but because of an injury I had to reschedule my racing plans. I met some runners who talked about this race and it really fit quite well into my schedule. So I got in touch with the organizer and here I am. And I have to tell you that people here have been very nice and shown such hospitality, I'm planning on coming back next year.

MM: Outstanding. Great performance. Congratulations. Thank you very much. OK, there you have it, Grete Waitz as advertised wins the race in a walk, if you'll pardon the pun. We're not sure about the women's record; it looks to be about 4 or 5 seconds under the women's record unofficially.

Tell Me About Your Bridge Run — 1989

By Cedric Jaggers, Originally appeared in the May-June 1989 Low Country Runner

(Bridge Run info for 1989 – 5,885 largest number of official finishers, 7,510 entrants, the largest number to date. Start time temperature 55 degrees and windy.)

After the Bridge Run while waiting for the awards ceremony held for the first time in Marion Square, I asked this question to club members as we bumped into each other. Club members are listed in the exact order they were interviewed. I added the overall place and time and noticed as people had told me, that some of the times were off from 11 to 22 seconds probably due to flipped stringers in the finish chute. CJ

Mary Alice Curtiss: About a half-mile into the race I was pushed from behind and fell. It shook me up. Then a half-mile later I tripped myself. I sprained my ankle and tore up my elbow and hand, but I said I've trained for 10 weeks and I'm not going to quit. It was my best Bridge Run at about 43:29. Overall place 744th, results time 43:19.

Stacie Novak: I followed Nina (Herndon) all the way until she blacked out. Then I decided to go on. My 42:40 was a PR for the Bridge Run, but not a regular PR. Overall place 639th, results time 42:41.

Jeffrey Herndon: It was pretty much what I hoped to do: 39:19. Considering that last year I didn't break 40 and this year I did, so that was good. Overall place 300th, results time 39:19.

Nina Parks Herndon: I felt bad on King Street. I felt like I was on PR pace, then turned the corner at Market and tried to kick it in from there. I went numb from head to toe, my knees buckled and I fell. So I started crawling because I was close to the finish line and suddenly these six 250 pound football players picked me up and I started screaming "No! I've got to finish!" and they set me down but I couldn't walk and they were sort of dragging me and some guy said "Take her to the hospital tent." And I said "No, take me through the chute." And they took me to the hospital tent instead and gave me 2 liters of intravenous fluid. DNF not in results.

Kathy Jaggers: I ran with Barbara Davidson the first 2 miles until I had an asthma attack and she got away. I was so disappointed. We were both in good shape and staying together and I think I would have run in the 44s. I ended up in the EMS tent after crossing the finish line. Overall place 1,270th, results time 46:25.

Bill Leopard: I took 2-and-a-half minutes off last year's time. That was quite an accomplishment. I managed to run the whole way this year. It was a Bridge Run PR but not a PR. Overall place 3,070th, results time 52:16.

Dick Linthicum: It was great other than having trouble getting out of the pack at the start. Great weather. I wanted to break 40 but it wasn't to be. Overall place 490th, results time 41:13.

Gary Eaton: I did great. I was real pleased: 34:05, over a minute better than any other Bridge Run. I'm very happy. The first span really hurt though. But overall I was very pleased. Overall place 38th, results time 34:07.

Jeff Hiott: A PR 42:35. My old PR was 45:20. The bridge was tough, especially the first span. I didn't think I'd make it. Overall place 651st, results time 42:36.

Beverly Hiott: I had my best Bridge Run ever. Overall place 1,813th, results time 48:40.

Dennis Hiott: 41:16, my best Bridge Run. I would have been happy if I'd broken 41 minutes. Those bridges just take too much out of your legs. Overall place 475th, results time 41:07.

Karen Caines: It was windy and insufferable. I thought I was doing okay until the second span. I thought, "Hey, I'm losing time." This race hurts more than any triathlon. I hurt from the very beginning. It's a tough run. I felt like I was holding up pretty well, but on King Street people were passing me like I was waiting on a bus. But I broke 40: 39:43. Overall place 313th, results time 39:29.

George Steele: My run was real good until some bald headed a… … passed me just past the 6-mile mark. (Note: An accurate if somewhat unflattering description of me, CJ.) But I ran 38:33 or 34 and I was pleased. Overall place 224th, results time 38:33.

Paul King: I did a Bridge Run PR 36:19 or 20, but who knows what will happen with the results. It was 50 seconds faster than last year. Overall place 94th, results time 36:09.

Tom Mather: I re-pulled a muscle right at the starting gun. I was facing the wrong way, unprepared for the start like 100-175 other people. (Note: the starting gun was fired with no warning, catching lots of runners unprepared. CJ) and when I tried to start, I pulled it. It hurt the whole way. Whenever I tried to make a push it really started to hurt. I won't be able to run for about two weeks. I'm glad I had planned to start my triathlon training and wasn't going to be running much anyway. I ran right at 32 flat. Marcus Newberry Award winner, results time 32:02.

Kathleen King: Three minutes off last year's time and all the other years. I'm too excited to talk, but I attribute this to swimming and biking. Losing weight didn't hurt. It was a real PR, just under 50 minutes, my first time; 49:52. Overall place 2,121, results time 49:50.

Irving Rosenfeld: I'm glad it wasn't duplicate bridges. I wouldn't want to do it twice. Overall place 2,031st, results time 49:38.

Stanley Feldman: Just grand. A perfect day: 50s, clear. I ran with a friend this year and had a real nice time. Overall place 3,731st, results time 55:47.

Sara Dorociak: The first span I thought I was not going too well. I thought I'd gone out too fast, but I was able to pick it up the last 2 miles. I wanted to break 38 but I can't complain about 5 seconds can I? Overall place 196th, results time 38:06.

Alex Morton: I had a great run today. It was better than last year: 43:07. I felt good on the hills. It's my best Bridge Run. I thought the weather was great. The wind only bothered me the first mile. It was a good race, but the start was a little squirrelly. Overall place 732nd, results time 43:14.

Ric Banning: Lousy. I felt sluggish and stale. I hadn't raced since the Reedy River Run and never got going. I ran about 32:21 and expected to be about a minute faster, but no such luck. Overall place 22nd, results time 32:31.

Linda Banning: I'm not going to talk about it. My shoe came untied going up the first span even though I had it double knotted. I had to stop and tie it and never got going again. Once I lost contact I never got it back. I ran about 40:40 or about 2 minutes off what I wanted. Results time 40:08.

Charles Stoyle: No comment. I hated it. I lost it at 2 miles, then I saw you and you were my inspiration. You looked terrible on King Street when I passed you. I can't explain how I feel. It was a minute and a half Bridge PR. Overall place 197th, results time 38:09.

David Shaw: Very bad. I was walking going up the first hill. My arms were cold and the wind really bothered me a lot. I was shooting for 38 and did 40:20 something. Overall place 400th, results time 40:23.

Weezie Shaw: It was so pretty. I think it was great going over the bridge. I wish the whole race had been over the bridge and not any on King Street. I ran the slowest I've ever done. I just died at the 5 mile mark. (Unable to find in the results. CJ)

Pat Rhode: It was great. If I hadn't died on King Street I'd have gotten the grand master's record. The first mile was good. The first span was really tough, but when I got on the flats I couldn't go. I still ran a minute faster than I did last year. Overall place 1,809th, results time 49:39.

Gail Bailey: I had a great race. I was elated with my time. I have done nothing of quality since November. I was all rested. I did it totally on memory. I knew how I had to feel to run a time and went out and did it. I've never run the Bridge Run before without quality running. I was forced into resting and it paid off. My time was almost the same as last year. Results time 39:20, Masters female winner.

Bob Walton: I did a 42:56. I enjoyed it. I always enjoy it. I didn't get boxed in this year. Overall place 749th, results time 43:20.

Mike Chodnicki: You had to ask. Five seconds slower than last year and last year was a Personal Worst. I really can't complain, it was about what I expected for the shape I'm in, 37:08. Overall place 140th, results time 37:03.

Susan Burditt: 39:46. I was afraid to blow it out on King Street because I'd seen that incorrect map in the race packet and I didn't know how far we had to go. I pushed it uphill and coasted down. I was very pleased. I didn't expect to break 40. It was a 2 minute PR on the bridge. Overall place 332nd, results time 39:36.

Ken Bible: Did somebody jack up the bridge? I wanted to run consistent splits but I ended up crawling uphill and flying down. On King Street I thought I'd have more left. I said I'd be happy with anything under 38 and it was 37:50 so I can't be unhappy. Overall place 186th, results time 37:56.

Barbara Davidson: There's nothing to say. This is my best Bridge Run. I felt great about it. The weather was perfect and the wind didn't bother me. Training on the bridge helped. I ran about 44:48. Overall place 1,008th, results time 44:50.

Blanche Todd: It was nice. The best one I've ever done. It was my first 10k. Overall place 5,869th, results time 82:57.

Mike Pate: Pretty good – 36:05 a Bridge Run PR. My legs kind of died on the first span but I was pleased with it. If the wind had just been a little less it would have been even better. Overall place 93rd, results time 36:09.

Sharon Chodnicki: It was absolutely great. It was my first 10k ever. The bridge didn't move. I feel good, I don't feel tired. Maybe that means I didn't run hard enough. Overall place 5,673rd, time 71:25.

Lucky Voiselle: I had a stress fracture, but I'm pleased with my time. Overall place 107th, results time 36:26.

Leon Locklear: Flowertown 10k created something faster in my mind. I thought I could go under 37. I ran comfortably and ran 36:48. Overall place 121st, results time 36:41.

Dan Clapper: It was great considering the cold weather. I'm a hot weather runner and I'd have done better if it had been warmer. I ran 37:08. Overall place 141st, results time 37:04.

Dupree Elvington: 37:20. I felt good all the way, never any pain. It was my best time in 5 years and I'm pleased. The reason I ran so well is I lost 35 pounds – from 170 down to 135. Overall place 154th results time 37:20.

Larry Strickland: 315 places and 6 minutes faster this year. I'm happy. That's it. My time was 35:30 or so. Overall place 73rd, results time 35:37.

Mike Hart: The slowest in 3 years but the easiest. I never hurt. I actually enjoyed it, but I had too much left afterwards. I ran 34:47. Overall place 50th, results time 34:49.

Connie Gruver: Oh, I wasn't happy. I wanted to break 40 and ran 40:05. I can't blame anyone but myself. I don't know what happened. Overall place 347th, results time 39:44.

Huey Inman: I was wanting to break 35 but I was satisfied with my 35:40. Overall place 77th, results time 35:47.

Jeff Gruver: Well, what can I say. It's my slowest one in 4 years. I went in the middle of the pack and thought I could break out, but I couldn't. I ran the first mile in 8:12; or walked it is more like it, on the sidewalk most of the way. Overall place 1,155th, results time 45:47.

Larry D'Ippollito: My time was 36:36, almost identical to last year. There was a little more wind than I wanted on the bridges. It was a taxing run for me. Overall place 112th, results time 36:37.

Franklin Wright: My first one. I thought the hills were going to be a lot easier than they were. I had trouble going up. I thought I was going to get about 40 minutes. I glided going down. I'm going to train on the bridge once or twice a month from now on. It was a lot of fun. My time was 36:20 something. Overall place 100th, results time 36:16.

Matt Fete: It was terrible, the hardest race I've run in my life. A minute slower than my norm and I hurt from the gun until the end, but I'm glad I did it. I'm not going to tell you my time because I'm too embarrassed. Overall place 55th, results time 34:59.

Bruce Taylor: It was terrible but it was what I expected. Overall place 229th, results time 38:37.

Therese Killeen: A good run, 43:25 or 26. It was definitely better than I expected to do. It's a tough run though. I don't like hills. Overall place 756th, results time 43:22.

Tommy Mullins: A PR on the bridge, 37:51. I have to credit . . . I don't know. I just enjoyed it. Overall place 184th, results time 37:55.

David Reese: It was fine. I ran about as well as I could run: 34:10. Both spans bothered me a lot. I didn't run very well uphill. Overall place 41st, results time 34:10.

Phillip Cook: I had a pretty good run. Uphills I liked a lot. Everybody passed me on the downhills. It was a 3 minute and 20 second PR for the bridge. Overall place 113th, results time 36:33.

John Atkinson: It was a PR for the Bridge Run, my third one. I enjoyed it. I felt like the wind was bad on the bridge. I thought I could make up time on King Street, but I couldn't. My time today: 38:16. I enjoyed the weather. Overall place 205th, results time 38:16.

Butch Cody: I was turned backwards when the gun went off. I was surprised they started it with no warning. I felt really good until midway up the first span when we hit the wind. I think it was a pacing race this year due to the wind. When I hit the flats I started picking it up. I ran the 4th and 5th miles faster than the first mile. For the kind of training I'm doing, I'm real happy. I ran 36:30. Overall place 129th, results time 36:47.

Bob Schlau: Adequate is the best way to describe it. I didn't run well, but I ran well enough to win the Masters Division. I couldn't keep up with the lead pack and had to run the bridge alone in the wind and it took it out of me. Out of all the races I've run traveling all over the U.S. this past year, this is probably the toughest 10k. My time was about 32:20, the slowest time since I turned 40. Results time 32:20 Masters winner.

Gordon Murray: Oh man. I trained for it like it was a marathon, tapered down, and felt good. It was my second best 10k I ever ran in my life. A bridge PR; 37:40. Overall place 169th, results time 37:37.

Howard Schomer: It was a lot of fun. It felt good at the beginning. I felt bad on the second hill, then felt good again on the flats and thought I could break 37. I ran 37:11 or 12, but I'm happy. Overall place 146th, results time 37:09.

David Bourgeois: Not the best time I've ever run, but I was real pleased. Except for the wind, it might have been better. This time I had enough left on King Street. I'm pleased with my overall time, about 35:57. Overall place 81st, results time 35:56.

Megan Othersen: 36:06, felt bad. I wanted to run in the 35s but the bridge killed me. I didn't expect the bridge to be that rough. It really got me. Wait till next time! Overall place 89th, results time 36:36.

Steve Caskie: 34:50. I felt strong. The wind kind of bothered me. I remembered how bad it was 2 years ago. It's the best worst race around. Overall place 53rd, results time 34:55.

Raleigh Wise: Don't come around me today. No, I just ran with a friend and had a relaxing time and enjoyed it. We finished in a little under an hour. Overall place 3,759th, results time 55:54.

Maurice Davidson: Terrible, I blew a foot. My plantar fascia acted up. I ran 43:17, a Personal Worst. My foot started hurting the day after the Flowertown race when I did an 18 mile run and went over the bridge a couple of times. Overall place 741st, results time 43:19.

Joyce Ploege: It was a PR on the bridge so I can't be too unhappy. I hoped to be a minute or so faster, but I ran a marathon 2 weeks ago and I'm running Boston in 2 weeks so I ran conservatively. Overall place 661st, results time 42:43.

Cedric Jaggers: Words can't describe how I felt about my run. Suffice it to say it was terrible, but my own fault. I felt bad before the start but went out too fast anyway and then felt really bad and hurt incredibly for over 5 miles. Overall place 219th, results time 38:29.

1989 Awards

Note: The race used an 'Invitational Division' – Elite Runners contesting for prize money – not eligible for age group awards.

Prize money winners:
Overall Male
1 Ashley Johnson .... Bowling Gr. KY .... 29:48 .. $2,000
2 Mike O'Reilly .... Boulder, CO .... 29:52 .. $1,000
3 Erik Hansen .... Gainesville, FL ...... 29:53 .. $700
4 Greg Beardsley .... Charlotte, NC .... 29:56 .. $500
5 Hans Koeleman .... Holland .... 30:05 .. $400
6 Espen Borge .... Gainesville, FL ...... 30:24 .. $350
7 Craig Thompson .... Knoxville, TN .... 30:33 .. $300
8 Rob Devlin .... Summerville, SC ...... 30:47 .. $250
9 Kevin Ruch .... Camp Hill, PA .... 30:58 .. $200
10 Doug Consiglio ...... Gainesville, FL ...... 31:14 .. $150

Overall Female
1 Grete Waitz .... Norway .... 33:29 .. $2,000
2 Carla Borovicka ...... Tala FL .... 34:01 .. $1,000
3 Joan Nesbit .... Durham NC .... 34:17 .. $700
4 Jo White .... Richmond, VA .... 34:35 .. $300
5 Teresa Ornduff .... Abingdon, VA .... 35:14 .. $200
6 M. Custy-Roben .... Denver, CO .... 35:26 .. $150

Masters Division Male
1 Bob Schlau .... Charleston, SC .... 32:20 .. $300
2 Wes Wessely .... Lilburn, GA .... 33:04 .. $200
3 Don Coffman .... Frankfort, KY .... 33:15 .. $100

Masters Division Female
1 Judy Greer .... Orlando, FL .... 37:38 .. $300
2 Claudia Ciaveralla ... Cary NC .... 37:52 .. $200
3 Gail Bailey .... Charleston, SC .... 39:20 .. $100

Special award:
Dr Marcus Newberry Award for first local Charleston Tri-County area finisher:
Male
Tom Mather .... Mt Pleasant, SC 32:02
Female
Megan Othersen .... Charleston, SC 36:06

Special award:
Dewey Wise Trophy for oldest finisher with time faster than his or her age in minutes:
James Sullivan, 82 ..... Mt Pleasant, SC 79:36

Age group award winners
(presented to top 25 or 5%, whichever is less) in each age group):

Male 12 & under (71 finishers, 4 awards)
1 Drew Anderson 45:53
2 Ryan Bonawitz 46:10
3 Chad Rogers 46:33
4 Tyler Garrison 46:50

Female 12 & under (14 fin., 3 awards)
1 Windi Sue Guntsch 47:43
2 Ciatlin Crow 53:44
3 Kimberly Deans 44:39

Male 13-17 (162 finishers, 8 awards)
1 Beau Fairbourn 36:31
2 Jack Murphy 37:07
3 Billy Beiner 37:37
4 Thomas Weeks 37:48
5 Brandon Kern 38:57
6 Thomas Fechhelm 38:57
7 Jason Michaels 38:58
8 Mike Strohm 39:03

Female 13-17 (55 finishers, 3 awards)
1 Leigh Jones 43:32
2 Billie Veber 44:04
3 Cara Schlegel 46:46

Male 18-21 (138 finishers, 7 awards)
1 Tex Sappenfield 35:51
2 Gregory Whipple 36:07
3 Lawrence Carrigan 36:34
4 Gerald Ellis 36:39
5 Rodney Gehman 37:19
6 William Fearn 37:36
7 Scott Vance 37:51

Female 18-21 (81 finishers, 4 awards)
1 Mary McEachern 42:22
2 Kimberly Kalista 45:55
3 Kay Breininger 46:03
4 Marlee Crosland 46:54

Male 22-25 (357 finishers, 18 awards)
1 Irv Batten 32:53
2 Edward Moore 33:47
3 Michael Brown 34:08
4 John Wheeler 34:22
5 Chris Legourd 34:51
6 Mitchell Embler 34:59
7 Matt Fete 34:59
8 Bobby Fary 35:09
9 Boy Jefferies 35:12
10 Steven Leopard 35:31
11 Chris Fleming 36:04
12 Ward Smith 36:31
13 William Gray 36:42
14 Richard Stephens 36:45
15 Brian Dowling 36:53
16 Edwin Givens 36:59
17 Jeffrey Hall 37:02
18 Mark Barton 37:02

Female 22-25 (160 finishers, 8 awards)
1 Megan Othersen 36:06
2 Janice DeHaye 38:14
3 Tracie Armold 39:02
4 Gina Latham 40:00
5 Lynn McCain 40:49
6 Carol Mann 42:25
7 Jane Stinley 45:12
8 Rebecca Jones 45:57

Male 26-29 (569 finishers, 25 awards)
1 Paul Kammerer 33:02
2 Jeff Milliman 33:09
3 Mark Teseniar 34:32
4 David Edwards 35:33
5 Scott Hirst 35:34
6 David Marshall 35:38
7 Jay Rao 35:38
8 Huey Inman 35:47
9 Patricia Kennedy 42:20
10 Terry Campbell 36:00
11 William Britton 36:18
12 Jeffrey Woods 36:26
13 Gene Hallman 36:34
14 James Kerby 36:37
15 Michael Anderson 36:42
16 Michael Milteer 36:43
17 Gary Peters 36:45
18 Patrick Keenan 36:49

19 Tom McLean ... 37:13
20 Dave Carney ... 37:29
21 Scott Teplica ... 37:32
22 Harold Brown ... 37:41
23 Jeff Parker ... 37:56
24 Madison Dye ... 38:02
25 Gary Araugo ... 38:04

Female 26-29 (258 finishers, 13 awards)
1 Jenny Glapinski ... 35:58
2 Betsy Veronee ... 37:14
3 Tracey Edwards ... 38:58
4 Karen Caines ... 39:28
5 Susan Foster ... 40:28
6 Susan Vujasin ... 41:07
7 Lynn Bustle ... 41:29
8 Robin Roughton ... 41:31
9 Steve O'Neill ... 35:59
10 Stacie Novak ... 42:41
11 Deborah McClure ... 43:53
12 Molly Strickland ... 44:10
13 Shelly McKee ... 44:19

Male 30-34 (859 finishers, 25 awards)
1 Tom Mather ... 32:02
2 Mark Hinson ... 32:57
3 Danny White ... 33:45
4 Virgil Griffin ... 34:05
5 Gary Eaton ... 34:07
6 Eddie Pennebaker ... 34:09
7 Robert Lowery ... 34:38
8 Mike Hart ... 34:49
9 Steve Caskie ... 34:55
10 Dave Kannewurf ... 35:18
11 Michael Fronsoe ... 35:29
12 Sam Swofford ... 35:31
13 Larry Strickland ... 35:37
14 David Bourgeois ... 35:56
15 Franklin Wright ... 36:16
16 Ronnie Floyd ... 36:19
17 George Howe ... 36:21
18 Phillip Cook ... 36:33
19 Brian Waldrep ... 36:41
20 Roland Butch Cody ... 36:47
21 David Dalhouse ... 36:50
22 Mike Chodnicki ... 37:03
23 Howard Schomer ... 37:08
24 Harry Ash ... 37:12
25 Greg Fagan ... 37:16

Female 30-34 (318 finishers, 16 awards)
1 Sara Dorociak ... 38:06
2 Janet Thiel ... 38:29
3 Pam Drafts ... 39:03
4 Susan Burditt ... 39:36
5 Debbie Mueller ... 39:52
6 Mika Savir ... 41:49
7 Beate Vogt ... 42:58
8 Mary-Alice Curtiss ... 43:19
9 Martha Cornett ... 43:21
10 Tami Dennis ... 43:24
11 Maria Griffith ... 43:44
12 Karen Burgoyne ... 44:05
13 Marian McCreight ... 44:06
14 Elizabeth Boineau ... 44:40
15 Cheryl Catton ... 44:56
16 Brenda Rautenkranz ... 45:29

Male 35-39 (839 finishers, 25 awards)
1 Ric Banning ... 32:31
2 Gordon English ... 33:54
3 Oliver Marshall ... 34:25
4 Leon Cook ... 34:53
5 Danny West ... 35:09
6 Ned Hettinger ... 35:11
7 Joseph Denney ... 35:15
8 Richard Markley ... 35:30
9 David Mauterer ... 35:36
10 Rusty Doyle ... 35:43
11 Gary Ricker ... 35:52
12 John Holzworth ... 36:05
13 Tommy Seymore ... 36:07
14 Michael Pate ... 36:08
15 Doc Bayne ... 36:10
16 Jack Todd ... 36:18
17 James Boyd ... 36:23
18 Larry D'Ippolito ... 36:32
19 David Jenkins ... 36:35
20 Leon Locklear ... 36:41
21 Ronald Gillespie ... 36:48
22 Charles Craft ... 36:58
23 Dan Clapper ... 37:04
24 Michael Moulden ... 35:07
25 Charles Kellner ... 37:10

Female 35-39 (265 finishers, 14 awards)
1 Nancy Grayson ... 36:34
2 Catherine Lempesis ... 39:01
3 Bonnie Long ... 39:11
4 Connie Gruver ... 39:44
5 Judy Rasnake ... 41:05
6 Mary Carbott ... 41:13
7 Marilyn Davey ... 43:16
8 Therese Killeen ... 43:22
9 Patricia Tavares ... 44:27
10 Alice McDaniel ... 45:10
11 Debbie Howard ... 45:20
12 Ginger Gregory ... 45:29
13 Sally Mincher ... 45:53
14 Deborah Estes ... 46:55

Male 40-44 (731 finishers, 25 awards)
1 Wes Wessely ... 33:04
2 David Reese ... 34:10
3 Jack Waitz ... 34:44
4 Phil Peterson ... 35:01
5 Bill Peay ... 35:54
6 Paul King ... 36:09
7 Reed Watson ... 36:13
8 Lucky Voiselle ... 36:26
9 Sandy Wetherhold ... 36:27
10 Robert Wilson ... 36:40
11 Scott Wilson ... 36:50
12 James Horne ... 36:58
13 Mickey Lackey ... 37:08
14 Clayton Krejci ... 37:13
15 Ronald Gorday ... 37:56
16 Jim Fields ... 38:05
17 Charles Stoyle ... 38:08
18 Cedric Jaggers ... 38:29
19 George Steele ... 38:33
20 Bruce Taylor ... 38:37
21 Thomas Jones ... 38:40
22 Ian Lester Reuben ... 38:44
23 Robert Murphy ... 38:48
24 Monty King ... 38:56
25 Tom Blankenship ... 38:56

Female 40-44 (168 finishers, 9 awards)
1 Claudia Ciavarella ... 37:52
2 Gail Bailey ... 39:20
3 Peggy Schug ... 41:56
4 Sharon Beal ... 42:08
5 Libby Neely ... 42:10
6 Phillis Mason ... 43:59
7 Judy Melton ... 44:02
8 Linda Miesch ... 44:23
9 Barbara Davidson ... 44:50

Male 45-49 (378 finishers, 19 awards)
1 Charles Teseniar ... 36:12
2 Dupree Elvington ... 37:20
3 Reginald Smith ... 37:25
4 James Adams ... 37:49
5 Russell Brown ... 38:13
6 Bill Seigler ... 38:15
7 Ray Hagan ... 38:30
8 William Mayer ... 39:28
9 Robert Welch ... 39:34
10 Dean Godwin ... 39:35
11 David McCann ... 39:39
12 Terrill McGee ... 40:16
13 Jack Wicks ... 40:23
14 Wendel Cribb ... 40:25
15 Ken Lewis ... 40:26
16 William Hollaway ... 41:03
17 Harold Dodd ... 41:06
18 Ron Sanders ... 41:10
19 Olin Hammond ... 41:16

Female 45-49 (62 finishers, 3 awards)
1 Joyce Ploeger ... 42:43
2 Linda Hendrix ... 47:33
3 Sallie Sinkler ... 48:03

Male 50-54 (178 finishers, 9 awards)
1 Jim Larson ... 35:59
2 Orbin Thompson ... 36:07
3 Adrian Craven ... 36:11
4 Rex Reed ... 36:13
5 Theron Cochran ... 39:00
6 Ed Guettler ... 39:10
7 Sammie Yarborough ... 39:30
8 Jerry Lyles ... 40:20
9 David Shaw ... 40:23

Female 50-54 (32 finishers, 3 awards)
1 Mary Anne Wehrum ... 41:16
2 Susie Kluttz ... 43:57
3 Marcia Herbst ... 46:20

Male 55-59 (71 finishers, 4 awards)
1 Charles Rose ... 38:50
2 Lee Swofford ... 41:54
3 Wayne Smith ... 42:28
4 Bob Walton ... 43:20

Female 55-59 (14 finishers, 3 awards)
1 Mary Anne Woodring ... 45:41
2 Garthedon Embler ... 50:09
3 Marge Hoffman ... 52:11

Male 60-64 (39 finishers, 4 awards)
1 Robert Gray ... 40:24
2 Gordon English Sr. ... 42:29
3 George Wilson ... 43:35
4 Griffith ... 45:33

Female 60-64 (3 finishers, 3 awards)
1 Faye Motley ... 1:08:44
2 Wyndall Henderson ... 1:17:49
3 Fran Wallace ... 1:19:03

Male 65-98 (14 finishers, 3 awards)
1 David Mellard ... 43:04
2 Dewey McMickle ... 46:53
3 Eldridge Lloyd ... 52:25

Female 65-98 (5 finisher, 3 awards)
1 Margaret Wright ... 1:01 40
2 Cecily Murdaugh ... 1:05:47
3 Evelyn Smith ... 1:06:34

Compiled by Cedric Jaggers from complete race results.

Bridge runners endure chilly rain and nervousness as they wait for the start in Mount Pleasant. Post and Courier photo by Stephanie Harvin

Chapter 13
1990
Unlucky 13? No Way, Rain Stops, No. 13 Wins

The 13th Bridge Run was held April 7, 1990. Is 13 an unlucky number? It sure seemed like it while all the runners were arriving and lining up for the 13th running of the Bridge Run. Shortly before the 8 a.m. start it was about 50 degrees with a northwest headwind blowing at 20 mph and rain coming down in sheets — terrible running conditions. Fortunately, as the runners lined up, the wind dropped to about 12 mph and shifted to a crosswind, and the rain stopped just as the race started. So maybe 13 wasn't unlucky after all. And it surely wasn't unlucky for the first time bridge runner wearing race number 13.

Race officials made sure there was no repeat of the confused start from 1989 and had all runners on the proper side of the starting line when the cannon fired to start the race. About 10 runners stuck together going over the bridge. Then four or five broke away on the overpass. Mike O'Reilly of Boulder, Colo., runner-up in '89 and winner in '85, took the lead and only Sam Obwacha, a Kenyan living in Van Nuys, Calif., went with him. At the 6-mile mark Obwacha kicked by O'Reilly and pulled away, but he turned off course at Calhoun. He was waved back on course and won in a record 29:20 with O'Reilly also under the old record in 29:23. Don Janicki of Louisville, Colo., was third in 29:30.

"At the 4-mile mark we were at 19 minutes and it was down to four people, and when we hit 5 miles at about 23 and a half, I knew we were going to be fast and close to the record," Obwacha, wearing race No. 13, told the *Post and Courier*.

"I figured if I slowed down going up the hills and used my energy going down the hills, I would do good. I knew I had a kick with 200 meters to go. With 50 meters to go I made a wrong turn, but then I just started sprinting again. This is the fastest I've run this year."

He was fast enough to take home the extra $1,000 bonus for setting a new course record.

Shelly Steely from Eugene, Ore., wasn't the women's favorite, but her 5:07 first mile gave her a lead she never surrendered as she went on to set a course record 32:57. "I've never won a big race like this before," she told the newspaper. "I'm kind of in shock still. My coach didn't really want me to run a 10k. He said before I left, 'At least come back with some big money!'"

The pre-race favorites finished second and third: Jody Dunston of San Antonio, Texas, 33:00, and Kellie Cathey of Fort Collins, Colo., 33:13. The top three were all under the old course record. "Shelly went off real fast once the gun went off," Dunston said. "Kellie and I decided to work together, trying to run her down. We didn't think she'd be able to keep up the pace with all the hills still to come."

Cathey said, "The hills on the bridge weren't that bad. They weren't the problem. Our problem was we just couldn't catch Shelly.

We saw her take off. We thought she would slow down, but she didn't."

Unbeknownst to them Steely wasn't comfortable in the lead. "It wasn't until late in the race I thought I would win or even set the record," she said. "I only felt in control at around the 5-mile mark. Then I figured if nobody else had caught me by now, I had a pretty good shot at winning and possibly setting a new record." She received a $1,000 bonus for setting a new course record.

Earl Owens of Dunwoody, Ga., almost missed the start of the race arriving just seconds before the start. He took off fast and built a huge lead to take the Masters title in 31:26. Defending champion Bob Schlau of Charleston was second in 31:53 while Lee Fidler of Stone Mountain, Ga., was third in 33:26.

The top three women Masters runners finished in the same order they had in 1989: Judy Greer of Orlando, Fla., won in 37:45, Claudia Ciavarella of Winter Park, Fla., second in 38:02, and Charleston's Gail Bailey third in her best Bridge Run time, 38:28.

The Dr. Marcus Newberry Award for first local finisher went to Michael Brown of Charleston, 19th overall in 32:04 and to Alison Roxburgh of Mount Pleasant, 10th female and 124th overall in 36:33. The Dewey Wise Trophy went to James Sullivan, 83, of Mount Pleasant, 76:39, for the second year in a row.

There were 7,820 entrants, and the results booklet listed 5,866 finishers: 4,432 male and 1,434 female. Seven runners broke 30 minutes, while 332 men and 28 women broke the 40-minute barrier. There were 2,264 runners who crossed the finish line under 50 minutes and a total of 4,744 who completed the race in less than an hour. The Sunday *Post and Courier* — the newspaper had merged its morning and evening editions in 1989 — listed the top 150 males, top 60 females and up to five deep in each age group, though it incorrectly included the invitational winners in the age groups.

The race was broadcast live on Channel 5 television for the fifth year in a row. Mark Blatchford was race director for the 13th through 15th Bridge Runs. The entry fee remained at $12. In 1990, *Runner's World* magazine named the Cooper River Bridge Run as one of its "Cream of the Crop" races.

Other voices
Tell Me About Your Bridge Run 1990
By Cedric Jaggers, Originally appeared in the May/June 1990 Low Country Runner

(Bridge Run info for 1990: 5,886 official finishers – second largest official number, 7,820 entrants, largest yet. Start time temperature 50 degrees and windy.)

Bridge Run morning. Marion Square. After the race. Clipboard in hand. Writing down exactly what each club member says. Sorry if I missed you. Okay, enough Ernest Hemmingway. Here are the post race interviews in the order that I happened to run into the folks. I've added the official place and time from the results.

Irving Rosenfeld: I was very happy with it. It was a PR Bridge Run for me. That's one bridge I won't have to cross 'till next year. 1,040th overall, 44:59

David Reese: It was fun. I was kind of pleased no more than I've run lately. 109th overall, 36:09

Mark Friedrich: Well, I didn't get knocked down this year (like year before last) so it was a very positive start. Then I got over excited and ran the first mile under 5 minutes; I'd planned a 5:20. Overall I thought it was a good run compared to some years. For the course – about 32:30, as good as I'd hoped or a little better. I'd hoped to break 33. 2nd overall, 32:30.

Kathy Jaggers: Aren't you going to ask me? I'd say it was an asthmatic's nightmare: rain, wind, cold and hills. The four things asthmatics can't handle. At least I ran easy this year and didn't end up in the hospital tent. 1,513th overall, 47:03

Paul King: I finally had a race I don't have any regrets about. It was better than running a PR. 99th overall, 35:50

Susan Burditt: I'll just say don't work the expo all day before the race and expect to run well. 337th overall, 39:46

Bob Walton: Very breezy. I ran about 43:51. It was enjoyable as usual. 856th overall, 43:52.

Whit Bailey: It was much tougher than the first one. I was very tired at the end. I think I barely beat the walkers. 5,150th overall, 63:13

Charles Stoyle: I saw that article Bob Schlau wrote yesterday in the newspaper and I followed it, but I just didn't push the uphills enough. My last 2 miles were sub 6. I wanted to break 38 but didn't. 212th overall, 38:12

Tommy Mullins: It was a PR for the bridge. I think I relaxed too much on the second span. I slowed too much but maybe it was a smart move. I thought it would be tougher than it was. I hope I get a plate (an award), I've never gotten one. (Note – he did. CJ). I'm pleased, I ran about 37:29. 170th overall, 37:30

Dan Clapper: It was my best one ever time wise, but I was more excited when the weather was better. I tried to follow the Pritikin diet again this year, but I wasn't as strict with it. I ran about 36:06. 106th overall, 36:07

Raleigh Wise: A real PR and a Bridge Run PR. It felt great. I like running in cold weather. 580th overall, 42:03

Jeffrey Herndon: The smoothest and easiest ever. I felt real comfortable. 494th overall, 42:06

Howard Schomer: I enjoyed it. The weather was nice, I thought. It was just great. I ran about 35:36. 88th overall, 35:36

Dennis Hiott: I felt good. The weather was better than I anticipated. The wind wasn't as bad as I expected. I ran about 41:05, the same as last year's run. 469th overall 41:08

Pat Rhode: I don't know what to say. It was pretty good. I figured I'd run 50 minutes and ran about 48:53 – only 20 seconds slower than last year, and this year I had to stop and tie my shoes. 1,957th overall, 48:54

Beverly Hiott: I actually felt human. I loved the down part on the bridge. 1,883rd overall, 48:34

Nina Parks Herndon: I actually finished it without fainting 100 feet in front of the finish line like last year. It was a PR for the bridge and running negative splits helped me. My last miles were the fastest. The best part was not to be delirious at then end. 621st place, 42:15

Mike Hart: I finally broke 34 minutes on the bridge. That's what I came 500 miles to do. (Note Mike moved to Washington, DC since the last race) I was happy with my time. 37th overall, 33:47

Larry D'Ippolito: A bit breezy at first, but it was a PR on the bridge. Being always surrounded by people – it motivated me to keep my pace up. 105th overall, 36:06

Jeff Hiott: It was good. I had stomach problems and at first the wind nearly kicked me, but then it benefited. I was proud of my time. A real PR, about 39:47. I was expecting to run 41 minutes. Not in my wildest dreams did I think I'd break 40. 346th overall, 39:51

Bill Leopard: My best ever. My fourth one. Not great by any means, 42:30, but my best Bridge Run. 3,020th overall, 52:50

Don Austell: About 42:46. I wanted to run 43 so I was pleased with it. On the fist span the wind was bad, but it wasn't bad after that. My last 2 miles were my fastest so that tells me I just don't want to hurt anymore. I enjoyed it. 690th overall, 42:44

Maria Griffith: It was my best Bridge Run time, about 43:23, but a minute slower than I wanted to be. I felt like the wind was going to blow me away on the bridge. I'll do better next year. 785th overall, 43:25

Mike Pate: It was a pretty good race, about 36:45. I feel like I'm out of shape. I'll get my legs back. Not bad for the way I feel. 133rd overall, 36:48.

Maurice Davidson: I thought it was very good as far as the weather. The wind was a little bit difficult. I just wish I was more conditioned for it. I was satisfied with my time, 41:42 and everything was well organized. 544th overall, 41:46

Dupree Elvington: I felt good all the way. I wanted to break 37 and ran 36:42 so I'm happy with it. 132nd overall, 36:45

John Atkinson: It was great. I came in faster than I thought I would for the training I put in. I didn't burn myself out in the first 2 miles. I felt good. I ran 38:07. 213th overall, 38:14

Gail Bailey: I ran my buns off. It was my best Bridge Run time. I felt real real good about it. The hills weren't that bad. When I got to mile 4 I was tired but managed to just hang in there. I just kept chugging, didn't run terrific, but enough to run a Bridge Run PR. My legs didn't get bad tired until 4 and a half. 321st overall, 38:28.

Matt Fete: I had a great experience this year. I ran a Bridge

Run PR by 2 minutes – 32:55. Mark Friedrich and I had a kind of battle on the bridges. I passed him on the downs and he passed me going up. We had a great race. 25th overall, 32:55

Tom Dority: The first 4 miles were a cinch. When I looked at the 5 mile mark everything went to rubber. You really should get to bed early the night before a race. I ran about 43:58 or so. I was happy, it was about what I planned. The Bridge Run is a fun run. 771st overall, 43:20

Larry Strickland: I ran 34:20 something. I didn't want to get beat by any women until the Boston Marathon next week. However, I ended up behind Carla Boravicka and a few others. I was happy with my race. 50th overall, 34:21

Tami Dennis: Let me think. I enjoyed this year's race, especially versus last year's when I ended up in the hospital tent. Even with the wind it was nice to finish on two feet versus on my hands and knees. I ran about 40:58. 447th overall, 40:58

Chris Fleming: I ran 34:18. It was a good run, my third fastest 10k run. My only two faster were on the track. I felt good. I was pleased – that says it all. 47th overall 34:18

Bob Schlau: I felt pretty good; I'm just over tired. This was my sixth weekend race in a row, and it's hard to get up so many times in a row. I'm going to take a few weeks off from racing. I was satisfied with my time, but not really happy. I'm in better shape than that. I just tried to do too much. The competition is getting too tough in the masters to run in the high 31's and expect to win. My next race is a marathon and that's my race. It's the smoothest I've seen a Bridge Run go, except maybe for the awards ceremony. 17th overall, 31:53.

Therese Killeen: It was a Bridge Run PR, about 42:05. What can I say? It was tough as usual. I'm pleased with my time definitely. I've been sick the past week so I didn't get to train. I might have done better since I was rested. 595th overall, 42:06

Charles Kellner: The best run of my life. A Bridge Run PR but I slipped on King Street and twisted my ankle. I decided it was an important race and finished. I got in about 35:52. Now I can't walk without limping. The medical attention in the tent was great. I loved all of it except that. 101st overall, 35:52

Dave Carney: It hasn't gotten any shorter. I think I was about 36:25. Coming off the second span I tried to stay with Nancy Grayson, but she just pulled away. I'm pretty happy with my time. 114th overall, 36:22.

Sharon Chodnicki: It was too cold. I don't run when it's cloudy, so it was a real challenge to run in the rain. 5,760th overall, 72:50

Leon Locklear: I just wonder if it's as windy as it seemed. It was comfortable, no pain. I kind of enjoyed the race this year. I ran 36:50 something. 141st overall, 36:58

Chuck Barton: It was great. I had one of my best times on the Bridge Run, about 36:21. I was surprised how quickly 2 miles went by considering the wind. I ran out of gas at 5 miles, but overall I'm pleased with how I'm coming back from my injury. 113th overall, 36:20

Alex Morton: I ran 43:35. I was real pleased with it since I've been marathon training, all slow stuff. This was only 20 seconds off my Bridge PR. 819th overall, 43:39

Benita Schlau: I was very pleased. I started back running on January 1st, keying for the bridge. I only took 3 days off. I think my time was 38:12 so I'm very pleased. 214th overall, 38:14

Franklin Wright: Terrible. I woke up this morning with a cold, but only ran 9 seconds slower than last year. I ran about 36:25. I enjoyed it though. 125th overall, 36:39

Huey Inman: About 35:40 or so. I was pretty content. I wanted to break 35, but I'll have to wait until next year. Don't I say that every year? I'm pretty satisfied. 93rd overall, 35:45

Bill Vetsch: I did better than I thought I'd do, about 42:10. I got up at 4 AM and drove down from Aiken. Other than being on medication for an abscessed tooth, I felt pretty good. 610th overall, 42:12

Dennis Bresnahan: I ran 36:53, I'm happy with it. It's my best Bridge Run by a minute and only 4 seconds off my PR. I'm real happy. 138th overall, 36:55

Brantley Arnau: A Bridge PR 41:59, not a great 10k, but okay for the bridge. One of the more enjoyable Bridge Runs with the wind behind us. 565th overall, 41:57

Joyce Ploeger: What can I say? It was a Bridge PR and fun as always. 533rd overall, 41:41

Larry Millhouse: Fun as usual. Chilly at the start but the run felt good. My time didn't show it though. I think PRs are a thing of the past. 1,330th overall, 46:21

Rob Ploeger: It was great. It's always great. I love coming back (from Norfolk) and running this race. I was racing as hard as anybody, but wasn't going as fast. 1,210th overall, 45:46

Ken Bible: What can I say? This was the best one ever. Charlie Kellner and I wanted to run conservatively to the bridge and over it. We did, and came to King Street feeling really good, then we let it fly. So 35:40, might be a PR. Never had a race like this in my life. Never. 89th overall, 35:40

Connie Gruver: Oh Cedric! What am I supposed to say? I just did terrible – 2 minutes slower than last year. I hope I'll do better next year. 617th overall, 42:14

Paul Snyderwine: Coming off the overpass I felt like I was dying and knew I needed to pick it up. I didn't feel like I was going faster, but somehow I did, and finished 13 seconds faster than last year. 41:38, my best Bridge Run so far. It may be a real PR too. 526th overall, 41:38

Stanley Feldman: It was great. I used it as a training run for the Pittsburgh Marathon. I felt good and finished strong. 3,831st overall, 55:59

Gordon Murray: What can I say about it? I ran about the same as last year, 37:37. I had trouble with my leg, but I'm looking forward to next week at the Boston Marathon and I didn't want to hurt it. 176th overall, 37:38

Terry Bartosh : That first span I hated. I'm shocked – happy with my time. I didn't think I could do it. When I hit the first span I wondered would the folks on my team kill me if I dropped out? I wished I was pregnant so I wouldn't have to run it. But I'm ecstatic with my time. 167th overall, 37:24

Mike Brown: I'm real happy. I ran about 32:03. I felt really good. It's my best Bridge Run, 2 minutes faster than last year. 19th overall, 32:04

Donnie Todd: I don't want to talk about it. I'm too fat. 494th overall, 41:18

David Dwiggins: I passed Cedric after the 5 mile mark and he looked terrible. Then Charles Stoyle passed me, but I finished my last race in Charleston with dignity. 221st overall, 38:19

Phillip Cook: I did real good: 35:44. Conditions were a lot better than I thought they'd be at the start. I was 50 seconds faster than last year, a Bridge Run PR. I didn't train much on the bridge this year. I don't know if that helped or not. 94th overall, 35:45

Cedric Jaggers: I was disappointed and shouldn't have been since I never run well when it is rainy. The first 4 miles were everything I hoped for; the last 2 were a nightmare beyond imagination. It felt like I was running backwards so many people were passing me. And what made it worse was it seemed like every one of them spoke to me and called me by name. I thought I ran 38:22 which was my best ever on a rainy day so I can't complain, but I will anyway. 230th overall, 38:27

1990 Awards

Awards: Note, the race used an Invitational Division – Elite Runners contesting for prize money – not eligible for age group awards.

Prize money winners
Overall Male
1 Sam Obwocha .... Kenya .... 9:20 ...$3,000
2 Mike O'Reilly .... Boulder, CO .... 29:23 ...$1,500
3 Don Janicki .... Louisville, CO ...... 29:30 .... $750
4 Jim Cooper .... Atlanta, GA .... 29:33 .... $500
5 Mark Curp .... Lee's Sum. MO .... 29:36 .... $400
6 Douglas Tolson ...... Powell, TN .... 29:39 .... $300
7 Stephen Kartazia .... Washingon MD .... 29:48 .... $200
8 Muriki Ngatia .... Kenya .... 30:29 .... $100

Overall Female
1 Shelly Steely .... Eugene, OR .... 32:57 ...$3,000
2 Jody Dunston .... San Antonio, TX ..... 33:00 ...$1,500
3 Kellie Cathey .... Ft Collins, CO ...... 33:13 .... $750
4 Carla Borovicka ..... Tallahassee FL ...... 34:11 .... $500
5 Elespth Turner ...... Tuscaloosa, AL ...... 35:12 .... $300

Masters Male
1 Earl Owens .... Dunwoody, GA .... 31:26 .... $500
2 Bob Schlau .... Charleston, SC ...... 31:53 .... $300
3 Lee Fidler .... Stone Mtn, GA .... 33:26 .... $100

Masters Female
1 Judy Greer .... Orlando, FL .... 37:45 .... $500
2 Claudia Ciavarella .. Winter Park FL ...... 38:02 .... $300
3 Gail Bailey .... Charleston, SC ...... 38:28 .... $100

Special award:
Dr Marcus Newberry Award for first local Charleston Tri-County area finisher:
Male
Michael Brown .... Charleston, SC 32:04
Female
Alison Roxburgh .... Mt Pleasant, SC 36:33

Special award:
Dewey Wise Trophy for oldest finisher with fastest time less than his or her age:
James Sullivan, 83 .... Mt Pleasant, SC 76:39

Age group award winners
(presented to top 3 to 5 in age group, with top 5% up to maximum of 25 awarded in each age group):

Male 12 & under (68 finishers, 5 awards)
1 Hamp Kennemore 41:38
2 Anthony Broad 42:53
3 Chad Rogers 44:13
4 Benjamin Townsend 44:55
5 Tony Rickman 48:43

Female 12 & under (19 fin., 5 awards)
1 Alison Schlegel 53:48
2 Tracey Butler 54:06
3 Stephanie McHerney 56:10
4 Kimberly Deans 58:01
5 Mary Buford Mayer 58:33

Male 13-17 (146 finishers, 8 awards)
1 Chalmers Johnson 37:58
2 Henry Othersen 38:03
3 Danny Huggins 38:46
4 Chad Brasington 39:00
5 Brad Taylor 39:34

Female 13-17 (45 finishers, 5 awards)
1 Caroline Bolt 42:54
2 Billie Veber 46:00
3 Jenna Ellwanger 46:24
4 Robin Messinger 49:21
5 Miranda Oakley 49:56

Male 18-21 (222 finishers, 8 awards)
1 Chris Many 33:52
2 Richard Lampe 34:22
3 David Eaton 34:48
4 Todd Jarman 35:11
5 Thomas McPhail 35:15
6 Paul Wright 36:50
7 Ed Charles 36:54
8 Chris Mackey 37:01

Female 18-21 (72 finishers, 5 awards)
1 Mickey Kawohl 39:06
2 Mary McEachern 41:40
3 Sheri Winningham 44:33
4 Kay Breininger 46:34
5 Rieppe Leigh Melton 46:35

Male 22-25 (344 finishers, 18 awards)
1 Michael Brown 32:04
2 Steve Conway 32:42
3 Matthew Fete 32:55
4 Thomas Trace 33:18
5 Robert Lee 34:00
6 John Wheeler 34:16
7 Paul Rearden 34:17
8 Christopher Fleming 34:18
9 James Page 34:29
10 Mitchell Embler 35:07
11 Fred Eaton 35:18
12 Michael Bowers 35:35
13 Robert Daley 35:50
14 Mark Hetrick 35:07
15 Timothy Lafon 36:18
16 Richard Stephens 36:57
17 Gerald Ellis 37:15
18 Joe Myers 37:19

Female 22-25 (178 finishers, 8 awards)
1 Jennifer Pappas 39:16
2 Susan Barbieri 40:05
3 Nancy Wubbenhorst 40:59
4 Ashley Thomason 41:04
5 Rhonda Morris 41:55
6 Elizabeth Graham 42:28
7 Anne Watkins 43:35
8 Joan Von Thron 44:08

Male 26-29 (503 finishers, 25 awards)
1 Larry Brock 31:45
2 Glenn Klassa 33:19
3 Jay Gottesman 33:31
4 Scott Hirst 34:36
5 Alan Gebert 34:54
6 Tom Mclean 35:23
7 Charles Shanks 35:24
8 Edwin Givens 35:34
9 Ken Bible 35:40
10 Huey Inman 35:45
11 Marshall Martin 35:47
12 Jeffrey Woods 35:49
13 Luke Barnwell 36:17
14 Dave Carney 36:22
15 Harold Brown 36:22
16 Ron Deramus 36:22
17 Brian Dowling 36:27
18 Billy Self 36:40
19 Chuck Spencer 36:53
20 Dennis Bresnahan 36:55
21 Michael Holzman 37:07
22 James Kerby 37:13
23 Milton Brown 37:45
24 Thomas Williams 37:51
25 Steve ONeill 37:51

Female 26-29 (260 finishers, 14 awards)
1 Terry Bartosh 37:24
2 Kim Ivey 37:53
3 Patt Kennedy-Loggins 38:24
4 Tracie Armold 39:21
5 Karen Caines 39:35
6 Mindy Gottesman 42:05
7 Meredith Thompson 42:17
8 Weezie Small 43:46
9 Kim Farmer 44:10
10 Laura Smith 44:29
11 Cynthia Lowery 44:37
12 Shelly McKee 45:14
13 Anna Blanton 45:28
14 Roberta Shropshire 46:08

Male 30-34 (856 finishers, 25 awards)
1 Danny White 32:01
2 Marshall Randall 32:12
3 Mark Hinson 32:26
4 Mark Friedrich 32:30
5 Johnny Devine 32:46
6 Cullan Crothers 33:12
7 Keith Johnson 33:42
8 Mike Hart 33:47
9 David Caborn 34:02
10 Bob Cramer 34:07
11 Gary Caton 34:19
12 Lawrence Propst 34:20
13 Larry Strickland 34:21
14 Holt Ivey 34:23
15 Ray Lewis 34:26
16 Jay Boland 34:49
17 Robert Lowery 35:08
18 Marc Embler 35:10
19 Cedric Singleton 35:22
20 David Bourgeois 35:26
21 Kyle Henson 35:28
22 Michael Fitzgerald 35:31
23 David Edwards 35:36
24 Howard Schomer 35:36
25 Phillip Cook 35:45

Female 30-34 (291 finishers, 17 awards)
1 Susan Burditt 39:46
2 Janet Thiel 40:19
3 Sara Dorociak 40:27
4 Susi Foster 40:56
5 Tami Dennis 40:58
6 Nina Parks Herndon 42:15
7 Mary Lou Day 42:34
8 Janice Cole 42:53
9 Anne Weston 43:02
10 Lynn Bustle 43:08
11 Rachel Allen 43:36
12 Annie Wetherhold 43:39
13 Lisa Niles 43:42
14 Waltraud Miller 43:46
15 Marian McCreight 44:09
16 Mary Alice Curtiss 44:30
17 MaryBeth Lees 44:31

Male 35-39 (765 finishers, 25 awards)
1 Gordon English 33:20
2 Ned Hettinger 35:06
3 David Jenkins 35:06
4 Roosevelt Mealing 35:17
5 David Mauterer 35:41
6 Randy Goins 35:42
7 Charles Kellner 35:52
8 Scott Wilson 36:03
9 Larry D'Ippolito 36:06
10 Dan Clapper 36:07
11 Gary Ricker 36:08
12 John Holzwoth 36:23
13 Jack Todd 36:44
14 Michael Pate 36:48
15 Leon Locklear 36:58
16 Larry Berglind 37:04
17 Jeff Dorociak 37:05
18 Michael Moulden 37:06
19 James Boyd 37:07
20 Ken Tuck 37:07
21 Butch Cody 37:09
22 John Sperry 37:14
23 Joe Marshall 37:16
24 Rusty Doyle 37:26
25 Stephen Johnson 37:31

Female 35-39 (263 finishers, 14 awards)
1 Benita Schlau 38:14
2 Carol Davis 40:41
3 Linda F Ray 42:01
4 Therese Killeen 42:06
5 Elizabeth Crowley 42:07
6 Mary Millar 42:24
7 Wendy Flath 43:18
8 Maria Griffith 43:25
9 Marilyn Davey 44:02
10 Ginger Gregory 44:42
11 Ellen Yatteau 45:11
12 Gail Carson 45:17
13 Mary Lesene 45:38
14 Gerri Antoniak 45:40

Male 40-44 (719 finishers, 25 awards)
1 Oliver Marshall 34:05
2 Phil Peterson 34:41
3 Russ Pate 34:47
4 Don Rowland 34:51
5 David Micale 35:00
6 Carl Howard 35:50
7 Paul King 35:50
8 Reed Watson 35:58
9 David Reese 36:09
10 Bill Peay 36:41

11	James Horne	37:08
12	Sandy Wetherhold	37:29
13	Thomas Mullins	37:30
14	Rod Whibley	37:35
15	William Dawson	37:57
16	Gene Thomas	37:59
17	William Harman	38:05
18	Charles Stoyle	38:13
19	Abe Gaspar	38:18
20	Phillip Dickert	38:18
21	Fred Oliver	38:18
22	Jerome Durkin	38:19
23	Willie Wright	38:22
24	Cedric Jaggers	38:27
25	Thomas Blankenship	38:44

Female 40-44 (176 finishers, 10 awards)

1	Linda Banning	38:55
2	Jane Millspough	39:23
3	Sharon Beal	40:12
4	Suzanne Puryear	40:13
5	Ellen Murphy	41:08
6	Anne Boone Reed	41:14
7	Betsy Reese	42:06
8	Connie Gruver	42:14
9	Andrea Pease	42:22
10	Andrea Berendt	42:35

Male 45-49 (419 finishers, 20 awards)

1	Tom Dooley	34:52
2	Gerry Carner	34:56
3	Fred Reinhard	35:51
4	Chuck Barton	36:20
5	Mickey Lackey	36:43
6	Dupree Elvington	36:45
7	Terry Van Natta	36:56
8	David McAdams	37:00
9	Bill Gernon	38:08
10	Walter Waddell	38:33
11	Richard Landsman	38:52
12	Sam Cathey	38:54
13	John Dillard	39:06
14	Jimmy Bagwell	39:32
15	Herb Smith	39:32
16	Ray Hagan	39:34
17	David Weekes	39:35
18	Paul Uriccuio	40:09
19	Kenneth Lewis	40:15
20	Tommy Farr	40:27

Female 45-49 (79 finishers, 5 awards)

1	Joyce Ploeger	41:41
2	Marilynn Martin	43:23
3	Barbara Davidson	46:40
4	Diane Deecheandia	48:12
5	Sallie Sinkler	48:13

Male 50-54 (202 finishers, 10 awards)

1	Sam Stone	35:44
2	Charles Teseniar	36:37
3	Orbin Thompson	36:42
4	James Tigner	37:02
5	Jim Larson	37:03
6	John Dunkelberg	37:47
7	Ed Ledford	38:11
8	James Adams	38:22
9	Dick Ruzicka	38:55
10	Keith Weaver	39:31

Female 50-54 (33 finishers, 5 awards)

1	Susie Kluttz	44:22
2	Mimi Oliveia	46:37
3	Pat Rhode	48:54
4	Marjorie Peterson	49:45
5	Jane McBryde	51:36

Male 55-59 (95 finishers, 5 awards)

1	Walter McDaniel	40:31
2	Phil Szczepanski	41:04
3	Wayne Smith	42:29
4	Bob Walton	43:52
5	Gordon Graham	44:46

Female 55-59 (12 finishers, 5 awards)

1	Barbara Neagley	56:04
2	Camille Daniel	56:27
3	Eileen Hallman	59:22
4	Mary Moore	1:00:52
5	Mary Trammell	1:01:52

Male 60-64 (33 finishers, 5 awards)

1	Jim Blount	39:00
2	George Wilson	42:36
3	Gordon English Sr.	43:51
4	Frank Blackett	46:37
5	Dick Griffith	46:53

Female 60-64 (4 finishers, 3 awards)

1	Garthedon Embler	52:17
2	Faye Motley	1:04:24
3	Wyndall Henderson	1:13:51

Male 65-98 (23 finishers, 5 awards)

1	David Mellard	43:55
2	Lawrence Moore	48:17
3	John Cuturilo	50:11
4	Carlyle Johnston	51:51
5	Eric Anderson	51:53

Female 65-98 (2 finishers, 2 awards)

1	Evelyn Smith	1:08:34
2	Lucy Jones	1:18:26

Compiled by Cedric Jaggers from complete results provided by Burns Computer Services April 7, 1990.

Runners make the last dash for the finish line. Post and Courier photo by Stephanie Harvin

Chapter 14
1991
Carolina Runners Surprise Favorites

The 14th Bridge Run was held April 6, 1991. It was a humid, foggy morning with the temperature at 64 degrees for the 8 a.m. start. The 15-mph crosswind blew the fog away before the runners reached the bridge.

It was a good year for Carolina runners as two of them surprised pre-race favorites U.S. Olympic Marathon Trials winner Mark Conover from San Luis Obispo, Calif., and John Tuttle of Douglasville, Ga. After running over the bridge with the lead pack, Steve Kartalia of Pendleton, S.C., and Jeff Cannada of Carrboro, N.C., pulled away. Cannada kicked past Kartalia to win by one second, 29:38 to 29:39. Cannada said he was more of a miler and was glad he had been able to hang on and use his speed at the finish. Conover and Tuttle were the only other runners to finish under 30 minutes in 29:43 and 29:53, respectively.

"Mark (Connover) and I thought it was over, but Stephen started coming back to us, and I was just in the right place at the right time," Cannada told the *Post and Courier*. "I just relaxed. Steve was so far ahead that I didn't think I could catch him. But before I knew it, I looked up and was in striking distance. I knew I could outkick him at the end if it was close."

Kartalia, who had broken away to a big lead at about 4 and a half miles, said, "I didn't know he was coming up on me until I heard the crowd and I knew he was coming, but I had nothing to answer with. By that time, my legs were fried. My kick was gone a mile and a half back. I raced well and ran faster than last year — when he finished seventh. I just didn't have it at the end. Not quite."

Cannada, running the race for the first time, concluded, "This was a very challenging course and I had a lot of fun. I'll be back." Third place finisher Conover said, "This race turned into a real strength test. At the end, it was a matter of who had the most left."

The women's field had a regional rather than a national flavor. Kim Bird of Newnan, Ga., was never challenged as she won in 34:49. She said she went out hard, with a 5:08 first mile as opposed to her usual 5:20 and then just tried to hang on. "I was excited when I figured out I could win, she told the newspaper. "After I got off the bridge, I looked to see where the next woman was, and I didn't see any." Sabina Wallace of Athens, Ga., was second in a Personal Best time of 35:24. Nancy Grayson of Columbia, S.C., was running as a Masters for the first time, but she didn't let that slow her down as she finished third overall, her highest finish since 1983 when she was runner-up. She ran a Masters course record 35:39.

John Campbell of New Zealand also took overall money and set a Masters course record as he finished seventh overall in 30:33. Kaare Osnes of Brighton, Mass., was second Masters in 32:52 while Charleston's Bob Schlau was third in 33:22. Nancy Oshier of Rush, N.Y., ran 36:21, and Jenny Kyle of Savannah, Ga., ran 37:45 to take second and third female Masters awards.

Mark Blatchford was race director for the second year in a row. The entry fee was raised to $13 and for the first time a late entry fee of $20 was added.

Channel 5 cancelled its scheduled live television coverage three weeks before the race. Channel 24 picked up the coverage and broadcast a one hour tape delay review of the race hosted by Steve Cooney with locals Benita Schlau and Frank Santangelo as commentators.

The Dr. Marcus Newberry Award for first local finisher went to Mark Friedrich

(1983 overall runner-up) of the Isle of Palms, 13th overall in 32:18 and to College of Charleston senior Micky Kawohl (Reger), who was fifth female, 68th overall in a personal best time of 35:48. The Dewey Wise Trophy was presented for the third year in a row to James Sullivan, 85, of Mount Pleasant, who ran a time of 76:09. The retired U.S. Army lieutenant colonel was a national track and field champion when he was young.

The Sunday *Post and Courier* listed the top 150 male runners and top 75 female runners, along with first five finishers in each age division. There were 6,527 entrants and the results booklet, which was mailed to all finishers, listed 5,503 finishers; 4,172 male and 1,331 female. Four runners broke 30 minutes, while 283 runners broke the 40-minute barrier, 19 of them female. There were 1,963 runners who completed the race in less than 50 minutes, with a total of 4,286 crossing the finish line under 60 minutes.

Other Voices

"Tell Me About Your Bridge Run" was not done in 1991. I had given up editorship of the *Low Country Runner* in preparation for my job-related move to Rock Hill, S.C. I assumed the new editor would continue the tradition and do the article. I was mistaken. I resumed doing "Tell Me" the next year.

— Cedric Jaggers

1991 Awards

Prize money winners

Overall Male
1. Jeff Cannada .... Carrboro, NC .... 29:38 ... $3,000
2. Stephen Kartalia ..... Pendleton, SC .... 29:39 ... $1,500
3. Mark Conover .... San Luis Obispo ...... 29:43 .... $750
4. John Tuttle .... Douglasville, GA ..... 29:52 .... $600
5. Jeff Smith .... Morrison, CO .... 30:06 .... $500
6. Glen Banker .... Newnan, GA .... 30:29 .... $400
7. John Campbell .... New Zealand .... 30:33 .... $300
8. Alison Roxburgh ..... MtPleasantSC .... 37:23 .... $100

Overall Female
1. Kim Bird .... Newnan, GA .... 34:49 ... $3,000
2. Sabina Wallace ...... Athens, GA .... 35:24 ... $1,500
3. Nancy Grayson .... Columbia, SC .... 35:39 .... $750
4. Karen Schotte .... Alpharetta, GA .... 35:45 .... $500
5. Micky Kawohl .... Charleston SC .... 35:48 .... $400
6. Nancy Oshier .... Rush, NY .... 36:21 .... $300
7. Gina Latham .... Greenville, SC .... 37:17 .... $200
8. Larry Clark .... Easley, SC .... 30:42 .... $200

Masters Male
Masters Female
1. John Campbell .... New Zealand .... 30:33 ... $1,000
1. Nancy Grayson .... Columbia, SC .... 35:39 ... $1,000
2. Kaare Osnes .... Brighton, MA .... 32:52 .... $500
2. Nancy Oshier .... Rush, NY .... 36:21 .... $500
3. Bob Schlau .... Charleston, SC .... 33:22 .... $300
3. Jenny Kyle .... Savannah, GA .... 37:45 .... $300
4. Bruce Kritzler ...... Gainesville, FL ...... 33:35 .... $200
4. Pat Aschinger-Lee ... Jacksonville, FL ..... 38:26 .... $200

Special award:
Dr Marcus Newberry Award for first local Charleston Tri-County area finisher:
Male
1. Mark Friedrich .... Isle of Palms, SC 32:18
Female
1. Micky Kawohl (Reger) ..... Charleston, SC 35:48

Special award:
Dewey Wise Trophy for oldest finisher with fastest time less than their age:
James Sullivan, 85 .... Mt Pleasant, SC 76:09

Age Group Award Winners

(presented to top 3 in age group, with top 5% up to maximum of 25 awarded in each age group):

Male 12 & under (68 finishers, 4 awards)
1. Jonathan Leggett 37:28
2. Hampton Kennemore 37:41
3. Anthony Broad 41:06
4. Chad Rogers 41:55

Female 12 & under (17 fin., 3 awards)
1. Helen Brew 50:09
2. Katherine Stephenson 58:23
3. Kimberly Deans 59:26

Male 13-17 (164 finishers, 9 awards)
1. Ray McMillian 36:16
2. Jack Murphy 36:47
3. William Leggett 37:20
4. Brad Taylor 37:54
5. Albert Hull 38:24
6. Billy Kirby 38:29
7. Jeff Hiott 38:37
8. Chris Jones 38:53
9. Phillip Simmons 39:09

Female 13-17 (44 finishers, 3 awards)
1. Jenny Musselwhite 42:29
2. Marie Earle 45:42
3. Jill Mieme 48:46

Male 18-21 (150 finishers, 8 awards)
1. Eric Ashton 30:53
2. Richard Lampe 32:32
3. Duane Wingate 37:37
4. Lawrence Carrigan 37:41
5. Jim Brigadier 37:47
6. Walter Dautenhahn 38:06
7. Mike Strohm 38:09
8. Chalmers Johnson 38:32

Female 18-21 (65 finishers, 4 awards)
1. Lisa Collier 45:44
2. Kay Breininger 46:19
3. Paula Patton 47:24
4. Sara Virella 47:26

Male 22-25 (307 finishers, 16 awards)
1. Ted Goodlake 30:55
2. James Curwen 32:34
3. Daniel Sturgill 34:05
4. Paul Readron 34:41
5. Rex Sappenfield 35:05
6. David Jackson 35:41
7. Jimmy Tassios 35:59
8. Paul Quick 36:10
9. Ricky Austin 36:45
10. Justin White 37:06
11. Layne Anderson 38:21
12. Timothy Lafon 38:27
13. Robert Mathis 39:07
14. Michael Christodal 39:21
15. Lew Robinson 39:27
16. Carl Buck 39:35

Female 22-25 (176 finishers, 9 awards)
1. Sarah Ottinger 39:51
2. Emily OBryant 41:07
3. Anne Watkins 42:40
4. Carrie Davis 44:33
5. Kay Smith 44:34
6. Susie Golemis 44:53

7 Cathy Messer 45:23
8 Stacey Paskey 46:03
9 Lisa Clark 46:24

Male 26-29 (501 finishers, 25 awards)

1 Rob Devlin 30:50
2 Adam Pinkston 31:24
3 Martin Mary 33:16
4 Jay Gottesman 33:39
5 Steve Conway 34:07
6 Stephen Morrell 34:37
7 Ron Deramus 34:52
8 Ken Bible 35:06
9 Alan Gebert 35:26
10 Timothy Jackett 35:34
11 Dave Carney 35:44
12 Marshall Martin 36:38
13 Glenn Sparkman 36:42
14 William David 36:59
15 Craig Bodkin 37:12
16 Jeffrey Swartz 37:30
17 Kevin Williams 37:33
18 Richard Crawford 37:36
19 Stephane Hennebert 37:43
20 Harold Brown 37:49
21 Keith Cunningham 37:56
22 Rodney Carroll 38:03
23 Kenny Hines 38:08
24 Dan Bliek 38:12
25 Roy Neal 38:18

Female 26-29 (245 finishers, 13 awards)

1 Leslie Fedon 38:12
2 Ute Jamrozy 38:19
3 Beverly Bennett 40:17
4 Angela Beckedorf 40:56
5 Allison Reeves 41:28
6 Karen Caines 41:29
7 Lisa Mosher 41:46
8 Toni Gariano 42:06
9 Rhonda Morris 43:27
10 Kim Farmer 43:31
11 Barbara Wagner 44:02
12 Virginia McCorkle 44:21
13 Cindy Dunn 44:30

Male 30-34 (769 finishers, 25 awards)

1 Mark Friedrich 32:18
2 Marshall Randall 32:41
3 Tom Gilligan 32:53
4 Ray Lewis 34:03
5 Paul Jessey 34:09
6 Tom Mahon 34:29
7 Robert Lowery 34:38
8 Roosevelt Mealing 34:40
9 Howard Schomer 34:41
10 David Bourgeois 35:14
11 Huey Inman 35:17
12 Randall Roland 35:21
13 David Moore 35:30
14 Sam Swofford 35:41
15 Bernie Pabon 35:42
16 Scott Hirst 35:45
17 Mike Dennis 35:57
18 Tom Luke 36:00
19 Harry Ash 36:13
20 Michael Desrosiers 36:41
21 Roy Estrada 36:46
22 Phillip Cook 36:51
23 Jay Boland 37:07
24 Mike Chodnicki 37:18
25 Brian Waldrep 37:26

Female 30-34 (283 finishers, 15 awards)

1 Terry Bartosh 38:22
2 Karen Dixon 38:52
3 Susi Foster 40:32
4 Courtney Moore 40:32
5 Rachel Allen 41:18
6 Janice Cole 41:34
7 Nina Parks Herndon 42:13
8 Mindy Gottesman 42:38
9 Elizabeth Boineau 43:10
10 Mary Kay Branch 43:23
11 Crystal Schafer 43:30
12 Mary Lou Day 43:44
13 Jean Craig 43:52
14 Nancy Farley 44:32
15 Tami Dennis 44:39

Male 35-39 (740 finishers, 25 awards)

1 Ric Banning 32:24
2 Gordon English 32:35
3 Bob Becker 33:21
4 Hank Brown 33:37
5 Mac Collie 34:17
6 Mike Hart 35:00
7 Duane Wolff 35:19
8 Joe Marshall 35:55
9 Dan Clapper 36:12
10 David Jenkins 36:18
11 Vic Fetter 36:29
12 Charles Kellner 36:32
13 George Howe 36:33
14 Rob Meade 36:48
15 Joe Mattingly 36:48
16 Jack Todd 36:56
17 Ben Burnsed 36:58
18 Ned Hettinger 37:13
19 Harold Fallis 37:24
20 Glen Lucas 37:25
21 Franklin Wright 37:35
22 Brad Palmer 37:38
23 David Dalhouse 37:39
24 Gary Ricker 37:51
25 Kelly Price 37:55

Female 35-39 (259 finishers, 13 awards)

1 Catherine Lempesis 38:50
2 Margie Clampitt 40:05
3 Mary-Alice Curtiss 41:15
4 Lisa Niles 42:14
5 Wendy Flath 42:25
6 Elizabeth Patterson 42:43
7 Waltraud Miller 42:55
8 Therese Killeen 43:00
9 Kathleen Whitcomb 43:07
10 Mary Millar 44:12
11 Judy Rasnake 44:17
12 Debbie Howard 44:38
13 Marilyn Davey 44:46

Male 40-44 (636 finishers, 25 awards)

1 Oliver Marshall 33:38
2 Bob Lunsford 33:42
3 Michael Crouse 34:27
4 Leon Cook 34:34
5 Herbert Rexrode 35:05
6 Francis Ruchugo 35:31
7 Tim Cosgrove 35:37
8 David Micale 36:00
9 John Sperry 36:15
10 Paul Brown 36:37
11 James Horne 36:59
12 David Kanners 37:03
13 Bill Peay 37:22
14 Pat Aschinger-Lee 38:26
15 David Ott 38:30
16 Jerome Durkin 38:33
17 Robert Schwamberger 38:38
18 Cedric Jaggers 38:50
19 Phillip Dickert 39:06
20 Jimmy Hadden 39:08
21 Ricky Vaughn 39:13
22 William Dawson 39:13
23 Terry Murphy 39:17
24 Johnny Masche 39:17
25 Guy Herring 39:26

Female 40-44 (170 finishers, 9 awards)

1 Claudia Ciavarella 38:33
2 Peggy Shug 42:29
3 Betsy Reese 43:42
4 Lynn Dobiel 44:29
5 Connie Gruver 44:35
6 Jan Crimin 45:09
7 Sallie Driggers 45:16
8 Kathy Jaggers 45:37
9 Susan Cahill 46:22

Male 45-49 (390 finishers, 20 awards)

1 Don Coffman 33:46
2 Gerry Carner 34:42
3 Chuck Greer 36:42
4 Terry Van Natta 36:47
5 Fred Reinhard 36:49
6 Mickey Lackey 36:53
7 Morris Williams 37:32
8 Dean Davis 37:56
9 Russell Brown 38:06
10 Richard Landsman 38:37
11 Bill Gernon 38:38
12 Charles Stoyle 38:40
13 Michael Taglio 38:44
14 Allen Hoven 38:52
15 Ronald Gorday 39:00
16 Blaine Ewing 39:39
17 David Howle 39:46
18 Herb Smith 40:11
19 Walter Waddell 40:38
20 Ken Lewis 40:53

Female 45-49 (77 finishers, 4 awards)

1 Gail Bailey 40:51
2 Sallie Sinkler 47:26
3 Martie Ulmer 47:54
4 Stephanie Hargrove 48:17

Male 50-54 (204 finishers, 11 awards)

1 Jerry McGath 35:46
2 Charles Tesniar 36:30
3 Orbin Thompson 37:05
4 Sam Stone 37:10
5 Alton Migues 37:30
6 Maurice Choquette 37:53
7 Dick Ruzicka 37:57
8 Ed Ledford 38:22
9 Frank Hannah 39:19
10 Tom Farr 39:50
11 George Kelly 40:11

Female 50-54 (32 finishers, 3 awards)

1 Susie Kluttz 43:35
2 Lucinda Clark 45:28
3 Pat Rhode 47:44

Male 55-59 (102 finishers, 5 awards)

1 Charles Williams 38:03
2 Bill Hendley 40:19
3 Norm McAbee 41:17
4 Jim Woodring 42:24
5 Phil Szczepanski 42:28

Female 55-59 (13 finishers, 3 awards)

1 MaryAnne Woodring 48:49
2 Suzanne Foster 50:37
3 Barbara Neagley 53:52

Male 60-64 (39 finishers, 3 awards

1 Lee Swofford 41:16
2 John Shoemaker 43:33
3 Neil Wilson 43:55

Female 60-64 (5 finishers, 3 awards)

1 Garthedon Embler 53:42
2 Nancy Bell 55:19
3 Dot Farley 59:39

Male 65-98 (29 finishers, 3 awards)

1 Dick Benson 40:38
2 Gordon English Sr. 44:11
3 David Mellard 45:31

Female 65-98 (3 finishers, 3 awards)

1 Margaret Wright 1:03:41
2 Margaret Hagerty 1:05:34
3 Ola Moody 1:10:26

Compiled by Cedric Jaggers from complete results provided by Burns Computer Services immediately after the race on April 6, 1991.

Leaders approach the top of the second span of the Grace Bridge. Post and Courier photo by Wade Spees

Chapter 15

1992
The Kenyans Begin A Long Winning Streak

The 15th Bridge Run, on April 4, 1992, had probably the most favorable conditions for any race so far. The sun was shining; it was 48 degrees and the wind was a crosswind so slight at 5 miles per hour as to be almost imperceptible at the 8 a.m. start.

A contingent of late entrants from Kenya led an assault on the course records, and three of the four would fall. William Mutwol, who had set a 5k road race world best of 13:12 the week before, led the first two miles. Then fellow Kenyan Dominic Kirui took the lead and hit the 3-mile mark in 13:53. He held the lead all the way to the 6-mile mark where Mutwol pulled even. Kirui kicked away to win by 2 seconds in a course record 28:24. William Sigei of Kenya ran 28:57. John Halvorsen of Norway 29:03 and Ondoro Osolo of Kenya 29:10 were also under the old course record.

"I was confident today," Kirui told the *Post and Courier*. "I relaxed too much in the last 10k (the Azalea Trail race where he had finished fourth)."

Mutwol said, "I knew he'd be strong, and he knows I'm strong. Today he was stronger than me."

Jill Hunter of England ran away from pre-race favorite and U.S. Olympic Marathon Trials winner Janis Klecker of Minnetonka, Minn. Hunter won in a course record 32:34 with Klecker second in 33:08 and Inna Poushkariva from St. Petersburg, Russia, third in 33:35. "The support from the people on the sidelines was great, and the weather conditions were very good," Hunter told the newspaper. "There was a bit of wind, but not too much. Today, the quality of the fields pushed you to better times. The competition was here."

Klecker wasn't too disappointed with her finish. She told the newspaper she planned to run an even pace and her time was about what she expected. "Jill went out and ran her race, and I just tried to keep her in sight most of the way," she said. "I'm in the middle of my (marathon) training, and I think I ran a strong race for me."

Nick Rose of England finished eighth overall and set a Masters male course record 29:52, becoming the first Masters Division runner to break the 30-minute barrier on any Bridge Run course. Kurt Hurst of Switzerland was second in 30:57 and Doug Kurtis of Northville, Mich., was third in 30:59. Rose told the newspaper he tried to keep the Kenyans in sight. "I just don't have the speed of 20 years ago – not to catch those guys," he said. "They used to run 13 miles every day to school. I admire those guys, but I can't compete with them."

Nancy Grayson of Columbia, S.C., missed her own course record by 11 seconds but repeated as Masters female champion in 35:50. Barbara Filutze of Erie, Pa., was second in 36:26 and Catherine Lempesis of Columbia, S.C., was third in 37:31.

The Dr. Marcus Newberry Award for first local finisher went to Tom Mather of Mount Pleasant, 23rd overall in 32:11 and to Patti Previtte-Clark, also of Mount Pleasant, who ran a personal best 38:58 to place 20th female and 258th overall. Cadwallader "Quaddy" Jones, 70, of Charleston, who ran a time of 69:13, won the Dewey Wise Trophy.

The *Post and Courier* said: "Kenyans cruise in Bridge Run". The paper listed the top 160 men's names and times and the top 80 women's names and times as well as listing five deep in each age group.

There were 7,602 entrants and 6,403 finishers; 4,675 male and 1,728 female, a record, to date, number of official finishers listed in the results booklet which was mailed to all finishers. The entry fee remained at $13 early, $20 late. The three Kenyans became the first runners ever to finish under the 29-minute mark, eight runners broke the 30-minute barrier and 332 runners, 28 of them female, broke the 40-minute barrier. There were 2,157 runners who finished the race under 50 minutes, while 4,915 managed to cross the line before the finish line clock flipped to 60:00. The untimed 4-mile Bridge walk had an estimated 6,400 walkers.

Channel 24 television, for the second year in a row, showed a one hour tape delay of the race. Mark Blatchford was race director for the third year in a row.

Other Voices
Tell Me About Your Bridge Run — 1992

By Cedric Jaggers, Originally appeared in the May 1992 'Bridge Run Issue' of the Low Country Runner

In 1991 since I had given up being Low Country Runner editor I assumed the new editor would do the 'Tell Me About Your Bridge Run' article. It didn't happen. So even though Kathy and I had moved to Rock Hill, S.C., a lot of people had asked me to do the article, so it was done. Here is pretty much what appeared in the LCR. I've added the overall finish place and official time which did not appear in the article that year.

Bridge Run morning in Marion Square right after the race. I tried to ask as many CRC members as I could find one question – then write down exactly what each said. These are in the order that we happened upon each other. Kathy insisted on making me answer the same question.

Jeff Hiott: A PR 38:38. I'm pleased. 235th overall, 38:38

Kathy Jaggers: I didn't have to go to the EMS tent this year. I wanted to run faster but got a side stitch early and it hurt every time I tried to pick up the pace. 1,429th overall, 47:29

Mike Chodnicki: 35:43. I was pleased with the time, but the effort was too much. I had to work too hard for the time – 30 seconds slower than at the Flowertown 10k. 91st overall, 35:43

Michael Desrosiers: 35:02. I can't remember it now. I had more fun than I did last year. Next year I'll catch Howie (Schomer). 70th overall, 35:00

Jeff Dorociak: 36:49. It cost. I thought I would be ready for the hills since we're living in Winston-Salem, but some things you can never conquer. We've had a lot going on with the triplets. We lost the boy, so with the two girls, and Maggie and Sara, even our pet is female. The women rule the world. 136th overall, 36:49

Sara Dorociak: I'm not telling my time, no way. I went slow enough that I enjoyed it. My back isn't even wet. It took me a minute and a half to get to the start. 2,451st overall, 51:09

Irving Rosenfeld: I've got nothing to say about my Bridge Run. It gets tougher every year. I think they jack it up. I ran about 49. 1,902nd overall, 49:06

Mike Nichols: It was great. A real PR 38:22. The quarters and the training program you gave me made the difference on the hills. I had plenty left. My fifth mile was 6:06. The first span makes you hurt so bad you can't gauge what you're doing. 219th overall, 38:23

Dan Clapper: 36:14. My goal was to break 36. I was a second faster than last year. It was great perfect weather for a PR, I just didn't do it. 113th overall, 36:14

Lennie Moore: The best one yet for me, about 37:30. I was at 5k at about what I've been racing them at. This is a marathon for me. I was happy with my race. 173rd overall, 37:33

Vic Fetter: It was excellent. The best BR I've ever had, a minute and a half faster. I woke up Ken and Howie when I caught up with them. This is my 10k PR – 34:58 on my watch. 69th overall, 34:58

Fred Reinhard: It was a good Bridge Run, better than last year, not as good as the year before. 36:11. I'm happy. I had a great first mile, good second mile, terrible third mile, then cruised in for the rest. 110th overall, 36:13

Micky Kawohl (Reiger): It was terrible. You want to know the truth? I'm working 9 hours a day, 6 days a week. I'm not allowed to sit. I can't train. After I work so much I can't go to the track, my legs won't move. I hate my job but I have to work. It is interfering with my running. I ran 37:11, a minute and a half slower this year than last. 153rd overall, 37:13

Howie Schomer: It doesn't get any better than this. A beautiful day and I ran well. Not as good as last year, but I didn't get lost on the course like I did at the race last week. Considering how I've been racing, I'm happy with my 34:56. 66th overall, 34:56

Maria Griffith: It was even slower than last year. My slowest in the last three years. I don't have any injuries. We had perfect weather. I'm not as upset as I was last year. I'm getting used to it. 46:12. 1,034th overall, 46:16

John Dallimonti: I hadn't been training a whole lot, only the last two or three weeks, but I was hoping to do a PR of sub 29 – finish before the 29th of April. But all in all I had a pretty good race. I managed to finish and that's the main thing. I ran 55 minutes exactly. 3,913th overall, 56:28

Eileen Stellifson: It was average. It was awful – no it wasn't, I had fun. I started back too far but had fun. 45:45. It wasn't my worst; twice I've run with first time runners. 1,191st overall, 46:08

Bernie Clark: Okay. My quickest Bridge Run. Terrible hamstrings on the up spans, no other excuses. An excellent day. 44:09, my first time under 45, a real PR. 827th overall, 44:10

Ken Bible: Pain, agony, screaming, yelling. I ran a little slower than I wanted to, but given the things going on at work and everything else in my life, it's okay. I got my PR at Flowertown: 34:49, here I ran 35:15. 78th overall, 35:14

Therese Killeen: 42:30. I think I ran pretty comfortably and once again I always leave room for improvement. 598th overall, 43:31

Jeff Gruver: 45:04. Probably the fastest in three or four years. I did good. I wanted to run under 45, but . . no guts, no speedwork or hills. I'm just keeping the streak alive, 13 Bridge Runs in a row. 997th overall, 45:05

Nina Parks Herndon: I must have a few enemies because all my friends who were going to go out at 7 minute pace – we all went out at 6:38. But the hills were great. I was dead when I came off them. I picked it up at the end. I finished and didn't end up in the EMS tent this year. 42:40. 600th overall, 42:37

Patti Clark: It was a PR 38:59. It went real well; I felt real good during the whole run. All the work I've put into it came together. I'll order the same weather next year. 258th overall, 38:58

Tom McGorty: It was great, I enjoyed it. Tommy Mullins helped me a lot. I passed him and he passed me, we helped each other. He got away after the last water stop. 41:33. 483rd overall, 41:33

Brian McGorty: I started out good. The bridge kind of hurt me. It was a pretty good run. 46:58. (Unable to find in results)

Chuck Wickersham: It was fun, a good day for it. I was a little disappointed in my time. I ran about a minute faster than last year, but not what I'm capable of. 42:05. 553rd overall, 42:11

Anne (Reed) Boone: You don't want to know. 42:20. About what I planned to run. I have yard work to do today. I'm not doing speed work so I run for fun these days. I'm making a comeback. I just wasn't pushing. 572nd overall, 42:19

Tom Mahon: 33:53. I was basically pleased. I wanted to break 34 and I did. It was a perfect day, no wind and good temperature. 43rd overall, 33:52

Stacie Novak: I'm not talking. I finished. I ran 44:20 so this isn't my worst. 883rd overall, 44:27

Larry D'Ippolito: The only thing that was different was I thought the first span would never end. I haven't had a good 10k this year, so this was good: 36:19. I expected 36:30 so I was pleased. 120th overall, 36:20

Owen 'Opie' Woolever: 38:40. My best in about four or five years. It felt real good; guess it was the adrenalin from Charleston. The first mile was 6:33, my slowest, the last mile was my fastest. 237th overall, 38:39

Jeffrey Herndon: The first span was devastating. The other two were okay. I ran about 42 flat. I was pleased for only running 10 miles a week or less. 533rd overall, 42:03

Pat Rhode: It was a good one; the best one I've had since I was 45. My time was 46:35 or so. I was real pleased. I wanted 46:59 so it was great. It felt like smooth sailing. 1,304th overall, 46:41

Bill Vetsch: I'm out of shape, overweight. 42:13. It was great conditions, but too many candy bars put my weight about 10 pounds over my usual running weight. 560th overall, 42:13

Benita Schlau: Please don't make me tell you. I enjoyed it. I never hurt. It seems like I can only run 6:30 pace now no matter what I do. I ran 40:16, 369th overall, 40:26

Charles Stoyle: A Bridge Run PR 37:42. Perfect weather, that's the key for me. The best weather I've ever seen for the Bridge Run. I felt good all the way, ran my own race with a 5:35 first mile. I felt so good I even ran back to my car after the race. 179th overall, 37:42

Chuck Greer: It was a Bridge Run PR 36:18. It hurt like hell as usual. Great conditions. Probably the best weather ever for the Bridge Run and the wind was not a factor. 119th overall, 36:17

Bob Walton: I enjoyed it. I wanted to break 45 and did; 44:29. I had my knee operated on back in September. I always enjoy this race. 893rd overall, 44:30

Lucky Voiselle: I'm just coming back from injury. Considering that and other things, my 37:19 is pretty good for what I'm doing. Traveling for my job makes it hard. 158th overall, 37:20

Leon Locklear: Struggle up and power down the spans. My body just took over and did it on memory. 38:40. I was surprised. 244th overall, 38:44

Huey Inman: Bridge Run PR 35:02. I'm very much satisfied. I wanted to break 35, but I'm satisfied with it. 73rd overall, 35:05

Mike Hart: My strategy was to follow Huey and go under 35, but he let me down. 35:02. Overall a comfortable run. 72nd overall, 35:03

Tommy Mullins: I tell you what, I had fun! I want everybody in my age group to know I'm on my way, I'm coming back. I hurt on the second hill and felt good the rest of the way. 40:24. 470th overall, 41:26

Dennis Hiott: My slowest and my most enjoyable. That sums it up. 44:44, 932nd overall, 44:45

Tom Mather: It was just about like all the other years. Show up in good shape and run 32, or show up in terrible shape and run 32 minutes. 32:05 is fine. I wanted 31:30 but couldn't get moving. 23rd overall, 32:11

David Mellard: 46:10. I actually felt stronger racing this year. My decline in time is just due to age. 1,201st overall, 46:08

Allen Hoven: Very tough. That first bridge just about got me. I was well up for it mentally, but something got me physically. I didn't do quite as well as I hoped, but I beat last year's time by 30 seconds. 38:23. 242nd overall, 38:42

Wade Ammons: 44:26. My best Bridge Run. My daughter Lynn ran 47:05, she's just starting to run. I hadn't run the Bridge Run since '86 due to National Guard conflict. 892nd overall, 44:30

Glenn Dennis: I set a Bridge Run PR 35:33. I was real happy with that. I was seventh in the Masters, sixth if you don't count Nick Rose. 85th overall, 35:33

Ronnie Yelton: I finished. It was 45:10 I think. I had problems with the uphills. 1,102nd overall, 45:38

Cecil Mack: My worst: 1:10. I haven't run in a whole week – a big mistake. I'm going to try to get back to 40 miles per week and break 50 minutes next year. 6,206th overall, 1:12:23

Jerome Durkin: I didn't run as well as I did last year, 39:52 today. It was my slowest 10k ever. I started working for SCE&G and have to work Saturday and Sunday. 331st overall, 39:58

Tami Dennis: 42:30. I'm pleased. I'm not training hard. 609th overall, 42:41

Ray Dennis: 52:30. I've been having trouble with asthma so I'm just happy to finish and not walk. 3,365th overall, 54:34

Gordon Murray: I was trying to break 40. I broke 41 so I was pretty pleased. Training on the bridge didn't help. 422nd overall, 40:58

Donna Lea Brown: 1:05:41. I ran 2 weeks ago. I haven't run a 10k in a year so I think it's super. It was best coming down the hill. 5,800th overall, 1:08:47

Larry Millhouse: I had a good time considering my age; about 45 minutes flat. The weather was ideal. For the first time I got at the right place at the start and didn't have to pass slow runners. 998th overall, 45:05

Cedric Jaggers: I'm surprised I did as well as I did due to a flare up of tendonitis which kept me from running much the past month. It was my slowest Bridge Run since 1981, but I was happy just to get 39:10. 280th overall, 39:11

1992 Awards

Prize money winners

Overall Male
1. Dominic Kirui........ Kenya............. 28:24 ...$5,000
2. William Mutwol..... Kenya............. 28:26 .. $2,000
3. William Sigai .... Kenya............. 28:57 .. $1,000
4. John Halvorsen ..... Canada........... 29:03 ... $750
5. Ondoro Osora....... Kenya..............29:10 ... $500
6. Jim Farmer .... Raleigh, NC ..... 29:28 ... $400
7. Steve Kartalia .... Pendleton, SC .. 29:35 ... $300
8. Nick Rose .... England........... 29:52 ... $200

Overall Female
1. Jill Hunter............ Albuquerque NM..... 32:34 ..$5,000
2. Janis Klecker .... Minnetonka MN... 33:08 .. $2,000
3. Irina Poushkariva ... Russia............. 33:55 .. $1,000
4. Wendy Frazier ...... Gainesville FL....... 34:46 ... $500
5. Maggie Kraft .... Columbia, SC ... 34:55 ... $300
6. Valerie McGovern... Lexington KY ... 34:56 ... $200
7. Kerry Robinson ..... Central, SC....... 35:13 ... $125
8. Gavin Gaynor .... Raleigh, NC......30:15 ... $125

Masters Division Male
1. Nick Rose .... England........... 29:52 ...$1,000
2. Kurt Hurst .... Switzerland ..... 30:57 ... $500
3. Doug Kurtis .... Northville, MI... 30:59 ... $300

Masters Division Female
1. Nancy Grayson...... Columbia, SC ..... 35:50 ..$1,000
2. Barbara Filutze ..... Erie, PA............ 36:26 ... $500
3. Catherine Lempesis Columbia SC ....37:31 ... $300

Special award:
Dr Marcus Newberry Award for first local Tri-County area finisher:

Male
Tom Mather..................... Mt Pleasant, SC 32:11

Female
Patti Previtte-Clark .... Mt Pleasant, SC 38:58

Special award:
Dewey Wise Trophy for oldest finisher with fastest time less than his or her age in minutes:
Cadwallader Jones, 70............ Charleston, SC 69:13

Age group award winners
(presented to top 3 in age group, with top 5% up to maximum of 25 awarded in each age group):

Male 12 & under (91 finishers, 5 awards)
1. Zachary Rutherford........................ 43:50
2. Hugh Knight 44:02
3. Michael Sieber 45:02
4. Ben Colgrove................................ 45:11
5. Ryan Hulland 45:33

Female 12 & under (22 fin., 3 awards)
1. Charity Fillmore............................ 39:08
2. Helen Brew 53:36
3. Anna Weatherford.......................... 56:19

Male 13-17 (156 finishers, 8 awards)
1. Jeff Gibbs 35:56
2. Brad Taylor 36:08
3. Hampton Kennemore 36:59
4. Jed Wiseman 37:43
5. Jake Johnson............................... 37:54
6. Danny Reeves.............................. 37:56
7. Shaun Traub 38:29
8. Patrick Sheehan............................ 38:40

Female 13-17 (58 finishers, 3 awards)
1. Melissa Jackobs 44:24
2. Carson Flowers 45:18
3. Trisha Watson.............................. 46:36

Male 18-21 (182 finishers, 10 awards)
1. Shawn Young 34:00
2. Wesley Littlejohn.......................... 35:25
3. Duane Wingate 36:15
4. Justin Hadley 35:32
5. Roderick Reeves........................... 37:07
6. Jonathan Morgan.......................... 37:24
7. Gregory Proctor 37:27
8. Thomas Howell............................. 37:33
9. Matthew Meyer 37:45
10. Mike Strohm.............................. 38:06

Female 18-21 (79 finishers, 4 awards)
1. Nicole Zevotek 43:08
2. Kimberly Wylie............................. 43:15
3. Gabrielle Lambert 45:02
4. Jill Miehe................................... 45:10

Male 22-25 (359 finishers, 18 awards)
1. Jorge Pardo 31:56
2. Mike Hedgecock........................... 33:38
3. Christopher Many 33:50
4. Paul Reardon 34:15
5. Mike Colaiacovo 34:37
6. Kenny Yeh 34:51
7. Dujuan Harbin............................. 35:15
8. Chip Owens 35:50
9. Victor Renard 36:09
10. Ben Farley 36:13
11. Justin White 36:16
12. Gerald Schauer 36:27
13. Will Mount 37:09
14. Mark Newnham.......................... 37:16
15. Jason Wells 37:22
16. Kirkland Davis 37:22
17. Steven Elton 37:30
18. Ed Charles 37:32

Female 22-25 (195 finishers, 10) awards)
1. Amy Kattwinkel 35:45
2. Micky Kawohl 37:13
3. Wilma Depiore 39:10
4. Denise Knickman 40:04
5. Kathy Fitzpatrick 42:43
6. Denise Lockett 42:48
7. Stacey Paskey 43:05
8. Courtney Griffith 44:23
9. Kim Ostrowsky 44:32
10. Maura Corcoran 44:44

Male 26-29 (547 finishers, 25 awards)
1. Chuck Lotz................................. 31:17
2. Howard Nippert 31:22
3. George Luke 31:45
4. John Caie 33:21
5. Ron Parker 33:23
6. Jay Gottesman 33:42
7. Galiano Floyd 33:43
8. Marshall Martin 34:03
9. Mark Scott 34:42
10. Edward Moore 34:54
11. Steven Leopard 35:02
12. Ken Bible 35:14
13. David Jessey 35:41

14	Chuck Hagan	35:58
15	Matthew Cooke	36:02
16	Jimmy Tassios	36:12
17	Dave Carney	36:14
18	Terry Spencer	36:52
19	Jeffrey Swartz	36:55
20	Kenny Hines	37:11
21	Byron Backer	37:44
22	Jeffrey Hall	37:59
23	Mark Rutledge	38:08
24	Damon Brown	38:15
25	Mark Johnson	38:23

Female 26-29 (326 finishers, 17 awards)

1	Brenda Bergum	40:13
2	Suzanne Lynch	40:41
3	Karen Tomlinson	40:52
4	Cindy Hedden	41:19
5	Shawn Baldy	41:59
6	Virginia McCorkle	43:01
7	Cindy Bryant	43:42
8	Susan Tedesco	44:06
9	Rebecca Hillman	44:14
10	Tricia Brown	45:03
11	Kathy Magor	45:11
12	Julia White	45:15
13	Lyn Smith	45:24
14	Suzanne Bacon	45:33
15	Lori Schumacher	45:44
16	Rhonda Morris	45:56
17	Lori Head	46:00

Male 30-34 (856 finishers, 25 awards)

1	Tom Mather	32:11
2	Jeff Milliman	32:38
3	Bill Fisher	33:31
4	Marshall Randall	33:35
5	Norman Blair	33:42
6	Tom Mahon	33:52
7	Danny White	34:01
8	Steve Shonts	34:06
9	Robert Lowery	34:31
10	David Moore	34:36
11	Reid Newmann	34:54
12	Michael Desrosiers	35:00
13	Huey Inman	35:05
14	Frank Lessue	35:21
15	Philip McGoff	35:23
16	Sam Inman	35:36
17	Craig Bodkin	35:39
18	Arnie Uvalle	35:45
19	Bruce Conrad	35:52
20	Eric Berry	36:31
21	Martin Royaards	36:33
22	John Holcomb	36:34
23	Joel Britton	36:37
24	Todd Hamilton	36:40
25	Roger Bowman	36:53

Female 30-34 (354 finishers, 18 awards)

1	Jenny Glapinski	35:14
2	Kim Bird	37:11
3	Sylvia Fisher	37:37
4	Patt Kennedy-Loggins	38:13
5	Patti Previtte-Clark	38:58
6	Lisa Roeber	39:07
7	Jean Strait	39:16

8	Susi Foster	39:31
9	Angela Moore	39:44
10	Allison Reeves	39:48
11	Terry Bartosh	40:18
12	Debra Caviness	40:48
13	Weezie Small	40:54
14	Rachel Allen	41:14
15	Carolyn Harrell	42:02
16	Martha Manning	42:03
17	Tammi Alderman	42:05
18	Luanne Coulter	42:26

Male 35-39 (812 finishers, 25 awards)

1	Jim Eastman	32:59
2	Tony Bateman	33:12
3	Perry Macheras	34:18
4	Brian Antonicelli	34:55
5	Howard Schomer	34:56
6	Vic Fetter	34:58
7	Mike Hart	35:03
8	Jim Brewer	35:07
9	David Bourgeois	35:08
10	Steven Pavik	35:12
11	Harry Ash	35:37
12	Gary Eaton	35:38
13	Joseph Denneny	35:44
14	Ned Hettinger	35:55
15	Joe Marshall	36:06
16	Dan Clapper	36:14
17	George Howe	36:16
18	Charles Kellner	36:29
19	Joseph Mattingly	36:34
20	Greg Fagan	36:38
21	Jeff Dorociak	36:49
22	Harold Fallis	36:54
23	Sam Swofford	37:05
24	Delmer Howell	37:17

Female 35-39 (297 finishers, 15 awards)

1	Patti Patterson	39:02
2	Becky Sox	40:06
3	Benita Schlau	40:26
4	Elizabeth Goeke-Patterson	41:13
5	Elizabeth Boineau	41:43
6	Therese Killeen	42:31
7	Sandra Stark	42:51
8	Donna Trask	43:05
9	Nitsa Calas	43:22
10	Annie Wetherhold	43:28
11	Mary Millar	44:25
12	Marilyn Davis	44:45
13	Ginger Gregory	44:51
14	Debbie Howard	44:57
15	Maria Griffith	45:16

Male 40-44 (742 finishers, 25 awards)

1	Gordon English	32:44
2	Bob Schlau	33:25
3	Bruce Kritzler	33:39
4	Lou Patterson	33:46
5	Barney Klecker	33:56
6	Francis Ruchugo	34:23
7	Danny West	34:39
8	Oliver Marshall	34:53
9	Jim Struve	35:17
10	Glenn Dennis	35:33

11	Clarence Cropps	35:47
12	John Sperry	35:52
13	David Mauterer	35:54
14	Larry D'Ippolito	36:20
15	Timothy Cosgrove	35:46
16	William Pierce	37:08
17	Randy Wall	37:11
18	Jack Todd	37:18
19	Lucky Voiselle	37:20
20	Herbert Taskett	37:21
21	James Boyd	37:35
22	Sandy Wetherhold	37:46
23	James Horne	37:53
24	Neil Derrick	38:19
25	Edward Kromka	38:24

Female 40-44 (210 finishers, 11 awards)

1	Barbara Ebers	41:51
2	Karen Erb	42:38
3	Peggy Schug	42:50
4	Betsy Reese	43:30
5	Neddie Legg	43:32
6	Sallie Driggers	43:40
7	Patricia Tavares	43:43
8	Tina Barber	44:21
9	Lynn Dobiel	44:27
10	Marilyn Davey	45:33
11	Nonie Hudnall	46:54

Male 45-49 (473 finishers, 24 awards)

1	Don Coffman	34:02
2	Terry Van Natta	34:56
3	Fred Reinhard	36:13
4	Chuck Greer	36:17
5	Bill Peay	36:36
6	Joe Gaglia	36:44
7	Dick Clarke	37:26
8	Charles Stoyle	37:42
9	Gerald Doeksen	37:46
10	Bill Seigler	37:52
11	Don Player	38:29
12	David Ott	38:37
13	Allen Hoven	38:42
14	Dupree Elvington	38:50
15	Will McKee	39:11
16	David Howle	39:46
17	Walter Waddel	39:48
18	Ronald Gorday	39:51
19	Lee Foster	40:06
20	James Lynn	40:09
21	Richard Horner	40:23
22	Wendel Cribb	40:39
23	Jerry Fussell	40:40
24	Herb Smith	40:41

Female 45-49 (111 finishers, 6 awards)

1	Anne Boone Reed	42:19
2	Judy Mays	44:55
3	Stephanie Hargrove	47:02
4	Sallie Sinkler	47:28
5	Kathy Jaggers	47:29
6	Joan Mulvihill	48:06

Male 50-54 (256 finishers, 13 awards)

1	John Benkert	35:28
2	Jim Adams	36:25
3	Charles Teseniar	36:51
4	Jimmy Bagwell	39:15

5	Keith Weaver	39:30
6	Theron Cochran	40:25
7	Joe Waters	40:36
8	Bill Vetsch	42:13
9	Thomas Brown	42:57
10	Dean Godwin	42:58
11	Olin Hammond	42:59
12	Pearce Connerat	43:04
13	Harold Dodd	43:06

Female 50-54 (39 finishers, 3 awards)

1	Ellen Nitz	44:05
2	Pat Rhode	46:41
3	Louise Merring	50:47

Male 55-59 (109 finishers, 6 awards)

1	Charles Rose	37:09
2	Ed Ledford	38:59
3	Norm McAbee	41:07
4	Arthur Semken	41:44
5	Toby Transou	42:39
6	James Allen	43:00

Female 55-59 (20 finishers, 3 awards)

1	Susie Kluttz	43:25
2	Dawn Owens	52:36
3	Barbara Neagley	52:49

Male 60-64 (58 finishers, 3 awards)

1	Lee Swofford	42:20
2	Phil Szczepanski	43:28
3	Richard Marsh	44:39

Female 60-64 (6 finishers, 3 awards)

1	Nancy Bell	56:42
2	Marilyn Griffith	58:20
3	Faye Motley	1:00:36

Male 65-69 (24 finishers, 3 awards)

1	Gordon English Sr.	44:27
2	Franklin Mason	45:49
3	David Mellard	46:08

Female 65-69 (2 finishers, 2 awards)

| 1 | Lynn Edwards | 53:35 |
| 2 | Lucy Jones | 1:15:41 |

Male 70 up (4 finishers, 3 awards)

1	Ed Shaffer	50:59
2	Arnold Hecht	54:17
3	Cadwallader Jones	1:09:13

Female 70 up (1 finisher, 1 award)

| 1 | Margaret Wright | 1:06:06 |

Compiled by Cedric Jaggers from complete results provided by Burns Computer Services immediately after the race.

Paul Bitok of Kenya (No. 1) leads early. Post and Courier photo by Wade Spees

Chapter 16
1993
Kenyans Take Top Three Spots

Excellent weather for the second year in a row greeted the runners of the 16th Bridge Run on April 3, 1993. It was a crisp, clear 50 degrees for the 8 a.m. start. A 10 mile per hour crosswind on the bridge made it feel much colder, but the wind became a tailwind as runners exited the Crosstown Overpass and headed down King Street.

The pre-race favorites were Kenyans, a contingent of three newcomers. Olympic 5,000 meter silver medalist Paul Bitok was favored, and he did not disappoint. He led the first mile in 4:29 then left the pack going up the first span and was never headed, though he had a couple of fellow Kenyans just 4 seconds back. He hit the 5-mile mark in 22:57 and fell just 7 seconds short of the course record, winning in 28:31. Fellow Kenyans Simon Chemoiywo and Jackson Kipngok sprinted to the finish with Chemoiywo winning by one second in 28:34. John Halvorsen had the identical finish and time as in '92: fourth in 29:03.

"It felt very good," Bitok told the *Post and Courier*. "It was so good. I'm pleased to win with my fellow athletes. The conditions were perfect. Before the race, I was fearing the bridge. But when I hit the bridge, it was not so bad."

Second place finisher Chemoiywo felt differently about the bridge. "I ran very good, but the bridge is very difficult," he said. "There was sometimes a lot of strong cold wind."

Nick Rose of England finished fifth overall to repeat as Masters winner in 30:21. Wilson Waigwa, a Kenyan living in El Paso, Texas, was second Masters in 31:09 followed by Charles McMullen of Rochester, N.Y., in 31:40.

The women's race was a battle between runners who had both complained that they were suffering from head colds. They battled for 4 and a half miles before Sabrina Dornhoefer of Minneapolis, Minn., broke away from Irina Pouskhariva of St. Petersburg, Russia, to win 33:53 to 34:05. Tamara Karlikova, of Russia, now residing in Carmel, Calif., was third in 34:48.

"These were the toughest hills I've ever run on," Dornhoefer said. "The first mile over the bridge was the worst." She had thought she probably would not win due to her cold. "I really just wanted to have a good showing and maybe place in the top three. I took Monday and Tuesday off (from running) and didn't think I'd be that strong. But the rest probably helped."

About her race with Pouskhariva, Dornhoefer said, "I could tell she was struggling at about 4 and a half miles. I decided it was better to make a move now than try to break away at the end." Pouskhariva said she didn't have the energy to stay with her. "I have a tickle in my throat. In my shape it was hard to breathe. She was much stronger than me today." Still, she was encouraged by her place since she had finished third in the '92 race. "Maybe next year I win," she said.

Carol McLatchie of Houston, Texas, took the female Masters title in 35:50 while defending champion and former South Carolinian Nancy Grayson, of Northville, Mich., was second in 36:16. Barbara Filutze of Erie, Pa., was third in 36:21.

The Dr. Marcus Newberry Award was sweetened by adding $500 for each winner. Tom Mather of Mount Pleasant repeated as winner by finishing 17th overall in 31:42. The female division saw the closest contest ever as two Charlestonians were credited with the same time of 39:56. Suzanne Lynch ran a personal best to edge Robin Roughton by a fraction of a second. Lynch was 27th female, 303rd overall.

The Dewey Wise Trophy went to Ed Shaffer, 74, of Walterboro, S.C., for his time of 54:23.

For the third year in a row, Channel 24 television broadcast a one hour tape delay of the race. Benita Schlau was the race director for the 16th Bridge Run only. The race entry fee was raised to $14 early, $20 late.

There were 7,544 entrants and 6,192 finishers. There were 4,405 males and 1,787 females listed in the official results booklet which was mailed to all finishers. There were three runners under 29 minutes and four runners under 30 minutes. A total of 307 runners, 28 of them female, broke the 40-minute barrier. There were 1,995 runners who completed the race in less than 50 minutes, with 4,566 runners crossing the finish line in less than an hour. The Sunday *Post and Courier* listed the top 125 males and top 60 female finishers and listed up to seven deep in each age division. There were an estimated 6,000 participants in the untimed 4-mile Bridge Walk. Runners from 49 states (only Alaska was missing) and a number of foreign countries made this Bridge Run the most cosmopolitan yet.

Other Voices
Tell Me About Your Bridge Run 1993

By Cedric Jaggers, Originally appeared in the May 1993 issue of the Low Country Runner

Marion Square after the Bridge Run. A clipboard, a pen, one question to ask and an erstwhile runner and journalist who annually writes down **exactly** what you say. I tried to stay around the Charleston Running Club tent and get as many club members as I could. Sorry if I missed you, catch me next year. I listed overall place and time from the preliminary official results given to me by Burns Computer Finish Line company in parenthesis. So, tell me about your Bridge Run . . . (listed in the order we bumped into each other.)

Irving Rosenfeld: About the same time as last year. When I don't lose any time to Father Nature I'm happy with 49:32. 1,886th overall, 49:34

Jeffrey Herndon: Nice and easy, even splits. 606th overall, 42:40

Nina Parks Herndon: 45:30. I ran it easier than normal but it was more fun. I knew I was in trouble when I looked down and saw my Kiawah Marathon splits were still on my watch. 1,033rd overall, 45:31

Patti Clark: It wasn't so bad. I was happy with my time. I haven't been running enough to run as fast as I'd like to. Plus I had a dog bite last week. I ran 40:30. 362nd overall, 40:28

Tami Dennis: I don't even want to tell you; 45:05. Oh, golly, I've been sick. 965th overall, 45:06

Ray Dennis: Well I've been sick for a week and a half. I enjoyed it as usual. Slower than ever; 56:40. My goal is to do it for another 42 years. 3,396th overall, 55:41

Eileen Stellefson: It was great. A PR 43:35. It was great fun. I'm not going to do like last year: somebody read it and said "That sounds just like you." 733rd overall, 43:38

Frank Blackett: I enjoyed it. I finished with a smile on my face. I really enjoyed it. 50:15. 2,086th overall, 50:25

Mark Newnham: Unbelievable. That's the best way to say it. It was a perfect day. The secret is to go up slow and come down fast. I ran 35:12, a Bridge Run PR by a minute twenty three. 59th overall, 35:11

Leon Locklear: This is the 16th Bridge Run, my 15th and they don't get any easier. I'm not sure of my time; I don't remember if I passed you back after you went by me going down the bridge. 291st overall, 39:48

Bernie Clark: A real PR, 43:53. I took it conservative the first 2 miles and had a good time. It was my kind of weather. 736th overall, 43:40

Tom McGorty: I'm just glad it's over. I'm going to London in 2 weeks to run a marathon. So this was a great run: 43:10. 652nd overall, 43:01

Henry Stilmack: Well it wasn't good and it wasn't bad. I did it in 56 but I was satisfied. (Unable to find in results)

David Anderson: I am in the 60-64 age group and was trying to get in 5th place based on last year's finishing list, but didn't make it. I got 48:05. 1,573rd overall 48:18

Vic Fetter: I was slow man. Plantar fasciitis and I stepped on a nail the other night. I'm down to 20 miles a week now, but I maintained but not improved. 36:06. 82nd overall, 36:05

Lennie Moore: I was off what I wanted to be. I had the flu but . . . I felt all considered I did about as well as I could 37:57 or so. 166th overall, 37:57

Bunny Owen: I felt great – Devil With The Blue Dress On – I had great music. I did 6 minutes faster than last year and should have run faster. I know why: Eileen the nutritionist fed me dinner last night. 55:26. It made me realize I can run 8 and a half minute miles instead of 10 minute miles. 3,327th 54:26

Bob Walton: I beat last year's time by 20 seconds so I'm pleased. I've had more fun since I retired. 44:11. 833rd overall 43:51

Mike Hart: I ran well, the fastest since 1990: 34:35. 44th overall, 34:34

Maria Griffith: It was my best in 3 years; 44:25. I wouldn't have survived if Bernie and Eileen hadn't pulled me the first 2 miles. 858th overall, 44:27

Pat Rhode: I don't know what to say except I did 30 seconds better. I felt pretty good running. It was a great day. 1,160th overall, 46:14

John Dallimonti: It was a good run. I was real pleased. I had a goal of 57 minutes or less. Overall I'm real pleased with how I ran considering I've been sick like a lot of other people; 56:43. 3,667th overall, 56:39

Huey Inman: Just like everybody else, I'm getting over the flu. Guess I'll have to wait till next year to break 35. The flu cost me a minute. I ran 35:56. 75th overall, 35:58

Ronnie Yelton: I had a 42:04, last year was 45:10. I improved 3 minutes and felt great. A real PR. The weather was good. 524th overall, 42:01.

Steven Barnes: Oh, it was nice. I'd forgotten what the slopes were like. The Charlotte Observer 10k has 1 slope, this one has 3. It felt good going down, it was effortless going down. 45:11. 982nd overall, 45:12

Dan Clapper: One of my best Bridge Runs ever. Not time wise, just enjoyment wise. The weather was great, the wind wasn't a factor, and it was sunny. 36:40. 105th overall, 36:40.

Steven Hunt: I did well; 45:35. I'm recovering from the flu so I felt good just being out there. Not my best, not my worst. 1,059th overall, 45:40

Mike Johns: I took 4 minutes off last year's Bridge Run. I felt good the whole run. Next year I'm going to take 4 more minutes off 43:30. 765th overall, 43:50

Bob Clawson: Fifty nine and a half minutes and lucky to get it. I did terrible. 4,468th overall, 59:30

Robin Roughton: Well, I went in with no expectations because I've had an injury. I was really pleased with it. It felt like hell. I don't train on hills. I didn't realize how bad it would hurt. Thanks to Leon Locklear and Fred Reinhard who came up on me at the 5th mile and pulled me through to 39:56. It's fun to be part of it. 304th overall, 39:56

Michael Desrosiers: It was great. I ran easy. I didn't have a watch and I couldn't hear the time splits. I surprised myself and ran a good time; 35:20 something. 63rd overall, 35:28

Cecil Mack: What are we going to do about those walkers? Shoot them off the bridge or something? I had to zigzag through them and lost 8 or 10 minutes. I ran 1:14, it took me 50 seconds to get to the start. 6,044th overall, 1:14:19

Kathy Jaggers: That's not fair. You're not supposed to ask me. I dropped my Ventolin inhaler (for asthma) on the bridge and had to go back and get it. That's worth 20 seconds isn't it? But it was better than last year and I didn't have to go to the EMS tent – don't write that down. 47:07. 1,344th overall, 47:07

Mike Chodnicki: Just average. I ran what I expected, no better, no worse. But I enjoyed it. 36:53. 117th overall, 36:53

Paul Bitok of Kenya crests the first span of the John P. Grace Memorial Bridge on his way to victory.
Post and Courier photo by Wade Spees

Bob Schlau: It was my best 10k time on any course in 2 years. To do it on the Bridge made me happy. There is life after 45. I ran 31:50 something. 19th overall, 31:55

Tom Mather: It was good. I was happy. I tried to run hard over all those hills. I've tried it all ways. The only way is to start out hard, not overly hard, and keep the rhythm. It felt like old times to turn around at 6 miles and see Bob Schlau right behind me. So I put in a good last quarter mile. 31:42. 17th overall 31:42

Weezi Small: Weezi was happy to start the Bridge Run today because I've had patella tendonitis all week. I've taken a hundred Advils and slept for the first time the night before the race because I knew I wasn't going to run it. But I got up and decided to try. I took 40 seconds off last year. I would have liked to break 40 like at Flowertown, but couldn't quite do it. I ran 40:15 or so. 342nd overall, 40:19

Chuck Greer: Well it was about as good as I could do this year. Some years you are in shape, some years you aren't. I'll take it. I had some asthma near the end of the race. 37:50. 157th overall, 37:50

Dennis Hiott and Beverly Hiott: I'm not in the club this year (said he). Well, I'll tell you I ran 57 something and he was 10 minutes in front of me (she said). 1,364th overall, 47:14; 3,890th overall 57:26

Bruce Adams: The best one I've had in years, 43:29. I felt good all the way, even on the spans. 708th overall, 43:30

Mary Frances Adams: 60:40. I've had diarrhea for several weeks. At least I got to run. Let me tell you about Crescent City two weeks ago – I couldn't leave the hotel room. 4,936th overall, 61:50

Bruce Taylor: Terrible. I was pretty good through the first mile; I was right behind you, but after the hills my legs went. I need to do some hill training. I can't be too disappointed. I'm lucky after all the problems and exploratory surgery last year. 40:28. 363rd overall, 40:28

Therese Killeen: Shall I say Lordy, Lordy next year thank God I'll be 40? (Just then Howie Schomer announced the masters women's winners and times). Oh, no. Be sure and say I said that before they called out their times. I had a good run and what else can I say? 42:30. 593rd overall, 42:31

Charles Kellner: It was a beauty. Jeff Dorociak was back and it was like the good old days except Ed Leford was injured and we miss him badly. We owe it all to Ed. I ran 36:57 and was very pleased to do so. I had a great time. 119th overall, 36:57

Dave Mellard: Well if the clock is right, I did 46:15. I ran better than I did last year. I didn't hit the bridge so fast, just tried to do a pace, and did it. I did great considering I'm 70 years old now. I felt good because of sensible pacing. 1,117th overall, 46:20

Lessie Snead: It was fun. This was especially fun because at Summerville Flowertown was my best and I was within 30 seconds of it. I felt good. It was a good experience and my husband was behind me. 45:35. 1,058th overall 45:39

Billy Wieters: 45:12. I went out slow and got slower, not wearing a watch for the first time in 15 Bridge Runs. I hit 1 mile in 7 minutes, knew it was too slow, got clogged up on the bridge. I figured I'd pick it up at 3 or 4 but it was never there. Lack of trackwork. 980th overall, 45:11

Ron Deramus: What do you want to know? From 2 years ago I was a minute and 30 second Bridge Run PR. I thought it was a beautiful day for it. I ran 33 flat I think. I was happy to be around Bob and Paul, but couldn't make it into the top 2 or 3 from Charleston. The Bridge is the Bridge. 29th overall, 33:04

Tami Varn: Very hectic because I worked packet pickup last night until real late and then again this morning and went straight to the starting line. I'm happy with my run. A lot of fun. I was glad to see that finish line. 45:40. 1,026th overall, 45:29

Margaret Wright: A total loss. I'm making a complete circle; my time this year is about my time in the first Bridge Run. I had an injury, a hamstring pull, but I did my best. What you wrote about getting old and falling apart is the truth. 70:45. 5,886th overall, 70:44

Bill Vetsch: I drove down from Aiken at 4 this morning, so I was pretty tight when I started the race. I did better than I thought I'd do. The race was well managed and well directed. 40:52. 399th overall, 40:53

Tom Dority: I started out at an easy pace until I hit the bridge. My strongest point going up and coming down worked for me. I leveled off after the bridge. 44:12. 807th overall, 44:03

Allen Hoven: My wheels fell off. I was a minute and a half slower than last year. I ran a 5:55 first mile, but lots of kids were up front and I had to dodge and work by them. I had to walk some on the second span. I thought I was ready when I ran in the 38's at the Flowertown 10k. It wasn't my day. I ran 40:05. 310th overall, 41:02

Keith Ambrose: It was . . . I knocked 3 minutes from last year. Now I'm catching up with Allen Hoven. I could see him up ahead of me this year. 40:10. 334th overall, 40:15

Cedric Jaggers: Kathy said I had to do this. I'm smiling even though it was my slowest Bridge Run since 1981 for the second year in a row. Like I told Dupree Elvington when he passed me at the Flowertown 10k, it's hard to run fast on 21 miles a week. I was over 30 seconds faster than I was afraid I was going to be. My watch said 39:27. 226th overall, 39:29

Female Overall Winner Sabrina Dornhoefer of Minneapolis.
Post and Courier photo by Roger Cureton

1993 Awards

Prize money winners
Overall Male
1 Paul Bitok .... Kenya .... 28:31 ... $3,000
2 Simon Chemoiyo ...... Kenya .... 28:34 ... $1,500
3 Jackson Kipngok ...... Kenya .... 28:35 ... $1,000
4 John Halvorsen .... Canada .... 29:03 ... $750
5 Nick Rose .... England .... 30:21 ... $500
6 Antoni Niemczak ..... Poland .... 30:28 ... $400
7 Eric Ashton .... Columbia, SC .... 30:31 ... $300
8 Michael Doborohotov Russia .... 30:34 ... $200
9 Selwyn Blake .... Columbia, SC .... 30:50 ... $100

Overall Female
1 Sabrina Dornhoefer ... Minneapolis .... 33:53 .. $3,000
2 Irina Pouskhariva ..... Russia .... 34:05 ... $1,500
3 Tamara Karlikova ..... Russia .... 34:48 ... $1,000
4 Betsy Schmid .... Chapel Hill, NC ...... 35:08 ... $750
5 Karen Hoffman .... Atlanta, GA .... 35:30 ... $500
6 Maggie Kraft .... Columbia, SC .... 35:43 ... $200

Masters Division Male
1 Nick Rose .... England .... 30:21 ... $1,500
2 Wilson Waigwa .... Kenya .... 31:09 ... $1,000
3 Charles McMullen ..... Rochester NY .... 31:40 ... $500

Masters Division Female
1 Carol McLatchie ...... Houston, TX .... 35:50 ... $1,500
2 Nancy Grayson .... Northville, MI .... 36:16 ... $1,000
3 Barbara Filutzie ...... Erie, PA .... 36:21 ... $500

Special awards:

Marcus Newberry award for first Tri-County, Charleston Area finisher (prize money awarded for the first time)
Male
Tom Mather .... Mt Pleasant, SC .... 31:42 ... $500
Female
Suzanne Lynch .... Charleston, SC .... 39:56 .... $500

Dewey Wise Trophy
For oldest finisher with time less than his or her age in minutes:
Ed Shaffer, 70 .... Walterboro, SC 54:23

Age Group Award Winners
(presented to top 3 in age group, with top 5% up to maximum of 25 awarded in each age group):

Male 12 & under (79 finishers, 4 awards)
1 Brantlee Milner 42:53
2 Ryan Holland 44:00
3 Robby Moore 45:27
4 Christopher Rivers 45:33

Female 12 & under (26 fin., 3 awards)
1 Charity Fillmore 39:16
2 Erin Burton 47:30
3 Terri Hubbard 54:55

Male 13-17 (147 finishers, 8 awards)
1 Brian Clark 34:28
2 Charlie Norris 35:46
3 Denis Fedulov 36:12
4 Ashley Ackerman 38:35
5 Russ Taylor 38:57
6 Timothy Gautreau 39:07
7 Adam Hare 39:16
8 Sean Chase 39:25

Female 13-17 (75 finishers, 4 awards)
1 Ellen Cogswell 42:51
2 Kathryn Weber 44:35
3 Leslie Tomlinson 46:18
4 Jenna Ellwanger 46:22

Male 18-21 (124 finishers, 7 awards)
1 Peter Kotland 34:54
2 Phillip Simmons 35:07
3 Todd Hammerstone 36:18
4 David Graham 36:31
5 Jonathan Morgan 37:19
6 Jim Baker 38:06
7 Zaid Subailat 38:19

Female 18-21 (84 finishers, 5 awards)
1 Gabrielle Lambert 41:03
2 Nicole Zevotek 42:09
3 Helen LaFaye 42:49
4 Sara Virella 43:30
5 Dustin Annan 46:21

Male 22-25 (356 finishers, 18 awards)
1 Jamie Barnes 31:17
2 Andrew Spaulding 33:25
3 Chip Owens 33:43
4 Pablo Sanchez 33:45
5 Paul Reardon 33:51
6 Michael Bowers 34:00
7 Michael Colaiacovo 34:03
8 John Raguin 34:42
9 Mark Newnham 35:11
10 Ben Farley 36:08
11 Michael Green 36:39
12 Philip Spotts 37:24
13 Brett Berry 38:43
14 Emmett Johnson 39:01
15 Rick Eitell 39:04
16 Clark Green 39:08
17 Jerome Santa 39:33
18 Walt Rooney 39:43

Female 22-25 (232 finishers, 12 awards)
1 Kelly McLaughlin 37:17
2 Lan Clayton 37:34
3 Kathy Fitzpatrick 40:07
4 Frances Armstrong 41:19
5 Heather Turnquist 42:17
6 Denise Lockett 42:36
7 Laura Willenborg 43:26
8 Anne Boger 43:45
9 Shawn Randolph 43:56
10 Jamie Oxendine 44:55
11 Laura Pierce 45:01
12 Carie Stefanou 45:48

Male 26-29 (504 finishers, 25 awards)
1 Chuck Lotz 31:04
2 George Luke 32:03
3 James Perry 32:30
4 Mark Scott 34:15
5 Marshall Martin 35:01
6 Rick Weiner 35:15
7 Jimmy Tassios 35:24
8 Timothy Sullivan 35:45
9 Dawson Cherry 35:48
10 Philip Ponder 36:25
11 Damon Brown 36:38
12 Mark Rutledge 36:45

13 Michael Craig	35:51
14 Buster McCoy	37:05
15 Paul Wismer	37:09
16 Daniel Bliek	37:27
17 Craig Boyer	37:36
18 Steven Elton	37:47
19 Douglas Richey	37:57
20 Kirkland Davis	38:02
21 Michael Parker	38:23
22 Alan Brown	38:25
23 Mitch Embler	38:26
24 Jonathan Meltzer	38:32
25 James Dwane	38:33

Female 26-29 (286 finishers, 15 awards)

1 Laura Glynn	37:37
2 Megan Othersen	38:29
3 Suzanne Lynch	39:56
4 Mary Jo Willard	40:35
5 Cindy Bryant	41:39
6 Janice Cooper	41:51
7 Laurie Sperry	41:53
8 Tracie Armold	42:22
9 Kimberly Woody	43:23
10 Tricia Brown	43:32
11 Rebecca Hillman	43:37
12 Lynne Smith	43:48
13 Kathy Magor	43:52
14 Sarah Dolven	44:01
15 Suzanne Hall	44:17

Male 30-34 (748 finishers, 25 awards)

1 Larry Brock	31:20
2 Alexander Reljaev	31:29
3 Tom Ratcliffe	31:55
4 Paul Jessey	32:00
5 Jeff Milliman	32:34
6 Ricardo Roman	32:40
7 Ron Deramus	33:04
8 Robert Lowery	34:27
9 Alan Gebert	34:45
10 Phillip McGoff	34:55
11 Michael Klatt	34:56
12 Michael Desrosiers	35:28
13 Dave Carney	35:35
14 Huey Inman	35:58
15 Sam Inman	35:58
16 Matthew Cooke	36:00
17 Joey Howard	36:01
18 David Jessey	36:04
19 Craig Bodkin	36:14
20 David Riddle	36:16
21 Steve Shonts	36:20
22 Roger Bowman	36:29
23 Paul Schmid	36:41
24 Blake Zemp	36:49
25 Charles Hagan	36:59

Female 30-34 (363 finishers, 19 awards)

1 Allison Reeves	37:04
2 Jean Strait	37:13
3 Patt Loggins	38:17
4 Lisa Roeber	38:20
5 Janice Cole	39:29
6 Robin Roughton	39:56
7 Weezi Small	40:19
8 Penny Bowman	40:23

9 Patricia Clark	40:28
10 Deborah McClure	42:29
11 Nina Cunningham	44:32
12 Tami Dennis	45:06
13 Cynthia Murphy	45:15
14 Allyson Mullins	45:15
15 Tami Varn	45:29
16 Nina Parks Herndon	45:31
17 Carrie Kelly	45:56
18 Jennifer Hales	46:40
19 Celia Griffin	46:44

Male 35-39 (746 finishers, 25 awards)

1 Tom Mather	31:42
2 Tony Bateman	32:18
3 Mark Friedrich	33:10
4 Marshall Randell	33:32
5 Perry Macheras	34:19
6 Mike Hart	34:34
7 Tim O'Brien	35:46
8 David Bourgeois	35:53
9 Bruce Conrad	35:58
10 Vic Fetter	36:05
11 Gregory Fagan	36:22
12 Art Bradham	36:25
13 Marc Judson	36:26
14 Scott Roark	36:35
15 Rod Sapp	36:39
16 Dan Clapper	36:40
17 Jeff Dorociak	36:41
18 Bobby Torri	36:43
19 John Ratier	36:44
20 Jim Brewer	36:49
21 Michael Chodnicki	36:53
22 Peter Orzech	37:00
23 Ray Krolewicz	37:08
24 Glenn Lucas	37:10
25 Paul Bullington	37:12

Female 35-39 (305 finishers, 16 awards)

1 Doris Windsand	39:04
2 Bonnie Poore Long	39:53
3 Debra Caviness	41:37
4 Theresa Killeen	42:31
5 Mary Millar	42:44
6 Stacie Goggans	43:03
7 Lisa Goodrich	43:05
8 Annie Wetherhold	43:25
9 Eileen Stellefson	43:38
10 Debbie Howard	44:18
11 Maria Griffith	44:27
12 Cindy Wright	44:45
13 Linda Davidson	45:01
14 Barbara Crumpler	45:40
15 Sally Drehmer	45:42
16 Michele Stutts	45:46

Male 40-44 (690 finishers, 25 awards)

1 Ric Banning	32:22
2 Chuck Smead	32:31
3 Danny West	35:00
4 Don Lucy	35:10
5 Oliver Marshall	35:52
6 Paul Brown	36:00
7 Joe Marshall	36:11
8 Mike Julian	36:24
9 Tommy Seymore	36:42

10 Glenn Tacy	36:45
11 Leon Cook	36:52
12 Jack Todd	36:55
13 Charles Kellner	36:57
14 Don Fraser	37:39
15 Sonny Hembree	37:44
16 Thomas Rowey	37:48
17 Rusty Doyle	37:54
18 Gary Ricker	38:03
19 Sandy Wetherhold	38:05
20 Dave Lemonds	38:22
21 Fred Teckleburg	38:31
22 Glen Eyhler	38:39
23 Mario Salas	38:42
24 Guy Herring	38:42
25 Dean Brooks	38:44

Female 40-44 (208 finishers, 11 awards)

1 Alendia Vestal	38:54
2 Becky Sox	40:18
3 Kiki Sweigart	41:32
4 Tina Barber	42:10
5 Donna Trask	42:31
6 Eileen Telford	42:41
7 Peggy Schug	43:40
8 Nonie Hudnall	43:45
9 Wanda Brooks	44:57
10 Marilyn Davey	45:35
11 Lessie Snead	45:39

Male 45-49 (496 finishers, 25 awards)

1 Greg Larson	34:43
2 Phil Peterson	34:52
3 Terry Van Natta	35:02
4 Brooke Meserole	37:15
5 Bill Peay	37:30
6 Russell Brown	37:48
7 Chuck Greer	37:50
8 Dan Young	37:56
9 Bill Seigler	38:30
10 Buddy Hyman	38:49
1 1 Phillip Dickert	39:00
12 David Ott	39:03
13 David Gelly	39:20
14 Arthur Smith	39:21
15 Cedric Joggers	39:29
16 Lee Foster	39:53
17 Fred Reinhard	39:58
18 Allen Hoven	40:02
19 Thomas Blankenship	40:09
20 Keith Ambrose	40:15
21 Bill Rogers	40:18
22 Walter Waddell	40:20
23 William Anderson	40:25
24 Bruce Taylor	40:28
25 Rick Cushing	40:32

Female 45-49 (119 finishers, 6 awards)

1 Anne Boone	44:02
2 Joan Mulvihill	46:30
3 Kathy Jaggers	47:07
4 Lyn Hammond	49:29
5 Carolyn Jarrell	50:02
6 Harriet Dubose	50:03

Male 50-54 (268 finishers, 14 awards)

1 Charles Teseniar	38:47
2 George Brandreth	40:05
3 Keith Weaver	40:07
4 Dean Godwin	40:14
5 Theron Cochran	40:40
6 Bill Vetsch	40:53
7 Dupree Elvington	41:04
8 Thomas Siegl	41:12
9 Wendell Cribb	41:22
10 Bob Farr	42:01
11 Harold Dodd	42:09
12 Will Hearn	42:09
13 David Moorhead	42:23
14 Sam Harrelson	43:16

Female 50-54 (43 finishers, 3 awards)

1 Pat Rhode	46:14
2 Louise Merring	49:14
3 Ann Marsh	52:03

Male 55-59 (129 finishers, 7 awards)

1 James Allen	40:50
2 Robert Cunningham	41:35
3 Toby Transou	43:08
4 Thomas Steele	44:08
5 John Nutt	44:19
6 John Thompson	44:25
7 Jim Wilson	44:31

Female 55-59 (20 finishers, 3 awards)

1 Susie Kluttz	44:05
2 Barbara Neagley	54:16
3 Faun Peters	54:29

Male 60-64 (63 finishers, 4 awards)

1 Charles Rose	36:37
2 Norm McAbee	40:51
3 Lee Swofford	42:33
4 Phil Szczepanski	43:51

Kenyans Simaon Karori (No.1) and Jackson Kipngok (No. 2) race for the finish line.
Post and Courier photo by Stephanie Harvin

Chapter 17
1994
This Was Oprah's race

The 17th Bridge Run on March 26, 1994, will probably be remembered as the year that a runner who finished 3,839th got more publicity than the winners. Talk show host Oprah Winfrey ran the race (under the pseudonym Francesca Kincaid) in a time of 55:48 and received massive publicity in the local papers and even nationally. Oprah was the talk of the town before, during and after the race. Runners and non-runners alike were talking about seeing her around town or running near her during the race. She had a big impact, and years later people still talk about the year Oprah ran the Bridge Run.

Race facts attracted less attention. It was the largest Bridge Run to date with 8,670 entrants and a record 7,355 official finishers. There were 5,063 males (68.8 percent) and 2,292 females (31.2 percent) listed in the results booklet. It had the largest number and highest percentage of female finishers. It also marked the first time over 2,000 women completed a race in the Carolinas.

The conditions were good for racing: about 60 degrees but rising at the 8 a.m. start. There was a slight crosswind as the runners went over the bridge. Once again Kenyans dominated the open division. Three Kenyans and one American took the first mile together in 4:25. The Kenyans were still together with no one else close when they reached the 5-mile mark. Simon Karori kicked away from Jackson Kipngok, who had finished third in '93, to win 28:35 to 28:37. Fellow Kenyan Gilbert Rutto was third in 28:57.

"I was strong for the finish. It's sweet to win," Karori told the *Post and Courier*.

Runner-up Kipngok said he couldn't match Karori's sprinting ability over the last 200 meters. "The conditions today were better than last year," he said. "Last year it was very cold. The only problem today was crossing the bridge."

Kenyan runners remained the only ones to have broken the 29-minute barrier in any Bridge Run. Eric Ashton of Columbia, S.C., was fourth overall and the first American in 29:56. England's Nick Rose ran 30:04 to take the Masters title for the third year in a row. His time was good for fifth place overall.

In the women's race, Elaine Van Blunk of Drexel Hill, Pa., led virtually from the start and won in 34:01. Lisa Vail of Pine Palms, N.Y., was second in 34:12 and despite receiving scorch marks on her legs when the starting cannon was fired — after the race she questioned why it was pointed at the runners — Irina Poushkariva of Russia was third in 34:21.

"I was hoping to run a little quicker, but considering the hills, I'm happy with it," Van Blunk told the newspaper. "I felt confident strength-wise, but you can never tell come race day. I enjoyed the course. It's definitely challenging, which right now is good for me because I think I'm stronger rather than faster, at this point. The hills weren't as bad as a lot of people had said. I just kept concentrating up the hills and working the downhill parts. I knew once we got to 4 miles, the last 2 were flat. That's where I kept saying, 'Just get to the 4-mile marker.' Coming off after 4 miles, I felt pretty strong coming in. I didn't see anyone around me."

Runner-up Vail said, "I figured my best chance was on the hills. I'm not strong on the flat part. We were close to start with, but Van Blunk pulled away right away. She didn't really gain on me, but she was always that much ahead of me."

Poushkariva, who finished third, had expressed her desire to win this year when she was runner-up last year. "I expected to run 33:10 to 33:15," she said. "I was only third, and I was prepared to try and win this race. I hope next year will be my year here."

Nick Rose repeated as Masters winner in 30:04, followed by Wilson Waigwa, a Kenyan now of El Paso, Texas, who repeated as second place Master in 31:31. Charleston's Bob Schlau ran his best Bridge Run time in a number of years, 31:47, to move up to third place Masters.

Female Masters winner was Rebecca Stockdale-Wooley from Chaplin, Conn., a recent convert from triathlon, in 36:32. Diana Tracy of Hermosa Beach, Calif., was second in 36:55. Catherine Lempesis of Columbia, S.C., repeated her third place finish from '93, improving her time to 37:07.

The Dr. Marcus Newberry Award for first Tri-County finisher again went to Tom Mather of Mount Pleasant, who finished ninth overall in 30:54, his fastest Bridge Run to date. Kathy Kanes of Charleston took the female division in 34:43 as the seventh female and 49th overall runner. The Dewey Wise Trophy went to Bill Forwood, 82, of Greenville, S.C., who ran 80:31.

Channel 24 television, for the fourth year in a row, showed a one hour tape delay of the race. The race entry fee remained at $14 early, $20 late; the walk entry fee was $9 early, $12 late.

There were three runners under the 29-minute barrier, and as in '93, a total of four runners under the 30-minute barrier. A total of 327 runners, 32 of them female, broke the 40-minute barrier. There were 2,005 runners who crossed the finish line in less than 50 minutes, and a total of 5,044 runners who finished the race in less than an hour. The *Post and Courier* listed the top 125 male finishers and top 75 female finishers along with up to 10 deep in each age division. Julian Smith was the new race director.

Other voices
The Bridge
By Michael Grybush, Originally appeared in the March 1994 issue of The Inside Lane Charlotte Road Runners Club Newsletter

The Cooper River Bridge Run in Charleston, S.C., is more than an ordinary 10k. Held near the first Saturday of April for the last 17 years, it is my ceremonial beginning of the summer racing season and the first noble reason to go to the beach. Moreover, it is an exceptionally challenging course, including consecutive 60-meter climbs over the two spans of the Cooper River Bridge. Runners cheer as they pass the crests, celebrating their annual defeat of the steel-and-concrete monster.

The greatest thrill came for me this past year on the Sunday morning after the race. Setting out for a long run at 5 a.m., I found myself a half hour later alone at the foot of the bridge. Three traffic lanes wide, it stands 50 meters from its older sister span and affords an elevated pedestrian walk two-thirds of a meter in width. A hip high rail separates a runner from the drop to the Cooper River below.

In the predawn darkness, the bridge took on a mysterious aura. Sparsely lighted, the steel structure above disappeared into the blackness of the sky, while the concrete pillars below disappeared into the blackness of the river.

Miles away, lights on the far bank reflected off the water to give some measure of where the land began, and above in the east, the first purple shades of dawn identified the sky. Lost between the two was a world that belonged to the bridge, a world in which I was intruding.

As I ran along the walkway, I was almost overwhelmed by exhilaration. It was the kind of fear induced adrenaline high which comes from roller coasters and high-speed driving. I could see some of the imposing steel above, and the proximity of the span on the other bridge gave me an idea of my height above the river. I felt like an insect, an infestation on some superior ferrous organism which could have flicked me off if it so chose. For the 15 minutes of the 2 miles on the bridge, I was at an almost unbearable level of excitement.

An hour later when I crossed back from Mount Pleasant to Charleston, it was daylight. The mystery of the bridge was gone. It was once again a big inanimate steel structure on concrete legs, dwarfed by the city and the sea on the horizon. But for that 15 minutes in the darkness, it was magical.

(Note: Michael completed the 1994 race in 44:23, CJ)

Tell Me About Your Bridge Run (1994)
By Cedric Jaggers, Originally appeared in the May-June 1994 issue of the Low Country Runner

If you were near the CRC tent or if I saw you in Marion Square right after the Bridge Run and I knew you as a CRC member, you got hit with the phrase: "Tell me about your Bridge Run." I wrote down exactly what you said. People are listed in the order we ran into each other. Sorry if I missed you - catch me next year. The place and time in parenthesis are from the preliminary uncorrected race day results which Burns Computer printed for me for Running Journal. The results show 7,288 finishers, 5,057 male and 2,231 female (the first time 2,000 females have finished a race in South Carolina and the most finishers ever for the Bridge Run).

Irving Rosenfeld: It was a cake walk. Sixty-one minutes. (5,445th overall, 61:24).

Ed Isaac: I think I did a little over 58 which isn't bad for an old man. I get a year older, the crowd gets bigger and it gets better. It's a good run. 58:02. Next year I'll be in the 60 age group at the bottom and have an advantage. (4,443rd overall, 58:01).

Larry D'Ippolito: I had a Bridge PR today. The first mile was fast; I purposely didn't look at my watch until mile 4. At 5 I was 29 flat and ran 35:47 on my watch. (75th overall, 35:49).

Kathy Jaggers: I went to the EMS tent after I finished. I don't know how I finished. I had an asthma attack on the bridge and my legs were shakey. Nina (Herndon Parks) and Therese (Killeen) were in the tent too; it was like a reunion — we meet there every other year. It must have something to do with the weather conditions. 46:30. (1,229th overall, 46:32).

Art Liberman: My slowest Bridge Run ever; 47:14. I wasn't properly trained. I'm not competing any more. I just came out to do it. It was more difficult because I haven't trained properly. (1,400th overall, 47:17).

Tami Dennis: It sucked wind. I ran with my brother who never runs, and he beat me by 30 seconds. 44:08. (841st overall, 44:09).

Ray Dennis: Well, I ran better than last year and I beat Oprah Winfrey; somebody said she ran 54. I ran 52:40. (2,874th overall, 52:47).

Bernie Clark: 43:38, a 10k PR! I felt great. We drove all night Thursday night, Don Austell and I did from New Orleans. We drove 1600 miles roundtrip to run 6 miles. I felt great and had a good time. (733rd overall, 43:38).

Kelly Walls: It was my first one. I didn't walk it. It was pretty good - all the exhilaration. I didn't have a panic attack and I didn't have to go to the bathroom in the bushes. 1:02. (5,791st overall, 1:02:57).

Ronnie Yelton: I think people in white numbers should have been further back at the start. Other than that it was beautiful. 43:04. (658th overall, 43:07).

Frank Blackett: I enjoyed it. What can I say? Same as I did last year with a smile on my face - a little slower, 53 minutes. (3,176th overall, 53:45).

Eileen Stellefson: Michael Desrosiers and I videotaped people for the running club while we ran and we had a ball. We got people smiling. We even stopped for a glass of champagne. We videotaped runners. 55 minutes. (3,719th overall, 55:26).

Steve Dykes: Don't even ask. I'm from the George Sheehan school of running for enjoyment. I came in under an hour. I whipped Oprah. (Unable to find in results).

Weezie Small: It was great, a beautiful day. I took it nice and easy and enjoyed helping everybody out along the way. I finished in about 44 minutes. I'm able to walk in this year instead of being carried. (812th overall, 44:00).

Gary Ricker: I felt good today the whole way. The cloud cover over the bridge really helped a lot. Doing the connectors the past few weeks really helped on the hills. 38:54. (219th overall, 38:53).

Tommy Mathewes: An aerobic pace and it was wonderful. Seven minute miles which meant I didn't have to get sick at the end. Just a beautiful, comfortable day. 44:20 (Unable to find in results)

Chuck Wickersham: Gosh, I don't know what to say. I couldn't figure out why they kept calling me Oprah. They kept saying "Oprah, Oprah." I must have been running close to her. It was a sprint at the finish and I nipped her by about 2 seconds. I just ran for fun this year. It was about 13 minutes off my bridge PR, 50 something. (3,459th overall, 54:36).

Billy Wieters: I cruised in at a 47 flat, my 16th Bridge Run. I took it easy, went out at 7:10, turned around and looked backwards. I watched the young bucks, male and female pass me. 47:00. (1,336th overall, 47:00).

Maria Griffith: It was the worst in four years. If I can't get better I'll never do it again. It was bad. 46:04, about 2 minutes slower than last year. (1,155th overall, 46:04).

Dan Clapper: I wish I had an excuse. Conditions were perfect. I had to pee after mile one. I was where I needed to be at mile 4 and let it slip. I picked up at mile 6. 37:10, respectable. (135th overall, 37:11).

Ginger Gregory: 43:15 which was the best since I had a baby in '88 or '89. I've been working hard at it trying to get back in triathlon shape for this summer. (691st overall, 43:19).

Jeffrey Herndon: I went out and the only thing I could see was the bouncing back of your bald head. Not good, Cedric. About 40:20. I had 100 people pass me on King Street and I couldn't pick it up. (357th overall, 40:28).

Helen Brew: It was a training run and Dad ran it with me. But I still got a PR 49:21. (1,907th overall, 49:26).

Charity Fillmore: I ran faster than I've run here before 38:15 or 38:20. When I was running up the bridge I'd pass people and they'd pass me back going down but I'd pass them again. After the bridge there was another big hill and I didn't like it. It was hard. I like this race because it is fun. (787th overall, 43:51 - note apparently an error as she ran the entire race and finished ahead of me, she should be have been 189th place with her time in the 38s. CJ).

Lennie Moore: It went well this year. We had the wind at our back for a change. I'm happy with my results 36:34 on a big 35 miles a week. A PR for me. (112th, 36:35).

Glenn Dennis: It was good. A good race. The thing that spurred me on was Larry D'Ippolito. He passed me at the corner of Meeting in the final stretch and I

Uphill on the second span. Post and Courier photo by Stephanie Harvin

out sprinted him. 35:43. (71st overall, 35:45).

Mike Desrosiers: Eileen and I ran with a camcorder. We were just having fun. We found out it's true; the bridge really does shake when you're back in the pack. We were trying to pass Oprah but we never did. (3,796th overall, 55:40).

Thomas Dority: The first span was the worst span. Once I got over it, it wasn't nearly as bad. It was a good race other than that. 45:35. (1,063rd overall, 45:30).

Harry Ricker: Oprah blocked me out on the first span, then tripped me going up the second span. But the weather was terrific and I finished in spite of it. 50:43. (2,290th overall, 50:53).

Ron Deramus: Well it came out better than I thought it would with no more training than I've had. I ran 33:14, only 10 seconds off last year and 2 places higher. I was just happy to break 34. (27th overall, 33:16).

Brian Harper: It was a good race but I didn't do as well as I thought because of the crowd. I usually run under 40 but ran 43 due to people up front who shouldn't have been there. But it was fun none the less. (924th overall, 44:37).

Leon Locklear: I can't complain; my best time in about 4 years. It got real tough about 4 miles. I saw Dr. (Chuck) Greer up there and couldn't hang with him. 37:58. (173rd overall, 37:59).

Bob Schlau: Great race. I felt good. It was a nice feeling. Tom Mather and I worked so hard this spring; when I got to the start I knew I was fit. This is the fastest start I've had in years. Ric Banning and I went 9:58 at 2 miles and really felt under control, like I could have run faster if I had to pick it up. It's the result of a lot of hard work this spring. We got on Meeting and I was closing on Wilson (Waigwa of Kenya). He looked around and saw me ... he has a gear I don't have. As long as I get 10 seconds faster every year I'll be happy. I'm so pleasantly surprised at this age to be running well. (14th overall, 31:47).

Harold Fallis: It was fun. I had an average race. I do a lot of coaching and my legs are heavy. I entered it to enjoy the festivities. The race was average but the finish area and facilities were above average. I've run slower and I've run faster. I'm happy to be running. 37:15. (142nd overall, 37:19).

Pat Rhode: I was going to be mad if you didn't ask me. Considering that I'm hurt, I'm very pleased. I ran 3 marathons in 3 months and still ran 48 minutes hurt so I'm fine. Thank you for doing this, we love you. (1,798th overall, 48:58).

Joe Allen: Terrible. I'm a fat old man. Too much Coors Light, not enough homework. I saw God when the bridge moved and shook. I said, "Lord, I'm coming to see you!" 48:08. (1,635th overall, 48:17).

Raleigh Wise: It was just very nice. I relaxed and had a good time. I'm going to wear a life preserver next year. About 64 minutes. (5,694th overall, 62:32).

Mike Chodnicki: Great. After a month of not being able to train, I was pleased with 37:21. My last mile was 6:10. From 5 miles in I was Jello. I was very, very pleased. (145th overall, 37:23).

Jarvie Young: I faced the hills and now I fear them no more. I was 38 and some change. I got a snapshot of me with the Kenyans after the race. It was like a family photo. (191st overall, 38:19).

Margaret Wright: I'm running with a handicap, a broken wrist last week when I fell at Summerville and also banged up knees. My biggest fear was that I'd fall down again today. I did all right, 70 something. (6,867th overall, 70:07).

Nina Parks: It's good to be back in Charleston. We were having a reunion in the EMS tent with Kathy and Therese. People kept passing me after I fell in the chute. I said, "She got my time." but they didn't do anything about it. 45 something. (1,262nd overall, 46:42 - note, Nina obviously was given the time of one of the slower runners who passed her. CJ).

Huey Inman: What can I say. The best ever. I broke 35, that's what counts. It was hard but I did it. Best of my 11 times. 34:56. (55th overall, 34:56).

David Mellard: I don't know what time I finished. It was a good race. I had a little trouble on the first span. It was difficult. Lack of training. (1,382nd overall, 47:11).

David Anderson: 47:45. It was a great run for me. Last year 48:07, my best this year. I'm 63 now. (1,515th overall, 47:46).

Bob Walton: Slower than last year, but I'm always glad to finish. 45:46. (1,107th overall, 45:47).

Lessie Snead: It was a hot uphill. I was not prepared for the incline. I was happy with my time definitely. Last year 45:39 so I took close to a minute off. I can't believe another one has come and gone. It is almost sad. (937th overall, 44:44).

Whit Bailey: I believe it was 1:07. It was good for my conditioning. I was well pleased. (6,654th overall, 68:00).

Arthur Smith: 39:02, a PR by 19 seconds. I went out a little too fast at 5:30, but I was trying my new training method: whatever it takes to beat Cedric. But it didn't work this year. (237th overall, 39:02).

Cedric Jaggers: I was really happy to be in the 38s. I told Ed Ledford at the start that I was going to run 38:50 and I was real happy to be within 8 seconds of it. I had to kick like crazy to keep it from flipping over to 39. My best Bridge Run since we moved to Rock Hill. Today is Kathy's and my wedding anniversary. It was a perfect anniversary present. (226th overall, 38:58).

1994 Awards

Prize money winners

Overall Male
1. Simon Karori .... Kenya .... 28:35 ... $3,000
2. Jackson Kipngok ...... Kenya .... 28:37 ... $1,500
3. Gilbert Rutto .... Kenya .... 28:57 ... $1,000
4. Eric Ashton .... Columbia, SC .... 29:56 ... $800
5. Nick Rose .... England .... 30:04 ... $600
6. Keith Johnson .... Dallas, TX .... 30:44 ... $500
7. Jamie Barnes .... Easley, SC .... 30:51 ... $400
8. Derek Mitchum .... Columbia, SC .... 30:52 ... $300
9. Tom Mather .... Mt Pleasant, SC ..... 30:54 ... $250
10. Scott Walshlager .... WinsSalem, NC .... 30:56 ... $150

Overall Female
1. Elaine Van Blunk ..... Drexel Hil PA .... 34:01 ... $3,000
2. Lisa Vaill .... Pine Plains, NY ..... 34:12 ... $1,500
3. Irina Poushkariva .... Russia .... 34:21 ... $1,000
4. Elena Vinitskaia ..... Russia .... 34:27 ... $800
5. Kirsten Russell ...... Boulder, CO .... 34:39 ... $600
6. Lynn Doering .... Atlanta, GA .... 34:41 ... $500
7. Kathy Kanes .... Charleston, SC ...... 34:43 ... $400
8. Debbi Kilpatrick ..... Berea, OH .... 34:43 ... $300
9. Betsy Schmid .... Chapel Hill, NC ..... 35:05 ... $250
10. Lorraine Hochella ... Wamsburg, VA .... 35:14 ... $150

Masters Division Male
1. Nick Rose .... England .... 30:04 ... $1,500
2. Wilson Waigwa .... Kenya .... 31:31 ... $1,000
3. Bob Schlau .... Charleston, SC ...... 31:47 ... $750
4. Ric Banning .... Alexandria, VA ...... 31:52 ... $500
5. Charl McMullen .... Rochester, NY .... 32:25 ... $250

Masters Division Female
1. Rebecca Stockdale .... Chaplin, CT .... 36:32 ... $1,500
2. Diania Tracy .... Hermosa B., CA ...... 36:35 ... $1,000
3. Catherine Lempesis ... Columbia SC .... 37:07 ... $750
4. Gretchen Maurer ...... Norfolk, VA .... 37:09 ... $500
5. Barbara Filutze ...... Erie, PA .... 37:16 ... $250

Special Awards:

Dr Marcus Newberry Award
For first Tri-County Charleston Area finisher
Male
Tom Mather .... Mt Pleasant, SC ...... 30:54 .... $500
Female
Kathy Kanes .... Charleston, SC .... 37:59 .... $500

Dewey Wise Trophy
For the oldest finisher with time faster than his or her age:
Bill Forwood, 82 .... Greenville, SC 80:31

Age group awards
(presented to top 3 in age group, with top 5% up to maximum of 25 awarded in each age group):

Male 12 & under (100 finishers, 5 awards)
1. Brantlee Milner 44:49
2. Jeremy Nordstrom 47:50
3. Zachary McKinney 47:58
4. Chris Dodds 48:06
5. David Southwick 48:25

Female 12 & under (28 fin., 3 awards)
1. Charity Fillmore 43:51
2. Helen Brew 49:26
3. Carol Weber 54:57

Male 13-17 (182 finishers, 10 awards)
1. Jake Johnson 34:48
2. William Silver 35:37
3. Eric Caldwell 35:48
4. Timothy Gautreau 36:00
5. Mike Wilson 36:13
6. Jay Glover 37:14
7. Jonathan Angelo 38:02
8. Benjamin Maddox 38:04
9. Mark Berglind 38:21
10. Russ Taylor 38:28

Female 13-17 (67 finishers, 4 awards)
1. Carson Flowers 42:14
2. Natali West 42:49
3. Sarah Judy 45:22
4. Kathryn Weber 45:22

Male 18-21 (188 finishers, 10 awards)
1. Peter Kotland 34:30
2. Wes Littlejohn 34:33
3. Phillips Simons 35:53
4. Carey Ketner 36:16
5. Matthew Meyer 36:34
6. Albert Hull 36:42
7. Jim Baker 37:18
8. Derren Burrell 37:36
9. Jason Annan 37:44
10. Eliot Cannon 37:47

Female 18-21 (125 finishers, 7 awards)
1. Gabrielle Lambert 40:31
2. Elizabeth Shea 44:07
3. Jennifer Bollerman 44:12
4. Rachelle Boxer 45:01
5. Leslie Tomlinson 47:26
6. Karen Carr 48:04
7. Kelly Camp 48:13

Male 22-25 (400 finishers, 20 awards)
1. Luis Molina 31:46
2. Michael Colaiacovo 33:00
3. Gerrit Riemer 33:42
4. John Raguin 34:27
5. Jeffrey Starke 34:41
6. Michael Green 35:27
7. Hunter Spotts 36:51
8. Jefferson Roberts 38:00
9. Paul Horner 38:07
10. Zaid Shubailat 38:15
11. Emmett Johnson 38:47
12. Clark Green 39:02
13. Brian Kistner 39:06
14. Richard Ried 39:20
15. Steven Cole 39:21
16. Jonathan Cook 39:46
17. Todd Sansbury 39:47
18. Gordon Sherard 40:18
19. Vincent Crum 40:23
20. Timothy McAuliffe 40:30

Female 22-25 (302 finishers, 15 awards)
1. Tamara Karliukova 35:45
2. Dodie Kocsis 36:37
3. Barbara Kannewurf 38:16
4. Virella 42:07
5. Heather Sutton 42:17
6. Wilma Depiore 42:30
7. Cindy Phillips 42:47
8. Kathy Stevens 43:40
9. J MaClure 43:50
10. Denise La Rocca 44:14
11. Christy VanValkenburg 44:47
12. Marcie Mott 46:08
13. Jamie Oxendine 46:25
14. Kimberly Tambini 46:43
15. Christy Tomlinson 46:52

Male 26-29 (547 finishers, 25 awards)
1. John Erickson 32:10
2. Frank Daniels 32:49
3. Andrew Ball 33:05
4. Cail Brown 34:46
5. Michael Walker 35:22
6. Robert Daley 36:00
7. John McCray 36:08
8. Kirkland Davis 36:14
9. Robyn Roberts 36:16
10. Michael Craig 36:22
11. Paul Reardon 36:26
12. William Mount 36:43
13. Jeffrey Dodrill 36:47
14. Jimmy Tassios 36:52
15. Alan Brown 37:33
16. Francisco Hamm 37:51
17. Joe Myers 37:53
18. David Simas 38:16
19. Ben Farley 38:22
20. Matthew Scheer 38:40
21. Brian Shelton 38:54
22. Richard Crawford 39:01
23. Brent Shirley 39:13
24. Damon Brown 39:14
25. William Bottoms 39:15

Female 26-29 (364 finishers, 19 finishers)
1. Amy Kattwinkel 35:54
2. Ute Jamrozy 36:14
3. Julie Jiskra 36:21
4. Larisa Witosmkin 38:19
5. Gina Latham 39:24
6. Katherine Konig 40:14
7. Kristen Moe 40:52
8. Nancy Dye 41:01
9. Laurie Sperry 42:16
10. Lori Nesbitt 42:41
11. Mechele Burns 43:01
12. Janet Norton 43:15
13. Amy Lee 44:10
14. Denise Lockett 44:18
15. Lynne Davis 45:06
16. Valerie Cavenaugh 45:31
17. Susan Roof 45:42
18. Cheri Gillilan 46:12
19. Eileen Bridges 46:26

Male 30-34 (864 finishers, 25 awards)
1. Larry Brock 31:00
2. Alexander Beljaev 31:45
3. Kaspar Solleberger 32:42
4. Ron Deramus 33:16
5. Thomas McCarthy 33:23
6. Tom Mahon 33:43
7. Michael Klatt 34:14
8. Alan Gebert 34:23
9. Huey Inman 34:56
10. James Carroll 35:02
11. Paul Davis 35:27
12. Mark Thomas 35:29
13. Stephen Shonts 35:31
14. Doug Harrell 35:48
15. Sam Inman 36:11
16. Layton Gwinn 36:17
17. Kenny Hines 36:17
18. Paul Schmid 36:24
19. John Varallo 36:29
20. David Addison 36:23
21. Bobby Aswell 36:33
22. John Holbrook 37:03
23. David Jessey 37:07
24. Peter Klatt 37:13
25. Jeffrey Swartz 37:28

Female 30-34 (460 finishers, 23 awards)
1. Clarice Marana 37:42
2. Betsy Veronee 37:53
3. Kay Weems 39:15
4. Patt Loggins 39:22
5. Janice Cole 39:29
6. Rachel Allen 39:32
7. Megan Othersen (Gorman) 39:54
8. Susi Foster 40:07
9. Karen McGee 41:21
10. Patricia Clark 41:29
11. Carolyn Harrell 41:42
12. Connie Grimes 41:45
13. Lori Hamilton 41:50
14. Mari Barrett 42:08
15. Beth Dixon 42:28
16. Tommy Ricks 42:49
17. Shelly McKee 42:53

18 Susan Hoffman	43:30	
19 Deborah Chaney	43:39	
20 Julia Smith	43:52	
21 Weezi Small	44:00	
22 Lisa Bowers	44:16	
23 Sheri Adams	44:41	

Male 35-39 (900 finishers, 25 awards)
1. Mark Friedrich — 32:40
2. Craig Virgin — 33:07
3. Tony Bateman — 33:10
4. Richard Ferguson — 33:13
5. Robert Lowery — 33:47
6. Steve Caskie — 33:52
7. Dave Kannewurf — 34:05
8. Mike Hart — 34:07
9. Jim Brewer — 35:26
10. Harry Ash — 35:39
11. Don Burckhardt — 35:42
12. David Bourgeous — 35:44
13. Kevin Nelson — 35:51
14. Andrew Ammon — 36:02
15. Bill Cavedo — 36:23
16. Lennie Moore — 36:35
17. Bobby Torri — 36:35
18. Glen Chamberlain — 36:54
19. Spider Gardner — 36:55
20. Paul Bullington — 36:57
21. Joe Panjada — 37:01
22. Glenn Lucas — 37:15
23. Harold Fallis — 37:19
24. Steve Staley — 37:21
25. Mike Chodnicki — 37:23

Female 35-39 (368 finishers, 19 awards)
1. Bonnie Poore Long — 41:09
2. Jean Kolbaba — 41:48
3. Tami Dennis — 44:09
4. Lisa Goodrich — 45:16
5. Nitsa Calas — 45:28
6. Sara Dorociak — 45:40
7. Melody Sliker — 46:03
8. Maria Griffith — 46:04
9. Lorraine Crosland — 46:13
10. Nina Zoe Parks — 46:42
11. Rick Widman — 46:48
12. Molly Noble — 47:14
13. Holly Konrady — 47:28
14. Nancy Sanders — 47:29
15. Kim Brattain — 47:58
16. Janet Judy — 48:00
17. Ann Arms — 48:24
18. Linda Davidson — 48:44
19. Marlene Barr — 48:55

Male 40-44 (703 finishers, 25 awards)
1. Jerry Clark — 33:28
2. Joseph Denneny — 34:39
3. Timothy McMullen — 34:43
4. Michael Amico — 34:44
5. Danny West — 35:42
6. Glenn Dennis — 35:45
7. Larry D'Ippolito — 35:49
8. David Mauterer — 36:02
9. Robert Rodriguez — 36:15
10. Joe Marshall — 36:23
11. Oliver Marshall — 36:34
12. Tommy Seymore — 36:39
13. David Freeze — 36:53
14. Charles Kellner — 36:58
15. Richard Benjamin — 37:09
16. Dan Clapper — 37:11
17. Thomas Roney — 37:19
18. Jack Todd — 37:35
19. Larry Milner — 37:49
20. Leon Locklear — 37:59
21. Fred Tecklenburg — 38:10
22. Chip Higginbotham — 38:16
23. Gary Joye — 38:26
24. Glenn Tacy — 38:34
25. Larry Berglind — 38:36

Female 40-44 (273 finishers, 14 awards)
1. Alendia Vestal — 38:51
2. Nonie Hudnall — 41:10
3. Donna Trask — 42:05
4. Mary Millar — 42:33
5. Libby Shipp — 43:02
6. Patricia Tavares — 43:14
7. Ginger Gregory — 43:19
8. Cynthia Reiser — 43:27
9. Bobbi Hackman — 43:34
10. Debbie Howard — 44:09
11. Janice Gannon — 44:10
12. Suzy Lorentz — 44:23
13. Lessie Snead — 44:44
14. Cathy Burton — 45:16

Male 45-49 (578 finishers, 25 awards)
1. Wayne Yarbrough — 35:34
2. Scott Taylor — 35:55
3. Steve Messier — 35:58
4. Mike Julian — 36:11
5. John Bernhardt — 36:20
6. Bill Peay — 36:32
7. Fred Reinhard — 36:45
8. Paul Brown — 36:50
9. Reed Watson — 37:16
10. Wallie Jones — 37:39
11. Chuck Greer — 37:47
12. Earl Jackson — 37:54
13. Charles Stoyle — 38:13
14. Herbert Taskett — 38:16
15. Thomas Jones — 38:45
16. David Ott — 38:46
17. Russell Brown — 38:58
18. Cedric Jaggers — 38:58
19. Bill Chasey — 39:00
20. Arthur Smith — 39:02
21. Jerome Durkin — 39:11
22. John Miller — 39:19
23. Dewey Sloan — 39:38
24. Phillip Dickert — 39:40
25. Dean Davis — 39:43

Female 45-49 (163 finishers, 10 awards)
1. Barbara Filutze — 37:16
2. Anne Yarbrough — 40:09
3. Barbara Ebers — 43:17
4. Peggy Schug — 44:26
5. Anne Boone — 44:39
6. Judy Mays — 45:23
7. Andrea Berendt — 45:37
8. Susan Houlton — 45:54
9. Karen Martin — 45:58
10. Kathy Jaggers — 46:32

Male 50-54 (324 finishers, 17 awards)
1. Gene Cassell — 37:05
2. Jim Adams — 37:23
3. Allan Gardner — 38:31
4. Bill Seigler — 38:42
5. Keith Ambrose — 39:08
6. Wallace Carr — 39:18
7. Dean Godwin — 39:54
8. T J Voss — 40:10
9. Paul Uricchio — 40:34
10. Bill Vetsch — 41:01
11. Fred Wood — 42:02
12. Tom Siegle — 42:47
13. David Moorhead — 43:23
14. Fred Robinson — 43:41
15. Will Hearn — 43:49
16. Kent Smith — 43:49
17. Sam Harrelson — 44:05

Female 50-54 (72 finishers, 4 awards)
1. Pauline Niilend — 48:52
2. Martie Ulmer — 51:07
3. Sallie Sinkler — 52:17
4. Mary Thompson — 52:36

Male 55-59 (133 finishers, 7 awards)
1. Ed Ledford — 39:26
2. Theron Cochran — 41:25
3. Bill Kehoe — 41:43
4. Keith Weaver — 41:46
5. Bob Cunningham — 41:53
6. Karl Andres — 42:04
7. Ron Findley — 42:51

Female 55-59 (38 finishers, 3 awards)
1. Pat Rhode — 48:58
2. Sally McKinney — 50:40
3. Suzanne Foster — 53:49

Male 60-64 (73 finishers, 4 awards)
1. Charles Rose — 36:34
2. Duncan Weeks — 42:07
3. Lee Swofford — 44:04
4. Phil Szczepanski — 44:28

Female 60-64 (10 finishers, 3 awards)
1. Garthedon Embler — 56:54
2. Nancy Bell — 58:53
3. Eileen Hallman — 1:03:11

Male 65-69 (28 finishers, 3 awards)
1. Herman Van Slooten — 46:57
2. Franklin Mason — 47:55
3. Ed Peters — 48:30

Female 65-69 (1 finishers, 3 awards)
1. Lucy Jones — 1:19:27

Male 70 up (11 finishers, 3 awards)
1. David Mellard — 47:11
2. John Cuturillo — 53:08
3. Leroy Stone — 56:06

Female 70 up (2 finishers, 2 awards)
1. Lynn Edwards — 58:10
2. Margaret Wright — 1:10:07

Compiled by Cedric Jaggers from complete results provided by Burns Computer Services immediately after the race on March 26, 1994.

Runners fill all three lanes of the Pearman Bridge. Post and Courier photo by Brad Nettles

Chapter 18

1995

Back On The 'New' Pearman Bridge; First Time Over 10,000 Finishers

The 18th Cooper River Bridge Run on April 1, 1995, marked the first course change since the 1987 return to the 1985 course. The new course was USATF certified #SC94030BS and returned to the "new" Silas Pearman Bridge, which was last used as part of the race course in 1979.

There was much pre-race speculation that the new course would prove to be faster because the "new" bridge is not as steep. After the race, consensus was that it was faster. The new course began in Mount Pleasant on Coleman Boulevard near Live Oak Street, proceeded across the Pearman Bridge and the Crosstown Overpass, turned left onto Coming, left onto Line then turned right onto King Street to follow the previous course across Market and up Meeting Street, finishing beside Marion Square in front of the Federal Building.

The 18th running was the largest Bridge Run to date with 12,406 entrants and 10,290 official finishers. All finishers' names and times were listed in the next day's Post and Courier, a first for the race. There were 6,841 males listed (66.5 percent) and 3,449 females (33.5 percent). For the second year in a row, it was the largest number and highest percentage of female finishers in race history. It was also the first time over 3,000 females ever completed a race in the Carolinas. In addition to the run, there was an accompanying untimed fun walk which attracted over 9,000 participants.

Despite weather forecasts predicting a 70 percent or higher chance of rain, skies were sunny and the temperature was 59 degrees and climbing when the race began. There was a slight crosswind, which was hardly noticeable on the wider bridge.

The race's start was delayed by about 5 minutes as hundreds of runners scrambled from the overloaded shuttle buses — the increased size of the field put unexpected demands on the transportation system — and rushed to get behind the starting line. For the first time, a voice command was used to start the race to prevent the problem caused by the cannon at the '94 race.

Once again Kenyans dominated. Before the race most people were saying that since the "new" Silas Pearman Bridge was not as steep as the "old" Grace Memorial Bridge that the course record 28:24 would probably be broken. They were right. Almost from the word go, a pack of Kenyans and one American (Travis Walter of Cary, N.C., who would finish as first American in seventh place overall), ran together all the way to the bridge. They went through the first mile in 4:29, hit 2 miles in 9:02 and 3 miles in 13:47. Joseph Kimani took control of the race by running 4:16 from mile marker 3 to 4. He passed 5 miles in 22:27 and got to the 6-mile mark in 26:52. He never let the lead go as he ran to a new course record 27:49 (4:29 pace). He became the first runner to break the 28-minute barrier in any Bridge Run. He led three other Kenyans, Francis Mbui, 28:13, Simon Chemoiywo, 28:21, and Ondoro Osoro, 28:23, under the old course record. Defending champion Simon Karori finished fifth in 28:41.

"I was confident because I've been training at high altitude in Kenya. Here it is low and I can run very fast," Kimani told the *Post and Courier*.

The top three women ran together, exchanging the lead until the last mile when Laura LaMena-Coll of Eugene, Ore., pulled away to win in 33:58. Cindi Girard of Red Bank, N.J., was second in 34:11 and defending champion Elaine Van Blunk of Drexel Hill, Pa., was third in 34:35. The first time to run the Bridge Run was charmed for LaMena-Coll, who told the newspaper, "I thought it was a good race. The bridge was long, but not as bad or as steep as I expected. It was a good experience for me." She had not seen the bridge until race day and said, "I thought maybe it was one of those little overpasses or something; I had no idea. I couldn't believe it when I saw it this morning. I was thinking it was not that long, but it definitely seemed longer running it than when we drove over it."

Second place finisher Gerard said, "Laura went past me and then we really started picking it up, but neither one of us had run this race before, and we weren't sure where the finish line was. I think she won because she was the stronger runner, and this is definitely a course for strong runners more than fast runners."

Wilson Waigwa, a Kenyan residing in El Paso, Texas, moved up from two consecutive second place Masters finishers to win the Masters title in 30:33. Former 5,000 meter world record holder David Moorcraft of England was second in 30:58 and Doug Kurtis of Northville, Mich., was third in 31:48. The female Masters title went to Irina Bondarchouck of Russia in a Masters female course record 35:13 followed by Rebecca Stockdale-Wooley of Chaplin, Conn., in 36:25 and Joanne Scianna of Savgus, Mich., in 36:42.

The Dr. Marcus Newberry Award for first area finisher again went to Tom Mather of Mount Pleasant, who finished 22nd overall in 31:14. Lynn MacDougall, also of Mount Pleasant, took the female division in 37:59 by finishing as 16th female and 197th overall. The Dewey Wise Trophy was won by Thomas King, 75, of Tucker, Ga., who crossed the finish line in 45:54.

The Sunday *Post and Courier* had a front page photo of runners coming down the three lanes of the Pearman Bridge with the headline "Thousands 'Get Over It'" the race motto printed on the T-shirt for 1995. The sports section had another color photo showing the eventual winner going up the bridge with the headline "Hill-humbling Kenyan" and 'Kimani rules Bridge Run in record 27:49." Inside the sports section, the paper listed the top 10 males and females, top five Masters males and females and up to 10 deep in each age division. For the first time all the official finishers' names and times were listed separately in the Sunday edition of the *Post and Courier:* 6,841 male and 3,449 female.

For the fifth year in a row, Channel 24 TV showed a one hour tape delay of the race. One runner broke the 28-minute barrier, with a total of five runners under 29 and a total of 12 runners under the 30-minute barrier. This compares to four runners breaking the 30-minute barrier in each of the previous two Bridge Runs. A total of 379 runners, 26 of them female, broke the 40-minute barrier. The 50-minute barrier was broken by a still standing record 2,692 runners. The 60-minute barrier was broken by 6,736 runners. The untimed Bridge Walk attracted an estimated 9,000 participants.

Race director for the second year in a row was Julian Smith. The race entry fee remained at $14 early, $20 late; the walk entry fee was $9 early, $12 late. In 1995, complete results were mailed to all finishers as a part of an issue of Carolina Action Sports magazine instead of in a separate results booklet.

Other Voices
Tell Me About Your Bridge Run (1995)
By Cedric Jaggers, Originally appeared in the May-July 1995 issue of the Low Country Runner

After my wife, Kathy, finished the race I rushed to the car to get my clipboard and she went to get some fruit. It was hours before I saw her again. The crowd, with 10,290 runners and 9,000 walkers, assorted vendors and spectators, was so huge in Marion Square that it was hard to find anybody. I feel like I missed a lot of club members, but if I saw you and you said you were a CRC member, you were asked the infamous "Tell me about your Bridge Run". I tried to write down exactly what you said. If we missed each other this year, look for me next year as always with a Running Journal T-shirt on and a clipboard in hand. People are listed in the order we bumped into each other. The places and times listed in parenthesis are those shown in the uncorrected race day results printed by Burns Computer immediately after the race.

Benita Schlau: Well it was a great race. It was my first time to run the race in 5 years and I ran my slowest Bridge Run ever, 42:24. But I had a great time. The only thing that bothered me was all the kids passing me and saying "Way to go Mrs. Schlau." (704th, 42:25)

Art Liberman: How about if I say I was in great shape and ran the race of my life? ... April Fool.(1,079th, 44:13)

Tom Dority: Great start, no problem, hit the bridge no problem. At the 4 mile mark I started getting tired and just gutted it out to the finish line. 45:02. (1,291st, 45:15)

Barbara Matheney: I actually had to walk a minute up the first span. My slowest and fattest. I'm 10 pounds heavier. 57:25. (5,637th, 57:26)

Eileen Stellefson: Put down what I said last year. No? It was great ..(can't read my writing, CJ) I just recovered from an injury. I love the new course. 44:49. (1,198th, 44:50)

Gary Ricker: Well, I was faster than last year which always pleases me. Leon

At the start on Coleman Boulevard. Post and Courier photo by Roger Cureton

Locklear is like a lighthouse. I saw him ahead of me and I knew if I followed that beam I'd have a good time. And I did and I did. 38:13. (223rd, 38:15)

Jeff Gruver: Sixteen in a row! About 3 minutes faster than last year unofficially. I didn't start my watch till I crossed the start line. I had dry heaves at the 3 mile mark. I like that new route. Probably ran 50:20 or something like that. (2,847th, 50:27)

Fred Reinhard: First mile in 5:16 right behind Steve Caskie and Marshall Randall. I managed to pick off Marshall but not Steve. I felt if I stayed with the two of them I might have a chance of winning the Grand Masters. Once on Meeting Street I saw Steve and started my final sprint and ran 35:02. I thought I'd won the age group and found out some guy from Savannah had run 34:57. The best 10k I've ever run in my life, a true PR at age 50. (75th, 35:15)

Sara Dorociak: Jeff (her husband) and I ran together. We took it easy, jogged through and talked. I like the new course. We ran about 46:10. (1,921st, 47:36)

Jeff Dorociak: I'm on call. I ran over from St. Francis Hospital and ran with Sara and had fun. I had my beeper in my pocket. I hate to say it, I had more fun than any year. 46:10. (unable to find in results)

Margaret Wright: It was okay. I ran the whole way, I didn't walk. 1:13. I felt good. It seemed like there were a lot more people. I couldn't move. The walkers got in the way and I had to keep going around them. (9,790th, 1:13:12)

Bernie Clark: A minute slower, a minute older and no speedwork. I drove 800 miles from New Orleans to get here and have to drive 800 miles back. It was a wonderful day. 44:36. (1,153rd, 44:38)

Kathy Jaggers: I don't wanta. I haven't even thought about what I was going to tell you. Go ask somebody else. Number 16 for me. About 2 seconds per pound per mile slower. Really, I had fun. I didn't push hard down King and Meeting because I knew if I did I'd have an asthma attack and end up in the EMS tent again. I felt like I could have run a minute faster; 46:50. (1,663rd, 46:40)

Larry D'Ippolito: I think I did okay. I ran a marathon two weeks ago. I can

handle the speed, but not the distance. 36:29. (127th, 36:29)

Jan Derrick: I had the best time - it was just great! I thoroughly enjoyed it. I had a smile on my face the whole way. 44:45. (1,613th, 46:29)

Gary Butts: My first one in eight years, it was super. Started out slow in the middle of the pack. Enjoyed it. Probably the slowest I've run the Bridge Run but I don't care. It's just great to be back. 48:26. (2,191st, 48:30)

Wendy Peiffer: What do I say? I ran a little faster, but there were more people where I was so it seemed slower. I beat last year by 2:40. 59:23 watch time. (unable to find in results)

Hunter Spotts: It was a P.W. (Personal Worst) for the bridge 40:14. I'm out of shape but I had a great time. I saw you for about half of it, then you pulled away. The Bridge Run was a very spiritual experience. (408th, 40:16)

Keith Ambrose: I probably beat you today but I ran terrible. I blew up after two and a half miles and ran about 39:12. Howie Schomer owes me free entry because I bet him that the Kenyans would break the record by 30 seconds on this new course. (295th, 39:12)

Leon Locklear: I love that course. There's something about the Bridge Run that makes me run on memory or something. I ran about a minute faster than I've been running 10ks. The bridge mystique; lots of inspiration out there, including you. 38:24. (238th, 38:28)

Lennie Moore: About 50 seconds off last year but I'm happy anyway. My training was going okay until about a month ago. 37:22. (161st, 37:23)

Irving Rosenfeld: 48:44. This is an easier Bridge Run than the other way. Except for one year, it's my best since 1988. The weather was a little too warm. I expected cool and rainy, got sunny and hot. The second span isn't as hard. I had a good time. (2,263rd, 48:44)

Dan Clapper: It was great. I finally did it - I broke 36! April Fools! I broke 39 - 38:46. I can live with that. I'm still under my age. (264th, 38:46)

Bunny Owen: I think my time was 57:30. Three weeks ago I twisted my ankle and I was on crutches, so I did okay. (unable to find in results)

Mike Johns: I think my time was 39:50. After a couple of injuries this year and recovery, I've got to work harder. (374th, 39:57)

Mike Hart: I've had better and I've had worse. It wasn't all that much easier. 34:55. (67th, 34:55)

Huey Inman: My best one ever. I can't complain. I love the new bridge; there's no comparison with the old one. 34:21. (60th, 34:23)

Tom Mahon: I did a lot better than I expected: hoping to break 34 and ran

33:43 give or take a little. (47th, 33:44)

Ron Deramus: Tickled to death with it. Out of shape due to a stress fracture earlier this year, I tried to keep up with Tom Mahon. I passed him, he started to come back and passed me on the first span, I passed him, we duked it out - he still got me in the last 50 yards. 33:44 (48th, 33:45)

Tommy Mullins: The easiest race I ever ran. I had a PR. I'm looking forward to next year 47:48. It's a new course so it's a course PR. (1,989th, 47:48)

Don Austell: So glad to be coming back. I ran 8 minutes faster than last year 47:49. (1,981st, 47:46)

Maria Griffith: 45:03. I wanted to be under 45 but I'm satisfied. (1,293rd 45:15)

Therese Killeen: Oh puh-leeze! I enjoyed it, the less intense hills definitely made a pleasant experience. I had a good time. 42:52 (784th, 42:54)

Tom Mather: It was pretty good. My second fastest. Not as fast as last year, but I ran well, 31:10. I don't know if it placed me in the top 20 or not. (22nd, 31:14)

Steve Caskie: It was a minute slower than last year and that was depressing since the course was easier. But doing the Iron Man took it out of me. 35:05 (76th, 35:11)

Sherri Adams: My best time thanks to my coach Benita Schlau. The first hill was a... UGH! It kicked my butt. 6:15 first mile, then I hit the hill and it was all downhill after that. 42:59. (819th, 43:04)

Pat Rhode: You're going to have to put down exactly what I say. I'm just praising God for the weather so all the really good runners could do well. 48:59 or 49:00. (2,339th, 48:57)

Phillip Cook: It was a lot easier course this year, but I wasn't in shape. 39:58. I lost you on those downhills. It is a good course, I like it. It's a lot faster than the old one. (382nd, 40:01)

Marc Judson: Don't publish my time, okay. Go ahead. I did about 38:07. I'm a little disappointed, but I'm glad I finished. I'm the medical director of lung transplantation at MUSC. We did eight transplants last year and four of them did the bridge walk today. That was more exciting for me than any race I've done. (221st, 38:14)

Nina Parks (Taylor): It was fun and I'll be back next year. I did enjoy being on the new bridge, but I still don't think it was any easier. 45:20. (1,312th, 45:21)

Bob Walton: I got across, that's the main thing. 46:43. (1,679th, 46:44)

Whit Bailey: I just barely finished. I wasn't pleased with my time. I was very tired - my worst 10k, 79 minutes. (10,177th, 1:22:00)

Tami Dennis: Um, I'm very pleased. I had a great run for not racing. I couldn't have done it without my baby brother. 41:48. (624th, 41:52)

Ray Dennis: I like the new bridge. If they can just figure out how to cut out the first hill I'd like it even more. 54:59. (4,919th, 55:35)

Cedric Jaggers: I had a terrible run. I felt bad the whole way. I think it's my slowest Bridge Run since the last time we used the new bridge back in '79. It seemed like I was moving backwards down King Street, especially when the guys in T-shirts started passing me. I kept chanting, "There's only a mile to go." I wouldn't have broken 40 on the old course. 39:31 and glad to get it. (333rd, 39:36)

1995 Awards

Prize money winners:

Overall Male

1	Joseph Kimani	Kenya	27:49	$3,000
2	Francis Mbui	Kenya	28:13	$1,500
3	Simon Chemoiywo	Kenya	28:21	$1,000
4	Ondoro Osoro	Kenya	28:23	$800
5	Simon Karori	Kenya	28:41	$600
6	Joseph Kamau	Kenya	29:02	$500
7	Travis Walter	Cary NC	29:16	$400
8	Cormac Finnerty	Atlanta GA.	29:28	$300
9	Simon Peter	Tanzania	29:35	$250
10	Eddy Hellebuyck	Albuquerque, NM	29:43	$150

Overall Female

1	Laura LaMena-Coll	Eugene,OR	33:58	$3,000
2	Cindi Girard	Red Bank NJ	34:11	$1,500
3	Elaine Van Blunk	Drexel PA.	34:35	$1,000
4	Tamara Karliukova	Russia	34:36	$800
5	Mary Alico	Orlando FL.	34:54	$600
6	Irina Bondarchouk	Russia.	35:13	$500
7	Karen Hoffman	Stone Mtn GA	35:49	$400
8	R Stockdale-Wooley	Chaplin CT	36:25	$300
9	Dee Goodwin	Cohulla, GA	36:33	$250
10	Joanna Scianna	Savgus, MA	36:42	$150

Masters Division Male

1	Wilson Waigwa	Kenya	30:33	$1,500
2	Dave Moorcroft	England	30:58	$1,000
3	Doug Kurtis	Northville, MI	31:48	$750
4	Charles McMullen	Rochester NY	31:59	$500
5	Pete Metzmaker	Whitefish MT	32:05	$250

Masters Division Female

1	Irina Bondarchouk	Russia.	35:13	$1,500
2	R Stockdale-Wooley	Chaplin CT	36:25	$1,000
3	Joanne Scianna	Savgus, MI.	36:42	$750
4	Nancy Grayson	Northville, MI	36:58	$500
5	Susan Segraves	Greer, SC	37:29	$250

Special Awards:

Dr. Marcus Newberry Award
For first Tri-County Charleston Area finisher

Male

Tom Mather .... Mt Pleasant, SC .... 31:14 .... $500

Female

Lynn MacDougall ..... Mt Pleasant, SC ...... 37:59 .... $500

Dewey Wise Trophy for oldest finisher with a time less than his or her age in minutes:

Thomas King, 75 .... Tucker, GA 45:54

Age Group Awards

(presented to top 3 in age group, top 5% up to maximum of 25 awarded in each age group):

Male 12 & under (111 finishers, 6 awards)

1 Brantlee Milner ... 39:30
2 Kevin Timp ... 41:28
3 Ryan Hulland ... 42:15
4 Ben Sherard ... 43:50
5 Steven Ubrik ... 45:22
6 David Southwick ... 46:36

Female 12 & under (37 finishers, 3 awards)

1 Michelle Milner ... 47:26
2 Lauren James ... 50:13
3 Meghan Gunderman ... 51:05

Male 13-17 (224 finishers, 12 awards)

1 Timothy Gaultreaux ... 33:58
2 Brian DeRoberts ... 36:33
3 Stuart Harrison ... 37:41
4 Chris Hornung ... 37:47
5 Joshua Wilson ... 37:50
6 Joey Jutzeler ... 38:01
7 James Wiley ... 38:25
8 Jeremiah Milliman ... 38:40
9 Robert Temple ... 38:57
10 Hamp Hennemore ... 39:06
11 Del Shaffer ... 39:17
12 Ricky Ward ... 39:50

Female 13-17 (107 finishers, 6 awards)

1 Kathryn Weber ... 44:08
2 Kelly Gordon ... 44:57
3 Rachel Decker ... 46:18
4 Melissa Lauffer ... 47:41
5 Jennifer Craig ... 48:15
6 Lara Caulder ... 49:26

Males 18-21 (243 finishers, 13 awards)

1 Albert Hull ... 35:24
2 Eliot Cannon ... 36:11
3 Stephen Saleeby ... 36:37
4 David Low ... 36:59
5 Jason Annan ... 37:20
6 Jef Titone ... 37:23
7 Jay Glover ... 37:36
8 Jason Turner ... 37:52
9 Jonathan Gee ... 38:00
10 Guy Berry ... 38:00
11 Kevin Croxton ... 38:06
12 John Tramel ... 38:21
13 Doug Tozzi ... 39:00

Female 18-21 (162 finishers, 8 awards)

1 Susan McLaughlin ... 41:36
2 Elizabeth Shea ... 42:31
3 Caroline Obosky ... 44:40
4 Jennifer Bollerman ... 44:55
5 Emily Walters ... 46:30
6 Marie Earle ... 47:18
7 Caraline Young ... 47:22
8 Ronna Zoucha ... 47:30

Males 22-25 (570 finishers, 25 awards)

1 Chad Newton ... 30:16
2 Mark Andrews ... 30:26
3 Jeff Campbell ... 30:36
4 Jamie Barnes ... 31:12
5 Mike Colaiacovo ... 32:31
6 Scott Drum ... 32:58
7 Guy McCrea ... 33:16
8 David Nelson ... 33:34
9 Peter Kotland ... 33:34
10 Wesley Littlejohn ... 33:37
11 Mike Monagle ... 34:12
12 Ole Heggheim ... 35:20
13 Rowdy Smith ... 35:32
14 Jonathan Morgan ... 36:10
15 Emery Lloyd ... 36:17
16 Jim Baker ... 36:31
17 Joshua Henderson ... 37:40
18 Paul Horner ... 38:10
19 Leslie Moore ... 38:44
20 Derek Kidd ... 38:47
21 Byron Pateras ... 39:04
22 Hal Crosswell ... 39:05
23 Richard Reid ... 39:21
24 Paul Wright ... 39:26
25 David Little ... 39:29

Female 22-25 (452 finishers, 23 awards)

1 Julie Seymour ... 37:21
2 Kathleen Gobbett ... 40:19
3 Tracy Center ... 40:22
4 Kimberly Haluski ... 41:27
5 Sara Virella ... 42:23
6 Kari Squillo (Staley) ... 42:38
7 Carol Barnett ... 43:01
8 Julie Oliver ... 43:35
9 Katie Aman ... 44:31
10 Christy VanValkenburgh ... 45:04
11 Marlee Crosland ... 45:13
12 Cara Balch ... 45:21
13 Dixie Baker ... 45:27
14 Diane Allen ... 45:32
15 Carey White ... 46:06
16 Meredith Swittenberg ... 46:10
17 Holly McKinney ... 46:26
18 Heather Tarpley ... 46:32
19 Gina Mauro ... 46:40
20 Monica Steffes ... 46:42
21 Kim Huffman ... 47:14
22 Brooks McAlister ... 47:22
23 Forrest Curran ... 47:43

Males 26-29 (759 finishers, 25 awards)

1 Dan Hostager ... 29:56
2 Randy Ashley ... 31:13
3 Todd Wells ... 31:22
4 David Brendle ... 32:10
5 Michael Bowers ... 33:05
6 Chris Carroll ... 33:06
7 Chris Legourd ... 33:08
8 Cail Brown ... 33:50
9 David Price ... 34:01
10 Dujuan Harbin ... 34:17
11 Brian Walter ... 34:28
12 Keith Hurley ... 34:55
13 Jay Hute ... 35:30
14 Tony Hawkes ... 35:39
15 David Gile ... 35:45
16 Steve Haire ... 35:54
17 Robert Daley ... 35:57
18 Brian Laprise ... 36:08
19 Karl Debate ... 36:12
20 Douglas Rickey ... 36:22
21 Greg Giddes ... 36:27
22 Jerry Rothschild ... 36:27
23 Paul Reardon ... 36:28
24 Eric Macklin ... 36:39
25 Buster McCoy ... 36:47

Females 26-29 (565 finishers, 25 awards)

1 Bonnie Dansky ... 40:51
2 Denise Lockett ... 41:33
3 Kristin Smith ... 41:56
4 Mary LaFrance ... 42:30
5 Katherine Jenrette ... 43:21
6 Nicole Marcelli ... 43:22
7 Kelley O'Donnell ... 43:23
8 Jane Ganey ... 43:33
9 Anne Mitchell ... 43:47
10 Andre Way ... 43:50
11 Marcie Mott ... 44:16
12 Elizabeth Holland ... 44:21
13 Susan Madlinger ... 44:25
14 Cindy Ostle ... 44:41
15 Cameron Sharbel ... 45:28
16 Laura Havrilesky ... 45:30
17 Debbie Wiklow ... 46:04
18 Joann Bradford ... 46:15
19 Constance Woods ... 46:19
20 Maury Bowen ... 46:24
21 Betsy McCutcheon ... 46:50
22 Suzanne Boyer ... 46:57
23 Rae Duke ... 47:04
24 Belinda Bernard ... 47:16
25 Brooks Fortson ... 47:19

Males 30-34 (1,189 finishers, 25 awards)

1 Paul Mbungua ... 29:49
2 Mark Smith ... 30:54
3 Paul Marmaro ... 31:07
4 Larry Brock ... 31:18
5 Scott Walschlager ... 31:49
6 Rob Wilder ... 31:55
7 Daniel French ... 33:02
8 Ron Deramus ... 33:45
9 Jim Bitsko ... 34:03
10 Huey Inman ... 34:23
11 John Varallo ... 34:35
12 Jack Murphy ... 34:38
13 Ned McDevitt ... 35:18
14 Thomas Poody ... 35:18
15 Charles McKeel ... 35:29
16 Mark Teseniar ... 35:35
17 Fred Gillen ... 35:36
18 Kevin Nelson ... 35:42
19 Sam Inman ... 35:53
20 Steven Mendelson ... 36:00
21 Lance Leopold ... 36:10
22 Blake Zemp ... 36:14
23 Steve Holt ... 36:17
24 Alan Gebert ... 36:19
25 Phil Ponder ... 36:22

Females 30-34 (685 finishers, 25 awards)

1 Sandy Bustamante ... 37:03
2 Lynn MacDougall ... 37:59
3 Jean Strait ... 38:29
4 Betsy Veronee ... 38:31
5 Anet Cooper ... 38:56
6 Patt Loggins ... 39:13

7	Lisa Roeber	40:14
8	Gina Latham	40:16
9	Megan Othersen (Gorman)	40:20
10	Kay Weems	40:34
11	Katherine Konig	40:49
12	Karen McGee	41:27
13	Julia Smith	41:36
14	Marcela Perkinson	41:40
15	Susan Gallas	41:55
16	Weezie Griffen	42:16
17	Laurie Sperry	42:34
18	Deborah Chaney	42:43
19	Elizabeth Carroll	42:45
20	Elizabeth Graham	42:56
21	Sheri Adams	43:04
22	Tracie Myers	43:05
23	Jan Johnson	43:36
24	Barbara Andrews	43:44
25	Belinda Cantwell	43:48

Males 35-39 (1,102 finishers, 25 awards)

1	Tom Mather	31:14
2	Mark Friedrich	32:39
3	Jeff Milliman	33:18
4	Tom Mahon	33:44
5	Tony Bateman	33:52
6	Robert Lowery	34:18
7	Danny White	34:29
8	George Howe	34:29
9	Mike Hart	34:55
10	Stephen Shonts	35:03
11	Gordon Smith	35:21
12	Harry Ash	35:22
13	James O'Brien	35:27
14	Todd Hamilton	35:44
15	Marshall Randall	35:52
16	Thomas Kelecy	36:06
18	Robert Anaya	36:21
19	Sam Swofford	36:26
20	David Clark	36:29
21	Glenn Lucas	36:32
22	Jeff Doherty	36:53
23	Mike Chodnicki	37:14
24	Lennie Moore	37:23
25	Michael Armor	37:54

Females 35-39 (565 finishers, 25 awards)

1	Danny Rudisill	39:36
2	Polly Rucker-Johns	39:38
3	Debbie Davis	40:50
4	Ruth Marie Milliman	40:54
5	Patti Patterson	41:10
6	Heather Roop-Garrison	41:35
7	Tami Dennis	41:52
8	Kathy Stewart	41:57
9	Sarah Gambrell	42:59
10	Elizabeth Boineau Lapham	43:16
11	Tammy Hovik	43:20
12	Nancy Farley	43:21
13	Vicki Black	43:28
14	Nancy Thomas	43:33
15	Jennifer Doles	44:07
16	Amy Matthews	44:36
17	David Bourgeois	36:09
17	Eileen Stellefson	44:50
18	Nina Zoe Parks (Taylor)	45:21

19	Sharon Bosch	45:30
20	Sissy Todd	45:38
21	Melody Sliker	45:49
22	Sharon Laudenslager	46:19
23	Lorraine Crosland	46:27
24	Jan Derrick	46:29
25	Ann Arms	46:34

Males 40-44 (986 finishers, 25 awards)

1	Joseph Nzau	32:15
2	David Geer	32:28
3	Terry Permar	32:29
4	Gordon English	32:42
5	Tim McMullen	34:30
6	Steve Caskie	35:11
7	Leon Cook	35:30
8	John Maness	35:30
9	Larry Milner	35:57
10	Steve Staley	36:15
11	Victor Rosado	36:21
12	Larry D'Ippolito	36:29
13	Michael Willoughby	36:47
14	Jack Todd	36:56
15	Bobby Torri	37:01
16	James Pannabecker	37:10
17	Charles Kellner	37:10
18	Del Rose	37:10
19	Michael Gant	37:37
20	John Sperry	37:44
21	Spyder Gardner	37:49
22	Joe Marshall	37:57
23	Marc Hoffman	38:11
24	Marc Judson	38:14
25	Gary Ricker	38:15

Females 40-44 (414 finishers, 21 awards)

1	Victoria Crisp	38:06
2	Alendia Vestal	38:08
3	Kay Harrison	38:18
4	Eileen Telford	41:53
5	Benita Schlau	42:25
6	Therese Killeen	42:54
7	Brenda Anderson	42:56
8	Debbie Judge	43:24
9	Janice Gannon	43:26
10	Sallie Driggers	43:35
11	Cathy Burton	43:53
12	Debbie Howard	44:09
13	Kiki Sweigart	44:20
14	Mary Millar	44:26
15	Nitsa Calas	44:26
16	Maria Griffith	45:15
17	Ginger Gregory	45:20
18	Judy Osborn	45:58
19	Helen Kapp	46:09
20	Susan Poulnot	46:11
21	Michi Pitts	46:14

Males 45-49 (787 finishers, 25 awards)

1	Bob Schlau	32:51
2	Russ Pate	34:43
3	Mike Julian	36:07
4	Tom O'Connor	36:16
5	Oliver Marshall	36:39
6	John Bernhardt	37:09
7	Barry Bishop	37:24
8	Gary Joye	37:28

9	Gary Cadle	37:43
10	Charles Stoyle	37:45
11	Bill Peay	38:05
12	Paul Brown	38:08
13	Wallie Jones	38:13
14	Rick Roy	38:22
15	Tom Jackson	38:44
16	Scott Wilson	38:46
17	David Gelly	38:50
18	John Miller	39:20
19	Sandy Wetherhold	39:28
20	Timothy Cosgrove	39:35
21	Cedric Jaggers	39:36
22	Phillip Dickert	39:38
23	Moses Williams	39:39
24	Guy Herring	39:42
25	Ward McAllister	40:04

Females 45-49 (234 finishers, 12 awards)

1	Barbara Filutze	37:55
2	Anne Yarborough	39:58
3	Barbara Blaszak	40:49
4	Libby Shipp	42:51
5	Patricia Tavares	43:40
6	Nonie Hudnall	43:53
7	Mary Ann Carbott	44:22
8	Peggy Schug	45:17
9	Marsha Mills	46:12
10	Judy Mays	46:23
11	Suzy Lorentz	46:33
12	Janet Musselwhite	46:40

Males 50-54 (467 finishers, 24 awards)

1	Anson Clapcott	34:57
2	Fred Reinhard	35:05
3	Gary Gray	38:02
4	Russell Brown	38:05
5	Richard Mauger	38:08
6	Allan Gardner	38:27
7	Keith Ambrose	39:12
8	Wallace Carr	39:48
9	Johnny Marcus	39:52
10	Robert Schottman	40:03
11	Joe Waters	40:08
12	Walter Waddell	40:08
13	Bill Seigler	40:54
14	Fred Wood	41:27
15	Thomas Siegle	41:40
16	Wendell Barker	41:49
17	Herb Smith	41:51
18	Edward Cassel	42:02
19	Robert Baker	42:27
20	Mick Fulkerson	42:30
21	Mickey Lackey	42:39
22	Will Hearn	42:54
23	Bruce Sprinkle	42:55
24	David Moorhead	43:05

Females 50-54 (122 finishers, 6 awards)

1	Pauline Niilend	45:17
2	Terry Klavohn	51:17
3	Diane Kohrman	51:19
4	Mary Thompson	51:21
5	Sallie Sinkler	51:50
6	Carole Schottman	51:54

Males 55-59 (191 finishers, 10 awards)

1	Rex Reed	36:36
2	Ed Ledford	37:45
3	James Adams	38:05
4	Larry Miller	39:40
5	Dean Godwin	40:27
6	Jim Duguay	41:08
7	Matt Ross	41:48
8	Alvin Walls	41:50
9	Keith Weaver	42:21
10	Roy Lamm	42:32

Females 55-59 (39 finishers, 3 awards)

1	Susie Kluttz	46:43
2	Pat Rhode	48:57
3	Barbara Edwards	53:16

Males 60-64 (105 finishers, 5 awards)

1	Charles Rose	37:15
2	Duncan Weeks	41:38
3	Toby Transou	42:32
4	John Thompson	43:25
5	Phil Szczepanski	44:28

Females 60-64 (14 finishers, 3 awards)

1	Camille Daniel	57:29
2	Barbara Nealey	58:21
3	Norma Phillips	1:01:54

Males 65-69 (25 finishers, 3 awards)

1	Lee Swofford	44:10
2	Edmond Peters	47:25
3	Lonnie Collins	51:33

Females 65-69 (2 finishers, 2 awards)

1	Garthedon Embler	55:41
2	Nancy Bell	1:00:14

Males 70-98 (15 finishers, 3 awards)

1	Thomas King	45:54
2	David Mellard	46:07
3	Carlyle Johnston	55:05

Females 70-98 (2 finishers, 2 awards)

1	Margaret Wright	1:13:12
2	Lucy Jones	1:25:24

Compiled by Cedric Jaggers from complete results provided by Burns Computer Services immediately after the race on April 1, 1995.

Runners pass by in a blur. Post and Courier photo by Robin Cornetet

Chapter 19
1996
Liz McColgan Of Scotland Takes Female Crown

The 19th Bridge Run was held on March 30, 1996. The new course for 1996 (USATF certified #SC96010BS) was basically the 1995 course with a few minor alterations: The finish line was moved from the front of the Federal Building to the corner of Meeting and Calhoun streets. This was done to help avoid congestion. The starting line was pushed back a corresponding distance on Coleman Boulevard in Mount Pleasant. Runners proceeded across the Silas Pearman Bridge and the Crosstown Overpass, turned left on to Coming, left on to Line then turned right on to King Street to follow the previous course across Market and up Meeting Street to the finish line.

The race again set a record for entrants and finishers with 14,030 entrants and 11,444 officially crossing the finish line. There were 7,362 men (64.3 percent) and 4,082 women (35.7 percent). For the third year in a row, it was the largest number and highest percentage of female finishers in race history. It also marked the first time over 4,000 women ever completed a race in the Carolinas.

For the second year in a row all of the official finishers' names and times were listed in the next day's *Post and Courier*. Results were later mailed to all finishers in a special edition of the *Low Country Runner,* the newsletter of the Charleston Running Club.

The weather forecast led to a lot of surprised runners as the predicted warm morning turned out to be an overcast, cool 50 degrees at start time with a steady 20 mile per hour wind making the temperature feel even colder. For only the second time in Bridge Run history, the wind was a tailwind for runners as they went over the first span of the bridge. Despite the fact that this made the wind a headwind as runners headed down King Street, there were very few complaints.

Once again Kenyans dominated, though not as completely as in 1995. Top seeded Joseph Kamau won in 28:32, followed by fellow countrymen Zakaria Kunyiha in 28:40 and Daniel Kihara in 28:59. Travis Walter of Wilmington, N.C., was the first American runner for the second year in a row, finishing fourth in 29:29. The Kenyans remained the only runners who had run under 29 minutes on any Bridge Run course.

Walter said he was surprised that the Kenyans had started out slowly (for them). "They usually go out fast," he told the *Post and Courier*, "and they just didn't. Last year, we went out extremely fast." The first mile this year was 4:40 with two miles coming in 9:22 and three passing in 14:03. He added, "Kamau made the decisive move right before the top of the second span and down the back side. During that fourth mile, they probably put 14 seconds on me. They left me to battle the wind on my own." The final three Kenyans hit the 4-mile mark in 18:32 with the winner pulling gradually away.

Liz McColgan of Scotland ran behind Kenya's Catherine Ndereba for almost 5 and a half miles before turning on the speed. McColgan set a new course record by 53 seconds, 31:41 (5:07 pace) with Ndereba also under the old record, finishing second in 31:48. Cathy O'Brien of Durham, N.H., who made the U.S. Olympic marathon team twice, finished third in 32:53.

"Because of the hills I went off really steady," McColgan told the newspaper. "I just wanted to get them out of the way. But then I must have caught 10 seconds running fast down the other side. I just sat about 5 seconds behind (Ndereba) the whole way. I knew I was going to catch her over the last stretch. I was running very relaxed and very controlled the whole way. In the final mile I got on her shoulder; then with about 3 minutes to go I passed her and that was it."

McColgan was easily recognizable with her hair pulled into a topknot on her head. She averaged 5:07 per mile and was planning to use the London Marathon the next month to qualify for the Scottish Olympic team. "Usually America is pretty flat," she said. "I about died when I saw the bridge. But the wind was behind us coming over; then it was slightly in our face when we came off the bridge and turned onto the street. I'm very pleased with my performance. I've never seen a race like it. I think the States is where it's at in running right now. This is where the good races are."

The Masters division went to Antoni Niemczak of Poland, who won handily in 30:14. Tom Stevens of Middleton, Md., was second in 30:48 and Paul Barron of Willowdale, Canada, was third in 31:29. The female Masters title went to Maureen de St. Croix of Ottawa, Canada, in 35:19. Rebecca Stockdale-Wooley of Chalin, Conn., in 35:56, was second for the second year in a row. Third place went to Irina Bondarchouk of Russia in 36:02. She had set the Masters course record in '95.

The Dr. Marcus Newberry Award for first area finisher went to Mark Friedrich of the Isle of Palms, who ran 31:59 and finished 19th overall. He said after the race that it was his best Bridge Run since his 29:58 which placed him second overall in 1983. Clarice Marana of Charleston ran 37:18, 20th female and 162nd overall, to take the female division. The Dewey Wise Trophy was won by Arnold Hecht, 75, of Greensboro, N.C., with a time of 63:38.

The *Post and Courier* had some interesting quotes from runners who didn't win the race. In fact, the paper used one as a headline. Garthedon Embler said, "It's not getting too big. It isn't a race; it's an event", with the last sentence appearing as a headline on Page 1. The paper also mentioned that Sallie Driggers, women's winner in 1982, had a cash incentive for her children as she told them, "I offer my children $100 apiece if they ever beat me." The paper reported that they still had not done so. Bill Vetsch of Aiken, S.C., told the newspaper he had run the race 17 times. "This time," he said, "the wind was behind you so it was pleasant."

For the sixth year in a row, Channel 24 TV showed a one hour tape delay of the race. Entry fee for the race and walk were unchanged. In 1996, three runners broke the 29-minute barrier with a total of six runners under the 30-minute barrier. A total of 357 runners, 315 male and a record 42 female, broke the 40-minute barrier. There were 2,329 runners who finished the race in less than 50 minutes. There were a total of 7,002 runners under the 60-minute barrier. Julian Smith was the race director for the third year in a row.

Other Voices
The Other Side Of The Bridge

By Kathy Jaggers, Originally appeared in the May-June 1996 issue of the Low Country Runner

At 6 o'clock in the morning we met friends, and 15 minutes later I waved them off with a lump in my throat as they headed to Mount Pleasant and what was to have been my 17th consecutive Cooper River Bridge Run. On Jan. 10 I had colon cancer surgery and did not run for nine weeks. I am not up to the challenge of the bridge yet, but I am feeling good and running daily, slowly building back my mileage.

I planned to run 3 or 4 miles and quickly shower before heading back to the finish with camera in hand. This was the first time I would have an opportunity to photograph the run as I had always been a participant in the past.

As I headed down Meeting Street past the finish line, a kind soul promptly informed me that the shuttle buses were in the other direction. I did not explain but felt like a truant cutting school, and I wanted to sneak through the rest of my run unseen. This was not to be. Before I reached Market, three more people tried to inform me of the error of my way.

At Broad, I turned right twice to head down King Street. As I ran, I drifted back to the memory of the last time I passed this way in agony in the last mile of the Turkey Day Run. That time I noticed nothing beyond my desire to run fast. This time I saw eye-catching window displays of stores which had gotten my money several times in the past.

I actually stopped to look at the ginkgo tree (one of only two in Charleston), probably the first time I have really seen that tree since I was a teenager and we had to get all kinds of special permission from the city to cut a few leaves from the tree. The trees had been the subject of a research project for science class, and I had been allowed a small cutting of my own. I suddenly remembered how pleased that had made me at the time.

As I ran down King toward Marion Square, I saw almost no one, and savored the quietness of the city as though it was just waiting for the siege. I looked in windows as I ran by and mentally spent next week's paycheck and then some.

At Calhoun, someone called my name and I was delighted to see an old friend and fellow Charleston Running Club member Bruce Adams, who is also on the sick and injured list. He had back surgery recently, a lot more recently than my cancer surgery, and he is not running at all yet. We talked a bit and I headed on my way across Calhoun and down Meeting again.

Somewhere I encountered the mounted police who said the shuttle buses were still running but they were "back there" — of course, in the other direction. Again I had the urge to pull the collar of my shirt up around my face to avoid being recognized. As I stopped to speak to them, the horse closest to me started chewing on his bit and acting like he wanted to take a bite out of me. I was bitten by a dog last summer and it hurt something awful. I could just imagine what it would feel like if a horse decided to chomp down on me, so I just waved and left – fast.

There were a lot of people walking and jogging toward the shuttle buses. I got a lot of quizzical looks as I plodded on.

On the other side of Market, I had the streets to myself. At Chalmers, I looked at the cobblestone road and remembered the years I had spent going down that road a few times each week to study ballet at Miss Maimee Forbes School of Ballet. I don't think of those days often now, but I suppose even then I had learned that I enjoyed pushing my body to its limits of endurance through training and discipline. Those lessons learned so early in life in those ballet classes have served me well through the years.

I ran on, totally enjoying my run and not at all feeling sorry that I was on the wrong side of the river. The other side of the bridge.

I passed a church and remembered (without being conscious of seeking the memory) my first few piano recitals held there when I was a mere child of 10. I had not thought of that in ages. I quit performing in public at 16 and now only play for my own enjoyment.

I ran on down a sleeping street as I plodded on the Battery where I gazed out at the harbor. I plan to describe the scene to my eighth-graders at Chester Middle School. I teach literature, and we have read stories about the Lowcountry and the history of South Carolina. I told the kids I would have a distant look at Fort Sumter so I could describe it to them one more time. I found the words of Charles Kuralt echoing in my head while running by quiet, well manicured gardens and private homes. His description of Charleston in his new book Charles Kuralt's America was freshly implanted in my mind since I had read it during my convalescence.

My 4-mile run turned into a pleasant trip down memory lane and I felt more than a little homesick for the city Cedric and I had left five years ago. Sometimes we talk about returning when we retire and are not both tied to jobs on which we are dependent. Charleston is a special place full of warm people, and we feel a special love for the running community in Charleston.

A little later at Marion Square the celebration began as finishers appeared. I heard about everyone's runs and enjoyed the tales immensely. I regret not being able to run the Bridge this year, but I am now healthy and getting stronger every day. There is no reason for sadness, and plenty of reason to be thankful that this has been only a minor setback in my life.

I am looking forward to 1997 and my first year of running as a Grand Master. Next year after the race, I'll be in Marion Square along with everyone else telling Cedric about my Bridge Run. Count on it. I do.

Other Voices
Tell Me About Your Bridge Run 1996
By Cedric Jaggers, Originally appeared in the May-July 1996 issue of the Low Country Runner

The Bridge Run is over. Thousands of folks are milling around waiting for the awards ceremony. Charleston Running Club members know what happens next. Since 1988 when I was editing this newsletter and started writing down exactly what club members said about the race they had just run, there is nowhere to hide in Marion Square. If I can find you there, you get the dreaded demand, "Tell me about your Bridge Run." If you tell me you are a member or if I know you as a member, you get included if I can find you. This year you even got warned in the last newsletter so - here are the people who didn't hide or go straight home.

As always club members are listed in the order we happened upon each other. I looked up the times and places listed from the uncorrected, unofficial race day results printed for me by Burns Computer Service immediately after the awards ceremony. There appear to be a number of discrepancies in the times of some club members which I hope will be corrected before final results are printed (apparently there were timing problems in one chute).

If anyone didn't tell me their time, I tried to remember to ask after they finished their story. If we missed each other this time, hunt me up next year. I'll be looking for you, as always with clipboard in hand and wearing a Running Journal T-shirt.

Nina Parks (Taylor): I'm training long mileage for the 100th Boston. It doesn't make running over the Bridge easy. I need to pay my dues. I ran 47 something. I enjoyed the scenery this year, ran in different spots and talked more. Overall 1,741st, 33rd a.g., official time 47:05

Ray Dennis: Oh Gawd. I just don't have anything to say. I'm here. I made it. I'm not going to give you any excuses. I enjoyed it as always. If they keep taking hills out of it I'll like it even better. I had a bandanna handkerchief over my face before the race and got interviewed for television. The interviewer asked me why

Joseph Kamau (1) and Zakaria Kunyiha celebrate.
Post and Courier photo by Robin Cornetet

I had it on. I told him I was going to steal the race from the Kenyans. I had fun. Overall 7,258th, 322nd a.g., official time 1:00:37

Tami Dennis: Oh darn. Wait, wait, wait. It was tougher this year than last because of the wind. When you're asthmatic like me, the wind will get you. I ran 3 minutes slower than last year, 43:15. Overall 915th, 17th a.g., official time 43:29

Mike Loggins: Shoot. This one was just waiting to get the knee cut on again. I still ran 40:12 but I wanted 38 minutes. Worked hard but the screw is coming out of my leg. Overall 274th, 48th a.g, official time 38:50

Loraine Sapp: I finished in 1:02. I felt really good and I feel too good now because I didn't try hard enough. Overall 8,826th, 24th a.g., official time 1:03:47

Keith Ambrose: I didn't have anything left. I couldn't catch you. You were about 10 yards ahead of me. I thought I could close but when I picked it up you picked it up as well. I ran 39:20-something. Overall 383rd, 7th a.g., official time 39:30

Dan Clapper: I always have a good Bridge Run. This is my 12th in a row. I still get excited when I see the Bridge. About two weeks before the race, I saw the Bridge and got butterflies in my stomach. I ran 38:58. Overall 304th, 51st a.g., official time 39:01

Lennie Moore: Oh, let me see . . . better than I thought. This morning I was hurting but I ran it out. 36:36 my time. I hung in down King Street. I'm happy. Overall 127th, 23rd a.g., official time 36:37

Leon Locklear: I went out with the Kenyans ... no. I had a good run until an aging friend from the past, C.J., passed me and said "Pick it up fat boy." [Yes, I am guilty - the devil made me do it since Leon has passed me at almost that same spot on the Overpass about 10 years in a row. What I actually said was, "Come on, fat boy." CJ] I tried to go with you but it just hurt too much. I ran about 39:35ish; it was the best I could do. I'm pleased. Overall 700th 96th a.g., official time 42:25

Mary Frances Adams: My slowest; 58:42. That's not what they're going to say, but it's what I've got. I push the watch button when I cross the start line. I don't count all that extra time. It was wild out there: more crowded. Overall 7,394th, 95th a.g., official time 60:59

Art Liberman: I've been thinking, what am I going to say since it isn't April Fool's this year like it was last time. I will tell you I'm happy to have the health to be able to do this. I was pleased with my time considering I haven't done any speedwork. 43:49. Overall 963rd, 331st a.g. official time 43:45

Jeffrey Herndon: Very pleased. A P.R. for the Bridge. The last was still a killer. I think the last 2 miles are harder than other races. 38:48. It was fun. Overall 293rd, 4th a.g., official time 38:51 [Later he came up to me and wanted to add something about my being behind him the whole way but I refused since it was after the fact and it was true. CJ]

Tom Mahon: I was pleased. I ran about 15 seconds slower than the last 2 years. But it was a good 40 seconds faster than Flowertown, so I'm happy. 34:09 I think. Overall 47th, 8th a.g., official time 34:14

Jill Pellerin: My two goals were to not walk and to pick up the last two miles and I got both of them so I'm pleased. 58:14. Overall 6,220th 139th a.g., official time 58:29

Frank Blackett: I'm like a Timex watch. I'm still ticking. I enjoyed it. I did what I wanted to do - I broke 60. It was 57 or 58 I forget. Overall 5,971st, 19th a.g., official time 57:54

Gary Ricker: 37:22. One of the few races where I've felt great the whole way. As usual having Ed Ledford in the race helped. You know if you run with him you'll have a good race. Suffering, running the Bridge on Sundays pays off in March.

Overall 165th, 31st a.g., official time 37:23

Terry Bartosh: Out of shape, no speed, but I'm happy. I ran about 39:24. I had Alison Roxburgh in my sights. Overall 340th, 13th a.g., official time 39:42

Mike Desrosiers: I ran it with Randy Brown; we were doing the video camera again. Unfortunately we ran out of battery power. It was fun. Overall 2,823rd, 404th a.g., official time 50:36

Robert Lowery: Great run. No training, who could ask for more. 34:52 approximately, after 6 months of injury I'm pretty happy. I've done a lot worse on more training. Overall 62nd, 11th a.g., official time 34:53

Irving Rosenfeld: 55:25. I would have run faster but I saw those 'Do Not Pass' signs and I tripped on the second hill. Overall 4,933rd, 82nd a.g., official time 55:49

Bernie Clark: 45:40. It took forever to start, but great weather. I enjoyed the social event. Overall 1,389th, 109th a.g., official time 45:41

Nancy Curry: You're going to write this down verbatim, right? This is a P.R. for me. Having the green number helped. I've never had a colored number before. This may be the apex of my running career. I'm not saying any more, Cedric. 46:46, 4 minutes faster than last year. Overall 1,755th, 9th a.g. official time 47:08

Mike Chodnicki: Fantastic considering I ran the first 50 yards with one of the balloons wrapped around my leg. Want me to start from the beginning? The median was right in front of me, so I moved over to the right a little, then a guy cuts left and runs right into the median barrel, I don't think he ever saw it, and knocks it over right in front of me. I hurdled the barrel and a brick holding the balloon down came flying right between my legs. It had a balloon attached and it wrapped around my leg. So I'm running with this balloon and brick dangling and I can't stop because all these people are right behind me. So I kept running until the balloon and brick came loose - I hope they didn't hit anybody else. If I hadn't been scared to death it would have been funny. I ran 36:49, 35 seconds faster than the Flowertown 10k. All the excitement at the start energized me. If you need a witness ask Opie Woolever, he was right beside me. Overall 137th, 24th a.g. official time 36:48.

Joyce Fleming: Today my run was terrible. I got back in the pack; my 58 minute run turned out to be an hour ten. I was a little afraid with the big crowd, but everybody was great. Overall 9,019th, 67th a.g., official time 1:04:21

Sue Bennet: It was great, slow but great. I finished. I'm still breathing. 1:12 or 1:13. Overall 10,741st, 228th a.g., official time 1:13:16

Duane Nicholson: I didn't have any unusual experiences. It was just right. 58 something. Overall 6,174th 135th a.g., official time 58:22

Nitsa Calas: I hope you don't want my time. It was good, it was fun, it was tough. I'm not going to tell you my time. Overall 1,592nd, 17th a.g., official time 46:32

Eileen Stellefson: Great ending, slow beginning. I ran negative splits. Considering the beginning, it was a great run. I ran 45:38. Overall 1,374th, 23rd a.g., official time 45:38

Marilyn Mattice: It was good overall. The temperature was great and I had a respectable time under an hour. It was 13 seconds over on the official clock, but I couldn't start running until 1 or 2 minutes after they started the race. Overall 7,271st, 91st a.g., official time 60:39

Randy Brown: Oh no! Shame on you for not warning me he was coming (said to Nina Parks). This was my first Bridge Run in 10 years and the only reason I ran it is because they didn't need my help with it since they were so well organized. Mike Desrosiers and I ran together, he with the video camera and me with the microphone, trying to interview people. But the camera kept cutting off. Our "official time" starting from when we crossed the starting line 49:59. We were about 30 seconds off the race clock. Overall 2,824th, 480th a.g., official time 50:36

Brantley Arnau: This is my first race since I got back from Uganda. I went to Frank's running camp this year. I'm coming back. I was able to maintain 7:30 miles. I was pleased. It must have been all that training that gave me the consistency. I ran 46:48. Overall 1,662nd, 220th a.g., official time 46:49

Wes Littlejohn: I got over the Bridge and felt like I was going to puke, but I pushed on to the finish. The crowd pulled me through. I ran 36:50 something. Overall 142nd, 10th a.g. official time 36:54

Tom Dority: Wonderful run, wonderful weather, wind to my back. 44:50. I love the race. Overall 1,200th, 13th a.g., official time 44:53

Lessie Snead: What can I say? I'm just thankful I was healthy and could run it. My number six Bridge Run. Ee-yow — 54:19, slower than my first Bridge time. Overall 4,341st, 37th a.g., official time 54:24

Cherry Smiley: My 11th year, but by far my most congested. It was still congested on King Street. I had a time of 57:14, just terrible. I'm glad I wasn't trying to set any P.R.s. I'm thankful that I was healthy and could run it. Overall 7,074th, 172nd a.g., official time 60:08

Ron Deramus: It was a great run ... about 4 minutes slower than last year. It felt good just getting over it. I ran 36:53, official - who knows? No complaints. I just haven't been running any. I put in 50 miles the last 5 or 6 weeks. Overall 141st, 24th a.g., official time 36:53

Ronald Charles: I thought it was pretty smart to run without a shirt because I like to run cool, made a good decision when I saw other people sweating - until

now at the awards ceremony I feel the cool North breeze and wonder about the decision. This is my best time, about 51:23, my 3rd time to run it. Overall 3,223rd, 116th a.g., official time 51:44

Kay Miller: It was great. My son Johnny and husband John and I ran together. We were married 10 years ago at the start of the Bridge Run, do you remember? [I did, and told her so since it was in the newspaper and on TV at the time, Cedric]. We started out too far back. We should have known better. My little boy was stepped on about 3 times. But it was great weather. Wish we could have started closer to the front. We ran 58:59. Overall 7,016th, 164th a.g., official time 1:00:02

Steven Hunt: Not my best, not my worst, just thankful I can get to the finish line. I ran 48:20. Overall 2,101st, 270th a.g., official time 48:23

Huey Inman: Well it shaped up pretty good. Running those hills in Virginia (where I live now) got me in shape. I ran another P.R, 34:19 or 20. Overall 51st, 9th a.g., official time 34:20

Larry D'ippolito: Not much to say. I'm training for Boston. I'm flat. The distance takes the speed away. I did 37:22. Overall 166th, 9th a.g., official time 37:23

Bunny Owen: I P.R.d. This my 14th year. My time by my watch was 52:02. I'm about to be Moore - I'm marrying Lennie in four more weeks. Overall 3,900th, 109th a.g., official time 53:21

Chuck Greer: I know you quote the things exactly. I just wanted to break 40 and things worked out - 37:36. I had 38:05 at the Flowertown 10k and thought I'd be a minute or a minute and a half slower here. Everything just went right. I think the tailwind helped. Overall 181st, 2nd a.g., official time 37:37

Mark Friedrich: It's been a long time since I had a race that went well. Usually I run pretty close to the shape I'm in. Today I was going out with the goal of under 33 flat. Usually Tom (Mather) is so far ahead it would hurt me just to stay with him. My legs were feeling lighter today - it was just one of those days. Without a plan I seemed to hit a peak. 31:59. I think it's my second fastest Bridge Run. I'm not sure if it is my second fastest [note in 1983 Mark was 2nd person to break the 30 minute barrier in any Bridge Run when he finished second overall in 29:58 CJ]. I told Keith Namm (of *The Post and Courier* newspaper) it was, then I told him I wasn't sure. Considering that I'm 39 now, it is my second best Bridge Run. I still wouldn't have finished in the top 5 Masters. Overall 21st, 3rd a.g., official time 31:59

Margaret Wright: It was fun. I enjoyed it. I didn't fall down. I didn't fall off the bridge. I ran about 1:15:39. Overall 10,698th, 2nd a.g., official time 1:12:55

Pat Rhode: The only good thing about it is I finished. I passed out at the 6 mile mark. Somehow I got up and finished. I don't have any idea what my time was. I spent 30 minutes in the medical tent after I finished. Overall 4,607th, 7th a.g., official time 54:59

Bob Schlau: Not one of my best. I just didn't feel good. I don't know if I had a bug or just felt kind of weak which is usually not my problem. I just have to come back next year and do better. 33:24. I just didn't feel strong. I'm not discouraged; I had a period like this a few years ago and came back. I'm not giving up. Overall 37th, 1st a.g., official time 33:27

Cedric Jaggers: Considering all we've been through this year with Kathy's colon cancer surgery and recovery, I'm really happy. I broke 40 for the 17th time on the Bridge and for the first time in a long time and I pushed hard the whole way. I was 14 seconds faster than last year when a month ago I wasn't even sure I could break 40 this year. I ran 39:22. Overall 334th, 27th a.g., official time 39:22

Overall winner Joseph Kamau at the finish line. Post and Courier photo by Robin Cornetet

1996 Awards

Prize money winners:

Overall Male
1. Joseph Kamau .... Kenya .... 28:32 ... $3,000
2. Zakaria Kunyiha ...... Kenya .... 28:40 ... $1,500
3. Daniel Kihara .... Kenya .... 28:59 ... $1,000
4. Travis Walter .... Wilmington, NC ..... 29:29 ..... $800
5. Valeri Pedotov .... Russia .... 29:34 ..... $600
6. Jerry Lawson .... Jacksonville FL .... 29:53 ..... $500
7. Antoni Niemczak ...... Poland .... 30:14 ..... $400
8. Amit Neeman .... Israel .... 30:22 ..... $300
9. Tom Stevens .... Middleton, MD ...... 30:48 ..... $250
10. Larry Brock .... Anderson, SC .... 31:01 ..... $150

Overall Female
1. Liz McColgan .... Scotland .... 31:41 ... $3,000
2. Catherine Ndereba .... Kenya 31:48 1,500
3. Cathy O'Brien .... Durham, NH .... 32:53 ... $1,000
4. Laura Mykytok .... Brevard, NC .... 33:24 ..... $800
5. Cindy Gerard .... Red Bank, NJ .... 33:30 ..... $600
6. Svetlana Vasilyeva ... Russia .... 33:33 ..... $500
7. Ludmilla Ilina .... Russia .... 33:41 ..... $400
8. Deanna O'Neal .... Canby, OR .... 34:10 ..... $300
9. Tamara Karlioukova ... Russia .... 34:35 ..... $250
10. Tania Jones .... Canada .... 34:55 ..... $150

Masters Male
1. Antoni Niemczak ...... Poland .... 30:14 ... $1,500
2. Tom Stevens .... Middleton, MD ...... 30:48 ... $1,000
3. Paul Barron .... Canada .... 31:29 ..... $750
4. Dave Kannewurf .... Portsmouth VA ...... 31:36 ..... $500
5. David Geer .... Clemson, SC .... 31:47 ..... $250

Masters Female
1. Maureen de St Croix .. Canada .... 35:19 ... $1,500
2. R Stockdale-Wooley ... Chaplin CT .... 35:56 ... $1,000
3. Irina Bondarchouk .... Russia .... 36:02 ..... $750
4. Diane Legare .... Canada .... 36:16 ..... $500
5. Nancy Grayson .... Northville, MI ..... 36:48 ..... $250

Dr. Marcus Newberry Award
Tri-County Local Winner Male:
   Mark Friedrich .... Isle of Palms SC ... 31:59 ..... $500
Tri-County Local Winner Female:
   Clarice Marana .... Charleston SC ...... 37:18 ..... $500

Special award:
Dewey Wise Trophy for oldest finisher with fastest time less than their age in minutes:
   Arnold Hecht, 75 .... Greensboro, NC 63:38

Age Group Award Winners
(presented to top 3 in age group, with top 5% up to maximum of 25 awarded in each age group):

Male 12 & under (107 finishers, 6 awards)
1. Scott Bytnar 41:07
2. John Carroll 41:23
3. Ben Sherard 41:52
4. Kevin Timp 42:32
5. Justin Higgins 43:04
6. Allan Donnellan 44:12

Female 12 & under (38 fin., 3 awards)
1. Michele Milner 46:12
2. Brittany Simpson 49:29
3. Marcie Milner 50:51

Male 13-17 (281 finishers, 14 awards)
1. Stewart Edwards 35:54
2. Mike Beigay 36:32
3. Jeremiah Milliman 36:36
4. Charlie Norris 36:43
5. Jordan Pritchard 37:17
6. Chris Douglas 37:34
7. Brian DeRoberts 37:38
8. Brantlee Milner 38:05
9. Kurt Wilson 38:22
10. Kevin Woodard 38:50
11. Ricky Ward 38:51
12. Christian Dawson 39:12
13. Nathan Cox 39:21
14. Dayton Dove 39:58

Female 13-17 (162 finishers, 8 awards)
1. Erin Burton 40:19
2. Cheri Scharff 42:05
3. Meridith Grimsley 43:24
4. Karen McChesney 45:55
5. Melissa Lauffer 46:09
6. Kathryn Weber 46:41
7. Shaw Hipsher 46:41
8. Rebecca Coffman 47:43

Male 18-21 (220 finishers, 11 awards)
1. Eric Roschick 31:38
2. Travis Dowdy 33:28
3. Josh Brashears 34:50
4. Jason Annan 34:57
5. Stanley Mdemu 35:01
6. David Low 35:20
7. Rahul Sharma 35:28
8. Kevin Croxton 35:34
9. Eliot Cannon 36:40
10. Derrick Williams 36:44
11. Jay Glover 36:56

Female 18-21 (203 finishers, 10 awards)
1. Jenna Bates 42:37
2. Natali West 43:02
3. Beth Shea 43:59
4. Erin Jacques 44:08
5. Becky Manfred 44:47
6. C Furlano 45:24
7. Rachelle Boyer 45:42
8. Andrea Simon 45:49
9. Karen Carr 47:21
10. Kimberly Powers 47:29

Male 22-25 (615 finishers, 25 awards)
1. Mark Cruz 31:04
2. Mark Donahue 32:14
3. Jonathan Ingram 32:33
4. Gregory Fennell 34:15
5. Lyn Rowland 34:19
6. Paterick Vanboden 35:39
7. Max Carroll 36:02
8. Justin Hadley 36:21
9. John Walz 36:33
10. Wesley Littlejohn 36:54
11. Zaid Shubailat 36:56
12. David Little 37:09
13. Paul Wright 37:46
14. Hal Crosswell 38:02
15. Alan Jenkins 38:04
16. Chris Pateras 38:04
17. Mike Mott 38:05
18. Matthew Biagioli 38:14
19. Richard Long 38:19
20. Michael Miller 38:21
21. Daniel Kuelker 38:50
22. Patrick Lemoine 38:50
23. Hunter Pierce 38:51
24. Jackson Rohm 39:20
25. Jason Michaels 39:21

Female 22-25 (559 finishers, 25 awards)
1. Ashley Holroyd 36:19
2. Tracy Center 38:33
3. Kari Squillo (Staley) 39:21
4. Cara Balch 41:13
5. Francois Trawalter 41:16
6. Julie Oliver 41:51
7. Kristen Albrecht 42:07
8. Erika Ellis 42:13
9. Monica Steffes 44:23
10. Jennifer Carman 44:42
11. Kim Huffman 44:51
12. Carey White 45:46
13. Julie Talbot 45:54
14. Stacy Meiler 46:04
15. Susan Moorehead 46:21
16. Tricia Erpelding 46:26
17. Liz Greer 46:32
18. Diane Karinshak 46:48
19. Sarah Lorge 46:50
20. Eileen Torres 47:05
21. Jody Zolman 47:10
22. Samantha Smith 47:10
23. Christy Vanvalkenburg 47:15
24. Liz Rossner 47:17
25. Yoshie Ihn 47:26

Male 26-29 (923 finishers, 25 awards)
1. Rob Darner 32:07
2. Greg McMillan 32:57
3. Cail Brown 33:19
4. David Nelson 33:23
5. Helmut Schmoock 34:04
6. Karl Debate 34:35
7. Dujuan Harbin 34:56
8. Timothy Decker 35:30
9. Kevin Vanboden 35:39
10. Bennett Cox 36:12
11. David Gile 36:24
12. Rick Garvais 36:46
13. John Frino 36:58
14. Brian Fancher 37:08
15. Ken Corsig 37:12
16. Michael Johnson 37:15
17. Richard De Guzman 37:20
18. Karl Johnson 37:29
19. Donat Auf Der Maur 37:37
20. Eric Wayner 37:51
21. Ben Vaughn 37:52
22. Bud Badyna 38:03
23. Jerry Rothschild 38:03
24. Paul Horner 38:15
25. Bryan Tinsley 38:17

Female 26-29 (679 finishers, 25 awards)
1. Tania Jones 34:55
2. Amy Kattwinkel 35:32
3. Mary Ellen Kelly 37:31
4. Jennifer Halsch 38:21
5. Alison Roxburg 39:39
6. Heather Sansbury 40:01
7. Nicole Marcell 40:17
8. Pam Mooring 40:59
9. Karen Neal 41:17
10. Jane Ganey 41:30
11. Saundi Theodossiou 41:35
12. Susan Madinger 42:08
13. Shelly Fulton 42:36
14. Michele Hall 42:40
15. Mylinda O'Quinn 42:48
16. K. Krehnbrink 42:49
17. Kelly O'Donnel 42:56
18. Molly Achille 43:20
19. Arlene Walker 43:27
20. Leslie Payne 43:34
21. Suzanne Boyer 44:23
22. Joni Hamilton 44:24
23. Tuba Malinowski 44:51
24. Nancy Madigan 45:10
25. Andrea Ziff 45:43

Male 30-34 (1,204 finishers, 25 awards)
1. Scott Walschlager 31:10
2. Jamey Yon 31:39
3. Daniel French 32:42
4. Keith Hurley 32:53
5. Mark Scott 34:19
6. Fred Gillen 34:26
7. Blake Zemp 34:26
8. Mickey Dechellis 35:13
9. Barry Fitts 35:31
10. James Wilbanks 35:38
11. Alan Gebert 35:44
12. Lance Leopold 35:47
13. Chandler Burns 35:56
14. Kevin Nelson 35:59
15. David Ariola 36:00
16. Bobby Aswell 36:00
17. Philip Barnhill 36:06
18. Paul Davis 36:13
19. Douglas Richey 36:16
20. Dawson Cherry 36:34
21. Jimmy Tassios 36:34
22. Terry Neuhart 36:36
23. Jim Madden 36:39

24 Jack Purdy ... 36:50
25 Ron Deramus ... 36:53
Female 30-34 (807 finishers, 25 awards)
1 Jean Strait ... 36:31
2 Mary Dunn ... 36:42
3 Clarice Marana ... 37:18
4 Patt Loggins ... 37:55
5 Laura Broon ... 38:21
6 Edie Brantley ... 38:47
7 Karen Pouch ... 38:49
8 Gina Latham ... 38:53
9 Elizabeth Graham ... 39:37
10 Cameron Sharbel ... 39:39
11 Terry Bartosh ... 39:42
12 Lisa Roeber ... 39:43
13 Patricia Foell ... 39:44
14 Katherine Forbes ... 39:49
15 Lynne Davis ... 41:01
16 Karen Caines ... 41:15
17 Suanne Hall ... 41:36
18 Karen Meader ... 41:40
19 Julia Smith ... 41:50
20 Betsy Veronee ... 41:55
21 Lynn Todd ... 42:00
22 Patti Bouvatte ... 42:38
23 Patricia Clark ... 42:51
24 Laurie Sperry ... 43:11
25 Mari Barrett ... 43:25
Male 35-39 (1,159 finishers, 25 awards)
1 Larry Brock ... 31:01
2 Selwyn Blake ... 31:58
3 Mark Friedrich ... 31:59
4 Tom Mather ... 32:30
5 Jeff Milliman ... 33:15
6 Steve Palladino ... 34:09
7 Tom Mahon ... 34:14
8 Huey Inman ... 34:20
9 Todd Hamilton ... 34:22
10 Marshall Randall ... 34:34
11 Robert Lowery ... 34:53
12 Tommy McAfee ... 35:11
13 Tom Clow ... 35:18
14 Jeff O'Neil ... 35:19
15 Danny White ... 35:25
16 Harry Ash ... 35:33
17 David Bourgeous ... 35:36
18 Jeff Wilmer ... 35:48
19 Steve Shonts ... 35:51
20 Carl Karpinski ... 36:29
21 Keith Winn ... 36:30
22 Lennie Moore ... 36:37
23 Mike Chodnicki ... 36:45
24 Bill Cavedo ... 36:49
25 Peter Edge ... 37:01
Female 35-39 (618 finishers, 25 awards)
1 Judy Walls ... 39:01
2 Ruth Marie Milliman ... 39:50
3 Eileen Clark ... 41:13
4 Jean Kolbaba ... 41:28
5 Gale Moore ... 41:42
6 Nancy Farley ... 41:51
7 Darlene Palmer ... 42:00
8 Clare Dillon-Palma ... 42:06
9 Pam Drafts ... 42:20
10 M Hollon ... 42:26
11 Sandra Legath ... 42:30
12 Janet Skinner ... 43:09
13 Kathy Berry ... 43:13
14 Jan Hagopian ... 43:16
15 Noriko Seiner ... 43:27
16 Weezie Griffen ... 43:28
17 Tami Dennis ... 43:29
18 Beth Dixon ... 44:10
19 Jennifer Doles ... 44:22
20 Belinda Cantwell ... 44:45
21 Tammy Hovik ... 45:07
22 Nancy Tucker ... 45:23
23 Eileen Stellefson ... 45:38
24 Karin Oehring ... 45:46
25 Julia Ralston ... 45:49
Male 40-44 (1,015 finishers, 25 awards)
1 Steve Winchel ... 32:23
2 Craig Virgin ... 33:09
3 Lloyd Boone ... 33:42
4 Jerry Clark ... 33:46
5 Dan Hyde ... 34:30
6 Alfie Cronin ... 34:45
7 Danny West ... 35:01
8 Tony Bateman ... 35:21
9 George Howe ... 35:43
10 Carlos Pignato ... 35:45
11 Larry Milner ... 35:54
12 Hal Hall ... 36:04
13 Michael Willoughby ... 36:15
14 Jack Todd ... 36:18
15 Del Rose ... 36:22
16 Andrew Ammon ... 36:23
17 Steven Kovach ... 36:28
18 Jim Wilhelm ... 36:44
19 Bobby Torri ... 36:48
20 Michael Drose ... 36:55
21 Steve Staley ... 36:57
22 Michael Stieglitz ... 37:02
23 Charles Kellner ... 37:07
24 Scott Roark ... 37:10
25 Mark Evans ... 37:15
Female 40-44 (470 finishers, 24 awards)
1 Alendia Vestal ... 37:39
2 Victoria Crisp ... 38:11
3 Catherine Lempesis ... 38:24
4 Lisa Schneiderman ... 41:14
5 Eileen Telford ... 41:23
6 Ginger Gregory ... 43:14
7 Cynthia White ... 45:07
8 Debbie Howard ... 45:27
9 Jo Haubenreiser ... 45:43
10 Brenda O'Shields ... 45:51
11 Sharon Cleveland ... 45:53
12 Maria Griffith ... 45:56
13 Annie Morehead ... 46:14
14 Nitsa Calas ... 46:32
15 Hilary Young ... 47:03
16 Deborah Lagaie ... 47:08
17 Kathy Revell ... 47:10
18 Debbie Ostrander ... 47:58
19 Barbara Carroll ... 48:09
20 Rosemary Sanford ... 48:14
21 Caroline Bailey ... 48:20
22 Martha White ... 48:24
23 Mary Millar ... 48:36
24 Sallie Chardukian ... 48:52
Male 45-49 (848 finishers, 25 awards)
1 Bob Schlau ... 33:27
2 Norman Ferris ... 34:25
3 Russ Page ... 35:09
4 Mike Julian ... 36:29
5 John Bernhardt ... 36:50
6 Larry Frederick ... 36:57
7 Herbert Rexrod ... 37:04
8 John Sperry ... 37:22
9 Larry D'Ippolito ... 37:23
10 Oliver Marshall ... 37:27
11 Harold Fallis ... 37:29
12 Reed Watson ... 37:30
13 Alan Abramowitz ... 37:44
14 Paul Brown ... 37:49
15 Buddy Hyman ... 37:58
16 Gary Cadle ... 38:06
17 Sandy Wetherhold ... 38:14
18 Dennis Crane ... 38:30
19 Jim Mercure ... 38:36
20 Chip Higginbotham ... 38:46
21 Theodore Taylor ... 38:50
22 William Dawson ... 38:50
23 Bill Peay ... 38:54
24 Phil Peterson ... 38:55
25 Phillip Dickert ... 39:05
Female 45-49 (299 finishers, 15 awards)
1 Nancy Grayson ... 36:48
2 Judith Hine ... 38:16
3 Betty Ryberg ... 40:06
4 Nonie Hudnall ... 42:02
5 Sallie Driggers ... 45:05
6 Wanda Brooks ... 47:00
7 Suzy Lorentz ... 47:06
8 Nancy Curry ... 47:08
9 Pamela Lestage ... 47:42
10 Judy Hierholzer ... 47:43
11 Lyn Smith Hammond ... 48:01
12 Peggy Schug ... 48:10
13 Joyce Lowe ... 48:29
14 Octavia Childress ... 49:22
15 Ruthie Tucker ... 49:26
Male 50-54 (535 finishers, 25 awards)
1 Terry Van Natta ... 35:04
2 Chuck Greer ... 37:36
3 Russell Brown ... 37:56
4 William Anderson ... 38:43
5 Kermitt Bowen ... 38:51
6 Charles Stoyle ... 39:02
7 Wallace Carr ... 40:10
8 Keith Ambrose ... 40:21
9 Walter Waddell ... 40:55
10 Allan Gardner ... 40:58
11 Robert Baker ... 41:01
12 Thomas Bolton ... 41:41
13 Arthur Smith ... 41:44
14 Herb Smith ... 42:00
15 Philip Watson ... 42:00
16 John Dillard ... 42:14
17 Will Hearn ... 42:17
18 Bill Vetsch ... 42:31
19 Thomas Siegle ... 42:32
20 Clay Walker ... 42:33
21 John Lestage ... 43:00
22 Edward Cassel ... 43:09
23 Kenneth Truelove ... 43:15
24 David Moorhead ... 43:19
25 Willie Wright ... 43:38
Female 50-54 (139 finishers, 7 awards)
1 Pauline Niilend ... 45:07
2 M. E. Morgan ... 49:00
3 Mary Thompson ... 50:22
4 Kathy Cusack ... 50:51
5 Sallie Sinkler ... 51:01
6 Carol Thomason ... 52:14
7 Sally McMillen ... 53:00
Male 55-59 (232 finishers, 12 awards)
1 James Adams ... 37:44
2 Charles Teseniar ... 38:43
3 Ed Ledford ... 38:50
4 Theron Cochran ... 41:52
5 Fred Wood ... 42:11
6 Richard Weatherford ... 42:18
7 Keith Weaver ... 42:20
8 Floyd Deandrade ... 43:07
9 Herman Hunt ... 43:50
10 Bill Bailey ... 43:51
11 Ben Sherman ... 44:10
12 Bill Ball ... 44:36
Female 55-59 (53 finishers, 3 awards)
1 Susie Kluttz ... 43:23
2 Diane Kohrman ... 49:23
3 Dawn Owens ... 52:33
Male 60-64 (122 finishers, 6 awards)
1 Charles Rose ... 37:16
2 Moe Bussino ... 41:10
3 Raymond Stone ... 43:22
4 Toby Transou ... 43:31
5 Phil Szczepanski ... 44:05
6 Charles Venning ... 44:52
Female 60-64 (17 finishers, 3 awards)
1 Suzanne Foster ... 53:02
2 Camille Daniel ... 58:17
3 Lois Johnson ... 58:57
Male 65-69 (39 finishers, 3 awards)
1 Duncan Weeks ... 38:28
2 George Wilson ... 42:44
3 Fred Steltmeier ... 45:36
Female 65-69 (6 finishers, 3 awards)
1 Marge Hoffman ... 54:12
2 Garthedon Embler ... 56:48
3 Nancy Bell ... 1:00:40
Male 70-98 (22 finishers, 3 awards)
1 David Mellard ... 47:33
2 Franklin Mason ... 48:38
3 Herman Lesslie ... 52:48
Female 70-98 (4 finishers, 3 awards)
1 Lynn Edwards ... 1:01:22
2 Margaret Wright ... 1:12:55
3 Ola Moody ... 1:25:45

Compiled by Cedric Jaggers from complete results provided by Burns Computer Services immediately after the race on March 30, 1996.

Hey, look everybody, it's Bill Murray. Post and Courier photo by Wade Spees

Chapter 20

1997

Elana Meyer Sets Female Course Record Of 31:19; First Chip Timing; No Americans In Top 10 For First Time

The 20th Cooper River Bridge Run was held on April 5, 1997. For the second year in a row the race grew by over a thousand in both entrants, 15,216, and finishers, 12,583, setting new records. With 7,839 male finishers (62.3 percent) and 4,744 female finishers (37.71 percent), the race increased female participation to its highest level yet. The race used the same USATF course #SC96010BS as in 1996, beginning on Coleman Boulevard in Mount Pleasant and finishing at the corner of Meeting and Calhoun streets in Charleston.

Actor Bill Murray (*Ghostbusters, Groundhog Day, Meatballs*, etc.) and comedian (*Saturday Night Live*) served as starter for the race. He made the race director nervous by showing up only 5 minutes before the start and made the crowd laugh when he said, "I'm going to be running in the middle of the crowd, so steer clear. I want to be identified later." Then he patted his gut and said, "There's nothing like a big, Southern breakfast." He ran in the race and after finishing 11,685th in a time of 1:25:19, made folks laugh again when he said, "The hardest part was going through the cup zones where people were throwing water at you."

The weather played a cruel trick on the runners. All week the Lowcountry and the entire state of South Carolina had enjoyed a string of unseasonably cool, crisp days with low humidity. But race morning arrived hot and humid. With clear skies and bright sunshine, the 68-degree start was the fourth hottest ever. Runners had a negligible wind, most unusual in itself. The conditions sent over 150 runners into the emergency treatment tents after the race, and 10 runners were hospitalized.

The heat did not seem to bother the large Kenyan contingent. Paul Koech won in 27:57 (4:30 pace), just 8 seconds off the course record. Tom Nyariki, also from Kenya was second in 28:13. For the first time, a non-Kenyan ran under 29 minutes as Khalid Khannouchi of Morocco was third in 28:15. Also for the first time, no Americans finished in the top 10. Travis Walter of Wilmington, N.C., was the first U.S. runner for the third year in a row, finishing 11th overall in 29:42.

"In every race, one has to work out a plan, and mine was to stay with my countrymen for the first 3 or 4 miles," Koech told the *Post and Courier*. "On the second hill, I started opening up to see if they were staying with me. I had to destroy (Nyariki) on the second hill."

Nyariki said, "I'm not disappointed I didn't win. He's strong. I want to come back here next year and improve my time. By then I'll have more experience on the course."

The women's race was perhaps the most exciting of the day, as pre-race favorite Elana Meyer of South Africa was as surprised as everyone else when Sally Barsosio, a 19-year-old Kenyan running her first Bridge Run, ran most of the first mile just behind the lead pack of male runners. In fact, it was not until the last 2 miles that Meyer overtook Barsosio. Meyer accelerated to a new female course record 31:19 (5:03 pace). Barsosio was second in 31:52 followed closely by defending race champion Liz McColgan of Scotland in 31:58.

"Sally took off like a jet, so for the first 2 miles I was a bit behind," Meyer, who was running her first Bridge Run, told the *Post and Courier*. "But I was sort of catching up slowly. On the last part of the bridge, I broke away. I was coming down as I passed her.

"We don't have bridges like this in South Africa. It was challenging. It was fun.

I enjoyed it."

Barsosio faded as the heat and humidity caught up with her near the end after her fast start. She said, "I knew she was going to beat me. It was too hot." McColgan was surprised at how fast the lead women started the race. "It was very fast at the start. I was hesitant to go out with the beginners. Last year my first mile was 5 minutes and this year it was 4:50. Those girls were running at 4:42 or something. It was really fast. I might have taken it too steady up the hills because I was trying to catch them the whole way. I let them get too far ahead."

The Masters division was again won by Antoni Niemczak of Poland, this year in 31:11. He held off Valery Svetegor of Russia, winning by just 2 seconds. Third place went to Dimitri Dmitriev, also of Russia, in 32:07.

Maureen de St. Croix from Canada, was female Masters winner for the second year in a row, this time in 37:31. Second place went to Claudia Kasen of Williamsburg, Va., in 37:54, with third going to Alendia Vestal of Brevard, N.C., in 38:14.

The Dr. Marcus Newberry Award for first area finisher went to Tom Mather of Mount Pleasant, who finished 21st overall in 31:42. Clarice Marana of Charleston ran a personal best 36:33 to finish as 16th woman and 134th overall. It was her second win in a row. The Dewey Wise Trophy was won by Arnold Hecht, 76, of Greensboro, N.C., with a time of 67:37.

For the seventh year in a row, Channel 24 television showed a one hour, tape delay of the race. Entry fees remained at $14 early, $20 late for the race, and $9 early $12 late for the walk.

For the first time, runners were timed using the ChampionChip computer timing chip. Since most runners were unfamiliar with how the system worked, here is the explanation given at the time: A quarter-sized computer chip pre-loaded with race number information is laced into each runner's shoe. This chip is activated when the runner crosses the special pad laid across the starting line and deactivated by a pad across the finish line. The chip transmits the runner's total running time and computed elapsed time to a master computer. Results can be (and were) printed out showing both times. The device eliminated the bottleneck of runners in chutes awaiting pull tab collection but created a chip-collection problem further down the road as runners had to remove and return the chips. Most runners, except the very small percentage whose chips malfunctioned — I calculated the failure rate at 1.28 percent — seemed to like the new system very much. The actual running time, called "gun time" was used for finish order and awards, while the "chip time" was shown for runners' personal interest.

For the third year in a row, all of the official finishers, except Masters division runner Tom Stevens, who had worn his computer chip on his race number instead of his shoe, were listed in the next day's *Post and Courier*. He was shown in the separate Masters box as one of the Masters overall winners, but not listed in the male/female separate finish order results. His name was never added to the official results and does not appear in the results posted on the race website, which was established a number of years later. Complete results were mailed to all finishers in a special supplement of the newspaper.

In 1997, only one runner broke the 28-minute barrier, six others broke the 29-minute barrier and a total of 13 runners broke the 30-minute barrier. A total of 330 runners broke the 40-minute barrier, 38 of them female. There were 2,398 finishers who completed the race in less than 50 minutes, while a still standing (after 33 races) record 7,111 runners (which totaled 56 percent of the finishing field) managed to cross the finish line in less than an hour. The accompanying 4-mile fun walk attracted an estimated 10,000 participants. The Sunday Post and Courier listed the finishers, showing 7,710 male and 4,812 female names and times. Julian Smith was the race director for the fourth year in a row.

Other Voices
Tell Me About Your Bridge Run 1997

By Cedric Jaggers, Originally appeared in the May-June 1997 issue of the Low Country Runner

Was it hot? Was it crowded? Was it Marion Square after the Bridge Run? Were you there? If you were not you should have been. If you were and you told me you are a Charleston Running Club member or I recognized you (those of you who were trying to avoid me) then you got asked. If I missed you this year, don't let it happen again next year. Look for the clipboard and the Running Journal T-shirt.

As always the names are listed in the order we happened to bump into each other. When I could find it, I've included the overall place, chip time, and official race time from the results Burns Computer Company printed for me immediately after the race. Since it also showed the difference i.e. the time it took each runner to reach the start line, I've included that data. I thought it was interesting that of all the club members I talked to after the race, only thee showed 0 seconds difference between chip and race time so they must have started right on the front line: Tom Mather, Patt Loggins and Irving Rosenfeld (Irving later told me this was a chip error as he did not start up front).

Cherry Smyly: According to my watch it was 56:20. I thought it was hard because of the heat. I'm glad it's over. 5,244th overall, Chip time 56:18, Race time 57:00, 42 seconds to start.

Ed Ledford: It was great, 38:40. I passed Cedric up the hill and he didn't pass me going down like he usually does. I don't know what happened. It was a great day. It wasn't as fast as I wanted but I'm older now. 250th overall, Chip time 38:39, Race time 38:44, 5 seconds to start.

Chuck Greer: I ran about the same as last year: 37:40s. I'm happy to be in the same time bracket. 181st overall, Chip time 37:38, Race time 37:43, 5 seconds to start.

Deanna Richard: It was entirely too hot. That cold spell came up this week and I was hoping it would be cool. I didn't catch my time. I think I was getting ready to go over - to have a heat stroke. I liked having a wide chute. Time? 48:49 maybe. 2,644th overall, Chip time 50:38, Race time 51:20, 42 seconds to start.

Jeffrey Herndon: It was okay but very hot. I panicked a little at the finish when I was approaching the line and heard the announcer say here comes Cedric Jaggers - finishing right behind me. 363rd overall, Chip time 40:25, Race time 40:31, 6 seconds to start.

Margaret Wright: It was too hot. I had to walk a lot but I finished. 11,664th overall, Chip time 1:14:44, Race time 1:19:18, 4 minutes 34 seconds to start.

Leon Locklear: My ankles were bleeding when I finished - no steam. 43:04. I never saw you this year. We've had some good battles. Wait till next year, I'll be 45. I'll finish school next month and dedicate a lot more time to training. 844th overall, Chip time 44:00, Race time 44:10, 10 seconds to start.

Don Austell: Don't ask me about my time. All you have to see is right here. (Shaking his large stomach as he grilled food at the CRC tent in Marion Square.) Unable to locate in results.

Lennie Moore: I felt okay until King Street as usual. It was a real effort just to hang on. Off from last year, but the best I could do. 36:43. It was warm. 142nd overall, Chip Time 36:42, Race time 36:44, 2 seconds to start.

Bill Lachiocotte: Another year of hard training and poor performance. I'm usually a better practicer than performer. But I survived it. No EMS is a good day for me. About 62 minutes. 10,442nd overall, Chip time 1:08:24, Race time 1:11:42, 3 minutes 17 seconds to start.

Tanis Manseau: I had a good run. I'm trying to learn the lesson you can't run 10k on 5k workouts. I thought the run went better this year. The organization at the start was better. I enjoyed it. 51:50. 3,117th overall, Chip time 51:47, Race time 52:44, 51:47, 57 seconds to start.

Jill Pellerin: Well when do I start? Do you want my runner's excuses? No? I was 4 minutes faster than last year, 54:30 this year. It was hotter than Hades, but I stayed steady. I'm very happy. 4,349th overall, Chip time 54:33, Race time 54:54, 21 seconds to start.

Mary Frances Adams: It was real nice. It was too hot. I ran it with a brother-in-law. We did 1:08. 10,517th overall, Chip time 1:08:43, Race time 1:10:20, 1 minute 37 seconds to start.

Tami Dennis: I'm pleased with as little training, racing - I don't race at all, 44:29. A minute off last year. With the heat I'm pleased. 929th overall, Chip time 44:28, Race time 44:48, 20 seconds to start.

Ray Dennis: Oh man. I decided I was going to do it this morning. I hurt my knee skiing. It was 12 in a row for me. That's the only reason I did it. My slowest time ever; 1:06. 9,884th overall, Chip time 1:06:23, Race time 1:08:36, 2 minutes 13 seconds to start.

Kathleen King: I felt strong the whole time but it wasn't fast: 57 minutes. I ran even the whole way. I ran with a friend who turned white - dehydrated. I did much better than last year. Training does help. 5,884th overall, Chip time 57:33, Race time 58:15, 42 seconds to start.

Tom Mahon: Same time as I did a year ago: 34:14. I was surprised I ran that as tough as I was feeling. I'm pleased with it since I was 35:04 at the Flowertown

Race starter, actor Bill Murray. Post and Courier photo by Wade Spees

10k. So I was basically pleased. 63rd overall, Chip time 34:12, Race time 34:14, 2 seconds to start.

Dan Clapper: I take back everything I said (we had talked before the race) about liking to race on the hills and in the heat with no breeze. I did relatively bad compared to you but relatively good compared to Leon. I ran right around 41 minutes: about 2 minutes slower than last year. 407th overall, Chip time 40:51, Race time 41:00, 9 seconds to start.

Keith Ambrose: 41:46. Just like I read in your last article in Running Journal - overtrained and getting slower than you. I'll be doing the 7 mile bridge in Florida next Saturday so I'm saving my time. 504th overall, Chip time 41:42, Race time 41:44, 2 seconds to start.

Stanley Feldman: It was very hot. I run over from town to the start and usually have a good run back, but I left it on the bridge this year. 55 minutes. 4,488th overall, Chip time 54:45, Race time 55:28, 43 seconds to start.

Bunnie Moore: I felt great. I had a good time with my girlfriend Cindy. It was hot but it was fun. This is my 15th year, don't I look it? I think my time was 56 minutes. (Unable to find time 2 minutes on either side of 56 minutes in the results, and not in the searchable results either. CJ).

Lily Andrews: I did fine if I was in the walk. That's all I can say. I have no clue what my time was but it was a long time from the start. You can't run 2 days a week and expect to do well. (unable to find in results).

Bernie Clark: Hot and slow. That's it. 51:39. 2,662nd overall, Chip time 50:40, Race time 51:40, 60 seconds to start.

Maria Griffith: Ha. It was slow and I started too far back. I went out slow and got slower. I finished. 48:30 on my watch. 1,750th overall, Chip time 47:55, Race time 48:34, 39 seconds to start.

Guy Hinson: Ditto for everybody else: hot and slow but I enjoyed it. It seemed more crowded than usual. 55:14. 4,674overall, Chip time 55:12, Race time 59:02, 3 minutes 50 seconds to start.

Jerome Durkin: My first race in a year and a half. I'm 48 now and ran 47:03, just glad to finish. I'm coming off double knee surgery and a torn hamstring. I'm coming back - I need speedwork. 1,522nd overall, Chip time 47:05, Race time 47:18, 13 seconds to start.

Eileen Stellefson: It was hot. I felt miserable. I almost stopped. 46:47. 1,432nd overall, Chip time 46:45, Race time 46:51, 5 seconds to start.

Bill Vetsch: A minute and a half slower than last year but I enjoyed it. It's a lot easier than on the old bridge. I'm interested to see how the chips work. My 18th straight Bridge Run. 43:49. 789th overall, Chip time 43:38, Race time 43:50, 12 seconds to start.

Irving Rosenfeld: It was muggy. It was so muggy that the police were kept busy all morning. That's all I have to say. About 57 minutes. 5,818th overall, Chip time 57:24, Race time 57:24, 0 seconds to start.

Ann Pye: It was great to be here. What? What else do you want to know? You're writing that down - I better be quiet. Oh, I had a good run. It was a good day. The first span was terrible. It was better organized this year than ever before. 44:30. 952nd overall, Chip time 44:33, Race time 44:51, 18 seconds to start.

Tom Dority: 46:02. I had a good start even though it was hot. It didn't bother me too much. I made it over both spans; I started feeling it about the fifth mile. 1,260th overall, Chip time 45:59, Race time 46:26, 32 seconds to start.

Bob Schlau: I thought it was good until I heard the awards. 32:46, 5th place masters was 32:40. I figured I was maybe 8th and took it too easy. I'm sick about giving away a finish in the masters but there is nothing I can do about it now. I look forward to next year, that's all I can do. 36th overall, Chip time 32:48, Race time 32:49, 1 second to start.

Tom Mather: I ran well, just a little over 31:30. I wanted to run well. I put a lot of pressure on myself. I want to get ready to be a masters runner in about 6 months. I won the Marcus Newberry award for the 6th or 7th time. I thought I was in shape to run 30:50 but the warm day slowed me down a little. I was tentative in the mid section of the race. I didn't know what I could take in the heat. 21st overall, Chip time 31:42, Race time 31:42, 0 seconds to start.

Pat Rhode: I've been eating on the Zone. (The diet book plan of the same name by Dr. Barry Sears. CJ) I don't know if I'm doing it right but I think it's helping me. It was a wonderful run. I felt good the whole time. Praise the Lord, I didn't pass out today. 51:30. 2,999th overall, Chip time 51:23, Race time 51:54, 21 seconds to start.

Michael Golemis: Man it was the most beautiful day we've had for the Bridge Run. I saw more people I know, maybe because I'm getting slower. I think they need a separate race for elites and normal people. 41:20. 459th overall, Chip time 41:19, Race time 41:23, 4 seconds to start.

Kathy Jaggers: Oh no. Okay, let's see. All right. When they started the race I was so happy I was grinning to be able to come back from cancer surgery. I grinned for a quarter mile until I got too hot. I didn't grin again until I finished it. But it felt good and I really enjoyed it. 45:38 when I went under the clock. For every year after you turn 45 it feels like they increase the angle of the bridge by 2 percent. 1,133rd overall, Chip time 45:29, Race time 45:40, 11 seconds to start.

Dave Mellard: It was good but I ran slower than I wanted. But I had a good one. Great day, great run. It was a great day for the walkers. About 50 or 51 minutes, it wasn't as good as Summerville. 3,009th overall, Chip time 51:30, Race time 51:55, 25 seconds to start.

Huey Inman: My best ever. It must be because of the hills in Virginia since I moved there and run them all the time. I held my speed in the heat. 34:02. 57th overall, Chip time 34:01, Race time 34:03, 2 seconds to start.

Nina Parks: It was great. I ran with Stacie Novak the whole way - a great team effort. A little warmer than North Carolina (where she lives now, CJ). That's all I can say. 1,240th overall, Chip time 45:52, Race time 46:11, 19 seconds to start.

Stacie Novak: It was great. For not training I'm happy with my time. 46:11. 1,270th overall, Chip time 46:01, Race time 46:20, 19 seconds to start.

Nancy Curry: I ran like a little old lady. I didn't do well. Excuses? Too hot, too crowded. I'll do better next time. By my watch 48:38 - a minute and a half slower than last year. 1,944th overall, Chip time 48:35, Race time 50:27, 1 minute 52 seconds to start.

Patt Loggins: A new PR. It was a PR that had stood since 1991; I thought those days were gone. A PR by 6 seconds and I felt good doing it. I didn't hurt until the last 1/4 mile. Last year I felt too much pressure. This year I didn't feel any pressure and that helped. 37:37. 180th overall, Chip time 37:38, Race time 37:38, 0 seconds to start.

William Snead: It was hot and I was prepared well enough and that's about my entire Bridge Run. If it had been 15 degrees cooler I'd have done better but so would everybody else. I feel like it might be getting too big. I know they are trying to grow with it. 52:50. 3,678th overall, Chip time 53:08, Race time 53:48, 40 seconds to start.

Lessie Snead: Oh dear, Cedric. Well it was going good until the finish got me. Is that what I'm saying? What a spastic. I don't know what happened. I think I stumbled over the pad. I was thinking I'm going to be pleased I'm healthy and happy and punch my watch and all of sudden I was down on the ground. (Note: Lessie fell and cut her knee at the finish, CJ) My time? Less than 52 minutes. 3,170th overall, Chip time 51:55, Race time 52:37, 42 seconds to start.

Cedric Jaggers: I was disappointed but not as badly as I would have been if most everybody else hadn't done worse than usual in the heat. I expected to break 40 and did not - I blew up in the heat, got a side stitch and really suffered worse than I have in any of the previous 18 Bridge Runs in a row that I've finished. 377th overall, Chip time 40:34, Race time 40:37, 3 seconds to start.

1997 Awards

Prize money winners:
Overall Male
1 Paul Koech .... Kenya .... 27:57 ... $5,000
2 Tom Nyariki .... Kenya .... 28:13 ... $3,000
3 Khalid Khannouchi .. Morocco .... 28:15 ... $1,500
4 John Kariuki .... Kenya .... 28:37 ... $1,000
5 Peter Githuka .... Kenya .... 28:43 .... $800
6 Simon Sawe .... Kenya .... 28:51 .... $600
7 Charles Mulinga ..... Zambia .... 28:55 .... $500
8 Phillimon Hanneck ... Zimbabwe .... 29:12 .... $400
9 James Bungei .... Kenya .... 29:24 .... $300
10 Joseph Kariuki ...... Kenya .... 29:35 .... $250
11 Travis Walter .... Wilmington NC ...... 29:42 .... $200
12 John Kagwe .... Kenya .... 29:56 .... $150
13 Francis Wanderi ..... Poland .... 29:58 .... $100
14 Vladimir Afanasiev ... Russia .... 30:22 ..... $75
15 Berthold Berger ..... Hulzen SC .... 30:24 ..... $50

Overall Female
1 Elana Meyer .... South Africa .... 31:19 ... $5,000
2 Sally Barsosio .... Kenya .... 31:52 ... $3,000
3 Liz McColgan .... Scotland .... 31:58 ... $1,500
4 Valentina Yegorova .. Russia .... 32:49 ... $1,000
5 Carol Howe .... Canada .... 33:22 .... $800
6 Ludmilla Petrova .... Russia .... 33:36 .... $600
7 Ludmilla Ilina .... Russia .... 33:59 .... $500
8 Lieve Siegers .... Belgium .... 34:02 .... $400
9 Tamara Karliovkova .. Russia .... 34:10 .... $300
10 Olga Yegorova ...... Russia .... 34:20 .... $250
11 Patty Pitcher .... Charlotte NC .... 34:47 .... $200
12 Svetlana Vasilieva ... Russia .... 35:19 .... $150
13 Tatiana Ivanova ..... Russia .... 35:24 .... $100
14 Mary Ellen Kelly .... Columbia SC .... 35:49 ..... $75
15 Stephanie Agosta .... Lancaster OH .... 36:27 ..... $50

Masters Male
1 Antoni Niemczak .... Poland .... 31:11 ... $1,500
2 Valery Svetegor ..... Russia .... 31:13 ... $1,000
3 Dmitri Dmitriev ..... Russia .... 32:07 .... $750
4 Tom Stevens .... Middleton MD ...... 32:09 .... $500
5 Mark Friedrich ...... IsleofPalms SC ..... 32:20 .... $250

Masters Female
1 Maureen de St Croix Canada .... 37:31 ... $1,500
2 Claudia Kasen ...... Willimburg VA ...... 37:54 ... $1,000
3 Alendia Vestal ...... Brevard NC .... 38:14 .... $750
4 Joyce Switzer .... Canada .... 38:41 .... $500
5 Victoria Crisp .... Nashville TN .... 38:35 .... $250

Dr. Marcus Newberry Award
Tri-County Local Area Winner Male:
  Tom Mather .... Mt Pleasant, SC ...... 31:42 .... $500
Tri-County Local Area Winner Female:
  Clarice Marana .... Charleston, SC .... 36:33 .... $500

Special award:
Dewey Wise Trophy for oldest finisher with time less than his or her age in minutes:
Arnold Hecht, 76 .... Greensboro, NC 67:37

Age group award winners
(presented to top 3 in age group, with top 5% up to maximum of 25 awarded in each age group):

Male 12 & under (76 finishers, 4 awards)
1 Jacob McCaskill 41:20
2 Wes Knight 44:00
3 Matthew Hardee 44:23
4 Michael Proctor 46:11

Female 12 & und (56 finishers, 3 awards)
1 Michele Milner 46:14
2 Langdon Smith 47:49
3 Marcia Milner 50:35

Male 13-17 (257 finishers, 13 awards)
1 David Scharff 36:49
2 Mark Berglind 37:03
3 Kevin Toth 38:13
4 Justin Walker 38:16
5 Kevin Timp 38:17
6 Brantlee Milner 39:05
7 Andrew Scharff 39:18
8 Kevin Patterson 39:57
9 Travis Smith 40:13
10 Graham Lovett 40:14
11 Ryan Hulland 41:47
12 Matthew Dexheimer 41:49
13 Jonathan Barnes 42:15

Female 13-17 (159 finishers, 8 awards)
1 Hana Syrorova 41:36
2 Megan Dexheimer 41:44
3 Erin Burton 42:38
4 Sarah Davis 43:24
5 Dale Alsbrooks 43:27
6 Meredith Grimsley 44:20
7 Annabelle Hunt 45:09
8 Kelly Compton 47:18

Male 18-21 (360 finishers, 18 awards)
1 Keith Woodman 31:36
2 Jason Putnam 34:20
3 Derrick Williams 34:34
4 Kevin Croxton 34:55
5 Dwayne Brown 36:26
6 Lee Kain 36:46
7 David Low 36:46
8 Jay Glover 37:00
9 Kurt Wilson 37:14
10 David Lee 37:46
11 Robbie Tigert 37:46
12 Chris Phillips 38:10
13 Chris Paes 38:31
14 Joey Parker 39:28
15 Nicholas Godfrey 39:44
16 Anthony Nardis 39:49
17 Cameron Brooks 40:11
18 Adam Hare 40:13

Female 18-21 (281 finishers, 14 awards)
1 Kelly Gordon 44:18
2 Taylor Hamilton 44:46
3 Heather Gallagher 46:09
4 Terri Cutler 46:25
5 Andrea Simon 46:35
6 Mary Gannt 47:25
7 Britney Cooke 48:19
8 Mary Thomason 48:26
9 Alicia Fuduric 48:39
10 Elizabeth Bancroft 48:44
11 Elizabeth Christovich 48:56
12 Corneilia Bihl 49:25
13 Sandra Godley 51:34
14 Robin Ridings 51:39

– Continued on next page

Continued from page 159

Male 22-25 (655 finishers, 25 awards)
1 Scott Laws ... 32:24
2 Kyle Armentrout ... 33:53
3 Brant Armentrout ... 34:03
4 Daniel Crooker ... 35:12
5 Jim Prussack ... 35:20
6 Jon Pruett ... 35:27
7 Jason Annan ... 35:46
8 Patrick Vanboden ... 35:47
9 Charles Rowland ... 36:08
10 Rayvis Key ... 36:40
11 Takayuki Sano ... 37:27
12 Wesley Littlejohn ... 37:33
13 Dan Schutt ... 38:04
14 Mike Miller ... 38:05
15 Glen Poklikuha ... 38:27
16 Robert Salomon ... 38:29
17 Jonathan Park ... 39:08
18 Chris Wozniak ... 39:16
19 Jeff Hiott ... 39:26
20 Mike McClaran ... 39:26
21 Robert Robinson ... 39:48
22 Alan Jenkins ... 39:59
23 Chris Pateras ... 40:23
24 Ryan Hernandez ... 40:35
25 Scott Crisp ... 40:39

Female 22-25 (609 finishers, 25 awards)
1 Christine Leaman ... 36:45
2 Kristin McCann ... 39:47
3 Erika Eliss-Harley ... 41:59
4 Betsy Page ... 43:08
5 Kimberly Stokes ... 43:56
6 Heather Tarpley ... 44:04
7 Trisha Watson ... 44:18
8 Heather Dobb ... 44:29
9 Jillion Stern ... 45:38
10 Jennifer Carman ... 45:47
11 Elizabeth Smith ... 45:49
12 Geneveeve Clissold ... 46:30
13 Elizabeth Hearon ... 46:45
14 Alice Osborn ... 47:02
15 Anne Welborne ... 47:20
16 Carol Burnett ... 47:25
17 Anne Wyman Fouche ... 47:26
18 Jeni McLane ... 47:59
19 Janice Lichniak ... 48:12
20 Sohee Park ... 48:12
21 Tracy Cordray ... 48:48
22 Laura Forster ... 49:13
23 Elizabeth Martin ... 49:17
24 Tammy Root ... 49:28
25 Jennifer Ellis ... 49:37

Male 25-29 (985 finishers, 25 awards)
1 Berthold Berger ... 30:24
2 Vince Howard ... 32:38
3 David Nelson ... 32:43
4 Jamie Barnes ... 33:05
5 Antonio Eppolito ... 33:46
6 Steve Venable ... 34:06
7 Robbie Smith ... 34:18
8 Ricky Harrison ... 34:43
9 Darol Timberlake ... 34:46
10 David Brown ... 34:53
11 Michael Colaiacovo ... 34:54
12 Kevin Stoots ... 35:00
13 John Wilson ... 35:30
14 Mo Burton ... 35:39
15 Andres Barron ... 35:45
16 Steve Desalvo ... 35:50
17 Tim Starets ... 36:09
18 Peter Sheldon ... 36:26
19 Karl Johnson ... 36:28
20 Timothy Decker ... 36:28
21 Ted Richardson ... 37:06
22 Abbott Whitney ... 37:11
23 Paul Horner ... 37:17
24 Hunter Pierce ... 37:25
25 Brian Fancher ... 37:37

Female 26-29 (856 finishers, 25 awards)
1 Gabriele Hauck ... 38:43
2 Amy Kattwinkel ... 38:50
3 Tracy Center ... 38:52
4 Julie Nielsen ... 39:08
5 Toni Leal ... 39:44
6 Kari Staley ... 40:40
7 Tania Jones ... 41:22
8 Judith Nwajiaku ... 41:24
9 Heather Sansbury ... 41:45
10 Cara Johnson ... 41:59
11 Susan Madlinger ... 42:09
12 Kristen Chesson ... 42:24
13 B. Thacker ... 42:33
14 Karl Krehnbrink ... 42:59
15 Lea Spaay ... 43:22
16 Kelly O'Donnell ... 43:26
17 Denise Lockett ... 43:51
18 Carey White ... 44:05
19 Lynn Pearson ... 44:26
20 Amy Stein ... 44:50
21 Julie Oliver ... 44:55
22 Pam Mooring ... 45:19
23 Kimberly Jones ... 45:26
24 Stephanie Horn ... 46:00
25 Yoshie Ihn ... 46:06

Male 30-34 (1,214 finishers, 25 awards)
1 Angus McBryde ... 31:45
2 Sergei Karasev ... 31:48
3 Paul Bonfiglio ... 32:21
4 George Walker ... 33:04
5 David Brendle ... 33:12
6 Shaun Walsh ... 33:16
7 Daniel Wallace ... 33:19
8 Jamey Yon ... 33:29
9 Scott Walschlager ... 33:49
10 Eddie Fagan ... 34:08
11 James Wilbanks ... 34:21
12 Karl Debate ... 34:23
13 Jonathon Ingram ... 34:29
14 Mike Mays ... 34:36
15 Blake Zemp ... 34:42
16 Irv Batten ... 35:03
17 Alan Gebert ... 35:21
18 Petri Huhtala ... 35:23
19 Keith Hurley ... 35:25
20 Marty Jones ... 35:32
21 Ricky Austin ... 35:44
22 Phil Ponder ... 35:59
23 Steve Hearn ... 36:01
24 Bobby Aswell ... 36:01
25 Bill Crooks ... 36:11

Female 30-34 (852 finishers, 25 awards)
1 Clarice Marana ... 36:33
2 Patricia Shaw ... 36:57
3 Laura Vroon ... 39:41
4 Megan Othersen Gorman ... 39:58
5 Nicole Marcelli ... 41:20
6 Saundi Theodossiou ... 41:21
7 Julia Smith ... 41:31
8 Jane Ganey ... 42:13
9 Karen Pouch ... 42:31
10 Suanne Hall ... 42:34
11 Cindy Dunn ... 42:51
12 Karen Meader ... 43:20
13 Traci Scarborough ... 43:51
14 Julie Boughn ... 44:15
15 Jessica Tisdale ... 44:21
16 Shelly McKee ... 44:22
17 Missy White ... 44:29
18 Pamela Mitchell ... 44:29
19 Deborah Chaney ... 44:38
20 Ann Gibson ... 44:41
21 Heather Wood ... 44:50
22 Lynne Todd ... 44:52
23 Elizabeth Graham ... 44:56
24 Almaz Smith ... 45:00
25 Mary Durando ... 45:35

Male 35-39 (1,102 finishers, 25 awards)
1 David O'Keefe ... 31:13
2 Tom Mather ... 31:42
3 Larry Brock ... 32:11
4 Alexander Beliaev ... 33:02
5 Huey Inman ... 34:03
6 Tom Mahon ... 34:14
7 Gregory Wimer ... 34:44
8 Norman Blair ... 34:51
9 David Moore ... 35:03
10 Gary Peters ... 35:19
11 David Agosta ... 35:20
12 Steve Shonts ... 35:24
13 Todd Hamilton ... 35:42
14 David Rourke ... 35:47
15 Thomas Cuff ... 35:51
16 John Schoen ... 36:13
17 Pete Edge ... 36:14
18 Bill Freeman ... 36:26
19 Keith Winn ... 36:36
20 Duane Dye ... 36:39
21 Chandler Burns ... 36:41
22 Sam Inman ... 36:50
23 Marc Embler ... 37:02
24 Eddie Pennebaker ... 37:25
25 Tommy McAfee ... 37:41

Female 35-39 (719 finishers, 25 awards)
1 Stephanie Agosta ... 36:27
2 Patt Loggins ... 37:38
3 Lisa Roeber ... 38:12
4 Susi Smith ... 38:50
5 Kerry Robinson ... 39:34
6 Patricia Clark ... 41:23
7 Susan Raridon ... 41:41
8 Allison Phillips ... 42:00
9 Vikki Saga ... 42:37
10 Darlene Palmer ... 42:49
11 Eileen Clark ... 43:22
12 Jean Kolbaba ... 43:22
13 Sally Knight ... 44:02
14 Peggy Kinney ... 44:12
15 Barbara Andrews ... 44:32
16 Beth Ritchey ... 44:44
17 Tami Dennis ... 44:48
18 Jennifer Hales ... 44:49
19 Nancy Thomas ... 44:49
20 Jennifer Doles ... 45:08
21 Eileen Peters ... 45:11
22 Christian Theodossiou ... 45:42
23 Lisa Krupp ... 45:43
24 Karen Murphy ... 45:44
25 Sandra Klatt ... 45:52

Male 40-44 (1,044 finishers, 25 awards)
1 Dan Lawson................................32:41
2 David Geer.................................32:51
3 Richard Ledoux...........................33:04
4 Pete Kaplan................................33:31
5 Vladimir Anissimov.....................33:37
6 Dan Hyde...................................33:41
7 David Renneisen.........................34:13
8 George Howe..............................35:28
9 Sam Swofford.............................35:33
10 Harry Ash..................................35:36
11 David Bougeois..........................36:14
12 Steve Caskie..............................36:16
13 James Wilhelm...........................36:22
14 Lennie Moore.............................36:44
15 Tony Bateman............................36:45
16 Joe Denneny..............................36:58
17 Rick Ingerson.............................37:01
18 Don Burckhardt..........................37:13
19 Dennis Moon..............................37:16
20 Thomas Lincul............................37:36
21 Bobby Torri................................37:37
22 Gary Ricker...............................37:54
23 Del Rose....................................38:00
24 Andrew Ammon.........................38:15
25 Michael Drose............................38:18

Female 40-44 (561 finishers, 25 awards)
1 Dian Ford..................................38:47
2 Kathy Ward...............................39:00
3 Lynn McFadden.........................39:17
4 Cathy Dwyer..............................41:46
5 Robin Smith...............................43:09
6 Cathy Burton.............................43:23
7 Jo Wenger..................................44:03
8 Ann Elish Pye.............................44:51
9 Nitsa Calas................................45:14
10 Jo Haubenreiser.........................45:40
11 Sharon Cleveland.......................46:13
12 Carol Grooters...........................46:37
13 Debbie Howard..........................47:09
14 Constance Caldwell....................47:12
15 Bobbi Hackman..........................47:20
16 Brenda O'Shields........................47:27
17 Annie Cruitt...............................47:58
18 Cheryl Catton.............................48:28
19 Maria Griffith.............................48:34
20 Debbie Ostrander.......................48:55
21 Holly Konrady............................49:13
22 Julia Baxter................................49:28
23 Betsy Walker..............................49:33
24 Sylvia Myrick..............................49:38
25 Rosemary Sanford......................49:38

Male 45-49 (819 finishers, 25 awards)
1 Gary Romesser..........................32:24
2 Bob Schlau.................................32:49
3 Devin Kelly................................36:33
4 Johnny Bernhardt.......................37:36
5 Mike Julian................................37:38
6 Jack Todd...................................37:48
7 Larry Frederick..........................38:15
8 Rob Kriegsharber.......................38:18
9 Gary Joye..................................38:20
10 Oliver Marshall..........................38:46
11 John Sperry...............................39:11
12 Ralph Veytia..............................39:27
13 Michael Willoughby...................40:14
14 David Gelly................................40:17
15 James Boyd...............................40:18
16 Gary Cadle.................................40:34
17 Cedric Jaggers...........................40:37
18 Vince Herran..............................40:37
19 John Smith.................................40:39
20 Richard Garrison........................40:41
21 Hisayoshi Sekino........................40:51
22 Louis Smith................................40:56
23 Martin Bunke.............................41:23
24 Sonny Hembree.........................41:30
25 Tom Shimbo..............................41:36

Female 45-49 (312 finishers, 16 awards)
1 Catherine Lempesis....................40:04
2 Rebecca Stockdale.....................40:54
3 Betty Ryberg.............................41:33
4 Nonie Hudnall............................42:19
5 Sallie Driggers...........................45:22
6 Karen Martin.............................46:46
7 Judy Gilman..............................48:14
8 Susie Black................................48:37
9 Suzy Lorentz..............................48:59
10 Heidi Bridges............................49:23
11 Marcella Farino.........................49:54
12 Joy Roschella............................50:32
13 Martha White............................51:02
14 Lucy Brown...............................51:10
15 Pamela Keeler...........................51:31
16 Jeannie Vinson..........................51:32

Male 50-54 (602 finishers, 25 awards)
1 Terry Van Natta.........................36:09
2 Bernard Wright..........................36:51
3 Scott Taylor...............................37:12
4 Chuck Greer..............................37:43
5 Bill Peay....................................37:48
6 Barry Bishop.............................38:23
7 Dave Roeber.............................38:24
8 Dewey Sloan.............................38:48
9 Russell Brown...........................38:54
10 Bruce McKinney........................38:56
11 Dave Kanners...........................39:09
12 Sam Davis.................................39:27
13 Keith Ambrose..........................41:44
14 Ray Kitchen..............................41:47
15 Earl Jackson..............................42:06
16 Isaiah Goodman........................42:10
17 T.D. Voss...................................42:54
18 Gary Butts.................................43:02
19 Ira Bradley................................43:02
20 Eric Elbel...................................43:05
21 Arthur Smith.............................43:07
22 Chuck Speight..........................43:23
23 Tom Ladewig............................43:25
24 Wallace Carr.............................43:27
25 Walter Waddell.........................43:30

Female 50-54 (187 finishers, 10 awards)
1 Kathy Jaggers...........................45:40
2 Kathleen Schmitt.......................46:18
3 Mary Thompson........................49:47
4 Nancy Curry..............................50:27
5 Pauline Niilend..........................51:17
6 Barbara Avant...........................53:43
7 Marilyn Craig............................53:45
8 Carol Thomason........................54:22
9 Kathy Seavers...........................55:33
10 Elizabeth Bugbee......................56:15

Male 55-59 (268 finishers, 14 awards)
1 Dean Godwin............................41:22
2 Keith Weaver............................41:53
3 James Adams............................42:59
4 Phillip Watson...........................42:59
5 Theron Cochran........................43:00
6 Floyde Deandrade.....................43:05
7 Richard Weatherford.................43:32
8 Bill Vetsch.................................43:50
9 James Hanlon............................43:57
10 Joseph McAlhany......................45:09
11 David Smith..............................45:35
12 Fred Motz.................................45:41
13 Gordon Heiser...........................46:07
14 Ron Sanders..............................46:09

Female 55-59 (67 finishers, 4 awards)
1 Pat Rhode.................................51:54
2 Diane Kohrman.........................53:28
3 Ann Schwacke..........................56:35
4 Evelyn Godley...........................56:43

Male 60-64 (127 finishers, 7 awards)
1 Ed Ledford................................38:44
2 Charles Rose.............................39:00
3 J Ayres......................................44:34
4 Raymond Stone........................45:33
5 Chuck Collins............................46:15
6 Donald Robinson.......................46:16
7 John Thompson.........................46:42

Female 60-64 (32 finishers, 3 awards)
1 Susie Kluttz...............................49:05
2 Suzanne Foster.........................57:05
3 Rebekah Stephens....................57:57

-Male 65-69 (33 finishers, 3 awards)
1 William Boulter.........................49:19
2 David Anderson........................49:53
3 Jack Lightle...............................55:11

Female 65-69 (4 finishers, 3 awards)
1 Garthedon Embler..................1:08:25
2 Nancy Bell..............................1:26:47
3 Wyndall Henderson................1:41:24

Male 70-74 (12 finishers, 3 awards)
1 Franklin Mason..........................50:41
2 David Mellard............................51:55
3 Ed Peters...................................53:09

Female 70-74 (3 finishers, 3 awards)
1 Janine Maltas.........................1:04:49
2 Lucy Jones.............................1:33:31
3 Ola Woody.............................1:40:49

Male 75-98 (7 finishers, 3 awards)
1 Arnold Hecht..........................1:07:37
2 Ed Shaffer..............................1:09:43
3 Cadwallader Jones.................1:20:14

Female 75-98 (2 finishers, 2 awards)
1 Francis Kelley........................1:05:30
2 Margaret Wright....................1:19:18

Compiled by Cedric Jaggers from complete results provided by Burns Computer Services immediately after the race.

A huge crowd prepares for the start in Mount Pleasant. Post and Courier photo by Robin Bass

Chapter 21

1998

Elana Meyer First Two-Time Female Winner Despite Windiest Race

The 21st Bridge Run was held on April 4, 1998. The number of entrants jumped to an all-time high 18,007, while the number of finishers increased only slightly, to 12,919. The race used the same USATF certified course #SC96010BS it had used since 1996. It started on Coleman Boulevard in Mount Pleasant, proceeded across the Silas Pearman Bridge and the Crosstown Overpass, turned left onto Coming, left onto Line then turned right onto King Street to follow the previous course across Market and up Meeting Street to the finish line at the corner of Meeting and Calhoun streets.

For the second year in a row, runners were timed by the ChampionChip computer timing chip system that proved to be 98.77 percent accurate.

The weather was probably the prime factor in the 71.7 percent finisher versus entrant percentage, which was the lowest in race history. More than 2 inches of rain fell the day before the race. Heavy rain, high wind and even some tornadoes struck nearby counties. Many runners decided not to make the trip.

For the second year in a row actor and comedian Bill Murray (a part owner of Charleston's minor league baseball team) was race starter and gave the runners a few humorous words before firing the starting gun. "There's no reason for any of you guys not to win this race," he said. "Just live by duty, honor, country, biscuits and gravy."

Race morning looked beautiful. Humidity was low; temperature at the 8 a.m. start was 64 degrees, but, oh, the wind. The Sunday *Post and Courier* headline borrowed the title of Bob Seger's song: "Against The Wind". With a steady 25 mile per hour wind which was gusting to 35 mph, runners ran directly into a headwind for virtually the first 4 and a quarter miles and last half-mile of the race. Going up the bridge spans into such a stiff headwind made the race much slower than usual. Almost every runner commented on being a minute or more slower than expected. It looked like no runners would break the 30-minute barrier. That had not happened since the last time the race had similar wind conditions in 1987.

Pre-race favorite Tom Nyariki of Kenya led the entire way. He took the pack through 1 mile in 4:49 and 2 miles in 9:39, and got to the 4-mile mark in 19:51. Over the bridge the leaders were running single file due to the wind. "Everybody was in a line so they would be protected from the wind force," Nyariki told the newspaper. "The course today wasn't the real obstacle. It was the wind. I felt good running today. I thought I was running very fast, but because of the wind it was more difficult for me."

Nyariki led the entire way except for one brief stretch right after the 4-mile mark when eventual second place finisher James Kariuki, also of Kenya, briefly took the lead. Nyariki moved back into first place and got to the 5-mile mark in 24:41. He had to turn on a powerful finishing kick to get under the 30-minute mark — he was the only runner to do so, winning in 29:58. Kariuki was second in 30:18. Kenyan James Bungei was third in 30:26. Craig Young of Colorado Springs, Colo., was the first American and second Masters runner in 31:29 as he finished ninth overall.

Defending champion Elana Meyer of South Africa did not leave it to the last minute this year. She jumped out quickly and settled in with the second pack of male runners. "It was a tough race," she told the newspaper. "The temperature was right and the other conditions were good, but it was quite a strong wind.

"The start is always a big part of this because you can get caught up with so many people here. I just found myself with the second lead group of guys and stuck with them. I never saw the second place woman."

Meyer was well off her own course record but won handily in 32:46. She said, "It's always a lot of fun. Charleston is a beautiful place, and it's really a world-class field. This is a one-of-a-kind race."

Sally Barsosio of Kenya, who had led Meyer for most of the 1997 race, was never a factor although she finished second for the second year in a row, this time in 34:31. "She (Meyer) just got out there with the men. I waited for the guys behind me to protect me, but by then Elana was gone," she told the newspaper. "After the bridge, I was thinking I could do something, but there were too many people in between us." Naomi Mugo, also of Kenya, was third in 34:37.

The Masters division had a new champion as Keith Anderson of England finished eighth overall in 31:04. He was followed by the next two overall finishers who were also Masters runners: Craig Young, 31:29, and defending champion Antoni Niemczak of Poland, 31:38. The female Masters division was won by Tatyana Pozdnyakova of Ukraine, who despite the windy conditions managed to set a new female Masters course record 35:09, 4 seconds under the old record. Patty Valadka 36:53 and Irina Bondarchouck 36:58, both of Russia, were second and third.

For the first time the race added prize money (three deep) for the Grand Masters (50 and over) division. Charleston runner Bob Schlau in his first year as a Grand Masters runner had suffered a severe hamstring injury. He ran the race anyway and was glad to be able to finish and win in 37:37. He admitted he was disappointed to have run 4 minutes slower than any of his previous Bridge Runs, but glad to win the division. Terry Van Natta of Greensboro, N.C., was second in 37:44, while Porter Reed of Elgin, Ill., was third in 39:15.

Betty Ryberg of Aiken, S.C., ran away from her competition to win handily in 42:44. Susie Kluttz of Winston Salem, N.C., was second in 46:59 and Kathy Jaggers of Rock Hill, S.C., was third in 47:19.

The Dr. Marcus Newberry Award for first area finisher went to Tom Mather of Mount Pleasant for the second year in a row. He finished 21st overall in 32:53. Female winner for the third year in a row was Charleston's Clarice Marana. She finished eighth female and 74th overall in 36:44. The Dewey Wise Trophy was won by Ed Shaffer, 79, of Walterboro, S.C., who ran 67:14.

For the eighth year in a row, Channel 24 television showed a one hour tape delay of the race. It was shown on Saturday night and repeated on Sunday morning.

Entry fee for the race was raised to $15 early, $20 late, and for the walk, $10 early, $12 late. In 1998, only one runner broke the 30-minute barrier. A total of 211 runners broke the 40-minute barrier, 21 of them female. There were 2,036 runners who crossed the finish line in less than 50 minutes, while 5,959 finished under 60. There were 7,916 men (61.3 percent of finishers) and 5,003 women (38.7 percent) listed in Charleston's Sunday Post and Courier, along with the top three from each age division. This was the third year in a row the newspaper printed complete results. It marked the first time over 5,000 women completed a race in South Carolina. This continued the race's pattern of increased female participation each year.

The accompanying untimed 4-mile fun walk drew an estimated 11,000 participants. Julian Smith was the race director for the fifth year in a row.

Other Voices
One View Over The Cooper's Best
By Dean Schuyler, Originally appeared in the May-June 1988 Low Country Runner

As much as we'd all like to change it, there can only be one first time. When a runner moves to Charleston, how soon does he know that he will do the Bridge Run? For me, I recall it taking about one week. Charlie Kellner, an early guide and confidante, said it first: "Of course, you'll do the Bridge Run next April."

I had not run the 10K distance in 15 years – but, I'd "train up." That's one way of looking at my life from Jan. 1 to April 2, 1998. But, the abstract way is frequently more fun. It didn't take long before I began to hear about the Bridge Run. "A lot of people do this." (What is it like to run with 30,000 people?) "It's one of the most scenic runs imaginable." (I drive the bridge twice daily – what would it be like to run the bridge?) "People come from everywhere to run this race." (Just to do the Bridge Run?)

Jungle Rain. Working at the Medical University of S.C. has been fun. Working at the Medical U. "during Bridge Week" is like doing group therapy with a large number of people suffering from the same obsession. Even I wanted to know about Saturday morning's weather one week earlier. (Why? I would've run whatever the weather. It only happens once a year.) They said it would be warm. They said a storm was coming. It would rain like hell on Friday and Saturday. Then, maybe just through Friday night, but the wind will blow you off the bridge. (The truth: There was "jungle rain" on Friday.)

Awakening Saturday, there was magically not a trace of the rain that fell. The sky was clear and blue. The sun was bright. The wind was a factor, but not nearly the gale that tried to blow me off the Isle of Palms Connector in a late March training run. When I awoke, I could not, at first, believe that the day was really here. I had

Elana Meyer on the way to her second win.
Post and Courier photo by Mic Smith

picked up my packet two weeks earlier, and Friday night I was formally introduced to my computer chip, ate pasta with my neighbor Marc Williams, pinned my number to my shirt, and then slept fitfully, listening to the thunder and seeing the lightning.

There was no preparation for arriving on Coleman Boulevard to get my initial glimpse of "the throng." Marc and I arrived about 7:30 a.m. and lined up "a respectable distance from the starting line." I met a teacher from North Carolina and a young woman doing the run for the first time. There was also the guy who would remark that the non-start when the gun sounded was "just his pace."

Where are you from? Bill Murray was funny; the trumpeter played a rousing anthem; the gun went off; and we stood there. We walked a bit, jogged a bit and (after 4 or so minutes) reached our first goal: the starting line. Things quickly opened up and I ran past my gas station and the cleaner. That's when I was engulfed by charging Marines (who, I was sure, were Citadel cadets). Turns out they were in the Highway Patrol corps from Columbia. They chanted, and the spectators cheered. I wondered at first why people I didn't know were cheering as I ran by. I thought maybe because I was doing something well, or just "lookin' good." Which reminds me: What are the most frequent comments heard among runners in this race? "Lookin' good!" and "Where you from?"

At Patriots Point, I actually locked eyes with Terry, my wife, awaiting the start of the Walk, and watching us runners go by. The sighting of the bridge begged for a camera. The first hill (and the wind) presented the first real obstacle. The view from the bridge was as awesome as I had imagined – and then some. Unforgettable! A tugboat greeted us with a horn blast and a rainbow of colors in its spray refracting the sun. A parasailor struggled with the wind above the Cooper. The well placed speakers on the last ramp down urged me on.

Lookin' good! There was the energy from the throng, the views and the spectators along the route. I remember the woman from Guam, the man wearing headphones to "control his breathing" and the woman who responded to my greeting with, "It's so nice to hear a voice." By mile 5, I was aware that my feet hurt. The pain was lost however, in the presence of the radio station, the named bricks on King Street, the photo takers on Market Street, and seeing the finish line on Meeting Street. Of course, I broke into an all-out run for the last two blocks.

Elite runners on the second span of the Pearman Bridge. Post and Courier photo by Brad Nettles

Times never matter a lot to me. And yet, I did two 10Ks in training at 79 and 77 minutes. On the big day, my chip said 68:55. Exhilarated wouldn't quite capture the feeling, but you get the idea. There will never be another first time. But I can't wait for next year.

Other Voices
Tell Me About Your Bridge Run 1998

By Cedric Jaggers. Originally appeared in the May-June 1998 issue of the Low Country Runner

Marion Square, April 4. After the 21st Bridge Run. Were you there? It was definitely a mob scene. I had my clipboard, my Running Journal T-shirt and my Charleston Running Club hat on. I had trouble finding you! I wanted to get every club member and only got about 10% of the club. Shame on you for leaving early or being too shy to come up and tell me about your Bridge Run. We stayed until the last award was handed out - Congratulations Margaret Wright. Next year I think they should do the oldest age groups first, what do you think? Anyway, here it is; the 10th edition of your words, written down EXACTLY as you say them, when you say them. People are listed in the order we happened to bump into each other. Times and places shown after each person are from the results Burns Computer printed for me during the awards ceremony.

Awards were presented by actual race time as required by USATF, chip time (which of course is only for fun) is also shown here. Kathy and I looked through the results up to 3 minutes on each side of the time you told me – the small print and 12,919 lines of times made it rough going. Sorry if we couldn't find you there.

Kathy Jaggers: Catch me, I'm going to fall down (in the finish chute - the rest was after we got out of the emergency tent, CJ). I'm not ready yet. Did you write that down? Stop it. It was the slowest second span I've ever run. I was more worried about the wind than the hills because of my asthma. Then once we got off the bridges it seemed to be over in 5 minutes, it went so quick. I was disappointed in my time because I felt like I worked a lot harder than that. 47:19. I've always said rain is a four letter word - so is wind. 3rd Overall Grand-Master Female, 1133rd overall, chip time 47:14, race time 47:19

Nina Parks: I was in the port-a-let line and let the runner with number 1 take my place and he wore my chip ... April Fool. 1,498th overall, chip time 43:30, race time 48:38

Leon Locklear: Bob Seger ruled the day – Against The Wind. A good effort 43 flat, maybe a little over. I had to work to get that. It was not what I wanted. It took me a long time to catch that race walking guy (note a sly reference to me which you can only understand if you know that I had been telling people about my hip problem and being asked during a race the previous week by another runner if I was race walking, CJ). It was my 20th Bridge Run. 412th overall, chip time 42:54, race time 43:01

Ray Dennis: I don't know that there is anything to tell. This is my 13th in a row. I just run it to run it. I thought the organization was a little lax. It was a personal worst, 1:08. 10,458th overall, chip time 108:35, race time 1:09:48

Tami Dennis: Oh. Ho, ho, ho, ho. Oh, don't put oh down. It was actually fun this year. I had surgery two weeks ago. I made a decision just to have fun with it. I ran it with a 10-year-old I coach. We ran 50:37. Hope it's good enough for her to place. 2,202nd overall, chip time 50:37, race time 50:37

Bob Schlau: I was happy just to be able to do it. I had trouble with my hamstrings. I ran about 37 minutes. Got to go, they are calling me to sign posters. 1st Overall Grand-Master Male, 104th overall, chip time 37:34, race time 37:37

Lennie Moore: Howie (Schomer) just said it (he had announced from the stage): wind blown. The wind got me like everybody else. I can't complain 38:11. 11th 40-44 male, 124th overall, chip time 38:08, race time 38:12

Frank Blackett: I finished with a smile on my face. I enjoyed it. That's important. I wish somebody knew how to change the wind direction. 24th 65-69, 7,336th overall, chip time 1:02:27, race time 1:02:45

Mike Johns: It was better than last year. The wind was brutal on the bridges. I ran as hard as I could. 41:15. 276th overall, chip time 41:09, race time 41:15

James Rion: Mile 1, 4, 5 and 6 were alright, but the middle was pretty tough. 44:20. 587th overall, chip time 44:17, race time 44:25

Jeffrey Herndon: Well, when I was passed by a racewalker ... at least that's what I felt like going up the first span. Near the finish it was nice to see Mike Chodnicki suffering as bad as I was. 40:14. 231st overall, chip time 40:12, race time 40:14

Keith Ambrose: Not worth talking about. The worst time I've ever run in my life. April comes around every year and I get sick. My worst: 49 something. 1,662nd overall, chip time 49:12, race time 49:17

Jill Pellerin: It was the worst, ha, ha, ha, ha. I was hoping you wouldn't find me. I'll just say I felt sick and dizzy. I don't mind telling you I walked some. I had an awful race. About 57:35. (unable to find in results, CJ)

Eileen Stellefson: No. I didn't have a good race. It's just something I think about all week, what will I say? It was fun compared to last year. I'd rather have the wind

than the heat. My time was the same as last year and I'm in a new age group. 47:40. 9th 40-44, 1232nd overall, chip time 47:26, race time 47:43

Robert Lowery: It was the year not to run. Ummm - I want to think of something positive. Lack of conditioning and the wind, pain, suffering and my slowest time ever by two minutes. 37:04. I didn't think I'd ever run slower than 35:40. 14th 35-39, 86th overall, chip time 37:03, race time 37:06

David Anderson: I'm 67 years old and missed first place in my age group by 30 seconds last year. I popped my hamstring, I even heard it and came across limping. Pretty good due to the circumstances. Next year I'm going to get faster. Pulled my hamstring 3 weeks ago, I shouldn't have been running it but I did. 2nd 65-69, 2,903rd overall, chip time 52:22, race time 53:18

Reg Horn: It wasn't too bad. It was pretty windy, pretty slow. I just ran a marathon 2 weeks ago. Today, about 49:45. 2,420th overall, chip time 49:47, race time 51:50

Delores Horn: I think the hills were less than I anticipated. I really enjoyed it a lot. It turned out good with the chip. It's a nice run. About 55 minutes. 4,688th overall, chip time 55:27, race time 57:30

Tom Dority: I just tore it up, around 45:40. A great race, windy but it didn't bother me. I had a great finish, couldn't ask for a better race. 811th overall, chip time 45:36, race time 45:49

Maria Griffith: I was happy with it considering the wind was so bad. I'd been training on the bridge. I ran about the same as last year, a little over 48 minutes. 13th 40-44, 1,468th overall, chip time 48:14, race time 48:32

Dan Clapper: Twenty-two seconds faster than last year. The only thing that could have made it better is a tailwind and if I could have beat Gary Ricker. 40:38. 244th overall, chip time 41:31, race time 40:38

Elizabeth Letourineau: It was beautiful, but it was painful. I've done it two other times, but it was never so painful. 57 minutes. I should have been a few minutes faster. (unable to find in results, CJ)

Steven Hunt: Just thankful I made it to the finish. I've had bronchitis twice in the past weeks. I ran about 48:10. 1,412th overall, chip time 48:13, race time 48:20

Lessie Snead: What do I say Cedric? I was just glad to get over the first span. The rest was alright. About 55:15. 3,735th overall, chip time 54:58, race time 55:18

John Vonderleith: Twenty seconds below my mark, which I'm proud of. 46:33.

1,041st, chip time 46:33, race time 46:53

Claudette Drawdy: I took 8 minutes off last year. 51:13. (unable to find in results, CJ)

Tom Mahon: Like everybody else—slow. I was hoping to run a minute and a half faster. Kind of disappointing. 35:24. 46th overall, 35:26 chip and race time

Gary Ricker: Thanks to Mike Chodnicki and Cedric, you two pulled me over that bridge. I can do without the wind next year. 40:02. My 19th one, and it was the hardest. 14th 45-49, 215th overall, chip time 39:58, race time 40:02

Dave Mellard: All I can tell you is I had a good time, no trouble with it, just slower. 52 minutes. In the 4th Bridge Run I ran 41:30, this year 10 minutes slower. 2nd 75up, 2,888th overall, chip time 52:58, race time 53:15

Pat Rhode: I finished. I fell, but I finished. I don't think I'm hurt. I've been running a lot better. It was windy. 52:58. This is my 19th one. 3rd 55-59, 2,900th overall, chip time 52:56, race time 53:17

Margaret Wright: I got stuck behind the walkers. They jumped in before they were supposed to. I had to walk, I couldn't get around them. That's aggravating. About 1:27. I had to walk almost the whole bridge because I couldn't get around all those people. Another year and I'm still here. 2nd 75up award, 1:27:00

Ed Ledford: There were 3 things: the Bridge, the wind, and I'm getting older. The wind was really bad, but I'm pretty pleased with my position. I usually can't sleep the night before the race but I did last night for the first time in five years. I hate being over 40 minutes. 1st 60-64, 223rd overall, chip time 40:07, race time 40:10

Mike Chodnicki: I was wondering how long it would take you to catch up with me. I thought it was the worst race in my life until I found out how bad everybody else did. It was just awful. That's about the bottom line, my worst Bridge Run ever. To me it was more punishment than fun. 40:15. 230th overall, chip time 3:08:57 - pretty slow huh? (Obviously a chip malfunction. CJ) race time 40:15

Cedric Jaggers: It was a nightmare, my worst Bridge Run. I felt bad the whole way. My hip bothered me and the wind just totally knocked me out. I honestly thought I wouldn't finish in the top 1,000 so many people passed me. I couldn't even kick. I usually kick like crazy and would have been under 43 if I could have kicked but I couldn't. 43:09. I was sure I hadn't placed in my age group. I was astonished when I got an age group mug for a higher place than I had placed in years. 9th 50-54, 423rd overall, chip time 43:05, race time 43:09

1998 Awards
Prize money winners:
Overall Male
1 Tom Nyariki .... Kenya .... 29:58 ... $5,000
2 John Kariuki .... Kenya .... 30:18 ... $3,500
3 James Bungei .... Kenya .... 30:26 ... $1,500
4 Steve Nyamu .... Kenya .... 30:43 ... $1,000
5 Simon Chemoiyo ...... Kenya .... 30:52 ... $800
6 John Mwai .... Kenya .... 30:55 ... $600
7 Joseph Kahuga .... Kenya .... 31:00 ... $500
8 Keith Anderson ...... Somerset UK .... 31:04 ... $400
9 Craig Young .... Colorado Sp CO ..... 31:29 ... $300
10 Antoni Niemczak .... Poland .... 31:38 ... $250
11 Eric Ashton .... Columbia, SC .... 31:40 ... $200
12 Paul Marmaro .... Delray Bch FL ...... 31:46 ... $150
13 Patrick Phillips.... WinSalem,NC .... 31:55 ... $100
14 Julius Rotich ...... Kenya .... 32:10 ... $75
15 Michael Tunget ..... Kenya .... 32:17 ... $50

Overall Female
1 Elana Meyer .... South Africa .... 32:46 ... $5,000
2 Sally Barsosio .... Kenya .... 34:31 ... $3,000
3 Naomi Mugo .... Kenya .... 34:37 ... $1,500
4 Teresa Wanjiku ...... Kenya .... 34:44 ... $1,000
5 Tatyano Pozdnyakova Ukraine .... 35:09 ... $800
6 Silvia Skvortsova..... Russia .... 35:20 ... $600
7 Tina Jensen .... Greenville SC ...... 36:35 ... $500
8 Clarice Marana .... Charleston SC ..... 36:44 ... $400
9 Patty Valadka .... Houston TX .... 36:50 ... $300
10 Irina Bondarchouk ... Russia .... 36:58 ... $250
11 Megan Flowers ...... Ft Collins CO ...... 37:21 ... $200
12 Amy Kattwinkel .... Charlotte NC .... 38:07 ... $150
13 Victoria Crisp ...... Nashville TN .... 38:41 ... $100
14 Mary Jo Ferrigan .... Athens GA .... 38:47 ... $75
15 Tracy Center .... Greenville SC ...... 38:49 ... $50

Masters Male
1 Keith Anderson .... Somerset, UK .... 31:04 ... $1,500
2 Craig Young .... Colorado Sp, CO .... 31:29 ... $1,000
3 Antoni Niemczak ..... Poland .... 31:38 ... $750
4 Ted Jaleta .... Canada .... 32:51 ... $500
5 Tom Mather .... Mt. Pleasant, SC .... 32:53 ... $250

Masters Female
1 Tatyana Pozdnyakova . Ukraine .... 35:09 ... $1,500
2 Patty Valadka .... Russia .... 36:53 ... $1,000
3 Irina Bondarchouk ... Russia .... 36:58 ... $750
4 Victoria Crisp .... Nashville TN .... 38:41 ... $500
5 Alendia Vestal .... Brevard NC .... 40:33 ... $250

– Continued on next page

1998 Award Winners, continued from page 169

Grand Masters

(prize money awarded for the first time)

Male

1	Bob Schlau	Charleston, SC	37:37	$750
2	Terry Van Natta	Greensboro NC	37:44	$500
3	Porter Reed	Elgin, IL	39:15	$250

Female

1	Betty Ryberg	Aiken, SC	42:44	$750
2	Susie Kluttz	Win. Salem NC	46:59	$500
3	Kathy Jaggers	Rock Hill SC	47:19	$250

Dr. Marcus Newberry Award

Tri-County Local Winners:

Tom Mather	Mt Pleasant, SC	32:53	$500
Clarice Marana	Charleston, SC	36:44	$500

Special award:

Dewey Wise Trophy for oldest finisher with time less than his or her age:

Ed Shaffer, 79 .... Walterboro, SC 67:14

Age group award winners

(presented to top 3 in age group, with top 5% up to maximum of 25 awarded in each age group):

Male 12 & under (82 finishers, 5 awards)

1 Ryan Deak ... 40:12
2 Jacob McCaskill ... 41:17
3 Ben Sherard ... 42:19
4 Wes Knight ... 46:24
5 David Poulnot Jr ... 47:47

Female 12 & under (68 fin., 4 awards)

1 Hailey Hymas ... 51:09
2 Ray Burns ... 51:40
3 Lexie Maravich ... 53:11
4 Sara Johannesmeyer ... 53:37

Male 13-17 (315 finishers, 16 awards)

1 David Scharff ... 37:03
2 Jeremiah Milliman ... 37:08
3 George Taylor ... 37:12
4 Brantlee Milner ... 37:24
5 Robert Killian ... 37:29
6 Andrew Scharff ... 38:40
7 Michael Proctor ... 38:45
8 Chad Zimmerman ... 39:18
9 Andrew Pifrrotti ... 39:54
10 Kevin Timp ... 40:00
11 Kevin Crosby ... 40:26
12 Keith Bagwell ... 40:48
13 Matt Smith ... 41:56
14 James Skelton ... 42:13
15 Chad Chism ... 42:25
16 Drew English ... 42:29

Female 13-17 (156 finishers, 8 awards)

1 Lauren Paige ... 44:14
2 Danielle Deines ... 46:27
3 Michele Milner ... 46:48
4 Kelly Compton ... 47:50
5 Meejin Hong ... 47:56
6 Summer Ford ... 49:29
7 Tiffany Griffin ... 49:32
8 Marcie Milner ... 50:06

Male 18-21 (291 finishers, 15 awards)

1 Gregg Bott ... 35:06
2 Derrick Williams ... 35:23
3 Kevin Croxton ... 35:24
4 Jay Glover ... 37:59
5 Travis Brady ... 38:01
6 David Lee ... 38:10
7 William Jutzeler ... 38:13
8 Chandler Conner ... 39:01
9 Kurt Wilson ... 39:27
10 Lee Kain ... 39:49
11 Brandon Duncan ... 40:23
12 Trey Mooring ... 40:25
13 Jason Birch ... 40:42
14 Wesley Jones ... 40:45
15 Jim Simson ... 41:44

Female 18-21 (315 finishers, 16 awards)

1 Angela Brown ... 41:27
2 Sarah Keen ... 44:28
3 Heather Varn ... 46:15
4 Julie Berlan ... 46:41
5 Traci Asti ... 46:50
6 Leslie Parker ... 47:33
7 Mollie McMahon ... 47:36
8 Laurie MacMillan ... 48:04
9 Noura Hibri ... 48:18
10 Daniela Srunk ... 48:57
11 Amanda Ping ... 49:32
12 Matalie Gaskill ... 49:40
13 Elisha Swett ... 50:11
14 Courtney Klemek ... 50:31
15 Britney Cooke ... 50:32
16 Laurel Crenshaw ... 50:33

Male 22-25 (668 finishers, 25 awards)

1 Daniel Moriasi ... 32:20
2 Brandt Armentrout ... 32:50
3 Lindsey Steele ... 34:50
4 Jason Annan ... 35:46
5 Bill Freeman ... 36:31
6 Mark Miller ... 37:00
7 Patrick VanBoden ... 37:23
8 Jonathan Stewart ... 37:38
9 Stephen Saleeby ... 38:12
10 Michael Gambrell ... 38:23
11 Eliot Cannon ... 38:44
12 Steve Coles ... 39:05
13 Michael Janech ... 39:05
14 Jeffry McCallum ... 39:08
15 Benji Keisler ... 39:32
16 Mark Polston ... 39:50
17 Stephen Hughes ... 40:02
18 Jaime Noel ... 40:08
19 Wesley Littlejohn ... 40:11
20 Johnathan Dobson ... 40:32
21 Jimmy Major ... 40:55
22 Chris Pateras ... 40:55
23 Greg Hall ... 40:56
24 Justin Howe ... 41:10
25 David Low ... 41:21

Female 22-25 (721 finishers, 25 awards)

1 Jennifer Sheets ... 42:08
2 Christina Hallenbeck ... 43:38
3 Heather Kempinger ... 44:01
4 Helen Lafaye ... 44:12
5 Sherril Wells ... 44:51
6 Joanna Morgan ... 44:59
7 Jennifer Freeman ... 45:11
8 Michelle Weber ... 46:12
9 Kimberly Morgan ... 46:17
10 Carol Burnett ... 46:20
11 Noelle Nolas ... 46:24
12 Zita Latona ... 47:20
13 Mason Best ... 47:25
14 Emily Redmon ... 47:27
15 Betsy Shaughnessy ... 47:28
16 Laura Forster ... 47:44
17 Maria Schnautz ... 47:53
18 Billi Veber ... 47:54
19 Bonnie Brooks ... 48:05
20 Lori Archer ... 48:10
21 Tara James ... 48:23
22 Jennifer Thompson ... 48:33
23 Anne Wyman Fouche ... 48:34
24 Sariah Toronto ... 48:36
25 Jennifer Carman ... 48:41

Male 26-29 (1,073 finishers, 25 awards)

1 Robert Adams ... 32:44
2 Jamie Barnes ... 34:33
3 Dan Crooker ... 35:00
4 David Brown ... 35:17
5 David Nelson ... 35:37
6 Joe Blackstone ... 35:45
7 Michael Haranzo ... 36:13
8 Jon Pruett ... 36:20
9 Brian Fancher ... 36:26
10 Byron Law ... 36:34
11 Darol Timberlake ... 36:38
12 Robbie Smith ... 36:44
13 Andres Barron ... 36:48
14 Nathan Stephens ... 36:50
15 Darius Deak ... 37:01
16 Tom Wakefield ... 37:02
17 Cory Fleming ... 37:17
18 Lyn Rowland ... 37:18
19 Steve De Salvo ... 37:34
20 Abbott Whitney ... 37:54
21 Sammy Owen ... 38:01
22 Chris Wozniak ... 38:15
23 Timothy Decker ... 38:17
24 Hunter Pierce ... 38:28
25 John Riordan ... 38:36

Female 26-29 (925 finishers, 25 awards)

1 Gabriele Hauck ... 39:07
2 Julie Seymour ... 39:21
3 Kristin McCann ... 40:43
4 Susan Madlinger ... 42:10
5 Julie Oliver ... 42:19
6 Cara Johnson ... 42:40
7 Carey White ... 44:36
8 Christina Clum ... 44:52
9 Dixie Baker ... 44:52
10 Katie Watson ... 45:04
11 Cindy Ostle ... 45:30
12 Karen Chovan ... 45:43
13 Sharon Stewart ... 45:43
14 Leslie Randall ... 46:29
15 Betsey Gallagher ... 46:57
16 Molly Hughes ... 47:03
17 Kathleen Mahoney ... 47:08
18 Tricia Erpelding ... 47:23
19 Kate Blaske ... 47:27
20 Heather Fogle ... 47:28
21 Kari Staley ... 47:44
22 Ellen Potts ... 47:55
23 Amy Stein ... 47:56
24 Cinda Miller ... 47:56
25 Sohee Park ... 48:08

Male 30-34 (1,220 finishers, 25 awards)

1 Jamey Yon ... 33:30
2 Irving Batten ... 33:53
3 Paul Bonfiglio ... 34:01
4 Keith Hurley ... 34:35
5 Keith Player ... 35:26
6 David Latimer ... 35:35
7 Scott Walschlager ... 35:49
8 Dale Carico ... 36:07
9 Michael Strickland ... 36:14
10 Mark Scott ... 36:26
11 Karl Debate ... 36:56
12 Kevin Tashleia ... 36:57
13 Karl Johnson ... 37:08
14 Chris Reilly ... 37:14
15 Kevin Nelson ... 38:01
16 James Doyle ... 38:03
17 Rick Garvais ... 38:34
18 David Malone ... 38:39
19 Mark Rutledge ... 38:42
20 Joe Bowman ... 38:44
21 Christopher Byers ... 38:51
22 Cail Brown ... 38:57
23 Hugh Myrick ... 39:06
24 Robert Denmark ... 39:19
25 Rorik Larson ... 39:20

Female 30-34 (863 finishers, 25 awards)

1 Renee Corsello ... 38:51
2 Elizabeth Graham ... 42:40
3 Julia Smith ... 42:52
4 Pamela Mitchell ... 42:55
5 Lorena Feree ... 42:59
6 Nancy Novelli ... 43:33
7 Jacqueline Miller ... 44:09
8 Kate Borg ... 45:06
9 Janet Norton ... 45:25
10 Almaz Smith ... 45:40
11 Mary Hunt ... 45:42
12 Heather Wood ... 45:55
13 Wendy Hunter ... 46:09
14 Beverly Veals ... 46:11
15 Lynn McCain ... 46:11
16 Ellen Smith ... 46:25
17 Maribeth Mortensen ... 46:26
18 Nyala Edwards ... 46:33
19 Christi Craft ... 46:38
20 Nancy Brennan ... 46:43
21 Kimberly Herrman ... 47:03
22 Melody Charles ... 47:20
23 Donna Durante ... 47:31

24 Susan Roof 47:53
25 Lynn Evans 48:07

Male 35-39 (1,065 finishers, 25 awards)

1 Paul Okerberg 34:42
2 Larry Brock 35:02
3 James Harris 35:05
4 Tom Cuff 35:30
5 Jamie Wilbanks 35:42
6 Joel Carpenter 35:49
7 James Youngquist 35:49
8 Angus McBryde 36:05
9 Paul Sax 36:23
10 Blake Zemp 36:30
11 David Moore 36:34
12 Pete Edge 36:43
13 Jonathan Bellingham 36:44
14 Robert Lowery 37:06
15 Chris Shockley 37:15
16 Lance Leopold 37:27
17 Randy Aldridge 37:30
18 Pender Murphy 37:33
19 Jeffrey Milliman 37:48
20 Alan Gebert 37:53
21 Billy Tisdale 37:55
22 Richard Kuehl 38:02
23 David Rourke 38:22
24 David Ariola 38:25
25 Jim Meadows 38:41

Female 35-39 (729 finishers, 25 awards)

1 Patti Bouvatte 38:55
2 Patt Loggins 38:57
3 Laura Vroon 39:18
4 Betsy Veronee 41:47
5 Alison Phillips 47:11
6 Deborah Chaney 43:14
7 Patty Fiero 44:10
8 Nancy Thomas 44:18
9 Eileen Clark 44:34
10 Barbara Wagner 44:58
11 Julie Boughn 45:01
12 Jane Banse 45:06
13 Marilee James 45:11
14 Lisa Krupp 45:12
15 Claudia Hapak 45:21
16 Patricia Clark 45:22
17 Jennifer Doles 45:25
18 Julia Ralston 45:43
19 Beth Ritchey 45:53
20 Jennifer Hales 46:13
21 Evelyn Long 46:19
22 Patricia Murphy 46:34
23 Pamela Peterson 46:39
24 Becky Droginske 46:45
25 Rhonda Cloinger 46:51

Male 40-44 (1,007 finishers, 25 awards)

1 Amit Ne'Eman 32:54
2 Jim Hage 33:03
3 Dave Geer 34:48
4 Randy Pochel 35:17
5 Paul Dawson 35:40
6 Harry Ash 37:14
7 Jim Wilhelm 37:19
8 David Bourgeois 37:58
9 Alan Blaszkiewicz 38:05
10 Hal Hall 38:11
11 Lennie Moore 38:12
12 George Howe 38:16
13 James Clayton 38:31
14 David Renneisen 38:33
15 Bob Foster 38:48
16 Clyde Sanders 39:06
17 Kurt Schaum 39:06
18 Andrew Ammon 39:12
19 Bobby Torri 39:15
20 Greg Fagan 39:17
21 Thomas Roberts 39:33
22 Jeff Dorociak 39:46
23 Anthony Pizzuti 39:58
24 Peter Brunnick 40:04
25 Dennis Kerwin 40:09

Female 40-44 (553 finishers, 25 awards)

1 Dian Ford 41:34
2 Sarah Overcash 45:11
3 Ann Gamba 45:29
4 Peggy Kinney 46:19
5 Cindy Brokens 46:31
6 Nancy Farlen 46:43
7 Ginger Foley 47:29
8 Eileen Stellefson 47:43
9 Patti Godsen 48:19
10 Patricia Marchand 48:22
11 Nitsa Calas 48:29
12 Maria Griffith 48:32
13 Beverly Grant 48:50
14 Michele Stutts 49:05
15 Gayle Kindschuh 49:29
16 Annie Cruitt 49:31
17 Kathleen Roberts 49:31
18 Mary Jane McGowan 49:39
19 Jill Smith 49:49
20 Mary Millar 49:58
21 Nancy Duff 50:02
22 Sallie Chardukian 50:07
23 Marilyn Wallace 50:16
24 Tricia Christie 50:19
25 Sue Porter 50:20

Male 45-49 (812 finishers, 25 awards)

1 Gordon English Jr 35:55
2 Norm Ferris 36:59
3 Ervin Reid 38:04
4 Donald Bergan 38:21
5 Danny West 38:25
6 Joseph Denneny 38:34
7 Marcal Marchand 38:40
8 David Reintjes 38:46
9 Leon Cook 38:50
10 John Bernhardt 38:57
11 Charles Kellner 39:01
12 Jim Boyd 39:05
13 Michael Drose 39:43
14 Gary Ricker 40:02
15 Ralph Veytia 40:07
16 Rob Krieghaber 40:53
17 Louis Smith 40:58
18 Larry Milner 41:04
19 John Sperry 41:12
20 Oliver Marshall 41:21
21 Vince Herran 41:35
22 Ned Hettinger 42:05
23 Dave Lemonds 42:05
24 Guy Herring 42:10
25 Paul Dixon 42:11

Female 45-49 (326 finishers, 17 awards)

1 Catherine Lempesis 41:45
2 Cheryl Brooks 42:10
3 Nonie Hudnall 44:06
4 Becky Sox 44:35
5 Sallie Driggers 46:14
6 Mary Carbott 47:06
7 Karen Martin 47:14
8 Cathy Burton 47:30
9 Pam Arnett 48:03
10 Susie Black 48:19
11 Jo Haubenreiser 48:41
12 Barbara Early 49:01
13 Helga Greim 49:25
14 Beth Schmid 49:51
15 Vera Tang 51:30
16 Judith Stanton 52:02
17 Judy Gilman 52:08

Male 50-54 (591 finishers, 25 awards)

1 Sam Davis 40:35
2 Dan Young 40:57
3 Gary Cadle 41:17
4 Phil Peterson 41:45
5 James Horne 42:14
6 Ray Kitchen 42:28
7 Robert Baker 42:37
8 Arnie Elton 42:40
9 Cedric Jaggers 43:09
10 Earl Jackson 43:21
11 John Johnson 43:51
12 Roy Pafenberg 43:53
13 Tai Sugimoto 43:55
14 Calvin Coetsee 44:28
15 Arthur Smith 44:44
16 Dick Brenner 44:44
17 Herb Smith 44:46
18 John Douglas 44:48
19 Mackie Johnson 44:57
20 Michael Clark 45:27
21 Gary Myers 45:29
22 Thomas Foster 45:42
23 James Greene 45:48
24 Steve Austin 46:00
25 Linny Moore 46:03

Female 50-54 (174 finishers, 9 awards)

1 Nancy Curry 47:37
2 Kathy Seavers 48:03
3 Lyn Hammond 49:02
4 Mary Milnarcik 50:03
5 Karen McMahon 51:35
6 Ann Macon-Ellis 52:38
7 Linda Simmons 53:26
8 Cheryl Ilderton 54:18
9 Mary Kay Benz 54:55

Male 55-59 (320 finishers, 16 awards)

1 Dick Ashley 41:51
2 Wallace Carr 43:00
3 Richard Weatherford 43:56
4 Eric Elbel Sr 44:05
5 Thomas Eison 44:23
6 Keith Weaver 44:29
7 Floyd Deandrade 44:57
8 Theron Cochran 45:00
9 Joseph McAlhany 45:20
10 Philip Watson 45:38
11 Dean Godwin 45:45
12 Thomas Dority 45:49
13 T J Voss 45:52
14 Thomas Zimmerman 46:16
15 Marshall Wakat 46:26
16 Roy Ingle 46:30

Female 55-59 (81 finishers, 5 awards)

1 Ashley Hurteau 47:59
2 Barbara Avant 51:25
3 Diane Kohrman 52:34
4 Pat Rhode 53:17
5 Mary Thompson 54:04

Male 60-64 (115 finishers, 6 awards)

1 Ed Ledford 40:10
2 John Dromsky 45:53
3 Toby Transou 46:34
4 Jack Schmid 47:30
5 Raymond Stone 48:03
6 John Thompson 48:23

Female 60-64 (28 finishers, 3 awards)

1 Cheyney Geren 58:17
2 E.K. Tolley Beeson 59:59
3 Camille Daniel 1:02:27

Male 65-69 (25 finishers, 3 awards)

1 Norm McAbee 50:13
2 Avery Goode Sr 52:54
3 David Anderson 53:18

Female 65-69 (10 finishers, 3 awards)

1 Garthedon Embler 52:21
2 Lois Gilmore 53:30
3 Nancy Bell 1:01:31

Male 70-74 (16 finishers, 3 awards)

1 William Fulton 51:17
2 Bill Kleber 56:26
3 Gene Priddy 1:03:07

Female 70-74 (3 finishers, 3 awards)

1 Kathleen Glancy 1:03:09
2 Mary Canty 1:30:38
3 Ola Moody 1:37:06

Male 75-99 (10 finishers, 3 awards)

1 Andrew Miller 52:03
2 David Mellard 53:15
3 Bob Wingard 1:00:54

Female 75-99 (2 finishers, 2 awards)

1 Lynn Edwards 1:10:31
2 Margaret Wright 1:27:00

Compiled by Cedric Jaggers from complete results provided by Burns Computer Services immediately after the race on April 4, 1998.

Elite runners approach the first of several spans, the bridge over Shem Creek. Post and Courier photo by Mic Smith

Chapter 22
1999
Eunice Sagero First Female Kenyan winner

The 22nd Bridge Run was held on March 27, 1999. Unseasonably cold rain during the week probably contributed to the decline in the number of race entrants: 15,349. The number of finishers also declined, though only slightly from the previous year, to 12,536. The race again used USATF certified course #SC96010BS. For the third year in a row, runners were timed by the ChampionChip computer timing chip system.

Race morning was cold, cloudy and windy — 35 degrees at dawn. Fortunately, the clouds blew away, and it was a sunny 45 degrees with a 10 mile per hour wind when the race began at 8 a.m.

The race itself was a Kenyan story again. Kenyans took 13 of the 15 spots including the first seven, and a Kenyan woman was a winner for the first time. The lead pack went through the mile mark in 4:35 and was down to six runners at the 2-mile mark in 9:15. Lazarus Nyakeraka began pulling away when he reached the top of the second span of the bridge. Nyakeraka and William Kiptum made a race of it, as Nyakeraka edged into the lead in the final miles and held off Kiptum to win by 5 seconds in 28:40. Daniel Kihara was third in 29:06. Johnathan Hume of Lakewood, Colo., was the first American finisher, running 29:39 to finish eighth overall.

"I was trying to make my move, but they are very fast," Nyakeraka told the *Post and Courier*. When Kiptum challenged him he was able to respond. "He runs good," Nyakeraka said, "but I didn't think he could outsprint me. It was cold today, and where I train it is very hot. But this is a good race and I hope to be back."

Eunice Sagero became the first Kenyan woman to win the Bridge Run as she ran 33:18. She was never challenged. "I'm used to the hills (in Kenya), so the bridge did not bother me," she told the newspaper. Tatyana Pozdnyakova of Ukraine smashed her own female course record set one year earlier as she finished second in 33:49. "I'm very happy with my results," she said. "The wind made it very tough, but I thought I ran well." Chris McNamara of Boulder, Colo., was third in 34:18.

John Tuttle of Douglasville, Ga., was male Masters winner in 30:27. David Geer of Clemson, S.C., was second in 33:11 with Randy Pochel of Charleston third in 33:22. Pozdnyakova's time of 33:49 set a female Masters course record. She was followed by Patty Valadka of Houston, Texas, in 35:52 and Lee Dipietro of Ruxton, Md., in 36:41.

Bob Schlau of Charleston won the Grand Masters for the second year in a row, this time in 34:48. Terry Van Natta of Greensboro, N.C., was second in 35:44 while Tom O'Connor of Smyrna, Ga., was third in 38:19. Female Grand Masters winner was Terry Mahr of Oregon, Ohio, in 39:24. She was followed by Betty Ryberg of Aiken, S.C., in 41:43 and Susie Kluttz of Winston Salem, N.C., 44:50.

The Dr. Marcus Newberry Award for first Tri-County finisher went to Eric Ashton of Mount Pleasant, who finished 18th overall in 30:32. Female winner was Sue Tandy of Goose Creek, 21st female overall, who ran 38:44. The Dewey Wise Trophy was won by Arnold Hecht, 78, of Greensboro, N.C., in a time of 75:42.

For the ninth year in a row, Channel 24 television showed a one hour tape delay of the race. It was shown on Saturday night and repeated on Sunday morning. Entry fees for the race and the walk were the same as the previous year.

In 1999, two runners broke the 29-minute barrier and 10 finished under 30 minutes. A total of 280 runners broke the 40-minute barrier, 29 of them female.

There were 2,008 runners who finished in less than 50 minutes and a total of 5,860 runners who crossed the finish line in less than an hour. The Sunday Post and Courier listed the top five in each age group (erroneously including prize money winners in the age groups) along with names and times for 7,523 men and 5,010 women. Complete results listed 7,524 men (60 percent) and 5,012 women (40 percent) finishers. The total number of male finishers decreased while female participation continued to increase. It was the second year in a row over 5,000 women finished the race. The untimed 4-mile walk, which begins near the foot of the bridge, drew more than 11,000.

Tell Me About Your Bridge Run 1999

By Cedric Jaggers, Originally appeared in the May/June 1999 Low Country Runner

Charleston Running Club members know the drill. Every year but one since 1988, after the Bridge Run in Marion Square an erstwhile journalist comes up to every CRC member he can find and asks them to "Tell me about your Bridge Run." Then he writes down exactly what they say. I tried to ask everyone's time so I could look up official time and place in the complete results which Burns Computer printed for me after the race. The results list all 12,536 finishers (7,524 male and 5,012 female) by age group.

For the second year in a row the Post & Courier listed the number of finishers incorrectly. The newspaper results, which apparently were printed 2 hours earlier than mine, listed 7,523 males and 5,010 females, yet the paper said there were 13,562 finishers.

I've tried to list everyone's official place and time, since it is a race, the results show real time, i.e. from the time the starting gun was fired until the runner crossed the finish line. USATF rules require real time for awards purposes; chip times, which will be in the mailed out results, are of course just for fun. Both times can be found in the results on the Internet: www.BridgeRun.Com. Here is everyone who told me about their Bridge Run, listed in the order we happened to bump into each other after the race.

Kathy Jaggers: They took me to the (Emergency Medical) tent. I crossed the line and I was stumbling and somebody came up and said, "Are you all right?" I said yes, then I stumbled again and he grabbed me and took me right to the tent. I couldn't talk. He asked if I had a problem. I showed him my inhaler and one of the ladies said, "I recognize you from last year." I had a good run, but then I couldn't breathe after I crossed the line. I worked real hard and ran over a minute faster than last year so I am happy. I ran 46:11. 1,078th overall, 2nd 50-54 46:11

Cherry Smiley: I'm so happy to have finished it. I ran all the inclines, I didn't walk. My knee didn't bother me ... I'm coming off a fractured knee cap. I'm happy to be here. I ran 1:07. 9,097th overall, 1:07:18

Steve Hunt: I'm very pleased, better than last year: 47:52. 1,464th overall, 47:56

Betsy Veronee: It was like the old days: I didn't catch you until after the first mile. I ran just over 40 minutes. 305th overall, top 5% a.g. award, 40:19

Lennie Moore: I usually think about what to tell you before I see you. All I can say is I'm happy. I had 36 flat, maybe my chip time will scoot me under. I felt I was going too fast the first quarter mile and felt like it was going to be a long day. I kept checking my splits and I just didn't slow down. 104th overall, top 5% a.g. award 40-44, 36:02

Jeffrey Herndon: I went out at 6:15 like I had good sense – finishing time 40:06, about 15 seconds faster than last year. Since I've gained about 20 pounds, I consider that pretty good. 291st overall, 40:08

Dan Clapper: It was great. The wind wasn't a factor but my lack of hill training was. I haven't done the bridge regularly like usual. 39:28. 245th overall, top 5% a.g. award 45-49, 39:29

Ronald Allan Charles: I really knew what to expect because I've done it before. It's interesting every year. I was intending to read Third Wind, a great article in the newsletter. It's different from second wind – go back and read the article. What I like about the chip, when you stop and go to the bathroom at one of the portable toilets it electronically stops running so you don't lose any time, or so I've been told. (Note: this is not factual, CJ) 1:00:11. 6,041st overall, 1:00:21

Keith Ambrose: I ran like the devil. The wind stopped me breathing. 43 something. I never do a good Bridge Run. I didn't hurt. 565th overall, 3rd 55-59, 43:02

Donna Lea Brown: It was great. I survived another one. 1:09. It took me 3 minutes to get to the start. 11,073rd overall, 1:13:59

Phil Cook: It was good. We just jogged with the rest of the crowd, about 54 minutes. The slowest I've ever run, but we enjoyed it. 3,586th overall, 54:50

Don Austell: I won't give you my time. They timed me with an hourglass. Less training and go faster? This makes 20 out of 22 Bridge Runs. I'm getting older but I love it anyway. About 1:05. (Unable to find in results)

Leon Locklear: One hour three minutes walking and jogging. My 21st Bridge Run. Missed the first one, had to ... (can't read my writing. CJ). The people who line up in the back don't lie about their pace. They are there for a reason. 9,772nd overall, 1:08:46

Maria Griffith: Whatever Phil said goes double for me. You really need to be racing before you run the Bridge Run. We were pretty far back. It took 10 minutes to get to the start, 42:37, officially about 55. It was more fun. 3,590th overall, 54:51

Jill Pellerin: I can't start talking yet because you'll write it down. Let's see ... well you know that I haven't been racing much or feeling good so I was happy with my race. I broke an hour. I jogged and ran and felt good the whole way. No pain and no gain. Like about an hour fifty-five. Under an hour running time. 6,361st overall 1:00:58

Frank Blackett: I enjoyed it because I knocked 3 minutes off last year's time: you're not supposed to do that. My time? 59:30 and I wanted to break 60. 6,223rd overall, 1:00:43

Mike Johns: I broke 40 and you can write what you want because I've been racing bad for about a year. I expected 41:30 or 42. I'm very happy to break 40. 39:56 or 58. I'm coming back. 248th overall 39:58

Bill Lachiocotte: This is Debbie (introducing me to her. CJ) We ran together. It was her first Bridge Run and her first 10k. We took a camera and took some pictures this year. Debbie, say something ...

Debbie: It was a great run. Time was 1:12 on my watch. 11,753rd overall 1:18:26

Tom Mahon: I was certainly pleased with it. I haven't been training hard and ran 34:11. Funny thing, I lost my watch at the starting line. The strap broke and I started to pick it up and said 'No way.' 50th overall, 5% a.g. award 35-39, 34:17

Bob Walton: It was 5 minutes better than last year. I got closer to the front. 52:39. I still need to get closer to the front. 2,774th overall, 52:39.

Gary Ricker: Well let's see. It was very good. I enjoyed it this time. The wind was not as bad as it was last year and it was an enjoyable experience. And I can say that because it is over now. My time was 38:43. 198th overall, top 5% a.g. award 45-49, 38:42

Lyn Hammond: Spectacular. You know, when you are editor you keep it short. 44:50. 836th overall, 1st 50-54, 44:51

Tom Dority: I was so impressed at the way it was organized, from the shuttles to the finish line. My time? 45:50 I think, I really don't know. It was just a great race. 972nd overall, top 5% a.g. award 55-59, 45:32

Nancy Curry: Let's see. My excuses: I've had plantar fasciitis the past year. I said I wanted to break 50 minutes and I did so I'm pleased as I can be under the circumstances. 1,773rd overall, 3rd 50-54, 49:11.

Margaret Wright: You found me. Well, I've been sick with the flu but I've run them all. I was back with the walkers. I ran 1:33 something. 12,345th overall 2nd 75-98, 1:31:42

Bob Schlau: They're getting better. I still want to do better. The recovery is a lot slower than I thought it would be from my injury. I still hope to run 33 again this year. 64th overall, 1st Grand Master overall award, 34:48

Pat Rhode: Well I ran the Bridge Run today with two people. I always run it with the Lord. Today I also ran with my mother who died two weeks ago. I didn't fall, and I did finish in about 52:51. 2,837th overall, 1st 60-64, 52:52

William Snead: I was under 8 minute miles at 4 miles, then my wheels fell off. 53 something. I hadn't run more than 4 miles in a long time. 3,425th overall, 54:24

Therese Killeen: Oh please. I always say the stupidest things. Don't, don't, don't write that down. (Attempts to grab my note pad, CJ). I had a good run. I'm satisfied. I think I was like 44:30, somewhere around there. I'm in a new age group. 800th overall, 2nd 45-49, 44:34

Nina Zoe Parks (Taylor): It was great, I'm training for the Boston Marathon. I ran negative splits. I've got to go, I finally won an age award (Awards announcement made by Howie Schomer so she had to go on stage and get it, CJ) It was my 16th in a row! 1,037th overall, top 5% a.g. award 40-44, 46:01

Dave Mellard: It was very good considering. It was a nice day, a nice run. I hope to be back next year. I ran 56 something. 4,298th overall, 1st 75-98, 56:33

Cedric Jaggers: (Note, Kathy grabbed the pad and wrote this down, so I know how everybody feels since she wrote down exactly what I said, CJ). Better than I expected, worse than I hoped for. It was what I was in shape to run, but I wanted to do better. Sometimes we can't complain but we do anyway. 421st overall, top 5% a.g. award 50-54, 41:36.

1999 Awards
Prize money winners:
Overall Male
1 Lazaru Nyakeraka ..... Kenya .... 28:40 ... $5,000
2 William Kiptum .... Kenya .... 28:45 ... $3,000
3 Daniel Kihara .... Kenya .... 29:06 ... $1,500
4 Julius Ondieki .... Kenya .... 29:10 ... $1,000
5 John Kariuki .... Kenya .... 29:21 .... $800
6 James Kariuki .... Kenya .... 29:34 .... $600
7 Kibet Cherop .... Kenya .... 29:39 .... $500
8 Jonathan Hume .... Lakewood CO ...... 29:39 .... $400
9 John Kagwe .... Kenya .... 29:47 .... $300
10 Ben Kimoundiu ...... Kenya .... 29:54 .... $250
11 Charles Mulinga ..... Zambia .... 30:02 .... $200
12 Simon Cherogony ... Kenya .... 30:07 .... $150
13 Cleophas Bor .... Kenya .... 30:08 .... $100
14 Jared Sagera .... Kenya .... 30:15 ..... $75
15 Jacob Kirwa .... Kenya .... 30:27 ..... $50

Overall Female
1 Eunice Sagero .... Kenya .... 33:18 ... $5,000
2 Tatyana Pozonyakova Ukraine .... 33:49 ... $3,000
3 Chris McNamara ...... Bolder CO .... 33:59 ... $1,500
4 Turena Johnson Lane Miami FL .... 34:18 ... $1,000
5 Marie Boyd .... Albuquerque .... 34:52 .... $800
6 Tina Jensen .... Greenville, SC ..... 34:55 .... $600
7 Patty Pitcher .... Charlotte, NC ..... 35:02 .... $500
8 Julia Kirtland .... Harpswell, ME .... 35:34 .... $400
9 Patty Valadka .... Houston, TX ...... 35:52 .... $300
10 Gail Pennachio ...... Greenville SC ..... 36:01 .... $250
11 Janice Addison ..... Columbia, SC ..... 36:33 .... $200
12 Lee Dipietro .... Ruxton, MD ...... 36:41 .... $150
13 Debra Wagner ...... Perrysburg, OH ... 36:49 .... $100
14 Farrell Burns .... Charlotte, NC .... 37:01 ..... $75
15 Patricia Bouvatte .... Jackson NC .... 37:02 ..... $50

Masters Male
1 John Tuttle .... Douglasville, GA ... 30:27 ... $1,500
2 David Geer .... Clemson, SC .... 33:11 ... $1,000
3 Randy Pochel .... Charleston, SC .... 33:22 .... $750
4 Paul Okenberg ...... Kiawah Isl, SC .... 33:27 .... $500
5 Paul Dawson .... Central, SC 34:33 $250

– Continued on next page

1999 Awards continued from page 175

Masters Female

1	Tatyana Pozdnyakova	Ukraine	33:49	$1,500
2	Patty Valadka	Houston, TX	35:52	$1,000
3	Lee Dipietro	Ruxton, MD.	36:41	$750
4	Debra Wagner	Perrysburg, OH	36:49	$500
5	Terry Mahr	Oregon, OH	39:24	$250

Grand Masters Male

1	Bob Schlau	Charleston, SC	34:48	$750
2	Terry Van Natta	Greensboro, NC	35:44	$500
3	Tom O'Connor	Smyrna, GA.	38:19	$250

Grand Masters Female

1	Terry Mahr	Oregon, OH	39:24	$750
2	Betty Ryberg	Aiken, SC	41:43	$500
3	Susie Kluttz	WinstonSalem NC	44:50	$250

Dr. Marcus Newberry Award

Local Tri-County Area Winners:

Male

Eric Ashton .... Mt Pleasant, SC ...... 30:32 .... $500

Female

Sue Tandy .... Goose Creek, SC ...... 38:44 .... $500

Special award:

Dewey Wise Trophy for oldest finisher with time less than his or her age:

Arnold Hecht, 78 .... Greensboro, NC 75:42

Age group award winners

(5% up to maximum of 25):

Male 12 & under (133 finishers 6 awards)

1	Mitch Chisholm	44:10
2	Mac McMahan	46:29
3	Zach Phillips	47:53
4	David Poulnot	47:54
5	David Johannesmeyer	49:10
6	Lowndes Sinkler	49:28

Female 12 & under (60 fin., 3 awards)

1	Erica Adams	46:21
2	Sarah Johannesmeyer	51:25
3	Haley Hymas	51:55

Male 13-17 (289 finishers, 15 awards)

1	Brantlee Milner	34:20
2	Robert Killian	34:32
3	Kevin Crosby	34:34
4	Derick Williamson	35:26
5	Kevin Timp	35:34
6	Michael Hatch	36:15
7	Aaron Reuwer	36:35
8	Nathan Crosby	38:01
9	Allen Stephenson	38:15
10	Henry Blackford	38:53
11	James Skelton	39:11
12	Thomas Bumgardner	39:52
13	Matthew Seel	40:16
14	Todd Walker	40:17
15	Stuart Campbell	40:47

13-17 Female (159 finishers, 8 awards)

1	Lauren Paige	44:09
2	Michele Milner	44:24
3	Marcie Milner	44:34
4	Shaw Hipsher	45:55
5	Margie Smith	46:25
6	Jennifer Chapman	47:43
7	Mary Runkie	48:17
8	Langdon Smith	49:44

Male 18-21 (249 finishers, 13 awards)

1	Brandon Cantrell	33:17
2	Derrick Williams	33:21
3	David Lee	34:13
4	Dwayne Brown	34:44
5	Shannon Stengel	35:01
6	Kurt Wilson	35:13
7	Stephen Eles	35:18
8	Nicholas Orenduff	35:22
9	Bradley Cantrell	35:57
10	Judson Ward	36:44
11	Hamp Kennemore	37:42
12	Shaun Byer	38:43
13	Daniel Bizzell	38:47

18-21 Female (290 finishers, 15 awards)

1	Angela Brown	40:48
2	Heather Varn	43:13
3	Megan Curran	43:21
4	Rachel Harder	43:35
5	Mara Vanderoord	44:35
6	Amy McCanless	45:26
7	Melissa Osean	45:37
8	Stephanie Anderson	46:14
9	Rebecca Hyde	46:43
10	Kelly Gordon	47:10
11	Sonja Reich	47:14
12	Laurie MacMillan	47:36
13	Emily Horton	47:45
14	Marilyn Pickard	47:48
15	Laurel Crenshaw	47:59

Male 22-25 (630 finishers, 25 awards)

1	Julius Rotich	30:52
2	Elly Rono	31:19
3	James Borir	32:23
4	Chad Sexton	32:52
5	Timothy Schubert	34:46
6	Charlie Middleton	34:50
7	Jason Annan	35:26
8	Aaron Linz	35:33
9	Bobby Wilder	36:10
10	Jonathan Edds	36:25
11	Michael Gambrell	36:36
12	Alexander Abess	36:45
13	Stephen Saleeby	37:38
14	John Stanley	37:54
15	Robert Mooring	37:58
16	Jeff Schenik	38:21
17	Jimmy Major	38:52
18	Thomas Webb	39:11
19	Peter Gallagher	39:28
20	Dustin Riccio	39:45
21	Greg Cameron	39:45
22	Chris Bolig	39:55
23	Andrew Powell	39:56
24	Jonathan Johnson	40:05
25	Franklin Estes	40:15

22-25 Female (808 finishers, 25 awards)

1	Petra Staskova	37:12
2	Heather Kempinger	41:04
3	Anne Wyman Cipolla	41:10
4	Lizi Coetsee	42:17
5	Christina Hallenbeck	42:59
6	Amy Giblin	43:06
7	Caroline Kondoleon	43:33
8	Sherri Wells	44:00
9	Adrienne Vredenburg	44:27
10	Linda Wood	45:21
11	Laura Green	45:29
12	Jennifer Sturgis	45:50
13	Veronica Goldmacher	46:04
14	Kimberly Blanchfield	46:05
15	Cara Lees	46:26
16	Becky Brown	46:30
17	Kristin Savery	47:05
18	Vera Landerer	47:11
19	Harriet Moore	47:12
20	Helen Lafaye	47:13
21	Mary Lynch	47:16
22	Miley McCarty	47:24
23	Julie Horsley	47:31
24	Kim Ulmer	47:49
25	Jennifer Sullivan	47:57

Male 26-29 (1054 finishers, 25 awards)

1	Eric Ashton	30:32
2	Chad Newton	30:52
3	Bill Baldwin	31:26
4	Matthew Gerard	31:35
5	Henno Haave	31:41
6	Gary Myers	32:33
7	Daniel Crooker	32:54
8	Pete Chenard	33:46
9	Scott Gordon	34:13
10	Timothy Starets	34:30
11	Andrew Barron	34:56
12	Nathan Sweet	34:57
13	Robbie Smith	34:58
14	Sammy Owen	35:19
15	Darol Timberlake	35:25
16	Conrad Orloff	35:26
17	John Anderson	36:03
18	Douglass Pratt	36:08
19	Nathan Stephen	36:14
20	Brian Kistner	36:18
21	Steve De Salvo	36:25
22	Martin Franklin	36:46
23	James Harris	37:12
24	Patrick Vanboden	37:18
25	Douglas Kugley	37:19

26-29 Female (917 finishers, 25 awards)

1	Lara Shaw	37:24
2	Tracy Center	38:07
3	Gabriele Hauck	38:18
4	Kate Forehand	39:02
5	Michelle Pomfrey	39:04
6	Kari Staley	40:32
7	Kimberly Morgan	41:17
8	Dixie Baker	41:51
9	Evelyn Schaniel	42:09
10	Cara Johnson	43:01
11	Lorie Elmore	43:24
12	Elizabeth Smith	43:33
13	Paula Walmet	44:35
14	Angie Hilsabeck	44:38
15	Laura Tischler	45:00
16	Leslie Randall	45:25
17	Tracey Malarkey	45:27
18	Cathy Spiess	45:27
19	Denise Walker	45:41
20	Sherilyn Hastings	45:43
21	Tammy Root	45:49
22	Christine Leader	46:04
23	Melissa Runey	46:07
24	Carey White	46:28
25	Meredith Tidwell	46:36

Male 30-34 (1238 finishers, 25 awards)

1	Robert Benjamin	32:24
2	Keith Hurley	33:33
3	Chris Klaes	33:44
4	Joseph Blackstone	34:16
5	Phil Ponder	34:54
6	Karl Debate	35:12
7	Andrew Jackler	35:23
8	Karl Johnson	35:25
9	Kevin Tashlein	35:55
10	John Riordan	36:01
11	Brian Fancher	36:03
12	Helmut Schmoock	36:21
13	Chaz Hinkle	36:32
14	Barry Fitts	36:42
15	Doug Cassidy	36:48
16	Cory Fleming	36:59
17	Kirk Corsello	37:15
18	Dale Carico	37:16
19	Michael Craig	37:18
20	Christopher Byers	37:23
21	Chip Owens	37:41
22	Eric Parker	38:01
23	John Planty	38:23
24	Dawson Cherry	38:48
25	Billy Jenkins	38:56

30-34 Female (857 finishers, 25 awards)

1	Amy Kattwinkel	37:37
2	Sarah Gray	38:58
3	Susan Madinger	41:33
4	Christie Hicks	41:38
5	Pamela Mitchell	42:31
6	Jackie Miller	42:34
7	Chris Gay	42:44
8	Almaz Smith	42:50
9	Elizabeth Graham	42:53
10	Adrienne Port	43:11
11	Molly Achille	43:18
12	Kara Grady	43:27
13	Nicole Marcelli	43:30
14	Clayton Griffin	43:34
15	Cindy Ostle	44:25
16	Wendy Hunter	44:32
17	Jo Halmes	44:32
18	Renee Heindel	44:45
19	Kate Borg	44:55
20	Susan Watts	44:57
21	Tuba Malinowski	45:12
22	Kathy Reilly	45:27
23	Naomi Hession	45:56
24	Missy Hunnicutt	46:06
25	Lynn Evans	46:19

Male 35-39 (1052 finishers, 25 awards)

1	Selwyn Blake	30:30
2	Bill Mariski	33:07
3	James Harris	33:34
4	Jamie Wilbanks	33:37
5	Blake Zemp	34:02

6 Tom Cuff	34:13
7 Chris Shockley	34:14
8 Tom Mahon	34:17
9 Huey Inman	34:24
10 Steve Shonts	34:43
11 Gary Judson	35:09
12 Randy Aldridge	35:27
13 Alan Gebert	35:28
14 Martin Harrison	35:41
15 Jeffrey Swartz	35:43
16 David Ariola	35:54
17 Wes Kessenich	36:04
18 Mark Scott	36:06
19 Dan Esser	36:11
20 Glenn Wells	36:37
21 Tom Wilson	36:38
22 Doug Godley	36:45
23 Michael Nichols	36:51
24 Gary Ledford	36:55
25 Jay Punke	36:59

35-39 Female (723 finishers, 25 awards)
1 Sue Tandy	38:44
2 Fe Atwater	39:11
3 Julia Ralston	39:28
4 Betsy Veronee	40:19
5 Karen Starets	41:52
6 Sue Shokes	42:31
7 Suzanne Lynch	43:22
8 Jennifer Doles	43:24
9 Liz Schick	43:40
10 Kim Long	43:40
11 Christi Craft	44:10
12 Therese Smythe	44:13
13 Heather Wood	44:15
14 Victoria Allen	44:18
15 Robin Tanner	44:44
16 Beth Ritchey	45:12
17 Pattie Paulett	45:19
18 Sylvia Herndon	45:27
19 Susan Graminski	46:07
20 Pamela Miller	46:11
21 Tom Wilson	36:38
21 Cynthia Lowery	46:20
22 Jamie Williams	46:50
23 Cindy Yager	47:05
24 Lynn McCain	47:15
25 Eileen Thames	47:25

Male 40-44 (915 finishers, 25 awards)
1 James Youngquist	34:33
2 David Renneisen	34:37
3 James Wilheim	34:50
4 George Moore	36:02
5 Lennie Moore	36:02
6 Adrian Pellegrini	36:03
7 Hal Hall	36:10
8 James Scheer	36:11
9 Marc Embler	36:19
10 Harry Ash	36:52
11 Stephen O'Neal	36:57
12 Eddie Pennebaker	36:59
13 Randolph Hennigar	37:09
14 Paul Marino	37:15
15 Billy Tisdale	37:16
16 Clyde Sanders	37:43
17 Marlowe Eldridge	37:48
18 Jim Clark	38:16
19 Mark Strohsacker	38:30
20 John Turner	38:32
21 Del Rose	38:35
22 Harold Fallis	38:55
23 Larry Harvey	38:58
24 Gregory Fagan	39:06
25 Andrew Ammon	39:13

40-44 Female (507 finishers, 25 awards)
1 Judy Walls	39:40
2 Ruth Marie Milliman	39:41
3 Tami Dennis	42:01
4 Nancy Farley	42:55
5 Mary Jaye McGowan	43:56
6 Barbara Edwards	44:32
7 Peggy Kinney	44:52
8 Colleen Rigley	45:28
9 Nina Zoe Parks	46:01
10 Beverly Grant	46:02
11 Nitsa Calas	46:33
12 Chrystal Fleishman	46:49
13 Tammy Hovik	46:56
14 Trudy Gale	46:57
15 Theresa Burst	46:57
16 Lynne Leroy	47:29
17 Jane Shelburn	47:48
18 Jill Smith	47:50
19 Valerie Wilson	48:07
20 Tricia Christie	48:24
21 B J Houchen	48:41
22 Debbie Ostrander	48:54
23 Becky Droginske	48:54
24 Penny Galbraith	49:00
25 Sue Porter	49:12

Male 45-49 (769 finishers, 25 awards)
1 Jerry Clark	34:45
2 Sam Lewis	34:51
3 Ervin Reid	35:50
4 Bill Bosmann	37:13
5 Jim Boyd	37:26
6 Jack Todd	37:58
7 Robert Ramser	38:05
8 Charles Kellner	38:12
9 Ronald Hutchison	38:42
10 Gary Ricker	38:42
11 Joe Denneny	38:43
12 Michael Drose	39:16
13 Oliver Marshall	39:11
14 Dan Clapper	39:29
15 Larry Milner	39:30
16 Dennis Moon	39:40
17 John Sperry	39:49
18 Lloyd Porterfield	40:17
19 Gary Joye	40:31
20 Steven Bennett	40:49
21 Tommy Seymore	40:54
22 David Lee	41:04
23 Orlando Consalvi	41:06
24 Greg Hoerich	41:18
25 Neil Derrick	41:25

45-49 Female (335 finishers, 17 awards)
1 Judith Hine	40:10
2 Therese Killeen	44:34
3 Sallie Driggers	45:44
4 Jill Force	46:24
5 Beth Schmid	46:59
6 Mimi Sturgell	47:03
7 Giulio Pescia	48:06
8 Nancy Duffy	48:07
9 Janice Wilkins	48:10
10 Susan Krepelka	48:17
11 Candace Aimers	48:18
12 Jo Habenreiser	49:05
13 Marlene Atwood	49:18
14 Debbie Howard	49:32
15 Mary Millar	50:03
16 Valerie Murrah	50:03
17 Andrea Kellner	50:31

Male 50-54 (606 finishers, 25 awards)
1 John Bernhardt	38:37
2 Marris Johnson	38:46
3 Ken Shipp	38:52
4 Sam Davis	39:14
5 Porter Reed	39:15
6 Sandy Weatherhold	39:16
7 Ben Millard	39:20
8 Sam Littlejohn	39:52
9 Robert Baker	40:01
10 Paul Brown	40:02
11 Chuck Greer	40:21
12 James Horne	40:39
13 William Harman	40:55
14 Russ Brown	41:00
15 Dave Lemonds	41:03
16 Bubba Gelly	41:16
17 Whitney Kemper	41:22
18 Cedric Jaggers	41:36
19 Phillip Dickert	41:48
20 Harry Reed	41:55
21 Mackie Johnson	42:02
22 John Johnson	42:26
23 Gary Myers	42:35
24 John Dillard	42:42
25 Timothy Cosgrove	43:00

50-54 Female (217 finishers, 11 awards)
1 Lyn Hammond	44:51
2 Kathy Jaggers	46:11
3 Nancy Curry	49:11
4 Katherine Boydston	49:36
5 Joan Mulvihill	50:56
6 Cathy Curtis	50:57
7 Myrna Meehan	51:27
8 Pamela Keeler	51:53
9 Marcella Farino	52:26
10 Lynda Heilmann	53:03
11 Clara Hogan	53:38

Male 55-59 (349 finishers, 18 awards)
1 Dick Ashley	40:56
2 Robert Watson	41:57
3 Keith Ambrose	43:02
4 Joe Waters	43:09
5 Dean Davis	43:18
6 Anthony Donachie	43:21
7 Bill Clayton	43:32
8 Johnnie Silon	43:52
9 Calvin Coetsee	43:56
10 Larry Seavers	44:05
11 Eric Eibel	44:16
12 Jim Strowd	44:33
13 Lou Wagner	44:48
14 Robin Vieyra	45:21
15 Ron Sanders	45:31
16 Thomas Dority	45:32
17 Bernard Loftis	46:19
18 Carter Bays	46:20

Female 55-59 (69 finishers, 4 awards)
1 Judy Stoller	50:02
2 Barbara Avant	51:23
3 Judy Ewing	55:55
4 Evelyn Sykes	55:57

Male 60-64 (119 finishers, 6 awards)
1 Ed Ledford	39:12
2 Theron Cochran	41:42
3 Floyd Deandrade	42:09
4 Art Morey	43:12
5 Fred Motz	43:15
6 Thomas McCorty	43:40

Female 60-64 (28 finishers, 3 awards)
1 Pat Rhode	52:52
2 Elfriede Tolley Beeson	57:53
3 Suzanne Foster	1:01:20

Male 65-69 (43 finishers, 3 awards)
1 David Duncan	47:22
2 David Anderson	49:06
3 John Thompson	51:11

65-69 Female (7 finishers 3 awards)
1 Therese Fanelli	1:05:33
2 Susie Bishop	1:12:51
3 Bobbie May	1:20:34

Male 70-74 (21 finishers, 3 awards)
1 Charles Scott	53:59
2 Bill Kleber	55:44
3 Franklin Mason	57:11

70-74 Female (4 finishers, 3 awards)
1 Wyndall Henderson	1:28:57
2 Mary Canty	1:32:08
3 Lucy Jones	1:33:47

Male 75-98 (10 finishers, 3 awards)
1 David Mellard	56:33
2 Bob Wingard	59:34
3 James Queeny	1:08:06

75-98 Female (2 finishers, 2 awards)
1 S. L. Huff	1:17:34
2 Margaret Wright	1:31:42

Compiled by Cedric Jaggers from complete results provided by Burns Computer Services on March 27, 1999.

The leader pack heads towards the second span of the Pearman Bridge. Post and Courier photo by Alan Hawes

Chapter 23
2000
James Koskei Wins In Course Record 27:40

The 23rd Cooper River Bridge Run began at 8:10 a.m. on April 1, 2000. It was unusually windy, a tailwind strong enough to be felt pushing on runners' backs as they climbed the first span of the bridge. The temperature was 61 degrees when the race began. There were 16,893 entrants, the second most ever, and there were a record 14,144 finishers. The Sunday *Post and Courier* listed the names and times of 8,201 men (58 percent) and 5,943 women (42 percent), the highest percentage yet for female participation.

For the fourth year in a row the race was timed with the ChampionChip computer timing chip system. The race used a new USATF Certified Course #SC00003BS. The course began further back on Coleman Boulevard in Mount Pleasant so the runners covered 2 miles before they reached the first span of the new bridge. The course went across the Crosstown Overpass, down King Street and turned left at Calhoun to finish at the corner of Alexander near East Bay Street. The awards ceremony was held in the new Calhoun Park. Some runners liked the new more spacious site while others preferred the old Marion Square finish.

Kenyan domination was the most thorough ever. For the second year in a row Kenyan men took 13 of the top 15 spots, including the first seven places. Kenyan women placed first and second and also took fourth through eighth and 11th. A Kenyan man was Masters overall winner as well.

James Koskei ran a new course record, 27:40. (It has stood through the 33rd running of the race.) Reuben Cheruiyot, 27:50, Joseph Kimani, 27:53, and Felix Limo, 27:58, also broke 28 minutes. Selwyn Blake of Columbia, S.C., was the first American in 29:46, running a personal best to take 21st place. Everyone felt that the 7 mile per hour tailwind over the first 4 miles of the course helped with times.

It looked to be a three-man race until the final 2 miles with Koskei and Cheruiyot exchanging the lead until Koskei surged away after the 6-mile mark. "I didn't have any idea it would be a record, but I knew we were going pretty fast," Koskei told the *Post and Courier*. "I was just trying to get to the finish line before everyone else." He did it by averaging a pace of 4:27 per mile for the entire race. "I wanted him (Cheruiyot) to come up with me so we could push together," Koskei said. "He was very tough, but I think he became a little winded."

Cheruiyot said, "I tried to keep up, but he's a strong man."

Catherine Ndereba became the second Kenyan woman in a row to win as she edged fellow Kenyan Sally Barsosio by 13 seconds to win in 31:42. This was Barsosio's third time to run the race and her third runner-up finish. She was second in 1997 and 1998. Colleen De Reuck, a South African living in Boulder, Colo., was third in 32:09. It was a two-woman race for the first 5 miles as Ndereba and Barsosio were together until about a half-mile was left in the race. At that point Ndereba took control.

"That's when I just took off," Ndereba told the newspaper. She ran the third best female time in race history and 6 seconds faster than she had run in the 1996 race. In 1997 she took a break from racing to have a child.

"It was tough when I tried to come back because there is a rhythm to running," she said. "It was difficult because I had a lot of pounds added to my weight. But I had that desire, plus it took patience. One must have patience. My running is getting better. I'm getting faster and my times are getting faster. Before I had my baby, my best time for a half-marathon was 1 hour and 10 minutes. Now it's 1 hour and 9 minutes.

Regarding the Bridge Run, she said, "The conditions were fine. I had a headwind from the fourth mile that made it difficult. The hard part is the bridges. The most challenging and fun part of the race was going downhill."

Barsosio said about Ndereba, "We're friends. We trained together and we're friends, but it surprised me because I didn't know she was coming (to the Bridge Run)." About finishing second for the third time, she added, "I have to train harder if I'm going to win here. I ran OK, and Catherine ran well. I ran my personal best which is good."

Kenyan Simon Kirori set a new male Masters course record, 29:13, breaking the mark that had stood for eight years. Kirori was the overall winner in 1994. Second place Master was David Chawane from South Africa in 30:03, while third went to John Tuttle of Douglasville, Ga., in 30:40. Marie Boyd of Albuquerque, N.M., was the female Masters winner in 35:25. She was followed by Janice Addison of Columbia, S.C., in 35:41 and Lee Di Petro of Ruxton, Md., in 36:12.

Bob Schlau of Charleston won the Grand Masters for the third time in a row, this year in 34:25. Norman Ferris of Columbia, S.C., took second in 34:51 followed by Ervin Reid of Campobello, S.C., in 35:19. Female Grand Masters winner was Terry Mahr of Oregon, Ohio, for the second year in a row, this time in 38:49. Judith Hine from New Zealand was second in 39:16 while Susie Kluttz of Winston Salem, N.C., was third in 45:07.

The Dr. Marcus Newberry Award for first Tri-County finisher went to Mike Aiken of Charleston, who finished 35th overall in 31:57. Kerry Robinson, now living in Megget, was the female award winner finishing as 24th overall female in 38:00. The Dewey Wise Trophy was won by Ed Shaffer, 81, of Walterboro, S.C., for his time of 73:47.

Television coverage was moved to cable. There was a one hour tape delay broadcast the night of the race. Entry fee remained $15 early, $20 late, for the walk $10 early $12 late.

In 2000, a record four runners broke the 28-minute barrier; another eight runners broke the 29-minute barrier, setting a record 12 runners under 29 minutes and another record total 21 runners broke the 30-minute barrier. There were 297 runners under the 40-minute barrier, 37 of them female. There were 1,850 runners under the 50-minute barrier and a total of 5,856 finished the race in less than an hour. There were runners from 48 states, with only North and South Dakota missing. The Sunday *Post and Courier* listed the top five in each age group, erroneously including the prize money winners in the age groups and listed the names and times of 14,144 runners: 8,201 male finishers and 5,943 female finishers. A record 12,407 walkers were registered for the 4-mile walk which began near the foot of the bridge on Coleman Boulevard.

Other Voices
Tell Me About Your Bridge Run 2000
By Cedric Jaggers. Originally appeared in the May/June 2000 Low Country Runner

Marion Square after the Bridge Run, wait, we weren't in Marion Square this year just like we weren't back in 1988 the first time I got Charleston Running Club members to tell me about their Bridge Run. We had been in Marion Square every other year since then though so it felt strange not to be there. This year we were in the new Calhoun Park at the end of the street across East Bay. What a day. Sunny, windy, warm at 61 degrees when we started 10 minutes late (did anyone else get hot and thirsty while we stood around and waited for all the folks who had waited for the last bus?). Just the kind of warm sunny day casual runners love, so voila: a record number of finishers this year: 14,144. I wish I could have found more club members, but below are the comments of all I could find. As happens every year I wrote down exactly what you said. I tried to find everyone in the results and found all but a few. The overall finish place and time are from the complete results, sorted by age group which Burns Computer printed for me after the race. If you want to see your chip time (as opposed to the real time shown below) it is available on the Internet: www.BridgeRun.Com.

Lyn Hammond: I had a good time. 1,160th overall, 1st age group award, 47:05.

Kathy Jaggers: My leg tightened up. I didn't think when I started out that I'd break 50. I ran about what I expected based on my lack of conditioning. 1,740th overall, 2nd age group award, 49:33.

Frank Blackett: I didn't run it, I walked it and I enjoyed the scenery. Walking it is different.

Mario Salas: First time I've run it in six years. I thought I could break 40: didn't quite make it 40:58. Training five days a week, it was the best I could do. 360th overall, top 5% age group award, 41:00.

Bill Blackett: Ah, the Bridge Run. I usually take it easy to the top then sprint down the Bridge. Further back I didn't get to do that. 53 minutes, my worst time in five years. 55:22

Dave Mellard: I did about 58 ½ minutes. It was good, it was great just as good as the first one. 5,105th overall, 2nd age group award, 58:36.

Leon Locklear: It was a good effort for me I had a 52:40 (laughed). It's about like a different race with 2 miles before the bridge. It changed the complexion of the race for the good. I enjoyed it. 2,967th overall, 53:42.

Wendy Roach: I knocked 3 minutes off by doing speedwork with those fast guys. Speedwork helps. 46:15. 1,051st overall, 46:28.

Steve Hunt: Much better than the last year: 47:15. I owe it to my chiropractor and the five pounds I lost when I had pneumonia in December. 1,212th overall, 47:18.

George Dunleavy: It was a great day, a beautiful day. I set my goal to break 39 and ran 38:01 so I am happy. 188th overall, 38:04.

Eric Parker: It was a good Bridge Run. It was a P.R. for me 36:19. I started out on my pace. The wind was pretty rough once we got off the bridge. 121st overall, top 5% age group award. 37:21.

Gary Ricker: Well here we are again. Let's see. I'm happy it's over. The wind sure cooperated. I did okay. Once we turned on Calhoun and I saw the finish it was fun again because I saw the finish. 38:47. 216th overall, top 5% age group 38:48.

Dan Clapper: Um, I loved the new course. I ran my fastest time in five years. I ran 38:40. Last year 39:26 so I'm happy. 210th overall, top 5% age group 38:40.

Joe Blackburn: It was a great day for the race. I was a little disappointed myself. I was hoping for 39 and endued up right at 40. I run the bridge about every day, but ran out of gas on the first span. 303rd overall, 40:06.

Jeffrey Herndon: 41:56, I really don't know what to say. Thank goodness there was a tailwind. If there had been a headwind I'd have been in a lot more trouble than I was. 444th overall 41:55.

Jill Pellerin: Earlier I was going, where is he? Where is he? I was on the starting line trying to make up a story, but it doesn't work that way. The logistics are harder for me having to go 2 miles before you get on the bridge was helpful. I worked hard the whole way and was better than last year so I'm happy. 53:47, big improvement over last year, about 6 minutes. 2,968th overall, 53:42.

Lennie Moore: I felt pretty good up through mile 4 and a half or so. I was about on par with last year but that last hill just cut my butt. I didn't have a lot left to get to the finish. I probably went out a little quick but I'm still happy. 37:26. 160th overall, top 5% age group, 37:29.

Ray Letellier: Well it was my second best time, just under 50 minutes which is great for me. I didn't think we'd ever get to the bridge. Then that headwind at the end was tough and it was hot as hell. 1,851st overall, 49:57

Michael Hughes: I got over it. I've been out for 3 months. I broke 50 minutes.

It's an event. I just came to do it. I'm one of the few people who likes the crowds. 1,991st overall, 50:29.

David Quick: Call me the April Fool in my heart. I wore this huge hat and it pushed me over the bridge. But it held me back on the kick - and Joe kicked past me. I'm blaming the hat. The weather was nice but you could definitely feel the wind pushing you up the bridge. Unfortunately that was my slowest mile: 7 minutes. I ran about 40:08. I hope with the chip I'll be under 40. I have the Boston Marathon in 16 days so I'm happy with it. 309th overall, 40:09.

Stuart Campbell: Um, it was tough enough. I didn't really train, I did like a 36:50 or so, a minute off my P.R. I was happy with my time. 146th overall, 3rd age group, 37:00.

Keith Ambrose: Don't talk to me. Go away. Go away. I had a really fantastic run for a cripple. I got nauseous on the bridge. Just another one of those Bridge Runs. I don't even know my time. I didn't clock it - it was that bad. 1,592nd overall, 48:54.

Bridge runners cross over Drum Island.
Post and Courier photo
by Mic Smith

Clara Hogan: It figures that the one time you find me it would be my worst year. Oh, I've got to watch what I say. I just haven't been running more than 2 or 3 miles and planned to walk it with my daughter. Then she didn't come. I got a free entry working at Chick-Fil-A. This is my first time walking the hills. 1 hour 2 minutes, it could turn out a minute longer. But it inspired me to do better. 6,825th overall, 1:02:04.

Pat Rhode: Well it's the worst time I've had except for the year I had my surgery. 55 minutes. The humidity hurt me. But I was happy I could do it. It isn't so bad for an old woman. 3,899th overall, 2nd age group, 56:01.

Jackie Bull: Full of or a lot of. I think I did well. I think I did under 50 which is good for me. I've enjoyed seeing all the people. I'm a new member. The next club meeting is going to be at my house and I want all the members to come. 2,342nd overall, 51:46.

Irving Rosenfeld: My watch said 53:08 but I started it a little late. It was a beautiful day - the best weather yet when you got off the bridge you had a breeze in your face. I enjoyed it. 2,878th overall, 53:26.

Eileen Stellefson: It was great. A minute and a half better than I'm trained for. I'm starting a new job and this is a great way to start my new job. 47:32. 1,318th overall, top 5% age group award, 47:44.

Bob Schlau: He's back. Hey, Cedric. I ran 34:26. It was OK. I really thought I could do better. I've had a good spring but I overdid my training this week. I guess I should have skipped that track workout. But I was faster than last year and at this age it's great to be going that way. 71st overall, 1st Grand Master award, 34:25.

Tom Mather: I was a little tired, a little over trained. But I enjoyed - that means I'll be in perfect shape for the next run. My second 10k in two years so I'm happy. 32:42. 46th overall, 5th overall Masters award, 32:42.

Nina Parks: (Taylor): My bridge run this year was wonderful. I ran very conservatively and finished in 41:30 - April Fools. 45:20. 883rd overall, top 5% age group award, 45:25.

Mark Taylor: I truly enjoyed the wind to my back. It was a unique experience, it truly was. 39:12. 236th overall, 39:09.

Cedric Jaggers: (My wife, Kathy, grabbed the pen and made me participate) I never thought I'd be glad just to be able to do it, beause a month ago I thought I wouldn't get to run the Bridge due to my injury. I was glad just to be able to do it and it doesn't even matter that it's my slowest ever. I started too fast and I paid for it on King Street. 760th overall, top 5% age group award, 44:40.

2000 Awards

Prize money winners:

Overall Male
1. James Koskei .... Kenya .... 27:40* ... $5,000
2. Reuben Cheruiyot ..... Kenya .... 27:50 ... $3,000
3. Joseph Kimani .... Kenya .... 27:54 ... $1,500
4. Felix Limo .... Kenya .... 27:58 ... $1,000
5. Philip Kirui .... Kenya .... 28:03 ... $800
6. Dominic Kirui .... Kenya .... 28:20 ... $600
7. David Makori .... Kenya .... 28:25 ... $500
8. Berhanu Adane .... Ethiopia .... 28:27 ... $400
9. Deresse Deniboba ..... Ethiopia .... 28:32 ... $300
10. John Kagwe .... Kenya .... 28:42 ... $250
11. John Kariuki .... Kenya .... 28:54 ... $200
12. Mattew Birir .... Kenya .... 28:56 ... $150
13. Simon Karori .... Kenya .... 29:11 ... $100
14. James Kariuki .... Kenya .... 29:13 ... $75
15. Peter Tanui .... Kenya .... 29:26 ... $50

*new course record earned an extra $1,000

Overall Female
1. Catherine Ndereba .... Kenya .... 31:41 ... $5,000
2. Sally Barsosio .... Kenya .... 31:54 ... $3,000
3. Colleen De Reuck ..... S Africa .... 32:09 ... $1,500
4. Grace Momanyi .... Kenya .... 32:37 ... $1,000
5. Jane Omoro .... Kenya .... 32:50 ... $800
6. Pauline Konga .... Kenya .... 32:59 ... $600
7. Teresa Wanjiku .... Kenya .... 33:10 ... $500
8. Naomi Wangui .... Kenya .... 33:47 ... $400
9. Michelle King .... Canada .... 34:26 ... $300
10. Tina Jensen .... Greenville, SC .... 34:29 ... $250
11. Miriam Wangari ...... Kenya .... 34:49 ... $200
12. Michelle LaFleur .... Savannah GA .... 35:08 ... $150
13. Marie Boyd .... Albuquerque .... 35:25 ... $100
14. Janeth Alder .... Columbus, GA .... 35:38 ... $75
15. Janice Addison ...... Columbia, SC .... 35:41 ... $50

Masters Male
1. Simon Karori .... Kenya .... 29:13 ... $1,500
2. David Chawane .... South Africa .... 30:03 ... $1,000
3. John Tuttle .... Douglasville, GA ...... 30:40 ... $750
4. Christopher Fox ...... Auburn, AL .... 31:26 ... $500
5. Tom Mather .... Mt Pleasant, SC .... 32:42 ... $250

Masters Female
1. Marie Boyd .... Albequerque .... 35:25 ... $1,500
2. Janice Addison .... Columbia, SC .... 35:41 ... $1,000
3. Lee Di Petro .... Ruxton, MD .... 36:12 ... $750
4. Kerry Robinson .... Megget, SC .... 38:00 ... $500
5. Terry Mahr .... Oregon, OH .... 38:49 ... $250

Grand Masters Male
1. Bob Schlau .... Charleston, SC .... 34:25* ... $750
2. Norm Ferris .... Columbia, SC .... 34:51 ... $500
3. Ervin Reid .... Campobello, SC .... 35:19 ... $250

*South Carolina state 50-54 age group record

Grand Masters Female
1. Terry Mahr .... Oregon, OH .... 38:49 ... $750
2. Judith Hine .... New Zealand .... 39:16 ... $500
3. Susie Kluttz .... Wins, Salem .... 45:07** ... $250

**national single age (63) record

Dr. Marcus Newberry Award:
For first local tri-county area finisher
Male
    Mike Aiken .... Charleston, SC .... 31:57 .... $500
Female
    Kerry Robinson ...... Megget, SC .... 38:00 .... $500

Special award:
Dewey Wise Trophy for oldest finisher with time less than his or her age:
    Ed Shaffer, 81 .... Walterboro, SC 73:47

Age group award winners
(5% deep maximum 25)

Male 12 & under (128 finishers, 7 awards)
1. Lowndes Sinkler 44:41
2. George McMahan 45:59
3. Andrew King 46:28
4. Bedford Tuten 47:00
5. Jacob Jett 47:42
6. Benjamin Althouse 48:24
7. Stephen Odom 50:00

Female 12 & under (98 fin., 6 awards)
1. Candice Johnson 42:35
2. Alicia Fuduric 43:50
3. J. Simkovich 50:14
4. Abby Osborn 50:25
5. Emily Wiles 55:45
6. Kristy Ritter 58:36

Male 13-17 (349 finishers, 18 awards)
1. Brantlee Milner 34:43
2. Henry Blackford 36:48
3. Stuart Campbell 37:00
4. Jovian Sackett 37:12
5. Kevin Felluer 37:15
6. Dan Homer 37:16
7. James Skelton 37:24
8. Conrad Shuler 37:50
9. Ben Sherard 38:21
10. Ben Jackson 38:54
11. Jeff Collins 39:12
12. Trey Rives 39:28
13. Carter Ridgeway 39:30
14. J. R. Knight 39:56
15. Robbie Phillips 40:40
16. Alex Hambacher 40:57
17. James McCutcheon 40:59
18. Robert Blain 41:01

– Continued on next page

2000 Award Winners, continued from page 183

Female 13-17 (220 finishers, 11 awards)

1 Ally Knight 38:54
2 Michele Milner 39:50
3 Jessica Carroll 43:53
4 Lauren Paige 45:23
5 Caitlin Heider 46:51
6 Sara Harris 47:21
7 Marcie Milner 47:47
8 Erica Adams 47:59
9 Jennifer Chapman 48:40
10 Rebecca Crawford 48:49
11 Juliee Boatwright 48:54

Male 18-21 (324 finishers, 18 awards)

1 Mike Aiken 31:57
2 Brandon Cantrell 32:29
3 Dave Lee 33:26
4 Tim Gibbons 33:45
5 Nick Grenduff 34:05
7 Travis Vaughn 34:48
8 Bradley Cantrell 34:50
9 Kevin Crosby 35:40
10 Daniel Bizzell 36:29
11 Greg Brown 36:34
12 Hudson Neely 36:46
13 Christopher Lamperski 37:33
14 Kurt Wilson 38:03
15 Steven Garner 38:09
16 Jonathan Whitlock 38:32
17 Laurie Sanders 39:00
18 Kenneth Borror 39:06

Female 18-21 (392 finishers, 20 awards)

1 Stephanie Feagin 39:17
2 Lane Condell 39:56
3 Sarah Keen 40:34
4 Sandy Page 43:48
5 Rebecca Hyde 48:07
6 Derrick Williamson 34:22
6 Brianna Stello 48:18
7 Jennie Brooks 48:31
8 Clare Whipple 48:58
9 Britt Ellis 49:07
10 Emily Keith 49:19
11 Mary Smutney 49:56
12 Natalie Rice 50:50
13 Missy Kergosien 50:54
14 Mary Davis 51:32
15 Kelli Buice 51:42
16 Erin Wells 51:43
17 Katherine Tumbleston 51:47
18 Danielle Baker 51:52
19 Kate Thompson 51:54
20 Jennifer Aulick 51:58

Male 22-25 (693 finishers, 25 awards)

1 Kibet Cherop 29:34
2 Julius Rotich 29:43
3 Sammy Nyamongo 30:09
4 Clephas Boor 30:16
5 Ben Hovis 32:37
6 Andrew Keel 33:49
7 Tom Wehr 34:02
8 Jason Putnam 34:03
9 Gin White 35:14
10 Michael Gambrell 35:26
11 Ryan Blaney 35:31
12 Lee Kain 35:48
13 Bobby Wilder 35:50
14 Kevin Croxton 36:44
15 Alexander Abess 36:48
16 Doug Godley 37:17
17 Jason Johnson 38:11
18 Brian Hamby 38:18
19 Markus Scheuermann 38:45
20 Frank Norcross 38:45
21 Axel Krieger 38:52
22 Jonathan Rowell 39:10
23 Jeffrey Krulick 39:11
24 Thomas Webb 39:12
25 Trent Humphreys 39:51

Female 22-25 (901 finishers, 25 awards)

1 Farrell Burns 37:08
2 Karen Gillespie 39:58
3 Anne Wyman Fouche 40:12
4 Trisha Stavinoha 42:34
5 Laura Forster 43:47
6 Laura Wise 44:09
7 Christina Rogers 44:46
8 Harriet Moore 44:49
9 Kimberly Blanchfield 45:28
10 Elizabeth Lightner 45:32
11 Isabel Ghowanly 45:35
12 Erin Fitzgerald 46:16
13 Laura Cisar 46:44
14 Erin Baker 47:01
15 Joy Fernandez 47:22
16 Nicole Mermans 47:33
17 Donna Dejong 47:34
18 Margaret Martin 47:36
19 Ximena Rebolledo 47:36
20 Holly Haemmerle 47:39
21 Kristin Shaffer 47:39
22 Julia Baskin 47:53
23 Nicki Breon 47:58
24 Jennifer Pryor 48:01
25 Amy Garrett 48:04

Male 30-34 (1,160 finishers, 25 awards)

1 Jeff Campbell 30:01
2 Simon Cherogony 30:50
3 William Baldwin 30:53
4 Timothy Donahugh 33:47
5 Jason Annan 33:50
6 Richard Dravenstott 34:04
7 William Freeman 34:46
8 James Harris 34:50
9 Michael Janech 34:54
10 Douglas Pratt 35:21
11 Brian Kistner 35:40
12 Keith Ellis 36:11
13 Nathan Stephens 36:38
14 Jered Haag 37:23
15 Jimmy Major 38:02
16 Chris Pateras 38:11
17 Scott Baskett 38:16
18 Jason Farmer 39:37
19 Timothy Mahon 39:47
20 Robert Matthews 40:06
21 Fumihiko Ishikawa 40:22
22 Urmo Jaanimagi 40:30
23 Garrett Dieck 40:34
24 Kurt Hollinger 40:36
25 Chris Wyckoff 40:52

Female 30-34 (1,086 finishers, 25 awards)

1 Gail Pennachio-Jervey 36:38
2 Lara Shaw 36:50
3 Tracy Center 37:56
4 Kate Forehand 38:45
5 Erin Engle 41:43
6 Kimberly Morgan 42:57
7 Linda Wood 43:15
8 Amy Giblin 43:15
9 Angie Lessis 43:56
10 Kimberly Sturkey 44:03
11 Courtney Moore 44:04
12 Carey Cochran 44:12
13 Sue Hall 44:15
14 Jennifer Occhipinti 44:34
15 Megan Parrott 45:00
16 Mary Hurteau 45:28
17 Tina Weiler 45:28
18 Jennifer Rothacker 45:32
19 Susan Barker 45:44
20 Paula Larson 45:50
21 Emily Hill 46:05
22 Maggie Corbett 46:12
23 Mellissa Runey 46:21
24 Jenny Bresnahan 46:23
25 Sonya Sprinkle 46:24

Male 30-34 (1,334 finishers, 25 awards)

1 David Kiptaras 29:41
2 Ben Kimondiu 29:42
3 Eric Ashton 30:27
4 Zach Kunyiha 31:06
5 Peter Githuka 31:42
6 Randy Ashley 31:52
7 Eric O'Brien 32:17
8 Robert Benjamin 32:28
9 Jamey Yon 32:35
10 David Brown 33:24
11 Ben Vaughn 33:40
12 Keith Hurley 34:41
13 Michael Haranzo 34:51
14 Emery Lloyd 34:57
15 Eric Vandervort 35:23
16 James Abercrombie 35:47
17 Dujan Harbin 36:08
18 John Riordan 36:10
19 Eric Parker 36:21
20 Morris Bodrick 36:27
21 Nick Felix 36:37
22 Helmut Schmock 36:50
23 Albert Marr 36:58
24 Will Barrett 37:09
25 Doug Cassidy 37:11

Female 30-34 (1,049 finishers, 25 awards)

1 Amy Kattwinkel 37:37
2 Sarah Gray 38:41
3 Saundi Theodossiou 40:08
4 Susan Madlinger 40:51
5 Alisa Tolley 41:19
6 Christine Gay 41:23
7 Pamela Mitchell 41:51
8 Nicole Marcelli 43:00
9 Christine Leader 43:01
10 Molly Achille 43:52
11 Laura Havrilesky 43:54
12 Cissy Bonifay 44:02
13 Cindy Ostle 44:03
14 Renee Johnson 44:12
15 Kristin Birirs 44:14
16 Pam Mooring 44:45
17 Lynn Evans 45:10
18 Olga Faison 45:14
19 Lisa Kay 45:23
20 Anita Charleston 45:26
21 Arlene Walker 45:46
22 Leslie Randall 45:54
23 Radonna Johnson 46:04
24 Denise Lockett 46:24
25 Janice Willey 46:27

Male 35-39 (1,084 finishers, 25 awards

1 Selwyn Blake 29:46*
2 Reuben Chesang 30:36
3 Darren De Reuck 32:08
4 Blake Zemp 34:23
5 Jamie Wilbanks 35:09
6 Jeffrey Swartz 35:34
7 Jeffrey Carson 35:40
8 Kevin Barry 35:42
9 Steve O'Hearn 35:47
10 Martin Harrison 36:11
11 Rob Burke 36:12
12 Bobby Aswell 36:28
13 Kevin Tashlein 36:28
14 Dave Kliphon 36:32
15 Chuck Howard 36:39
16 George Patterson 36:51
17 Lance Leopold 37:04
18 Christopher Byers 37:34
19 Eric Emerson 37:46
20 Ivo Maia 37:58
21 Sam Inman 38:15
22 Layton Gwinn 38:19
23 Bobby Harper 38:24
24 John Rowley 38:30
25 Dawson Cherry 38:52

*state 35-39 age group record

Female 35-39 (805 finishers, 25 awards)

1 Laura Vroon 37:29
2 W. Macy 37:37
3 Fe Atwater 38:19
4 Lee Berlinsky 39:09
5 Nancy Brennan 39:20
6 Gina Latham 39:38
7 Laura Landes 40:09
8 Jean Aswell 41:31
9 Janet Good 42:12
10 Patt Loggins 42:18
11 Bev Veals 42:29
12 Christi Craft 42:31
13 Karen Murphy 43:12
14 Susan Dunlap 43:48
15 Suzanne Lynch 44:01
16 Suanne Hall 44:12
17 Patti Paulett 45:04
18 Lisa Powell 45:06

19 Nyala Edwards ... 45:06
20 Heather Wood ... 45:16
21 Annie Stevenson ... 45:24
22 Barbara Wagner ... 45:32
23 Ashley Reynolds ... 45:37
24 Carol Snyder ... 46:04
25 Rhonda Cloinger ... 46:05

Male 40-44 (965 finishers, 25 awards)
1 Robert Murray ... 33:16
2 Randy Pochel ... 33:47
3 Marc Embler ... 33:49
4 Richard Ferguson ... 34:00
5 Chris Shockley ... 34:06
6 Gerald Hutchinson ... 34:33
7 Dan Kimaiyo ... 34:41
8 Tom Mahon ... 34:54
9 Jim Wilhelm ... 35:00
10 John Taylor ... 35:04
11 Pete Edge ... 35:23
12 Paul Marino ... 35:49
13 Randy Aldridge ... 35:49
14 Clyde Sanders ... 36:36
15 Tom Kelecy ... 36:44
16 George Howe ... 36:45
17 Jim Shimberg ... 36:49
18 David Bourgeios ... 36:51
19 Bruce Herman ... 37:03
20 Lennie Moore ... 37:29
21 James Bailey ... 37:33
22 Tom Rossi ... 37:41
23 David Renneisen ... 37:45
24 James Scheer ... 37:55
25 Mike Hart ... 38:01

Female 40-44 (580 finishers, 25 awards)
1 Clare Dillon-Palma ... 40:20
2 Debbie Knight ... 41:26
3 Lee Patterson ... 41:51
4 Mary Jaye McGowan ... 42:29
5 Tami Dennis ... 43:20
6 Beverly Grant ... 44:48
7 Nancy Thomas ... 44:51
8 Nina Zoe Parks (Taylor) ... 45:25
9 Sue Porter ... 46:17
10 Michele Stutts ... 47:35
11 Ann Elish ... 47:36
12 Trudy Gale ... 47:40
13 Eileen Stellefson ... 47:44
14 Jill Smith ... 47:52
15 Bluette Brooks ... 48:13
16 Cyndy Lehmann ... 48:19
17 Cheryl Spillman ... 48:20
18 Lynne Leroy ... 48:41
19 Linda Fairey ... 48:47
20 Dallys Kulynych ... 48:48
21 S.J. Drehmer ... 48:54
22 Elizabeth Lierley ... 49:17
23 Susan Lambreth ... 49:35
24 Joyce Thompson ... 49:39
25 Lynn Leatherman ... 49:52

Male 45-49 (653 finishers, 25 awards)
1 Dave Geer ... 32:55
2 Roy Kulikowski ... 34:10
3 Paul Dawson ... 35:19
4 Bill Bosmann ... 36:17
5 Jim Knight ... 37:16
6 Charles Kellner ... 37:33
7 Bob Foster ... 37:37
8 Dan Richardson ... 37:40
9 P. Michael Cunningham ... 37:59
10 Joe Denneny ... 38:10
11 Tim Kerr ... 38:21
12 James Pannabecker ... 38:35
13 Dan Clapper ... 38:40
14 Del Rose ... 38:43
15 Gary Ricker ... 38:48
16 Larry Milner ... 39:15
17 Jeff Dorociak ... 39:18
18 Michael Drose ... 39:22
19 Mark Howell ... 39:24
20 Shawn Nettles ... 39:57
21 Marc Hoffman ... 40:31
22 Jim Boyd ... 40:43
23 Jamie Robinson ... 40:48
24 Bill Edwards ... 40:56
25 Mario Salas ... 41:00

Female 45-49 (385 finishers, 20 awards)
1 Mary Gail Murphy ... 44:28
2 Sallie Driggers ... 45:05
3 Therese Killeen ... 45:56
4 Debbie Howard ... 46:01
5 Jo Haubenreiser ... 46:29
6 Betsy Henderson ... 46:46
7 Susan Colquitt ... 47:31
8 Nancy Duffy ... 48:03
9 Barbara Warner ... 49:48
10 Starr Hazard ... 49:53
11 Harriett Woodson ... 50:24
12 Judy Osborn ... 50:24
13 Lewanna Caldwell ... 50:27
14 Laura Russell ... 50:40
15 Carol Hahn ... 50:59
16 Judith Stanton ... 51:42
17 Nancy Anderson ... 51:44
18 Marie Santos ... 51:48
19 Caroline Burns ... 51:51
20 Mary Turner ... 51:53

Male 50-54 (674 finishers, 25 awards)
1 Johnny Bernhardt ... 38:29
2 David Lawson ... 39:19
3 James Horne ... 39:40
4 Paul Brown ... 39:59
5 Chuck Greer ... 40:07
6 Bill Peay ... 40:15
7 Steven Annan ... 41:14
8 Richard LaChance ... 41:27
9 Terry Murphy ... 41:45
10 Steve Rogers ... 42:37
11 Jim Suber ... 42:47
12 Linny Moore ... 42:50
13 Bubba Gelly ... 43:01
14 Gary Richardson ... 43:02
15 Mackie Johnson ... 43:03
16 Wally Kastner ... 43:22
17 John W. Johnson ... 43:26
18 Douglas Blackford ... 43:30
19 William Anderson ... 43:39
20 Mike Mahaney ... 43:42
21 Joseph Siever ... 44:14
22 Boyd Haile ... 44:18
23 Ricky Barnes ... 44:23
24 Don Whelchel ... 44:30
25 Cedric Jaggers ... 44:40

Female 50-54 (241 finishers, 13 awards)
1 Lyn Hammond ... 47:05
2 Kathy Jaggers ... 49:33
3 Brenda Cooter ... 50:11
4 Judy Gilman ... 50:14
5 Claudette Herman ... 52:15
6 Charla Thomas ... 52:16
7 Linda Romero ... 52:19
8 Nancy Curry ... 52:34
9 Marcella Farino ... 52:34
10 Pamela Keeler ... 52:34
11 Kari Sprecher ... 53:01
12 Judy Campbell ... 53:24
13 Mary Frazier ... 54:08

Male 55-59 (392 finishers, 20 awards)
1 Tom Dooley ... 36:52
2 Terry Van Natta ... 37:13
3 Fred Reinhard ... 37:34*
4 Robert Baker ... 39:28
5 Sam Littlejohn ... 39:33
6 Russ Brown ... 40:19
7 Dick Ashley ... 40:33
8 Ray Kitchen ... 42:00
9 Bill Clayton ... 42:00
10 Tai Sugimoto ... 42:16
11 Johnnie Silon ... 42:22
12 Joe Waters ... 42:35
13 Robert Watson ... 42:45
14 Anthony Donachie ... 43:00
15 Frank Frazier ... 43:13
16 Bill Thompson ... 43:25
17 Dean Davis ... 43:47
18 James Richardson ... 44:07
19 Fred Wood ... 44:33
20 Jim Strowd ... 44:43

*state 55-59 age group record

Female 55-59 (133 finishers, 7 awards)
1 Patricia Guthrie ... 50:09
2 Joan Mulvihill ... 51:11
3 Sissy Logan ... 54:25
4 Kim Wells ... 54:34
5 Muff Harner ... 55:33
6 Barbara Avant ... 55:52
7 Janice Hicks ... 55:57

Male 60-64 (152 finishers, 8 awards)
1 James Adams ... 39:42
2 Ed Ledford ... 42:01
3 Dean Godwin ... 43:39
4 Floyd Deandrade ... 43:47
5 Fred Motz ... 44:16
6 Carter Bays ... 44:52
7 Frank Nicholson ... 45:57
8 Alan Shufet ... 46:40

Female 60-64 (36 finishers, 3 awards)
1 Mae Cleveland ... 53:10
2 Pat Rhode ... 56:01
3 Barbara Crosher ... 57:38

Male 65-69 (53 finishers, 3 awards)
1 John Thompson ... 48:49
2 David Anderson ... 51:55
3 Bob Walton ... 54:12

Female 65-69 (15 finishers, 3 awards)
1 E.K. Tolley Beeson ... 58:46
2 Eileen Hallman ... 64:30
3 Ann Trammell ... 64:47

Male 70-74 (17 finishers, 3 awards)
1 William Boulter ... 48:22
2 Bill Kleber ... 54:57
3 Lonnie Collins ... 57:27

Female 70-74 (5 finishers, 3 awards)
1 Nancy Bell ... 66:13
2 Janine Maltas ... 77:00
3 Mabel Velge ... 81:28

Male 75-98 (12 finishers, 3 awards)
1 Franklin Mason ... 56:40
2 David Mellard ... 58:36
3 Bob Wingard ... 66:55

Female 75-98 (3 finishers, 3 awards)
1 Mary Canty ... 1:30:26
2 Lucy Jones ... 1:37:21
3 Margaret Wright ... 1:41:46

Compiled by Cedric Jaggers from complete results provided by Burns Computer Services immediately after the race on April 1, 2000.

Joggers make their way across the first span of the Silas Pearman Bridge during the 24th Annual Cooper River Bridge Run. Post and Courier photo by Mic Smith

Chapter 24
2001
Warm Weather Slows All Runners

The 24th Cooper River Bridge Run was held April 7, 2001, and began just after 8 a.m. The story was the heat. There had only been four Bridge Runs with a temperature higher than the 65 degrees (and going up fast) in 2001, but what really created a problem for many runners was the added burden of high humidity and a tailwind for the first 2 mile which caused many to overheat. It even affected the elite runners, as one of the invited Kenyans dropped out of the race going up the first span. Eighty-one runners had to be treated for heat-related problems.

For the fifth year in a row the race was timed with the ChampionChip computer timing chip system. The race used the same USATF Certified course #SC00003BS as the 2000 race, beginning on Coleman Boulevard and finishing at the corner of Alexander near East Bay Street. The awards ceremony was again held in Calhoun Park.

Not surprisingly, the race was dominated by Kenyans. Five Kenyans went over the bridge together, and three ran together for almost 6 miles. For the first time, both defending champions repeated as overall race winners, though both were about a minute slower than the previous year. James Koskei won in 28:45, ahead of fellow Kenyans Tom Nyariki, Olympic Steeplechase winner in 1992, whom he outkicked by 3 seconds, and Matthew Birir, whom he beat by 7 seconds. Kenyans took the first 16 places in the race with the top American, Scott Dvorak of Charlotte, N.C., 17th in 31:32.

"We were going against the wind up there, and when you tried to push you didn't move," Koskei told the *Post and Courier*.

Nyariki talked about going over the bridge and said Koskei talked about the finish. "That group I was running with was very strong," he said, "but my kick is strong. I knew in the last 300 yards that I had it." Nyariki said about Koskei, "We train together and I know him. He is strong at the end, but he is fresh because he just came from home. This is my third race here (in the U.S.) and maybe I'm a little exhausted right now."

Catherine Ndereba repeated as female champion in 32:33. She was followed by two Kenyans. Sally Barsosio stayed with the winner for the first 5 miles, and was second for the second year in a row in 32:56. She holds a special place (though perhaps not the one she would want) in Bridge Run history as this was her fourth time to run the race and the fourth time she has finished second. She has finished second to Catherine Ndereba twice and to Elana Meyer twice. Third place went to Martha Nyambura Komu in 33:23.

Nderaba and Barsosio, who are friends, talked about the race afterwards. Nderaba said, "Sally and I took the lead and it was a two-person race, shoulder to shoulder. I was able to break away from her to win. She's a true competitor. Running across the bridge was hard because of the headwind, but overall, it was a good race."

Barsosio said, "I don't know what it will take to win." She laughed and added, "Maybe my only chance is if Catherine doesn't enter it. My run was OK. She left me at the last mile. We were together all the way."

Masters winner was Simon Karori of Kenya, 1994 overall Bridge Run winner and Masters winner for the second year in a row, finishing seventh overall in 29:21, just 8 seconds off his Masters record established a year earlier. Andrew Masai of

Kenya was second Masters in 29:44, while Selwyn Blake of Columbia, S.C., was third Masters in 31:51.

Female Masters winner was Viazova Elena of Russia in 34:48. Sabrina Robinson of Tempe, Ariz., was second in 35:11, followed by two-time Masters winner Tatyana Pozdnyakova of Ukraine in 35:53.

Grand Masters prize money went to Gary Romesser of Indianapolis, Ind., for his time of 33:18, while three-time Grand Masters winner Bob Schlau of Charleston was second in 35:06, and Ervin Reid of Campobello, S.C., third in 35:13. Terry Mahr of Oregon, Ohio, was female Grand Masters winner for the fourth year in a row, this time in 39:10. She was followed by Judith Hine of Marietta, Ga., in 40:53, and by 1982 overall female winner, Sallie Driggers of Hanahan, S.C., in 46:03.

The Dr. Marcus Newberry Award for first Tri-County finisher went to Irv Batten of Summerville, S.C., who ran 33:13 to finish 26th overall. The female division award went to Amy Clements of Charleston, 14th female, in 36:14. For the second year in a row, the Dewey Wise Trophy went to Ed Shaffer, 82, of Walterboro, S.C., in 77:50.

Television coverage was again a one-hour tape delay broadcast on cable. Julian Smith again was race director. The race entry fee was raised to $20 early, $25 late; the walk to $15 early, $20 late.

In the 2001 race, three runners broke the 28-minute barrier, another eight broke the 30-minute barrier for a total of 11 runners finishing under 30 minutes. A total of 229 runners finished under the 40-minute barrier: 201 men and 28 women. There were 1,604 runners who finished the race under 50 minutes, and a total of 5,375 who finished under an hour. There were 16,432 official race entrants, 13,993 of whom finished. This was the second largest number of finishers for the race, just off the previous year's record.

The Charleston Sunday *Post and Courier* included the top five in each age division, erroneously including the prize money winners in the age divisions and listed the names and times of all the finishers: 7,932 males (56.7 percent) and 6,061 females (47.2 percent). This marked the first time over 6,000 females had finished any race in South Carolina, and was again the highest percentage of female finishers in any Bridge Run. Complete results were later mailed to all finishers as a supplement to the newspaper.

There were runners from every state except Hawaii. There were 10,406 walkers registered for the 4-mile walk which began at the foot of the bridge on Coleman Boulevard.

Other Voices
Running The Cooper River Bridge Run

By Katie Bowen. Originally appeared in the May-June Rock Hill Striders Newsletter

Charleston is one of my favorite places to visit. I had wanted to combine a trip with a race in Charleston for some time. I just happened to be on business in the area the weekend of the Cooper River Bridge Run. I missed not helping Ernie LaCasse with the PawPrint race but I am glad I had a chance to experience the Bridge Run.

At my level of racing, I prefer the larger races (not so much pressure on being the last person). I love these larger ones mostly because they are more of a social event than a race. I am not for sure of the total number of runners/walkers. I heard about 25,000. I just know there was a crowd!

The starting area was very organized. There was plenty of water for everyone, which was great because it was beginning to get warm. There were also plenty of "facilities". The pre-race entertainment kept you from getting bored waiting for the start. We arrived at 6:30 and the start wasn't until 8.

Finally the start. As always, I have pre-race butterflies. Those seemed to disappear as U2's "It's a Beautiful Day" blasted out over the speakers. Everyone was pumped! It took me about 5 minutes to get to the starting line. I assumed by this time the Kenyans were across the bridge.

The first 2 miles were fine. It was the bridge that was the challenge. The battle to get across was not only the uphill, but also trying to maneuver around the other runners. Some people would actually stop in front of me and I would almost fall over them.

One thing I would suggest the organizers of this race should do next year is to insert a flier advising "runner's etiquette". So many people would shove and bump without saying, "Excuse me" (people are not as polite as they used to be no matter where they are). Also, the bridge was moving. It felt like an earthquake or like I was running under the influence of a couple of margaritas! Yes, just a couple. It doesn't take much for me).

So due to the crowded conditions, I gave up on speed and decided to just enjoy the "social" event. As I looked around I saw Bat Man, a girl with fairy wings, two girls with hula skirts and coconut "jogging bras", and plenty of different T-shirts to read. My favorite was - I'm slow, I know it, so get over it! See what you guys up front are missing!

As I came off the bridge and turned the corner on King Street, I got a much-needed jolt to push me through to the finish. Led Zeppelin was blasting from the speakers. So cool!

This got me down King Street to the finish line on Calhoun. The finish line was a welcome site due to the heat. There were a lot of good refreshments and "freebies" at the tents in Calhoun Park. So we loaded up our bags with things to bring home.

The next thing to do was get back to Mount Pleasant to the car. We were told to go to where the shuttle buses would pick us up and take us back across the bridge. Everything else with the race had been going smoothly up until this point. There was already a group of people (including Jill Smith and Bob Ferguson) anxiously awaiting the shuttle.

What disorganization! I will not go into all details. But just imagine a large group of tired, hot and smelly people... you get where I'm going. The natives were getting restless. A fight almost broke out. It seemed some guys behind me were pushing and shoving each other. Luckily the doors to the bus opened at that time and all was avoided. After about an hour and a half wait, we were on our bus to the car.

So all in all, I did enjoy the Bridge Run. I am glad I decided to run this year. I understand that they are going to be building a new bridge in the near future. I can at least say that I ran the old one. It was "A Beautiful Day" for a race!

Tell Me About Your Bridge Run 2001

By Cedric Jaggers. Originally appeared in the May/June 2001 Low Country Runner

(Bridge Run info for 2001 – 13,993 second largest number of official finishers at the time, 16,432; third largest number of entrants. Start time temperature 65 degrees and very humid.)

On telling me about your bridge run. Well, things didn't work out like we had planned. In fact, the article did not happen. We were not ready for the heat and humidity. It has been a really cold winter and spring "way up North" in Rock Hill where we live now. As a result, Kathy and I had no heat acclimatization built up. So we both overheated big time in this year's Bridge Run. I slowed down to 8 minute miles and Kathy passed out after she crossed the finish line. She was taken to the EMS emergency tent and I couldn't find her.

Ken Wong, a friend from Charlotte (whom Kathy usually outruns) told me that he had passed her at mile 5 and she was in trouble. I headed, or should I say tried to head back to the finish line to get her. I couldn't get there. The monitors were doing too good a job of turning back people trying to go that way. I can't complain about that because with so many people coming in to finish, they don't need people bucking the tide.

So I went to the emergency tent inside the park in case she was there. She wasn't.

They told me about the other EMS tent near the finish line and I walked around a couple of blocks the back way, and finally got to it.

To make a long story short, I went back to our hotel, and by the time she was recovered enough for me to get back to the park, the awards ceremony was almost over. I talked to Jeff Herndon and the four or five people left at the Running Club tent. I decided not to do the article, headed to the finish line and got complete results from Burns Computer for Running Journal, and headed back to the Hampton Inn.

Kathy has recovered okay, but it sure took a lot of the joy out of our weekend. We both enjoy talking to all the club members and hearing what everyone has to say about the race and about their race. We really missed doing that this year. Note added years later – we did not know it, but this was probably the first Multiple Sclerosis attack which would lead to her diagnosis the next year. CJ)

So there is not a 'Tell Me About Your Bridge Run' article this year. You will have to imagine how most folks would have commented on the heat, humidity and headwind and how much slower they were than last year. I sure missed chasing people down, listening to their tales of triumph or tragedy and writing them down. There would probably have been more pathos than joy this year, but maybe not. Maybe you were the exception and had a great race. If so, good for you!

Since Burns gave me the information, here are some statistics. The race had the highest number, 6,016, and percentage, 43.3 percent, of female finishers ever. The number and percentage of women goes up every year.

If someone had said back in 1978 after the first Bridge Run when 113, i.e. 14.8 percent of the finishers were female, that someday over 6,000 females would finish the Bridge Run, anyone hearing it would probably have fallen over laughing. No more. Now the question looks like, how many years, or how few, will it be before females make up over 50 percent of the field?

Runners and walkers make their way up the first span of the Silas Pearman Bridge from Mt. Pleasant.
Post and Courier photo
by Mic Smith

2001 Awards

Prize money winners:

Overall Male
1 James Koskei .... Kenya .... 28:45 ... $5,000
2 Tom Nyariki .... Kenya .... 28:48 ... $3,000
3 Matthew Birir .... Kenya .... 28:52 ... $1,500
4 John Kiriuki .... Kenya .... 29:07 ... $1,000
5 John Thuo Itati .... Kenya .... 29:08 ... $800
6 Leonard Mucheru .... Kenya .... 29:09 ... $600
7 Simon Kirori .... Kenya .... 29:21 ... $500
8 Amos Gitagama .... Kenya .... 29:26 ... $400
9 Kibet Cherop .... Kenya .... 29:34 ... $300
10 Andrew Masai .... Kenya .... 29:44 ... $250
11 Francis Kirwa .... Kenya .... 29:58 ... $200
12 Thomas Omwenga ...... Kenya .... 30:19 ... $150
13 Jared Segera .... Kenya .... 30:34 ... $100
14 Silah Misoi .... Kenya .... 30:54 ... $75
15 Peter Tanui .... Kenya .... 31:07 ... $50

Overall Female
1 Catherine Ndereba ... Kenya .... 32:33 ... $5,000
2 Sally Barsosio .... Kenya .... 32:56 ... $3,000
3 Martha Komu .... Kenya .... 33:23 ... $1,500
4 Margaret Ngotho ..... Kenya .... 34:03 ... $1,000
5 Tatiana Maslova ...... Russia .... 34:12 ... $800
6 Ramilia Burangulova Russia .... 34:17 ... $600
7 Anna Brzezinska ...... Russia .... 34:18 ... $500
8 Naomi Wangui ...... Kenya .... 34:27 ... $400
9 Viazova Eleana ...... Russia .... 34:48 ... $300
10 Olga Markova ...... Russia .... 35:03 ... $250
11 Sabrina Robinson ..... Tempe, AZ .... 35:11 ... $200
12 Gabrielle O'Rourke .... New Zealand .... 35:37 ... $150
13 Tatyana Pozdyakova Ukraine .... 35:53 ... $100
14 Amy Clements .... Charleston, SC .... 36:14 ... $75
15 Janice Addison .... Columbia, SC .... 36:37 ... $50

Masters Male
1 Simon Karori .... Kenya .... 29:21 ... $1,500
2 Andrew Masai .... Kenya .... 29:44 ... $1,000
3 Selwyn Blake .... Columbia, SC .... 31:51 ... $750
4 Gary Romesser ...... Indianapolis, IN .... 33:18 ... $500
5 Larry Brock .... Anderson, SC .... 33:24 ... $250

Masters Female
1 Viazova Elena .... Russia .... 34:48 ... $1,500
2 Sabrina Robinson ..... Tempe, AZ .... 35:11 ... $1,000
3 Tatyana Pozdyakova Ukraine .... 35:53 ... $750
4 Janice Addison .... Columbia, SC .... 36:37 ... $500
5 Lee Di Pietro .... Ruxton, MD .... 37:00 ... $250

Grand Masters Male
1 Gary Romesser Indianapolis, IN .... 33:18 ... $750
2 Bob Schlau .... Charleston, SC .... 35:06 ... $500
3 Ervin Reid .... Campobello, SC .... 35:13 ... $250

Grand Masters Female
1 Terry Mahr .... Oregon, OH .... 39:10 ... $750
2 Judith Hine .... Marietta, GA .... 40:53 ... $500
3 Sallie Driggers .... Hanahan, SC .... 46:09 ... $250

Dr. Marcus Newberry award:
First local Tri-Country area finisher

Male
Irv Batten .... Summerville, SC .... 33:13 ... $500

Female
Amy Clements .... Charleston, SC .... 36:14 ... $500

Special award:
Dewey Wise Trophy for oldest finisher with time less than his or her age in minutes:
Ed Shaffer, 82 .... Walterboro, SC 77:50

Age group awards:
5% deep up to maximum of 25:

12 & und Male (145 finishers, 7 awards)
1 Andrew King 43:16
2 Lowndes Sinkler 43:41
3 Tommy Wilson 45:06
4 Cameron Moore 45:58
5 Andrew Adams 46:02
6 Edward Ball 46:56
7 Matt Buening 49:20

12 & under Female (79 fin., 4 awards)
1 Abby Osborn 46:47
2 Erin Carroll 49:12
3 Elizabeth Tempel 49:50
4 Peggy Busbee 54:50

13-17 Male (307 finishers, 16 awards)
1 Johnny Mitchell 35:56
2 Trevor Beesley 36:35
3 David Hill 37:15
4 Ricky Johnson 37:51
5 Robbie Phillips 38:11
6 Trey Rives 38:21
7 Kenny Supplee 39:04
8 Austin Brown 39:12
9 David Johannesmeyer 39:16
10 James McCutcheon 39:18
11 Jacob Morris 39:27
12 Stuart Campbell 39:42
13 Adam Young 40:41
14 Neil Ballentine 41:28
15 Eugene Zahoruyko 42:01
16 Aaron Schrock 42:16
17 Zachary Phillips 42:18
18 Jordan Lybrand 42:21

13–17 Female (219 finishers, 11 awards)
1 Michele Milner 41:05
2 Marcie Milner 42:23
3 Jessica Carroll 44:31
4 Lauren Paige 45:01
5 Ashley McCauley 45:43
6 Candice Johnson 46:08
7 Erica Adams 46:56
8 Katie Qualls 50:12
9 Chelsey Wilson 50:22
10 Jamie Mussman 51:12
11 Corrie Austin 51:12

18-21 Male (334 finishers, 17 awards)
1 Brandt Wallace 34:13
2 Brandon Cantrell 34:15
3 Travis Smith 34:33
4 Vince Bechtel 34:57
5 Tim Gibbons 35:08
6 Clark Davis 35:13
7 Derick Williamson 35:14
8 John Boettcher 35:49
9 Travis Vaughn 35:56
10 Henry Blackford 36:03
11 Robert Lowrey 36:17
12 Eric Cannon 36:30
13 Bradley Cantrell 36:50
14 Christopher Lamperski 37:05
15 Aubrey Florence 37:14
16 Jason Vanvaerenewyck 37:26
17 Robert Petree 37:30

18–21 Female (413 finishers, 21 awards)
1 Stephanie Feagin 39:47
2 Jill Hawley 41:20
3 Sharon Hacker 44:06
4 Mary Davis 46:15
5 Rebecca Hyde 46:45
6 Alison McGlinn 47:00
7 Ehrin Irvin 47:06
8 Becky Witkop 47:44
9 Maria Malatanos 48:10
10 Hillary Trudell 48:12
11 Kate Thompson 48:31
12 Angela Wiseman 50:27
13 Beth O'Brien 50:39
14 Allie Unger 50:52
15 Rachel Boyer 51:03
16 Lena Weinman 51:06
17 Jobeth Stephens 51:16
18 Ashley Hawkins 51:18
19 Margie Smith 51:42
20 Emiline Fricke 51:59
21 Hillary Goode 52:03

22-25 Male (668 finishers, 25 awards)
1 Samuel Mangusho 31:13
2 Drew Macaulay 32:14
3 David Njuguna 32:26
4 Isaac Kariuki 32:26
5 Mike Aiken 33:33
6 Jake Johnson 33:51
7 Andrew Keel 34:01
8 Jason Putnam 34:06
9 John McDaniel 34:22
10 Michael Ryan 34:33
11 Paul Wiesner 34:43
12 Patrick Dillon 35:12
13 Bobby Wilder 36:07
14 George Linney 36:11
15 Palmer Thomas 36:18
16 Ryan Blaney 37:02
17 Hamp Kennemore 37:10
18 Jonathan Gee 38:17
19 Thomas Manganiello 38:38
20 Jonathan Rowell 39:27
21 Steven Stivers 39:39
22 David Chambless 39:51
23 Travis Brady 39:52
24 Dean Milne 40:08
25 Matthew Valle 40:25

22–25 Female (884 finishers, 25 awards)
1 Jennifer McConeghy 38:46
2 Maryclaire Barry 39:06
3 Farrell Burns 39:17
4 Sara Jenkins 41:02
5 Sarah Lemley 41:56
6 Deina Velasco 42:04
7 Jennifer Johnson 42:06
8 Angie Paprocki 42:20
9 Jennifer Lakas 42:53
10 Alison Rogers 43:02
11 Megan Auger 43:16
12 Sarah Keen 43:41
13 Heather Houseknecht 44:01
14 Emily Keller 44:16
15 Laura Cisar 44:46
16 Jenny Techey 45:18
17 Allison Bumgardner 45:45
18 Clare Whipple 46:14
19 Anne Stowell 46:46
20 Jamie Reichert 46:52
21 Allison Gordon 46:53
22 Rachelle Tomlin 46:54
23 Ginger Applegate 47:05
24 Heather Gallagher 47:05
25 Linda Garrett 47:24

26-29 Male (1,027 finishers, 25 awards)
1 Christian Muentener 34:41
2 Jason Annan 34:50
3 Tim Donahugh 35:16
4 Bradly Fowler 35:44
5 Byron Buckley 35:54
6 Karl Kaiser 36:26
7 James Harris 36:35
8 Michael Janech 36:42
9 Thomas Walls 37:00
10 Alexander Abess 37:06
11 William Freeman 37:07
12 Brian Hamby 37:32
13 Jamie Griggs 37:59
14 Eliot Cannon 38:01
15 Andrew Powell 38:07
16 Matt Pryor 38:18
17 David Stewart 38:43
18 Jimmy Major 38:44
19 Jon Van Order 38:45
20 Kemp Burdette 38:52
21 Andrew Stroupe 39:03
22 Scott Baskett 39:41
23 Robert Matthews 39:53
24 Wesley Littlejohn 39:58
25 Michael Marcharg 40:02

26–29 Female (1,083 finishers, 25 awards)
1 Gail Pennachio Jervey 37:04
2 Kristin McCann 40:49
3 Karen Gillespie 41:40
4 Giblin Giblin 42:19
5 Helen Lafaye 42:55
6 Joanna Cox 43:18
7 Amy Clark 43:52
8 Erin Kuhn 44:09
9 Stephanie Baumgarner 45:11
10 Deb Kamzol 45:48
11 Lori Archer 46:20
12 Billi Veber 46:34
13 Donna Dejong 47:01
14 Jenny Bresnahan 47:23
15 Betsy Wallace 47:26
16 Dillard Dillard 47:51
17 Mia Griggs 48:12
18 Cara Lees 48:16
19 Jolee Robbins 48:16
20 Jennifer Schneider 48:18
21 Lisa Vondracheck 48:22

– Continued on next page

2001 Awards, continued from page 191

22 Deborah Kuo … 48:30
23 Julie Tashlein … 48:35
24 Beth Mitchell … 48:37
25 Christian Altman … 48:43

30-34 Male (1,396 finishers, 25 awards)
1 Scott Dvorak … 31:32
2 John Charlton … 33:05
3 David Lively Jr. … 34:47
4 Emery Lloyd … 35:27
5 Eric Parker … 35:34
6 Brian Fancher … 35:41
7 Darol Timberlake … 35:44
8 Tim Starets … 35:52
9 Karl Johnson … 36:04
10 Sean Dollman … 36:06
11 James Abercrombie … 36:23
12 Patrick Materna … 36:38
13 Guy Scheiwiller … 36:40
14 Scott Smith … 36:58
15 James J. Ruiz … 37:01
16 Eric Vandervort … 37:03
17 Stephen Redmond … 37:29
18 Bob Teachman … 37:30
19 Nick Felix … 37:39
20 John Riordan … 38:03
21 Rip Oldmeadow … 38:07
22 Steve Hudzik … 38:16
23 Daniel Budd … 38:17
24 Bill Miller … 38:21
25 Daniel Kehoe … 38:22

30-34 Female (1,115 finishers, 25 awards)
1 Irina Suvorova … 38:52
2 Francine Carpenter … 38:53
3 Tracy Foss … 40:42
4 Tara Gurry … 41:37
5 Arlene Walker … 42:19
6 Lisa Tolley … 42:30
7 Karen Killeen … 42:38
8 Collin Franceschi … 43:16
9 Katie Watson … 43:44
10 Beth Nabers … 43:54
11 Shannon Johnson … 44:14
12 Leslie Randall … 44:17
13 Lynette Greene … 44:24
14 Molly Achille … 44:30
15 Kim Russell … 44:58
16 Sara Alba … 45:09
17 Jacqueline Miller … 45:14
18 Stephanie Horn … 45:21
19 Kate Ledford … 45:28
20 Cara Johnson … 45:31
21 Kristi Burkhardt … 45:33
22 Julia Umbreit … 45:33
23 Shelley Dean … 45:42
24 Michele Hobson … 45:46
25 Jessica Gray … 45:50

35-39 Male (1,047 finishers, 25 awards)
1 Jamey Yon … 33:01
2 Irving Batten … 33:13
3 Blake Zemp … 34:56
4 Kevin Barry … 35:22
5 Craig Kingma … 35:32
6 Peter Esser … 35:45
7 Chaz Hinkle … 36:31
8 Sven Rieoesel … 37:26
9 Bobby Aswell … 37:31
10 Daniel Edwards … 37:31
11 Jeff Hass … 37:43
12 Iva Maia … 37:53
13 Robert Landrum … 38:09
14 Lance Leopold … 38:19
15 Christopher Byers … 38:24
16 Chris Reilly … 38:24
17 Leighton Lord … 38:37
18 David Quick … 38:59
19 Gregory Jones … 39:08
20 George Patterson … 39:14
21 Barry Fitts … 39:24
22 Kenneth Foster … 39:30
23 Layton Gwinn … 39:31
24 Lynne Sherron … 47:14
25 Kevin Tashlein … 39:58

35–39 Female (855 finishers, 25 awards)
1 Tatiana Titova … 36:52
2 Laura Vroon … 39:10
3 Missy White … 40:21
4 Patt Loggins … 40:45
5 Elizabeth Graham … 41:18
6 Marie Sumnicht … 42:07
7 Christi Craft … 43:04
8 Nancy Brennan … 43:13
9 Suanne Hall … 43:27
10 Barbara Wagner … 43:31
11 Keely Churchill … 43:56
12 Catherine Mirando … 44:11
13 Lisa Powell … 44:42
14 Karen Strarets … 44:54
15 Kelly Hazel … 45:01
16 Frannie Reese … 45:34
17 Cindy Overton … 45:48
18 Eileen Thames … 46:19
19 Julie Hendrix … 46:39
20 Patti Paulett … 46:41
21 Elizabeth Jones … 46:44
22 Heather Wood … 46:53
23 Renee King … 47:14
24 Skip Persick … 39:45
25 Judy Grist … 47:20

40-44 Male (901 finishers, 25 awards)
1 Pete Edge … 35:19
2 Chris Shockley … 35:45
3 Richard Ferguson … 36:02
4 Paul Marino … 36:49
5 Marc Embler … 37:22
6 Scott Duncan … 37:31
7 David Bourgeois … 37:36
8 George Dunleavy … 38:07
9 Lennie Moore … 38:08
10 Robert Lowrey … 38:28
11 Doug Godley … 38:36
12 Mike McConeghy … 39:32
13 James Scheer … 39:36
14 Steve Feltman … 39:37
15 Jack Dusenberry … 39:41
16 Mark Taylor … 39:51
17 Steven Rudnicki … 39:55
18 Bob Wilson … 40:00
19 Mike Armor … 40:04
20 Dunn Neugebauer … 40:08
21 Eddie Pennebaker … 40:09
22 Stewart Banner … 40:25
23 Andy Barker … 40:25
24 Mike Griffin … 40:32
25 David Gee … 40:51

40–44 (577 finishers, 25 awards)
1 Kerry Robinson … 39:13
2 Susi Smith … 39:47
3 Joanne Collins … 40:27
4 Mary Jaye McGowan … 43:18
5 Lee Patterson … 43:24
6 Tami Dennis … 43:35
7 Nancy Thomas … 44:26
8 Beverly Grant … 45:05
9 Evelyn Long … 45:12
10 Caroline Lemelin … 45:51
11 Lynn Olson … 45:55
12 Sheila Roebuck … 46:06
13 Tammy Hovik … 47:25
14 Lynne Leroy … 47:26
15 Trudy Gale … 47:31
16 Anna Johnson … 47:45
17 Jane Godwin … 47:47
18 Linda Smith … 47:53
19 Eileen Myers … 48:09
20 Penny Galbraith … 49:24
21 Janet Daniel … 49:28
22 Linda Fairey … 49:32
23 Deborah Edwards … 49:41
24 Leslie Poujol-Brown … 49:49
25 Sandra Smith … 49:56

45–49 Male (752 finishers, 25 awards)
1 Jim Wilhelm … 35:17
2 David Renneisen … 35:59
3 Paul Dawson … 36:20
4 Jim Freid … 36:50
5 John Cash … 38:13
6 Jack Todd … 38:32
7 Joseph Denneny … 39:00
8 James Halsch … 39:04
9 Ron Collins … 39:07
10 Gary Ricker … 39:41
11 Samuel Jenins … 40:56
12 George Howe … 40:57
13 Michael Drose … 41:06
14 Chuck Bishop … 41:09
15 Bill Edwards … 41:19
16 Mark Greenway … 41:31
17 Jim Boyd … 41:33
18 Joe Lockman … 41:51
19 Bill Maddux … 41:52
20 Rob Meade … 42:13
21 Michael Loggins … 42:19
22 Larry Milner … 42:35
23 Dan Clapper … 42:39
24 William Whitman … 42:49
25 Bob Foster … 42:58

45–49 Female (411 finishers, 21 awards)
1 Barbara Holman … 44:02
2 Catherine Lempesis … 44:08
3 Sarah Bell … 45:33
4 Betsy Henderson … 46:29
5 Sue Porter … 47:21
6 Jo Haubenreiser … 47:45
7 Debbie Howard … 48:48
8 Sara Drehmer … 49:31
9 Judy Osborn … 50:06
10 Valerie Murrah … 50:11
11 Deby Shirk … 50:21
12 Brenda O'Sheilds … 50:46
13 Ellen Gower … 51:13
14 Tricia Christie … 51:16
15 Debbie Ostrander … 51:43
16 Cynthia Weckbacher … 51:44
17 Jeany Zuhde … 51:47
18 Caroline Bailey … 51:57
19 Barbara Warner … 52:04
20 Nancy Douglas … 52:23
21 Judith Stanton … 52:30

50-54 Male (686 finishers, 25 awards)
1 Richard Trammell … 36:28
2 Wes Wessely … 36:38
3 Oliver Marshall … 39:09
4 Phil Peterson … 39:22
5 Tim Kerr … 40:13
6 John Bernhardt … 40:40
7 John Sperry … 40:58
8 Douglas Blackford … 41:44
9 David Lee … 41:58
10 Mike Decamps … 42:05
11 Terry Murphy … 42:17
12 James Horne … 42:25
13 Paul Brown … 42:31
14 Norman Green … 42:41
15 Linny Moore … 43:43
16 Francis Burriss … 43:44
17 Dean Leroy … 44:47
18 Mackie Johnson … 45:02
19 Ricky Barnes … 45:22
20 David Anderson … 45:38
21 Mike Mahaney … 45:39
22 Bubba Gelly … 45:39
23 Don Whelchel … 45:40
24 William Hendrickson … 45:46
25 Frederick Hancock … 45:49

50–54 Female (239 finishers, 12 awards)
1 Brenda Cooter … 49:09
2 Nancy Curry … 49:50
3 Diane O'Donnell … 50:46
4 Judy Gilman … 50:58
5 Charla Thomas … 51:09
6 Kathy Jaggers … 51:45
7 Pamela Keeler … 52:18
8 Marianne Rice … 54:07
9 Beverly Stovall … 54:24
10 Dixie Dunbar … 54:52
11 Marcella Farino … 55:15
12 Patricia Kotila … 56:12

55–59 Male (393 finishers, 21 awards)
1 Terry Van Natta … 37:51
2 Tom Dooley … 38:10
3 Steve Annan … 38:45
4 Russ Brown … 40:19
5 Frank Eichstaedt … 41:21
6 Peter Mugglestone … 41:30

7	Jim Strowd	43:14
8	Charles Stoyle	44:09
9	Jim Kruse	44:15
10	Chuck Speight	44:25
11	Ray Kitchen	44:42
12	William Anderson	44:48
13	Tai Sugimoto	44:50
14	Elbert Howard	45:33
15	Dean Davis	45:52
16	Anthony Donachie	46:10
17	Bill Vetsch	46:16
18	David Moorhead	46:23
19	Tom Swanson	46:42
20	Donald Albert	46:43
21	Keith Ambrose	46:55

55–59 Female (101 finishers, 6 awards)

1	Mary Thompson	49:46
2	Joan Mulvihill	49:56
3	Nita Eichstaedt	50:57
4	Gail Bailey	51:34
5	Sissy Logan	51:50
6	Muff Harner	55:17

60-64 Male (155 finishers, 8 awards)

1	Gerald Friedman	42:52
2	Dean Godwin	43:47
3	Floyd Deandrade	43:50
4	Thomas Dority	47:02
5	Fred Wood	49:54
6	Bud Parker	51:03
7	Jack Marlowe	51:29
8	Bill Blizard	51:37

60–64 Female (39 finishers, 3 awards)

1	Pat Rhode	56:51
2	Robin Johnson	1:06:00
3	Helen Botti	1:06:11

65-69 Male (59 finishers, 3 awards)

1	Raymond Stone	47:28
2	Joe Nettles	48:39
3	Clyde Mizzell	48:57

65–69 Female (14 finishers, 3 awards)

1	Joyce Huguelet	59:48
2	Elfriede Tolley Beeson	1:04:43
3	Camille Daniel	1:07:11

70-74 Male (20 finishers, 3 awards)

1	William Boulter	50:35
2	David Anderson	50:53
3	Lonnie Collins	54:21

70–74 Female (5 finishers, 3 awards)

1	Garthedon Embler	1:10:53
2	Wyndall Henderson	1:36:30
3	Mabel Velge	1:37:19

75 & up Male (14 finishers, 3 awards)

1	John Cahill	47:32
2	Franklin Mason	58:50
3	David Mellard	1:01:54

75 & up Female (3 finishers, 3 awards)

1	Mary Canty	1:31:10
2	Lucy Jones	1:57:48
3	Margaret Wright	1:58:46

Compiled by Cedric Jaggers from complete results provided by Burns Computer Services on April 7, 2001.

Shadows fall across the Silas Pearman Bridge as runners make their way up the first span.
Post and Courier photo by Mic Smith

Runners make their way through the second span of the Silas N. Pearman bridge. Post and Courier photo by Yalonda M. James

Chapter 25
2002
All Finishers Get 25th Anniversary Race Medallions

The 25th Cooper River Bridge Run was held April 6, 2002, and began at 8 a.m. The 25th anniversary running will be remembered by the then record 14,338 runners, 8,079 male and 6,259 female who crossed the finish line, and for the near perfect sunny, crisp, 51 degree morning. They will also remember the race since each finisher was given a silver anniversary Olympic-style medal when they turned in their ChampionChip after crossing the finish line. The chips were used for timing the race for the sixth year in a row. The morning was made even better by a tailwind for the start of the race which became a crossing headwind on the first span of the bridge and became a tailwind as runners turned up the second span of the bridge.

The race used USATF certified course #SC00003BS for the third year in a row. It began on Coleman Boulevard in Mount Pleasant and finished at the corner of Alexander near Bay Street in Charleston.

It appeared the course record would be shattered as two Kenyans were on record pace when the unforeseen happened. The lead vehicle hesitated as it came to the turn off the bridge. The runners went past it and down the wrong ramp. The third place runner took the right path, and when the other two realized it, they had to stop and jump a rail to get back on the right road. John Itati of Kenya retook the lead and won in 28:06 with 1998 champion Tom Nyariki, also of Kenya, second in 28:11. Dejene Berhanu of Ethiopia was third in 28:14.

"I think it would have been under 28 minutes and that's what I wanted to run," winner Itati told the *Post and Courier*. "I know I could have made it if we had not taken that wrong turn there." Second place finisher, for the second year in a row, Nyariki said, "It cost me. I can't say for sure that it cost me the race, but it probably did. The man who won, we had left him behind earlier in the race." He estimated the mistake cost him 16 to 18 seconds and added, "once you lose your rhythm, it's hard to get it back. When you are running these races, you have to trust the lead car to be accurate. I have seen these things happen before, but it's the first time it's happened to me. But I am not upset; I'm satisfied with what I have."

Third place finisher Berhanu, who took the lead for awhile due to the error, said, "But it was not that much of an advantage. The two runners who went the wrong way, they had run this race before and I have not. So at first I thought they were right and I was wrong. I hesitated until I saw them coming over the side. If I had not, I might have had even a bigger lead."

Defending champion Catherine Ndereba of Kenya became the first person to ever win three Bridge Runs, missing her own course record by just 12 seconds to win in 31:53. She was followed by Ethiopians Ejegayehu Dibaba in 32:07 and Merima Hashim in 32:58.

"God is good for giving me this win," Ndereba told the *Post and Courier*. "I have kept my health, and it is because of God. With him, all things are possible." She said the wind became a crossing headwind on the bridge. "The wind is too much," she said. "When I ran on the bridge there was a very strong headwind. That makes it a challenge. I'm very happy with my time. The competition was very strong. The Ethiopians, Europeans and Americans ran well. So it wasn't just me and the other Kenyans who ran well."

Masters winner Eddy Hellebuyck of Albuquerque, N.M., set a U.S. Masters

Women's top finisher Catherine Ndereba crosses the finish line.
Post and Courier photo by Alan Hawes

men's record 29:23 to win as he was just 10 seconds off the course Masters record. He was also the first American to finish and 10th overall. "With the wind today, it was a good opportunity to go out for a fast time," he told the newspaper. "I've been running very well, so I didn't want to let this opportunity go. This race really supports the Masters runner. The money goes five deep in the Masters. I like to support races that think about the older people, too. Out of the 30,000 people here, probably more than half are over the age of 40. They are a big part of the race." Gennady Temnikov of Russia was second Masters in 29:29 followed by Andrew Masai of Kenya in 29:50.

Female Masters winner was Lyubov Kremleva of Russia in 34:04. Two-time Masters winner Tatyana Pozdnyakova of Ukraine was second in 34:22 with U.S. Olympian Joan Nesbit-Mabe of Chapel Hill, N.C., third in 36:10.

Grand Masters prize money went to Gary Romesser of Indianapolis, Ind., in 33:22 for the second year in a row. Three-time Grand Masters winner Bob Schlau of Charleston was second for the second year in a row, this time in 35:42. New Grand Master Danny West of Myrtle Beach, S.C., was third in 36:22.

Female Grand Masters winner was Debra Wagner of Fort Myers, Fla., in 37:14. Three-time Grand Masters winner Terry Mahr of Oregon, Ohio, was second in 38:44 while Catherine Wides of Durham, N.C., was third in 40:54.

The Dr. Marcus Newberry Award for first Tri-County finishers went to Sean Dollman of Charleston, 28th overall in 31:45. Dollman had retired from running in 1996 after running in the Olympics twice for Ireland. He moved to Charleston and started running again. Laurie Sturgell of Kiawah Island was the female winner, finishing 21st in a time of 36:41. The Dewey Wise Trophy was won by David Mellard, 79, of North Charleston with a time of 63:23.

For the first time since 1985 there was no television coverage. The race entry fee was again $20 for early registration and $25 for late entry. The walk fee was $15 early and $20 late.

A total of 286 runners broke the 40-minute barrier in the 2002 race. The breakout: 249 men and 37 women. There were 14 runners under 30 minutes, seven of them under the 29-minute barrier. The 50-minute barrier was broken by 1,955 runners, with a total of 6,007 crossing the finish line before the clock hit 60:00.

All the finishers' names and times were listed in the Sunday *Post and Courier*, and complete results were again mailed to all finishers as a supplement to the newspaper. The 16,802 runners who had registered for the race was not a new record. There was a wheelchair exhibition in 2002, with the two wheelchair participants beginning at the 7K walk start 15 minutes before the run began. Dan Pilon won in a time of 18:48 with Eugene Wellon second in 23:18. The untimed 7 kilometer walk had 10,021 registrants.

The Bridge Run established a Hall of Fame to honor runners who had contributed to the race. The initial six inductees were: Sallie Driggers, runner and local resident female overall race winner (1982); Ed Ledford, runner, four-time Masters winner; Cedric Jaggers, runner and race historian; Marcus Newberry, race founder; Bob Schlau, runner, overall race runner-up in 1979, two-time Marcus Newberry Award winner for first local Tri-County finishers, one-time Masters winner, three-time Grand Masters winner; and Margaret Wright, runner, oldest female finisher of the inaugural race and again the oldest female finisher at age 80 in 2002 when she set a South Carolina state age group record.

Other Voices
Tell Me About Your Bridge Run 2002

By Cedric Jaggers. Originally appeared in the May-June 2002 Low Country Runner

(Bridge Run info for 2002 – 14,338 largest number of official finishers at the time; 16,779 second largest number of entrants. Start time temperature 51 degrees.)

After the Bridge Run every year since 1988 (with only 2 exceptions) Charleston Running Club members get hit with a simple demand: Tell me about your Bridge Run. As everyone has been warned in the newsletter, I write down EXACTLY what you say. No one gets to come back later and add or change anything they said (and every year 5 or 6 people ask for changes).

The first batch of interviews was done immediately after the race in Calhoun Park, mostly at the CRC tent. Since the awards ceremony was unfortunately held much later that day at a separate location, I've indicated the interviews done there since folks had more time to reflect on what they would say (but it still seemed to take some people by surprise).

It was actually fun to do this article this year. As you know it did not happen last year for reasons beyond my control. I hope it will always happen from now on. Hey, you are a fun bunch of people to talk to, even the folks I did not know. Next year I still want to get a hundred – we only got 40% of the way there this year.

This year's 14,338 finishers was a record number, though the 16,779 entrants was not a record. If a person did not tell me their time, I tried to ask when they were through talking so I could find them in the results. I've listed everyone's overall place and official time I could find from the complete results Burns Computer printed for me after the race.

Pat Rhode: Well, we were talking before the race about how runners haven't improved … but I did better this year. Having asthma, I was having trouble, but everybody was so encouraging. At the end a black guy came up and said "Come on, Mom." It was so nice. I was hoping I'd see you this year. 55 twenty or so. 3,854th overall, 1st 60-64, 55:25

Jeffrey Herndon: Probably the easiest Bridge Run ever. Did the first mile in 6:25. The tailwind helped tremendously. 41:25, slow, but went out easy. 444th overall, 41:51

Ed Isaac: I'm 67 and it gets harder every year. I enjoyed it. About 67 minutes. 12,704th overall, 76:54

Eileen Stellefson Myers: Very fun. Slower and slower and slower. A consistent runner and not doing anything with speed anymore. It was a great day. My 15th Bridge Run. 49:12. 1,737th overall, 49:12

Brantley Arnau: I chose to run 10 minute pace this time and it was the most comfortable run I've had. It was my 20th Bridge Run and I was there at the first one. 62 minutes. (Unable to locate in results. CJ) 67:51 per BridgeRun.Com

Keith Ambrose: (Shakes head). I have nothing to say. I'm getting older and slower. 45:44. 1,005th overall, top 5% 55-59, 45:42

Dan Clapper: I had all these excuses ready for you but I actually ran pretty well. Let me look at my watch 41:27. 400th overall, top 5% 45-49 41:25

Gary Ricker: Let's see. What can I say? 40:43. I certainly can't blame the weather – it was ideal. I have to blame it on age. 324th overall, 40:42

Julie Deibel: Oh, don't say that … it was great. The best ever. 57 minutes for me is excellent. 5,179th overall, 58:29

Nancy Curry: Uh … perfect day. I was well prepared and I'm pleased with my time. And that is all this little old lady is going to say. 48:32. I'm pleased. 1,609th overall, top 5% 55-59, 48:35

Patrice Katsonevakis: You're going to be sorry you asked my name. (Note: I made her spell it. CJ) It was great. Great time. Great day. Great people. 48:06. 1,509th overall, 48:09

Debbie Eckles: I ran the whole thing and that was a feat for me because I haven't run 3 miles since last year. I didn't even stop at the water table; I brought my own. 1:02. 7,945th overall, 1:03:51

Wendy Roach: It was the best one ever. The tailwind pushed me over the hills. All the training pays off. A P.R. 44:44. 871st overall, top 5% 30-34, 44:58

Wayne Todd: Tell you about it? It was a P.R. of course. I wanted to go faster

Crossing the Pearman bridge with the Grace bridge in the background.
Post and Courier photo by Yalonda M. James

but ... 43:06. 614th overall, 43:14

Jim Madden: 41:30. Pleased with it. Trying to get back in shape. 426th overall, 41:41

Lennie Moore: I'm happy. I did better than last year and that was my goal. The temperature and the wind kind of helped everybody. 37:25. 153rd overall, top 5% 45-49, 37:25

Scott Smith: It was awesome. I knocked 45 seconds off last year. It was just a great day man. 36:12. 107th overall, top 5% 30-34, 36:12

Bob Kohn: I just got back from the Rome Marathon two weeks ago. This was just a survival thing. I just barely broke 59 minutes. This is my 18th time. I love it. 5,482nd overall, 59:03.

Joe Blackburn: I was very happy with the Bridge Run this year. The past couple of times I've been disappointed. My best Bridge Run ever. I realize maybe I didn't run hard enough. 39:25. It was a lot of fun. 238th overall, 39:23

Glen Braddock: It was okay. I had a great time. The time wasn't as fast as it has been. It's just hell to get old. 48:30. 2,017th overall, 50:14

Anne Maguire: It was good. I was pleased. Do I have to say anything more than that? My time? It was 47:10 which was a P.R. so I'm happy with that. 1,317th overall, 47:18

Gary Myers: You don't need me in here. It's the worst one I've ever done. I had a fun race. I ran it with Eileen until she ran off and left me – this is off the record, of course. 49:30. (Unable to locate in results. CJ) 49:29 per BridgeRun.Com

Bernie Clark: I survived. Now that I'm a retired person I need to get back in shape. I set a goal of minutes and I made it under 59 chip time. 1:02 clock. 7,172nd overall, 1:02:17

David Quick: Well like everybody, I had a PR 37:35. I'm very happy – it set me up pretty good for the Boston Marathon in nine days. Nice tailwind. I wish we had one every year. My Kenya shirt helped. 159th overall, top 5% 35-39, 37:35

Kathy Jaggers: Oh, you always get me when I'm not expecting it ... Don't write that down. It was a lot of fun. Actually about as much fun as the first year I did it. I noticed a lot of stuff I never noticed before. I never looked at the city of Charleston before. I never talked to anybody before while we ran the run. 2,544th overall, top 5% 55-59, 51:53.

Cedric Jaggers: (To Kathy who wrote this down) Mine goes last. Well, I'll put it last. I enjoyed it because I ran with my wife who has just been diagnosed with multiple sclerosis. It's a whole different experience being in the crowd, but I never felt like I was racing. I've never seen the city before from the bridge, and never felt fresh before at the finish. 2,543rd overall, 51:53

Interviews conducted at the awards ceremony:

Steve Annan: It was the best run I've ever had 36:45. As far as the race, it couldn't have been better. Conditions were perfect. A lot of people I'd been working out with ran sort of as a group. It was good to have them run well and inspire you to run well too. 128th overall, 1st 55-59, 36:47.

Ed Ledford: Well I was pretty happy with it. One of these days I'd like to finish a race feeling like I'm alive. It was hard, just really hard. One of the hardest ones I've ever had – even back when I was chasing you. 48:30. 1,691st overall, top 5% 65-69, 49:00

Alan Campbell: I'm a year older and 3 minutes faster so I wasn't complaining. Keep it short and simple. 43:20. 650th overall, 43:33

Irv Batten: Tell me about your Bridge Run? What do you want to know? I had a good time. I'm 38 years old and ran 32:24. We've got 5 guys who run for the store and they were the first 4 local runners. 35th overall, 1st 35-39, 32:24

David Mellard: What do you want to know? I thought it was marvelous because I ran all the spans. Last year I had to walk some but I ran it all this year. My time was about the same. Now I'm looking forward to the next one when I'll be 80. 7,682nd overall, 3rd 75-98, 1:03:23

Terry Hamlin: 48 minutes. My run sucked, it was expectedly slow. I've only been running again since Jan. 17. But I wasn't unhappy with it. It was cold and girls wear a lot less than they used to back in the '70s. 1,278th overall, 48:14

Margaret Wright: It was okay but I had to walk with the walkers again as usual. It was a good day for a run. 13,984th overall, 2nd 75-98, 1:53:42

Irving Rosenfeld: Strong tailwind, cool temperature, a winning combination. Everybodys been telling you that right? 56:40. 5,647th overall, 59:21.

David Bourgeois: I entered a new age group and my thing is last man standing. If my time gets slower and my place higher I figure if I live to 96 I'll win. 36:37. 124th overall, 36:39.

Patt Loggins: Very good considering I had a stomach virus and severe Montezuma all week. I'm happy. No complaints. I ran about 39:56 or 57 unofficially. 283rd overall, top 5% 40-44, 39:57

Mike Loggins: I'm mad that I got a side stitch, but I'm happy with my time. 40:20 something 26 or 29. 323rd overall, top 5% 45-49, 40:32

Lyn Hammond: Spectacular. Best one ever. Safe start, smooth finish. Good tailwind 48:30. 1,547th overall, 3rd 50-54, 48:21

Donna Lea Brown: It was wonderful. I'm going to keep trying until I win a place in my age group. That sounds good. We had a great time. Ran 1:06 or 1:09. 10,551st overall, 1:09:12.

Betsy Rivers: I had a good day. I thought it was fun. The weather was great, I felt real good. I had a good time. You've never asked me before. I ran 1:08 something. 10,361st overall, 1:08:46

2002 Awards
Prize money winners:
Overall Male
1 John Itati . . . . Kenya . . . . 28:06 . . . $5,000
2 Nyariki . . . . Kenya . . . . 28:11 . . . $3,000
3 Dejene Berhanu . . . . Ethiopia . . . . 28:14 . . . $1,500
4 Benjamin Limo . . . . Kenya . . . . 28:26 . . . $1,000
5 Sammy Nyamongo . . . . Kenya . . . . 28:38 . . . $800
6 Kibet Cherop . . . . Kenya . . . . 28:41 . . . $600
7 John Kariuki . . . . Kenya . . . . 28:53 . . . $500
8 Karl Rasmussen . . . . Norway . . . . 29:04 . . . $400
9 Sammy Ng'eno . . . . Kenya . . . . 29:14 . . . $300
10 Eddy Hellebuyck . . . . . . Albuquerque . . . . 29:23 . . . $250
11 Gennady Temnikov . . . Russia . . . . 29:29 . . . $200
12 David Njuguna . . . . Kenya . . . . 29:44 . . . $150
13 Andrew Masai . . . . Kenya . . . . 29:50 . . . $100
14 Andrey Kuznetsov . . . . Russia . . . . 29:56 . . . $75
15 Vincent Pemu . . . . Kenya . . . . 30:06 . . . $50

Overall Female
1 Catherine Ndereba   Kenya . . . . 31:53 . . .$5,000
2 Ejegayehu Dibaba . . . . . Ethiopia . . . . 32:07 . . . $3,000
3 Merima Hashim . . . . Ethiopia . . . . 32:58 . . . $1,500
4 Dorota Gruca . . . . Poland . . . . 33:00 . . . $1,000
5 Amy Yoder Begley . . . . . Kendallville IN . . . . 33:02 . . . $1,000
6 Gladys Asiba . . . . Kenya . . . . 33:19 . . . $800
7 Atelelech Kitema . . . . . Ethiopia . . . . 33:30 . . . $600
8 Bente Landoy . . . . Norway . . . . 33:30 . . . $400
9 Jeanne Hennessy . . . . . Mahopac, NY . . . . 33:59 . . . $300
10 Lyubov Kremleva . . . . . Russia . . . . 34:04 . . . $250
11 Martha Komu . . . . Kenya . . . . 34:06 . . . $200
12 Tatyana Maslova . . . . . . Russia . . . . 34:10 . . . $150
13 Tatyana Pozdnyakova Ukraine . . . . 34:22 . . . $100
14 Beth Old . . . . Douglasville, GA . . . . . 34:33 . . . $75
15 Monica Hostetler . . . . . Kendallville, IN. . . . . . . 34:45 . . . $50

Masters Overall Male
1 Eddy Hellebuyck . . . . . . Albuquerque . . . . 29:23 . . . $1,500
2 Gennady Temnikov . . . Russia . . . . 29:29 . . . $1,000
3 Andrew Masai . . . . Kenya . . . . 29:50 . . . $750
4 Andrey Kuznetsov . . . . Russia . . . . 29:56 . . . $500
5 Simon Karori . . . . Kenya . . . . 30:21 . . . $250

Masters Overall Female
1 Lyubov Kremleva . . . . . Russia . . . . 34:04 . . . $1,500
2 Tatyana Pozdnyakova   Ukraine . . . . 34:22 . . . $1,000
3 Joan Nesbit-Mabe . . . Chapel Hill, NC . . . . . . .36:10 . . . $750
4 Janice Addison . . . . Columbia, SC . . . . 36:26 . . . $500
5 Debra Wagner . . . . Ft Myers, FL . . . . 37:14 . . . $250

Grand Masters Overall Male
1 Gary Romesser . . . . Indianapolis, IN . . . . . . 33:22 . . . $750
2 Bob Schlau . . . . Charleston, SC . . . . . . .35:42 . . . $500
3 Danny West . . . . Myrtle Beach, SC . . . . . 36:22 . . . $250

Grand Masters Overall Female
1 Debra Wagner . . . . Ft Myers, FL . . . . 37:14 . . . $750
2 Terry Mahr . . . . Oregon, OH . . . . 38:44 . . . $500
3 Catherine Wides . . . . . . Durham, NC . . . . 40:54 . . . $250

Dr. Marcus Newberry Award
For First Local Tri-County Area Finisher
Male
 Sean Dollman . . . . Charleston, SC . . . . 31:45 . . . . $500
Female
 Laurie Sturgell . . . . . . Kiawah Island, SC . . . . . 36:41 . . . $500

Special award:
Dewey Wise Trophy for oldest finisher time less than his or her age in minutes:
 David Mellard, 79 . . . . N Charleston, ... 63:23

Age division winners
resented three deep, then top 5% up to a max. of 25
Males 12 & under (146 fin., 8 awards)
1 Alex Kingsley . . . . Swansea, SC 39:05
2 Camden Shealy . . . . Spartanburg, SC 43:54
3 Matt Buening . . . . Matthews, NC 45:00
4 Cameron Moore . . . . Anderson, SC 46:44
5 Trey Parker . . . . Sumter, SC 46:48
6 Hampton Graham . . . . Columbia, SC 46:53
7 Harrison Cabiness . . . . Charleston, SC 47:06
8 Zachary Flickinger . . . . Roswell, GA 49:42

Females 12 and under (79 fin., 4 awards)
1 Alexis Philips . . . . Spartanburg, SC 47:27
2 Stephanie Ruff . . . . Greenville, SC 48:39
3 Lillian Williams . . . . Chandler, NC 50:07
4 Cara Browning . . . . Goose Creek, SC 50:59

Males 13 - 17 (368 finishers, 19 awards)
1 Matthew Cregger . . . . Chapin, SC 33:49
2 Trevor Beesley . . . . Greenwood, SC 33:54
3 Jacob Morris . . . . Aiken, SC 34:16
4 Will Williams . . . . Lexington, VA 35:18
5 David Johannesmeyer . . . . Summerville, SC 36:27
6 Adam Taylor . . . . Simpsonville, SC 36:57
7 Ben Lassiter . . . . Charlotte, NC 37:33
8 Stuart Campbell . . . . Johns Island, SC 37:41
9 Christopher Butler . . . . Hilton Head Is, SC 37:41
10 Neil Ballentine . . . . Cornelius, NC 37:49
11 Andrew Symmes . . . . Greenville, SC 38:25
12 Zachary Phillips . . . . Spartanburg, SC 38:45
13 Will Jeffries . . . . Summerville, SC 38:56
14 Robbie Phillips . . . . Greenville, SC 39:39
15 Eric Howell . . . . Columbia, SC 39:41
16 Erik Clark . . . . Greenville, SC 39:44
17 Mac Mcmahan . . . . Anderson, SC 39:59
18 Trey Rives . . . . Moore, SC 39:59
19 Douglas Engleman . . . . Hanahan, SC 40:15

Females 13 - 17 (277 finishers, 14 awards)
1 Michele Milner . . . . Aiken, SC 38:35
2 Marcie Milner . . . . Aiken, SC 41:00
3 Elizabeth Tempel . . . . Beaufort, SC 43:01
4 Erin Smith . . . . Greenwood, SC 44:01
5 Lauren Jaynes . . . . Summerville, SC 44:49
6 Kelsey Jones . . . . Summerville, SC 44:57
7 Julia Bisschops . . . . Johns Island, SC 45:15
8 Chelsey Wilson . . . . Candler, NC 45:37
9 Sarah Atkins . . . . Charleston, SC 45:40
10 Erica Adams . . . . Spartanburg, SC 45:55
11 Abby Osborn . . . . Charlotte, NC 46:08
12 Andrea L Stokes . . . . Aiken, SC 46:12
13 Jane Spears . . . . Greenville, SC 46:55
14 Kaci McCall . . . . Greenville, SC 48:38

Males 18 - 21 (273 finishers, 14 awards)
1 Charles Kamindo . . . . Kenya 31:40
2 Brandon Cantrell . . . . Inman, SC 32:14
3 Clark Davis . . . . Spartanburg, SC 33:57
4 Brandon Downey . . . . Greenwood, SC 34:31
5 Kevin Timp . . . . Chapel Hill, SC 34:34
6 Travis Smith . . . . Spartanburg, SC 34:56

– Continued on next page

2002 Awards, continued from page 199

7	Eric Cannon	Newberry, SC	35:06
8	Daniel Lowrey	Clemson, SC	35:11
9	Hunter Hicklin	Greenville, SC	36:03
10	Ricky Johnson	Clinton, SC	36:24
11	Hudson Belk	Charleston, SC	36:57
12	Drew Brannon	Clinton, SC	36:57
13	Benjamin Galizi	Charleston, SC	37:12
14	Bradley Cantrell	Inman, SC	37:15

Females 18 to 21 (404 fin., 21 awards)

1	Elspeth Hamilton	Chapel Hill, NC	40:54
2	Krystle Short, FL	etcher, NC	41:10
3	Holly Bednarek	Charleston, SC	42:57
4	Renee High	Goose Creek, SC	43:10
5	Jessica Carroll	Charlotte, NC	43:33
6	Becky Witkip	Charleston, SC	43:38
7	Meg Austin	New Bern, NC	45:02
8	Lindsay Macpherson	Charleston, SC	45:09
9	Cheryl Ewing	Charleston, SC	45:18
10	Jennifer Gratton	Charleston, SC	45:18
11	Lace Cosgrove	Greer, SC	45:38
12	Kasey Favinger	Charleston, SC	45:50
13	Aaryn Munson	Charleston, SC	45:50
14	Jamie Mussman	Greer, SC	46:23
15	Elizabeth Rose	Charlotte, NC	46:46
26	Tonya Henderson	Spartanburg, SC	47:02
17	Stephanie Miller	Chapel Hill, NC	47:03
18	Lauren Bates	Mt Pleasant, SC	47:06
19	Rachel Robinson	Chapel Hill, NC	47:30
20	Casey Hannifin	Greenville, SC	47:37
21	Emiline Fricke	Charleston, SC	47:50

Males 22 - 25 (672 finishers, 25 awards)

1	Samuel Mangusho	Savannah, GA	30:42
2	Kevin Hill	Advance, NC	31:08
3	Andrew Begley	Kendallville, IN	31:42
4	Mike Aiken	Charleston, SC	32:07
5	Jake Johnson	Atlanta, GA	32:12
6	Christopher Westerkamp	Greenville, NC	32:47
7	Palmer Thomas	Charleston, SC	33:40
8	Tim Gibbons	Spartanburg, SC	33:43
9	Blake Benke	Emerald Is., NC	34:05
10	Kurt Wilson	Candler, NC	34:21
11	Devin Langguth	Goose Creek, SC	35:02
12	Andrew Cawood	Marietta, GA	35:53
13	Michael Houlihan	Harrisonburg, VA	36:15
14	David Lee Jr	Columbia, SC	36:31
15	Jamie Williams	Charleston, SC	36:49
16	Travis Brady	Spartanburg, SC	37:07
17	Wallace Brandt	Charleston, SC	37:54
18	Richard Galinski	Chapel Hill, NC	38:18
19	Steven Alexander	Buies Creek, NC	38:22
20	Ben Schluckebier	Charleston, SC	38:29
21	Hamp Kennemore	Greenwood, SC	38:51
22	Jacob Millican	Hanahan, SC	39:01
23	William Gray	Athens, GA	39:20
24	Tom Stone	Mt Pleasant, SC	39:42
25	Kris Kitzke	Charleston, SC	39:50

Females 22 - 25 (939 finishers, 25 awards)

1	Agnes Ngunjiri	Kenya	35:07
2	Naomi Wangui	Kenya	35:51
3	Laurie Sturgell	Kiawah Island, SC	36:41
4	Jill Marie Hawley	Surfside Beach, SC	39:19
5	Emily Keller	Athens, GA	39:48
6	Corey Burgoyne	Charleston, SC	40:16
7	Jessica Kennedy	Athens, GA	40:57
8	Emily Eades	Mt Pleasant, SC	41:38
9	Suzanne Clemmer	Gastonia, NC	41:52
10	Ligeia Bricken	Columbia, SC	42:11
11	Kimberly Timberlake	Carrboro, NC	42:27
12	Carlajane Costantini	Charleston, SC	42:57
13	Elizabeth Johnson	N Charleston, SC	43:44
14	Holly Munnis	Charleston, SC	43:48
15	Kate Thompson	Chapel Hill, NC	43:48
16	Jenna Shive	Mt Pleasant, SC	44:17
17	Diana Epstein	Charleston, SC	44:26
18	Allison Bumgardner	Charlotte, NC	44:39
19	Desiree Pittman	Chapel Hill, NC	44:43
20	Elizabeth Weaver	Columbia, SC	44:46
21	Jennifer Emblidge	Charleston, SC	45:01
22	Melissa Hersh	Charleston, SC	45:03
23	Allison Gordon	Winston-Salem, NC	45:20
24	Alison Andrews	Charleston, SC	45:25
25	Roberta McCue	Charleston, SC	45:35

Males 26 - 29 (1,003 finishers, 25 awards)

1	Ben Kapsoiya	Kenya	30:37
2	Jared Segera	Kenya	30:49
3	Bill Baldwin	Brevard, NC	31:41
4	Christian Muentener	Yarmouth, ME	32:16
5	Charles Wangondu	Kenya	32:39
6	Francis Friedman	Camp Lejeune, NC	33:38
7	Jason Annan	Chapel Hill, NC	33:58
8	Mark Evans	Lynchburg, VA	34:18
9	Andrew Keel	Marietta, GA	34:23
10	Joshua Reid	Charlotte, NC	34:26
11	Peter Brown	Matthews, NC	34:29
12	Chad Myers	Lancaster, OH	34:31
13	Andrew Bartle	Camp Lejeune, NC	34:36
14	Matthew Johnson	Rock Hill, SC	35:17
15	Bradley S Fowler	Win.-Salem, NC	35:37
16	Mark Gelazela	Emerald Isle, NC	36:35
17	Philip Tannheimer	Isle of Palms, SC	36:37
18	Bobby Wilder	Myrtle Beach, SC	36:46
19	Janek Kazmierski	Columbia, SC	36:59
20	Jorum Nyakeraka	Howard , KY	37:34
21	Jimmy Major	Chapin, SC	37:43
22	Roger Fagala	Blenheim, SC	37:59
23	Matthew Pryor	Unknown	38:18
24	Andrew Stroupe	Charlotte, NC	38:32
25	Stephen Hughes	Charleston, SC	38:43

Females 26 - 29 (1,067 fini., 25 awards)

1	Farrell Burns	Charlotte, NC	37:08
2	Amy Clements	Charleston, SC	38:56
3	Amanda Charlton	Columbia, SC	40:35
4	Marty Raines	Inman, SC	40:58
5	Carol Brunson	Spartanburg, SC	41:34
6	Carrie Hunoval	Winston-Salem, NC	41:35
7	Helen Lafaye	Columbia, SC	41:56
8	Ginny Carson	Charleston, SC	43:11
9	Kimberly Morgan	Greenville, SC	43:29
10	Leesa Wells	W. Columbia, SC	43:59
11	Linda Wood	Marietta, GA	44:08
12	Amy Landers	Charleston, SC	44:50
13	Sara Lawrence	Chapel Hill, NC	45:09
14	Thomissa Wallwork	Charlotte, NC	45:14
15	Claire Penton	Marietta, GA	45:25
16	Tanya M Dillard	Greenville, SC	45:35
17	Dixie McCutchen	Win.-Salem, NC	45:46
18	Danni Owens	Mt Pleasant, SC	45:47

19	Shontel Jung	Chapel Hill, NC	45:48
20	Lynn Sykes	Atlanta, GA	45:55
21	Linda Anderson	Charlotte, NC	46:23
22	Melissa Reich	Piedmont, SC	46:44
23	Brittany Olson	Columbia, SC	46:54
24	Melissa Moore	Charlotte, NC	46:54
25	Paige Walker	Charlotte, NC	47:00

Males 30 - 34 (1,392 finishers, 25 awards)

1	Stephen Kenny	Columbia, SC	31:09
2	Keith Matiskella	Columbia, SC	31:18
3	Sean Dollman	Charleston, SC	31:45
4	Larry Evans	Augusta, GA	32:29
5	Byron Law	Cary, NC	33:28
6	Bob Ferguson	Johnstown, OH	34:06
7	David Lively Jr	Blythewood, SC	34:43
8	David Mccombs	Jacksonville, NC	34:57
9	Karl Kaiser	Columbia, SC	35:01
10	Darol Timberlake	Matthews, NC	35:11
11	Dan Holland	Pittsburgh, PA	35:19
12	Emery Lloyd	Moncks Corner, SC	35:29
13	Scott Smith	Charleston, SC	36:12
14	Doug Long	Huntersville, NC	36:13
15	Paul Reardon	Hartsville, SC	36:23
16	Nick Felix	Hilton Head, SC	36:25
17	Dave Popik	Lexington, SC	36:33
18	Paul Harris	Martinez, GA	36:38
19	Bo Butler	Mooresville, NC	36:50
20	Stephen Hudzik	Charlotte, NC	36:54
21	Mark Harrell	Unknown	37:26
22	Daniel Kehoe	Atlanta, GA	37:30
23	Elijah Kosgei	South Bend, IN	37:39
24	Michael Haranzo	Roanoke, VA	37:40
25	Scott Baskett	Summerville, SC	37:48

Females 30 - 34 (1,097 fin., 25 awards)

1	Karen Killeen	Winston-Salem, NC	38:29
2	Tracy Foss	Greenville, SC	40:30
3	Christine Conrad	Charleston, SC	41:30
4	Winn Elliott	Charlotte, NC	41:49
5	Laurie Deputy	Richmond, VA	42:09
6	Ginger Carter	Greenville, SC	42:30
7	Kimberly L Sturkey	Charlotte, NC	43:03
8	Jacqueline Miller	Pineville, NC	43:28
9	Carey Cochran	Charleston, SC	43:48
10	Tammy Root	Hagerstown, IN	43:59
11	Tricia Parish	Charlotte, NC	44:23
12	Debra Brown	Mt Pleasant, SC	44:24
13	Jeanne Marie Kenny	Columbia, SC	44:28
14	Wendy Roach	Mt Pleasant, SC	44:58
15	Megan Parrott	Greer, SC	45:06
16	Renee Johnson	Spartanburg, SC	45:08
17	Anita Charleston	Charlotte, NC	45:14
18	Cara Balch	Charlotte, NC	45:14
19	Terri Conroy	Atlanta, GA	45:19
20	Missy Hunnicutt	Columbia, SC	45:27
21	Leslie Randall	Charlotte, NC	45:32
22	Samantha Roberts	Mt Pleasant, SC	45:42
23	Stephanie Horn	Charlotte, NC	45:51
24	Julie Law	Cary, NC	46:09
25	Corey Goldman	Charlotte, NC	47:03

Males 35 - 39 (1,067 finishers, 25 awards)

1	Irv Batten	Summerville, SC	32:24
2	Eric Parker	Mt Pleasant, SC	34:44
3	Sean Kileen	Win.-Salem, NC	34:59
4	Eric Vandervort	Clinton, TN	35:16
5	Rob Blaszkiewicz	Monroe, GA	36:08
6	Peter Esser	Summerville, SC	36:20
7	Dave Pratt	Salinas, CA	36:48
8	Robert Landrum	Port Royal, SC	36:52
9	Lance Leopold	Simpsonville, SC	37:03
10	Eddie Parsley Jr	Richmond, VA	37:04
11	Toby Brown	Greenville, SC	37:05
12	Craig Kingma	Jenison, MI	37:08
13	Mike Ohara	Summerville, SC	37:12
14	Lee Willard	Greenville, SC	37:34
15	David Quick	Mt Pleasant, SC	37:35
16	James Doyle	Charlotte, NC	37:42
17	Paul Thauer	Unknown	37:42
18	George Patterson	Kings Mtn., NC	38:08
19	Jim Daniel	Greenville, SC	38:13
20	Roman Pibl	Salisbury, NC	38:30
21	Chris Hicks	Sumter, SC	38:40
22	Richard West	Tulsa, OK	38:45
23	Helmut Schmoock	Murrells Inlet, SC	38:47
24	Jeff Wolfson	Marietta, GA	38:52
25	Cail Brown	Charleston, SC	39:03

Females 35 - 39 (871 finishers, 25 awards)

1	Donna Anderson	Pawley's Is. SC	35:29
2	Cynthia Anzalone-Fox	Cleveland, OH	39:39
3	Saundi Theodossiou	Asheville, NC	40:04
4	Lisa Tolley	Seneca, SC	40:28
5	Tracy Steele	Atlanta, GA	41:32
6	Missy White	Unknown	41:41
7	Kelly Hazel	Summerville, SC	42:43
8	Pamela Mitchell	Wilmington, NC	43:29
9	Christi Craft	Simpsonville, SC	43:31
10	Tracy Rogers	Simpsonville, SC	44:17
11	Carol Malnati	Charlotte, NC	44:37
12	Jane Few	Greenville, SC	44:51
13	Ann Coggiola	Isle of Palms, SC	45:27
14	Keely Churchill	Raleigh, NC	45:32
15	Suanne Hall	Greenville, SC	45:34
16	Lynne Takac	Charlotte, NC	45:58
17	Kathy Murray	Jacksonville, FL	45:58
18	Angela Brose	Mt Pleasant, SC	46:18
19	Diane Lancaster	Charlotte, NC	46:22
20	Monica Fichman	Matthews, NC	46:25
21	Elizabeth Graham	Columbia, SC	46:52

22 Lynn McCain..............Mt Pleasant, SC......47:02
23 Karen Karwowski.........Richmond, VA.........47:07
24 Dawn McCarthy...........Cornelius, NC........47:09
25 Kelly Adams.............Mt Pleasant, SC......47:17

Males 40 - 44 (935 finishers, 25 awards)
1 Paul Mbugua..............Kenya................30:24
2 John Tuttle..............Douglasville, GA.....30:53
3 Volodymyr Bukhanov.......Ukraine..............32:55
4 Tom Mather...............Mt Pleasant, SC......33:42
5 John Patterson...........Charlotte, NC........34:45
6 Andrew Wheeler...........Fayetteville, NC.....35:03
7 David Agosta.............Lancaster, OH........35:28
8 Peter Edge...............Simpsonville, SC.....35:35
9 Dwight Jacobs............Greensboro, NC.......35:36
10 Dan Wellbaum............Rock Hill, SC........36:14
11 Rob Burke...............Wilmington, NC.......36:26
12 Clyde Sanders...........Beaufort, SC.........36:42
13 Billy Tisdale...........Sumter, SC...........37:03
14 Sam Inman...............Greenville, SC.......37:06
15 Mike Yawn...............Gainesville, GA......37:24
16 Robert Curci............Levittown, PA........37:40
17 Eddie Pennebaker........Clemson, SC..........37:41
18 George Dunleavy.........Sullivans Isl, SC....37:44
19 David Gee...............Gaffney, SC..........38:26
20 Marc Embler.............Summerville, SC......38:33
21 John Moylan.............Columbia, SC.........39:10
22 Steven Rudnicki.........Columbia, SC.........39:15
23 Jack Dusenbery..........Mt Pleasant, SC......39:23
24 Joseph Blackburn........Charleston, SC.......39:23
25 Luke Egan...............Rock Hill, SC........39:27

Females 40 - 44 (615 finishers, 25 awards)
1 Lee Di Pietro............Ruxton, MD...........37:18
2 Janice Reilly............Cary, NC.............38:22
3 Patti Stewart-Garbrecht..Jacksonville, NC.....38:34
4 Ruth-Marie Milliman......Greenville, SC.......38:52
5 Susi Smith...............Taylors, SC..........39:14
6 Patricia Loggins.........Charleston, SC.......39:57
7 Joanne Collins...........Westlake, OH.........40:50
8 Lee Patterson............Summerville, SC......42:31
9 Mary Jaye McGowan........Wilmington, NC.......42:45
10 Barbara Wagner..........Mt Pleasant, SC......43:01
11 Tami Dennis.............Spartanburg, SC......43:25
12 Nancy Tholmas...........Mt Pleasant, SC......43:35
13 Robin Tarpinian.........Greer, SC............43:45
14 Mary H Roebuck..........Fernandina Bch, FL...43:49
15 Diane Deems.............Hendersonville, NC...44:08
16 Lori Reinhardt..........Sullivan's Isl, SC...44:32
17 Kathy Abernethy.........Matthews, NC.........44:57
18 Debbie Edwards..........Denver, NC...........45:11
19 Trudy Gale..............Spencer, NC..........45:54
20 Tammy Hovik.............Charlotte, NC........46:12
21 Lynne Leroy.............Goose Creek, SC......47:22
22 Jan Millsaps............Knoxville, TN........47:45
23 Marsha Alterman.........Charleston, SC.......47:52
24 Connie Rink.............Mt Pleasant, SC......48:05
25 Jane Godwin.............Greer, SC............48:15

Males 45 - 49 (820 finishers, 25 awards)
1 David Renneisen..........Goose Creek, SC......33:50
2 Jim Wilhelm..............Canton, OH...........34:58
3 Pete Kaplan..............Charlotte, NC........35:19
4 David Bourgeois..........Summerville, SC......36:39
5 Lennie Moore.............Mt Pleasant, SC......37:25
6 George Howe..............Raleigh, NC..........38:19
7 Samuel McNeill...........Kuttawa, KY..........38:37
8 Jim Halsch...............Greensboro, NC.......39:01
9 Bob Foster...............Goose Creek, SC......39:15
10 Peter Hertl.............Jamestown, NC........39:21
11 Gregory Fagan...........Win.-Salem, NC.......39:30
12 Lyn Short...............Fletcher, NC.........39:42
13 Gregory Baker...........Williamsburg, VA.....40:19
14 Michael Loggins.........Charleston, SC.......40:32
15 Thomas Horn.............Mt Pleasant, SC......40:33
16 Gary Ricker.............Charleston, SC.......40:42
17 Don O'Quinn.............Tybee Island, GA.....40:58
18 Rick King...............Anderson, SC.........41:00
19 Bill Edwards............Florence, SC.........41:00
20 Bobby Wynn..............Carrollton, GA.......41:05
21 Bill Maddux.............Mt Pleasant, SC......41:12
22 Tom Alvey...............Lexington, SC........41:18
23 Peter O'Boyle...........Columbia, SC.........41:20
24 Dan Clapper.............N Charleston, SC.....41:25
25 Larry Milner............Aiken, SC............41:28

Females 45 - 49 (438 finishers, 22 awards)
1 Nancy Stewart............Atlanta, GA..........38:28
2 Diana Cushing............Clemmons, NC.........41:17
3 Trish Vlastnik...........Peachtree City, GA...41:42
4 Sarah Ball...............Charleston, SC.......43:21
5 Beverly Grant............Weaverville, NC......44:00
6 Sheila Roebuck...........San Rafael, CA.......44:07
7 Jo Haubenreiser..........Kernersville, NC.....46:48
8 Nitsa Calas..............N Charleston, SC.....46:56
9 Patrice Katsanevakis.....Mt Pleasant, SC......48:09
10 Sandra Smith............Powder Sprs, GA......48:10
11 Therese Killeen.........Isle of Palms, SC....48:25
12 Brenda O'Shields........Beaufort, SC.........48:52
13 Judy Osborn.............Charlotte, NC........49:02
14 Debra Peters............Myrtle Beach, SC.....49:08
15 Carol Mosher............Anderson, SC.........49:10
16 Jean Sellers............Trinity, NC..........49:28
17 Mary Millar.............Hickory, NC..........49:28
18 Elizabeth Lierley.......Mt Pleasant, SC......49:42
19 Susan Krepelka..........Charlotte, NC........50:02
20 Nancy Duffy.............Charlotte, NC........50:07
21 Beth Atkins.............Charleston, SC.......50:38
22 Sally Drehmer...........Charlotte, NC........50:41

Males 50 - 54 (674 finishers, 25 awards)
1 Jack Todd................Spartanburg, SC......37:50
2 Rick Boyle...............Ringoes, NJ..........38:00
3 William Papa.............Pocono Pines, PA.....38:53
4 Fred Corpuz..............Strongsville, OH.....38:57
5 Jim Boyd.................Mt Pleasant, SC......39:38
6 Tim Kerr.................Charlotte, NC........39:47
7 Patrick Gaughan..........Jacksonville, FL.....40:18
8 Rob Kriegshaber..........Columbia, SC.........41:02
9 Douglas Blackford........Todd, NC.............41:09
10 James Horne.............Taylors, SC..........41:30
11 Gary Joye...............Columbia, SC.........41:40
12 Bob Perkins.............Charleston, SC.......42:05
13 Larry Berglino..........Simpsonville, SC.....42:44
14 James Greene............Kings Mtn, NC........42:58
15 Mike Mahaney............Kannapolis, NC.......42:59
16 Paul Brown..............Goose Creek, SC......43:28
17 David Lee...............Columbia, SC.........43:31
18 David Johnson...........Sarasota, FL.........43:47
19 Kenneth Flowers.........Marion, SC...........44:00
20 Albert Anderson.........Eastover, SC.........44:07
21 Bill Allen..............Charlotte, SC........44:32
22 Nick Ramsdell...........Summerville, SC......44:33
23 John Smith..............Hilton Head, SC......44:34
24 Sam Culbertson..........Kingsport, TN........44:51
25 Bubba Gelly.............Win.-Salem, NC.......44:54

Females 50 - 54 (252 finishers, 13 awards)
1 Catherine Lempesis.......Irmo, SC.............42:57
2 Sallie Driggers..........Hanahan, SC..........46:19
3 Lyn Hammond..............Charleston, SC.......48:21
4 Neddie Legg..............Arvada, CO...........49:41
5 Valerie Murrah...........Chapel Hill, NC......50:29
6 Janice Wilkins...........Greenville, SC.......51:33
7 Diane Spicer.............Tampa, FL............52:00
8 Judith Stanton...........Aiken, SC............52:13
9 Judy Gilman..............McClellanville, SC...52:34
10 Marianne Rice...........McMurray, PA.........52:59
11 Judy Greenhill..........Columbia, SC.........53:07
12 Mary Vish...............Levittown, PA........53:24
13 Jeannie Vinson..........Chapin, SC...........53:43

Males 55 - 59 (414 finishers, 21 awards)
1 Steve Annan..............Mt Pleasant, SC......36:47
2 Scott Taylor.............Beaverton, OR........37:57
3 Earl Jackson.............Rock Hill, SC........41:06
4 Tai Sugimoto.............Charleston, SC.......41:08
5 Charles Stoyle...........Augusta, GA..........41:16
6 Peter Mugglestone........Charlotte, NC........42:16
7 Mackie Johnson...........Conover, NC..........42:27
8 Linny Moore..............Greer, SC............42:49
9 William Anderson.........Wadmalaw Isl, SC.....43:04
10 Elbert Howard...........Jamestown, SC........43:32
11 Thomas Henkel...........Orange Park, FL......44:11
12 Roddy Whitaker..........Swansea, SC..........44:18
13 Richard Landsman........Summerville, SC......44:30
14 Larry Seavers...........Charlotte, NC........44:33
15 Gary Melville...........Charleston, SC.......44:57
16 Eric Elbel..............Marietta, GA.........45:07
17 John Johnson............Greenville, SC.......45:10
18 Keith Ambrose...........Mt Pleasant, SC......45:42
19 Roger Arthur............Red House, WV........45:52
20 Don Albert, FL..........etcher, NC...........46:16
21 James Troknya...........Perrysburg, OH.......46:44

Females 55 - 59 (129 finishers, 8 awards)
1 Susie Hamilton...........Fairview, NC.........43:59
2 Kathy Seavers............Charlotte, NC........46:29
3 Sissy Logan..............Salem, VA............48:05
4 Nancy Curry..............Mt Pleasant, SC......48:35
5 Gail Bailey..............Charleston, SC.......48:53
6 Joan Mulvihill...........Charleston, SC.......49:43
7 Brenda Cooter............Grovetown, GA........50:15
8 Kathy Jaggers............Rock Hill, SC........51:53

Males 60 - 64 (195 finishers, 10 awards)
1 Jim Strowd...............Mt Pleasant, SC......41:09
2 Anthony Donachie.........Mt Pleasant, SC......43:50
3 Dean Godwin..............Aiken, SC............43:54
4 George Luke..............Greenville, SC.......46:48
5 Bill Vetsch..............Aiken, SC............46:48
6 Thomas Dority............Charleston, SC.......46:59
7 Riley Floyd..............St George, SC........47:39
8 Ron Sanders..............Columbia, SC.........48:08
9 Larry Crosby.............Anderson, SC.........48:08
10 Donald Jones............Columbia, SC.........48:36

Females 60 - 64 (38 finishers, 3 awards)
1 Pat Rhode................Walterboro, SC.......55:25
2 Barbara Lindeman.........Oregon, OH...........58:11
3 Shirley Salvo............Kiawah Island, SC....58:20

John Itati of Kenya (#3) passes Tom Nyariki for the win.

Post and Courier photo by Alan Hawes

Males 65 - 69 (60 finishers, 4 awards)
1 Raymond Stone............Simpsonville, SC.....48:09
2 John Thompson............Taylors, SC..........48:22
3 Clyde Mizzell............Charleston, SC.......48:42
4 Ed Ledford...............Folly Beach, SC......49:00

Females 65 - 69 (19 finishers, 3 awards)
1 Susie Kluttz.............Win.-Salem, NC.......46:23
2 E. K. Tolley-Beeson......Sumter, SC...........54:52
3 Joyce Huguelet...........Wilmington, NC.....1:03:14

Males 70 - 74 (17 finishers, 3 awards)
1 William Boulter..........Charleston, SC.......48:36
2 Lonnie Collins...........Gilbert, SC..........50:35
3 Ken Walls................Mt Pleasant, SC......53:48

Females 70 - 74 (2 finishers, 2 awards)
1 Garthedon Embler.........Isle of Palms, SC..1:14:39
2 Wyndall Henderson........Walterboro, SC.....1:33:12

Males 75 - 98 (15 finishers, 3 awards)
1 Franklin Mason...........Mullins, SC..........56:53
2 Charles Scott............Atlanta, GA..........56:58
3 David Mellard............N Charleston, SC...1:03:23

Females 75 - 98 (2 finishers, 3 awards)
1 Lore McCoy...............W. Columbia, NC....1:38:11
2 Margaret Wright..........Folly Beach, SC....1:53:42

Compiled by Cedric Jaggers from complete results provided by Burns Computer Services April 6, 2002.

Runners and walkers near the top of the first span. Post and Courier photo by Mic Smith

Chapter 26
2003
Heat Sends Record 200 To Medical Treatment

The 26th Cooper River Bridge Run began at 8 a.m. on April 5, 2003. It was a great morning for standing around but not for running. With the temperature at 66 degrees with high humidity and bright sunshine at the start, fifth warmest in the race's history, it soared to near 80 before the then record 17,071 entrants and 14,623 runners (8,039 male and 6,584 female) crossed the finish line. There was a cooling headwind as runners crossed the 2-mile bridge, but it was a tailwind, mostly blocked out by buildings for the last mile in downtown Charleston. As a result, over 200 runners required medical treatment with six hospitalized. All runners were again timed by ChampionChip computer timing chip.

Two Kenyans ran virtually shoulder to shoulder through downtown Charleston. Tom Nyariki, 1998 champion, had finished second the past two years and was determined not to let that happen again. At the 6-mile mark, he kicked to take a short lead over Linus Maiyo and held it to the finish where both were timed in 28:57, the slowest winning time since 1998. Defending champion John Itati, also of Kenya, was third in 29:12, over a minute slower than his winning time from 2002. Nyariki said, "Last time we raced, he beat me. Last time I kicked (early) and did not lose him, so this time, I think, I will not kick too early. He tried to kick and I went with him, and then I had the last kick to the finish."

The headline in the Sports section of the *Post and Courier* said: "No wrong turn for Nyariki this year," referring to his having been led off course by the lead vehicle in 2002. Nyariki was watching out this year and was really glad that the wrong turn was blocked by a truck. He laughed as he said, "I was very keen to see that mark, so that I would not get lost again." The hot day even affected the winners. He said, "The time is not good for Kenyans in this run; I was expecting much better."

Second place finisher Maiyo echoed the sentiment. "I can say that this time was not good for Kenya. We have to run faster times so that we can be invited to more races. At the start, the pace was very slow; it was too slow. But we increased the pace. If we had not, we would have finished in 30 minutes, and that's not good for Kenya."

The slow start was mentioned by other runners as Masters Division runners Selwyn Blake of Columbia, S.C., and Eddy Hellebucyck of Albequerque, N.M., led most of the first mile. Blake said, "I don't know if they (the Kenyans) knew the course that well. A lot of them were here for the first time. Eddy knows the course and is always going to run the shortest part, so I just went with him." Hellebuyck said, "They were sleeping the first mile. I was very surprised it went out so slow." Blake, who finished 19th, added "The first mile was slow, and then they throw in a 4:14 mile, an unbelievable pace. They crushed everyone after that. They crushed me."

Kenyans also swept the top three women's positions, as first time Bridge Runner Edna Kiplagat won in 33:41. "I really didn't know about the bridge. I only saw the map of the course," she said. "I knew there were bridges, but I didn't know they would be so big. The first hill was so very long and very steep. The second hill wasn't as long, but it was a challenge." She was happy with her win and added, "It wasn't about times today. Today was about winning. It's running your best race and beating the best runners in a race like this." Gladys Asiba, 33:58, and Emily Samoei, 34:01, were second and third.

Master's winner was Andrew Masai of Kenya in 30:49. Defending Masters champion Eddy Hellebuyck of Albequerque, N.M., who set a pending U.S. Masters record 29:23 last year, had come back hoping to break the Masters course record 29:05, but said after the race that the heat and having just set a 10-mile record the previous weekend, took a toll and he finished second in 31:06. Russian Lyubov Kremleva repeated as female Masters winner in 33:58. Grand Masters winner for the thrd year in a row was Gary Romesser of Indianapolis, Ind., in 33:36. Terry Mahr of Oregon, Ohio, was female Grand Masters winner in 40:42.

The award for the first finisher from the Tri-County is named for race founder Dr. Marcus Newberry. Nicholas Iauco of the Isle of Palms won it as he was 17th overall in 32:24. Lizl Kotz of Charleston was the 22nd female finisher and first local in 41:22. Winner of the Dewey Wise Trophy for the second year in a row was David Mellard, 80, of North Charleston, who finished in a time of 64:06.

Bridge Run Hall of Famer Margaret Wright, 81, of Folly Beach, who in the inaugural 1978 race was the oldest female finisher, was the oldest female finisher in the 26th running as well. She also set a South Carolina state 10K age group 80-84 record which was ratified as 1:53:42.

For the second year in a row there were runners from all 50 states, the District of Columbia and a large number of foreign countries. After a one-year absence, television coverage returned – as local Channel 5 showed a live 90-minute broadcast.

There were a total of 155 runners finishing under the 40-minute barrier, 139 males and 16 females. There were 1,383 runners who finished the race in less than 50 minutes, with a total of 4,526 crossing the finish line in less than an hour. Race entry fee remained $20 early and $25 late with the walk fee $15 early and $20 for late entry. Julian Smith served as race director again.

The Sunday *Post and Courier* listed the top three in each age division, erroneously including the prize money winners in the age award list. The paper also listed the names and times of all 14,653 runners: 8,039 male finishers and 6,584 female finishers. In addition to the runners, another 11,481 walkers registered for the untimed 7-kilometer walk. The walkers started at the foot of the bridge, just before the runners' 2-mile mark and provided a huge cheering section. The walk begins after the last runners pass. Between the events, a then record 29,293 participants were registered.

The Bridge Run Hall of Fame installed its second group. Inductees were: Keith Hamilton, race director of the inaugural race; Terry Hamlin, runner, and measurer of the inaugural course; Chuck Magera, runner and former finish line director; Dr. Brian Smith, runner and former race director; and Gary Wilson, race volunteer and lead bicyclist for the first race.

Other voices
Tell Me About Your Bridge Run 2003
By Cedric Jaggers. Originally appeared in the 2003 Volume 26, Issue 2, Low Country Runner

(Bridge Run info for 2003 – 14,623 largest number of official finishers; 17,071 second largest number of entrants. Start time temperature 66 degrees.)

After the Bridge Run, milling around in Marion Square with the 14,623 official finishers, the 11,000 walkers and who knows how many others, it took me a while to find the CRC tent, so I didn't get to talk to as many club members as I would have liked. Nevertheless, here, in the order we bumped into each other, are all the club members I could find. As always, I wrote down exactly what you said, but didn't get too many really wild ones this year. The quick find search engine for finishers (available at the www.BridgeRun.Com site and *Running Journal's* Running.Net site) made finding people's finish place and times easier than in the past when I had to look them up in the complete printed results provided again this year by Burns Computer. Since it was the fifth hottest Bridge Run ever, it was interesting to hear what people had to say about the weather.

Pat Rhode: Well, next year ... that's all I can say. I've been hurt, but I finished ... a horrible time. I don't want to be negative. Time? 1:03. I never ran a race that slow in my life. It was hot today. 6,080th overall, 3rd age group, time 1:03:46, chip 1:03:35.

Lynn Leroy: Not very good. Slow, comfortable (laughed). 56 minutes. 3,234th overall, time 56:49, chip 54:10.

Clyde Mizzell: It was hot with no wind. I thoroughly enjoyed it. I have no idea what my time was. I didn't look at the clock, but for me it was a perfect day. 1,540th overall, 1st age group, time 50:48, chip 50:43.

Nancy Curry: Two minutes slower than my Flowertown 10k time. The hill was a killer. It was hot. 49:56. 1,359th overall, 2nd age group, time 49:55, chip 49:51.

Patrice Katsanevakis: Two minutes off what I'd like to have run. Two minutes off what I'd planned to run. Happy at the end that I broke 49. 1,165th overall, time 48:50, chip 48:46.

Michael Hughes: It was lousy, it was hot, too many people. Time? No, I refuse to admit that I had 54 minutes. I have never been behind as many people and couldn't get around them. 3,235th overall, time 56:49, chip 54:37.

Jeffrey Herndon: This was an experiment. Not running for 10 days prior. Time? 52:30, what can you expect? 1,920th overall, time 52:24, chip 51:57.

Eileen Myers: I felt bad from the beginning and got worse. Still glad I did it. That's it. I ran about 53:00. 2,079th overall, top 5% award, time 53:00, chip 52:34.

Dan Clapper: Every year while I'm running I think about what to tell (I interrupted – no rehearsed speeches I said. CJ) At mile 4 I am usually at 24 minutes, at mile 4 I was 27:30. My time was 42:27, about the same as the Flowertown 10k. My goal was to get in under 42, but I'll take the 42:27. 281st overall, top 5% award, time 42:25, chip 42:29.

Lennie Moore: Not so hot. I was about where I wanted to be up through 4, then I completely lost it. 2 minutes off last year. 39:20 or something like that. 128th overall, top 5% award, time 39:24, chip 39:22.

Gary Ricker: Hot, hot, hot, but very happy to do another one and I'm looking forward to next year because I think I'll be able to beat this time. It was 42 something; fortunately my watch messed up so I'm not sure. 276th overall, top 5% award, time 42:22, chip 42:16.

Leon Locklear: It's a ritual of spring. Just under 46 minutes, a good effort. It was a beautiful day and it was good to see old friends. That's what makes this race special. 795th overall, time 46:43, chip 46:28.

George Dunlevy: Very hot, slow, not as fast as last year, but I'm happy. I'm getting ready for Boston in two weeks. About 39:15. 124th overall, time 39:15, chip 39:17.

Tom Rossi: I enjoyed it, the weather was perfect, the weather was great. I didn't have a great time. My focus was on Boston until last night. 213th overall, top 5% award, time 41:06, chip 41:05.

Barbara Clayton: The only thing I have to say: my beer tasted mighty good. It was warm, it was warm, what other excuse can I come up with. 55 something, I was hoping to do sub 50. 2,845th overall, time 55:38, chip 53:59.

Wendy Roach: I started out way too fast – like a 5K. I wanted to stop but I didn't. I did close to what I did last year. Not a P.R. but okay; 44:52. Slightly delirious at the end of the race. 541st overall, top 5% award, time 44:55, chip 44:51.

Debra Brown: It was hotter than last year but I did a P.R. 43:00, a minute faster than last year. I'm glad it's over for another year. 344th overall, top 5% award, time 43:03, chip 43:00.

Greg Brown: I went out a bit too fast caught up in the Bridge Run fun. The fast first mile made me hurt on the bridges. Then I hung on and tried to beat my wife ... she's a bit too fast. 338th overall, time 43:00, chip 42:55.

Joan Mulvihill: My worst one ever, but I got a good spot, a good 8 min pace group. A beautiful day. A nice day for me; my girlfriend from San Francisco's

daughter ran it with me. I love the end of the race with all the people. The last mile coming down Calhoun just didn't have that tough mind set. Just one of those days. 53 minutes. 2,029th overall, time 53:02, chip 52:48.

Note, the names above are everyone I interviewed in the park after the race. My wife, Kathy, who couldn't participate due to her multiple sclerosis, grabbed the clipboard when I got back to the hotel room and made me answer:

Cedric Jaggers: Hot and horrible. I suffered as much as if I were running fast, but I wasn't. It was scary to see people fall out during the race – I saw two on King Street, and heard people say, "Get a doctor! Get a medic!" When I turned the corner and saw the clock I wanted to kick and get in under 49 but I couldn't make my

Going up the first span of the Pearman bridge with the new Ravenel bridge under construction in the background. Post and Courier photo by Tom Spain

legs go. My worst competitive Bridge Run ever. Wait till next year! And that's it. It was fun, but I didn't enjoy seeing everyone I knew out run me, or at least it seemed that way. 1,207th overall, time 49:05, chip 48:39.

The following interviews were conducted at the awards ceremony that evening:

Margaret Wright: I've got to figure out how to say this in a few words. I ran slower than most people walk. My son Ralph was with me. He said, "I'm going to pick you up if you fall." It was sweet of him. I was fine when I finished, but I felt a little woozy and had to sit down. My time was over 2 hours. 14,558th overall, 3rd age group. Pending South Carolina 80-84 age group record time of 2:04:21, chip 1:59:44.

David Mellard: My run? I really don't know what to say. It was a gorgeous day and I thought I ran well, but I was 2 minutes slower than last year. I hope I can do it next year. I'll be 81 this month. 6,340th overall, 2nd age group, time 1:04:06, chip 1:03:53.

Bill Boulter: It was hot and hard. My time was off today. I did the Flowertown 10k in 47; today I was 49. 1,261st overall, 1st age group, time 49:25, chip 49:04.

Jim Daniel: Let's see. I don't know what to say. It was hot. I've enjoyed the media exposure – you know, the picture in the paper. I felt pretty good until I got water at the end of the bridge. It really got hot once we got in town. That's when the racing usually begins and it didn't this year. 121st overall, top 5% award, time 39:16, chip 39:16.

Lyn Hammond: Excellent day. A little hot. It started to go downhill when I was passed by Nancy Curry going uphill. I never caught her. So the day and my competition were hot. 1,484th overall, 3rd age group, time 50:28, chip 50:20.

Steve Hunt: I'm old, I'm fat. My second worst time, 51:15. I was just glad to get to the finish line. 1,632nd overall, 51:13, chip 51:09.

Charles Stoyle: It was lots of fun with my wife Roseanne. It was my slowest one. I slowed down in the beginning, I realized the heat was going to get me and I didn't let it. 44 something. 454th overall, top 5% award, time 44:11, chip 44:01.

Andy Barker: I ended up in the arms of a police officer at mile 6 saying, "Just let me finish, I promise I'll go straight to medical." I was pumped full of IVs and I realize I'm not as indestructible as I thought. The heat I think and (can't read my writing, CJ) last week and working shifts, I was more exhausted than I thought. It is quite an experience when the mind says drive on and the body refuses. I was touched by the concern shown by members of the Charleston Running Club and medical services and want to say thank you.

2003 Awards

Prize money winners:

Overall Male
1. Tom Nyariki .... Kenya .... 28:57 ... $5000
2. Linus Maiyo .... Kenya .... 28:57 ... $3000
3. John Itati .... Kenya .... 29:12 ... $1500
4. Moses Mwangi .... Kenya .... 29:40 ... $1000
5. Patrick Nthiwa .... Kenya .... 30:07 ... $800
6. David Kipngetich .... Kenya .... 30:08 ... $600
7. Jared Segera .... Kenya .... 30:26 ... $500
8. David Ngigi Karanjia . Kenya .... 30:32 ... $400
9. Andrzej Kryscin ...... Poland .... 30:36 ... $300
10. Gabriel Muchiri ...... Kenya .... 30:41 ... $250
11. Andrew Masai .... Kenya .... 30:49 ... $200
12. Eddy Hellebuyck ..... Albuquerque NM .... 31:06 ... $150
13. Gennady Temmnikov .. Russia .... 31:12 ... $100
14. Leszek Biegala .... Poland .... 31:37 ... $75
15. Eric Ashton .... Columbia SC .... 31:53 ... $50

Overall Female
1. Edna Kiplagat .... Kenya .... 33:41 ... $5000
2. Gladys Asiba .... Kenya .... 33:58 ... $3000
3. Emily Samoei .... Kenya .... 34:01 ... $1500
4. Lyubov Kremlyova ... Russia .... 34:07 ... $1000
5. Tatyana Pozdnyakova . Ukraine .... 35:21 ... $800
6. Agnes Ngunjiri .... Kenya .... 36:18 ... $600
7. Farrell P Burns ...... Charlotte NC .... 37:01 ... $500
8. Lee Dipietro .... Ruxton MD .... 37:17 ... $400
9. Terri Bradley .... Fayetteville, NC .... 38:32 ... $300
10. Anne Wyman Cipolla .. Columbia SC .... 38:38 ... $250
11. Velda Balmer .... Mechanicsville VA .. 38:43 ... $200
12. Janice Reilly .... Cary NC .... 39:02 ... $150
13. Sheila J Wakeman .... Cornelius NC .... 39:09 ... $100
14. Laura Jo Vroon ...... Wyoming MI .... 39:12 ... $75
15. Nancy Stewart .... Atlanta GA .... 39:30 ... $50

Masters Male
1. Andrew Masai .... Kenya .... 30:49 ... $1500
2. Eddy Hellebuyck ..... Albuquerque NM .... 31:06 ... $1000
3. Gennady Temmnikov .. Russia .... 31:12 ... $750
4. Selwyn Blake .... Columbia SC .... 33:23 ... $500
5. Gary Romesser .... Indianapolis IN .... 33:36 ... $250

Masters Female
1. Lyubov Kremlyova ... Russia .... 33:58 ... $1500
2. Tatyana Pozdnyakova . Ukraine .... 35:21 ... $1000
3. Lee Dipietro .... Ruxton MD .... 37:17 ... $750
4. Velda Balmer .... Mechanicsville VA .. 38:43 ... $500
5. Janice Reilly .... Cary NC .... 39:02 ... $250

Grand Masters Male
1. Gary Romesser .... Indianapolis IN .... 33:36 ... $750
2. Jerry Clark .... Charlotte NC .... 34:51 ... $500
3. William Dixon .... Brattleboro VT ..... 35:39 ... $250

Grand Masters Female
1. Terry Mahr .... Oregon OH .... 40:42 ... $750
2. Trish Vlastnik .... Peachtree City GA .. 41:57 ... $500
3. Eddie Muldrow .... Chapin SC .... 45:03 ... $250

Marcus Newberry Award:
First Local (Tri-Country) Finisher Award

Male
Nicholas Iauco .... Isle of Palms SC ... 32:24 ... $500

Female ....
Lizl Kotz .... Charleston SC ...... 41:22 ... $500

Dewey Wise Trophy
Oldest finisher with time less than his or her age in minutes:
David Mellard, 80 .... N Charleston, SC 64:06

Age division winners
Presented 5% deep up to a maximum of 25 (engraved silver plates)

Male 12 & Under (102 finishers, 5 awards)
1. Matt Buening .... Matthews SC 43:40
2. Reid Cabiness .... Charleston SC 44:56
3. Samuel P Henry .... Mt Pleasant SC 53:40
4. Corey Clawson .... Charleston SC 53:47
5. Adam King .... Charlotte NC 55:19

Female 12 & under (92 finishers, 5 awards)
1. Jessica Brooke Wood ..... Johns Island SC 52:43
2. Cayla Campbell .... Johns Island SC 58:06
3. Nakita Kappel .... Charleston SC 58:42
4. Leslie Semken .... James Island SC 59:30
5. Jan Lynn Woods .... Boone NC 1:00:51

Male 13 - 17 (319 finishers, 16 awards)
1. Trevor Beesley .... Greenwood SC 35:13
2. Ben Sherard .... Williamston SC 37:35
3. Jacob Morris .... Aiken SC 37:46
4. Jefferson Waugh .... Statesville NC 38:41
5. Andrew Symmes .... Greenville SC 38:42
6. Will Jeffries .... Summerville SC 39:24
7. Jordan Lybrand .... Greer SC 39:32
8. James Sweeney .... Savannah GA 40:32
9. Stephen Sykes .... Spartanburg SC 40:37
10. Brian Mcguffee .... Taylors SC 41:13
11. Andrew King .... Anderson SC 41:38
12. David Hodges .... Clinton SC 41:41
13. Daniel Vincent .... Mt Pleasant SC 41:45
14. Stuart Guthrie .... Central SC 42:05
15. Christopher Fallis .... Awendaw SC 42:22
16. Quintin Washington ...... Charleston SC 42:29

Female 13 - 17 (238 finishers, 12 awards)
1. Emily Hollings .... Charleston SC 46:47
2. Andrea Downey .... Greenwood SC 49:25
3. Martha Ferebee .... Charlotte NC 49:27
4. Katie Anderson .... Goose Creek SC 49:53
5. Sarah Kizer .... Charleston SC 50:27
6. Corrie Austin .... Charleston SC 51:17
7. Danielle Franklin .... Greer SC 51:37
8. Jenny Chiarelli .... Pawleys Island SC .. 52:06
9. Stacey Austin .... Charleston SC 52:27
10. Heather Lisle .... Summerville SC 52:32
11. Ashley Hodges .... Columbia SC 52:55
12. Adrienne Brenner .... Lancaster CA 52:57

Male 18 - 21 (295 finishers, 15 awards)
1. Garrett Johnson .... Savannah GA 37:14
2. Adam Taylor .... Simpsonville SC 37:55
3. Daniel Lowrey .... Clemson SC 37:57
4. Eric C Cannon .... Newberry SC 38:06
5. Chip Perkins .... Charleston SC 40:35
6. Matthew McKeown ...... Wellford SC 40:41
7. Greg Self .... Clemson SC 40:47
8. Joseph M Petrocorro .... Brick, NJ 40:57
9. Matthew E Supple .... Charleston SC 42:18
10. David Gibbons .... Charleston SC 42:34
11. Harry E Cromer .... Charleston SC 42:36
12. Scott Peevy .... Charleston SC 42:50

– Continued on next page

2003 Awards, continued from page 207

13	Shaun Sullivan	Conway SC	43:09
14	Adam Cone	Goose Creek SC	43:10
15	Eric M Brandner	Charleston SC	43:23

Female 18 - 21 (394 finishers, 20 awards)

1	Krystle Short	Fletcher NC	40:28
2	Michele Milner	Fletchere NC	40:55
3	Marcie Milner	Aiken SC	43:37
4	Julia C Bisschops	Johns Island SC	45:31
5	Ross J Magee	Raleigh NC	47:04
6	Ismailia Ferguson	Charleston SC	47:19
7	Maria Malatanos	Charleston SC	47:45
8	Erin Smith	Greenwood SC	47:58
9	Ashley Leuck	Greer SC	49:43
10	Kristen Sanders	Winston-Salem NC	50:08
11	Stefanie Farris	Charleston SC	50:18
12	Julie Livingston	Florence SC	50:21
13	Kristin Williamson	Greenwood SC	51:05
14	Jennifer Wassell	Charleston SC	51:29
15	Stephanie Stalnaker	Charleston SC	51:32
16	Ryan Cozens	Davidson NC	51:35
17	Carina Hermann	Matthews NC	51:55
18	Lisa Hassard	Charlestown RI	52:09
19	Ashley Platt	Charleston SC	52:14
20	Joey M Lee	Irmo SC	52:15

Male 22 - 25 (678 finishers, 25 awards)

1	Daniel Hughes	Columbia SC	32:18
2	Nicholas Iauco	Isle of Palms SC	32:24
3	Palmer Thomas	Charleston SC	35:04
4	Jason Putnam	Central SC	36:11
5	Brooks Keys	Belton SC	36:27
6	William Whiteside	Charleston SC	37:05
7	Hudson G Belk	Charleston SC	37:09
8	Lee Kain	N Charleston SC	37:52
9	Richard Velazquez	New York NY	38:29
10	John T Yow	Goose Creek SC	38:35
11	Matthew Terrio	Florence SC	38:58
12	Kris Kitzke	Charleston SC	39:00
13	Joshua Clarke	Goose Creek SC	39:07
14	Danny White	Charleston SC	39:57
15	Nicholas Orenduff	Goose Creek SC	40:29
16	Ward Burgess	Spartanburg SC	40:35
17	Jonathan Tetirick	Charlotte NC	40:55
18	Mark Tibshrany	Columbia SC	40:57
19	Eric S Grenier	Fayetteville NC	41:28
20	Scott Esher	N Charleston SC	41:40
21	George J Hild	Charlotte NC	41:41
22	Garrett Anderson	Charleston SC	41:44
23	Andrew Delmas	Columbia SC	41:50
24	Colin M Crowley	N Charleston SC	41:58
25	Kirk Jenkins	Anderson SC	42:08

Female 22 - 25 (1,031 finishers, 25 awards)

1	Suzanne Clemmer	Gastonia NC	40:59
2	Megan Curran	Naperville IL	41:41
3	Emily Eades	Mt Pleasant SC	42:12
4	Mary S Brosche	Athens GA	42:58
5	Scarlet Day	Greenville SC	43:02
6	Emma C Batchelor	Charleston SC	43:58
7	Kinsey Eschenburg	Charleston SC	44:00
8	Becca Beverly	Mt Pleasant SC	44:13
9	Holly Munnis	Charleston SC	44:27
10	Kelly Clark	Sumter SC	44:35
11	Misty Davis	Columbia SC	45:08
12	Holly Moye	Virginia Beach VA	45:14
13	Katherine England	Charleston SC	45:19
14	Amy Ward	Columbia SC	45:32
15	Dana Jo Smith	Bluffton SC	45:48
16	Malgorzata Wawrzak	Hanahan SC	46:10
17	Darby H Tucker	Huntersville NC	46:17
18	Mary P Stokes	Charleston SC	46:50
19	Sylvia Dodd	Mt Pleasant SC	46:53
20	Wendy Mcintosh	Atlanta GA	47:12
21	Sarah Glenn	New York NY	47:19
22	Katie Hoeft	Mt Pleasant SC	47:33
23	Alison Andrew	Charleston SC	47:33
24	Angela Finley	Charleston SC	47:38
25	Heather Trembley	Charleston SC	47:38

Male 26 - 29 (1,007 finishers, 25 awards)

1	Christian Muentener	Yarmouth ME	33:46
2	Brian Johnson	Mt Pleasant SC	34:28
3	Andy Keel	Marietta GA	34:54
4	Thomas M Walls	Fort Mill SC	36:40
5	Jason Annan	Chapel Hill NC	36:48
6	Bobby Wilder	Myrtle Beach SC	36:59
7	Matthew Johnson	Rock Hill SC	37:46
8	Rob Pearce	Charleston SC	37:55
9	Galen Holland	Asheville NC	37:56
10	Matt Pryor	Greenville SC	38:02
11	Dennis Albaugh	Chapel Hill NC	38:11
12	Eliot Cannon	Winston-Salem NC	38:40
13	Chad Brittingham	Charleston SC	39:08
14	Mark Richardson	Charleston SC	39:26
15	Benjamin Schwartz	Charlotte NC	39:36
16	Kevin Croxton	Charleston SC	40:15
17	Stephen Hughes	Charleston SC	40:19
18	Jimmy Major	Chapin SC	40:27
19	Jonathan Rowell	Charleston SC	40:50
20	Andrew Stroupe	Huntersville NC	40:51
21	Shawn Donovan	N Charleston SC	40:52
22	Brently Whitaker	Myrtle Beach SC	41:07
23	Jason Michaels	Asheville NC	41:15
24	Doug Hellinger	Sumter SC	41:42
25	Jason Forche	Mt Pleasant SC	41:45

Female 26 - 29 (1,094 finishers, 25 awards)

1	Lizl Kotz	Charleston SC	41:22
2	Carrie Hunoval	Winston-Salem NC	42:18
3	Sarah Reed	Summerville SC	42:51
4	Mary-Claire Cox	Columbia SC	43:04
5	Jennifer Edwards	Columbus OH	43:27
6	Karen Gillespie	Greenville SC	43:31
7	Laura Cisar	Summerville SC	44:12
8	Rachelle B Tomlin	Columbia SC	44:13
9	Renee White	Charlotte NC	44:29
10	Colleen M Angstadt	Charlotte NC	45:29
11	Stacey A Willging	Charlotte NC	45:45
12	Gretchen Bielmyer	Central SC	46:16
13	Allison Bumgardner	Charlotte NC	46:27
14	Rosemary Ferguson	Charlotte NC	46:28
15	Erika Marie Britt	Clinton NC	46:37
16	Jennifer Kimbrell	York SC	47:06
17	Helen Cary Lafaye	Columbia SC	47:16
18	Sara Lawrence	Chapel Hill NC	47:35
19	Jennifer Osborne	Charleston SC	48:02
20	Sandra Valbuena	Greensboro NC	48:15
21	Nicki Breon	Columbia SC	48:23
22	Isabel Gnowanlu	Charleston SC	48:46
23	Roxanne Migne	Charlotte NC	48:48
24	Kristen L Overcash	Charleston SC	48:50
25	Julie Tashlein	Athens GA	49:08

Male 30 - 34 (1,454 finishers, 25 awards)

1	Everett Whiteside	Pensacola FL	33:09
2	Larry Evans	Augusta GA	33:57
3	Charles Wangandu	Kennesaw GA	36:24
4	James Harris, Jr	Maineville OH	36:33
5	Karl Kaiser	Columbia SC	36:35
6	Bryan Benitez-Nelson	Columbia SC	36:36
7	Mark Harrell	Raleigh NC	36:50
8	Boen Butler	Huntersville NC	36:52
9	Darol Timberlake	Matthews NC	36:57
10	Nathan Weber	Charleston SC	37:18
11	Gregg Cromer	Summerville SC	37:22
12	Michael Cipolla	Columbia SC	37:29
13	Emery Lloyd	Moncks Corner SC	37:33
14	Gerry Schauer	Charleston SC	38:22
15	Jason Philbin	Charlotte NC	38:24
16	Coates Kennerly	Brevard NC	38:27
17	Brad Schneider	Bowling Green KY	38:29
18	Roger Fagala	McColl SC	38:54
19	Doug Long	Huntersville NC	39:07
20	Michael Mason	Charlotte NC	39:19
21	G Fallon	Charlotte NC	39:21
22	Stephen W Hudzik	Charlotte NC	39:21
23	Robert Ross	Charleston SC	39:46
24	Gregory S Sisson	Myrtle Beach SC	39:50
25	Hardy Bryant	Roanoke VA	39:53

Female 30 - 34 (1,203 finishers, 25 awards)

1	Janet Urbanski	Frederick MD	41:53
2	Charlotte Thomason	Charlotte NC	42:31
3	Rebecca Crowder	Charlotte NC	42:38
4	Onika Kerber	Greenville SC	42:56
5	Debra Brown	Mt Pleasant SC	43:03
6	Kristin McCann	Quantico VA	43:30
7	Jennifer D Curtin	Raleigh NC	43:55
8	Leslie Randall	Royersford PA	44:28
9	Gabriele Hauck	Savannah GA	44:44
10	Ginger Carter	Greenville SC	44:58
11	Tunde Gergosky	Myrtle Beach SC	45:29
12	Sara Vaughn	N Charleston SC	45:43
13	Elizabeth Ransom	Williamsburg VA	46:06
14	Mary Medlin	Winston-Salem NC	46:06
15	Alethea Setser	Mt Pleasant SC	46:13
16	Renee Johnson	Spartanburg SC	46:14
17	Chatherine Alley	Charleston SC	46:29
18	Molly Hughes	Charleston SC	46:41
19	Tracy McKee	Charleston SC	46:48
20	Dede Griesbauer	Boston MA	47:03
21	Cara Leigh Balch	Charlotte NC	47:05
22	Belynda Veser	Johns Island SC	47:07
23	Betsey Stewart	Davidson NC	47:22
24	Lynn H Cecil	Rock Hill SC	47:43
25	Leslie Messisco	Salisbury NC	47:56

Male 35 - 39 (1,117 finishers, 25 awards)

1	John Charlton	Columbia SC	33:40
2	Eric Vandervort	Clinton TN	35:12
3	Craig R Kingman	Jenison MI	35:37
4	Eric Parker	Mt Pleasant SC	35:57
5	Sean Killeen	Winston-Salem NC	37:02
6	Ben Vaughn	N Charleston SC	37:07
7	David Quick	Mt Pleasant SC	37:59
8	Daniel Kehoe	Atlanta GA	38:02
9	James Morse	Virginia Beach VA	38:14
10	Jeffrey L Wolfson	Marietta GA	38:35
11	Jim Daniel	Mt Pleasant SC	39:16
12	Helmut Schmoock	Murrells Inlet SC	39:37
13	Michael D Smith	Goose Creek SC	39:40
14	Karl Johnson	Spartanburg SC	39:44
15	Martin Guthrie	Wallace NC	39:48
16	John D Barry	Wilmington NC	39:54
17	Jeff Urbanski	Frederick MD	40:17
18	Stephen Trabucco	Huntersville NC	40:18
19	Roman Carl Pibl	Salisbury NC	40:20
20	Scott Smith	Charleston SC	40:31
21	Nate Ross	Birmingham AL	40:44
22	Randall Hrechko	Columbia SC	40:50
23	Chris Hicks	Sumter SC	40:55
24	Esser Peter	Summerville SC	40:57
25	Larry Clark	Easley SC	40:58

Female 35 - 39 (916 finishers, 25 awards)

1	Bonnie McDonald	Roanoke VA	40:35
2	Lisa Tolley	Seneca SC	41:32
3	Keely Churchill	Raleigh NC	42:30
4	Christi Craft	Simpsonville SC	42:40
5	Pamela Mitchell	Wilmington NC	43:15
6	Suanne Hall	Greenville SC	43:42
7	Molly Achille	Greenville SC	43:45
8	Arlene Walker	Charlotte NC	43:57
9	Missy Hunnicutt	Columbia SC	44:22
10	Carleen J Davis	N Charleston SC	44:30
11	Wendy Roach	Mt Pleasant SC	44:55
12	Diane Lancaster	Charlotte NC	45:34
13	Sandy Wallsch	Conover NC	46:09
14	Missy White	Wilmington NC	46:25
15	Brooks Fortson	Mt Pleasant SC	46:40
16	Bev Veals	Newton NC	46:53
17	Monica Fichman	Matthews NC	46:56
18	Beth Coe	Simpsonville SC	47:21
19	Lynne Takac	Charlotte NC	47:29
20	Heather Wood	Johns Island SC	47:32
21	Linda Cannon	Conway SC	47:35
22	Cathie Miller	Dunwoody GA	47:47
23	Megan Gorman	Charleston SC	48:02
24	Kelly Dobson	Mt Pleasant SC	48:37
25	Beth T Pierpont	Charlotte NC	48:49

Male 40 - 44 (847 finishers, 25 awards)

1	Wieslaw Perszke	Albuquerque NM	33:45
2	Peter Edle	Simpsonville SC	35:32
3	Huey Inman	Harrisonburg VA	36:55
4	Tim Stewart	Simpsonville SC	37:06
5	John Black	Atlanta GA	37:28
6	Billy Tisdale	Sumter SC	38:17
7	Sam Inman	Greenville SC	38:20
8	Michael Parker	Goose Creek SC	38:24
9	Lance Leopold	Simpsonville SC	39:18
10	George Dunlevy	Mt Pleasant SC	39:19
11	David Gee	Gaffney SC	39:39
12	Andree Colvin	Hanahan SC	39:45
13	Eric Sabin	Columbia SC	39:50
14	Nicholas Simontis	Cayce SC	40:22
15	Robert Lowery	Charleston SC	40:24
16	Steven Rudnicki	Columbia SC	40:25
17	Till Kohlmey	Swisttal ??	40:38
18	Mike Armor	Greer SC	40:46
19	Steve Shonts	Charlotte NC	40:55
20	Jamie Riggins	Charlotte NC	41:01
21	Rob Burke	Wilmington NC	41:03
22	Tom Rossi	Mt Pleasant SC	41:06

Post and Courier photo by Mic Smith

23 Tommy Bedenbaugh .... Charlotte NC 41:41	15 Derek Appleton .... Valley Sheffield UK 40:07	9 Ricks Boyle .... Ringoes NJ 39:31	11 Peter Mugglestone .... Columbia SC 44:34
24 Randy Smith .... Myrtle Beach SC 41:44	16 Lyn Short .... Fletcher NC 40:59	10 Gary Adkins .... Salem VA 39:32	12 David Henry .... Cloverdale VA 44:38
25 Peter Godley .... Charlotte NC 42:01	17 Tate Phillips .... Myrtle Beach SC 41:03	11 Jack Todd .... Spartanburg SC 40:07	13 Linny Moore .... Greer SC 45:00

Female 40 - 44 (664 finishers, 25 awards)

1 Patti Stewart-Garbrecht .... Jacksonville NC 39:37	18 Dan Bradley .... Winston-Salem NC 41:29	12 Joseph Denneny .... Edwardsville IL 40:15	14 Steve Middleton .... Boones Hill VA 45:12
2 Jean Aswell .... Cornelius NC 43:04	19 Bill Maddux .... Mt Pleasant SC 42:10	13 Patrick Gannon .... Mt Pleasant SC 41:25	15 Elbert Howard .... Jamestown SC 45:12
3 Lee Patterson .... Summerville SC 43:09	20 Paul Smith .... Cumming GA 42:10	14 Gary Ricker .... Charleston SC 42:22	16 Chuck Speight .... Doraville GA 45:51
4 Kelly Hazel .... Jacksonville FL 44:25	21 Scott Roark .... Greenville SC 42:19	15 James Boyd .... Mt Pleasant SC 43:39	17 William Anderson .... Wadmalaw Isl SC 45:59
5 Lisa Powell .... Columbia SC 44:31	22 Harold Fallis .... Awendaw SC 42:21	16 Robert Perkins .... Charleston SC 43:52	18 Thomas Blankenship .... Anoka MN 46:05
6 Nancy Thomas .... Mt Pleasant SC 44:35	23 Jim Fann .... Charleston SC 42:23	17 David Furman Lee .... Columbia SC 44:09	19 Richard Landsman .... Summerville SC 46:19
7 Ann Remmers .... Ann Arbor MI 44:48	24 Daniel Clapper .... N Charleston SC 42:25	18 Buddy Rabun .... Marietta GA 44:24	20 Thom Henkel .... Orange Park FL 46:23
8 Kathy Abernethy .... Matthews NC 45:37	25 Rick King .... Anderson SC 42:52	19 Gary Richardson .... Greensboro NC 44:41	21 Larry Seavers .... Charlotte NC 46:32
9 Tracy Rogers .... Simpsonville SC 45:47	**Female 45 - 49 (459 finishers, 23 awards)**	20 Francis Burriss .... Chapin SC 44:41	22 John Babineau .... Arlington VA 46:35
10 Noriko Seiner .... Beaufort SC 46:37	1 Cherry Croker .... Anderson SC 45:58	21 Mark Yoffe .... Raleigh NC 44:54	23 James Richardson .... Charlotte NC 46:51
11 Leslie Graves .... Pawleys Isl SC 46:51	2 Debbie Howard .... Mt Pleasant SC 46:16	22 David Sweet .... Knoxville TN 44:55	**Male 60 - 64 (211 finishers, 11 awards)**
12 Kathy Murray .... Jacksonville FL 47:09	3 Nitsa Calas .... Charleston SC 46:21	23 Samuel Jenkins .... N Charleston SC 45:11	1 George Luke .... Greenville SC 41:23
13 Diane Cash .... Landrum SC 47:25	4 Nancy Duffy .... Charlotte NC 47:39	24 Kenneth Hanger .... Charleston SC 45:15	2 Frank Shea .... Charlotte NC 41:50
14 Trudy Carolyn Gale .... Spencer NC 47:26	5 Darla Bennett .... Mt Dora FL 47:40	25 David Graber .... Indianapolis IN 45:15	3 Gerald Friedman .... Atlanta GA 44:51
15 Jane Foy .... Roswell GA 48:16	6 Anne Marie Moncure .... Camden SC 47:55	**Female 50 - 54 (292 finishers, 15 awards)**	4 James Salvo .... Kiawah Island SC 45:47
16 Tracey Wagner .... Afton VA 48:19	7 Laurel Easterson .... Hampton VA 48:24	1 Catherine Lempesis .... Irmo SC 45:25	5 Donald Snowdon .... Brevard NC 46:43
17 Tami Dennis .... Isle ofPalms SC 48:25	8 Sallie J Chardukian .... Simpsonville SC 48:44	2 Mimi Sturgell .... Kiawah Island SC 46:08	6 Anthony Donachie .... Mt Pleasant SC 46:47
18 Sara Major Schultz .... Greer SC 48:40	9 Patrice Katsanevakis .... Mt Pleasant SC 48:50	3 Betsy Henderson .... Roanoke VA 46:55	7 James Hanlon .... Folly Beach SC 48:10
19 Barbara Neale .... Yonges Island SC 48:40	10 Michelle Withers .... Charlotte NC 49:44	4 Marie Hollings .... Charleston SC 48:10	8 Thomas Eison .... Greenville SC 50:10
20 Susan McKee .... Charlotte NC 48:45	11 Sarah Ball .... Charleston SC 49:49	5 Susan Bratton .... Charlotte SC 48:14	9 Donald Jones .... Columbia SC 50:52
21 Sandy Austin .... Asheville NC 48:45	12 Linda Rodarte .... Columbia SC 50:14	6 Sallie Driggers .... Hanahan SC 48:39	10 Gene Cater .... Easley SC 51:05
22 Eileen Thames .... Mt Pleasant SC 49:08	13 Beverly Grant .... Weaverville NC 50:57	7 Toni Cruz .... Charlotte NC 49:06	11 David Moorhead .... Simpsonville SC 51:25
23 Marsha Alterman .... Charleston SC 49:09	14 Mary McDonald .... Rome GA 51:04	8 Judy Osborn .... Charlotte NC 50:29	**Male 65 - 69 (62 finishers, 4 awards)**
24 Connie Rink .... Mt Pleasant SC 49:19	15 Kathleen Roberts .... Mt Pleasant SC 51:09	9 Valerie Murrah .... Chapel Hill NC 52:28	1 Clyde Mizzell .... Charleston SC 50:48
25 Robin Tarpinian .... Taylors SC 49:36	16 Donna Joyce .... Mt Pleasant SC 51:19	10 Deby Shirk .... Mt Pleasant SC 52:31	2 Bill Blizard .... Kiawah Island SC 51:26
Male 45 - 49 (804 finishers, 25 awards)	17 Maryjane Eubank .... Roanoke VA 51:34	11 Martha White .... Columbia SC 53:14	3 Joe Nettles .... Savannah GA 51:34
1 Tom Mather .... Mt Pleasant SC 35:15	18 Susan Krepelka .... Matthews NC 51:37	12 Judy Gilman .... McClellanville SC 53:53	4 Ed Ledford .... Folly Beach SC 54:12
2 David Renneisen .... Goose Creek SC 37:10	19 Brenda O'Shields .... Beaufort SC 52:00	13 Judy Greenhill .... Columbia SC 54:41	**Male 70 - 74 (23 finishers, 3 awards)**
3 Alfred Cronin .... Decatur GA 38:26	20 Nancy Susan Sumner .... Simpsonville SC 52:06	14 Christian M Patton .... West Columbia SC 55:01	1 William Boulter .... Charleston SC 49:25
4 James Wilhelm .... Canton OH 38:30	21 Cheryl Cheek .... Martinez GA 52:27	15 Rosemarie Kuhn .... Spartanburg SC 55:01	2 Moe Buccino .... Anderson SC 50:22
5 David Bourgeois .... Summerville SC 39:01	22 Dawn Betz .... Carolina Bch NC 52:46	**Male 55 - 59 (453 finishers, 23 awards)**	3 Ken Walls .... Mt Pleasant SC 56:18
6 James Scheer .... Charleston SC 39:02	23 Eileen Myers .... Charleston SC 53:00	1 Bob Schlau .... Charleston SC 36:30	**Male 75 - 98 (15 finishers, 3 awards)**
7 John Ewing, Jr .... Asheville NC 39:20	**Male 50 - 54 (633 finishers, 25 awards)**	2 Fred Corpuz .... Strongsville OH 39:42	1 Charles Scott .... Atlanta GA 1:00:34
8 Lennie Moore .... Mt Pleasant SC 39:24	1 Ervin Reid .... Campobello SC 35:52	3 Steve Annan .... Mt Pleasant SC 39:49	2 Franklin Mason .... Mullins SC 1:00:59
9 Jim Halsch .... Greensboro NC 39:25	2 Danny West .... Myrtle Beach SC 36:50	4 James Horne .... Taylors SC 42:30	3 David Mellard .... N Charleston SC 1:04:06
10 Clyde Sanders .... Beaufort SC 39:34	3 David Olson .... Peachtree City GA 37:15	5 Charlie Padgett .... N Charleston SC 42:38	Compiled by Cedric Jaggers from complete results provided by Burns Computer Services on April 5, 2003.
11 Marc Embler .... Summerville SC 39:41	4 Claude Grenier .... Harrington ?? 37:54	6 Russ Brown .... Midway GA 42:41	
12 Chris Farrell .... Poland IN 39:45	5 John Cash .... Landrum SC 38:13	7 Dewey Sloan .... Charlotte NC 42:53	
13 Keith Hertling .... Greenville SC 39:59	6 Larry Milner .... Aiken SC 38:41	8 Tai Sugimoto .... Charleston SC 43:39	
14 Mike Griffin .... Hampton SC 40:02	7 Bill Bosmann .... Sparta NJ 38:44	9 Charles Stoyle .... Augusta GA 44:11	
	8 Walt Rider .... Germantown TN 38:49	10 Douglas Blackford .... Todd NC 44:27	

Runners stream across the finish line on Calhoun Street. Post and Courier photo by Mic Smith

Chapter 27

2004

Sallie Barsosio Female Winner After Four Second-Place Finishes

The 27th Cooper River Bridge Run began at 8 a.m. on April 3, 2004. It was a crisp, sunny, moderately windy morning with the temperature at 48 degrees when the race began.

The race set a record for number of finishers as 15,229 were listed in the results printed at the finish. The Sunday *Post and Courier* printed 15,179 names and times: 8,269 male and 6,910 female. BridgeRun.Com shows 15,184 finishers: 8,272 male and 6,912 female. Regardless of the number, it was a record for finishers. The race had the second largest number of entrants: 17,311. There were a record 12,619 entrants for the walk. This brought the total entrants to a record 29,930. When entrants for the children's run were included, it pushed the number of registrants over the 30,000 mark for the first time.

Charleston's Sunday *Post and Courier* headline read "Kipkosgei wins largest Bridge Run in history". And indeed Luke Kipkosgei of Kenya, who was running the Bridge Run for the first time and battling fellow Kenyan Linus Maiyo virtually the entire race, did win in 28:13 to 28:14. It was the second year in a row Maiyo had finished second, and the second year in row that he had fallen just short in a sprint to the finish. Kiposgei continued the Kenyan dominance as he was one of 13 of 15 top finishers from Kenya, including the first 12 places. Ben Limo, 28:27, Boniface Songok, 28:45, John Itati, 28:51, Yevgen Bozhko, 28:59, all finished under the 29-minute mark.

During the race Kiposgei noticed what all the other runners couldn't help but notice: construction of the new bridge. He told the *Post and Courier*, "It was very exciting to see the new bridge going up. It's going to be very steep and very hard, I think." He enjoyed the race, saying, "It was a difficult race, but a fun race. I was able to look around on the bridge, to look out at the beautiful bay and the boats. I definitely want to come to the Bridge Run again." Second place finisher Maiyo said, "I felt good about my position throughout the race. From the start through mile 6, I was in good position. It was just at the finish where I lacked."

Female winner Sallie Barsosio of Kenya had finished second each of her four previous races — behind Catherine Ndereba twice and Elana Meyer twice. She made sure it did not happen again. Barsosio ran 32:28 to win with Russian Tatyana Chulakh just 8 seconds back for second place. Jane Kiptoo of Kenya was third in 33:09.

"I didn't think it would ever happen," Barsosio told the newspaper. "I didn't know if I was going to win, but I knew I could finish in the top three. In the past, Catherine would win and I would finish second. There always was someone ahead of me." Neither Catherine nor Elana were in the race this year. The Russian Chullakh felt lack of experience in the race hurt her. "I can beat her, but today, I really was disappointed that I lost first place," she told the newspaper. "I ran too slowly down the hills of the bridge. I've never run in a race like this. The bridge makes it unique. Oh yes, I'll be back. The new bridge looks very challenging."

Masters winner was Dennis Simonaitis of Kenya in 31:44. Selwyn Blake of Columbia, S.C., was second in 32:20 while Irv Batten of Summerville, S.C., was third in 32:37. Chris Chattin of Columbia, Md., was fourth in 33:43 while Grand Masters division winner Gary Romesser was fifth Master in 33:45.

Female masters winner was Tatyana Pozdnyakova of Ukraine in 34:55 – she had also won this title in 1998 and 1999. Lyubov Kremleva of Russia, who had won this title the past two years, was second in 35:11. Janice Addison of Columbia, S.C., ran 37:17 to take third place Masters money. Janice Reilly of Cary, N.C., was fourth in

38:10, while Laura Jo Vroon of Grand Rapids, Mich., was fifth, also timed in 38:10.

The male Grand Masters division was again dominated by Gary Romesser of Indianapolis, Ind., as he won for the fourth year in a row, this time in 33:45. Richard "Dick" Berkle of Atlanta, Ga., was second in 35:15, while Steve Annan of Mount Pleasant took third place prize money in 37:29.

The female Grand Masters winner was also a familiar name. Terry Mahr of Oregon, Ohio, ran 40:24 and won for the second year in a row, her fifth win in the last six years. Judith Hine of Marietta, Ga., was second in 43:35 and Toni Cruz of Charlotte, N.C., was third in 44:04.

The Dr. Marcus Newberry Award for first Tri-County finisher went to runners from Summerville. Irv Batten, male winner, finished 23rd overall in 32:37. Sarah Reed, was the 19th female finisher in 39:29. The Dewey Wise Trophy was won for the third year in a row by David Mellard, 81, of North Charleston, who finished the race in 65:18.

A tragedy occurred during the race as James Scott, 47, of Charleston, who was running with his 20-year-old daughter, had a heart attack and died going up the first span of the bridge. His was the first death of a participant.

For the second year in a row there was live television coverage as local Channel 5 showed a two-hour broadcast that was rebroadcast later so the participants could see it. A total of 214 runners broke the 40-minute barrier: 192 male and 22 female. A total of eight runners finished under the 30-minute barrier with seven of them being under 29 minutes. There were 1,653 runners who finished the race in less than 50 minutes and a total of 5,366 runners who crossed the line before the clock flipped to 60:00. The entry fee schedule for both the run and the walk remained the same as the previous year: $20 early and $25 late entry for the run, with the walk fee $15 early and $20 for late entry.

The Bridge Run Hall of Fame installed its third group. Inductees were: Betty Bell, Gil Bradham and Emelyn Commins, all race volunteers, and Mike Chodnicki, runner and race volunteer.

Other Voices
Tell Me About Your Bridge Run 2004

By Cedric Jaggers. Originally appeared in the May-June 2004 Low Country Runner

Since 1988 CRC members have had the chance to "Tell Me About Your Bridge Run". One question after the race where I write down exactly what you say. This year hardly anyone was very talkative. But it was still a pleasure to talk to as many of you as were still on hand when I got to the CRC tent. This year the race had more finishers than ever: 15,229. The Sunday *Post and Courier* listed the first 15,184 finishers. The crisp morning, just under 50 degrees when the race started promised great things. But the headwind for the first 2 miles on Coleman slowed everyone more than they expected. It was great to see and talk to everyone again.

Mike Hart: I just tried to stay with Huey (Inman) but he got away from me at the end. Ran about 38 minutes. 127th O.A. top 5% a.g. 37:48.

Huey Inman: Enjoyed it. Not as fast as we wanted but it was just 37:50 something or so. 120th O.A. top 5% a.g. 37:40.

Kathy Jaggers: I did a little better than I thought I'd do. I ran it on memory. I thought I'd do 65 minutes, but got about 61:18. I'm proud we ran and didn't have to walk. 6,011th O.A. 61:15.

Frank Blackett: All I can say is I finished with a smile on my face, and I did. It was 5 years since I did the last one. No idea what my time was, somewhere in the 70s. 11,967th O.A. 1:13.54.

Gary Ricker: It was my 25th straight so it was very special to me. 40:34. Very happy just to be able to do it. The wind was not a factor. It was very enjoyable, especially the last 6.2 miles. I'm looking forward to next year. 255th O.A. top 5% a.g. 41:36.

Eric Malinowski: Excellent. We ran slow. My brother came to town and we ran it together. Our fastest splits were going uphill. About 52 minutes. 2,241st O.A. 52:17.

David Quick: It was terrible. People I usually beat, beat me. It was humiliating but that's good because I'm taking names and they'll be around later. I ran 38 something. I ran 37s at Summerville and thought I'd do better than that. 147th O.A. top 5% a.g. 38:21.

Mario Salas: It was – probably worst ever 44:34 – the Bridge got my butt. The last time I ran a 10k was this race in 2000. I'm starting to race again; maybe next year it'll be easier. 625th O.A. top 5% a.g. 44:32.

Wendy Roach: Good weather, 3 seconds chip time faster than last year. Started out slower and picked it up. But I wanted to break 44 and didn't. 698th O.A. top 5% a.g. 45:03.

Wayne Todd: It was okay. 44:10 but it was a good run. I guess I'm pleased. 604th O.A. 44:21.

Pat Rhode: Well, you know my husband had a heart attack a month ago. This is my 25th Bridge Run and I'm glad just to do it. I did this race totally for James – he's doing better. 6,895th O.A. 3rd a.g. 1:03:02.

Leon Locklear: I just had a great morning. Great weather. My 26th race so I had to get up and be here. Ran about 48:05. 1,259th O.A. 48:16.

Bob Schlau: Well, it was my slowest one ever, Cedric. I never felt good the whole day. I never felt good warming up or in the race. We all have those days, but I hate it happened at the Bridge Run. 180th O.A. 1st a.g. 39:21.

Mike Chodnicki: I didn't run but I had fun. I drove the lead vehicle and it went very smoothly.

Clyde Mizzell: It felt good. It was a perfect day. My time couldn't have been too good – I felt too good. 49 something. 1,481st O.A. 3rd a.g. 49:21.

Dan Clapper: It was okay. I'm pleased. It was my 20th and I haven't come full circle. My first one is still my slowest. Today 41:26. 308th O.A. top 5% a.g. 41:30.

Jeffrey Herndon: Good Bridge Run. Missed the first mile split, 2 at 13:55 ran as even as I possibly could, 43:58 chip. I felt really good, instead of going out too fast like we usually do. 566th O.A. 44:03.

Marc Embler: It was good. Older, fatter but I ran faster than I have run in 3 years. Great weather. Good crowd, it's always the best. 143rd O.A. top 5% a.g. 38:18.

Betsy Rivers: I thought it was great. The weather was perfect; it was as windy as I thought. I took pictures, stopped 9 times and my IT band didn't seize up on me. Now it's wonderful in the park to drink beer and enjoy. 10,301st O.A. 1:09:46.

Margaret Wright: It was okay. My son ran with me so if I fell down he'd pick me up. 15,097th O.A. 2:07:22.

James Cronin: Well it was good this year, slower than last. The wind that was blowing down King Street helped out – that was a big plus. Did it in about 56 minutes. 3,512th O.A. 56:00.

Steven Hunt: I made it. 50:15 that's all I have to say. It was beautiful weather. 1,722nd O.A. 50:19.

Lennie Moore: Older and slower, Cedric but still under 40. 39:33 I think that's about it. 191st O.A. top 5% a.g. 39:35.

Steve Annan: I had a great, wonderful run. It was great weather, a perfect day to run. I ran about 37:24. 112th O.A. 3rd Grand Masters 37:29.

Ed Isaac: I don't know what my time was. About 75 minutes. I pulled a calf muscle in the last mile. It's still a lot of fun though. I'm having as much fun as I did when I first ran it 18 years ago. 14,146th O.A. 1:26:41.

Keith Ambrose: Same as always – bad. Stopped up breathing. I don't know what time I ran, something over about 48 flat. 1,227th O.A. 48:07.

Cedric Jaggers: I'm just glad that Kathy and I got to do it together. (I ran it with her due to her Multiple Sclerosis.) Feeling the Bridge move, since we were back in the crowd was a new experience for me. We really appreciated just getting to do it. It was the slowest of my 26 in a row. 6,011th O.A. 1:01:15.

2004 Awards

Prize money winners:

Males Overall
1. Luke Kipkosgei .... Kenya .... 28:13 ... $5000
2. Linus Maiyo .... Kenya .... 28:14 ... $3000
3. Ben Limo............. Kenya .... 28:27 ... $1500
4. Boniface Songok...... Kenya .... 28:45 ... $1000
5. John Itati............. Kenya .... 28:51 ... $800
6. Yevgen Bozhko .... Kenya .... 28:52 ... $600
7. Henry Kipchirchir ..... Kenya .... 28:59 ... $500
8. Albert Okemwa....... Kenya .... 29:52 ... $400
9. Kip Muneria .... Kenya .... 30:03 ... $300
10. Patrick Nithwa....... Kenya .... 30:04 ... $250
11. Jared Segera .... Kenya .... 30:06 ... $200
12. Sammy Nyamongo..... Kenya .... 30:30 ... $150
13. Juan C Gutierrez ..... Columbia............... 30:46 ... $100
14. Kennedy Ondimu ..... Kenya .... 30:59 ... $75
15. Joe Gibson .... Asheville, NC........... 31:29 ... $50

Females Overall
1. Sallie Barsosio .... Kenya .... 32:28 ... $5000
2. Tatyana Chulakh ..... Russia .... 32:36 ... $3000
3. Jane Kiptoo .... Kenya .... 33:09 ... $1500
4. Galina Alexandrova ... Russia .... 33:32 ... $100
5. Gladys Asiba .... Kenya .... 34:28 ... $800
6. Tatyana Pozdnyakova . Ukraine .... 34:55 ... $600
7. Sonya Friend-Uhl ..... W Chester, PA .... 35:02 ... $500
8. Lyubov Kremleva ..... Russia .... 35:11 ... $400
9. Valerie Young .... Marietta, GA .... 35:24 ... $300
10. Ute Jamrozy......... College Station, TX ..... 36:29 ... $250
11. Janice Addison....... Columbia, SC .... 37:17 ... $200
12. Megan Weis......... Columbia, SC .... 37:33 ... $150
13. Anne Wyman Cipolla .. Columbia, SC .... 37:53 ... $100
14. Janice Reilly .... Cary, NC............... 38:10 ... $75
15. Laura Jo Vroon....... Grand Rapids, MI ...... 38:10 ... $50

Male Masters
1. Dennis Simonaitis..... Kenya .... 31:44 ... $150
2. Selwyn Blake .... Columbia, SC .... 32:20 ... $100
3. Irv Batten .... Summerville, SC .... 32:37 ... $75
4. Chris Chattin .... Columbia, MD.......... 33:43 ... $50
5. Gary Romesser ...... Indianapolis, IN .... 33:45 ... $25

Female Masters
1. Tatyana Pozdnyakova . Ukraine .... 34:55 ... $1500
2. Lyubov Kremleva ..... Russia .... 35:11 ... $1000
3. Janice Addison....... Columbia, SC .... 37:17 ... $750
4. Janice Reilly .... Cary, NC............... 38:10 ... $500
5. Laura Jo Vroon....... Grand Rapids, MI ...... 38:10 ... $250

Male Grandmasters
1. Gary Romesser ...... Indianapolis, IN .... 33:45 ... $750
2. Richard Buerkle...... Atlanta, GA .... 35:15 ... $500
3. Steve Annan........ Mt Pleasant, SC .... 37:29 ... $250

Female Grandmasters
1. Terry Mahr .... Oregon, OH........... 40:24 ... $750
2. Judith Hine......... Marietta, GA.......... 43:35 ... $500
3. Toni Cruz........... Charlotte, NC .... 44:04 ... $250

Marcus Newberry Award
First Local (Tri-County) Finisher
Male
  Irv Batten .... Summerville, SC ..... 32:37 ... $500
Female
  Sarah Reed........... Summerville, SC ..... 39:29 ... $500

Special award:
Dewey Wise Trophy for oldest finisher with fastest time less than their age in minutes:
  David Mellard, 81 .... N Charleston SC 65:18

Age division winners
Presented to top 3 in each division; top 5% awards presented up to a maximum of 25 per division.

Male 12 & under (111 finishers, 6 awards)
1. Matt Buening........ Matthews, NC.......... 42:43
2. Ryan Atkinson .... Greer, SC 42:57
3. Conley Bryan .... Mt Pleasant, SC........ 44:18
4. Benjamin Green ..... Union, SC............. 46:27
5. Parker Ellison .... Conyers, GA........... 48:15
6. Brandon Rhodes ..... Anderson, SC.......... 49:50

Female 12 & under (64 finishers, 4 awards)
1. Ismailia Ferguson ..... Charleston, SC......... 48:13
2. Jamie Lynn Reichert ... Charleston, SC......... 48:46
3. Hilary McHugh ...... Boston, MA 49:29
4. Jessica Wood .... Johns Island, SC........ 50:40

Male 13 - 17 (292 finishers, 15 awards)
1. Jacob Morris .... Aiken, SC............. 36:48
2. Stephen T Powell .... Fort Mill, SC........... 36:59
3. Jordan Lybrand ..... Greer, SC 37:02
4. Stephen Sykes ...... Spartanburg, SC........ 37:12
5. Bryan Brooks .... West Columbia, SC..... 37:16
6. Andrew C Symmes .... Greenville, SC......... 37:36
7. Chris R Powell ...... Fort Mill, SC........... 38:29
8. Chris Fallis......... Awendaw, SC.......... 38:52
9. Thomas Shealy ..... Spartanburg, SC........ 39:03
10. Jefferson Waugh..... Statesville, NC......... 39:49
11. Thomas G Wilson.... Salisbury, NC.......... 40:17
12. Michael Depp....... Travelers Rest, SC...... 40:24
13. Joseph Laurendi .... Summerville, SC........ 40:27
14. Alan Ford.......... Huntersville, NC........ 40:34
15. Samuel Godfrey..... Rutherfordton, NC...... 41:01

Female 13 - 17 (252 finishers, 13 awards)
1. Danielle Franklin..... Greer, SC 45:13
2. Janet E Durst .... Greer, SC 47:29
3. Julia Baldwin .... Greer, SC 47:52
4. Erin Wendel .... Union, SC............. 47:54
5. Adrienne Brenner .... Lancaster, CA 48:04
6. Abby Osborn........ Charlotte, NC 48:24
7. Kerry Klimecki ...... Mt Pleasant, SC........ 48:32
8. Jenny Chiarelli ..... Pawleys Isl, SC......... 49:03
9. Megan Umphlett .... Charleston, SC......... 49:38
10. Laura Steele .... Alpharetta, GA 50:33
11. Caroline Leary ..... Mt Pleasant, SC........ 50:36
12. Stacia Streetman.... Greer, SC 50:47
13. Ashlyn Bristle...... Waynesville, NC........ 50:52

Male 18 - 21 (367 finishers, 19 awards)
1. Trevor A Beesley .... Greenwood, SC........ 33:47
2. Andrew A Powell.... Charleston, SC......... 36:22
3. Matthew Elliott..... Greensea, SC.......... 37:14
4. Paul Deyonker ...... Athens, GA............ 37:44
5. Bradley Sisk .... Easley, SC............. 38:04
6. Michael Guthrie..... Charleston, SC......... 38:06
7. Arnold Wood .... Goose Creek, SC........ 38:11
8. Matthew Greco ..... Chapel Hill, NC 38:12
9. Adam Taylor....... Simpsonville, SC........ 38:13
10. Dan Homer .... Lexington, SC.......... 38:40
11. Chip Perkins .... Charleston, SC......... 38:41
12. John Young......... Indianapolis, IN 38:42

– Continued on next page

2004 Awards, continued from page 213

13	William Coggins	Gramling, SC	38:45
14	Matthew Oakley	Chapel Hill, NC	39:07
15	Jesse Berger	Indianapolis, IN	39:28
16	Brad Topper	Wingate, NC	39:36
17	Jonathan Atkinson	Charleston, SC	39:47
18	Jon Duggins	Cowpens, SC	39:54
19	Arthur Sherry	Charlotte, NC	39:58

Female 18 - 21 (514 finishers, 25 awards)

1	Renee Keydoszius	Clemson, SC	41:52
2	Emily Cupito	Greensboro, NC	44:07
3	Sarah Melissa Kizer	Charleston, SC	44:44
4	Kristi Carlson	Charleston, SC	45:12
5	Natasha Darwent	Mt Pleasant, SC	45:45
6	Erin Smith	Greenwood, SC	45:59
7	Natalie Creech	Wingate, SC	46:02
8	Chelsey Wilson	Wingate, NC	46:02
9	Katie Bloemeke	Chapel Hill, NC	46:42
10	Kathryn Boettcher	Charleston, SC	46:51
11	Meredith Craig	N Charleston, SC	46:51
12	Ashley N Leuck	Columbia, SC	46:59
13	Kyle Palmquist	Charleston, SC	47:14
14	Elizabeth Rose	Charleston, SC	47:14
15	Stephanie Stalnaker	Charleston, SC	47:28
16	Stephanie Kurtz	Chapel Hill, NC	47:38
17	Miley White	Greer, SC	48:14
18	Ashley Adamson	Chapin, CA	48:20
19	Carla R Davison	Pawleys Island, SC	48:22
20	Andrea McGinn	Charleston, SC	48:56
21	Sarah Carrier	Wingate, SC	49:00
22	Stephanie Miller	Chapel Hill, SC	49:04
23	Anna Stark	Charleston , SC	49:27
24	Helen Fout	Myrtle Beach, SC	49:29
25	Nancy S Wilson	Mt Pleasant, SC	49:44

Male 22 - 25 (776 finishers, 25 awards)

1	Ryan Emry	Atlanta, GA	31:55
2	Daniel Hughes	Columbia, SC	32:25
3	Mike Aiken	Mt Pleasant, SC	33:00
4	Shawn Evans	Buies Creek, NC	34:00
5	Michael McCauley	Greenville, SC	34:02
6	Brooks Keys	Central, SC	34:25
7	Scott Penick	Atlanta, GA	34:41
8	Matt Legrand	Birmingham, AL	34:56
9	Brian Reinhardt	Charleston, SC	36:29
10	James Church	Greenville, SC	36:50
11	Hudson Belk	Charleston, SC	36:55
12	Zachary Hollis	Winston-Salem, NC	37:11
13	Jeffrey Schimizze	Sumter, SC	37:15
14	Matt Terrio	Florence, SC	37:28
15	Jonathan Kuiper	Crofton, MD	37:47
16	Jack Carmody	Clinton, SC	37:56
17	Danny White	Blacksburg, VA	38:00
18	William Whiteside	Charleston, SC	38:54
19	Joshua Clarke	Summerville, SC	38:57
20	Kurt Wilson	Unknown	38:58
21	Doug Cook	Ardmore, PA	39:01
22	John Boettcher	Columbia, SC	39:02
23	Aref Jallali	Wingate, NC	39:35
24	Joey Jutzeler	Charleston, SC	39:46
25	Daniel Thomas	Bergton, VA	41:18

Female 22 - 25 (1,093 finishers, 25 awards)

1	Shannon Smith	Potsdam, NY	38:43
2	Sara M Jenkins	Columbia, SC	39:52
3	Suzanne Clemmer	Gastonia, NC	39:55
4	Mary Dressler	Decatur, GA	40:00
5	Lynley Roberts	Atlanta, GA	40:19
6	Elizabeth Taylor	Salisbury, NC	40:55
7	Emily Johnson	Mt Pleasant, SC	41:23
8	Katherine Thurmond	Charleston, SC	42:24
9	Jennifer Emblidge	Charleston, SC	42:32
10	C J Donovan	Charleston, SC	42:54
11	Jessica Millican	Mt Pleasant, SC	43:08
12	Jill Hawley	Mt Pleasant, SC	43:42
13	Kate Veazey	Richmond, VA	43:45
14	Katie Swint	Decatur, GA	44:00
15	Meredith A Spears	Lillington, NC	44:07
16	Jennifer Skinner	Irmo, SC	44:28
17	Misty Davis	Columbia, SC	44:43
18	Jennifer Leiser	Charleston, SC	45:01
19	Sylvia Dodd	Mt Pleasant, SC	45:12
20	Emma Batchelor	Charleston, SC	45:30
21	Meredith L Evans	Charleston, SC	45:43
22	Sasha Azevedo	Charleston, SC	45:45
23	Becky Witkop	Charleston, SC	46:09
24	Laura Church	Greenville, SC	46:11
25	Angela Finley	Charleston, SC	46:28

Male 26 - 29 (975 finishers, 25 awards)

1	Orinthal Striggles	Columbia, SC	32:13
2	Palmer Thomas	Charleston, SC	33:17
3	Loic Laforet	Flat Rock, NC	34:16
4	Aaron Bowman	McLeansville, NC	34:31
5	Cornelius Mason	Charleston, SC	34:35
6	Jason Putnam	Anderson, SC	34:47
7	Blake Donald Benke	Emerald Isle, NC	34:58
8	Patrick Hamper	St Marys, GA	35:14
9	Thomas Walls	Fort Mill, SC	35:31
10	Shawn Donovan	N Charleston, SC	35:48
11	Matthew Johnson	Rock Hill, SC	36:36
12	Travis Brady	Spartanburg, SC	36:38
13	Brad Scott Fowler	Winston-Salem, NC	36:52
14	Jay Upchurch	Charleston, SC	37:03
15	Philipp Rittershaus	Charleston, SC	37:07
16	Johnnie Pearson	Virginia Beach, VA	37:19
17	Chris Jones	Davidson, NC	37:21
18	Bobby Wilder	Myrtle Beach, SC	37:32
19	Jeremy Becraft	Mt Pleasant, SC	37:41
20	Rob Pearce	Charleston, SC	37:55
21	Galen Holland	Asheville, NC	38:01
22	Doug Lake	Charleston, SC	38:34
23	Will Brumbach	Asheville, NC	38:53
24	Jonathan Skelley	Florence, SC	39:03
25	Jake Raser	Folly Beach, SC	39:39

Female 26 - 29 (1,094 finishers, 25 awards)

1	Laurie Knowles	Atlanta, GA	38:57
2	Sarah Reed	Summerville, SC	39:29
3	Jennifer Freeman	Maywood, NJ	40:16
4	Karen Gillespie	Greenville, SC	41:42
5	Mary Shell Brosche	Mt Pleasant, SC	41:54
6	Kelly Greene	Atlanta, GA	41:59
7	Wendy Moeller	Charlotte, NC	42:03
8	Emily Mountain-Geiger	Howard, OH	42:11
9	Sarah Hallenbeck	Charlotte, NC	42:29
10	Kristin Ann Cooley	Atlanta, GA	42:53
11	Kelly Spears	Beaufort, SC	44:34
12	Brooke Asselta	Mt Pleasant, SC	44:37
13	Titilola Iyun	Catonsville, MD	44:46
14	Elizabeth Weaver	Charlotte, NC	44:57
15	Ami Dewar	Raleigh, NC	45:07
16	Rives Poe	Athens, GA	45:10
17	Julia Baskin	Charleston, SC	45:14
18	Betsy Wallace	Mt Pleasant, SC	45:26
19	Isabel Ghowanlu	Charleston, SC	45:44
20	Colleen Angstadt	Charlotte, NC	46:16
21	Nancy Padgett	Charleston, SC	46:20
22	Gretchen Haufler	Knoxville, TN	46:32
23	Amy Clark O'Reilly	Pinehurst, NC	46:37
24	Shontel Jung	Asheville, NC	46:53
25	Heather Brumbach	Asheville, NC	46:56

Male 30 - 34 (1,392 finishers, 25 awards)

1	Julius Montanya	Columbia, KY	31:31
2	Christian Muentener	Yarmouth, ME	33:04
3	Jason Dressler	Decatur, GA	33:25
4	Todd Bibb	Woodstock, GA	34:01
5	Todd Martin	North Canton, OH	34:33
6	Jason Annan	Chapel Hill, NC	35:10
7	Coates Kennerly	Brevard, NC	35:16
8	Brad Schneider	Bowling Green, KY	35:27
9	Robert Wolfe	Washington, DC	35:30
10	Mark Harrell	Raleigh, NC	35:39
11	Jason Philbin	Charlotte, NC	36:09
12	Roger Fagala	Blenheim, SC	36:20
13	Emery Lloyd	Moncks Corner, SC	36:26
14	Darol Timberlake	Matthews, NC	36:45
15	Matt Pryor	Greenville, SC	36:55
16	Karl Kaiser	Columbia, SC	36:58
17	Nathan Weber	Charleston, SC	37:15
18	Jeffery Massey	Greenwood, SC	37:26
19	Jimmy Major	Chapin, SC	37:32
20	Gerald Griffitts	Hartsville, SC	37:35
21	Phillip Doiron	Hartsville, SC	38:12
22	Kevin Kelly	Charlotte, NC	38:28
23	Ellsworth Bergan	Silver Spring, MD	38:45
24	M W Mason	Charlotte, NC	38:46
25	Andres Powell	Decatur, GA	39:14

Female 30 - 34 (1,238 finishers, 25 awards)

1	Eileen Torres	Decatur, GA	40:13
2	Charlotte Thomason	Charlotte, NC	40:47
3	Debra Brown	Mt Pleasant, SC	42:05
4	Megan Davis Parrott	Simpsonville, SC	42:10
5	Kristin McCann	Jacksonville, NC	42:18
6	Dian Berry	Lexington, SC	42:38
7	Leslie Randall	Royersford, PA	42:53
8	Willa Patricia Veber	APO	42:55
9	Rebecca Crowder	Charlotte, NC	43:06
10	Tracy Dewitt	Charleston, SC	43:40
11	Sandy Weston	Simpsonville, SC	44:06
12	Alethea Setser	Mt Pleasant, SC	44:26
13	Ruth Halter	Charlotte, NC	44:53
14	Tammy Root	Richmond, IN	45:02
15	Lane McLeod Perry	Hendersonville, NC	45:11
16	Molly Hughes	Charleston , SC	45:30
17	Jennifer Wilkinson	Huntersville, NC	45:39
18	Ellen Smith	Charleston, SC	45:44
19	Claire Veber	Charlottesville, VA	46:33
20	Jennifer Kalich	Charlotte, NC	46:34
21	Laura Mullis	Charlotte, NC	46:51
22	Irene Draesel Todd	Charleston, SC	47:00
23	Martha Howard	Raleigh, NC	47:10
24	Linda Anderson	Charlotte, NC	47:18
25	Tracy McKee	Charleston, SC	47:24

Male 35 - 39 (1,136 finishers, 25 awards)

1	Eric Ashton	Columbia, SC	32:18
2	David Honea	Raleigh, NC	32:50
3	John Charlton	Columbia, SC	33:23
4	Eric Vandervort	Clinton, TN	34:07
5	Keith Batten	Clearwater, FL	34:10
6	Sean Killeen	Richmond, VA	35:26
7	Pat McCallion	Greer, SC	35:58
8	Craig Kingman	Jenison, MI	36:07
9	Martin Guthrie	Wallace, NC	36:13
10	Chris Hicks	Sumter, SC	36:34
11	Joseph Derajtys	Alpharetta, GA	37:11
12	Daniel Kehoe	Atlanta, GA	37:19
13	Jim Daniel	Mt Pleasant, SC	37:46
14	James Morse	Virginia Beach, VA	38:15
15	John Riordan	Charleston, SC	38:33
16	Helmut Schmoock	Murrells Inlet, SC	38:50
17	Alan Pogroszewski	Rochester, NY	39:12
18	Todd Siczek	Charlotte, NC	39:22
19	Greg Brown	Mt Pleasant, SC	39:30
20	Nicholas Taylor	Gilbert, SC	39:36
21	Randy Ashley	Asheville, NC	39:46
22	Peter Hastings	Goose Creek, SC	39:51
23	Ron Hutchins	Belmont, NC	39:55
24	Joe Helwig	Atlanta, GA	40:09
25	Maciej Nowak	Sumter, SC	40:12

Female 35 - 39 (900 finishers, 25 awards)

1	Sheila Wakeman	Cornelius, NC	38:48
2	Lisa Tolley	Seneca, SC	39:35
3	Saundi Theodossiou	Asheville, NC	40:14
4	Keely Churchill	Raleigh, NC	40:37
5	Wendy Shuping	Mooresville, NC	41:35
6	Karen Killeen	Richmond, VA	42:54
7	Diane Lancaster	Charlotte, NC	43:09
8	Molly Achille	Greenville, SC	43:10
9	Kathe Klein	Columbia, SC	43:20
10	Christine Conrad	Hillsborough, NC	43:46
11	Pamela D Mitchell	Wilmington, NC	44:04
12	Lanita Carpenter	Charlotte, NC	44:30
13	Wendy Roach	Mt Pleasant, SC	45:03
14	Lisa Anderson	Summerville, SC	45:34
15	Missy Hunnicutt	Columbia, SC	45:42
16	Lynne Takac	Matthews, NC	46:03
17	Beth Pierpont	Charlotte, NC	46:04
18	Betsy Jessup	Mt Pleasant, SC	46:07
19	Shanon Kay Duling	Greenville, SC	46:23
20	Gezelle H Macon	Seagrove, NC	46:33
21	Julie McArdle	Charlotte, NC	46:45
22	Stacey Johnson	Isle of Palms, SC	46:55
23	Robin Siczek	Charlotte, NC	46:56
24	Kelly Dobson	Mt Pleasant, SC	47:17
25	Rachel Cooter	Greenville, SC	47:31

Male 40 - 44 (943 finishers, 25 awards)

1	Dave Berardi	Baltimore, MD	34:04
2	John Anderson	Moore, SC	36:34
3	Michael Parker	Goose Creek, SC	36:39
4	David Ariola	Asheville, NC	36:54
5	Eric Sabin	Columbia, SC	36:58
6	James Alan Harris	Wilmington, NC	37:01
7	Sam Inman	Greenville, SC	37:38
8	Huey Inman	Mt Pleasant, SC	37:40
9	David Quick	Mt Pleasant, SC	38:21
10	Lance Leopold	Simpsonville, SC	38:30
11	Steven Rudnicki	Columbia, SC	38:47
12	Gary Ledford	Hickory, NC	39:00
13	Paul Baczewski	N Charleston, SC	39:37

14	Lennie Davis	Kettering, OH	39:43
15	Rob Newton	Mooresville, NC	40:04
16	Stephen Trabucco	Huntersville, NC	40:20
17	Chris Handal	Charleston, SC	40:30
18	Kenneth Clyburn	Beaufort, SC	40:33
19	Andy Barker	Isle of Palms, SC	40:37
20	Rob Burke	Wilmington, NC	40:41
21	Thomas Hayden	Greenville, SC	40:47
22	E Hood Temple	Florence, SC	40:50
23	Randall Fisher	Goose Creek, SC	40:52
24	Thomas McDonald	Anderson, SC	41:16
25	Dwayne Hellard	Raleigh, NC	41:16

Female 40 - 44 (728 finishers, 25 awards)

1	Mary Dore	Charlotte, NC	40:10
2	Kelly Hazel	Summerville, SC	42:16
3	Patt Loggins	Charleston, SC	42:28
4	Christi Craft	Simpsonville, SC	43:00
5	Suanne Hall	Greenville, SC	43:47
6	Lisa Powell	Columbia, SC	43:59
7	Carleen J Davis	N Charleston, SC	44:28
8	Kathy Gettys	Columbia, SC	45:23
9	Jean Aswell	Cornelius, NC	45:26
10	Megan Gorman	Melrose Park, PA	46:03
11	Linda Smith	Mt Vernon, OH	46:29
12	Eileen Thames	Mt Pleasant, SC	46:46
13	Jane Godwin	Greer, SC	46:46
14	Sue McKee	Charlotte, NC	47:12
15	Noriko Seiner	Beaufort, SC	47:45
16	Jennifer S Byrd	Greenville, SC	48:16
17	Simone Kleist	N Charleston, SC	48:42
18	Tracey Wagner	Afton, VA	48:45
19	Janice Sides	Concord, NC	49:17
20	Polly Shoemaker	Columbia, SC	49:48
21	Cindy Keys	Miamisburg, OH	49:52
22	Ann Doggett	Forest City, NC	50:00
23	Cynthia McDonald	Anderson, SC	50:01
24	Lita Gatlin	Matthews, NC	50:06
25	Janet Harris	Matthews, NC	50:08

Male 45 - 49 (753 finishers, 25 awards)

1	Tom Mather	Mt Pleasant, SC	34:23
2	Peter Edge	Simpsonville, SC	35:29
3	Alan Blackwell	Moore, SC	36:37
4	James Wilhelm	Canton, OH	36:40
5	Fesshaye Haile	Virginia Beach, VA	37:41
6	Mark Friedrich	Isle of Palms, SC	37:42
7	Mike Hart	Washington, DC	37:48
8	James Scheer	Charleston, SC	37:58
9	Clyde Sanders	Beaufort, SC	37:59
10	Marc Embler	Summerville, SC	38:18
11	David Bourgeois	Summerville, SC	38:19
12	Billy Tisdale	Sumter, SC	38:20
13	David Renneisen	Goose Creek, SC	38:22
14	Alfie Cronin	Decatur, GA	38:25
15	Lennie Moore	Mt Pleasant, SC	39:35
16	David Gee	Gaffney, SC	39:49
17	Michael Cannon	Fayetteville, NC	39:58
18	Keith Hertling	Taylors, SC	40:01
19	Derek Appleton	Cornelius, NC	40:08
20	Richard Gerardi	Charlotte, NC	40:16
21	Tim Carter	Greer, SC	40:17
22	Bill Edwards	Florence, SC	40:23
23	Harold Fallis	Awendaw, SC	40:32
24	Peter Hertl	Jamestown, NC	40:42
25	Dan Bradley	Winston-Salem, NC	40:43

Female 45 - 49 (475 finishers, 24 awards)

1	Sarah Ball	Charleston, SC	43:33
2	Kathy Abernethy	Matthews, NC	44:59
3	Debbie Davis	Charlotte, NC	45:36
4	Anne Marie Moncure	Camden, SC	45:55
5	Pam Drafts	Beaufort, SC	46:09
6	Tami Dennis	Isle of Palms, SC	46:19
7	Jan Odonnell	Lantana, FL	46:22
8	Colleen Adams	Daniel Island, SC	47:07
9	Tammy Hovik	Jonestown, TX	47:12
10	Beverly Grangt	Weaverville, NC	47:13
11	Sara Major Schultz	Greer, SC	47:39
12	Trudy Carolyn Gale	Spencer, NC	48:08
13	Marilyn Adamson	Chapin, SC	48:20
14	Ann Douglas	Chapin, SC	49:13
15	Dell Toomer	Summerville, SC	49:24
16	Pamala Jordan	Snellville, GA	49:34
17	Sue Jane Porter	Columbia, SC	49:46
18	Laurel Easterson	Hampton, VA	49:59
19	Carol S Hermann	N Wilkesboro, NC	50:35
20	Tacey Penland	Laurens, SC	50:42
21	Debby Moore	Simpsonville, SC	51:15
22	Anette Putnam	N Augusta, SC	51:37
23	Caroline Bailey	Mt Pleasant, SC	51:39
24	Joannie Essler	Nunda, NY	51:46

Male 50 - 54 (638 finishers, 25 awards)

1	Rick Boyle	Ringoes, NJ	38:49
2	Jack Todd	Spartanburg, SC	39:24
3	Jim Boyd	Mt Pleasant, SC	40:09
4	Gary Ricker	Charleston, SC	40:36
5	Michael Drose	Mt Pleasant, SC	40:38
6	Rick King	Anderson, SC	40:40
7	Jim Freid	Tega Cay, SC	41:05
8	Fernando R Puente	Raleigh, NC	41:30
9	Dan Clapper	N Charleston, SC	41:30
10	Randal Greg Price	Horseshoe, NC	41:44
11	Robert D'Italia	Mt Pleasant, SC	41:59
12	Ronald Stanley	Charlotte, NC	43:09
13	Samuel Jenkins	N Charleston, SC	43:11
14	Ken Hanger	Charleston, SC	43:43
15	Mark Greenway	Anderson, SC	44:03
16	Rusty Doyle	Marion, SC	44:22
17	Mario Salas	Mt Pleasant, SC	44:32
18	Eddie Muldrow	Chapin, SC	44:33
19	Mark Yoffe	Raleigh, NC	44:38
20	Jack Spanner	Charlotte, NC	44:38
21	Jeronimo Lopez	N Charleston, SC	44:39
22	Neil Derrick	Columbia, SC	44:58
23	Will Jones	Atlanta, GA	45:00
24	Don Whelchel	Charlotte, NC	45:08
25	Jonathan Anderson	Charleston, SC	45:13

Female 50 - 54 (289 finishers, 15 awards)

1	Catherine Lempesis	Irmo, SC	45:28
2	Michelle Withers	Charlotte, NC	46:41
3	Mimi Sturgell	Kiawah Island, SC	46:57
4	Patrice Katsanevakis	Mt Pleasant, SC	47:00
5	Kathy Ward	Raleigh, NC	47:05
6	Susan Krepelka	Matthews, NC	48:27
7	Debbie Howard	Mt Pleasant, SC	48:55
8	Sallie Driggers	Hanahan, SC	49:21
9	Therese Killeen	Isle of Palms, SC	49:28
10	Judy Osborn	Charlotte, NC	49:32
11	Jo Haubenreiser	Kernersville, NC	49:39
12	Susan Bratton	Charlotte, NC	49:51
13	Cathy Burton	Isle of Palms, SC	51:00
14	Martha White	Columbia, SC	52:12
15	Deby Shirk	Mt Pleasant, SC	52:54

Male 55 - 59 (504 finishers, 25 awards)

1	Bob Schlau	Charleston, SC	39:21
2	Russ Brown	Midway, GA	42:23
3	David Cromer	Dallas, TX	42:42
4	Fred Reinhard	Charleston, SC	42:56
5	Paul Gordon	Concord, NC	43:37
6	William Anderson	Wadmalaw Isl, SC	44:25
7	Mackie Johnson	Conover, NC	45:00
8	Peter Mugglestone	Columbia, SC	45:14
9	Tony Hill	High Point, NC	45:20
10	David Anderson	N Charleston, SC	45:58
11	Ed Vinson	Chapin, SC	46:05
12	Charles Stoyle	Augusta, GA	46:09
13	Roddy Whitaker	Swansea, SC	46:10
14	Barnard Gesing	Mooresville, NC	46:15
15	Byron Trotter	Decatur, GA	46:36
16	Frank Mcleod	Fitzgerald, GA	46:53
17	Albert Anderson	Eastover, SC	46:59
18	Gary Melville	Charleston, SC	47:01
19	Doug Matthews	Winterville, GA	47:34
20	Herbie Blackwell	York, SC	47:36
21	Ben Grant	Weaverville, NC	47:47
22	William Reece	Centerville, IN	48:28
23	Jim Musselwhite	Atlanta, GA	48:30
24	Bruce Snow	Lexington, SC	49:02
25	Roger Arthur	Red House, WV	49:10

Female 55 - 59 (165 finishers, 9 awards)

1	Lyn Hammond	Charleston, SC	48:06
2	Kathy Seavers	Charlotte, NC	50:51
3	Sissy Logan	Salem, VA	51:40
4	Brenda Cooter	Grovetown, GA	52:46
5	Lillian Cheshire	Charlotte, NC	53:04
6	Anita Cohen	Hilton Head, SC	53:16
7	Marcella Farino	Lancaster, SC	53:56
8	Ruth Uhlhmann	Mt Pleasant, SC	54:07
9	Dorothy Anderson	Kiawah Island, SC	55:28

Male 60 - 64 (244 finishers, 13 awards)

1	George Luke	Greenville, SC	42:21
2	Jim Strowd	Mt Pleasant, SC	43:31
3	James Salvo	Kiawah Island, SC	43:55
4	Richard Landsman	Summerville, SC	44:49
5	Donald Snowdon	Brevard, NC	44:52
6	Ned Lesesne	Canton, NC	45:06
7	James Adams	N Augusta, SC	45:14
9	Thomas Eison	Greenville, SC	46:20
10	Ed Sessions	N Charleston, SC	46:39
11	Larry Seavers	Charlotte, NC	46:44
12	Anthony Donache	Mt Pleasant, SC	48:00
13	Keith Ambrose	Mt Pleasant, SC	48:07

Female 60 - 64 (62 finishers, 3 awards)

1	Pauline Niilend	Charlotte, NC	54:18
2	Kim Wells	Columbia, SC	54:36
3	Kay Chandler	Isle of Palms, SC	58:02

Male 65 - 69 (73 finishers, 4 awards)

1	Harvey McCormick	Charleston, SC	46:29
2	Floyd Deandrade	Johns Island, SC	47:09
3	Clyde Mizzell	Charleston, SC	49:21
4	Ed Ledford	Folly Beach, SC	52:19

Female 65 - 69 (19 finishers, 3 Awards)

1	E. K. Tolley-Beeson	Sumter, SC	1:00:12
2	Faye Davis	Mt Pleasant, SC	1:01:52
3	Pat Rhode	Walterboro, SC	1:03:02

Post and Courier photo by Yolanda M. James

Male 70 - 74 (17 finishers, 3 awards)

1	William Boulter	Charleston, SC	50:38
2	Lonnie Collins	Gilbert, SC	54:24
3	Ken Walls	Mt Pleasant, SC	56:17

Female 70 - 74 (3 finishers, 3 awards)

1	Pep Logan	Johns Island, SC	1:16:11
2	Garthedon Embler	Isle of Palms, SC	1:23:22
3	Elizabeth Rebl	Summerville, SC	1:42:51

Male 75 - 79 (13 finishers, 3 awards)

1	William Fulton	Greenvile, SC	57:38
2	Franklin Mason	Mullins, SC	58:08
3	Bill Kleber	Knoxville, TN	59:06

Female 75 - 79 (3 finishers, 3 awards)

1	Mary Canty	Orlando, FL	1:34:00
2	Wyndall Henderson	Walterboro, SC	1:41:16
3	Ola Moody	Augusta, GA	1:45:19

Male 80 - 98 (5 finishers, 3 awards)

1	David Mellard	N Charleston, SC	1:05:18
2	William Pennebaker	Charleston, SC	1:33:27
3	Tellis Martin	Penney Farms, FL	1:33:46

Female 80 - 98 (1 finisher, 1 award)

1	Margaret Wright	Folly Beach, SC	2:07:22

Compiled by Cedric Jaggers from complete results provided by Burns Computer Services on April 3, 2004.

The leaders on a rain-drenched Pearman bridge. Post and Courier photo by Sarah Bates

Chapter 28

2005

Last Bridge Run On The Pearman Bridge Draws Over 20,000; First Rain During Race

Post and Courier headlines trumpeted: "28th Annual Cooper River Bridge Run END OF AN ERA. Pearman farewell attracts record number of runners." And the headlines were correct. At 8 a.m. on April 2, 2005, the 28th Cooper River Bridge Run began and it went over the Silas Pearman Bridge for the last time. In fact, both of the "old" bridges the race used during its 28-year history were scheduled to be torn down. They were to be replaced by a taller, $620 million Arthur Ravenel single span suspension bridge.

There was a certain poetic symmetry between the first and the "last Bridge Run" as some people called it. The first Bridge Run used one lane of the Silas Pearman Bridge. The "last", actually the 28th Bridge Run, used all three lanes. Weather for the first race was generally regarded as terrible: record heat, 82 degrees, with bright sunshine. The weather for the "last" race was generally regarded as terrible: record rain and wind gusting to 40 miles per hour, making the 63-degree morning feel much colder.

It was the first time rain fell during the actual running of any Bridge Run. The rain stopped 20 minutes after the race began and the sky was a cloudless blue by the time the last runners crossed the finish line. In the first race, only 73.6 percent of the registrants finished the race, the lowest percentage ever. In the "last" race, only 74.9 percent of the entrants finished the race, the third lowest percentage in race history. But there the similarities end.

There were record numbers of entrants (later eclipsed); 24,663 and record 18,480 finishers listed in the results printed at the finish line after the last runner crossed the ChampionChip timing pad. This included all the finishers.

The Sunday *Post and Courier* printed the names and times of 10,187 male finishers and 8,256 female finishers but could not include the 37 entrants who had not shown their gender on their entry form. The race website www.BridgeRun.Com used the same file and showed 18,446 finishers, in a searchable format. ChampionChip timing was used and runners used special commemorative chips, emblazoned with the same design printed on the race T-shirt, which they were allowed to keep.

There were a then record 24,663 entrants for the run and a record 17,200 entrants for the untimed walk. For the first time, race entrant numbers were capped, with the number set at 42,000. Perhaps due to the weather a record of another kind was set as 6,183 did not finish the race. A number of runners said that when they got up that morning and saw all the rain and wind, they decided to stay home. Observers estimate that about half the registered walkers did not participate due to the weather.

The weather affected the race leaders as they had to contend with the ferocious headwind on the bridge. Members of the lead pack stayed together until they hit an unexpected obstacle at the foot of the bridge: a street-wide pool of water. Kenyan Linus Maiyo, who had been outkicked at the finish the previous two years, did not want to lose a step so he splashed right through while some others tried to avoid it. Maiyo said, "In Kenya, we are used to running through water; for me, it was not a problem."

The puddle did create a problem for slower runners. There was a small, dry area on the right edge near a retaining wall. Some runners stopped running and tried to wade into it and this caused a bottleneck. The elite runners were unaffected and probably unaware of any problem.

The lead pack thinned out over the spans and Thomas Kiplitan, also of Kenya, took the lead in the flats of downtown Charleston. When Kiplitan made the final turn onto Calhoun Street and could see the finish banner approximately a half-mile ahead, he had a 50-yard lead.

Maiyo was determined not to be the runner-up for the third year in a row. He made a powerful move and overtook Kiplitan at just about the 6-mile mark. Linus Maiyo won the race in 29:30 with Kiplitan finishing second in 29:40. Michael Aish of New Zealand was third in 29:46, with David Korir of Kenya and Ryan Kirkpatrick of Augusta, Ga., finishing at 29:49 and 29:50. They were the only runners to break the 30-minute barrier. The winning time was the slowest since 1998.

Maiyo seemed disappointed with his time but not his win. "We didn't run fast the way we were supposed to, and that was because of the weather," he told the *Post and Courier*. "I'm very happy to finally win this race. I've been second twice, so I thought this year would be my year." Kenyans took six of the top eight spots but did not have any others in the top 15 as in previous years.

Kenyan women did not dominate the female division this year either. Winner Olga Romanova of Russia was not too upset with her time of 34:04. "The weather, it was miserable," she told the newspaper. "The weather made it impossible to break the record. It was windy going up the hill, and that made it impossible." She didn't know this would be the last run over the "old bridge" and said about her win, "It's a great honor then. It's important that I did it." Galina Alexandrova, another Russian, took second in 34:39. Breeda Willis of Ireland was third in 34:52.

"The rain wasn't a problem but the wind was," Willis said. "It slowed everyone down and that surprised me. It was tough, very tough." Tatyana Pozdnyakova of Ukraine (a familiar name at the Bridge Run) was fourth in 35:34, and Donna Anderson of Pawleys Island, S.C., was fifth in 35:39. It was the slowest female winning time since 1994 and the first time a non-Kenyan woman had won since 1998.

Masters winner was Paul Aufdemberg of Redford, Mich., in 31:22. Last year's winner, Dennis Simoaitis of Kenya, was runner-up in 32:36, while last year's runner-up, Selwyn Blake of Columbia, S.C., finished third in 32:48. Tom Mather of Mount Pleasant took fourth place Masters money in 32:53. David Matherne of Cartersville, Ga., took home fifth place money for his 34:38.

Female Masters winner for the second year in a row was the overall fourth place finisher Tatyana Pozdnyakova of Ukraine in 35:34. She was followed by Valentina Egorova of Russia in 36:12, Lee DiPietro of Ruxton, Md., in 38:06, Maria Spinnier of Hagerstown, Md., in 39:03 and Janice Reilly of Cary, N.C., in 39:10.

Male Grand Masters runner Gary Romesser of Indianapolis, Ind., won for the fifth year in a row, this time in 36:02. Jerry Clark of Charlotte, N.C., was second in 37:25 while Wes Wessely of Clermont, Ga., took home the final Grand Masters money in 39:13.

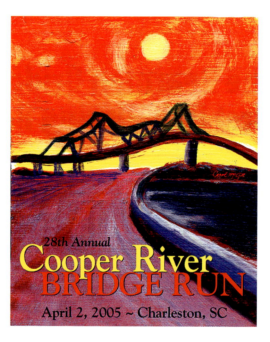

The female Grand Masters had a new but familiar name as winner. Tatyana Pozdnyakova of Ukraine, who had recently turned 50, tripled up in prize money by winning this division in a new Grand Masters record 35:34. Debra Wagner of Perrysburg, Ohio, was runner-up in 40:43 while Catherine Wides of Durham, N.C., was third in 43:58.

The Dr. Marcus Newberry Award for first Tri-County finisher went to Tom Mather, 47, of Mount Pleasant. He won the award for and unprecedented ninth time by placing 18th overall in 32:53. After the race he told the Post and Courier how tough conditions were. "It was the wind and the direction of the wind," he said. "It was a strong headwind through about mile 5, and then it turned a little bit more to the side. But boy, at that point you had already gone up and down hills into the wind. It was tough." Carre Joyce of Summerville, S.C., took home the female award with her time of 37:22, 12th place female. John Noble, 75, of Charleston ran 69:52 to win the Dewey Wise Trophy.

For the third year in a row live television coverage was broadcast on Channel 5. The two-hour broadcast was shown again Sunday evening so that participants could watch it.

Only five runners broke the 30-minute time barrier with none under 29 minutes – a fact attributed to the strong headwind. A total of 199 runners broke the 40-minute barrier: 174 male and 25 female. There were 1,889 runners under the 50-minute barrier, with a total of 5,775 under 60 minutes.

The entry fee was raised to $25 for early race registration, $30 after March 12, and $15 early entry for the walk, $20 after March 26. Julian Smith continued as race director. Complete race results were mailed to all finishers. This was a good year for runners who were interested in seeing previous race results: the Bridge Run Committee borrowed all the pre-computerized paper race results for the race from race historian Cedric Jaggers (since he had the only known complete set), scanned/retyped and posted them on the www.bridgerun.com website.

The 2005 Hall of Fame inductees were Tom Mather, runner and nine-time winner of the race's Marcus Newberry Award for first local Tri-County finisher; Tom O'Rourke, volunteer; and Thomas Dewey Wise, former state senator who pushed through legislation allowing use of the bridge for the race.

Other Voices
A View From The Bridge

By Kenneth Bible, CRC Bridge Run Representative. Originally appeared in the May-June 2005 Low Country Runner

Rain, puddles, mud. . . we had it all, and a lot of fun on April 2nd for the last Cooper River Bridge Run over the Pearman Bridge. The Charleston Running Club was well represented amongst race participants, as well as in the ranks of volunteers helping make this record setting event possible. With a sold out registration of 42,000 participants, it is estimated that a record crowd between 37,000 and 38,000 came out for race day despite the weather!

We had a lot of folks help with the activities leading up to the race. Whether packet stuffing, helping with packet pick-up, staffing the club's Bridge Run Expo table on Thursday and Friday, volunteering with the Children's Run, or helping after the race with the awards ceremony, it was great to see so many members getting involved in the race. What follows is part chronology, and part impressions from this milestone year in the event.

My day Friday was spent setting out mile markers, helping move supplies to the Children's Run, and participating in the various functions leading up to the race. I started at Hampton Park in the morning, where there was a good crew of people setting up. The park venue is perfect for this type of event, and Liz Sheridan and Mike Desrosiers were busily organizing volunteers, setting up tents and signs, and preparing for the many events. The need for some additional supplies for the Children's Run sent me packing off to Galliard Auditorium next, but I was able to put mile markers 5 and 6 in place en route.

After completing my rounds downtown, and returning to Hampton Park to drop off the materials they needed, it was off to Mount Pleasant to check on the start line and miles 1 and 2. Work on the scaffolding on Coleman Boulevard for the run and walk start lines was just beginning. Mount Pleasant had helped get some posts driven in the ground for the 1 and 2 mile marks. This really helped keep me from having to play in traffic! The road crew from Mount Pleasant was hard at work on the pavement near the 2-mile mark. I had my fingers crossed that they would be finished before the predicted rain moved in.

Next it was off to the press conference at noon. I didn't have time to change into some nicer clothes, so I had to go as I was. There was a great crowd at the Maritime Center – one of the best I have ever seen. It was really gratifying to have Gary Santos (representing Mount Pleasant) and Mayor Joe Riley (of Charleston) recognize the significance of the day. The Mayor and Mr. Santos read a proclamation naming race day as Cooper River Walk and Run Day in Charleston and Mount Pleasant, and April as Fitness Awareness Month in the two municipalities.

We had made it through the whole morning without rain. After the press conference, I made a quick stop back into Hampton Park to see some of the Children's Run activities underway. Then I went to Ansonborough Field to check on the finish festival set-up. The Bi-Lo crew was hard at work offloading thousands of pounds of fruit and other food in the park. This crew is amazing to watch, and have made the set up in the park a real pleasure. Rather than hand-carrying hundreds of cases of water, fruit and other food as we have done in the past, their forklift driver now deftly plucks pallet after pallet out of the several track-trailers assembled. After making a quick check with the City of Charleston and Charleston County Parks and Recreation Commission representatives overseeing the operations, I knew that the finish festival would be a success, even if it was wet.

I had seen a brochure for a "come as you are" worship service at the Second Presbyterian Church organized by Clyde and Jan Mizell. With the inclement weather holding off all day, and the challenges ahead on Saturday, thanking a higher power for 30 minutes was an enjoyable break from the pace of the day.

Next, I was able to meet up with my wife at the Expo, and we had a chance to break bread with Frank Hunt and a number of others at the pasta dinner. Then it was off to meet up with a police escort in the rain just after rush hour to go place the bridge mile markers and medical zone signs. The medical signage was a new addition to the race this year to help officials locate injured runners more precisely during the race. However, putting them in place significantly increased the time we were exposed to the rapidly intensifying rain, not to mention many impatient drivers!

The sound of the rain on the roof kept me awake most of Friday night. Needless to say, the thunder very early in the morning really made me nervous. As I left the house on my way to the finish line to meet up with the crew helping with the race timing, I was able to get a report from one of the ham radio crew that was watching the weather radar on a web site on their home computer. This reassured me that the rumbles of thunder were the end of the storm, and not signs of continuing trouble.

Glenn Braddock, Mike Chodnicki and I met at the Renaissance Hotel and proceeded over the bridge with the elite athlete shuttle so we arrived at the start line in good time. But the rain was still falling, and it was clear that water on the road would be an issue for the runners. Further, the rain seemed to be causing some of the electronics at the start and finish line to interfere with our communications network so everyone had to be especially alert.

The ride to the start line was surreal. In the 12 or so years that I have been involved with the Cooper River Bridge Run, we have never had rain of the intensity of that morning. Instead of the usual elbow-to-elbow crowds on Coleman Boulevard, the street was nearly empty. The same was true at the run start. However, careful observation revealed that every overhang and doorway was crammed with people. And amazingly, they all seemed to be smiling.

Despite all of the weather issues I was relieved to get that final "All Clear" over the radio at just a couple of minutes before 8 a.m. We quickly got the race off to an on time start.

From there, you can tell the story better than I can, and I hope you will write about your experiences. It means a lot to those who organize and work on a race to know that the effort is appreciated, and to hear your feedback.

Thanks to the work of club members like Glenn Braddock, Mike Chodnicki, Nancy Curry, Mike Desrosiers, Clyde and Jan Mizell, Gary Ricker and many others, we are able to enjoy races of the quality of the Bridge Run.

As you can see from the above, there are a lot of parts to a race the size and scope of the Cooper River Bridge Run and many ways to contribute. The action is not all on the run. I look forward to working with many of you over the next year as we plan for the first race on the "New Bridge".

Other Voices
Tell Me About Your Bridge Run 2005

By Cedric Jaggers. Originally appeared in the July-August 2005 Low Country Runner
(Bridge Run info for 2005 – 18,480 largest number of official finishers; 24,663 largest number of entrants. Start time temperature 63 degrees, rained until 20 minutes after the starting gun was fired.)

Back in 1988 a 40-year-old CRC member had a great idea. Get CRC members to "Tell Me About Your Bridge Run". One question after the race where I would write down exactly what you say. Is it really 17 years later and I'm still doing it? Time flies when you are having a good time, but like I warned you in the last newsletter it was going to take me a long time to waddle the distance and get to the CRC tent. I wish more club members had still been there, but after the horrible rain and wind I sure understood why so many people went home quickly. It was still a pleasure to talk to as many of you as were still on hand when I got to the CRC tent.

Again this year the race had more finishers than ever: 18,480. The Sunday *Post and Courier* listed 10,187 male and 8,256 female finishers. I was hoping for 20,000 finishers or more on the final trek over the "old new bridge" and we would have had that many if over 6,000 registered entrants hadn't been fair weather runners (or should that read "smarter than us runners") and stayed home. The 63-degree morning sure felt a lot colder and the headwind on the bridge was the worst ever. But hey, it was a tailwind on King Street. Anyway, it was great to see and talk to everyone who was still there; sorry if I missed you. Here are the names and stories, in the order I bumped into people. If folks didn't tell me their time, I tried to ask them after they had finished talking. I entered names on the www.BridgeRun.Com to get place and chip and race time.

John Hughes: It was windy and wet (laughs). Very much fun as usual. I'll miss the old bridge; seeing and running it. It'll be a challenge next year. Next year I will have done all three bridges. Time 55:40. 2,570th Overall, chip time 54:58, race time 55:07.

Melanie Hughes: It was windy. It was an experience. It was the first time I've ever felt like I was flying. Ran about 1:01. 5,916th Overall, chip time 1:01:00, race time 1:03:00.

Therese Killeen: Oh, God. Oh, please don't do that (as I wrote down exactly what she said). Well, I got up and tackled the run because I know some people who didn't. The race? Slow but satisfying. About 50 minutes and some change. 2,277th Overall, 50:11 chip time, 50:20 race time, top 5% award.

Mike Chodnicki: No wrong turns and you can quote me on that. (Mike drove the lead truck.) 29:00 minutes truck time (ha, ha).

Michael Hughes: I stayed with my wife. We had fun. We were looking for you. (Note: we started the race side by side). Time about 1:01. 5,917th Overall, 1:01:00 chip time, 1:03:00 race time.

Thomas McGorty: (Laughs.) I don't know what to say. I was hoping to do better. At least I did it. 44:25. 609th Overall, 44:26 chip time, 44:28 race time.

William Boulter: Well I had a good run. I felt good about it. I may have been a minute or less off last year. I won my age group: 75 and above. Ran 51:50 or so.

1,680th Overall, 51:31 chip time, 51:50 race time 1st 75-79 a.g. award.

George Dunleavy: Windy, windy, windy. It was always great to run the bridge. I was 2 minutes slower than two weeks ago at the Flowertown 10k, but it's to be expected. 39:40. 180th Overall, 39:49 chip time, 39:49 race time, top 5% award.

Sasha Azevedo: Wet and very traditional. I enjoyed the run. I started out pretty fast. Got a little slow going up the bridge. I enjoyed the race. 51 something. Did not locate on website.

Tom Rossi: My son and I ran together, it was the best Bridge Run I ever had; the most fun. We started out slow and got progressively slower. We made it together. 50 flat. 1,591st Overall, 51:23 chip time, 51:27 race time.

Gary Ricker: It was more like a walk. I got to the starting line at 20 after 8 because the buses were slow. I wanted to break 40 – I broke an hour twenty. It was the land of the strollers and walkers. There's always next year though. There were lots of buses behind me – there had to be lots more people. 12,328th Overall, 56:28 chip time, 1:15:50 race time.

Clyde Mizzell: A little windy on the second span. It about stood me up. I never knew what my time was. It must not have been too good because I enjoyed the run. 1,666th Overall, 51:45 chip time, 51:47 race time, top 5% award.

Ed Ledford: Worst and terrible. I had to walk a lot. Ten minutes slower than last week at the Flowertown 10k. At 4 miles I was slower than I did the race in 5 years ago. I should have entered the walk. 58:37. 3,860th Overall, 58:26 chip time, 58:35 race time.

Lennie Moore: Considering what I've been though (Note: refer to Lennie's article about the dog attack in the Jan-Feb newsletter). I guess I'm happy with my results. A little under 40. 198th Overall, 39:55 chip time, 39:58 race time, top 5% award.

Dan Clapper: Well I was 16 seconds late getting to mile 3 and just tried to hang on after that. I actually enjoyed the rain. Ran a little bit faster than last year, about 41:11. I was pleased. 265th Overall, 40:08 chip time, 41:14 race time, top 5% award.

Keith Ambrose: I had a good run for a change. It would have been better if I could find some doctor who could get rid of the crap that gets in my throat when I run. I have trouble breathing. 47:35. 1,009th Overall, 48:28 chip time, 48:31 race time, top 5% award.

Joan Mulvihill: Great start, right behind the Kenyans. They ran a little faster than me, but you have those days. Nobody around me, I felt a little sick but didn't throw up. Now my feet are soaking wet and muddy. I have on brand new shoes – my chip was on my new shoes and I had to run in them. 54:09. 2,273rd Overall, 54:09 chip time, 54:11 race time, 2nd 60-64 a.g. award.

Female winner, Olga Romanova from Russia, blows kisses to the crowd before she crosses the finish line. Post and Courier photo by Sarah Bates

Jeffrey Herndon: It sucked. I think I ran 46:20. This is one year I don't even know what to say. I ran about a 7:30 pace. At two miles I was at 14:20 and just ran it to finish it. 721st Overall, 46:15 chip time, 46:20 race time.

David Quick: I had a great Flowertown 10k race at 36:20 and hoped it would translate into a 36-something Bridge Run. I knew at the 3-mile mark when I ran a 6:30 it wouldn't happen. It was good, but I had some people around me – Carre Joyce was one - I couldn't quite catch up to her. It was a P.R. on the Pearman Bridge by 12 seconds so I'll take it. I remember when breaking 40 was a milestone. When you get in the top 100 it's great. It's only the second time I've done that. So there are always good things about the race. 93rd Overall, 37:30 chip time, 37:31 race time, top 5% award. –––

Cedric Jaggers: Kathy said I should add myself. Unfortunately she had to stay in the hotel room for health reasons due to her multiple sclerosis and could not take the notebook from my hand and make me tell her about my Bridge Run and write it down as she has done in the past. I actually ran about what I should have run based on my lack of training. It took exactly 11 minutes to get to the 1-mile mark after taking 1:56 to get to the start line. I had on a huge plastic bag from the hotel which I shed just before the mile mark even though it was still raining. I was surprised when we stopped at the foot of the bridge – the puddle made the joggers in front of me stop so their feet wouldn't get wet. I was hoping to get in under an hour so getting in just under 59 minutes (about 22 and a half minutes slower than my best B.R.) actually didn't upset me like it would have in the old days. 4,011th Overall, 57:00 chip time, 58:56 race time.

Post and Courier photo by Mic Smith

2005 Awards

Prize money winners:

Males Overall

1	Linus Maiyo	Kenya	29:30	$5000
2	Thomas Kiplitan	Kenya	29:40	$3000
3	Michael Aish	New Zealand	29:46	$1500
4	David Korir	Kenya	29:49	$1000
5	Ryan Kirkpatrick	Augusta, GA	29:50	$800
6	Patrick Nithwa	Kenya	30:17	$600
7	Henry Kipchirchir	Kenya	30:30	$500
8	Yevgen Bozhko	Kenya	30:59	$400
9	Joe Gibson	Greenville, SC	31:13	$300
10	Paul Aufdemberg	Redford, MI	31:32	$250
11	Scott Wietecha	Columbia, SC	31:36	$200
12	Eric Ashton	Columbia, SC	31:51	$150
13	Devin Swan	Raleigh, NC	32:16	$100
14	Malcolm Campbell	Great Britain	32:21	$75
15	Daniel Hughes	Greenville, SC	32:26	$50

Females Overall

1	Olga Romanova	Russia	34:04	$5000
2	Galina Alexandrova	Russia	34:39	$3000
3	Breeda Willi	Ireland	34:52	$1500
4	Tatyana Pozdnyakova	Ukraine	35:34	$1000
5	Donna Anderson	Pawleys Island, SC	35:39	$800
6	Denise Costescu	Wixom, MI	35:42	$600
7	Teresa Wanjiku	Kenya	35:44	$500
8	Ann McGranahan	Newport, VA	35:51	$400
9	Valentina Egorova	Russia	36:12	$300
10	Elena Orlova	Russia	36:35	$250
11	Laura Rhodes	Raleigh, NC	37:11	$200
12	Carre Joyce	Charleston, SC	37:22	$150
13	Genet Gebregiorgia	Ethiopia	38:01	$100
14	Lee DiPietro	Ruxton, MD	38:06	$75
15	Amanda Tate	Bristol, VA	38:14	$50

Male Masters

1	Paul Aufdemberg	Redford, MI	31:32	$1500
2	Dennis Simonaitis	Draper, UT	32:36	$1000
3	Selwyn Blake	Columbia, SC	32:48	$750
4	Tom Mather	Mt Pleasant, SC	32:53	$500
5	David Matherne	Cartersville, GA	34:38	$250

Female Masters

1	Tatyana Pozdnyakova	Ukraine	35:34	$1500
2	Valentina Egorova	Russia	36:12	$1000
3	Lee DiPietro	Ruxton, MD	38:06	$750
4	Maria Spinnier	Hagerstown, MD	39:03	$500
5	Janice Reilly	Cary, NC	39:10	$250

Male Grandmasters

1	Gary Romesser	Indianapolis, IN	36:02	$750
2	Jerry Clark	Charlotte, NC	37:25	$500
3	Wes Wessely	Clermont, GA	39:13	$250

Female Grandmasters

1	Tatyana Pozdnyakova	Ukraine	35:34	$750
2	Debra Wagner	Perrysburg, OH	40:43	$500
3	Catherine Wides	Durham, NC	43:58	$250

Marcus Newberry Award:

First local (Tri-Country) finisher award

Male

Tom Mather . . . Mt Pleasant, SC . . . 32:53 . . . $500

Female

Carre Joyce . . . Charleston, SC . . . 37:22 . . . $500

Dewey Wise Trophy

Oldest finisher with time less than his or her age in minutes:

John Noble, 75 . . . Charleston, SC . . . 69:52

Age division awards

Presented to top 3 in each division. Top 5% awards presented in each division up to a maximum of 25 per division.

Male 12 & Under (173 finishers, 8 awards)

1	Ethan Ruckel	Mt Pleasant, SC	43:30
2	Martin Tiller	Pauline, SC	44:38
3	Ronnie Dennis	Columbia, SC	44:58
4	Dan Bradley	Winston-Salem NC	45:06
5	Trent Carpenter	Conyers, GA	49:48
6	Brandon Wood	Mt Pleasant, SC	50:30
7	Brandon Rhodes	Anderson, SC	51:50
8	Nathan Bourdeau	Summerville, SC	51:52

Female 12 Under (125 finishers, 7 awards)

1	Melissa Fairey	Mt Pleasant SC	50:12
2	Hannah Anderson	Goose Creek SC	50:57
3	Mary Miles Fewell	Greenville CA	56:03
4	Anna Fairey	Mt Pleasant SC	56:23
5	Makenzy Landay	Mt Pleasant SC	56:24
6	Ellen Klimecki	Mt Pleasant SC	57:39
7	Noelle A Blum	Summerville SC	57:44

Male 13 - 17 (468 finishers, 24 awards)

1	Bryan Brooks	W Columbia, SC	36:12
2	Hudson Belk	Charleston, SC	36:23
3	Alan Ford	Huntersville, NC	36:30
4	Dan Wagoner	Moore, SC	37:04
5	Jefferson Waugh	Statesville, NC	37:27
6	Stephen Powell	Fort Mill, SC	37:31
7	Jonathan Stone	Pinehurst, NC	37:32
8	Tyler Dennis	Indianapolis, IN	38:30
9	Andrew King	Anderson, SC	38:37
10	Joey Baldwin	Greer, SC	38:40
11	Christopher Fallis	Awendaw, SC	38:57
12	Samuel Godfrey	Rutherfordton, NC	39:15
13	Stephen Usery	Easley, SC	39:17
14	Jordan Plumblee	Taylors, SC	39:26
15	Taylor Stroud	Spindale, NC	39:34
16	Joshua Fitts	Mt Pleasant, SC	39:58
17	Chris Powell	Fort Mill, SC	40:07
18	Patrick Beckman	Charleston, SC	40:19
19	Adam Romesser	Indianapolis, IN	41:20
20	Robbie Mullen	Charleston, SC	41:44
21	McClain Stoneburner	Avon Lake, OH	42:24
22	Taylor Padgett	Moore, SC	42:26
23	Sam Keesler	Huntersville, NC	42:35
24	Benjamin Griswold	Moore, SC	43:02

Female 13 - 17 (355 finishers, 19 awards)

1	Carey L Phillips	Chesnee, SC	43:46
2	Kimberly Spano	Huntersville , NC	44:51
3	Meghan Kirwan	Mt Pleasant, SC	45:01
4	Stacia Streetman	Greer, SC	45:14
5	Cara Browning	Goose Creek, SC	46:07
6	Katie Anderson	Goose Creek, SC	47:06
7	Danielle Franklin	Greer, SC	47:06
8	Elisabeth Elliott	Tryon, NC	47:40
9	Mary Laurens	Greer, SC	48:52
10	Taylor Harvey	Moore, SC	49:02
11	Harrison Tiller	Pauline, SC	49:04
12	Sarah Williamson	Charlotte, NC	49:08
13	Julie Baldwin	Greer, SC	49:42
14	Jennifer Johnson	Mt Pleasant, SC	49:58
15	Anne Breeden	Spartanburg, SC	50:19
16	Kerry Klimecki	Mt Pleasant, SC	50:23
17	Darla Browning	Goose Creek, SC	50:35
18	Whitney Stanton	Mt Pleasant, SC	50:43
19	Jean Walker	Blythewood, SC	51:05

Male 18 - 21 (436 finishers, 22 awards)

1	Harrison Johnson	Charleston, SC	35:20
2	Matthew Elliott	Green Sea, SC	35:29
3	Ben Sherard	Charleston, SC	35:40
4	Michael Rella	Summerville, SC	35:49
5	Kevin Timp	Chapel Hill, NC	37:01
6	Alex Leveen	Charleston, SC	37:11
7	Todd Laurhridge	Wingate, NC	37:26
8	Stephen Sykes	Spartanburg, SC	37:44
9	Anthony Howard Guy	Mt Pleasant, SC	38:09
10	John-Michael Gerlach	Charleston, SC	38:17
11	George Tozer	Charleston, SC	38:28
12	Brad Topper	Wingate, NC	39:19
13	Ryan Boggs	Seneca, SC	39:35
14	Jordan Lybrand	Greer, SC	39:50
15	Joseph Petraccoro	Brick, NJ	40:01
16	Eric Owensby	Spartanburg, SC	40:07
17	Arnold E Wood	Summerville, SC	40:19
18	Jonathon Black	Rock Hill, SC	40:30
19	Eric Bilbrey	Nashville, TN	40:44
20	Wayne Driscoll	Greenville, SC	41:15
21	James Kimball	Grand Rapids, MI	41:15
22	Ryan Clark	Cincinnati, OH	41:17

Female 18 - 21 (494 finishers, 25 awards)

1	Marcie Milner	Aiken, SC	40:50
2	Lauren Jaynes	Summerville, SC	43:48
3	Mary Claire Utsey	Columbia, SC	44:32
4	Chelsey Wilson	Wingate, NC	45:13
5	Laura Berry	Wingate, NC	45:13
6	Jane Spears	Charleston, SC	45:40
7	Julie Livingston	Mt Pleasant, SC	48:35
8	Karen Porter	Wingate, NC	49:24
9	Katherine Camp	Columbia, SC	49:38
10	Jobeth Schmiesing	Fort Mill, SC	49:58
11	Molly Ball	Charleston, SC	50:09
12	Jameela Johnson	N Charleston, SC	50:19
13	Katherine Stange	Greensboro, NC	50:43
14	Casey Weir	Charleston, SC	51:03
15	Natalie Creech	Wingate, NC	51:26
16	Sarah Carrier	Wingate, NC	51:26
17	Natasha Darwent	Mt Pleasant, SC	51:36
18	Tristan Rackow	Columbia, SC	53:39
19	Anna Kate Clayton	Unknown	53:39
20	Dana Lee Dodds	Simpsonville, SC	54:00
21	Bailey R Reue	Winston-Salem, NC	54:06
22	Stephanie Lyons	Simpsonville, SC	54:18
23	Emily Cupito	Greensboro, NC	54:20
24	Kristy Nix	Charleston, SC	54:36
25	Johanna Lee	Irmo, SC	54:36

Male 22 - 25 (841 finishers, 25 awards)

1	Jason Woolhouse	Lawrence, KS	33:25
2	Kevin Crosby	Matthews, NC	34:07
3	Drew Brannon	Athens, GA	34:49
4	Brooks Keys	Central, SC	35:08
5	Robert Christopher	Charleston, SC	35:58
6	Chris Lamperski	Charlotte, NC	36:26
7	Adam Casseday	Elkins, WV	37:15
8	Jordon David Hoort	Charleston, SC	37:28
9	Andrew Morgan	Mt Pleasant, SC	37:49
10	Michael McCauley	Greenville, SC	38:02
11	Douglas Moody	Charleston, SC	38:07
12	Dana Homer	Lexington, SC	38:26
13	Matt Terrio	Florence, SC	38:28
14	David Jirousek	Beaufort, SC	38:36
15	Josh Myers	Cochran, GA	38:50
16	Kyle Rusthoven	Atlanta, GA	39:19
17	Michael Griffin	Goose Creek, SC	39:46
18	William Leppard	Charleston, SC	39:54
19	John Blevins	Mt Pleasant, SC	40:29
20	Brett Mclane	Lake Wylie, SC	41:11
21	Mark Tibshrany	Columbia, SC	41:49
22	Brent Francese	Stanley, NC	42:10
23	Michael Whitley	Oakboro, NC	42:12
24	Trevor Douglas	Charleston, SC	42:39
25	Michael Arrigo	Raleigh, NC	42:59

Female 22 - 25 (1,260 finishers, 25 awards)

1	Emily Johnson	Johns Island, SC	41:40
2	Heather Nichols	Mt Pleasant, SC	41:55
3	Kinsey Eschenburg	Mt Pleasant, SC	42:54
4	Emily Campbell	Greensboro, NC	43:25
5	Kathryn Cavanaugh	Columbia, SC	43:35
6	Bethany Harry	Winston-Salem, NC	43:36
7	Jackie Seibert	Roswell, GA	43:44
8	Meghann Gardner	New York, NY	45:00
9	Meredith Spears	Lillington, NC	45:20
10	April Coldiron	Lexington, KY	46:18
11	Stephanie Stalnaker	Charleston, SC	46:25
12	Kory Thompson	Columbia, SC	47:14
13	Jennifer Warolin	Charleston, SC	47:43
14	Lee Bugay	Lexington, SC	47:51
15	Katherine Ticknor	Greer, SC	48:12
16	Emiline Fricke	Charleston, SC	49:11
17	Michelle Keel	Marietta, GA	49:13
18	Tiffany Fore	Columbia, SC	49:27
19	Meredith Evans	Charleston, SC	49:42
20	Katherine Clarke	Martinez, GA	49:56
21	Becky Lynn Witkop	Charleston, SC	50:05
22	Kristen Champion	Charleston, SC	50:09
23	Ruberta McCue	Charleston, SC	50:27
24	Stephanie Miller	Chapel Hill, NC	50:35
25	Kim Weselak	Charleston, SC	50:37

Male 26 - 29 (1,158 finishers, 25 awards)

1	Brian Johnson	Johns Island, SC	32:55
2	Orinthal Striggles	Elgin, SC	34:04
3	Aaron Bowman	Mcleansville, NC	34:13
4	Mike Aiken	Charleston, SC	34:19
5	Karl Walsh	Mt Pleasant, SC	35:23
6	Jason Putnam	Anderson, SC	35:52
7	Elijah Shekinah	Knoxville, TN	36:03
8	Blake Benke	Emerald Isle, NC	36:08
9	Patrick Shaw	Buies Creek, NC	36:08
10	Shawn Donovan	Charleston, SC	36:36
11	David Lee, Jr	Charleston, SC	36:46
12	Philipp Rittershaus	Charleston, SC	36:55
13	Travis Brady	Spartanburg, SC	37:02
14	Andy Keel	Marietta, GA	37:16
15	Jeremy Becraft	Mt Pleasant, SC	37:20
16	Kurt Wilson	Candler, NC	37:21
17	Chris Jones	Davidson, NC	37:35
18	Chad Brittingham	Charleston, SC	37:56
19	Lee Kain	N Charleston, SC	37:56
20	Sims Key	Clemson, SC	38:09

– Continued on next page

2005 Awards, continued from page 223

21	Russel Drylie	Cockeysville, MD	38:18
22	Andrew Goodwin	Taylors, SC	38:39
23	Bobby Wilder	Myrtle Beach, SC	38:39
24	Charlie Epperson	Wrightsville, NC	38:44
25	Tommy Boles	Greensboro, NC	38:47

Female 26 - 29 (1,203 finishers, 25 awards)

1	Megan Weis	Columbia, SC	38:41
2	Shannon Schoppman	Greenville, SC	38:54
3	Laurie Knowles	Atlanta, GA	38:58
4	Farrell Hudzik	Charlotte, NC	39:01
5	Maryshell Zaffino	Mt Pleasant, SC	41:28
6	Sara M Jenkins	Elgin, SC	42:19
7	Elizabeth Weaver	Charlotte, NC	43:21
8	Dana Hayden	Mt Pleasant, SC	43:56
9	Rachelle Tomlin	Columbia, SC	44:31
10	Rives Poe	Mt Pleasant, SC	44:42
11	Shontel Jung	Asheville, NC	45:03
12	Isabel Ghowanlu	Charleston, SC	45:06
13	Holly Munnis	Charleston, SC	45:40
14	Sarah Wilde	Chapel Hill, NC	45:59
15	Andrea Pietras	Charleston, SC	46:12
16	Heidi Broerman	Greer, SC	46:35
17	Ginny Carson	Charleston, SC	47:22
18	Margaret Florence	New York, NY	47:40
19	Jennifer Martin	Alpharetta, GA	48:11
20	Kimberley Patterson	Jacksonville, FL	48:13
21	Blake Ellis	Charleston, SC	48:19
22	Curry Smoak	Rockville, SC	48:27
23	Molly Hughes	Charlotte, NC	48:47
24	Allison Gordon	Winston-Salem, NC	48:54
25	Lauren Carr	Charlotte, NC	48:56

Male 30 - 34 (1,465 finishers, 25 awards)

1	Justin Lee Ratike	Tega Cay, SC	34:18
2	Conrad Hall	Durham, NC	34:53
3	Jason Annan	Chapel Hill, NC	35:09
4	Jason Philbin	Charlotte, NC	36:38
5	Richard Cooney	Waxhaw, NC	36:47
6	Roger Fagala	Blenheim, SC	37:02
7	Bradley Fowler	Winston-Salem, NC	37:25
8	Alan Black	Hillsboro, GA	37:42
9	Brad Schneider	Charleston, SC	37:42
10	Thomas Walls	Fort Mill, SC	37:44
11	Roberto Quiroga	Bluffton, SC	38:03
12	Derrick Stamey	Huntersville, NC	38:04
13	Gerald Griffitts	Hartsville, SC	38:08
14	Carl Buckner	Charleston, SC	38:09
15	Mark Harrell	Raleigh, NC	38:25
16	Ladd Lumpkin	Columbia, SC	38:46
17	Matt Pryor	Greenville, SC	38:52
18	Jimmy Major	Chapin, SC	39:00
19	Kevin Kelly	Charlotte, NC	39:41
20	Ryan Rybolt	Cincinnati, OH	40:03
21	Anthony Goldman	Charleston, SC	40:06
22	Jason Farmer	Greenville, SC	40:11
23	David Rogers	Charleston, SC	40:14
24	Scott Putnam	Knoxville, TN	40:25
25	Robert Matthews	Columbia, SC	40:37

Female 30 - 34 (1,356 finishers, 25 awards)

1	Anne-Wyman Cipolla	Charleston, SC	38:45
2	Rebecca Crowder	Charlotte, NC	39:30
3	Charlotte Thomason	Charlotte, NC	40:44
4	Karen Gillespie	Greenville, SC	40:55
5	Amanda Charlton	Columbia, SC	41:07
6	Carol Brunson	Spartanburg, SC	41:59
7	Jennifer Lepori	Maywood, NJ	42:36
8	Debra Brown	Mt Pleasant, SC	43:50
9	Linda Beth Wood	Seabrook, SC	44:10
10	Janet Regnier	Daniel Island, SC	44:30
11	Meghan Schwartz	Marblehead, MA	44:46
12	Carey Cochran	Charleston, SC	45:07
13	Stephanie Gross	Charlotte, NC	45:11
14	Stephanie Miller	Charlotte, NC	45:40
15	Jennifer Jensen	Providence, RI	45:58
16	Ruth Straley	Charlotte, NC	46:16
17	Tracy Foss	Greer, SC	46:28
18	Rosemary Ferguson	Cornelius, NC	46:36
19	Shannon Iriel	Mt Pleasant, SC	46:38
20	Karin Linner	Brooklyn, NY	46:45
21	Megan Parrott	Simpsonville, SC	46:51
22	Rachel Gammel	Georgetown, SC	47:07
23	Jennifer Wilkinson	Huntersville, NC	47:31
24	Amy Nelson	Mt Pleasant, SC	47:39
25	Lynn Cecil	Rock Hill, SC	47:57

Male 35 - 39 (1,384 finishers, 25 awards)

1	David Honea	Boone, NC	33:49
2	John Charlton	Columbia, SC	34:46
3	Robert Benjamin	Chapel Hill, NC	34:48
4	Eric Vandervort	Clinton, TN	34:58
5	Rob Anderson	Summerville, SC	36:04
6	Darol Timberlake	Matthews, NC	36:28
7	Kristian Blaich	Decatur, GA	36:35
8	Ben Cheek	McPherson, KS	36:38
9	Pat McCallion	Greer, SC	37:17
10	Michael Haranzo	Beaverton, OR	37:29
11	Sean Killeen	Richmond, VA	37:57
12	Martin Guthrie	Wallace, NC	38:05
13	Daniel Kehoe	Atlanta, GA	38:09
14	Chris Hicks	Florence, SC	38:41
15	Emery Lloyd	Moncks Corner, SC	38:44
16	Michael Cipolla	Charleston, SC	38:51
17	Timothy T Tenne	Mt Pleasant, SC	38:52
18	Jim Daniel	Mt Pleasant, SC	39:14
19	Corbett Thomason	Charlotte, NC	39:17
20	Greg Brown	Mt Pleasant, SC	39:25
21	Glenn Douglas	Nashville, TN	39:36
22	John Riordan	Charleston, SC	39:37
23	Chris Egger	Wilmington, NC	39:39
24	Karl Johnson	Spartanburg, SC	39:48
25	Cliff McHenry	Mooresville, NC	40:02

Female 35 - 39 (1,042 finishers, 25 awards)

1	Carla Pinkerton	N Wilkesboro, NC	40:01
2	Lisa Tolley	Seneca, SC	41:12
3	Saundi Theodossiou	Asheville, NC	41:16
4	Molly Achille	Greenville, SC	44:22
5	Keely Churchill	Raleigh, NC	44:43
6	Rachel Cooter	Greenville, SC	45:28
7	Mijanou Spurdle	Miami Beach, FL	45:37
8	Karen Killeen	Richmond, VA	45:38
9	Catherine Mirando	Greenville, SC	46:21
10	Laura Dechamplain	Georgetown, SC	46:26
11	Lana Torkildsen	Matthews, NC	46:28
12	Hannah Mo Dodson	Sullivans Isl, SC	46:53
13	Kim Blankenbeckler	Lexington, SC	47:10
14	Diane Lancaster	Unknown, NC	47:20
15	Sharryn Whitmore	Mt Pleasant, SC	47:25
16	Cyndy Dail	Mt Pleasant, SC	47:32
17	Stacey Johnson	Isle of Palms, SC	47:36
18	Carol Hauss	Salisbury, NC	48:00
19	Maria Lipsitz	Columbia, SC	48:46
20	Melissa Coleman	Mt Pleasant, SC	48:53
21	Gezelle Macon	Seagrove, NC	48:54
22	Patricia Johnson	Asheville, NC	49:05
23	Liesl Hintz	Mauldin, SC	49:30
24	Sunnie McGonigal	N Myrtle Beach, SC	49:33
25	Anna Calkins	Raleigh, NC	49:39

Male 40 - 44 (1,197 finishers, 25 awards)

1	Angel Roman	Garden Grove, CA	35:08
2	John Anderson	Moore, SC	36:56
3	Paul Holyko	Daytona Beach, FL	37:12
4	Eric Ruckel	Mt Pleasant, SC	37:27
5	David Quick	Mt Pleasant, SC	37:31
6	Michael Parker	Goose Creek, SC	37:47
7	Lance Leopold	Simpsonville, SC	38:03
8	Pierre-Yves Page	Greenville, SC	38:06
9	Allen Acken	Charlotte, NC	38:28
10	Bobby Aswell	Cornelius, NC	38:57
11	Kevin Barry	Shelter Island, NY	39:50
12	Christopher Spano	Huntersville, NC	39:51
13	Stephen Morrell	Arlington, VA	40:02
14	James McDaid	Charlotte, NC	40:13
15	Peter Esser	Summerville, SC	40:16
16	Jim Bitsko	Doraville, GA	40:36
17	Chris Handal	Charleston, SC	40:37
18	Bratton Fennell	Mt Pleasant, SC	40:38
19	Richard Stephens	Summerville, SC	40:39
20	Michael O'Hara	Summerville, SC	40:47
21	William Macy	Statesville, NC	40:53
22	Dwayne Hellard	Raleigh, NC	40:54
23	Huey Inman	Mt Pleasant, SC	40:55
24	Rob Newton	Mooresville, NC	40:56
25	Barrett Kitch	Belmont, MA	41:08

Female 40 - 44 (878 finishers, 25 awards)

1	Sheila Wakeman	Cornelius, NC	39:24
2	Laura Vroon	Wyoming, MI	40:37
3	Mary Dore	Charlotte, NC	40:52
4	Susan Rogers	Spartanburg, SC	40:57
5	Betsy Veronee	Charleston, SC	43:30
6	Michelle Beaulieu	Summerville, SC	43:37
7	Patt Loggins	Charleston, SC	43:48
8	Kelly Hazel	Summerville, SC	44:01
9	Suanne Hall	Greenville, SC	44:04
10	Lisa Powell	Columbia, SC	44:16
11	Christi Craft	Simpsonville, SC	44:40
12	Inga Sullivan	Mt Pleasant, SC	46:13
13	Donna D Robinson	Hartsville, SC	46:52
14	Beth Cavanaugh	Sullivans Isl, SC	47:17
15	Beth Pierpont	Charlotte, NC	47:22
16	Lynne Elliott	Summerville, SC	48:47
17	Janice Sides	Concord, NC	49:09
18	Martha Armstrong	Asheville, NC	49:14
19	Susan McKee	Charlotte, NC	49:27
20	Linda Serkiz	Aiken, SC	50:08
21	Kerrie Sijon	Greer, SC	50:11
22	Amy Sue Pearson	Mt Pleasant, SC	50:53
23	Susan Whitman	Orangeburg, SC	51:16
24	Michele Moore	Tallulah Falls, GA	51:19
25	Karen Clark	Jericho, VT	51:29

Male 45 - 49 (1,014 finishers, 25 awards)

1	Mark Friedrich	Isle of Palms, SC	37:24
2	Mike Hart	Washington, DC	37:36
3	Tim Dunlap	Lancaster, PA	37:42
4	David Renneisen	Goose Creek, SC	37:59
5	David Bourgeois	Summerville, SC	38:27
6	Billy Tisdale	Sumter, SC	38:42
7	Alan Blackwell	Moore, SC	38:52
8	Marc Embler	Summerville, SC	39:28
9	George Dunleavy	Mt Pleasant, SC	39:42
10	Alfie Cronin	Decatur, GA	39:47
11	Richard Keating	Milford, NH	39:47
12	James Wilhelm	Canton, OH	39:48
13	Gerald Hutchinson	Charlotte, NC	39:52
14	Andrew Ammon	Statesville, NC	39:56
15	James Scheer	Charleston, SC	39:58
16	Lennie Moore	Mt Pleasant, SC	39:58
17	Derek Appleton	Cornelius, NC	40:56
18	Clyde Sanders	Beaufort, SC	41:10
19	Gary Wayne Edwards	Goose Creek, SC	41:12
20	Frank Storniolu	Gainesville, GA	41:44
21	Jeff Armstrong	Talbott, TN	41:51
22	Jim Fann	Charleston, SC	42:06
23	Bill Ehrhorn	Florence, SC	42:23
24	Michael Wilson	Winston-Salem, NC	42:23
25	George Sykes	Spartanburg, SC	42:30

Female 45 - 49 (643 finishers, 25 awards)

1	Janice Addison	Columbia, SC	39:50
2	Darla Bennett	Mt Dora, FL	45:21
3	Kathy Abernethy	Matthews, NC	45:44
4	Laurie Will	Charlotte, NC	45:59
5	Kay Sanborn	Huntersville, NC	46:16
6	Nancy Thomas	Mt Pleasant, SC	46:36
7	Pam Hood Drafts	Beaufort, SC	46:58
8	Tami Dennis	Isle Of Palms, SC	47:05
9	Trudy Carolyn Gale	Salisbury, NC	48:26
10	Adele Mecionis	Sumter, SC	49:21
11	Sue Jane Porter	Columbia, SC	50:05
12	Tammy Hovik	Jonestown, TX	50:09
13	Colleen Adams	Daniel Island, SC	50:22
14	Barbara Edwards	Chesapeake, VA	50:36
15	Nicki Hutchens	Collierville, TN	50:39
16	Dell Toomer	Unknown, SC	50:49
17	Joan Cleary	Florence, SC	51:29
18	Nancy Flynn Sanders	Dillon, SC	51:39
19	Jane Godwin	Greer, SC	52:10
20	Lucy Hawk Banks	Holden, MA	52:14
21	Carla McGinty	Concord, NC	52:15
22	Linda Fairey	Mt Pleasant, SC	53:08
23	Constance Caldwell	Winston-Salem, NC	53:15
24	Eileen Myers	Nashville, TN	53:32
25	Bunny Deas Hicks	Columbia, SC	53:55

Male 50 - 54 (873 finishers, 25 awards)

1	Jack Todd	Spartanburg, SC	39:29
2	David Forrest	Charlotte, NC	39:30
3	Larry Milner	Aiken, SC	39:53
4	Harold Fallis	Awendaw, SC	40:55
5	Jim Freid	Tega Cay, SC	41:00
6	Paul Smith	Greer, SC	41:03
7	Dan Clapper	N Charleston, SC	41:14
8	Wayne Foster	Burlington, NC	41:38
9	Barry Schniderman	Mt Pleasant, SC	42:02
10	Bradley Matthiesen	Madison, WI	42:33
11	Richard King	Anderson, SC	42:42
12	David Branner	Tupelo, MS	42:48
13	Greg Price	Horseshoe, NC	43:10
14	Patrick Gannon	Mt Pleasant, SC	43:24
15	George Henehan	Chapel Hill, NC	43:37

16	Vasan Neovakul	Atlanta, GA	43:41
17	Billy Hardin	Chapin, SC	44:05
18	Samuel Jenkins	N Charleston, SC	44:37
19	Joseph Mazurkiewicz	Conway, SC	44:41
20	Gabriel Lugo	Wilmington, NC	44:44
21	J J Anderson	Charleston, SC	44:51
22	Richard Jacques	Greenville, SC	45:02
23	Eddie Muldrow	Chapin, SC	45:10
24	Bob Barrett	Florence, SC	45:13
25	Vincent Pastore	Mooresville, NC	45:15

Female 50 - 54 (429 finishers, 22 awards)
1	Sarah Ball	Charleston, SC	45:22
2	Catherine Lempesis	Irmo, SC	45:37
3	Toni Cruz	Concord, SC	45:53
4	Michelle Withers	Charlotte, NC	47:09
5	Mimi Sturgell	Kiawah Island, SC	48:01
6	Debbie Howard	Mt Pleasant, SC	48:06
7	Sallie Driggers	Hanahan, SC	48:56
8	Glenda Chapman	Kingsport, TN	50:01
9	Therese Killeen	Isle of Palms, SC	50:20
10	Cathy Burton	Isle of Palms, SC	50:47
11	Judy Osborn	Charlotte, NC	51:08
12	Mary Howk	Columbia, SC	51:09
13	Jo Haubenreiser	Kernersville, NC	51:37
14	Terry Maluk	Easley, SC	51:43
15	Judith Stanton	Aiken, SC	52:23
16	Nitsa Calas	N Charleston, SC	52:27
17	Sharon Allen	Charlotte, NC	54:45
18	Carol Goehring	Greenville, NC	54:56
19	Janice Wilkins	Greenville, SC	55:07
20	Marty Smith	Greenville, SC	55:09
21	Linda Eckstrom	Columbia, SC	55:58
22	Kristine Cuprys	Perrysburg, OH	56:51

Male 55 - 59 (635 finishers, 25 awards)
1	John Rinker	Decatur, GA	40:01
2	Donald Brown	Unknown	41:30
3	James Horne	Taylors, SC	43:52
4	Steve Annan	Mt Pleasant, SC	43:53
5	Chuck Greer	Charleston, SC	44:16
6	Jan Hardwick	Dillon, SC	44:39
7	James Rich	Asheboro, NC	44:52
8	Mackie Johnson	Conover, NC	44:52
9	Glenn Dennis	Raleigh, NC	45:31
10	Linny Moore	Greer, SC	46:46
11	William Anderson	Wadmalaw Isl, SC	46:51
12	Don Whelchel	Charlotte, NC	47:15
13	Roger Arthur	Red House, WV	47:40
14	Terry Murphy	Dansville, NY	48:12
15	Hoot Gibson	Folly Beach, SC	48:18
16	John Johnson	Greenville, SC	48:21
17	Robert Schlau	Charleston, SC	48:38
18	Alan Shufelt	Spartanburg, SC	48:40
19	Gary Richardson	Greensboro, NC	48:53
20	Larry Butler	Fletcher, NC	48:57
21	James Lynn	Easley, SC	49:19
22	Bruce Snow	Lexington, SC	49:26
23	Robert Lee	Charleston, SC	49:51
24	Tony Hill	High Point, NC	50:02
25	Roddy Whitaker	Swansea, SC	50:19

Female 55 - 59 (210 finishers, 11 awards)
1	Lyn Hammond	Charleston, SC	49:45
2	Kathy Seavers	Charlotte, NC	49:47
3	Betty Ryberg	Aiken, SC	51:12
4	Gail Bailey	Charleston, SC	52:41
5	Anne Boone	Hollywood, SC	53:23
6	Marlene McCraw	King, NC	54:28
7	Brenda Cooter	Grovetown, GA	54:49
8	Lucy Hinson	Greenville, SC	55:08
9	Kari Sprecher	F?, VA	57:13
10	Judy Gilman	McClellanville, SC	58:33
11	Brenda Bishop	Charlotte, NC	59:01

Male 60 - 64 (345 finishers, 18 awards)
1	Russ Brown	Midway, GA	44:08
2	Dick Ashley	Myrtle Beach, SC	46:49
3	Don Perkins	Snellville, GA	47:56
4	Richard Landsman	Summerville, SC	48:18
5	Keith Ambrose	Mt Pleasant, SC	48:31
6	John Sneed	Mt Pleasant, SC	48:40
7	Eric Elbel, Sr	Marietta, GA	48:59
8	Larry Crosby	Anderson, SC	49:26
9	Elbert Howard	Jamestown, SC	49:42
10	Ralph Ogden	Mt Pleasant, SC	49:55
11	Phil Mead	Edisto Beach, SC	51:04
12	Thomas Dority	Charleston, SC	51:25
13	James Troknya	Perrysburg, OH	51:53
14	Patrick Morgan	Clemson, SC	52:19
15	Harry Peeples	Summerville, SC	52:26
16	George Geils	Charleston, SC	52:59
17	Rex McNeely	Yonges Island, SC	53:08
18	Thomas Eberhardt	Roswell, GA	53:24

Female 60 - 64 (95 finishers, 5 awards)
1	Sissy Logan	Salem, VA	53:48
2	Joan Mulvihill	Charleston, SC	54:11
3	Kay Chandler	Isle of Palms, SC	58:31
4	Barbara Lindeman	Oregon, OH	58:50
5	Barbara Avant	Boone, NC	1:00:51

Male 65 - 69 (118 finishers, 6 awards)
1	George Luke	Greenville, SC	42:35
2	Norman Hankins	Jonesborough, TN	45:20
3	Harvey McCormick	Charleston, SC	47:04
4	James Adams	N Augusta, SC	49:37
5	Gil Gilmore	Perrysburg, OH	50:30
6	Clyde Mizzell	Charleston, SC	51:47

Female 65 - 69 (27 finishers, 4 awards)
1	E. K. Tolley-Beeson	Sumter, SC	1:04:50
2	Faye Davis	Mt Pleasant, SC	1:06:08
3	Carole McCrary	Charleston, SC	1:08:34
4	Pat Rhode	Walterboro, SC	1:12:59

Male 70 - 74 (30 finishers, 3 awards)
1	Gordon Peoples	Greensboro, NC	50:50
2	Jim Wilson	Anderson, SC	59:59
3	Ken Walls	Mt Pleasant, SC	1:00:47

Female 70 - 74 (15 finishers, 3 Awards)
1	Mary Purvis	Charlotte, NC	55:37
2	Jane Gregorie	Yemassee, SC	1:15:56
3	Camille Daniel	Summerville, SC	1:16:17

Male 75 - 79 (14 finishers, 3 Awards)
1	William Boulter	Charleston, SC	51:50
2	Lonnie Collins	Gilbert, SC	55:58
3	Dick Mandell	Columbia, SC	1:04:18

Female 75 - 79 (2 finishers, 3 Awards)
| 1 | Garthedon Embler | Isle of Palms, SC | 1:39:53 |
| 2 | Ola Moody | Augusta, GA | 1:43:18 |

Male 80 - 98 (3 finishers, 3 Awards)
1	David Mellard	N. Charleston, SC	1:23:00
2	Franklin Mason	Mullins, SC	1:37:46
3	Leroy Miller	N Charleston, SC	2:29:55

Female 80 - 98 (2 finishers, 3 Awards)
| 1 | Eleanor Jerdan | Irvine, CA | 1:32:55 |
| 2 | Mary Canty | Orlando, FL | 1:40:24 |

Compiled by Cedric Jaggers from complete results provided by Burns Computer Services on April 2, 2005.

Post and Courier photo by Grace Beahm

A ship named "Charleston" makes its way under the new Ravenel bridge after passing the demolition of the old bridges. Post and Courier photo by Mic Smith

Chapter 29

2006
First Race On New Ravenel Bridge Draws Record 33,742 Finishers

The new era for the Bridge Run began at 8 a.m. on April 1, 2006, as the 29th Cooper River Bridge Run got underway. This was the first year the race crossed the new, larger, higher $620 million Arthur Ravenel Jr. Bridge.

The 28 previous races had been run over one of two old bridges. The Silas Pearman Bridge was used for the first two races and from 1995 through 2005, while the other years the race was run over the older two-lane Grace Memorial Bridge. Both of the older bridges were in the process of being torn down due to completion of the new span.

In the new era for the "first Bridge Run" as some people were calling it, record numbers of runners and walkers signed up. In 2006, for the first time, the walkers started behind the runners, completed the entire course and were timed. This resulted in a record number of combined total entrants: 45,497. The *Post and Courier* had a front page headline "Running the Ravenel" since runners were crossing the Ravenel Bridge for the first time.

The new USATF Certified Course #SC05039BS moved the starting line in Mount Pleasant near Moultrie Middle School. Runners had a near flat first mile and then began climbing over the new Ravenel Bridge. Runners took the Meeting Street ramp and went towards downtown to John Street where a right turn took them on to King Street where they turned left. The next turn was at Wentworth Street where runners reached the 6-mile mark, then made another left to Meeting Street where the final left turn was made. The new finish line was just south of George Street.

Conditions for the race were not ideal as the 83 percent humidity made the 65-degree starting time temperature seem much warmer. There was also a steady 10 to 15 mile per hour quartering headwind which made crossing the new bridge more difficult than expected. There was also the difficulty factor of the mile-long, 4 percent uphill grade on the bridge. Course records had been predicted for the first race on the new bridge, but none came about. In fact, after the race many runners talked about their times being slower than expected.

Despite conditions, there were a record number of finishers: 33,742 (15,461 male and 18,135 female and 82 who did not indicate their sex). This was the first time in race history that female finishers outnumbered males. For the second year in a row, timing was done using a special commemorative ChampionChip computer timing chip displaying the same design as the race T-shirt. The runners were allowed to keep the chip and this meant they did not have to stop after crossing the finish line and remove it.

The race again belonged to Kenyan men as they took the first nine places. Ten of the top 15 (prize money) finishers were Kenyan. After a 4:19 first mile, a pack of runners ran together to the new bridge, then the separation began. When the runners came off the bridge it was a two-man race between Sammy Kipketer and Abraham Chebii. Chebii probably was well aware that Kipketer held the road race 5K world record so he wanted to get away from him and not have the race decided by a sprint. Each time he would pull away, Chebii would pull back even. Kipketer mistook a race banner for the finish line and began his sprint before the final two turns and the 6-mile mark. When he slowed and Chebii caught him they turned the corner and came to the 6-mile mark. Chebii turned on his sprint and kicked away to win 28:16 to 28:35. "I looked overhead and thought I saw the finish line," he told the *Post and Courier*. "I sprinted too soon." Third place went to Julius Koskie in 28:52 and fourth place to Shadrack Kosgei in 29:01. Defending champion Linus Maiyo finished fifth in 29:08.

Sally Barsosio returned Kenyan women to the winner's circle after a one-year absence. She won in 33:35, edging Russians Tatiana Chulakh 33:40 and Lyubov Denisova in 33:52. This was the sixth time Barsosio had run the race. She had won for the first time in 2004 after finishing second in four earlier attempts. "The course is very different," she told the *Post and Courier*, "and it is still very difficult. The hill was hard and another hard thing was the wind. It was very windy today."

About racing over the new bridge, she said, "I really didn't know what to expect because of the new hill. The course was different. There wasn't two hills like in the past. I didn't know how the other runners would plan their strategy."

She liked the view from the bridge, saying "I enjoyed it. I got off to a good start and the competition was behind me. I was hot, but oh, I feel good. I've been here several times and finished either 1 or 2. I feel at home here."

Master's winner was Albert Okema of Kenya in 31:20 while new Zealand's Sean Wade was second in 31:47 with Phillip Walkins of Coconut Creek, Fla., third in 32:42. Ukranian Tatyana Pozknyakova again defended her female Masters title taking her third title in a row, this year in 35:16, edging Russian Lyubov Kremleva, who ran 35:18.

"It is a very nice new bridge," she said. "It was a little bit harder than last year because of the such strong wind. Going up and down twice (as on the old bridge) might be good for the legs, but I enjoyed this one more. I'm tired after I run, but it was a good day for me." Sheila Wakeman of Cornelius, N.C., was third in 39:51.

Grand Masters winner for the sixth year in a row was Gary Romesser of Indianapolis, Ind., who ran 34:30; former Charlestonian Mike Hart, now of Washington, D.C., was second in 37:18. For the second year in a row Tatyana Pozdnyakova of Ukraine doubled up by taking Grand Masters and Masters prize money. This year she broke her own year old record to set a new female Grand Masters course record 35:16. Debra Wagner of Perrysburg, Ohio, was runner-up for the second year in a row, this time in 41:01. Dian Ford of Piedmont, S.C., was third in 41:14.

The race added an official wheelchair division in 2006. Tyler Byers of Reston, Va., was first of the eight finishers in 26:43.

The award for the first finisher from the Tri-County is named for race founder Dr. Marcus Newberry. Mount Pleasant resident Neil McDonagh was 16th overall to win it in 31:38. It was the first time he had run the Bridge Run. "It was tough," he told the *Post and Courier*. "I figured we'd get a little bit of a break coming downhill on the bridge, but the wind was still in our face. It wasn't even that helpful. It's a nice downhill, but with the wind in your face it's still tough."

Anne Wyman Cipolla of Charleston was the 19th female finisher and first local in 39:02. She said she was "definitely happy to win." She added about the new course, "It was very tough, but it was fun. The hill killed me. It's longer. You are going uphill so long." The Dewey Wise Trophy was won by David Mellard, 83, of North Charleston for his time of 80:50.

A water main break could have created a major water supply problem for the running of the race. Race director Julian Smith was called at about midnight and told that due to the break there would be no water from the spigots used every year during the race. He ordered 70,000 extra bottles of water to go along with the 80,000 already ordered. It worked, as runners had no problem getting water during and after the race.

For the fourth year in a row live television coverage was broadcast on Channel 5. The two-hour broadcast was shown again on Sunday evening.

Seven runners (all male) broke the 30-minute barrier with three of them under 29 minutes. A total of 262 runners broke the 40-minute barrier: 234 male and 28 female. There were 1,884 runners who crossed the finish line under 50 minutes. Despite the record number of finishers, only the third largest number of participants finished in under an hour: 6,767, a new low of 20 percent of the total who finished. Of course, this was due to timing the walkers for the first time, since in the past they had been untimed and uncounted.

The *Post and Courier* published the names and times of the 12,180 male and 10,426 female competitors who crossed the finish line in 1:45:00 or faster in the Sunday, April 2, edition. The paper also showed the top five finishers in each group, though it erroneously included the prize winners (who were excluded from the age groups) in the age group awards list. Complete results were later mailed to all finishers.

The race entry fee was $25 for early race registration, and $30 after March 11. This meant the entry fee for runners remained the same, but was an increase of $10 in each category for walkers who were being timed and included in the official race results for the first time. Julian Smith was again the race director.

The 2006 Hall of Fame inductees included the mayors or former mayors of the cities that helped sponsor and support the race: Charleston Mayor Joe Riley, Mount Pleasant Mayor Harry Hallman and former Mount Pleasant Mayor Cheryll Woods-Flowers. Other inductees were: the only local overall winner of the Bridge

Run (1981), Marc Embler; longtime endurance athletes and fitness advocates Cadwallader "Quaddy" Jones and Lucy Jones; and former Bridge Run Chairman John Smyth, who was also the former director of the U.S. Olympic Training Centers.

Other voices
Tell Me About Your Bridge Run 2006

By Cedric Jaggers. Originally appeared in the May-June 2006 Low Country Runner

(Bridge Run info for 2006 – 33,678 largest number of official finishers, 45,663 largest number of entrants to date. Start time temperature 65 degrees.)

Another Bridge Run, but wait, not the same old same old. The first time over the new, really new, Arthur Ravenel Bridge; but the more things change, the more they stay the same. Seems like we were talking about it in Marion Square again instead of that field at the end of Calhoun Street. Having the roped off Charleston Running Club area made it easier for me to find club members this year – I just talked to the people with the purple club armbands inside the area. Got more folks this year as a result, missed a few however, and if you were one of them – sorry – catch me next year. As I have since the '80s when I first started doing this, I asked each runner to "Tell Me About Your Bridge Run" and tried to write down exactly what each person said. Everyone is listed in the order I talked to them. I added the overall place and official gun and chip times and awards placement.

Female runnerup Tatyana Chulakh. Post and Courier photo by Sarah Bates

Lyn Hammond: It was tough. About 51 minutes. 2,221st place overall, gun time 51:13, top 5% 55-59 a.g. award, chip time 51:04.

Jeffrey Herndon: When I was about 5 miles and saw Cedric I knew I was having a great day. I thought it was easier. 54:37. 3,334th place overall, gun time 54:37, chip time 54:11.

Pat Rhode: It wasn't as bad as I thought. I didn't feel the Bridge move. I wasn't as slow as I thought; I'm glad to be over it. 1:07. 9,925th place overall, gun time 1:07:07, chip time 1:06:20, 3rd 65-69 a.g. award.

Joanne Herndon: It was ... well ... I just wasn't ready for it. I did worse than last year I think. I don't think I was prepared. I've had some problems with my running the past few weeks. I'm glad I did it. 1:04:10. 8,655th place overall, gun time 1:04:59, chip time 1:04:11.

Anne Boone: Well I walked about 6 times going up the incline I haven't been training worth a doodle. I loved the end. It was so hot. I've just been jogging around out in the country. Ran about 56 minutes. 4,015th place overall, gun time 56:25, chip time 56:00, top 5% 55-59 a.g. award.

Glen Dennis: Good run. I felt good. Running with a stress fracture of the foot – a stress fracture of the brain. You inspire me. I read your articles, got out there and trained hard. 39:31. 220th place overall, gun time 39:32, chip time 39:29, 1st 55-59 a.g. award.

Joan Mulvihill: Great day, good run. I miss racing Kathy. Same time as last year. I lost 4 pounds, worked hard to get that time. 54:20. 3,258th place overall, gun time 54:25, chip time 53:56, top 5% 60-64 a.g. award.

Palmer Thomas: It was good place wise, slow time wise. You know the course will be fast with so much downhill – if we get a day with a tailwind. Ran a 5:06 first mile trying to hold back. Ran 33:20 something – not satisfied with it. 29th place overall, gun time 33:24, chip time 33:23, 2nd 26-29 a.g. award.

Carol Thomason: After the climb it was just a great run. What can you say? I think they did a real good job with volunteers this year. 1 hour 2 minutes. I'm sad about that, but that's okay. 7,350th place overall, gun time 1:02:41, chip time 1:04:45, top 5% 60-64 a.g. award.

Huey Inman: I broke 38 minutes and that was my goal. 37:55 or something. With 3 kids, coaching basketball and baseball I just do the best I can. 146th place overall, gun time 37:55, chip time 37:52, top 5% 45-49 a.g. award.

Therese Killeen: (Made faces and wouldn't say anything until I threatened to write down a description of the faces she was making. CJ) Well, I have an injury so I jogged it. I did it slow and nice and got to enjoy the new bridge. I didn't get overheated like I usually do. Ran about 55 minutes. 3,569th place overall, gun time 55:14, chip time 54:37, top 5% 50-54 a.g. award.

Mike Chodnicki: Drove the lead truck again this year, another smooth year. It's amazing to watch those guys – the Kenyans. Enjoyed the heck out of it. (Truck time 28 minutes?)

Marc Embler: I did okay. Went out too quick in 5:23. Finished 36:40s. My legs just haven't responded since I ran a half marathon in February. I had hoped to break 36. I never recovered on the downhill. 96th place overall, gun time 36:48, chip time 36:48, top 5% 45-49 a.g. award.

Turner Boone: I didn't run what I wanted to do. Thought I'd feel better coming down the bridge, but it never felt better. The wind didn't help either. Ran 38:48. 181st place overall, gun time 38:48, chip time 38:47.

Jan Embler: I did kind of a jog walk. My first time over the new Bridge. I've had 5 back surgeries and I was just glad to do it without pain. 1:26:06. 20,359th place overall, gun time 1:32:44, chip time 1:26:09.

Gena Henry: It was awesome. I did it a minute faster than last year. 68 minutes. 14,814th place overall, gun time 1:16:58, chip time 1:08:02.

Jim Kempert: A little disappointed. Every year I tell myself I'm going to get a donut, but I get to the Krispy Kreme guy (handing out free donuts as you come off the bridge) and can't make myself do it. I wanted to break 50 – the donut might have been the key, but I ran 50:12. 2,960th place overall, gun time 53:52, chip time 50:11.

Fred Reinhard: I like the start even though the gun didn't go off. I did reasonably well. I really liked the downhill. I ran as fast as I could, maybe too fast. When I came up to the 5 mile I was looking over my shoulder for Russ (Brown). Ran 43, almost 44. 588th place overall, gun time 43:55, chip time 43:46, top 5% 60-65 a.g. award.

Russ Brown: 44:05. I was right behind Fred. We ran out of finish line before I could catch him. I like the course. It's a lot faster than the other 2 courses. 621st place overall, gun time 44:10, chip time 44:08, top 5% 60-64 a.g. award.

John Bradley: Just moved here two weeks ago from New York. My first 10K in 5 years. I thought it was a great race, well organized, fantastic course, lots of nice folks. Just over 46 minutes. 999th place, gun time 46:23, chip time 46:15, top 5% 60-64 a.g. award.

David Quick: Fast run, fast course, my a**! Thirty eight 0 something. I'm off. 150th place overall, gun time 38:03, chip time 38:02, top 5% 40-44 a.g. award.

Rives Poe: I don't wanna. I got a P.R. 40:20 something. It was hard; the wind was hard. I didn't feel great, I wanted to puke the whole time. But it was fun to be on the new Bridge. 295th place overall, gun time 40:37, chip time 40:33. (note sex/age were wrong in race day results so she was not included in the original awards list. Results on www.BridgeRun.Com now show her 2nd in 26-29 a.g. CJ)

Wendy Roach: I just did it for fun. Enjoyed. 48:33. 1,544th place overall, gun time 48:49, chip time 48:33.

Bratton Fennell: I had a very bad race, but I'm running Boston in 2 weeks and didn't push myself. My worst 10k in a couple of years, but I'll be back ... need to embarrass yourself every once in a while. Still, a nice event. 42 almost on the dot. 413th place overall, gun time 42:04, chip time 42:04.

Dan Clapper: I'd have done better if I hadn't spent too much time trying to think up something clever to say to you. I thought it would be faster, but the hill took more out of me than I thought and the downhill wasn't as good. I usually run the same time here as at the Flowertown 10k, but I was 2 minutes off. 42:09. 421st place, gun time 42:09, chip time 42:02, top 5% 50-54 a.g. award.

Keith Ambrose: I had a good one for a change. I got rid of all my medicine and can get through without hurting myself. Not as fast as I used to be, but still got a trophy in the old farts brigade, 15th in the age group 48:26. 1,453rd place, gun time 48:28, chip time 48:23, top 5% 60-64 a.g. award.

Gary Ricker: It was number 27 for me. A little warm, it could have been 20 degrees cooler. The wind wasn't really much of a factor. I enjoyed the cloud cover – it helped a lot. Just happy to complete another one. Ran about 42. 411th place overall, gun time 42:02, chip time 41:39, top 5% 50-54 a.g. award.

Kay Chandler: To be honest, it was bittersweet. I started running the Bridge when we ran the old bridges in '84. It was faster but I felt a little sadness for the old bridges. I won an award and enjoyed it. It was fun, ran about 57:48 or 58:24 on the clock. 4,956th place overall, gun time 58:28, chip time 57:57, top 5% 60-64 a.g. award.

Joyce Rasberry: The Bridge Run - I just went into it as an event. I did have some goals, I wanted to take time off from last year and enjoy it. Used it as a training run. I'm doing my first marathon, this is no big deal. I was overwhelmed with a 5% award in my age group. About 1:02. Took 3 minutes off last year. Just happy. Overwhelming experience. 7,148th place overall, gun time 1:02:21, chip time 1:01:50 top 5% 60-64 a.g. award.

Jim Chandler: First Bridge run in about eight years. I didn't run for 7 or 8 years. I ran the early bridges and went over the humps and thought it was over and then

First time over the new Ravenel bridge. Post and Courier photo by Grace Beahm

the overpass would kill me. But this year at the crest I said "It's all downhill from here." For the first time I wasn't jammed up by walkers in front of me. Ran about 1:05. 10,595th place, gun time 1:08:15, chip time 1:04:57.

Anne Wyman Cipolla: My run? It was a little slow, but overall I was happy. I was okay on the Bridge, felt great on the downhill, got to Meeting Street and my legs ... just gave out. I really slowed down the last miles. I finally got the Newberry award. 39:02. 196th place overall, gun time 39:02, chip time 39:01, Marcus Newberry Award for first area female finisher, 1st 30-34 a.g. award.

Mike Cipolla: Well I had a pretty good Bridge Run considering last year I had to walk some. Hats off to the people who put it together. I was expecting it to be worse with the heat. 37:30. 117th place overall, gun time 37:29, chip time 37:27, top 5% 35-39 a.g. award.

Irving Rosenfeld: Truth was the course was easier. I didn't get to Meeting Street without going up the ramp. Thank God for the wind – it was too hot otherwise. I'm happy with my time – I lined up with the Kenyans – couldn't stay with them. 1:00:22. 5,980th place overall, gun time 1:00:24, chip time 1:00:16.

Donna Lea Brown: I really enjoyed the new course and my time was acceptable. Next year I'll do better, I'll be in a new age group – look out world! I'm glad I survived it. 1:23 I think. 17,887th place overall, gun time 1:24:32, chip time 1:23:58.

Jim Denning: Well, disappointing time, but I like the new Bridge; it's gotten a lot of people interested in running. It really kicked my butt, but I'll be ready next year. 44:03 – a minute slower than last year. 620th place overall, gun time 44:10, chip time 44:06.

David Anderson: Age 75. I did it in 62 minutes and got 3rd place. I had some injuries the last couple of years, but came back – and I'm encouraged to improve. 7,223rd place overall, gun time 1:02:29, chip time 1:02:24, 3rd 75-79 a.g. award.

Tracy Oetgen: The weather was gorgeous, we appreciate it. It wasn't as organized as it could have been better organized – there were too many walkers up front. All in all it was really fun. I did it in a little under an hour. 11,949th place overall, gun time 1:10:46, chip time 1:01:04.

Viki Maddox: I finished. I'm really happy. I was concerned about getting tripped at the finish. Ran about an hour chip time. (unable to locate in results or on web-site. CJ)

Irv Batten: I went out a bit too fast, cramped up on the Bridge, got caught in no man's land and slithered to the finish. I mean I slithered. 33:59. Disappointed – I'm in a lot better shape, but whatever. 37th place overall, gun time 34:01, chip time 34:01, 1st 40-44 a.g. award.

Ed Brinkley: 65-59 first place. It was hard to me. I'm not used to running hills. I'm pleased with my time. After the first 3 miles I thought I was done for. I can't run hills. I ran 41:43. 388th place overall, gun time 41:43, chip time 41:40, 1st 65-69 a.g. award.

Bill Boulter: I had 51:33. Great. A great run. I enjoyed it. Gradual rise in height was awesome, but I managed it. A little slower than the Flowertown 10k but I won my age group. 2,283rd place overall, gun time 51:23, chip time 51:19, 1st 75-79 a.g. award.

Clyde Mizzell: Man it was a great run. I'm so pleased with my time. I had to pace myself, but coming into the city I felt great. Because it felt so good I'm surprised with my time 51:08. Good enough. 2,205th place overall, gun time 51:09, chip time 51:07, 1st 70-74 a.g. award.

Jan Mizzell: I thought the race was really great. First span probably the toughest run across it. The whole race was well organized. 1 hour 20 minutes. I was trying to get a 5% award, but so many competitors I didn't quite make it. 16,356th place overall, gun time 1:20:35, chip time 1:18:04.

Steven Hunt: It was good, right under 52 - as long as I keep it under my age. It was tougher than I thought it was going to be. 2,438th place overall, gun time 51:54, chip time 51:32.

Cedric Jaggers: It was really about what I expected time wise due to my hip trouble, but I had hoped to be faster. The unbroken uphill just killed me. I've always been a good downhill runner and when we topped the bridge it didn't seem to go downhill, just to flatten out and I barely speeded up. Then on Meeting and King Street my legs turned to rubber and I suffered to the finish. I was sorry my wife Kathy was unable to participate this year due to her multiple sclerosis. 3,541st place overall, gun time 55:09, chip time 54:47.

Cooper River Bridge Run — Charleston, SC - 29th Annual 10K - April 1, 2006

2006 Awards

Prize money winners:

Males Overall

1	Abraham Chebii	Kenya	28:16	$5000
2	Sammy Kipketer	Kenya	28:35	$3000
3	Julius Koskei	Kenya	28:52	$1500
4	Shadrack Kosgei	Kenya	29:01	$1000
5	Linus Maiyo	Kenya	29:08	$800
6	Nathan Kosgei	Kenya	29:08	$600
7	Julius Kiptoo	Kenya	29:50	$500
8	George Kirwa Misoi	Kenya	30:06	$400
9	Stephen Koech	Kenya	30:12	$300
10	Kyle King	Blowing Rock, NC	30:53	$250
11	Malcolm Campbell	Marietta, GA	30:57	$200
12	Eric Ashton	Columbia, SC	30:59	$150
13	Michael Green	Atlanta, GA	31:09	$100
14	Albert Okemwa	Kenya	31:20	$75
15	Thomas Morgan	Blowing Rock, NC	31:26	$50

Females Overall

1	Sally Barsosio	Kenya	33:35	$5000
2	Tatiana Chulakh	Russia	33:40	$3000
3	Lyubov Denisova	Russia	33:52	$1500
4	Janet Cherobon	Norcross, GA	34:16	$1000
5	Gladys Asiba	Kenya	34:25	$800
6	Adriana Pirtea	Romania	34:27	$600
7	Florence Jepkosgei	Kenya	35:02	$500
8	Rebbie Koech	Kenya	35:14	$400
9	Tatyana Pozdnyakova	Ukraine	35:16	$300
10	Lyubov Kremleva	Russia	35:18	$250
11	Heather Lee	Shelby, NC	35:29	$200
12	Donna Anderson	Pawleys Island, SC	35:59	$150
13	Michelle LaFleur	Savannah, GA	36:07	$100
14	Laura Rhoads	Raleigh, NC	36:11	$75
15	Tina Jullerat	Charlotte, NC	37:12	$50

Male Masters

1	Albert Okemwa	Kenya	31:20	$1500
2	Sean Wade	New Zealand	31:47	$1000
3	Phillip Walkins	Coconut Creek, FL	32:42	$750
4	Jamey Yon	Gainesville, GA	33:18	$500
5	Eric Morse	Berlin, VT	33:20	$250

Female Masters

1	Tatyana Pozdnyakova	Ukraine	35:16	$1500
2	Lyubov Kremleva	Russia	35:18	$1000
3	Sheila Wakeman	Cornelius, NC	39:51	$750
4	Laura Vroon	Wyoming, MI	40:17	$500
5	Mary Williams	Conway, SC	40:57	$250

Male Grand Masters

1	Gary Romesser	Indianapolis, IN	34:30	$750
2	Mike Hart	Washington, DC	37:18	$500
3	Jim Wilhelm	Canton, OH	37:36	$250

Female Grandmasters

1	Tatyana Pozdnyakova	Ukraine	35:16	$750
2	Debra Wagner	Perrysburg, OH	41:01	$500
3	Dian Ford	Piedmont, SC	41:14	$250

Marcus Newberry Award:

First Local Charleston (Tri-Country) Finisher

Male

Neil McDonagh .... Mt Pleasant, SC .... 31:38 .... $500

Female

Anne Wyman Cipolla .. Charleston, SC .... 39:02 .... $500

Special Awards:

Wheelchair Division

1 Tyler Byers .... Reston, VA 26:43

Dewey Wise Trophy

Oldest finisher with time less than his or her age in minutes:

David Mellard, 83 .... N Charleston, SC 80:50

Age division winners

Presented to top 3 in each dividsion. Top 5% awards presented in each division up to a maximum of 25 per division

Males 12 & under (468 Finishers, 24 Awards)

1	Jack Felix	Hilton Head, SC	45:55
2	William Dodds	Charlotte, NC	46:43
3	Miren Ivankovic	Clemson, SC	47:03
4	Felix Hadtstein	Isle Of Palms Sc	47:09
5	Grier Sponenberg	Greenwood, SC	47:35
6	Sidney Houting	Mt Pleasant, SC	49:21
7	Damian Woods	Union, SC	49:47
8	Tanner Wood	Johns Island Sc	51:26
9	John L Sanford	Columbia, SC	51:49
10	Langdon Fennell	Mt Pleasant, SC	52:19
11	Gary Mathis	Summerville, SC	52:35
12	Andre Ivankovic	Clemson, SC	52:43
13	Brandon Wood	Mt Pleasant, SC	52:54
14	Timothy Kennedy	Summerville, SC	53:24
15	Brandon Cook	Summerville, SC	54:48
16	Dylan Morone	Unknown, SC	54:53
17	Chaz Schuck	Mt Pleasant, SC	54:57
18	Eric Davidson	Mt Pleasant, SC	55:08
19	Michael Reamer	Mt Pleasant, SC	55:09
20	P J Loheide	Crestwood, KY	55:13
21	Andy Toussaint	Clinton, SC	55:24
22	Brandon Smith	Chesterfield Sc	56:11
23	Sam Wingate	Mt Pleasant, SC	56:23
24	Adam Austin	Moncks Corner Sd	56:35

Females 12 & under (441 Finishers, 23 Awards)

1	Anna Fairey	Mt Pleasant, SC	47:43
2	Kelsy Dawsey	Milner, GA	48:42
3	Kelley Strong	Union, SC	50:08
4	Megan Duncan	Ladson, SC	50:45
5	Melissa Fairey	Mt Pleasant, SC	50:52
6	Christa Green	Union, SC	51:42
7	Kristen Cain	Abbeville, SC	53:26
8	Merry Pierpont	Charlotte, NC	56:26
9	Tara Hadtstein	Isle Of Palms SC	56:33
10	Katherine Gore	Summerville, SC	56:35
11	Brianna Eaton	Easley, SC	56:36
12	Kelsey Orvin	Summerville, TX	56:36
13	Sydney Grobowsky	Tryon, NC	56:47
14	Sarah Loheide	Crestwood, KY	56:48
15	Ansley Shultz	Atlanta, GA	57:17
16	Katharina Koch	Mt Pleasant, SC	57:27
17	Caitlin Rowe	Spartanburg, SC	59:57
18	Caitlyn Fairey	Mt Pleasant, SC	1:00:22
19	Anna Stockman	Mt Pleasant, SC	1:01:54
20	Rhianna Sherlock	Goose Creek, SC	1:02:46
21	Courtney Wood	Mt Pleasant, SC	1:04:36
22	Ellen Klimecki	Mt Pleasant, SC	1:04:37
23	Alex Bailey	Bluffton, SC	1:07:14

Males 13 - 17 (742 Finishers, 25 Awards)

1	Justin Ruppe	Forest City, NC	35:14
2	Jefferson Waugh	Statesville, NC	35:27
3	David Huckaby	Fort Mill, SC	35:58
4	Taylor Stroud	Spindale, NC	36:00
5	Sam Godfrey	Rutherfordton NC	37:09
6	Stephen Usery	Easley, SC	37:36
7	Mike Lambert	Aiken, SC	37:42
8	Matthew Ellison	Charleston, SC	37:44
9	Mark Bowers	Ladson, SC	37:59
10	Joshua Fitts	Mt Pleasant, SC	38:16
11	Robert Padgett	Moore, SC	38:38
12	Joey Baldwin	Greer, SC	39:15
13	Parker Wade	Greer, SC	39:38
14	Alan Ford	Huntersville NC	39:48
15	Joseph Laurendi	Summerville, SC	39:50
16	Conley Bryan	Mt Pleasant, SC	39:52
17	Adam Burrell	Campobello, SC	40:09
18	Ben Miller	Chesnee, SC	40:10
19	Nathaniel Hayes	Fort Mill, SC	40:16
20	James Carroll	Isle Of Palms Sc	40:21
21	Sean Kelley	Canton, OH	40:27
22	Forrest Parker	Goose Creek, SC	40:32
23	James Jackson	Aiken, SC	40:42
24	Dennis Randar	Fort Mill, SC	40:45
25	Reid Cabiness	Charleston, SC	40:47

Females 13 - 17 (701 Finishers, 25 Awards)

1	Cara Browning	Goose Creek SC	43:39
2	Rindi Wood	Charleston SC	43:49
3	Alexa Gellman	Charlotte, NC	45:51
4	Julia Baldwin	Greer, SC	47:01
5	Meghan Kirwan	Mt Pleasant, SC	47:59
6	Abby Osborn	Charlotte, NC	48:07
7	Taylor Hughes	Greer, SC	48:55
8	Stacey Austin	Charleston, SC	49:00
9	Lesley Sweat	Summerville, SC	49:28
10	Kelly Maw	Raleigh, NC	49:40
11	Hannah Anderson	Goose Creek ,SC	49:40
12	Darla Browning	Goose Creek, SC	49:44
13	Connor Suggs	Mt Pleasant, SC	49:47
14	Katie Anderson	Goose Creek ,SC	49:51
15	Amy Laughlin	Aiken, SC	50:02
16	Amanda Sinclair	Buffalo, SC	50:08
17	Kelly Caldwell	Greenville, SC	50:18
18	Peggy Busbee	Unknown	50:33
19	Annie Pendleton	Fort Mill, SC	50:56
20	Lauren Bishop	Pinehurst, NC	51:03
21	Darby Kirven	Darlington, SC	51:05
22	Paisley Lewis	Easley, SC	51:10
23	Mary Crawford	Cheraw, SC	51:22
24	Ashley Lisle	Summerville, SC	51:36
25	Emily Willoughey	Mt Pleasant, SC	51:41

Males 18 - 21 (511 Finishers, 25 Awards)

1	Brock Phillips	Chapel Hill, NC	34:04
2	Harrison Johnson	Charleston, SC	34:17
3	Thomas Sullivan	Chapel Hill, NC	34:34
4	Charles Kutz	Anderson, SC	34:47
5	Nathan Blat	Moreland Hills, OH	34:47
6	Jayce Watson	Wingate, NC	35:07
7	Alexander Leveen	Charleston, SC	35:48
8	Matthew Elliott	Greensea, SC	36:00
9	Stephen Sykes	Spartanburg, SC	37:29
10	John-Michael Gerlach	Charleston, SC	37:32
11	Austin Brown	Hodges, SC	38:08
12	William Huff	Summerville, SC	38:10
13	Cory Kvartek	Aiken, SC	38:40
14	Chris Powell	Fort Mill, SC	38:56
15	Mark Schandel	N Augusta, SC	39:01
16	John Schandel	N Augusta, SC	39:02
17	Stephen Powell	Fort Mill, SC	39:06
18	Todd Hines	Union, SC	39:18
19	Kevin Lane	Asheville, NC	39:38
20	Jonathan Foote	Marietta, GA	39:41
21	Thomas Moore	Spartanburg, SC	39:45
22	Zachary Johnson	Charleston, SC	39:52
23	Paul Testa	Wingate, NC	39:51
24	Nick Holt	Spartanburg, SC	39:54
25	Patrick Beckman	Charleston, SC	39:58

Females 18 - 21 (895 Finishers, 25 Awards)

1	Margaret Brinson	Greenville, SC	41:42
2	Marcie Milner	Aiken, SC	42:08
3	Megan Jenkins	Charleston, SC	42:16
4	Lauren Clark	Raleigh, NC	43:18
5	Laura Berry	Wingate, NC	44:27
6	Chelsey Wilson	Wingate, NC	44:59
7	Bergen Holzworth	Sullivans Isl, SC	45:34
8	Erin Smith	Greenwood, SC	46:22
9	Kyle Palmquist	Charleston, SC	46:39
10	Elizabeth Browning	Broad Run, VA	46:51
11	Amy Singer	Vienna, Wv	47:14
12	Lindsay Decken	Clemson, SC	47:16
13	Meredith Spry	Chapel Hill, NC	47:39
14	Theresa Verostek	Rock Hill, SC	47:41
15	Taylor Harvey	Moore, SC	47:46
16	Mary Laurens	Greer, SC	47:53
17	Virginia Haden	Rutherfordton, NC	48:22
18	Ashley Hubbard	Wingate, NC	48:51
19	Holly Ballenger	Tucker, GA	49:22
20	Anna Griffis	Salisbury, NC	49:23
21	Carla Stanley	Charleston, SC	49:49
22	Kim Hutter	Raleigh, NC	49:56
23	Cascy Wcir	Germantown, MD	49:56
24	Brett Miller	Dunkirk, MN	49:56
25	Ashley Godwin	Irmo, SC	50:09

Males 22 - 25 (1,141 Finishers, 25 Awards)

1	Neil Mcdonagh	Mt Pleasant, SC	31:38
2	Devin Swann	Raleigh, NC	31:59
3	Mike Earle	Buies Creek, NC	32:49
4	Kevin Crosby	Chapel Hill, NC	33:05
5	Hudson Belk	Charleston, SC	33:54
6	Brooks Keys	Charleston, SC	35:34
7	Marc Quesenberry	Charleston, SC	35:50
8	Ethan Coffey	Goose Creek, SC	35:56
9	Jovian Sackett	Columbia, SC	36:14
10	Kevin Timp	Chapel Hill, NC	36:35
11	Alan Woodruff	Carrboro, NC	36:51
12	Joel B Cantrell	Inman, SC	37:05
13	Elliott Taylor	Greenville, SC	37:36
14	Brett Mclane	Charlotte, NC	37:51
15	John Aleman	Greenwood, SC	38:07
16	Ian Seeney	Fort Mill, SC	38:35
17	Rajesh Manickam5	Unknown, NC	38:38
18	Ruskin Vest	Portwentworth, GA	38:51
19	Patrick Kelly	Charlotte, NC	39:16
20	Ryan Clark	Cincinnati, OH	39:22
21	Alan Gibson	Columbia, SC	39:25
22	Edward Moseley	Charlotte, NC	39:36
23	Joseph Petraccoro	Brick, NJ	39:46
24	Laurie Sanders	Edisto Beach, SC	40:02
25	Matthew Brownlee	Charlotte, NC	40:07

– Continued on next page

2006 Awards, continued from page 233

Females 22 - 25 (2,150 Finishers, 25 Awards)

1	Stephanie Feagin	Fort Mitchell, AL	38:46
2	Heather Nichols	Mt Pleasant, SC	40:00
3	Kathryn Cavanaugh	Columbia , SC	40:28
4	Kelly Fleming	Sanford, NC	40:33
5	Stephanie Lundeby	Ladson, SC	41:41
6	Jenny Mcdonagh	Mt Pleasant , SC	41:52
7	Leanne Sagmeister	Jacksonville , SC	41:52
8	Elizabeth Metherell	Greenville, SC	42:04
9	Jennifer Montano	Norfolk, VA	42:41
10	Michelle Johnston	Columbia, SC	43:35
11	Lynn Takala	Greenville, SC	44:22
12	Shenna Kevorkian	Charlotte, NC	44:59
13	Erin Burdette	Clemson, SC	45:25
14	Jamie Stewart	Charleston, SC	45:36
15	Margaret Banks	Mt Pleasant, SC	46:10
16	Meredith Evans	Mt Pleasant, SC	46:25
17	Kristen Champion	Charleston, SC	46:48
18	Jessica Jank	Gastonia, NC	46:56
19	Emiline Fricke	Simpsonville, SC	47:01
20	Nicole SaUnders	Sylva, NC	47:02
21	Rachel Weightman	Charlotte, NC	47:10
22	Cara Musumeci	Kannapolis, NC	47:21
23	Nicole Rager	Charleston, SC	47:38
24	Emily Cupito	Chapel Hill, NC	47:41
25	Carly Costanza	Rochester, NY	47:49

Males 26 - 29 (1,693 Finishers, 25 Awards)

1	Daniel Hughes	Greenville, SC	31:50
2	Palmer Thomas	Mountville, SC	33:24
3	Mike Aiken	Mt Pleasant, SC	33:29
4	Jason Putnam	Anderson, SC	34:38
5	Patrick Shaw	Buies Creek, NC	35:16
6	Joseph Ryan	Charleston, SC	35:16
7	Eric Bonnette	Haddenfield, NJ	35:27
8	Blake Benke	New York, NY	35:30
9	Jeremy Becraft	Mt Pleasant, SC	35:31
10	David Lee, Jr	Charleston, SC	35:35
11	Robert Christopher	Charleston, SC	35:39
12	Kevin Lisska	Fletcher, NC	36:19
13	Jay Upchurch	James Island, SC	36:20
14	Michael Mccauley	Greenville, SC	36:26
15	Tomasz Baginski	Waynesville, NC	37:01
16	Sims Key	Clemson, SC	37:05
17	Jamie Lippert	Savage, MN	37:18
18	Travis Brady	Spartanburg, SC	37:26
19	Kurt Wilson	Candler, NC	37:40
20	Chad Brittingham	Charleston, SC	37:47
21	Andrew Cawood	Summerville, SC	37:52
22	Matthew Tooman	Charleston, SC	38:24
23	James Powell	Charleston, SC	38:26
24	Andy Gordon	Kannapolis, NC	38:35
25	Dylan Wiek	Columbia, SC	38:38

Females 26 - 29 (2,347 Finishers, 25 Awards)

1	Jc Hanley-Pinto	Jacksonville, FL	37:50
2	Rives Poe	Mt Pleasant, SC	40:37
3	Emily Johnson	Johns Island, SC	41:07
4	Katie Thurmond	Charleston, SC	41:10
5	Darby H Tucker	Charlotte, NC	41:51
6	Maryshell Zaffino	Mt Pleasant, SC	42:07
7	Erin Ritter	Raleigh, NC	43:01
8	Sarah Wilde	Chapel Hill, NC	43:11
9	Elizabeth Weaver	Charlotte, NC	43:23
10	Dana Hayden	Mt Pleasant, SC	43:28
11	Sarah Reed	Daniel Island, SC	43:53
12	Jennifer Leiser	Charleston, SC	44:44
13	Colleen Angstadt	Charlotte, NC	44:46
14	Blake Ellis	Charleston, SC	44:53
15	Staci Jenkins	Pope Afb, SC	45:16
16	Isabel Ghowanlu	Charleston, SC	45:18
17	Jill Hawley	Mt Pleasant, SC	45:38
18	Curry Smoak	Charleston, SC	45:54
19	Francesca Bosco	Mt Pleasant, SC	45:56
20	Gretchen Haufler	Knoxville, TN	46:12
21	Karen Courington	Charleston, SC	46:21
22	Chappell Hughes	Greenville, SC	46:25
23	Meredith Daves	Cary, NC	47:06
24	Katie Hoeft	Nashville, TN	47:18
25	Kate Crofton	Columbia, SC	47:24

Males 30 - 34 (2,054 Finishers, 25 Awards)

1	Silah Misoi	Kenya	32:30
2	Orinthal Striggles	Columbia, SC	32:38
3	Brian Johnson	Johns Island, SC	33:11
4	Jonathan Kraas	Mt Pleasant, SC	33:24
5	Aaron Bowman	Mcleansville, NC	33:48
6	Karl Walsh	Mt Pleasant, SC	34:20
7	Coates Kennerly	Brevard, NC	35:18
8	Roger Fagala	Blenheim, SC	35:29
9	Justin Ratike	Charlotte, NC	35:33
10	Mike Moran	Stanley, NC	36:00
11	Brad Schneider	Bowling Green, KY	36:16
12	Jason Annan	Charlotte, NC	36:37
13	Thomas Walls	Fort Mill, SC	36:58
14	Kevin Mosteller	Mt Pleasant, SC	37:31
15	Douglas Pratt	Charleston, SC	37:42
16	Brian Tullis	Silver Spring, MD	37:43
17	Brad Fowler	Winston-Salem, NC	37:44
18	Robert Stanfield	Atlanta, GA	37:50
19	Bobby Wilder	Myrtle Beach, SC	37:53
20	Carl Buckner	Charleston, SC	37:53
21	Scott Kennedy	Rock Hill, SC	38:06
22	David Rogers	Charleston, SC	38:18
23	Ferald Griffitts	Hartsville, SC	38:20
24	Rob Dee	Charleston, SC	38:28
25	Timothy Limbert	Ann Arbor, MI	38:32

Females 30 - 34 (2,470 Finishers, 25 Awards)

1	Anne Wyman Cipolla	Charleston, SC	39:02
2	Colleen Nicoulin	Port Orange, FL	39:34
3	Angie Slappey	Carrollton, GA	40:12
4	Rebecca Crowder	Charlotte, NC	40:36
5	Kristin Mccann	Jacksonville, NC	41:51
6	Jennifer Lepori	Maywood, NJ	42:01
7	Carol Brunson	Spartanburg, SC	42:24
8	Tina-Marie Poulin	New York, NY	42:32
9	Christine Twining	Columbia, SC	42:54
10	Tracy Mckee	Charleston, SC	43:17
11	Paige Hauff	Charlotte, NC	43:38
12	Helen Lafaye	Columbia, SC	44:00
13	Stephanie Hall	Hickory, NC	44:05
14	Dian Berry	Lexington, SC	44:34
15	Melissa Spacek	Chapel Hill, NC	44:36
16	Linda Wood	Marietta, GA	44:52
17	Allison Cook	Charleston, SC	45:05
18	Heather Alexander	Columbia, SC	45:19
19	Christy Sheppard	Mt Pleasant, SC	46:06
20	Kim Mendoza	Summerville, SC	46:09
21	Stephanie Mascia	Charlotte, NC	46:38
22	Carrie Manson	Charleston, SC	46:44
23	Lori Sheridan-Wilson	Mt Pleasant, SC	47:05
24	Doreen Mccormick	Huntersville, NC	47:07
25	Rhonda Huggins	Murrells Inlet, SC	47:08

Males 35 - 39 (2,020 Finishers, 25 Awards)

1	Gregg Cromer	Summerville, SC	34:39
2	Eric Vandervort	Clinton, TN	35:05
3	Nick Felix	Hilton Head, SC	36:32
4	Douglas Long	Charlotte, NC	36:35
5	Daniel J Mcdowell	Beckley, WV	36:57
6	Emery Lloyd	Moncks Corner, SC	37:00
7	Jason Philbin	Charlotte, NC	37:11
8	Eric Sullivan	Birmingham, AL	37:13
9	Joseph Pinto	Jacksonville, FL	37:29
10	Michael Cipolla	Charleston, SC	37:29
11	Mark Widmann	Mt Pleasant, SC	37:34
12	Darol Timberlak	Matthews, NC	37:39
13	Michael Kulling	Stillwater, OK	37:43
14	Timothy Tenne	Mt Pleasant, SC	37:48
15	Mike Pryor	New Bern, NC	37:51
16	Ben Cheek	Mcpherson, KS	37:57
17	Chip Owens	Atlanta, GA	38:00
18	Mark Harrell	Raleigh, NC	38:37
19	Bo Butler	Mooresville, NC	38:43
20	Billy Estes	Isle Of Palms, SC	38:54
21	David Creel	Mt Pleasant, SC	38:58
22	Gregory Brown	Mt Pleasant, SC	39:02
23	Rick Cota	Wakefiled, RI	39:16
24	Alan Brown	Charleston, SC	39:29
25	Alan Pogroszewski	Rochester, NY	39:40

Females 35 - 39 (2,177 Finishers, 25 Awards)

1	Charlotte Ratike	Charlotte, NC	40:55
2	Kathy Stewart	Mt Pleasant, SC	41:43
3	Debra Brown	Mt Pleasant, SC	42:19
4	Molly Achille	Greenville, SC	42:40
5	Kristi Wise	Mt Pleasant, SC	43:42
6	Janet Regnier	Daniel Island, SC	44:14
7	Jeanette Mohl	Cleveland, SC	44:25
8	Elizabeth Mccaleb	Mt Pleasant, SC	45:01
9	Laura Mullis	Mooresville, NC	45:23
10	Jennifer Stabene	Mt Pleasant, SC	45:40
11	Susanne Gaus-Zikel	Charlotte, NC	45:50
12	Irene Draesel	Charleston, SC	46:04
13	Molly Hughes	Charleston, SC	46:09
14	Stacey S Johnson	Isle Of Palms, SC	46:32
15	Janice Willey	Mt Pleasant, SC	46:44
16	Leslie Randall	Royersford, PA	47:00
17	Missy Hunnicutt	Columbia, SC	47:02
18	Alethea Setser	Mt Pleasant, SC	47:08
19	Maria Lipsitz	Columbia, SC	47:11
20	Lana Torkildsen	Matthews, NC	47:12
21	Karen Howard-Goss	Myrtle Beach, SC	47:19
22	Carey Cochran	Charleston, SC	47:27
23	Mary M Mceachern	Wilmington, NC	47:29
24	Kirsten Baggett	Tallahassee, FL	47:34
25	Jenny Hickey	Wellsboro, PA	47:35

Males 40 - 44 (1,630 Finishers, 25 Awards)

1	Irv Batten	Summerville, SC	34:01
2	David Matherne	Cartersville, GA	34:22
3	Sean O'donnell	Ozark, AL	34:26
4	John Anderson	Greenville, SC	36:19
5	Craig Kingma	Jenison, MI	36:46
6	Eric Ruckel	Mt Pleasant, SC	36:51
7	Chris Hicks	Florence, SC	37:17
8	Michael Parker	Goose Creek, SC	37:41
9	Lance Leopold	Simpsonville, SC	37:49
10	David Quick	Mt Pleasant, SC	38:03
11	Dale Waters	Leland, NC	38:22
12	Steve Morrell	Arlington, VA	38:24
13	Roman Pibl	Cary, NC	39:02
14	Dawson Cherry	N Charleston, SC	39:24
15	Marshall Martin	Cary, NC	39:31
16	Mark Rutledge	Mt Pleasant, SC	39:48
17	Kenneth Clyburn	Beaufort, SC	39:52
18	Rob Newton	Mooresville, NC	40:03
19	Tracy Schooler	Cross, SC	40:06
20	Chris Handal	Charleston, SC	40:19
21	Darrell Stone	Wilkesboro, NC	40:33
22	Peter Esser	Summerville, SC	40:37
23	Don Aschenbrenner	Cornelius, NC	40:46
24	Michael Smith	Painesville, OH	40:52
25	Jeffrey Stockdale	Goose Creek, SC	40:55

Females 40 - 44 (1,910 Finishers, 25 Awards)

1	Mary Dore	Charlotte, NC	41:05
2	Keely Churchill	Raleigh, NC	42:01
3	Michelle Beaulieu	Summerville, SC	42:18
4	Brian Roberts	Myrtle Beach, SC	42:41
5	Terri Marshall	Fort Mill, SC	43:20
6	Jean Aswell	Cornelius, NC	43:20
7	Beth Pierpont	Charlotte, NC	44:32
8	Inga Sullivan	Mt Pleasant, SC	45:22
9	Lisa Powell	Columbia, SC	45:33
10	Carol Hauss	Salisbury, NC	45:33
11	Laura Kelecy	Colorado Springs, CO	46:03
12	Kay Weems	Charlotte, NC	46:30
13	Kathy Bunting	Mt Pleasant, SC	46:37
14	Suanne Hall	Greenville, SC	46:48
15	Sharon Hasty	Spartanburg, SC	47:06
16	Karen Clark	Jericho, VT	47:08
17	Laura Casscaddan	Winter Park, FL	47:27
18	Gina Latham	Greenville, SC	47:30
19	Lynne Elliott	Summerville, SC	47:36
20	Jane Byrne	Charleston, SC	47:42
21	Anne Maguire	Mt Pleasant, SC	47:43
22	Lynne Takac	Matthews, NC	48:04
23	Angela Greenlee	Albemarle, NC	48:30
24	Pamela Doreen	Wilmington, NC	48:31
25	Peggy Rhodes	Anderson, SC	48:46

Males 45 - 49 (1,456 Finishers, 25 Awards)

1	Tom Mather	Mt Pleasant, SC	33:57
2	Ken Youngers	Decatur, GA	35:52
3	Pierre-Yves Page	Greenville, SC	36:20
4	Bill Gibbs	Winston-Salem, NC	36:44
5	Marc Embler	Summerville, SC	36:48
6	Alan Blackwell	Moore, SC	37:09
7	Jeremy Tomlinson	St Andrews, Fi	37:13
8	Gerald Hutchinson	Charlotte, NC	37:46
9	Huey Inman	Mt Pleasant, SC	37:55
10	Pete Edge	Simpsonville, SC	38:30
11	David Bourgeois	Summerville, SC	38:33
12	Derek Appleton	Cornelius, NC	38:37
13	John Walton	Charlotte, NC	38:48
14	James Scheer	Charleston, SC	38:59
15	Billy Tisdale	Sumter, SC	39:19
16	Matt Crabbe	San Antonio, TX	39:25
17	Keith Hertling	Lexington, SC	39:42
18	Charles Schirmer	Southern Pines, NC	39:57
19	Luke Egan	Rock Hill, SC	40:10
20	Fleetwood Fleming	Mt Pleasant, SC	40:14

21 Richard Keating ... Milford, NH ... 40:15
22 Randy Smith ... Myrtle Beach, SC ... 40:24
23 Cesar Gamez ... Mt Pleasant, SC ... 40:30
24 Andy Crowley ... Greer, SC ... 41:13
25 George Sykes ... Spartanburg, SC ... 41:23

Females 45 - 49 (1,633 Finishers, 25 Awards)

1 Tami Dennis ... Isle Of Palms, SC ... 44:56
2 Darla Bennett ... Longwood, FL ... 45:15
3 Nancy Thomas ... Mt Pleasant, SC ... 45:22
4 Helen Hiser ... Mt Pleasant, SC ... 45:24
5 Mary Ellen Mcmanus ... Charlotte, NC ... 45:38
6 Jennifer Doles ... Mt Pleasant, SC ... 45:51
7 Barbara Neale ... Yonges Island, SC ... 47:17
8 Cherry Kent ... Belton, SC ... 47:33
9 Trudy Gale ... Salisbury, NC ... 47:39
10 Adele Mecionis ... Sumter, SC ... 47:52
11 Janice Sides ... Concord, NC ... 47:55
12 Pam Drafts ... Beaufort, SC ... 48:49
13 Lela Wakin ... Hickory, NC ... 49:01
14 Linda Fairey ... Mt Pleasant, SC ... 49:09
15 Elizabeth Keating ... Charlotte, NC ... 49:13
16 Amy Herold ... N Charleston, SC ... 49:15
17 Barbara Whitmire ... Lake Toxaway, NC ... 49:19
18 Nicki Hutchens ... Collierville, TN ... 49:37
19 Jane Godwin ... Greer, SC ... 49:50
20 Dell Toomer ... Summerville, SC ... 50:03
21 Katherine Owens ... Summerville, SC ... 50:24
22 Joannie Essler ... Nunda, NY ... 50:40
23 Laurie Will ... Charlotte, NC ... 51:16
24 Theresa Smythe ... Charleston, SC ... 51:20
25 Colleen Adams ... Daniel Island, SC ... 51:20

Males 50 - 54 (1,379 Finishers, 25 Awards)

1 Dave Forrest ... Charlotte, NC ... 39:22
2 Jack Todd ... Spartanburg, SC ... 39:58
3 Paul Smith ... Greenville, SC ... 41:45
4 Fred Mullen ... Columbia, SC ... 41:49
5 Andrew Ammon ... Statesville, NC ... 41:54
6 Bill Edwards ... Florence, SC ... 42:00
7 Gary Ricker ... Charleston, SC ... 42:02
8 Dan Clapper ... N Charleston, SC ... 42:09
9 Rick Ingerson ... Port Orange, FL ... 42:41
10 Ron Chappell ... Greer, SC ... 42:44
11 Victor Rosado ... Salisbury, NC ... 42:45
12 Joe Howell ... Harrisburg, NC ... 42:58
13 Rob Kriegshaber ... Columbia, SC ... 43:04
14 David Sweet ... Knoxville, TN ... 43:09
15 Gabriel Lugo ... Wilmington, NC ... 43:09
16 Harold Fallis ... Awendaw, SC ... 43:26
17 Karl Dearnley ... Denver, NC ... 43:49
18 William Rowell ... Peoria, AZ ... 44:04
19 Michael Loggins ... Charleston, SC ... 44:07
20 Jim Boyd ... Mt Pleasant, SC ... 44:10
21 Timothy Williams ... Macclenny, FL ... 44:13
22 John Holzworth ... Sullivans Island, SC ... 44:18
23 Richard Jacques ... Greenville, SC ... 44:19
24 Joe Dipiro ... Mt Pleasant, SC ... 44:22
25 Bill Maddux ... Mt Pleasant, SC ... 44:22

Females 50 - 54 (1,427 Finishers, 25 Awards)

1 Sarah Ball ... Charleston, SC ... 45:49
2 Toni Cruz ... Concord, NC ... 45:52
3 Catherine Lempesis ... Irmo, SC ... 46:05
4 Michelle Withers ... Charlotte, NC ... 47:22
5 Hope Young ... Winnsboro, SC ... 48:41
6 Debbie Howard ... Mt Pleasant, SC ... 49:31
7 Sharon Allen ... Charlotte, NC ... 49:51
8 Judy Osborn ... Charlotte, NC ... 50:17
9 Patricia Ryan ... Middletown, CT ... 51:02
10 Martha White ... Columbia, SC ... 51:30
11 Pamela Manuel ... Savannah, GA ... 51:39
12 Antoinette Palmisano ... Mt Pleasant, SC ... 51:43
13 Nitsa Calas ... N Charleston, SC ... 52:30
14 Elizabeth Lierley ... Mt Pleasant, SC ... 52:56
15 Carol Ervin ... Charleston, SC ... 53:25
16 Nan Copeland ... Charlotte, NC ... 53:51
17 Jeanne Mckittrick ... Charlotte, NC ... 53:56
18 Valerie Murrah ... Chapel Hill, NC ... 54:00
19 Nancy Duffy ... N Charleston, SC ... 54:02
20 Mary Turner ... Charlotte, NC ... 54:19
21 Linda Gunshor ... Atlanta, GA ... 54:38
22 Carol Corson ... Roebuck, SC ... 55:06
23 Therese Killeen ... Isle Of Palms, SC ... 55:14
24 Carol Goehring ... Greenville, NC ... 55:23
25 Claudia Broome ... Dacula, GA ... 55:43

Males 55 - 59 (1,167 Finishers, 25 Awards)

1 Glenn Dennis ... Raleigh, NC ... 39:32
2 John Rinker ... Decatur, GA ... 39:58
3 Jan Hardwick ... Dillon, SC ... 42:26
4 Bob Schlau ... Charleston, SC ... 42:41
5 David Frith ... Trefriw, CO ... 42:55
6 James Horne ... Taylors, SC ... 42:59
7 Pooh Neovakul ... Atlanta, GA ... 43:01
8 David Lee ... Columbia, SC ... 44:13
9 Jim Osborne ... Concord, NC ... 44:40
10 Paul Gordon ... Concord, NC ... 44:48
11 James Rich ... Asheboro, NC ... 44:49
12 Wes Wessely ... Clermont, GA ... 45:18
13 Mackie Johnson ... Conover, NC ... 45:25
14 Tony Hill ... Greensboro, NC ... 46:10
15 Kaarman Richburg ... Mt Pleasant, SC ... 46:34
16 Don Whelchel ... Charlotte, NC ... 46:51
17 Paul Brown ... Goose Creek, SC ... 46:58
18 Hoot Gibson ... Folly Beach, SC ... 47:11
19 George Rolling ... Johnson City, TN ... 47:14
20 Jerry Sofley ... Gastonia, NC ... 47:14
21 Bill Barfield ... Charleston, SC ... 47:33
22 David Wingard ... Greenville, SC ... 47:38
23 Linny Moore ... Greer, SC ... 47:38
24 Eric Peltosalo ... Annapolis, MD ... 47:43
25 Peter Walters ... Muncie, IN ... 47:47

Females 55 - 59 (997 Finishers, 25 Awards)

1 Catherine Wides ... Durham, NC ... 43:14
2 Mimi Sturgell ... Kiawah Island, SC ... 44:48
3 Sallie Driggers ... Hanahan, SC ... 48:53
4 Betty Ryberg ... Aiken, SC ... 49:32
5 Lyn Hammond ... Charleston, SC ... 51:13
6 Diane Thomas ... Altamonte Spring FL ... 52:00
7 Nancy Anderson ... Spartanburg, SC ... 53:28
8 Marcella Farino ... Lancaster, SC ... 53:43
9 Patricia Kotila ... Johns Island, SC ... 54:57
10 Doreen Tylak ... Winston-Salem, NC ... 55:35
11 Marlene Mccraw ... King, NC ... 55:43
12 Brenda Cooter ... Grovetown, GA ... 56:25
13 Anne Boone ... Hollywood, SC ... 56:25
14 Lucy Hinson ... Greenville, SC ... 56:31
15 Janice Wilkins ... Greeenville, SC ... 56:58
16 Lynn Dobiel ... Knoxville, TN ... 57:24
17 Jan Metherell ... Greenville, SC ... 58:03
18 Patty Obrien-Dorner ... Yorktown, VA ... 58:17
19 Isabel Arrington ... Omaha, NE ... 59:35
20 Judy Gilman ... Mcclellanville, SC ... 59:45
21 Ann Scruggs ... Statesville, NC ... 1:00:28
22 Teenia Henderson ... Grover, NC ... 1:00:31
23 Linda Lemons ... Lenoir, NC ... 1:00:31
24 Katherin Mcnamara ... Springfield, IL ... 1:00:34
25 Mary Hamrick ... Belmont, NC ... 1:01:49

Males 60 - 64 (635 Finishers, 25 Awards)

1 Steve Annan ... Mt Pleasant, SC ... 38:57
2 Terry Van Nata ... Sugar Grove, NC ... 40:31
3 Robert Henderson ... Grover, NC ... 43:48
4 Fred Reinhard ... Sullivans Isl, SC ... 43:55
5 Russ Brown ... Midway, GA ... 44:10
6 Jim Strowd ... Mt Pleasant, SC ... 44:25
7 William Hunt ... Beaufort, SC ... 46:01
8 John Sneed ... Mt Pleasant, SC ... 46:13
9 John Bradley ... Goose Creek, SC ... 46:23
10 Ned Lesesne ... Canton, NC ... 46:40
11 Don Perkins ... Snellville, GA ... 47:08
12 Eitan Rosen ... W Palm Beach, FL ... 47:40
13 Elbert Howard ... Jamestown, SC ... 47:59
14 Vito Scarafile ... Mt Pleasant, SC ... 48:14
15 Keith Ambrose ... Mt Pleasant, SC ... 48:28
16 Ralph Ogden ... Isle Of Palms, SC ... 48:40
17 Larry Crosby ... Anderson, SC ... 49:25
18 John Dillard ... Columbia, SC ... 49:27
19 Glenn Ragsdale ... W Columbia, SC ... 49:36
20 Eric Elbel ... Marietta, GA ... 49:52
21 Steve Comer ... Charleston, SC ... 50:20
22 David Myer ... Ladson, SC ... 50:30
23 Arnold Floyd ... Hartsville, SC ... 50:54
24 Donald Jones ... Columbia, SC ... 51:29
25 C D Smith ... Charleston, SC ... 52:28

Females 60 - 64 (541 Finishers, 25 Awards)

1 Kathy Seavers ... Charlotte, NC ... 48:35
2 Jeryll Perlmutter ... Sullivans Island, SC ... 50:55
3 Sissy Logan ... Salem VA ... 52:50
4 Jean Littlejohn ... Pacolet, SC ... 53:45
5 Gail Bailey ... Charleston, SC ... 54:23
6 Joan Mulvihill ... Charleston, SC ... 54:25
7 Barbara Lindeman ... Oregon, OH ... 56:40
8 Kay Chandler ... Isle Of Palms, SC ... 58:28
9 Motria Benson ... St Augustine, FL ... 58:41
10 Joyce Rasberry ... Isle Of Palms, SC ... 1:02:21
11 Carol Thomason ... N Charleston, SC ... 1:02:41
12 Marydavis Riddle ... Charlotte, NC ... 1:03:11
13 Jean Sims ... Charleston, SC ... 1:03:17
14 Barbara Avant ... Boone, NC ... 1:03:37
15 Vickie Sessions ... Charleston, CA ... 1:04:05
16 Sally Kaiser ... Myrtle Beach, SC ... 1:04:35
17 Jewell Patterson ... Columbia, SC ... 1:05:55
18 Gwen Greenwalt ... Summerville, SC ... 1:07:06
19 Suzanne Hewitt ... Chester, VA ... 1:07:22
20 Joyce Ploeger ... Virginia Beach, VA ... 1:07:42
21 Mary J Hall ... Brandon, FL ... 1:09:33
22 Ellen Dehihns ... Marietta, GA ... 1:09:49
23 Betty Burrell ... Pendleton, SC ... 1:09:56
24 Nancy Mckeown ... Atlanta, GA ... 1:10:42
25 Jan Mcalhany ... Dewees Island, SC ... 1:11:11

Males 65 - 69 (295 Finishers, 14 Awards)

1 Ed Brinkley ... Charleston, SC ... 41:43
2 Sonny Barber ... Falls Church, VA ... 47:11
3 Jimmy Adams ... North Augusta, SC ... 47:17
4 Thomas Dority ... Charleston, SC ... 47:35
5 Michael Murphy ... Concord, NC ... 48:36
6 David Pike ... Cleveland, SC ... 48:52
7 Donald Snowdon ... Brevard, NC ... 50:44
8 Floyd Riley ... St George, SC ... 51:03
9 Fred Wood ... Waynesville, NC ... 51:03
10 Gil Gilmore ... Perrysburg, OH ... 53:08
11 Thomas Eison ... Greenville, SC ... 54:02
12 Jim Wilson ... Aiken, SC ... 54:14
13 Gordon Heiser ... Columbia, SC ... 54:27
14 Patrick Fitzgerald ... Gainesville, FL ... 54:28

Females 65 - 69 (191 Finishers, 10 Awards)

1 E K Tolley-Beeson ... Sumter, SC ... 1:03:09
2 Patricia Thompson ... Hilton Head, SC ... 1:06:01
3 Pat Rhode ... Walterboro, SC ... 1:07:07
4 Ann Hicks ... Greenville, SC ... 1:08:43
5 Barbara Crosher ... Mt Pleasant, SC ... 1:09:21
6 Karen Yossef ... Mt Pleasant, SC ... 1:09:50
7 Ruby Collins ... Harrodsburg, KY ... 1:10:40
8 Robin Johnson ... Travelers Rest, SC ... 1:11:03
9 Faye Davis ... Mt Pleasant, SC ... 1:12:27
10 Lynn Hopkins ... Charleston, SC ... 1:12:28

Males 70 - 74 (111 Finishers, 6 Awards)

1 Clyde Mizzell ... Charleston, SC ... 51:09
2 George Hilton ... Dewees Island, SC ... 52:02
3 Jerry Lardinois ... Port Orange, FL ... 52:11
4 John L Thompson ... Taylors, SC ... 54:31
5 Ken Walls ... Mt Pleasant, SC ... 59:29
6 Joe Nettles ... Tybee Island, GA ... 59:51

Females 70 - 74 (77 Finishers, 4 Awards)

1 Myron Ingram ... Huntersville, NC ... 1:01:57
2 Joyce Huguelet ... Wilmington, NC ... 1:12:22
3 Jane Gregorie ... Yemassee, SC ... 1:14:46
4 Alice Colhoun ... Hendersonville, NC ... 1:17:57

Males 75 - 79 (38 Finishers, 3 Awards)

1 William Boulter ... Charleston, SC ... 51:23
2 Lonnie Collins ... Gilbert, SC ... 59:32
3 David Anderson ... Charleston, SC ... 1:02:29

Females 75 - 79 (17 Finishers, 3 Awards)

1 Garthedon Embler ... Isle Of Palms, SC ... 1:36:59
2 Kay Biddlecomb ... Hanahan, SC ... 1:51:50
3 Almeria Turner ... Mt Pleasant, SC ... 1:57:22

Males 80 - 98 (20 Finishers, 3 Awards)

1 Alex Clarson ... Mt Pleasant, SC ... 54:52
2 David Pearlstone ... Mt Pleasant, SC ... 1:08:26
3 David Mellard ... N Charleston, SC ... 1:20:50

Females 80 - 98 (11 Finishers, 3 Awards)

1 Ola Moody ... Augusta, GA ... 1:46:19
2 Elsie Heehuk ... N Charleston, SC ... 2:26:17
3 Pecolia Dykes ... Charleston, SC ... 2:34:54

NOTE: 101 runners with age & sex not listed were excluded from awards

Compiled by Cedric Jaggers from complete results provided by Burns Computer Services on April 1, 2006, with corrections.

At the starting line, 2007. Post and Courier photo by Sarah Bates

Chapter 30
2007
All Finishers Of 30th Annual Race Get Gold Medallions

At 8 a.m. on March 31, 2007, the 30th Cooper River Bridge Run got underway, crossing the Arthur Ravenel Jr. Bridge. For the second time, both runners and walkers were timed. The number of participants who completed the race was second only to the 2006 race as 28,952 (14,420 female, 12,960 male and 472 who did not list their sex) crossed the finish line. After they finished, participants were handed a special Olympic-style golden medallion, emblazoned with the new bridge logo and "30th Annual Cooper River Bridge Run 2007". The 37,161 entrants was also the second largest number in race history.

The race again used USATF Certified Course #SC05039BS with the starting line in Mount Pleasant near Moultrie Middle School. Runners had a nearly flat first mile and then began climbing over the Ravenel Bridge. Runners took the Meeting Street ramp and went towards downtown Charleston to John Street where a right turn took them onto King Street where they turned left. The next turn was at Wentworth Street, shortly after which runners reached the 6-mile mark, then made another left to Meeting Street where the final left turn was made. The finish line was just south of George Street.

For the fourth year in a row everyone was timed using commemorative ChampionChip computer timing chips emblazed with the same design which appeared on the race T-shirt. Using this type chip meant the runners did not have to stop and remove the chip after finishing the race.

Weather conditions for the race were very good, with a start time temperature of 58 degrees and a slight, under 4 mile per hour, tailwind as the runners headed up the span with its mile-long, 4 percent grade. Since the runners usually have a headwind to contend with, it made going up the bridge much easier. As a result, a number of runners ran Personal Best times including the race winner.

With no returning champions the race was wide open. A pack of six runners stayed together over the entire bridge and raced the flat downtown section together until 24 minutes into the race. Unlike recent years, the pack was not all Kenyan. As the pace increased the pack fell off one by one.

With about a quarter mile to go, Richard Kiplagat of Kenya turned on a tremendous finishing kick and won in a Personal Best time of 28:35, with teammate Stephen Koech second in 28:42, edging Ethiopian Woeku Beyi by one second. Fourth place went to Soloman Molla, also from Ethiopia, in 28:47 who was just 1 second ahead of Patrick Nithwa of Kenya, as the first five all finished in under 29 minutes.

"The guys were right there together, so we pushed each other and I knew we would finish strong," Kiplagat told the *Post and Courier*. "We were together for a very long time, so I knew the other runners were strong. I think my kick made the difference. When it came down to the last 800 meters, I was just a little stronger."

It was Kiplagat's first time to run the race, and he was very happy with his win. "All my teammates who have run here told me the crowds were unbelievable, and they were right. The crowds were unbelievable. I've never run in front of crowds like that before," he said.

The women's favorite was last year's second place finisher, Tatiana Chulakh of Russia, but she fell off the pace after 2 miles and Redhima Kedir, an Ethiopian who was running the race for the first time, pulled away to win in 32:05, with fellow Ethiopian Amane Gobina second in 32:12. Chulakh was third in 33:14. Sylvia Mosqueda of Rosemead, Caif., was fourth in 33:40 to also top the Masters division. Fifth place went to Rose Kosgei of Kenya in 33:43.

"It was a very good race, there was no question about that," Kedir told the newspaper. "This is my first time in this race and I didn't feel anything different when I ran that bridge. I won last week, and that race helped me win today."

Pre-race favorite Chulakh said, "This time it was two very strong girls from Ethiopia. After the second mile, I just don't know what happened. This year I had a little trouble with my knee and didn't train for 10 days because of the pain. Ten days is a long time for a professional, but it was a good race."

Master's winner was New Zealand's Sean Wade, moving up from second place last year to win in 31:12. Summerville's Irv Batten took second place in 32:53 with Jamey Yon of Gainesville, Ga., third in 33:27. Female Masters winner Sylvia Mosqueda's time of 33:40 was a new female Masters course record. She was followed by two Russians, Lyubov Kremleva in 34:08 and Ramilia Burangulova in 34:56.

Grand Masters winner was Jerry Clark of Charlotte, N.C., in 34:04. With Gary Romesser of Indianapolis, Ind., second in 34:41 and Sam Swofford of Matthews, S.C., third in 35:42. Ukrainian Tatyana Pozdnyakova again defended her female Grand Masters title, this year in 35:16. She was followed by Toni Cruz of Concord, N.C., who ran 45:25 and Catherine Lempesis of Irmo, S.C., in 46:34.

The award for the first finisher from the Tri-county area is named for race founder Dr. Marcus Newberry. Neil McDonagh of Mount Pleasant won for the second year in a row. He was 18th overall in 32:06. Rives Poe of Charleston ran a Personal Best time 37:33 to place as the 25th female finisher and first local. The Dewey Wise Award went to William Fulton, 79, of Greenville, S.C., for his time of 73:19.

For the fifth year in a row live television coverage was broadcast on Channel 5. The two-hour broadcast was repeated on Saturday night. In the 2007 race, a total of 278 runners broke the 40-minute barrier (16 more than in 2006): 246 male and 32 female. A total of eight runners, all male, broke the 30-minute barrier (one more than in 2006) and five of them (up from three the previous year) broke the 29-minute barrier. There were 2,063 runners who managed to cross the finish line under 50 minutes. A total of 6,122 participants crossed the finish in under an hour.

The Sunday *Post and Courier* listed the top five finishers in each age group, erroneously including the prize money winners as age group winners. The paper also published the names and times of the 10,943 males and 9,982 females who completed the race in less than 1 hour and 45 minutes. Complete results were later mailed, as a special insert in the newspaper, to all participants. Out of those participants there are only five who are known to have run all 30 races. They are Ed Ledford, Owen Meislin, Bob Schlau, Bob Walton and John Weeks.

The race entry fee of $25 for early race registration and $30 after March 4 was the same as the previous year. Julian Smith was again the race director.

For only the second time, the race had a wheelchair division. This year the winner was defending champion Tyler Byers of Sterling, Va., in 24:30.

For the sixth year in a row there were runners from all 50 states, the District of Columbia and a large number of foreign countries.

The 2007 Hall of Fame was made up of three inductees: Anne (Reed) Boone, well known local runner who was the third place overall female in the 1980 race; Richard Godsen, race volunteer who handled the finish line for the inaugural race and later wrote a computer program to help handle the growing number of race finishers; Jimmy Seignious, race volunteer, former Mount Pleasant Recreation director and former member of the Bridge Run Executive Committee.

OTHER VOICES
The Bridge Run Experience 2007
By Shane T. McKevlin

It's 6 a.m. on Saturday morning, and I was sitting on a school bus with people way too old to be in high school. Still dark outside that last day of March, and 48 degrees, I waited inside the bus on Calhoun Street until all the buses on the block were loaded up with people in shorts and t-shirts and numbered like cattle. We were all ready to run or walk 6.2 miles in the 30th Annual Cooper River Bridge Run.

I had woken up at 4:30am and had my breakfast of champions, Cheerios with bananas, as I had the last 5 times I had run this race. I guess it's like one of those sports superstitions, or maybe the fact that if it ain't broke me the last few years, don't fix it. Except for the run, I'm never up at this hour, especially on a Saturday. In college when my marching band had to be up at such an hour for a road trip football game, the easiest way to get up at 4:30 in the morning was to never go to sleep. Get a group of friends and watch movies all night and say you're going to shave the eyebrows of those that fall asleep. Of course the noise of the electric razor near their ear was all we needed to make them jump to attention. Of course back then, we had hours to ride on the bus to get to our destination, and to catch up on the missed sleep the night before. In this race, you could only get 30 minutes of sleep before the bus had forced its way through the traffic to the other side of the long and high suspension bridge we would be running in just a couple of hours.

The night grew into morning as we drove up East Bay Street in downtown

Charleston towards the Ravenel Bridge, and into the sunrise over Mount Pleasant. You could hear the awe of those that had never ridden, run, or walked over this giant before. As the bus' engine roared up the incline, I heard one anonymous voice shout, "If a school bus is having problems getting up this monster, what do you think my chances are?"

Over the river and through the woods to Chuck Dawley Boulevard we go. We're let off the bus right at the Mustard Seed and have to walk a good mile to the starting line at Moultrie Middle School on Coleman Boulevard. Once there, I find one of the three Budget Trucks that will take my book bag, filled with my warm-up pants, fleece, and long sleeve shirt I had been sweating through on the well-heated school bus, over the bridge at 6:45am. It's not called a sweat shuttle for nothing.

Now begins the waiting game. Waiting in line for the Port-A-Lets, waiting at the starting line for the race to start. It's now 7:30 in the morning and I'm in my correct colored race number section. The color-coded race numbers are based on when you said you would finish the race. To get around the slow people I had to deal with last year, I fudged a little and got a green number instead of the red. If you said you'd finish in 45 minutes or under, you had to submit a race time to prove it, so I was just above that section. From where I stood, I could see the elite runners in the section ahead of me running back and forth, warming up. My warm-up is to just do my stretches. I hear a gun, and the wheelchair race begins. Those guys are fast, as updates are soon announced that they're at the 5-mile mark already. The national anthem is sung, and then played on trumpet before the start, and after the applause the nervous chitchat takes place as friends are talking. "That guy up there near the front has gray hair, and he's going to beat me!" I overheard, and he probably did, since he was seeded in the next section up.

Finally the moment had arrived. Mayor Harry Hallman starts the race. The race begins, and if you want to ever see the Kenyans again, watch the news that night. Though it may take some several seconds or even minutes to reach the starting line, it won't penalize you. Everyone has a piece of plastic with a 2007 logo of the Cooper River Bridge Run fastened to their shoe tops, and that little piece of plastic is a computer chip that will give the time you run, from start to finish. Even if you finish at 1:00:02 as you pass under the finish line you still beat an hour because that clock is Kenyan Standard Time, which is started at the time the elites crossed the starting line, not when you crossed the starting line. In fact, you have to walk just to get to the starting line.

It's funny running down the street with 40,000 of my closest friends. I look to my left, and then to my right, and it's like one of those movies where aliens are attacking, yet the people in the movies never run this fast; if they had, they may have survived the attack. The run is fun, even over Shem Creek, until you get to the Cooper. The people are forced into the two-lane off ramp of the Ravenel, and you're running into where cars would normally be coming from. Climbing upward at such a fast pace, the whole crowd begins to slow down. Any chattering you may have heard before isn't heard anymore. No more crowds on the sidewalks on your left and right cheering you on, no water stations on the bridge. All you can hear is the pitter-patter of thousands of feet pounding the pavement up almost 200 feet in just a mile's distance. This is the slowest mile for most. This is where so many start walking. This is where my mind is yelling over my MP3 player at me to "STOP OR YOU'LL DIE!" My inspiration is when I see either a 10 year old or an 80 year old pass me and my body speaks back to my mind with a defying "NO!"

Then the hill goes flatter, and then it starts to slope the other way. The Kenyans have now finished their race as my body is given a vacation, and I fly closer to the 4-mile marker. The terrain is getting flatter as the runners exit towards Meeting Street, and what a long street it is. Once you turn on John Street, and then King, you know it's almost over. Several water stations are passed, and I run across Calhoun now having a wet t-shirt as a result of them. Down to the narrowest streets of the race, I hop up on the sidewalk on Wentworth, and try to get that second wind. Once I get around to Meeting again, now running north, I can see the big yellow

Sprinting for the finish line. Post and Courier photo by Sarah Bates

banner with big red letters of F-I-N-I-S-H L-I-N-E! This is where I kick into the high gear, knowing I had to finish strong, to prove though I'm not as fast as those from Kenya, I can hit their speed the last tenth of this race (just can't keep it up for the other 6.1 miles like they do).

I cross the line, and hear yells of "Keep on going" as I walk towards my free stuff at Marion Square. I get my blue ribbon "30th Anniversary Cooper River Bridge Run" medal that everyone else got too, to add to my first year running it and "25th Anniversary Cooper River Bridge Run" medal. I get my water first, then bananas, oranges, and apples. I get power drinks, boxes of cookies and crackers, cups, pencils, and lots of other free stuff including bratwursts. There's one tent there that gives free stuff, but you have to work for it. It's the Marines' tent, and they have a bar you must either do chin-ups on or see how long you can hang with your chin up there for a prize. The prizes could be anything from a t-shirt, hat, a sticker or a poster. While you hang on that bar, shaking with defiance to drop, the marines yell at you, but not in a mean way like in Full-Metal Jacket, but to encourage you do keep going.

As I walk through Marion Square, I hear sounds from a live R&B band singing and playing anything from Usher and Outkast, to the Drifters and Earth, Wind, and Fire. Next to the stage with the band is a tent with people holding these long yellow poles, of which one of them referred to as a magic wand. These magicians point this three foot stick at a runner's computer chip on their shoe, and like groceries scanned over the supermarket counter, it beeps, and then it prints a sticker with your name, and actual race time (not Kenyan Standard Time) on it. There are also tents with my personal favorite, massages. There's nothing like a massage after running a 10K to relax me. The price? Also free.

Marion Square is where it all ends, and the thousands eventually end up, but not for long. By noon you'd never know anything had happened except for all the litter that's being picked up by volunteers and street sweepers. All the costumed crazies, like a bowling ball and pins, men in formal gowns, people with snorkels, goggles, and floatation devises made for 2 year olds, people dressed liked the 70's and 80's or even the person dressed as a carton of cigarettes, are all gone. Those that parked in Mount Pleasant load the buses to get back to the other side, while some, still full of energy, walk or run back over the bridge. Those running it again, are obviously marathon runners who are used to doing 26 miles in a race rather than only 6. For me, I had survived, again running the race in under an hour, and had gotten enough free stuff from both the 2-day packet pick-up expo at Galliard Auditorium on Thursday and Friday and the post-race freebies that I may skip my weekly trip to the grocery store. I may not have gotten 1st place, but I'm the 4,789th person to cross the finish line in the 2007 Cooper River Bridge Run, and proud of it. There may only be one true winner, but all who finished what they started have the feeling of accomplishment that makes all who participated, winners in the end.

Other Voices
Tell Me Abour Your Bridge Run 2007
By Cedric Jaggers. Originally appeared in the May-June 2007 Low Country Runner

(Bridge Run info for 2007 – 28,953 second largest number of official finishers; 37,161 second largest number of entrants. Start time temperature 58 degrees)

After the Bridge Run every year since 1988 (with only two exceptions) Charleston Running Club members get hit with a simple demand: Tell me about your Bridge Run. As everyone has been warned in the newsletter I write down exactly what you say. No one gets to come back later and add or change anything they said (and every year five or six people ask for changes).

So despite telling everyone what was going to happen in the last newsletter, some people didn't want to cooperate and some club members (obviously the ones who only glance at the newsletter) didn't even know what I was doing. That was okay. It made it a lot of fun, and I talked to more new club members whom I didn't know than ever before. It makes it easier to find CRC members since the roped in club area has been used these past 2 years. The race crowd was slightly smaller than last year: only 28,953 finishers of the race this year, but it was hard to tell any difference if you were running it. The 58 degree morning and tailwind over the bridge made a lot of people happy. I stayed in the club's roped in area after the race to do these interviews, and these are the folks I talked to in the order I talked to you. Sorry if I missed you. I added the overall place, official time and chip time at the end of each person's comments.

Pat Rhode: I ran it, that's all I can say. Better than I thought. Not as many people who ran that I know. They are all younger than me. 1:10:45. Overall place 11,797th, time 1:10:41, chip time 1:10:03.

Bob Walton: It was good, a little bit slower than last year. I wanted to run under my age and I did, my time 68 minutes. It took 3 minutes to get to the start. Overall place 12,321stl, time 1:11:41, chip time 1:08:31.

Jeffrey Herndon: I'm gonna let you put what you want. I walked the first 2 miles with Joanne, then jogged the last 4. Chip time 1:16:57 real – 1:23 ish. Overall place 17,346th , time 1:21:41, chip time 1:16:53.

Susan Ziman: Um, (laughs). What do you want me to tell you? I enjoyed it. I ran exactly what I thought I'd run. I almost didn't make it to the start. 1:00:37, I wanted to get under an hour. Overall place 6,444th, time 1:00:42, chip time 59:47.

Lennie Moore: Well, a little off what I wanted to be, but all in all I'm happy. I missed it last year and I'm glad to be back. 38:50 something. Overall place 218th, time 38:50, chip time 38:48.

Steve Annan: I had a great Bridge Run. It was good: 38:15. I just faded a little at the end. Perfect race, I had a great time. Overall place 179th, time 38:08, chip time 38:06.

Walt Jabolinski: Um, well. I'm running with an injury that recurred; I pretty much worked my way through it. Are you going to edit this? Hurt my calf on top of the bridge, stretched, walked, ran but lost about 5 minutes. No way I wasn't going to run it. Ran about 48 minutes, I wanted 43.(Unable to find on internet site)

Bob Kohn: You don't want to hear about mine. It was a jog walk: 1hr 12 minutes and I was pleased with it. It's turned into a good event. Overall place 13,366th, time 1:13:57, chip time 1:12:23.

Mike Cipolla: I thought I went okay and then I finished under 37 minutes, my fastest 10k. These were the best conditions we've had in 7 or 8 years. Overall place 121st, time 36:47, chip time 36:46.

Nancy Curry: I'm thankful Cedric; I ran a minute faster than I thought I was going to. I'm not saying anything else. 50:46. I took your advice about the corrals and it worked. I ran an even pace, still had something left. Not as fast as my best 46 minutes. I didn't get to do it the last 3 years. Overall place 2,342, time 50:54, chip time 50:43.

Marc Embler: (Overall race winner in 1981, CJ) Well, I hadn't run in 7 weeks since I've got plantar fasciitis. I said I've got to run under 40 and I ran 37:20. My feet didn't hurt until 4 and a half miles. Can you find a more perfect day to run the Bridge? Overall place 151st, time 37:26, chip time 37:25.

Janice Pearce: My 25th Bridge Run. I ran the entire way, real slow. It took me 10 minutes to get to the starting line, but once I got there I ran the whole way. 85 minutes, 75 chip time. Overall place 17,511, time 1:25:23, chip time 1:15:29.

Dirk Pflieger: First time I've run it. I'm from Orlando. They don't have hills in Florida. I suffered but it was tough going up it. It was great. I loved the (illegible) it was fun. 55:43. (Unable to find on website)

Steven Hunt: It was wonderful. My time was 46:55, 5 minutes under last year. Thanks to my aerodynamic haircut (lifts hat) and to Betsy Rivers for the 10 pounds I lost and gave to her. Overall place 1,206th, time 46:54, chip time 46:48.

Fred Reinhard: Very good Bridge Run this year. I liked the fact that we didn't have a headwind. The easiest time in the Bridge Run 41:50 something. Overall place 418th, time 41:51, chip time 41:47.

George Dunleavy: It was a good day. The weather was perfect – no wind. A minute faster than last year. I'm getting ready for Boston in 2 weeks. 38:22. Overall place 188th, time 38:20, chip time 38:14.

Chuck Magera: (Didn't run it) It's all about the hashing. We set up the (Charleston Running Club) area this morning: 4 kegs, 200 hamburgers.

Joan Mulvihill: Great weather. Same time as last year, but I felt good downhill, not too steep that you can't run it. I started a little too fast, but it wasn't too bad, about an 8:10 and then 9:10 on the uphill. About 54:35. Overall place 3,616, time 54:35, chip time 54:23.

Dan Clapper: I took the wind and ran with it. I really didn't expect to do as well as I did. Ran a minute slower than last year, but 2 minutes faster than the Flowertown 10k and I usually run about the same here as there. Thankful for the tailwind. 43:06. Overall place 543rd, time 43:02, chip time 42:57.

Sherril Bean: I was about 1:09:13.and happy. I thought the weather was great. It was the best run Bridge Run they've had. Having the walkers in the back was great. I did a half marathon last month or I'd have been faster. That's my excuse and I'm sticking to it. Overall place 11,423rd, time 1:10:02, chip time 1:09:13.

Lisa Guerrino: No.No No. No. It was an okay Bridge Run. It was a lot harder going up the Bridge than I thought it was. I was wanting to break 50 but I didn't. I was close: 50:14. (Unable to locate on website)

Kay Chandler: I've been running it since '85. My Bridge Run was good. I took close to 2 minutes off last year's time and I'm in the grand masters category. 56:47. Overall place 4,799, time 57:16, chip time 56:46.

Huey Inman: I did what I wanted to do – I broke 37 minutes. I can't say much more. 36:45. Overall place 116th, time 36:45, chip time 36:44.

Larry Schrecker: A little slower than I wanted. I'm training for the Boston Marathon. No speed in the legs. I just didn't want to get hurt. 42 even. Overall place 479th, time 42:20, chip time 42:14.

Joanne Herndon: It was a walk, and not my best. Today I walked it. Time? I don't know if I can even count that high 1 hour 36 minutes and that's a long walk. I tried to run one time and got sharp pain in my knee cap. Overall place 20,850th, time 1:44:30, chip time 1:36:43.

Leon Locklear: One I did on memory – it was just hard work. I worked hard the whole way. 58 minutes. Glad to do my 29th consecutive. Overall place 5,851st, time 59:29, chip time 58:50.

Gary Ricker: Well it's no easier for me and my slowest. Conditions were good but it could have been a little cooler. I'm happy to be able to do another one. 45:11. Overall place 868th, time 45:08, chip time 44:42.

Bruce McGowan: Oh is this the Bridge Run? I thought it was a beer drinking contest. I had a great time, my 3rd one. I hadn't run in 3 weeks. I had hurt myself at the Myrtle Beach Marathon. 65 minutes. Overall place 9,619th, time 1:06:37, chip time 1:05:03.

Vicky Whalen: It was spectacular. It was not a personal best. No, no, no, you're not printing this in the paper are you? The post race party is the best part of the Bridge Run. 47:00. (Unable to locate on website)

Craig Coleman: Painful. Sore foot from the half mile mark to the end. A recurring injury. Perfect weather 43:24. Overall place 603rd, time 43:27, chip time 43:24.

Melissa Coleman: I enjoyed it. I think it was a P.R. for me but I'm just here for the beer. 47:27. Overall place 1,394th, time 47:40, chip time 47:27.

Clyde Mizzell: I ran out of steam on Meeting Street. 2 minutes slower than last year, but I felt good. It must be age. I have no idea whether I placed or not but I had a lot of fun. 53:14. Overall place 3,124th, time 53:14, chip time 53:13.

Jan Mizzell: Considering we didn't get much sleep it was not great. I struggled going up the Bridge but I felt good. Clyde woke up at 3:30 this morning. When we got to the end of the Bridge, it seemed a long way to the visitor's center. 1:33 was good considering the lack of sleep. Overall place 17,035th, time 1:23:42, chip time 1:21:11.

Gale Fennell: This is my first run. I don't want to be in this. I ran for the first time and finished and didn't have to walk. 1 hour 16 minutes. I don't want that in the newsletter. Overall place 14,720th, time 1:17:08, chip time 1:09:34.

Betsy Rivers: Well, I had a PSR – a Personal Slow Record and I'd like to thank Steve Hunt for the 10 pounds he gave me to help contribute to that. I had a pinched nerve in my foot and 2 recurring injuries this winter. Other than that, it was a great day, 1:29:22, and I'm humbled by the Marines (referring to the injured Marines who ran. CJ). Overall place 18,492nd, time 1:29:19, chip time 1:27:07.

Mimi O'Brien: It's always hard. I'm glad to finish, but I enjoy it. I thought it was good weather this year. It wasn't really windy. I thought it was going to be cold, but it turned out to be real good. It's always great to see that finish line. 1:06. Overall place 11,040th, time 1:09:20, chip time 1:06:34.

Clara Hogan: Well I got lined up too far from the start, but I had a comfortable run. Always wishing for a better time. Glad I got over it. 1:06:45. Slowest ever. Overall place 9,724th, time 1:06:47, chip time 1:04:46.

Monica Kimbler: I had a great run. I was real happy with it. Faster than last year.

A course P.R. for me, 55:59. I'm hoping to win an award. Overall place 4,224th, time 55:59, chip time 55:52.

Robert Aydelotte: I had a good run. My best part was the church when I saw the 5 mile mark. I thought I had a shot at under 48 but missed it by 13 seconds. I just flat got tired. I held the pace as long as I could. Overall place 1,552nd, 48:12, chip time 48:00.

Michael Early: My first Bridge Run. I was invited to train with the CRC by Eric Reddick. Both my wife and me – our first Bridge race. My goal was 45 minutes and I ran it in 43:44. I've run Peachtree (in Atlanta) four times and this was as good as any of them. 1983 was the last time I was here at the Bridge Run and I saw Frank Shorter finish. Overall place 750th, time 44:24, chip time 43:44.

Cherie Early: My first Bridge Run, my first race. I enjoyed it. I had a great time. I trained 3 months with Eric Reddick of the CRC and went from walking up to running and told myself it's a big achievement. I'm kind of proud of myself. My husband and I running together was one of my 2007 goals. 1:10:26. Overall place 13,746th, time 1:14:51, chip time 1:10:26.

Mike Chodnicki: I finished in front of all the Kenyans again this year. I drove the lead truck. It was great: 6 Kenyans came off the Bridge together. Then they dropped off one by one.

Sharon Chodnicki: My (illegible) was a little bad. It was okay on the way. I enjoyed it. I was in the middle of the pack. It's the second year I've walked it. The weather was good. 1:53 or 1:54. Overall place 22,131st, time 1:51:46, chip time 1:44:18.

Brendan Silver: 38:40. It was a P.R. by over a minute. My first time ever to break 40. I don't want to give you any B.S. I was hoping to break 40 before I got too old. Overall place 216th, time 38:48, chip time 38:44.

David Quick: My fastest time ever despite the fact I ran the Inaugural Georgia Marathon last week with my brother. I was only 11 seconds off the P.R. I set at the Flowertown 10k on a faster course. I'm pleased. I'd like to score a Masters award, but you have to run a 33:00. Overall place 77th, time 35:30, chip time 35:29.

Cedric Jaggers: I'm happy. I broke an hour. Never thought I'd say that but it is true. Surgeries take a lot out of you and I suffered after we got off the Bridge, but it was my 29th Bridge Run in a row and I can't complain. About 55:40. Overall place 4,042nd, time 55:35, chip time 55:17.

2007 Awards

Prize money winners:

Male overall

1	Richard Kiplagat	Kenya	28:35	$5000
2	Stephen Koech	Kenya	28:42	$3000
3	Woeku Beyi	Ethiopia	28:43	$1500
4	Soloman Molla	Ethiopia	28:47	$1000
5	Patrick Nithwa	Kenya	28:48	$800
6	Jacob Chamar	Kenya	29:02	$600
7	John Itati	Kenya	29:26	$500
8	Haron Lagat	Kenya	29:30	$400
9	Joseph Mutisya	Kenya	30:19	$300
10	Sammy Nyamongo	Kenya	30:32	$250
11	Devin Swann	Raleigh, NC	30:39	$200
12	Eric Ashton	Columbia, SC	30:45	$150
13	Sean Wade	New Zealand	31:12	$100
14	Alan Black	Hillsboro,GA	31:26	$75
15	OJ Striggles	Columbia, SC	31:27	$50

Females Overall

1	Rehima Kedir	Ethiopia	32:05	$5000
2	Amane Gobena	Ethiopia	32:12	$3000
3	Tatiana Chulakh	Russia	33:14	$1500
4	Sylvia Mosqueda	Rosemead, CA	33:30	$1000
5	Rose Kosgei	Kenya	33:43	$800
6	Janet Cherobon	Kenya	33:45	$600
7	Lyubova Denisova	Russia	33:55	$500
8	Gladys Asiba	Kenya	34:01	$400
9	Lyubov Kremleva	Russia	34:08	$300
10	Denisa Costescu	Romania	34:53	$250
11	Ramilia Burangulova	Russia	34:56	$200
12	Atalelech Ketema	Ethiopia	35:09	$150
13	Laura Swann	Raleigh, NC	35:22	$100
14	Lydia Kurgat	Kenya	35:28	$75
15	Firaya Sultanova Zhdanov	Russia	35:44	$50

Male Masters

1	Sean Wade	New Zealand	31:12	$1500
2	Irv Batten	Summerville, SC	32:53	$1000
3	Jamey Yon	Gainesville, GA	33:27	$750
4	Jerry Clark	Charlotte, NC	34:04	$500
5	Eric Vandervort	Clinton, TN	34:06	$250

Female Masters

1	Sylvia Mosqueda	Rosemead Ca	33:30	$1500
2	Lyubov Kremleva	Russia	34:08	$1000
3	Ramilia Burangulova	Russia	34:56	$750
4	Firaya Sultanova Zhdanov	Russia	35:44	$500
5	Donna Anderson	Pawleys Island, SC	35:50	$250

Male Grand Masters

1	Jerry Clark	Charlotte, NC	34:04	$750
2	Gary Romesser	Indianapolis, IN	34:41	$500
3	Sam Swofford	St. Matthews, SC	35:42	$250

Female Grand Masters

1	Tatyana Pozdnyakova	Ukraine	36:48	$750
2	Toni Cruz	Concord, NC	45:25	$500
3	Catherine Lempesis	Irmo, SC	46:34	$250

Marcus Newberry Award

First local (Tri-Country) finisher award

Male

Neil McDonagh	Mt Pleasant, SC	32:06	$500

Female

Rives Poe	Charleston, SC	37:33	$500

Dewey Wise Award

Oldest Runner With Time Under His Or Her Age In Minutes

William Fulton, 79	Greenville, SC	73:19

Wheelchair Top 3

1	Tyler Myer	Sterling, VA	24:30
2	Jordan Bird	Witchita, KS	26:43
3	Grant Berthiamume	Tuscon, AZ	27:58

Age division awards

Presented to top 3 In Each Division, With additional top 5% awards presented in each division up to a maximum of 25 per division

Males 9 & Under (117 Finishers, 6 Awards)

1	Cash High	Chesnee, SC	50:26
2	Alex Cothran	Anderson, SC	51:40
3	Boyce Haigler	Isle Of Palms, SC	54:18
4	Chase Mcdonald	Mt Pleasant, SC	54:29
5	Jack Serkiz	Aiken, SC	58:36
6	Matthew Dennis	Summerville, SC	59:34

Females 9 & Under (106 Finishers, 6 Awards)

1	Katherine Gore	Summerville, SC	50:38
2	Marni Berger	Asheville, NC	59:25
3	Kristin L Fairey	Mt Pleasant, SC	1:00:32
4	Terri Stafford	Isle Of Palms, SC	1:02:01
5	Scarlett Andrews	Mt Pleasant, SC	1:06:44
6	Lorraine Burke	Mt Pleasant, SC	1:08:17

Males 10 - 14 (485 Finishers, 25 Awards)

1	Timothy Tyler	Mt Pleasant, SC	37:18
2	Braxton Sheriff	Easley, SC	37:49
3	Drew Marshall	Fort Mill, SC	42:13
4	Lukas Hadtstein	Isle Of Palms, SC	42:13
5	Leland Rayner	Spartanburg, SC	42:21
6	Michael Kitchens	Union, SC	43:11
7	Brandon Rhodes	Piedmont, SC	43:18
8	Grier Sponenberg	Greenwood, SC	43:23
9	Todd Page	Johns Island, SC	43:59
10	Stephen Hurlbutt	Charleston, SC	44:17
11	Alex Holliday	Belton, SC	45:07
12	Sidney W Houting	Mt Pleasant, SC	45:29
13	Matthew S Wright	Mt Pleasant, SC	45:48
14	Felix Hadtstein	Isle Of Palms, SC	46:18
15	Joshua Minton	Charleston, SC	46:20
16	Garth Maree	Camden, SC	46:27
17	Chase Mann	Raleigh, NC	46:51
18	Jordan Napier	Williamson, GA	46:57
19	Martin Morrow	Moore, SC	47:00
20	Alexander N Buhle	Summerville, SC	47:09
21	Michael Wegner	Columbia, Md	47:46
22	Patrick Quinif	Goose Creek, SC	47:47
23	Brandon H Wood	Mt Pleasant, SC	48:04
24	Dylan Brown	Hickory, NC	48:04
25	Parker Cromley	Pawleys Island, SC	48:25

Females 10 - 14 (432 Finishers, 22 Awards)

1	Taylor Stubbs	Charleston, SC	43:13
2	Lucy Rummler	Mt Pleasant, SC	43:51
3	Caroline Duer	Greenville, SC	47:01
4	Anna Few	Greenville, SC	47:10
5	Brittany Best	Union, SC	47:21
6	Kirsten Sanders	Union, SC	48:09
7	Tara Hadtstein	Isle Of Palms, SC	48:54
8	Stephanie Hulme	Alpharetta, GA	49:14
9	Alexis Prickett	Columbia, SC	49:16
10	Rhianna Sherlock	Goose Creek, SC	49:49
11	Kelley Strong	Union, SC	50:38
12	Amanda Sinclair	Buffalo, SC	50:38
13	Catherine Smith	Murrells Inlet, SC	50:50
14	Allison Beam	Greer, SC	51:06
15	Kristen Cain	Abbeville, SC	52:22
16	Kelsey Orvin	Summerville, SC	53:32
17	Hannah Anderson	Goose Creek, SC	53:35
18	Amanda Bumeder	Summerville, SC	53:38
19	Mary Fewell	Greenville, SC	54:20
20	Elise Cox	Taylors, SC	54:40
21	Darby Woodard	Greenville, SC	54:40
22	Kendall Pace	Summerville, SC	54:50

Males 15 - 19 (575 Finishers, 25 Awards)

1	Brock Phillips	Chapel Hill, NC	32:14
2	Maxwell Gustaitis	Charleston, SC	33:37
3	Mick Francis	Lake Wylie, SC	33:54
4	Jefferson Waugh	Statesville, NC	34:04
5	Matt B Henderson	Inman, SC	34:17
6	Chris Bailey	Charlotte, NC	34:51
7	Daniel Knight	Elgin, SC	35:00
8	Jake Dialesandro	Ravenna, OH	35:13
9	Mark Bowers	Ladson, SC	36:33
10	Josh Brooks	Unknown	36:34
11	Paul Bowers	Summerville, SC	36:40
12	Adam Burrell	Campobello, SC	36:56
13	Robert Padgett	Moore, SC	37:15
14	Josh Cain	Union, SC	37:19
15	Craig Simpkins	Boiling Springs, SC	37:19
16	Erik Myers	Beaverton, OR	37:34
17	Parker Wade	Greer, SC	38:01
18	Drew Sayce	Greer, SC	38:07
19	Chris Siers	Granite Falls, NC	38:29
20	Andrew King	Anderson, SC	38:39
21	Nathaniel Hayes	Fort Mill, SC	38:49
22	Adam Standley	Greenwood, SC	39:12
23	Taylor Christiansen	Jamestown, NC	39:20
24	Daniel Yeakley	Locust, NC	39:24
25	Tyler Dawson	Charleston, SC	39:25

Females 15 - 19 (778 Finishers, 25 Awards)

1	Cara Browning	Goose Creek, SC	42:20
2	Elizabeth Tempel	Beaufort, SC	42:59
3	Raven Campbell	Westminster, SC	44:01
4	Sarah Williamson	Charlotte, NC	46:12
5	Stacia Streetman	Greer, SC	46:18
6	Kimberly Demetriou	Alpharetta, GA	47:21
7	Jade Gurlanick	Goose Creek, SC	47:47
8	Bekah Henderson	Lexington, SC	47:52
9	Reed Few	Greenville, SC	47:53
10	Laura Brichler	Charleston, SC	47:55
11	Alix Pommerenke	Sumter, SC	47:59
12	Heather R Lisle	Summerville, SC	47:59
13	Elizabeth Holman	Greenwood, SC	48:05
14	Elizabeth High	Chesnee, SC	48:06
15	Darla Browning	Goose Creek, SC	48:11
16	Ilana Mcquinn	Charleston, SC	48:13
17	Jessica Franklin	Greer, SC	48:18
18	Abbie Ormond	Sumter, SC	48:43
19	Claire Hobbs	Asheville, NC	48:44
20	Taylor Hughes	Greer, SC	49:09
21	Taylor Walker	Waxhaw, NC	49:13
22	Kelly Maw	Raleigh, NC	49:16
23	Brittany Jones	Summerville, SC	49:17
24	Marina Fleming	Charleston, SC	49:17
25	Allie Wagner	Salisbury, NC	49:21

Males 20 - 24 (1,099 Finishers, 25 Awards)

1	Michael Earle	Greenville, NC	32:12
2	Jayce Watson	Wingate, NC	32:36
3	Brian Mcneil	Charlotte, NC	32:55
4	Matt Holmes	Charleston, SC	34:15
5	Matthew Elliott	Green Sea, SC	34:21
6	Josh Myers	Unknown	35:19
7	William Huff	Summerville, SC	35:20
8	Cody Angell	Belmont, NC	35:33
9	John Sell	Simpsonville, SC	35:37
10	John Young	Charleston, SC	36:17
11	Nick Gastley	Marietta, GA	36:17
12	Bentley Hankins	Jonesborough, TN	36:22
13	Patrick Braxton-Andrew	Davidson, NC	36:41
14	Chas Biederman	Asheville, NC	36:46
15	Stephen Sykes	Spartanburg, SC	36:47
16	James Alexander	Charleston, SC	37:07
17	Ryan Boggs	Seneca, SC	37:10
18	Aubrey Darnell	Charleston, SC	37:11
19	Kevin Timp	Chapel Hill, NC	37:23
20	Alan Gibson	Columbia, SC	38:07
21	Adam Melson	Cherry Hill, NJ	38:19
22	Patrick O'brien	Statesboro, GA	38:23
23	John Leeds	Goose Creek, SC	38:26
24	Craig Thompson	Cayce, SC	38:29
25	Joseph Whiteley	Charleston, SC	38:30

Females 20 - 24 (1,919 Finishers, 25 Awards)

1	Jobeth S.	North Mankato, MN	36:28
2	Josie Hahn	Charleston, SC	39:53
3	Heather Knight	Mt Pleasant, SC	40:34
4	Jenny Mcdonagh	Mt Pleasant, SC	41:55
5	Kelsey Jones	Summerville, SC	42:02
6	Amanda Rawl	Charleston, SC	42:08
7	Laura Hewston	Summerville, SC	42:51
8	Margie Smith	Spartanburg, SC	43:21
9	Marcie Milner	Aiken, SC	43:36
10	Sarah Sentlinger	Mt Pleasant, SC	44:00
11	Laura Berry	Wingate, NC	44:26
12	Amy Sulser	Elon, NC	44:31
13	Charissa Skuza	Fort Gordon, GA	44:39
14	Haley Chura	Athens, GA	44:40
15	Andrea Klocko	Spartanburg, SC	44:48
16	Mary Legare Whaley	Charleston, SC	44:53
17	Stephanie Lundeby	Ladson, SC	45:17
18	Bree Ruppert	Charleston, SC	45:31
19	Erin Burdette	Clemson, SC	45:33
20	Sarah Goodstein	Mt Pleasant, SC	45:46
21	Casey Phillips	Greenville, SC	45:54
22	Nicole Rager	Folly Beach, SC	45:54
23	Stephanie Luther	Charleston, SC	45:55
24	Stefanie Wadsworth	Simpsonville, SC	46:28
25	Lillian Lampe	Chapel Hill, NC	46:31

Males 25 - 29 (1,931 Finishers, 25 Awards)

1	Neil McDonagh	Mt Pleasant, SC	32:06
2	Chan Pons	Arlington, VA	32:30
3	Robert Killian	Charleston, SC	32:41
4	David Cisewski	Mt Pleasant, SC	32:47
5	Patrick Hopewell	Florence, SC	33:42
6	Kurt Wilson	Asheville, NC	34:11
7	Christopher Lamperski	Charlotte, NC	34:14
8	Hudson Belk	Charleston, SC	34:16
9	Joseph Ryan	Winston Salem, NC	35:01
10	Dave Lee	James Island, SC	35:23

– Continued on next page

2007 Awards, continued from page 243

11	Elliott Taylor	Greenville, SC	35:32
12	Michael Beigay	Kannapolis, NC	35:56
13	Jeremy Duncan	Savannah, GA	35:59
14	Brooks Keys	Charleston, SC	35:59
15	Matt A Hopper	Goose Creek, SC	36:28
16	Justin Braune	Charleston, SC	36:48
17	Michael Mccauley	Greenville, SC	37:14
18	Jake Raser	Altus, OK	37:22
19	Leo Foley	Savannah, GA	37:25
20	Oliver Sendall	Charleston, SC	37:28
21	Rob Hambrecht	Orlando FL	37:37
22	Kurt Braeckel	Charleston, SC	38:16
23	Timothy Townsend	Raleigh, NC	38:27
24	John Berger	Summerville, SC	38:46
25	Zach Stroud	Charleston, SC	38:56

Females 25 - 29 (2,848 Finishers, 25 Awards)

1	Heather Lee	Clayton, NC	36:11
2	Amanda Cooley	Fountain Inn, SC	36:25
3	Rives Poe	Charleston, SC	37:33
4	Amy Crain	Cooperstown, NY	39:38
5	Alice Rogers	Charlotte, NC	40:17
6	Katie Ballagh	Blacksburg, VA	41:08
7	Marie Knight	Isle Of Palms, SC	41:17
8	Nicole SaUnders	Sylva, NC	42:03
9	Jenny Leiser	Charleston, SC	42:04
10	Erin Ritter	Raleigh, NC	42:14
11	Kristin Janson	Baltimore, MD	42:22
12	Darby H Tucker	Folly Beach, SC	42:27
13	Sarah Oliver	Simpsonville, SC	43:38
14	Karen Courington	Charleston, SC	43:41
15	Carter Monroe	New York, NY	43:45
16	Rebecca Wein	Glendale, AZ	43:53
17	Christine Swofford	Greenville, SC	44:05
18	Christy Paine	Holly Springs, NC	44:24
19	Kelly Compton	Charleston, SC	44:49
20	Stephanie Young	Spartanburg, SC	44:59
21	Amy Smith	Asheville, NC	45:04
22	Sara Couse	Charlotte, NC	45:23
23	Clare Whipple	Mt Pleasant, SC	45:37
24	Regina Nesseler	Charlotte, NC	45:41
25	Katherine Kelly	Greenville, SC	45:50

Males 30 - 34 (1,792 Finishers, 25 Awards)

1	Emisael Favela	Cicero, IL	31:47
2	Sam Volkman	Lansing KS	33:29
3	Jonathan Kraas	Mt Pleasant, SC	33:41
4	Trent Humphreys	Greenwood, SC	34:03
5	Coates Kennerly	Brevard, NC	34:05
6	Karl Walsh	Mt Pleasant, SC	34:29
7	Trent Kirk	Charlotte, NC	34:39
8	Jeremy Becraft	Columbia, SC	34:44
9	Mike Moran	Stanley, NC	34:51
10	Roger Fagala	Blenheim, SC	34:55
11	Jason Annan	Charlotte, NC	35:02
12	Matthew Muspratt	Ann Arbor, MI	36:20
13	Michael Gambrell	Fayetteville, NC	36:31
14	Tim Limbert	Ann Arbor, MI	36:38
15	Patrick Shaw	Clayton, NC	36:43
16	Thomas Walls	Ft Mill, SC	36:46
17	Jarett Prady	Unknown	36:47
18	Bradley Fowler	Winston-Salem, NC	36:55
19	Matt Pryor	Greenville, SC	37:00
20	Jimmy Major	Clarksville TN	37:08
21	Bobby Wilder	Myrtle Beach, SC	37:11
22	Scott Putnam	Knoxville TN	37:37
23	Jim Baker	Alpharetta, GA	37:40
24	David Rogers	Charleston, SC	37:40
25	Xan Abess	Lebanon, NH	37:49

Females 30 - 34 (2,068 Finishers, 25 Awards)

1	Jennifer Pryor	Greenville, SC	37:01
2	Sarah Hallenbeck	Chapel Hill, NC	38:08
3	Caroline Blatti	Chapel Hill, NC	38:29
4	Colleen Nicoulin	Port Orange, FL	40:35
5	Christine L Twining	Columbia, SC	40:51
6	Dana Hayden	Mt Pleasant, SC	41:00
7	Tracy Mckee	Charleston, SC	41:19
8	Jessica Zichichi	Johns Island, SC	42:03
9	Lara Byers	Scottsdale, AZ	42:18
10	Fiona Lufton	Irmo, SC	42:47
11	Carmen Zimeri	Greenville, SC	43:05
12	Mary Resseguie	Unknown	43:05
13	Arden Stelly	Anderson, SC	44:24
14	Ellen Smith	Charleston, SC	44:30
15	Shannon Iriel	Newberry, SC	45:09
16	Maleia Lake	Charleston, SC	45:37
17	Lori Wilson	Mt Pleasant, SC	45:42
18	Rachelle Tomlin	Columbia, SC	45:45
19	Lynn Cecil	Rock Hill, SC	45:54
20	Andrea Pietras	Charleston, SC	46:04
21	Curry Smoak	Charleston, SC	46:24
22	Kristin Steuerle	Beaufort, SC	46:40
23	Amie Sweet	Bluffton, SC	46:47
24	Angela R Torgerson	Summerville, SC	46:48
25	Kelley Wells	Columbia, SC	47:11

Males 35 - 39 (1,683 Finishers, 25 Awards)

1	Reuben Chebutich	Kenya	32:57
2	Gregg Cromer	Summerville, SC	33:30
3	Kevin Mosteller	Mt Pleasant, SC	34:24
4	James Varra	Charleston, SC	35:13
5	Emery Lloyd	Moncks Corner, SC	35:58
6	John Webb	Columbia, SC	36:01
7	Darol Timberlake	Matthews, NC	36:26
8	Michael Cipolla	Charleston, SC	36:47
9	Bo Butler	Mooresville, NC	36:51
10	Doug Long	Charlotte, NC	36:55
11	Mike Pryor	Cramerton, NC	37:13
12	Turner Boone	Charleston, SC	37:58
13	Greg Brown	Mt Pleasant, SC	38:07
14	Mason Ferratt	N Charleston, SC	38:15
15	Mark Harrell	Raleigh, NC	38:27
16	Brent Shealy	Lexington, SC	38:28
17	Harry Efird	Troutman, NC	38:37
18	Billy Estes	Mt Pleasant, SC	38:38
19	Calin Maniu	Charleston, SC	38:43
20	Giuseppe Gumina	Charleston, SC	38:45
21	Brendan Silver	Mt Pleasant, SC	38:48
22	Nicholas Mayernick	Asheville, NC	39:06
23	Kevin Adcock	N Charleston, SC	39:14
24	Garrett Dieck	Mt Pleasant, SC	39:18
25	Kevin Kelly	Charlotte, NC	39:25

Females 35 - 39 (1,876 Finishers, 25 Awards)

1	Elizabeth Mccaleb	Mt Pleasant, SC	40:38
2	Laura Mullis	Mooresville, NC	42:22
3	Jeanette Mohl	Cleveland, SC	43:36
4	Debra Brown	Mt Pleasant, SC	43:50
5	Karen Killeen	Richmond, VA	43:57
6	Andrea Haschker	Charleston, SC	43:58
7	Stuart James	Columbia, SC	44:08
8	Charlotte Ratike	Charlotte, NC	44:29
9	Terri Mahoney	Okatie, SC	44:33
10	Julie Jacobs	Moore, SC	44:50
11	Melanie Stuart	Goose Creek, SC	44:58
12	Missy Hunnicutt	Columbia, SC	45:06
13	Pamela Piper	Unknown	45:19
14	Leslie Randall	Royersford, PA	45:35
15	Rebecca Thomason	Charlotte, NC	45:35
16	Molly Hughes	Charleston, SC	45:43
17	Rebecca Farsaci	Charlotte, NC	46:02
18	Kathrine Wall	Charlotte, NC	46:10
19	Beth Wease	Kings Mountain, NC	46:19
20	Gezelle Macon	Seagrove, NC	46:41
21	Jennifer L Stabene	Mt Pleasant, SC	46:45
22	Martha Bertscha	Charleston, SC	46:50
23	Stacey Griffith	Forest City, NC	46:57
24	Jennifer Sabin	Houston, TX	46:58
25	Catherine Mccullough	Mt Pleasant, SC	47:40

Males 40 - 44 (1,255 Finishers, 25 Awards)

1	Craig Kingma	Jenison, MI	35:15
2	David Quick	Mt Pleasant, SC	35:30
3	Chris Hicks	Florence, SC	35:36
4	Sean Killeen	Richmond, VA	35:40
5	James Harris	Wilmington, NC	35:50
6	Antonio N Holguin	Seneca, SC	35:56
7	Rob Blaszkiewicz	Loganville, GA	36:04
8	Nicholas Fleming	Spartanburg, SC	36:31
9	Keith Hurley	Charlotte, NC	37:12
10	Tracy Schooler	Sullivans Isl Sc	37:12
11	Lance Leopold	Simpsonville, SC	37:49
12	Jim Daniel	Mt Pleasant, SC	37:54
13	Dale Waters	Leland, NC	38:08
14	Todd Siczek	Charlotte, NC	38:12
15	Alan Brown	Charleston, SC	38:41
16	Jeff Dubis	Raleigh, NC	39:01
17	Paul Greene	Apex, NC	39:08
18	Uriel Lara	Seneca, SC	39:29
19	Kenneth Clyburn	Beaufort, SC	39:39
20	Andrew Krueger	High Point, NC	39:50
21	Rob Newton	Mooresville, NC	39:53
22	Dan Bensimhon	Greensboro, NC	39:59
23	Richard Stephens	Summerville, SC	39:59
24	Bratton Fennell	Mt Pleasant, SC	40:18
25	Dawson Cherry	Mt Pleasant, SC	40:22

Females 40 - 44 (1,513 Finishers, 25 Awards)

1	Lisa Tolley	Seneca, SC	37:14
2	Tatania Titova	Russia	37:32
3	Lori Hageman	Charlotte, NC	38:11
4	Laura Vroon	Wyoming, MI	38:56
5	Sheila Wakeman	Cornelius, NC	39:13
6	Terri Marshall	Fort Mill, SC	40:27
7	Kelly Hazel	Summerville, SC	41:51
8	Suanne Hall	Greenville, SC	42:56
9	Susan Saint	Atlanta, GA	43:10
10	Molly Achille	Greenville, SC	43:29
11	Keely Churchill	Raleigh, NC	43:58
12	Julie Murphy	Greer, SC	44:54
13	Diane Lancaster	Waxhaw, NC	44:55
14	Sharryn Whitmore	Mt Pleasant, SC	45:30
15	Lana Torkildsen	Matthews, NC	45:31
16	Sharon Hasty	Spartanburg, SC	45:44
17	Susie G Cump	Johns Island, SC	45:56
18	Michelle E Beaulieu	Summerville, SC	46:34
19	Kathy Bunting	Mt Pleasant, SC	46:35
20	Usa Mcclamrock	Columbia, SC	47:21
21	Jane Byrne	Daniel Island, SC	47:35
22	Deborah Baumgarten	Atlanta, GA	47:39
23	Melissa Coleman	Mt Pleasant, SC	47:40
24	Angela Greenlee	Albemarle, NC	47:44
25	Lisa Royer	Dekalb, IL	48:04

Males 45 - 49 (1,122 Finishers, 25 Awards)

1	Pierre-Yves Page	Greenville, SC	35:28
2	Ed Hughes	Greenville, SC	36:09
3	Tom Mather	Mt Pleasant, SC	36:19
4	Huey Inman	Mt Pleasant, SC	36:45
5	Peter Edge	Simpsonville, SC	36:51
6	Bill Gibbs	Winston-Salem, NC	37:02
7	Marc Embler	Folly Beach, SC	37:26
8	Lance E Kinsey	Myrtle Beach, SC	37:56
9	Paul Holyko	Daytona Beach FL	38:19
10	George Dunleavy	Mt Pleasant, SC	38:20
11	Cesar Gamez	Mt Pleasant, SC	38:35
12	Billy Tisdale	Sumter, SC	38:46
13	Fleetwood Fleming	Mt Pleasant, SC	39:03
14	Armando Aguilar	Woodruff, SC	39:51
15	William Macy	Statesville, NC	40:09
16	Henry Mccullough	Greenville, SC	40:45
17	Gregg Cox	Mt Pleasant, SC	40:46
18	Bermain Bolvin	Terrebonne, CA	40:47
19	Richard Keating	Milford ,NH	40:50
20	Michael Seekings	Charleston, SC	41:22
21	Jeffrey Stockdale	Goose Creek, SC	41:41
22	Dan Bradley	Winston-Salem, NC	42:33
23	Tony Da Silva	Charleston, SC	42:42
24	Michael Huff	Columbia, SC	42:43
25	Rick Little	James Island, SC	42:56

Females 45 - 49 (1,380 Finishers, 25 Awards)

1	Patt Loggins	Charleston, SC	41:32
2	Chantale Mercier	Terrebonne , CA	43:46
3	Dell Toomer	Summerville, SC	44:21
4	Tami Dennis	Isle Of Palms, SC	44:23
5	Jane Godwin	Greer, SC	44:52
6	Lee Patterson	Summerville, SC	45:25
7	Barbara Wagner	Mt Pleasant, SC	45:29
8	Mary Jaye Mcgowan	Wilmington, NC	47:03
9	Jennifer Doles	Mt Pleasant, SC	47:04
10	Lisa E Powell	Columbia, SC	47:22
11	Laurie Will	Charlotte, NC	47:43
12	Adele Mecionis	Sumter, SC	47:44
13	Trudy Gale	Salisbury, NC	48:03
14	Barbara Whitmire	Lake Toxaway, NC	48:41
15	Lisa Saladin	Mt Pleasant, SC	49:55
16	Rachel Caldwell	Lexington, SC	50:02
17	Elizabeth Chura	Gallatin Gatew, MT	50:06
18	Laura Blevins	Charleston, SC	50:18
19	Anne Boyd	Charlotte, NC	50:30
20	Lisa Guerrino	Charleston, SC	50:30
21	Beth Cavanaugh	Sullivans Isl, SC	50:41
22	Gigi Wallace	Mt Pleasant, SC	50:51
23	Leanne Johnston	Charlotte, NC	50:54
24	Donna Johnston	Mt Pleasant, SC	50:55
25	Paula Fernandez	Cowpens, SC	51:31

Males 50 - 54 (1,097 Finishers, 25 Finishers)

1	David Smith	Flagstaff, AZ	35:47
1	Mike Hart	Washington, DC	36:02
3	David Renneisen	Goose Creek, SC	36:36
4	David Bourgeois	Summerville, SC	37:05
5	Greg Leblanc	Charlotte, NC	37:17

6	Jim Wilhelm	Canton, OH	37:29
7	Lennie Moore	Mt Pleasant, SC	38:50
8	Peter Hertl	Jamestown, NC	39:33
9	James C Scheer	Charleston, SC	39:34
10	Dave Forrest	Charlotte, NC	39:48
11	Andrew Ammon	Statesville, NC	40:13
12	George Sykes	Spartanburg, SC	40:17
13	Fred Mullen	Columbia, SC	40:19
14	Bill Edwards	Florence, SC	40:48
15	Peter O'boyle	Columbia, SC	41:02
16	Rick L Carter	Eutawville, SC	41:14
17	Ken Cherry	Moline, IL	41:16
18	Michael Cunningham	Newton, MA	41:22
19	Jim Fann	Charleston, SC	41:27
20	Victor Rosado	Salisbury, NC	41:36
21	Sanders Lee	Spartanburg, SC	41:47
22	Jerry Donohue	Columbia, MO	42:27
23	Michael Drose	Mt Pleasant, SC	42:41
24	Bill C Maddux	Mt Pleasant, SC	43:02
25	Daniel Clapper	N Charleston, SC	43:02

Females 50 - 54 (1,169 Finishers, 25 Awards)

1	Ginny Moore-Bradley	Goose Creek, SC	47:15
2	Judy Osborn	Charlotte, NC	47:57
3	Sue Porter	Columbia, SC	49:05
4	Helen Hiser	Mt Pleasant, SC	49:08
5	Susan Walker	Charlotte, NC	49:48
6	Sharon Allen	Charlotte, NC	50:27
7	Debbie Howard	Mt Pleasant, SC	50:30
8	Michelle Withers	Charlotte, NC	50:46
9	Jo Haubenreiser	Kernersville, NC	51:34
10	Lori Pope	Charleston, SC	51:36
11	Myong Dunn	Durham, NC	51:38
12	Kathy Maschka	Saint Helena, SC	51:49
13	Mary Turner	Charlotte, NC	51:57
14	Kathy Adams	Martinez, GA	52:12
15	Elizabeth Boineau	Charleston, SC	52:39
16	Betty Floyd	Marion, SC	53:01
17	Paula Greiner	York, SC	53:32
18	Barbara Babb	Lexington, SC	53:32
19	Beth Bumgardner	Lancaster, SC	53:42
20	Kathy Tomasello	Weddington, NC	53:45
21	Rita Hobi	Sumter, SC	54:03
22	Patrice Katsanevakis	Mt Pleasant, SC	54:09
23	Sarah Mcneill	Salisbury, NC	54:12
24	Marty Smith	Greenville, SC	54:20
25	Mary Mccain	Nashville, TN	54:23

Males 55 - 59 (852 Finishers, 25 Awards)

1	Kirk Larson	Atlanta, GA	37:33
2	Charlie Galloway	Coconut Grove FL	37:35
3	Bob Schlau	Charleston, SC	38:37
4	Bill Brackin	Peachtree City, GA	40:14
5	Jack Todd	Spartanburg, SC	40:41
6	Vasan Pooh Neovakul	Atlanta, GA	40:45
7	Vince Herran	Greenville, SC	42:05
8	Rob Kriegshaber	Columbia, SC	42:36
9	David Lee	Columbia, SC	43:05
10	Glen Farr	Knoxville TN	43:40
11	Paul Brown	Goose Creek, SC	43:54
12	Paul Gordon	Concord, NC	44:21
13	Kenneth Hanger	Charleston, SC	44:24
14	Raymond Willard	Summerville, SC	44:37
15	John Northen	Chapel Hill, NC	44:40
16	Stephen Parrish	Fairview, NC	44:46
17	Kaarman Richburg	Mt Pleasant, SC	45:04
18	Philip Blyskal	Princeton NJ	45:06
19	J J Anderson	Charleston, SC	45:10
20	Bob Lee	Charleston, SC	45:18
21	David Wingard	Greenville, SC	45:28
22	Steve Hart	Andrews, SC	45:55
23	King Grant-Davis	Charleston, SC	45:58
24	Neil Derrick	Columbia, SC	46:01
25	Steve Moree	Wilkesboro, NC	46:29

Females 55 - 59 (764 Finishers, 25 Awards)

1	Toni Cruz	Concord, NC	45:25
2	Catherine Lempesis	Irmo, SC	46:34
3	Kathy Cole	Suquamish, WA	49:01
4	Lyn Hammond	Charleston, SC	50:30
5	Cindy Grant	Southport, NC	50:33
6	J Stewart	Aiken, SC	50:45
7	Janice Wilkins	Greenville, SC	51:16
8	Sallie Driggers	Hanahan, SC	51:43
9	Sherry F Barfield	Mt Pleasant, SC	53:00
10	Valerie Murrah	Chapel Hill, NC	53:43
11	Doreen Tylak	Winston-Salem, NC	54:45
12	Patricia Kotila	Johns Island, SC	55:13
13	Martha S White	Columbia, SC	56:38
14	Karel Keel	Sunset, SC	57:02
15	Judy Greenhill	Columbia, SC	57:54
16	Dolores Coughlin	Concord, NC	57:54
17	Patty Ostner	Orlando, FL	58:12
18	Karen Curran	Keene, NH	58:26
19	Marsha Joy	Unknown	58:38
20	Deb Bergren	Carmel, ID	59:47
21	Sissy O'daniel	Mt Pleasant, SC	1:00:39
22	Mary Cady	Savannah, GA	1:00:45
23	Chris Blake	Mt Pleasant, SC	1:01:27
24	Marsha Young	Atlanta, GA	1:01:42
25	Marcella Farino	Lancaster, SC	1:01:54

Males 60 - 64 (570 Finishers, 25 Awards)

1	Steven Annan	Mt Pleasant, SC	38:08
2	Rick Stetson	Duxbury, MA	41:24
3	Jan Hardwick	Dillon, SC	41:48
4	Fred Reinhard	Sullivans Island, SC	41:51
5	Joseph Bennett	Conway, SC	42:40
6	Earl Jackson	Rock Hill, SC	43:13
7	Russ Brown	Midway, GA	43:50
8	Robert Aby	Worthington, MN	44:07
9	Alan Mcgillivray	Charlotte, NC	44:32
10	Mackie Johnson	Conover, NC	44:51
11	Elbert Howard	Jamestown, SC	45:50
12	Linny Moore	Greer, SC	46:08
13	Jerry Sofley	Gastonia, NC	46:24
14	Richard Poremba	Corpus Christi, TX	46:28
15	John Sneed	Mt Pleasant, SC	46:59
16	Keith Ambrose	Mt Pleasant, SC	47:13
17	Eitan Rosen	W Palm Beach FL	47:57
18	Arnold Floyd	Hartsville, SC	48:06
19	Rich Welker	Okatie, SC	48:09
20	William Reece	Centerville, IN	48:28
21	Glenn Ragsdale	W Columbia, SC	48:42
22	John Johnson	Greenville, SC	48:54
23	John Dillard	Columbia, SC	49:14
24	Gary Butts	Statesville, NC	49:28
25	Larry Seavers	Charlotte, NC	49:58

Females 60 - 64 (425 Finishers, 22 Awards)

1	Nancy Curry	Mt Pleasant, SC	50:54
2	Kathy Seavers	Charlotte, NC	51:38
3	Sissy Logan	Salem, VA	52:31
4	Joan Mulvihill	Charleston, SC	54:35
5	Jean Sims	Charleston, SC	56:33
6	Kay Chandler	Isle Of Palms, SC	57:16
7	Connie Vogt	Stone Mountain, GA	58:43
8	Dorothy Anderson	Kiawah Island, SC	59:20
9	Janet Hursey	Greenville, SC	59:22
10	Marydavis Riddle	Charlotte, NC	59:46
11	Sooja Sung	Mt Pleasant, SC	59:58
12	Joyce Ploeger	Virginia Beach, VA	1:00:46
13	Vickie Sessions	Charleston, SC	1:01:13
14	Sheri Flower	Mooresville, NC	1:01:38
15	Kay Lackey	Mt Pleasant, SC	1:04:17
16	Hiddy Morgan	Collowhee, NC	1:04:29
17	Donna Wuelzer	Herndon, VA	1:05:41
18	Nancy Mckeown	Johns Island, SC	1:05:58
19	Monika Wells	Greer, SC	1:06:35
20	Iris Hill	Goose Creek, SC	1:06:36
21	Sally Anne Kaiser	Myrtle Beach, SC	1:06:51
22	Dianne Gregory	Edisto Isl, SC	1:07:34

Males 65 - 69 (257 Finishers, 13 Awards)

1	Jim Strowd	Mt Pleasant, SC	44:06
2	Steve Comer	Charleston, SC	45:35
3	Sonny Barber	Falls Church VA	46:08
4	Thomas Eison	Greenville, SC	49:11
5	Ernst Lenz	High Point, NC	50:35
6	George Geils, Sr	Charleston, SC	51:03
7	Roman Marks	Charleston, SC	51:34
8	Floyd Riley	St George, SC	52:40
9	Thomas Dority	Charleston, SC	52:48
10	Amblick Smith	Salisbury, NC	54:22
11	Edmund Miller	Hendersonville, NC	55:11
12	Wally Goode	Shipman VA	56:07
13	Bill Lindeman	Oregon, OH	56:13

Females 65 - 69 (155 Finishers, 8 awards)

1	Barbara Lindeman	Oregon, OH	55:36
2	Heide-Marie Lenz	High Point, NC	1:00:32
3	Bobbye Faucette	Sparatanburg, SC	1:02:54
4	Jan Mcalhany	Dewees Island, SC	1:04:03
5	Florence Gatto	Pawleys Island, SC	1:04:19
6	Patricia Thompson	Hilton Head, SC	1:04:55
7	Faye Davis	Mt Pleasant, SC	1:05:05
8	Karen Yossef	Mt Pleasant, SC	1:05:51

Males 70 - 74 (89 Finishers, 5 Awards)

1	Clyde Mizzell	Charleston, SC	53:14
2	George Hilton	Dewees Island, SC	55:24
3	Branch Worsham	Old Westbury, NY	55:37
4	Ed Ledford	Folly Beach, SC	58:08
5	Jacob Cooter	Grovetown, GA	58:12

Females 70 - 74 (64 Finishers, 4 Awards)

1	Susie Kluttz	Winston Salem, NC	51:00
2	E.K. Tolley-Beeson	Sumter, SC	1:04:18
3	Jane Gregorie	Yemassee, SC	1:14:13
4	Camille Daniel	Summerville, SC	1:16:10

Males 75 - 79 (25 Finishers, 3 Awards)

1	William Boulter	Charleston, SC	52:01
2	Jack Lightle	Cocoa, FL	58:11
3	John Noble	Charleston, SC	1:01:35

Females 75 - 79 (15 Finishers, 3 Awards)

1	Garthedon Embler	Isle Of Palms, SC	1:37:54
2	Marilyn Griffith	Asheville, NC	1:53:10
3	Kay Biddlecomb	Hanahan, SC	1:53:51

Males 80 - 98 (11 Finishers, 3 Awards)

1	Ralph Kennedy	Summerville, SC	1:32:10
2	Franklin Mason	Mullins, SC	1:36:36
3	Charles Farmer	Beckley, WV	1:40:31

Females 80 - 98 (8 Finishers, 3 Awards)

1	Ola Moody	Augusta, GA	1:48:04
2	Stephanie Schnegmann	Charleston, SC	1:51:20
3	Mary Canty	Orlando, FL	1:53:32

Compiled by Cedric Jaggers from complete results provided by Burns Computer Services on March 31, 2007.

A birds-eye-view. Post and Courier photo by Grace Beahm

CHAPTER 31
2008
Kenyans Take First Nine Places

The 31st Cooper River Bridge Run got underway at 8 a.m. on April 5, 2008. It was the third time the race was run over the Arthur Ravenel Jr. Bridge, and the third year both runners and walkers were timed. The number of participants who completed the race was second only to the 2006 race (the first time over the Ravenel Bridge) as 29,247 (16,419 female, 12,828 male; an increase in female numbers and a decrease in males) of the 37,666 entrants finishing the race. The 37,666 entrants was also the second largest number in race history.

The race again used USATF Certified Course #SC05039BS which starts in Mount Pleasant near Moultrie Middle School. The first mile is practically flat and then the course begins climbing over the Ravenel Bridge. Runners took the Meeting Street ramp and went toward downtown to John Street where a right turn took them onto King Street for a left turn. The next turn was also left onto Wentworth Street, shortly after which runners reached the 6-mile mark, then made another left to Meeting Street where the final left turn was made. The finish line was just south of George Street.

For the fifth year in a row everyone was timed using commemorative ChampionChip computer timing chips emblazoned with the same design appearing on the race T-shirt. Use of this type chip meant the runners did not have to stop and remove the chip after finishing the race, something experienced runners really appreciate.

Conditions for the race were oppressive, with a start time temperature of 66 degrees and a tailwind for most of the first 2 miles. As runners took on the mile-long, 4 percent uphill grade, they were greeted with a 15 mile per hour crosswind which pushed them from their left shoulder. When runners came off the bridge they turned into that stiff headwind.

Returning race champion Richard Kiplagat of Kenya was favored. He led a pack of eight over the entire bridge. When they got about a half-mile from the finish, the six Kenyans began racing for real and all of them finished under 29 minutes. Kenyans took nine of the top 10 places.

Robert Letting kicked to win in 28:46.8, with John Itati second in 28:49.3, Moses Kigen third in 28:49.8, defending champion Kiplagat was fourth in 28:50.2. Twelve of the 15 male overall prize money winners were Kenyan. "It was a tough run, very tough," Letting told the *Post and Courier*. Second place finisher Itati concurred. "It was," he said, "very difficult conditions for us."

A year after being shut out of the top two women's overall places, Kenyans took first and second. Leah Malot was running the race for the first time and was pleased to win in 33:22.6. Eleven of the top seeded women had previously run the distance in under 33 minutes. "The competition was quite OK," she told the newspaper. "There were many good runners and it was very nice for me to run here for the first time. It was very nice for me to win." Asked about the bridge she said, "The race was quite good. I enjoyed the bridge even though it was a bit windy. I didn't look out and enjoy the view. I didn't look at anything because when you are running, you are just concentrating on the race. So maybe I'll go out another time and look." Janet Cherobon, last year's sixth place finisher, moved up to second place in 33:36.8. Russian Lyudmila Biktasheva was third in 33:57.9.

Sean Wade of New Zealand repeated as Master's winner, just three tenths of a second slower than last year in 31:12.3. Eric Ashton of Columbia, S.C., took second place in 31:30.8 while Kenyan Gideon Mutisya was third in 32:43.3.

Female Masters winner was Firaya Sultanova-Zhdanova from Russia in 35:42.9. Donna Anderson of Pawleys Island, S.C., took second place in 37:33.1. Tatyana Pozdnyakova from Ukraine, who won the Grand Masters female division, took third in the Masters division in 38:18.4.

Grand Masters winner for the second year in a row was Jerry Clark of Charlotte, N.C., who ran 34:47.8. South Carolina runners took second and third: David Bourgeois of Summerville in 35:23.6, and Danny West of Myrtle Beach in 38:27.8.

Ukrainian Tatyana Pozdnyakova was female Grand Masters winner for the fourth year in a row in 38:18.4. Second place went to Jane Elizabeth Harlan of Greenville, S.C., in 46:02.7. Third place was taken by Betty Floyd of Marion, S.C., in 46:48.5.

The award for the first finisher from the Tri-county is named for race founder Dr. Marcus Newberry. Kurt Russell (not the movie star) of nearby Ladson, won in 33:31.3, placing 33rd overall. "I wasn't feeling that good," he told the newspaper, "and I think the humidity got to people a lot more than they thought it would. There was a little headwind all day, and over 6 miles that will get to you."

Rives Poe of Mount Pleasant was female winner for the second year in a row and ran her best Bridge Run time of 37:15.9. This was the third time she had run a personal best time in the Bridge Run. She also placed as the 15th female finisher to double up on prize money. She told the newspaper she was surprised to be in the top 15 women, saying, "No way. I never expected it. I am kind of in shock that I was in the top 15. It's the first time I finished in the top 15, so it was a big day. It was great. I had a good race the whole time. It was windy, but I felt good." The Dewey Wise Award was won by James Lamarre, 75, of Charleston, whose time was 63:02.

For the fifth year in a row live race morning television coverage was broadcast on Channel 5. The two-hour broadcast was replayed on Saturday night. In the 2008 race, a total of 200 runners broke the 40-minute barrier: 172 male and 28 female. Nine runners, all male, broke the 30-minute barrier with six of them under the 29 minutes. There were 1,564 runners who crossed the finish line under 50 minutes. A total of 5,410 participants managed to cross the line under an hour.

Charleston's Post and Courier showed the top 5 in each age division, once again erroneously including the prize money winners in the age divisions from which they are excluded. The paper also published the names and times of the top 10,000 male and top 10,000 female finishers in the Sunday edition. Complete results were mailed to all participants in June, as a special insert in the newspaper.

The race entry fee of $25 for early race registration and $30 after March 15 was the same as in 2007. Julian Smith was again the race director.

For the third time, the race had a wheelchair division. The winner, for the third time in a row, was defending champion Tyler Byers of Sterling, Va., in 24:31.

For the seventh year in a row there were runners from all 50 states, the District of Columbia and a large number of foreign countries.

The 2008 Hall of Fame was made up of five inductees: Roy Hills, former race director and Bridge Run Committee member; Margaret Konecky, composer of the Bridge Run theme music; Lee Newton, Bridge Run water station organizer and director; and Bryce and Jenny Myers, Charleston Amateur Ham Radio Club members who have broadcast the split times for every Bridge Run.

Other Voices
Tell Me About Your Bridge Run 2008
By Cedric Jaggers. Originally appeared on the Charleston Running Club website April 2008

(Bridge Run info for 2008 29,247 official finishers – second largest official number, 37,666 entrants, second largest. Start time temperature 66 degrees and rising with high humidity.)

I had to look it up. When David Quick asked me when I started doing this article (for his article about it in the *Post and Courier*) I couldn't remember the exact year. So I dug out the May-June 1988 newsletter and there it was. The very first "Tell Me", inspired by tedium and the long delay for the awards ceremony which for some obscure reason was held at the State Ports Authority that year instead of at Marion Square. Only Dan Clapper and Mike Chodnicki were among the 40 interviewees that year who also appear in this year's version. Not much has changed (ha, ha). I just ask all the club members I can find to "Tell Me About Your Bridge Run" and then write down exactly what you say. Sorry it took me so long to get to the club area (yes I ran 20 minutes slower than I did back in '88) so way too many people were already gone. I'm glad I talked to as many of you as I did. Sure hope to get more next year. Overall place, chip time and official race clock time were added from printed results given me by Burns Computer and online search of the www.BridgeRun.Com website. CJ

Anne Boone: It took me 3 minutes to get to the start. Even when I got to the start, I wasn't able to start running; we were walking. The run was good after that. It was fun. I was frustrated about the start. Now I know how the average runner

Kathy Owens: It was tough – warmer than I wanted. I didn't run as well as last year. Last year I left my chip at home and ran 2 minutes faster than this year. 51:20. Overall place 50:59

Joanne Herndon: I'm so happy I finished. I took the fastest I ever ran – 69 minutes and said I have to do better than that and I did. Chip 1:08:39 about 2 and a half minutes faster. Overall place 11,814th, chip time 1:08:38, official Clock Time 1:12:13.

Joan Mulvihill: All right. My worst Bridge Run time but I loved the day. 8 minutes slower than my slowest. I don't know why. 1 hour flat. Overall place 5,426, chip time 59:44, official Clock Time 1:00:03.

Mike Chodnicki: I got to lead for the whole race until the final mile but had to drop out at the 6 mile mark. I drove the lead truck again this year. It was neat to see the 6 of them still together until Calhoun Street and then they started racing.

Keith Ambrose: The same old crap. I fought my way through it and came across the line with the best looking girl in town. (As he gestured to the girl next to him) Time 51:25. Overall place 1,952nd, chip time 51:16, official Clock Time 51:21.

Jill Pellerin: I've moved to Atlanta. I was excited today, adrenaline is what you need. So anyway, a bunch of sweat at the base of the bridge. All I wanted to do was holler. 59:58. Overall place 5,391st, chip time 59:37, official Clock Time 59:58.

John Sneed: 45:16. The humidity was more than I expected. I was looking for something quicker than that. Don't know how I did in the age group. Hope I'm finally in the top 3. Overall place 641st, chip time 45:11, official Clock Time 45:16. 1st 65-69 age group award.

Fred Reinhard: Flat day. Combination of a little bit of wind and more heat than expected but it was still fun. 44:30. Overall place 547th, chip time 44:33, official Clock Time 44:38, top 5% age group award.

Rives Poe: It started off with a bang – no one was lined up. I went out too fast. This is the first time I learned how to draft. I felt a little bad I did draft on King Street. I P.R.ed again at the Bridge. I was hoping to be in the 36's. 37:17 (Note: she was the Marcus Newberry Award winner for the second year in a row.) Overall place 101st, chip time 37:14, official Clock Time 37:16. 15th place overall female prize money winner.

Richard Ruth: My first one. 58 to about an hour I guess it was good for me. The downhill was harder than I thought. I expected I could rest the whole way down but I couldn't. I'm happy with my time, glad the rain didn't get us. Overall place 4,538th, chip time 56:43, official Clock Time 58:15.

Lennie Moore: Well I did another one. The time wasn't so swift. My slowest since I began racing. Wild heat. 40:15. Overall place 215th, chip time 40:14, official Clock Time 40:17. 3rd place 50-54 age group award.

Anne Wyman Cipolla: I started out a little fast. It's not my fastest run, but I'm pretty happy about 38:51. Overall place 150th, chip time 38:48, official Clock Time 38:51. 1st place 30-34 age group award.

Jeffrey Herndon: One hour 13 minutes.38 seconds. Just ran it slow. It took 6 or 7 minutes to get to the start. It's what you get when you get old and do no training. Overall place 12,532nd, chip time 1:06:26, official Clock Time 1:13:58.

Gary Ricker: My 29th one. It's my worst time so far. I'm happy to be out here and doing it. It was too hot. The wind was not a factor. No hill work this year. Even though it was my worst I thoroughly enjoyed it. 46:26. Overall place 805th, chip time 46:21, official Clock Time 46:25. Top 5% age group award.

Donna Lea Brown: I did wonderful considering I got hit by a truck on Easter Sunday. The race was great. I walked and ran 15 minute miles and it brought me in at 1:32:48. Overall place 19,323rd, chip time 1:31:09, official Clock Time 1:32:51.

Steve Hunt: 53 and some change. I wouldn't have been out here without my podiatrist's help. I had plantar fasciitis. Just thankful to be here. Overall place 2,463rd , chip time 52:51, official Clock Time 53:03.

Dan Clapper: It was great. I set my goal 43 if felt real well, 46 if harder. I ran 43:23 by my watch drafting off people – I stayed with one bunch then I'd move up to the next. Overall place 420th, chip time 43:10, official Clock Time 43:22. Top 5% age group award.

Leann Reigart: I thought it was the best organized. It seemed further but I felt great. I'm getting old but it is still exciting. Time? 1:15. Overall place (note: I could not find in the results or searchable online.)

Jay Reigart: It was good. A little warm today. I've got a blister. I ran pretty good. I finished my 24th Bridge Run. My first one was '84. I stopped and had a Red Bull (Note: they were handing them out when we came off the Bridge. CJ) 1:02:07. Overall place 7,846th, chip time 1:02:02, official Clock Time 1:04:43.

Dawn Allen: It was the warmest Bridge Run of the five I've done. I enjoy the camaraderie and I enjoy being with my friends. 1:22 something or 1:23:05. Overall place 16,583rd, chip time 1:15:24, official Clock time 1:23:06.

Maria Cunningham: It was fun except for the humidity. I was pouring water on me all the time and I came in soaking wet 5 minutes slower than last year. Overall place 16,582nd, chip time 1:15:24, official Clock Time 1:23:06.

Clyde Mizzell: I was fine at the start except they waited until the gun went off to take the divider (between time groups) down. Other than that it was fantastic.

I felt good. I always run out of steam on Meeting Street. I felt good at the start and all the way down King Street. 54 something. Overall place 3,151st, chip time 54:49, official Clock Time 54:54. 2nd place 70-74 age group award.

Michael Hughes: I was walking and running right behind you. All I tried to do was keep your bald spot in sight. 56:36 (Note: at this point I asked him his time and he told me his chip time instead of his Clock Time and when I told him my Clock Time 57:33 he added this) A wonderful run. I finally beat you. (Sorry, Michael I got you! Clock time and chip time. CJ) Overall place 4,710th, chip time 56:35, official Clock Time 58:35.

Melanie Hughes: It was a Bridge walk. We partied all the time. I forgot to stop my watch. Overall place 25,419th, chip time 1:56:48, official Clock Time 2:04:21.

Art Zimmerman: It was a good run. I tried to get under 10 minute miles and just did it: 61:09. The new bridge is tougher; that 1 mile uphill. They tried to keep the walkers from up front. Overall place 6,344th, chip time 1:01:06, official Clock Time 1:01:54.

Jan Mizzell: It was great. The wind got me on the span. It was great to be out in the open and I feel better now that I'm done. 1 hour 23 minutes. Overall place 17,481st, chip time 1:23:23, official Clock Time 1:25:48.

David Quick: I was pretty happy with my 35:35. Overall place 68th, chip time 35:36, official Clock Time 35:36. Top 5% age group award.

Cedric Jaggers: I said before the race I'd be happy if I beat my age since I haven't trained much this year due to my cataract surgery in February and the flu in March. So even though it was one of my slowest I have to be happy. I suffered today. It felt like an oven the first 2 miles with the wind behind us and then my legs turned to rubber when we got off the Bridge and into the headwind. Still it was fun. Overall place 4,365th, chip time 56:23, official Clock Time 57:53.

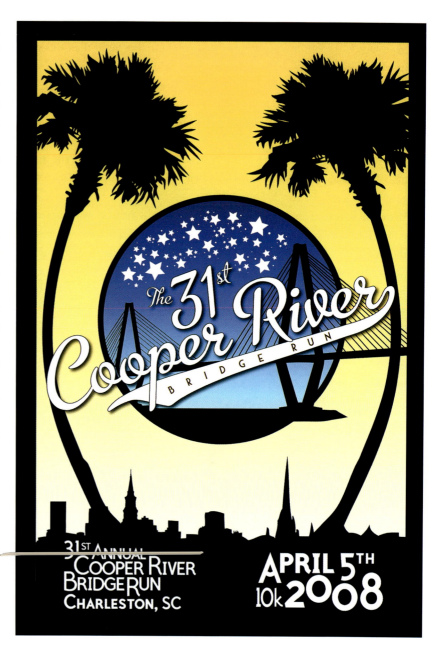

2008 Awards

Male Overall
1. Robert Letting........ Kenya........... 28:46.8 .... $5000
2. John Itati............. Kenya........... 28:49.3 .... $3000
3. Moses Kigen........ Kenya........... 28:49.8 .... $1500
4. Richard Kiplagat..... Kenya........... 28:50.2 .... $1000
5. George Misoi........ Kenya........... 28:57.1 ..... $800
6. Linus Maiyo......... Kenya........... 28:59.0 ..... $600
7. Daniel Kipkoech..... Kenya........... 29:09.9 ..... $500
8. Philip Koech........ Kenya........... 29:29.8 ..... $400
9. Lamech M Mokono... Kenya........... 29:39.3 ..... $300
10. Wegayehu Girma .... Ethiopia......... 30:14.4 ..... $250
11. Worku Beyi......... Ethiopia......... 30:16.9 ..... $200
12. Joel Melly.......... Kenya........... 30:19.4 ..... $150
13. Wesley Ochoro...... Kenya........... 30:39.3 ..... $100
14. Genna Tufa......... Ethiopia......... 30:44.1 ...... $75
15. Francis Kiprop...... Kenya........... 30:55.1 ...... $50

Female Overall
1. Leah Malot.......... Kenya........... 33:22.6 .... $5000
2. Janet Cherobon...... Kenya........... 33:36.8 .... $3000
3. Lyudmila Biktasheva.. Russia.......... 33:57.9 .... $1500
4. Irene Limika........ Kenya........... 34:00.0 .... $1000
5. Margaret Chirchir.... Kenya........... 34:23.2 ..... $800
6. Caroline Chepkorir ... Kenya........... 34:35.2 ..... $600
7. Firehiwot Tesfaye.... Ethiopia......... 35:18.1 ..... $500
8. Caroline Kiptoo..... Kenya........... 35:23.6 ..... $400
9. Eunice Orwaru...... Kenya........... 35:25.1 ..... $300
10. Genet Gebregiorgis ... Ethiopia......... 35:39.3 ..... $250
11. Firaya Sultanova-Zhdanova Russia..... 35:42.9 ..... $200
12. Laura Swann........ Raleigh, NC ..... 35:49.4 ..... $150
13. Meskerem Legesse.... Ethiopia......... 36:22.3 ..... $100
14. Maggie Chan-Roper... Shaw AFB, SC .... 36:27.7 ...... $75
15. Rives Poe .... Mt Pleasant, SC ... 37:15.9 ...... $50

Male Masters
1. Sean Wade.......... New Zealand ..... 31:12.3 .... $1500
2. Eric Ashton......... Columbia, SC .... 31:30.8 .... $1000
3. Gideon Mutisya..... Kenya........... 32:43.3 ..... $750
4. Sergei Kaledin...... Russia.......... 33:03.2 ..... $500
5. Philip Walkins ..... Coral Gabels, FL ... 33:08.7 ..... $250

Female Masters
1. Firaya Sultanova-Zhdanova Russia..... 35:42.9 .... $1500
2. Donna Anderson..... Pawleys Island, SC. 37:33.1 .... $1000
3. Tatyana Pozdnyakova . Ukraine .... 38:18.4 ..... $750
4. Lori Hageman ...... Charlotte, NC .... 38:35.9 ..... $500
5. Lisa Tolley......... Seneca, SC....... 38:57.1 ..... $250

Male Grand Masters
1. Jerry Clark........ Charlotte, NC .... 34:47.8 ..... $750
2. David Bourgeois .... Summerville, SC ... 35:23.6 ..... $500
3. Danny West .... Myrtle Beach, SC ... 38:27.8 ..... $250

Female Grand Masters
1. Tatyana Pozdnyakova . Ukraine .... 38:18.4 ..... $750
2. Jane Elizabeth Harlan . Greenville, SC .... 46:02.7 ..... $500
3. Betty Floyd.......... Marion, SC...... 46:48.5 ..... $250

Marcus Newberry Award
First Local Tri-County finisher-
  Male
   Kurt Russell .... Ladson, SC...... 33:31.3 ..... $500
  Female
   Rives Poe .... Mt Pleasant, SC ... 37:15.9 ..... $500

Dewey Wise Award
Oldest runner with time under his or her age in minutes
    James Lamarre, 75 .... Charleston, SC 63:02

Male overall wheelchair
1 Tyler Byers .... Sterling, VA 24:31.0

Female overall wheelchair
1 Maggie Frederick .... Kennesaw GA 39:12.5

Male overall Masters wheelchair
1 Matt Davis .... Bowling Green KY ... 28:57.3

Female overall Masters wheelchair
1 Jacqui Kapinowski .... Pt Pleasant NJ....... 41:52.5

Age group results
(Presented to top 3 in each division; Top 5% awards presented in each division up to a maximum of 25 per division)

Male 9 and under (97 finishers, 5 awards)
1 Noah Spencer............... Mt Pleasant, SC 46:35.1
2 Tyler Fish .... Boiling Springs, SC 54:23.7
3 Erich Wilklow.............. Greenville, SC 1:00:39.8
4 Preston Rubenstein .... Simpsonville, SC 1:01:40.3
5 Jacob Swartz .... Summerville, SC 1:09:04.4

Female 9 and under (83 finishers, 5 awards)
1 Kristin Fairey .... Mt Pleasant, SC 56:29.9
2 Julia Ann Kennedy .... Mt Pleasant, SC 1:05:39.9
3 Riley Reinhard .... Charlotte, NC 1:06:36.1
4 Maci Rebecca Bolin........ Rock Hill, SC 1:16:33.8
5 Elizabeth Lonon .... Eastover, SC. 1:20:28.3

Male 10 - 14 (428 finishers, 22 awards)
1 Todd Page .... Johns Island, SC....... 42:09.1
2 Brent Demarest............ Charleston, SC 43:19.6
3 Brandon Rhodes .... Anderson, SC 43:55.0
4 Jesse Luttner .... Buffalo, SC 44:24.2
5 Langdon Fennell .... Mt Pleasant, SC 44:57.6
6 Jacob Spencer .... Mt Pleasant, SC 45:34.6
7 Cooper Donoho .... Mt Pleasant, SC 45:37.3
8 Samuel Littlejohn.......... Blowing Rock, NC 45:48.3
9 Boyce Haigler.............. Isle of Palms, SC 45:50.7
10 Sam Stout .... Gastonia, NC 46:22.8
11 Robert Hunter .... Summerville, SC 46:39.3
12 Zach Robinson .... Spartanburg, SC 47:24.7
13 Ian Dibble .... Charlotte, NC 47:35.1
14 Austin Pendergist......... Charleston, SC 48:45.4
15 Christopher Kennedy ..... Summerville, SC 49:50.1
16 Matthew Gaines .... Charleston, SC 49:51.5
17 William Glenn .... Charlotte, NC 50:23.0
18 Logan Spencer .... Mt Pleasant, SC 50:32.0
19 Aubrey Smith............. Newberry, SC 50:34.2
20 Martin Morrow .... Moore, SC 50:53.7
21 Thomas Davant .... Columbia, SC 50:55.3
22 Tradd Teigen.............. Charleston, SC 51:05.3

Female 10 - 14 (449 finishers, 23 awards)
1 Tara Hadtstein .... Isle of Palms, SC 46:32.1
2 Anna Todd................. Spartanburg, SC 47:43.6
3 Megan Duncan .... Ladson, SC 48:35.9
4 Hunter Quinn .... Greenville, SC 49:42.1
5 Christa Green .... Union, SC 50:42.9
6 Danielle Marie Sams....... Charleston, SC 52:16.5
7 Rhianna Sherlock .... Goose Creek, SC 52:47.6
8 Emmeline Wheeler .... Troy, SC 52:56.4
9 Kelly Knutson............. Travelers Rest, SC 52:58.8
10 Anna Davis .... Cowpens, SC 53:04.0
11 Kristen Cain .... Abbeville, SC 53:32.4
12 Emily Lewis............... Easley, SC 54:08.8
13 Carly Caldwell .... Greenville, SC 54:35.0
14 Stephanie Herlong .... Sullivan's Isl and, SC ... 54:58.3
15 Grace Chambless .... Lincolnton, NC 55:06.1
16 Jessie Bridgham .... Isle of Palms, SC 55:34.9
17 Stephanie Hulme .... Alpharetta, GA 56:06.7
18 Danna Edu .... Ladson, SC 56:19.8
19 Ashton Lee Johnson ...... Summerville, SC 57:01.5
20 Jordan Pierpont........... Charlotte NC 57:12.8
21 Elizabeth Willingam....... Mt Pleasant, SC 57:52.4
22 Yasmin Alvarez-Garcia..... Mt Pleasant, SC 57:57.0
23 Caty Reville Hueske .... Charleston, SC 58:10.7

Male 15 - 19 (610 finishers, 25 awards)
1 Brad Meyer................. Charleston, SC 33:55.0
2 Bryan Brooks .... West Columbia SC 34:53.5
3 Sean Kelley................ Canton, OH 35:45.8
4 Trevor Sprague .... Charleston, SC 35:57.4
5 Braxton Sheriff .... Easley, SC 35:58.6
6 Jefferson Waugh........... Statesville NC 35:59.7
7 Andrew King .... Anderson, SC 36:44.2
8 Bobby Obrien............. Goose Creek, SC 36:49.8
9 Nicholas Baer .... Easley, SC 37:02.5
10 Austin High................ Chesnee, SC 37:05.7
11 David Cason .... Clemmons, NC 37:25.3
12 Taylor Christiansen........ Jamestown, NC 37:27.2
13 Tim Hawkins .... Aiken, SC 37:57.4
14 Ross Kimball .... Chapel Hill, NC 38:05.8
15 Parker Wade .... Greer, SC 38:18.1
16 Chris Sovacool .... Canton, OH 39:41.8
17 Chad Reynolds .... N Augusta, SC 39:59.1
18 Brandon Rabon .... Goose Creek, SC 40:10.9
19 Douglas Coats .... Wingate, NC 40:17.2
20 Chance Reynolds .... Clinton, SC 40:21.7
21 Cody Polzin............... Lexington, KY......... 40:23.0
22 Kip Thompson .... Charleston, SC 41:02.4
23 Ty Henderson .... Moore, SC 41:13.2
24 Daniel Williamson .... Summerville, SC 41:30.0
25 Jesse Crouch.............. Clemmons, NC 41:30.5

Female 15 - 19 (861 finishers, 25 awards)
1 Jamie Sires .... W Columbia, SC 40:48.1
2 Jade Guralnick .... Goose Creek, SC 42:23.4
3 Taylor Hughes .... Greer, SC 43:38.2
4 Janelle Sittema .... Matthews, NC......... 43:48.9
5 Karen Jayne .... Charleston, SC 44:18.6
6 Amanda Weekes .... Simpsonville, SC 44:40.2
7 Elizabeth Tempel .... Clemson, SC 45:06.6
8 Kimberly Ruck .... Greer, SC 45:34.0
9 Michelle Anderson .... Mauldin, SC 45:37.1
10 Mary Fewell .... Greenville, SC 46:01.1
11 Ali Cupito .... Greensboro, NC 46:01.2
12 Lesley Sweat .... Summerville, SC 46:29.2
13 Anna Few .... Greenville, SC 46:31.1
14 Kelly Maw .... Raleigh, NC 46:51.8
15 Sarah Williamson .... Charlotte, NC 46:59.1
16 Cierra Burchfield .... Clemson, SC 47:07.0
17 Martha Sampson .... Mt Pleasant, SC 47:11.1
18 Erin Becker .... Chapel Hill, NC 47:12.3
19 Alexandria Dibble .... Charlotte, NC 48:03.2
20 Kelsey Armstrong .... Talbott, TN. 48:03.4
21 Sarah Turman .... Taylors, SC 48:08.2
22 Logan Fry .... Charlestown, IN. 48:25.2
23 Caroline McDonough ..... Simpsonville, SC 48:30.3
24 Taylor Stubbs .... Charleston, SC 48:39.8
25 Melissa B Smith .... Easley, SC 48:59.7

Male 20 - 24 (1,205 finishers, 25 awards)
1 Andres Zamora .... Uruguay 31:42.0
2 Brock Phillips .... Chapel Hill, NC 33:36.1
3 Martin Cuestas .... Uruguay 33:48.2
4 Tom Clifford .... Wrightsville Bch, NC ... 33:57.6
5 Jayce Watson .... Wingate, NC 34:20.1
6 Jonathan Kinsey .... Myrtle Beach, SC 34:55.8
7 TJ Sullivan................. Chapel Hill, NC 35:11.0
8 Max Gustaitis .... Charleston, SC 35:52.7
9 Robert Isaac .... Charleston, SC 36:06.7
10 Josh Shumaker .... Bristol TN. 36:32.6
11 Adam Harris .... Clinton, SC 36:41.9
12 Nathan Bergeron .... Charleston, SC 37:14.7
13 Ben Sherard .... Charleston, SC 37:30.0
14 Colt Brock .... N Charleston, SC 37:37.9
15 Adam Jones .... Goose Creek, SC 37:48.6
16 Matthew Morrisette....... Mt Pleasant, SC 37:58.4
17 Stephen Sykes .... Spartanburg, SC 38:40.8
18 James Alexander .... Charleston, SC 38:47.4
19 Alex Sanders .... Charlotte, NC 38:52.9
20 Jake Barwick .... Clemson, SC 39:37.7
21 Todd Williamson .... N Charleston, SC 39:43.0
22 Hunter Barnhardt......... Clinton, SC 39:44.0
23 Anthony Westmoreland ... Wingate, NC 40:00.7
24 Harry Ehlies .... Belton, SC 40:15.8
25 Jonathan Riffle .... Augusta, GA 40:24.2

Female 20 - 24 (2,175 finishers, 25 awards)
1 Buzunesh Deba .... Ethiopia 37:52.7
2 Jocelyn Sikora .... Charlotte, NC 40:02.1
3 Josie M Hahn .... Charleston, SC 40:27.6
4 Casey Jeanne Phillips ...... Greenville, SC 41:34.6
5 Kristen Lisek .... Summerville, SC 41:37.4
6 Caitlin Renee Quinn .... Chesapeake, VA. 41:47.3
7 Anna Dukes .... Charleston, SC 42:08.5
8 Catherine Garrett .... Charleston, SC 42:13.3
9 Kelsey Jones .... Summerville, SC 42:18.9
10 Chelsea Van Horn .... Charleston, SC 43:25.4
11 Brittany Owens .... Merritt Isl, FL 43:48.2
12 Ashleigh Dane .... Charleston, SC 43:58.1
13 Laura Hodges .... Mt Pleasant ,SC 44:34.2
14 Anna Petrov .... Columbia, SC 44:36.8
15 Nicole Breves .... Charleston, SC 44:42.6
16 Sarah Dowd .... Chapel Hill, NC 45:05.6
17 Lauren Janarella .... Greenville, SC 45:24.9
18 Kelly Michele Urso .... Mauldin, VA 45:44.2
19 Michele Milner .... Charleston, SC 45:47.1
20 Alexandrea Dachenhaus ... Leesville, SC 46:00.2
21 Kimberly Parkhill .... Charleston, SC 46:16.5
22 Emily Williams............ Clemmons, NC 46:27.3
23 Kimberly Demetriou...... Athens, GA. 46:37.9
24 Jani Linde .... Columbia, SC 46:51.4
25 Mary Legare Whaley ...... Charleston, SC 46:55.4

Male 25 - 29 (1,923 finishers, 25 awards)
1 Devon Swann.............. Raleigh, NC 31:21.9
2 Vincent Longei............. Kenya 32:16.9
3 Birhanu Wukaw........... Fayetteville, GA 32:17.3
4 Garick Hill .... Winston-Salem, NC ... 32:52.0
5 Timothy Briles .... Greenville, SC 33:55.6
6 Kevin Crosby .... Chapel Hill, NC 34:10.8
7 Ethan Coffey.............. Goose Creek, SC 35:22.2
8 Jany Deng .... Phoenix, AZ. 35:25.4
9 Hunter Hicklin............ Charleston, SC 35:35.0
10 Anthony Fleg .... Chapel Hill, NC 35:53.2
11 Hudson Belk .... Charleston, SC 36:17.9
12 Kurt Wilson............... Asheville, NC. 36:20.0
13 Ryan Thompson .... Charleston, SC 36:21.1
14 Dave Lee .... James Island, SC....... 36:28.7
15 Robert Christopher........ Charleston, SC 36:54.6

— Continued on next page

2008 Awards continued from page 251

16	Matt Hopper	Goose Creek, SC	37:12.5
17	Lat Purser	Charlotte, NC	37:35.1
18	Colby Broadwater	Charleston, SC	38:34.8
19	Matt King	Durham, NC	38:35.1
20	David Bunge	Wake Forest NC	38:42.5
21	Brooks Keys	Anderson, SC	38:44.8
22	Michael Simpson	Charleston, SC	38:48.5
23	Todd Mayes	Cornelius, NC	38:51.3
24	James Wolf	Mt Pleasant, SC	39:10.4
25	Hudson Neely	Spartanburg, SC	39:14.4

Female 25 - 29 (3,029 finishers, 25 awards)

1	Tara Gruskiewicz	Lakewood, OH	38:46.5
2	Katherine Cavanaugh	Columbia, SC	39:02.7
3	Margie Smith	Spartanburg, SC	39:07.0
4	Alice Rogers	Charlotte, NC	39:30.5
5	Sara Jenkins	Alpharetta, GA	39:55.8
6	Emily Johnson	John's Island, SC	40:19.8
7	Katie Thurmond	Charleston, SC	40:41.2
8	Heather Knight	Mt Pleasant, SC	40:59.9
9	Erin Deleo	Wrightsville Bch NC	42:27.9
10	Anne Clinton	Greenville, SC	42:30.9
11	Andrea Stehman	Spartanburg, SC	42:38.8
12	Nicole SaUnders	Charlotte, NC	43:10.2
13	Katherine Kelly	Greenville, SC	43:52.3
14	Melissa Bell	Charlotte, NC	44:11.5
15	Jamie Ryan Turner	Mt Pleasant, SC	44:26.8
16	Jennifer Leiser	Charleston, SC	44:35.4
17	Jessica Claflin	Mt Pleasant, SC	44:36.8
18	Sandy O'Keefe	Summerville, SC	44:43.1
19	Nicole Rager	Johns Island, SC	45:15.4
20	Marion Minaudo	Asheville, NC	45:19.8
21	Mitty Frenzel	Mt Pleasant, SC	45:31.3
22	Mary Rebok	Myrtle Beach, SC	45:36.3
23	Kelly Compton	Charleston, SC	45:57.8
24	Rebecca Mayernick	Fletcher, NC	46:35.3
25	Erin Ritter	Raleigh, NC	46:41.7

Male 30 - 34 (1,664 finishers, 25 awards)

1	Tamrat Ayalew	Ethiopia	31:03.7
2	Sammy Nyamongo	Kenya	31:10.6
3	Tadesse Abebe	Ethiopia	31:38.7
4	Orinthal Striggles	Elgin, SC	33:18.9
5	Channing Pons	Mt Pleasant, SC	33:19.9
6	Jay Upchurch	James Island, SC	33:52.9
7	Palmer Thomas	Mountville, SC	34:03.2
8	Brian Johnson	John's Island, SC	34:29.6
9	Jason Putnam	Simpsonville, SC	35:27.5
10	Jeremy Becraft	Columbia, SC	35:29.0
11	Moran Mike	Stanley, NC	36:15.1
12	Trent Aaron Kirk	Charlotte, NC	36:23.7
13	Thomas Walls	Fort Mill, SC	37:24.8
14	Jake Raser	Altus, OK	37:28.5
15	Chris Cummins	Charlotte, NC	37:37.5
16	Jason Annan	Charlotte, NC	37:45.4
17	Chris Paes	Fredericksburg VA	38:02.1
18	Jeff Baxter	N Charleston, SC	38:17.2
19	Douglas Rappoport	Charlotte, NC	38:23.1
20	Charlie Epperson	Wrightsville Bch NC	38:32.9
21	Bobby Wilder	Myrtle Beach, SC	38:33.0
22	Tim Limbert	Mt Pleasant, SC	38:41.7
23	Oliver Sendall	Charleston, SC	38:45.5
24	Peter Mueller	Greer, SC	38:51.0
25	Joshua Rogers	Beaufort, SC	39:02.4

Female 30 - 34 (2,351 finishers, 25 awards)

1	Anne Wyman Cipolla	Charleston, SC	38:50.6
2	Farrell Hudzik	Charlotte, NC	39:55.3
3	Marie Domin	Isle of Palms SC	40:46.5
4	Arden Stelly	Anderson, SC	43:50.3
5	Amy McDonaugh	Irmo, SC	43:59.2
6	Sarah Wilde	Charlotte, NC	44:10.4
7	Sarah Blackwell	Columbia, SC	45:32.2
8	Evie Tashie	Asheville, NC	46:08.3
9	Lori Sheridan-Wilson	Mt Pleasant , SC	46:10.9
10	Colleen Angstadt	Charlotte, NC	46:15.1
11	Francesca Mosteller	Greenville, SC	46:27.2
12	Charmaine Howell	Columbia, SC	46:28.9
13	Jennifer Broadwell	Wilmington, NC	46:29.7
14	Sally Amanda Garner	Charleston, SC	46:41.7
15	Emily Heflin	Simpsonville, SC	46:43.4
16	Linda Beth Wood	Marietta, GA	46:46.5
17	Christian Altman	Walterboro, SC	46:52.4
18	Kari Graser	Charlotte, NC	46:57.4
19	Andrea Pietras	Charleston, SC	47:32.5
20	Jennifer Casey	Arlington, VA	47:38.7
21	Linn Hall	Irmo, SC	47:51.9
22	Jennifer Stillman	St Simons Isl GA	48:17.7
23	Curry Smoak	Charleston, SC	48:34.0
24	Marie Schmader	Charlotte, NC	48:45.4
25	Brandy Jade Englert	Charleston, SC	48:50.8

Male 35 - 39 (1,664 finishers, 25 awards)

1	Zachary Nyambaso	Kenya	33:21.0
2	Gregg Cromer	Summerville , SC	35:23.3
3	James Vavra	Charleston, SC	35:26.8
4	Roger Fagala	Blenheim, SC	37:06.2
5	Jason Philbin	Charlotte, NC	37:21.2
6	Emery Lloyd	Moncks Corner SC	37:27.4
7	Brian Fancher	Charleston, SC	37:38.8
8	Mark Widmann	Mt Pleasant , SC	38:04.0
9	Maurice Davis	N Charleston, SC	38:22.4
10	Mason Ferratt	N Charleston, SC	38:35.4
11	Gregory Brown	Mt Pleasant , SC	39:22.8
12	Giuseppe Gumina	Charleston, SC	39:30.0
13	Brent Shealy	Lexington, SC	39:34.6
14	Stephen Hudzik	Charlotte, NC	39:37.3
15	Michael Haranzo	Beaverton, OR	39:42.3
16	David Roper	Athens, GA	39:51.2
17	Shaun McDonald	Mt Pleasant , SC	39:54.5
18	David Barnes	Myrtle Beach, SC	40:04.0
19	Mark Harrell	Raleigh, NC	40:05.4
20	Billy Estes	Mt Pleasant , SC	40:22.1
21	Jeff Meier	Charlotte, NC	40:24.9
22	Turner Boone	Mt Pleasant , SC	40:31.4
23	Andrew Renton	Wilmington, NC	40:31.7
24	Greg Vigil	N Charleston, SC	40:50.3
25	Glenn Lankowski	Bluffton, SC	40:56.2

Female 35-39 (1,998 finishers, 25 awards)

1	Carol Brunson	Spartanburg, SC	41:28.5
2	Rebecca Browne	Virginia Beach VA	41:49.7
3	Rebecca Thomason	Charlotte, NC	42:37.8
4	Kelly Ruggles	Tampa, FL	43:57.3
5	Julie Jacobs	Moore, SC	43:58.6
6	Anne Stewart	Lexington, SC	44:48.5
7	Tina Juillerat	Chapel Hill, NC	44:54.4
8	Araby Ammons	Mt Pleasant, SC	44:56.6
9	Terri-Marie Mahoney	Okatee, SC	45:09.3
10	Cindy Ann Lyday	Goose Creek, SC	45:15.9
11	Claire Veber	Charlottesville VA	45:45.2
12	Cameron Wannamaker	Mt Pleasant, SC	46:05.3
13	Molly Hughes	Charleston, SC	46:22.6
14	Ellen Smith	Charleston, SC	46:26.4
15	Sally Tippett	Raleigh, NC	46:32.7
16	Kelly Owen	Charleston, SC	46:58.0
17	Mary Orr	Charlotte, NC	47:14.0
18	Kathleen Werkheiser	East Hartford CT	47:31.7
19	Lynn Hendricks Cecil	Rock Hill, SC	47:32.8
20	Debra Brown	Mt Pleasant, SC	47:36.3
21	Stephanie Morgan	Flowery Branch GA	48:02.9
22	Kelli Lyman	Charleston, SC	48:04.2
23	Kathrine Wall	Matthews, NC	48:07.7
24	Rebecca Brown	Charlotte, NC	48:14.1
25	Amie Sweet	Bluffton, SC	48:17.7

Male 40-44 (1,326 finishers, 25 awards)

1	Matthew Whitis	Columbus, OH	33:38.8
2	Jamey Yon	Charlotte, NC	34:44.9
3	Eric Vandervort	Clinton, TN	35:29.9
4	Chris Hicks	Florence, SC	35:31.8
5	David Quick	Mt Pleasant , SC	35:35.9
6	Chip Owens	Marietta, GA	35:47.6
7	Hank Risley	Cedar Springs MI	35:55.4
8	Craig Kingma	Jenison, MI	37:10.9
9	John Anderson	Greenville, SC	37:34.5
10	Tim Long	Charlotte, NC	38:11.4
11	Dan Rodell	Mt Pleasant , SC	38:38.6
12	Kevin Murphy	Columbia, SC	39:19.9
13	Harry Carl Efird	Troutman, NC	39:20.3
14	Greg Dudra	Hobe Sound, FL	39:22.1
15	Dale Waters	Leland, NC	39:26.3
16	Michael Desantis	Charleston, SC	39:27.7
17	Marshall Martin	Cary, NC	39:28.4
18	Martin Guthrie	Houston, TX	39:34.8
19	Paul A Reardon	Hartsville, SC	39:40.9
20	Alan Neil Brown	Charleston, SC	39:45.4
21	Jody McAuley	Mt Pleasant , SC	39:53.7
22	Kenneth Clyburn	Beaufort, SC	40:00.0
23	Paul Greene	Apex, NC	40:03.7
24	Alan Pogroszewski	Hilton, NY	40:07.1
25	Jim Daniel	Mt Pleasant , SC	40:16.4

Female 40 - 44 (1,523 finishers, 25 awards)

1	Sheila Wakeman	Cornelius, NC	40:54.4
2	Meredith Nelson	Sullivan's Isl SC	42:03.2
3	Anita Freres	Reston, VA	42:03.8
4	Janice Long	Clinton, SC	42:23.9
5	Michelle Beaulieu	Summerville, SC	42:55.3
6	Suanne Hall	Greenville, SC	43:26.9
7	Beth Pierpont	Charlotte, NC	43:45.2
8	Camelia Marculescu	Charleston, SC	45:33.2
9	Missy Hunnicutt	Columbia, SC	45:56.0
10	Anne Ainslie	Pelham, NY	47:35.7
11	Michelle Baggett	Goose Creek, SC	47:53.2
12	Sharryn Whitmore	Mt Pleasant, SC	47:57.1
13	Betsy Jessup	Mt Pleasant, SC	48:21.7
14	Kathy Bunting	Mt Pleasant, SC	48:23.6
15	Betsy Houck	Charlotte, NC	48:37.9
16	Beth Webster Wease	Kings Mountain NC	48:44.3
17	Jane Lockwood	Charlotte, NC	48:54.9
18	Keely Churchill	Raleigh, NC	49:56.8
19	Danna Brown	Taylors, SC	50:12.8
20	Stacey Renee	Farish Newtown, PA	50:20.2
21	Sue Echavarria	Mt Pleasant, SC	50:39.8
22	Michelle Pavlakos	Fort Mill, SC	51:18.9
23	Dana Ehde	Beaufort, SC	51:19.5
24	Dawn Ferguson	Greer, SC	51:24.7
25	Heather Wood	Johns Island , SC	51:48.1

Male 45 - 49 (1038 finishers, 25 awards)

1	Ed Hughes	Greenville, SC	37:15.5
2	James Harris	Wilmington, NC	37:36.4
3	Alan Thomas	Florence, SC	37:53.2
4	Lance Leopold	Simpsonville, SC	37:59.4
5	Michael Seekings	Charleston, SC	38:49.6
6	Huey Inman	Mt Pleasant, SC	39:57.5
7	Jim Bertrand	Charlotte, NC	40:01.3
8	Philip J Iuliano	Matthews, NC	40:13.2
9	David Edwards	Pownal, ME	40:21.3
10	Fleetwood Fleming	Mt Pleasant, SC	40:25.2
11	Billy Tisdale	Sumter, SC	40:40.8
12	David Kitchens	Union, SC	41:05.6
13	Cesar Gamez	Mt Pleasant, SC	41:25.8
14	Josiah Will	Bessemer City NC	41:52.8
15	Armando Aguilar	Woodruff, SC	41:58.9
16	Eric Smith	Greenwood, SC	42:03.0
17	Andrew White	Mt Pleasant, SC	42:05.0
18	Timothy Welch	Westlake, OH	42:07.5
19	Jeffrey Knapp	Hickory, NC	42:14.8
20	Jeffrey Stockdale	Goose Creek, SC	42:41.3
21	Donald Silleman	Matthews, NC	42:44.0
22	Andrew Krueger	Summerfield NC	43:25.8
23	Edwin Holler	Morganton, NC	43:58.7
24	Randy Nolff	Columbia, SC	43:58.9
25	Steve Bunecke	Simpsonville, SC	44:08.0

Female 45 - 49 (1,321 finishers, 25 awards)

1	Laura Jo Vroon	Wyoming, MI	40:33.3
2	Pamela Lovett	Newport News VA	42:22.3
3	Kelly Hazel	Summerville , SC	43:22.4
4	Patt Loggins	Charleston, SC	43:52.2
5	Nancy Thomas	Greenville, SC	45:42.0
6	Jane Godwin	Greer, SC	46:29.2
7	Lisa Powell	Columbia, SC	46:54.0
8	Tami Dennis	Isle of Palms SC	46:56.8
9	Deborah Baumgarten	Decatur, GA	47:20.4
10	Laura Blevins	Charleston, SC	48:05.9
11	Leslie Knapp	Hickory, NC	48:37.9
12	Amy Herold	N Charleston, SC	49:12.0
13	Trudy C Gale	Salisbury, NC	49:15.5
14	Elizabeth Riley	Columbia, SC	49:15.8
15	Nina Parks-Taylor	New York, NY	49:20.9
16	Barbara Neale	Yonges Island SC	49:22.5
17	Kim Walton	Charlotte, NC	49:29.7
18	Cheryl Lynn Quinn	Greenville, SC	50:15.5
19	Katherine Owens	Summerville , SC	51:21.1
20	Lesly Davidson	Isle of Palms SC	51:26.6
21	Barbara Whitmire	Lake Toxaway NC	51:29.3
22	Barbara Young	Greensboro, NC	51:46.8
23	Danher Wang	Mt Pleasant , SC	52:14.6
24	Penny Galbraith	Spartanburg , SC	52:40.4
25	Sandra Austin	Asheville, NC	52:50.0

Male 50 - 54 (1,026 finishers, 25 awards)

1	Keith Hertling	Lexington, SC	39:25.8
2	James Wilhelm	Canton OH	39:44.6
3	Lennie Moore	Mt Pleasant, SC	40:16.7
4	George Sykes	Spartanburg, SC	41:40.6
5	Marc Embler	Folly Beach, SC	41:46.1
6	Dan Bradley	Winston-Salem NC	42:02.3
7	David Renneisen	Goose Creek, SC	42:20.4
8	Bill Edwards	Florence, SC	42:23.0
9	Andy Tedesco	Mt Pleasant, SC	42:42.5

10	Jim Fann	Charleston, SC	43:10.5
11	Daniel Clapper	N Charleston, SC	43:21.3
12	Barry Schneiderman	Mt Pleasant, SC	43:25.2
13	Danny Morgan	Pawleys Island, SC	43:31.5
14	Felipe Mejia	Mt Pleasant, SC	43:32.7
15	Reagan Rice	Gainesville, FL	43:42.3
16	William O Young	Greensboro, NC	43:57.0
17	Richard Lee Carter	Eutawville, SC	43:59.9
18	William Rowell	Peoria, AZ	44:01.7
19	Will Jones	Atlanta, GA	44:10.9
20	Paul Coombs	Rock Hill, SC	44:13.3
21	Tony Da Silva	Ponte Vedra Bch FL	44:31.7
22	James Bradley	Rockwall, TX	44:33.5
23	Paul Caldwell	Lexington, SC	45:02.3
24	Frederick Ingerson	Port Orange, FL	45:07.5
25	Bill Miller	Summerville, SC	45:16.9

Female 50-54 (1,111 finishers, 25 awards)

1	Betty Floyd	Marion, SC	46:48.5
2	Mary McGowan	Wilmington, NC	47:04.7
3	Connie Young	Hurricane, WV	47:21.8
4	Helen Hiser	Mt Pleasant, SC	47:34.0
5	Lori Pope	Charleston, SC	48:12.4
6	Myong Dunn	Durham, NC	48:51.9
7	Cherry Kent	Belton, SC	49:00.2
8	Susan Jones	Atlanta, GA	49:02.9
9	Sarah Ball	Charleston, SC	49:23.3
10	Rachel Caldwell	Lexington, SC	50:02.3
11	Paula Fernandez	Cowpens, SC	51:43.6
12	Therese Killeen	Mt Pleasant, SC	51:59.1
13	Toni Paylor	Greenville, SC	52:11.6
14	Debbie Howard	Mt Pleasant, SC	52:21.8
15	Debra Grubbs	Belmont, SC	53:07.1
16	Kathy Tomasello	Weddington, NC	53:40.3
17	Gigi Lacey	Charlotte, NC	53:44.0
18	Rebecca Fairey	St Matthews, SC	53:54.9
19	Lynn Myers	Goose Creek, SC	54:22.7
20	Kathy Adams	Martinez, GA	54:50.9
21	Dallys Kulynych	Vero Beach, FL	54:53.1
22	Beth Smith	Spartanburg, SC	55:17.3
23	Aline Laing	Anderson, SC	55:24.3
24	Rita Hobi	Sumter, SC	56:14.9
25	Beverly Grant	Asheville, NC	56:15.6

Male 55-59 (805 finishers, 25 awards)

1	Dave Forrest	Charlotte, NC	40:47.6
2	Stan Wheeler	Charleston, SC	44:38.3
3	Raymond Willard	Summerville, SC	44:58.0
4	Pat Barfield	Ontario, OR	45:09.7
5	Richard Knight	Inman, SC	45:15.1
6	Paul Myers	Charlotte, NC	45:23.7
7	Gary Ricker	Charleston, SC	46:24.9
8	J J Anderson	Charleston, SC	46:30.6
9	Gary Richardson	Greensboro, NC	46:38.9
10	David Lee	Columbia, SC	46:39.8
11	John Northen	Chapel Hill, NC	46:49.0
12	Larry Milner	Aiken, SC	47:03.6
13	Glenn C Johnson	Charleston, SC	47:05.5
14	Neil Derrick	Columbia, SC	47:08.9
15	Robert A Fyfe	Montreal QC, CA	47:27.8
16	Eddie Muldrow	Chapin, SC	48:05.6
17	Samuel Jenkins	N Charleston, SC	48:18.0
18	Micahel Scardato	Charleston, SC	48:23.2
19	Donald Nugent	Belmont, MI	48:27.3
20	Bayne Selby	Sullivan's Island, SC	48:32.6
21	Robert Lee	Charleston, SC	48:34.6
22	Paul A Gordon	Concord, NC	48:35.3
23	David Wingard	Greenville, SC	48:36.2
24	Paul Brown	Goose Creek, SC	48:36.4
25	Jack Todd	Spartanburg, SC	48:40.8

Female 55-59 (825 finishers, 25 awards)

1	Deborah Stuart	Columbia, SC	46:45.8
2	Judith Osborn	Charlotte, NC	49:28.5
3	Rebecca Morgan	Chapin, SC	51:47.8
4	Sallie Driggers	Hanahan, SC	52:59.2
5	Patricia Kotila	Johns Island, SC	54:04.5
6	Kristine Serkedakis	Marietta, GA	54:11.7
7	Sally McNeill	Salisbury, NC	54:13.5
8	Valerie Ann Murrah	Chapel Hill, NC	54:31.1
9	Martha White	Columbia, SC	56:26.1
10	Janice Wilkins	Greenville, SC	57:17.9
11	Karel Keel	Sunset, SC	57:48.3
12	Jane Mayer	Columbia, SC	59:08.8
13	Cynthia Brown	Sullivan's Isl, SC	59:50.7
14	Jill Pellerin	Alpharetta, GA	59:57.2
15	Trisha Griffin	Summerville, SC	1:00:22.3
16	Judith Anderson	Summerville, SC	1:00:37.4
17	Kathleen Teryl Koss	Dewitt, NY	1:00:56.2
18	Debbie Rutan	Charleston, SC	1:00:56.9
19	Brenda Mary Hunter	Montreal QC, CA	1:00:57.2
20	Gail Newton	Mt Pleasant, SC	1:00:57.2
21	Patty Ostner	Orlando, FL	1:02:01.5
22	Bridget-Anne Hampden	Charlotte, NC	1:02:32.0
23	Gaye Milling	Ridgeway, SC	1:02:51.2
24	Susan Minck	Georgetown, SC	1:02:51.3
25	Pamela Garbarino	Columbia, SC	1:03:03.0

Male 60 - 64 (556 finishers, 25 awards)

1	Bob Schlau	Charleston, SC	39:27.7
2	Jan Hardwick	Dillon, SC	41:05.8
3	Steven Annan	Mt Pleasant, SC	43:49.4
4	Fred Reinhard	Sullivan's Island, SC	44:37.8
5	James Rich	Asheboro, NC	45:55.3
6	Linny Moore	Greer, SC	46:26.5
7	Joseph Siever	Bradenton, FL	49:04.7
8	Elbert Howard	Jamestown, SC	49:05.7
9	Eitan Rosen	West Palm Bch, FL	49:09.2
10	John W Johnson	Greenville, SC	50:03.8
11	George Bolton	Phoenix, AZ	50:31.3
12	Richard Landsman	Summerville, SC	50:51.0
13	Herbert Blackwell	Rock Hill, SC	51:16.8
14	Peter Mugglestone	Columbia, SC	51:18.2
15	Keith Ambrose	Mt Pleasant, SC	51:20.8
16	Robert M Ott	Mt Pleasant, SC	51:35.1
17	William Buchanan	Atlanta, GA	51:40.1
18	Glen Ragsdale	W Columbia, SC	51:51.4
19	Benn Grant	Asheville, NC	53:04.2
20	David Myer	Ladson, SC	53:08.1
21	Joseph Losek	Mt Pleasant, SC	53:13.5
22	Willis Burkett	Chesnee, SC	53:21.4
23	Patrick Welch	Charleston, SC	53:29.6
24	Lawrence Devoe	Augusta, GA	53:37.2
25	Donald Smith	Buffalo, NY	53:43.3

Female 60 - 64 (410 finishers, 21 awards)

1	Nancy Curry	Mt Pleasant, SC	53:31.0
2	Lyn Hammond	Charleston, SC	54:28.5
3	Vickie Sessions	Charleston, SC	58:15.4
4	Anne Boone	Hollywood, SC	58:22.6
5	Dorothy Anderson	Kiawah Island, SC	59:56.7
6	Joan Mulvihill	Charleston, SC	1:00:02.5
7	Dixie Dunbar	Sullivan's Isl, SC	1:00:56.6
8	Joyce Ploeger	Virginia Beach, VA	1:01:35.9
9	Connie Vogt	Knoxville, TN	1:03:39.2
10	Cynthia Gardner	Hartsville, SC	1:03:40.9
11	Barbara Riffle	Martinez, GA	1:05:07.2
12	Celine Blais	Montpelier, VT	1:05:48.6
13	Brenda Bouvier	Charleston, SC	1:06:23.1
14	Kari Sprecher	Fairfax, VA	1:07:06.2
15	Monika Wells	Greer, SC	1:07:19.2
16	Suzanne Hewitt	Chester, VA	1:09:37.8
17	Grace Rowe	Middletown, NJ	1:09:39.8
18	Ellie Bobilin	Sarasota, FL	1:10:05.8
19	Iris Hill	Goose Creek, SC	1:10:25.2
20	Marion Thompson	Lumberton, NC	1:10:41.2
21	Brenda Bruce	Greenville, SC	1:11:18.3

Male 65 - 69 (236 finishers, 12 awards)

1	John Sneed	Mt Pleasant, SC	45:15.7
2	Sonny Barber	Falls Church VA	45:46.9
3	Steve Comer	Charleston, SC	47:53.8
4	Marshall Wakat	Charleston, SC	48:12.1
5	Arnold Floyd	Hartsville, SC	48:57.6
6	Harry Ong	Roxbury, CT	48:58.1
7	Charles Sanders	Monroe, GA	49:45.9
8	Rohan Marks	Charleston, SC	52:40.9
9	James Adams	N Augusta, GA	53:54.5
10	George Geils	Charleston, SC	54:13.4
11	Ronald Rowland	Folly Beach, SC	54:42.4
12	Peter Rowe	Middletown, NJ	55:10.6

Female 65 - 69 (156 finishers, 8 awards)

1	Ricki Vadset	Seattle, WA	53:20.9
2	Kay Chandler	Isle Of Palms, SC	57:56.7
3	Sally Anne Kaiser	Myrtle Beach, SC	1:08:11.0
4	Linda McLaughlin	Marblehead, MA	1:10:03.3
5	Bobbye Faucette	Spartanburg, SC	1:11:33.0
6	Ruth Bruhns	Snellville, GA	1:11:51.7
7	Helga Hulett	Chapin, SC	1:16:57.8
8	Carolyn Banks	Cary, NC	1:17:32.0

Male 70 - 74 (82 finishers, 5 awards)

1	George Hilton	Dewees Island, SC	54:08.2
2	Clyde Mizzell	Charleston, SC	54:53.9
3	Jim Wilson	Aiken, SC	58:37.4
4	Floyd Riley	St George, SC	58:58.5
5	Art Pue	Charlotte, NC	59:28.9

Female 70 - 74 (61 finishers, 4 awards)

1	Susie Kluttz	Winston-Salem, NC	55:13.2
2	Faye Davis	Mt Pleasant, SC	1:02:31.2
3	Patricia Thompson	Hilton Head, SC	1:11:59.6
4	E.K. Tolley-Beeson	Sumter, SC	1:15:16.9

Male 75-79 (29 finishers, 3 awards)

1	Jack Lightle	Cocoa, FL	59:22.8
2	Ken Walls	Mt Pleasant, SC	1:00:31.6
3	James Lamarre	Charleston, SC	1:03:02.0

Female 75 - 79 (14 finishers, 3 awards)

1	Winifred Shrift	Jacksonville, FL	1:01:55.9
2	Garthedon Embler	Isle of Palms, SC	1:47:41.7
3	Barbara Klippel	Hayward, WI	1:49:28.7

Male 80 & Over (11 finishers, 3 awards)

1	Camil Toulouse	Sherbrook, Canada CA	1:21:00.8
2	Franklin Mason	Mullins, SC	1:25:31.3
3	Ralph Kennedy	Leesville, SC	1:33:39.5

Female 80 & Over (5 finishers, 3 awards)

1	Alice Wood	Elgin, SC	2:09:14.9
2	Alene B Parker	Camden, SC	2:13:54.0
3	Claire G Willett	Charleston, SC	2:16:55.1

Elite runners chase their shadows over the Ravenel bridge. Post and Courier photo by Grace Beahm

CHAPTER 32
2009
Ethiopian Tilahun Regassa Ends Kenyan Winning Streak

The 32nd Cooper River Bridge Run began at 8 a.m. on April 4, 2009. It was the fourth time the race was run over the single span Arthur Ravenel Jr. Bridge. It was also the fourth year that walkers as well as runners were timed. The field of finishers was second only to the first time in 2006 over the Ravenel Bridge in the number of entrants and finishers with 31,460 finishers (17,882 females, 13,578 males) of the 37,617 entrants finishing the race.

Conditions for the race were near perfect, with a clear crisp morning and a start time temperature of 54 degrees with a trace of wind as runners ran the first 2 miles in Mount Pleasant while they headed toward the bridge. As runners took on the mile-long 4 percent uphill grade, they were greeted with a 5 to 10 mile per hour head wind. When runners came off the bridge they enjoyed a tailwind.

Kenyans had dominated the race for years and last year's champion Robert Letting was favored to win again. However, 20-year-old Tilahun Regassa from Ethiopia had other ideas. Since he had not run the race before, he ran with the lead pack. During the race he would surge ahead, rejoin the pack and then pull away to win in 28:24, becoming the first non-Kenyan to win since 1991. Mark Kiptoo edged defending champion Letting as the two Kenyans finished second and third in 28:28 and 28:29. There were four Ethiopians and six Kenyans in the top 10.

The Sunday *Post and Courier* sports section headline read, "Regassa ends Kenyan reign". Regassa did not speak any English but smiled in satisfaction after the race. Second place finisher Kiptoo said about Regassa, "He used the tactics very well. There was no one to really push the pace consistently. He was trying to see who was strong. He ran a smart race. I felt like I had to do a lot of the work myself, and at the end, he just sprinted away."

It was a good year for Ethiopians as 26-year-old Amane Gobena was female winner in 32:25, just 3 seconds ahead of another Ethiopian, Teyba Naser. Jane Murage of Kenya was third in 32:59. It was only the third time in the past 11 years that a Kenyan did not win the race. There were five Ethiopians and five Kenyans in the top 10 female finishers.

"It feels good to win," Gobena told the *Post and Courier*. "It was a very tough course and I'm happy to win. I know this race is hard because I finished second two years ago. I trained hard and wanted to win because the bridge is so big and hard to run."

Elarbi Khattabi of Morocco was Masters winner in 31:40. Female Masters winner was Firaya Sultanova-Zhdanova from Russia, who repeated as female Masters winner, this year in 35:37. Tom Mather of Mount Pleasant proved he had overcome the serious bike/car collision injuries he suffered a few years ago and won the Grand Masters division in 36:03. Ukrainian Tatyana Pozdnyakova was female Grand Masters winner for the fifth year in a row, this time in 39:40.

The Dr. Marcus Newberry Award for the first local finisher from the Tri-County is named for the race founder. Brian Johnson, who has been runner-up for this award several times, won it in 32:41 and placed 30th overall. Sopagna Eap, who had moved from California to Johns Island for medical studies at the Medical University in Charleston, (and will be returning to California in July) won by running 36:04 and placed 15th female overall. The Dewey Wise Award was won by William Boulter, 79 of Charleston, whose time was 57:38 and his chip time was 57:32.

For the fourth time, the race had a wheelchair division. This year the winners were Krige Schabort of Cedartown, Ga., in 23:48 and female winner Shannon Franks of College Park, Md., in 40:30.

The race again used USATF Certified Course #SC05039BS which started in Mount Pleasant near Moultrie Middle School. The first mile is practically flat and then the course begins climbing over the Ravenel Bridge. Runners took the Meeting Street ramp and went towards downtown to John Street where a right turn took them onto King Street where they turned left. The next turn was at Wentworth Street, shortly after which runners reached the 6-mile mark, then made another left to Meeting Street where the final left turn was made. The finish line was just south of George Street.

For the first time the race presented age group awards by chip time (elapsed race time and place calculated by computer) rather than by gun time (actual time and finish place) as USATF rules require. Also for the first time everyone was timed using D-chip disposable computer timing chips. Like the commemorative chips used the previous five years, runners did not have to stop and remove the chip after finishing the race.

For the first time in five years there was no unbroken live race morning television coverage on Channel 5, which did broadcast four live segments — 18 minutes that included the start and coverage of the overall winner. A 30-minute program of delayed race coverage was shown on the evening of the race and several other times on cable Comcast Channel 2.

In the 2009 race, using actual finish place by gun time, a total of 249 runners broke the 40-minute barrier: 216 males and 33 females. An additional 19 males ran under the 40-minute barrier using chip time re-arranged finish order. There were 2,303 runners who crossed the finish line in less than 50 minutes, while 6,480 managed to cross the line before the clock flipped to 60:00. A total of 13 runners, all male, broke the 30-minute barrier with five of them under the 29-minute barrier. Charleston's *Post and Courier* listed the top five in each age division, again erroneously including the prize money winners, who are excluded from age division awards, in the listing. The paper also published the names and times of the top 10,105 male and top 9,834 female finishers in the Sunday April 5, 2009, edition. Complete results were mailed to all participants in June, as a special insert in the newspaper.

The race entry fee was raised to $30 for early race registration and $40 after March 14. Julian Smith was again the race director.

The 2009 Hall of Fame was made up of two inductees: Karl Gueldner, the first paid race director, and Al Hawkins, medical director for the past 18 years.

For the eighth year in a row there were runners from all 50 states, the District of Columbia and a large number of foreign countries. South Carolinians made up 23,954 of the entrants.

Other Voices
Tell Me About Your Bridge Run 2009
By Cedric Jaggers. Written for the Charleston Running Club newsletter in April 2009

Marion Square after the 32nd Cooper River Bridge Run: It was the second largest number of finishers ever at 31,430 and it has gotten really hard to find club members after the race. Of course, it doesn't help that I was slow to finish the race and to get to the club tent. But here are the answers from the people I could find and talk to. As virtually every year since 1988 when I started doing this article, I asked each person to do one thing "Tell me about your bridge run" and wrote down exactly what the person said. I looked up the official times and places and added them after each person's response. I was surprised when I picked up the results from Burns Computer after the race that the Bridge Run Committee had decided (and informed Steve, the computer programmer of Burns Computer at 10:30 P.M. the night before the race) to use chip time rather than the USATF recognized gun time for age division award order for the first time this year.

Tom Mather: It was my first 10k in a year and a half recovering from a torn tendon. Good run. 36:03. Official results time; chip and gun 36:03, chip and gun finish place 89th Grand Masters winner.

Anne Boone: You beat me! I think I beat everybody local in my age group. I shouldn't say that but it was my goal. I bought racing flats a couple of weeks ago and the racing flats felt really good. I've been trying to get in shape. 51:25. Official results time; gun 51:27, chip 51:23, gun finish place 2,441st, chip finish place 3,512th. 3rd 60-64 age group.

Keith Ambrose: I finished. I came to my 20th one. Suffered again but made it through another one. Just under 53:50. Official results time; gun and chip 53:58, gun finish place 3,470th, chip finish place 5,105th .

Gary Ricker: It was 46:24. The 30th one for me. It was hot. I was just happy to do it. I just didn't have it today. Official results time; gun 46:22, chip 46:15, gun finish place 1,028th, chip finish place 1,284th. Top 5% age group award.

Jeffrey Herndon: I couldn't do nothing, running one day a week – I think my time was 55:45. I don't remember the hill being that long. All in, another good Bridge Run. First time in three years I broke an hour. Unable to find in results (note: I saw Jeff put on his number and computer D chip so I know he was registered. CJ)

More that 30,000 participants jam the Coleman Boulevard starting corrals.
Post and Courier photo by Tom Spain

Lyn Hammond: A better run than last year. A gorgeous day. It's great to see everybody. A wonderful Bridge Run. 53:33. Official results time; gun 53:38, chip 53:33, gun finish place 3,301st, chip finish place 4,823rd. Top 5% age group award.

Tom Dority: I had old shoes on and no injuries. I had a good run. 52:27. Official results time; gun 52:21, chip 52:16, gun finish place 2,746th, chip finish place 4,025th. Top 5% age group award.

Pat Rhode: It was my 30th, I just wanted to finish. I didn't walk at all and thought about Kathy several times. 1:30:30. Official results time; gun 1:30:31, chip 1:26:54, gun finish place 20,788th, chip finish place 22,649th.

Jeff Gruver: 30th in a row. I'm dedicating it to my very sick mother. I felt good the entire distance. I've never been able to say that before. 53:17. Official results time; gun 53:17, chip 52:36, run finish place 3,138th, chip finish place 4,236th.

Gary Butts: My bridge run was super because I got to help Gail Bailey because she was struggling. Came in about 50:18 or 49:49. It was great to see the people; that's what I like about it. Official results time; gun 50:13, chip 49:49, gun finish place 2,063rd, chip finish place 2,656th.

Anne Wyman Cipolla: I did a P.R. today. I thought I was going slow because it was so windy and we were running uphill. Windy on the bridge. I couldn't believe I ran that fast, about 37:55 – not exactly sure. It was a good day. Official results time; gun and chip 37:52, gun finish place 140th, chip finish place 144th. 2nd 30-34 age group.

Joanne Herndon: I finished. It was good. I never … the 5th and 6th mile my side hurt so bad, but I just kept moving. I just ran a good pace. I didn't get too hyped up about it. 1:12 I think. Official results time; gun 1:13.26, chip 1:09:50, gun finish place 13,.082nd, chip finish place 17,085th.

Leon Locklear: Number 31. I ran it on memory; the first mile in about 10 minutes. The first 4 miles at a steady 10-minute pace, the old knees started aching. About 1:05 on my watch. Official results time; gun 1:09:15, chip 1:05:26, gun finish place 11,724th, chip finish place 14,250.

Bob Schlau: This was one of the difficult ones. I never felt good. I felt lousy from the start. No idea why I felt that way, my training has been going good, but I've had some knee pain and took 3 days off in a row before the race and I was stale. 41:15. Official results time gun and chip 41:25, gun finish time 340th, chip finish place 371st. 1st 60-64 age group.

Marc Embler: You don't wanna know. Bad. Three minutes slower than the Flowertown 10k two weeks ago. I'm dealing with this breathing issue I've been having for several months. The last couple of weeks have been really rough. I actually walked going up the bridge. I'm happy to be out here. There will be another day. 40:30. Official results time; gun and chip 40:42, gun finish place 292nd, chip finish place 309th. Top 5% age group award.

Note: Rives Poe grabbed the notepad out of my hands and said she was going to make me tell about my bridge run so here's what she wrote down:

Cedric Jaggers: It wasn't what I wanted but it was what I got. I blew up after the bridge. I wanted, wanted, wanted under 50 minutes. I told Kathy I'd kiss the ground if the clock said 49:59 after I crossed the finish line, but it didn't happen. 51:20. Official results time; gun 51:20, chip 51:09, gun finish place 2,411th, chip finish place 3,368th.

Bob Walton: I was one minute faster than last year. If I can beat my age I'm doing good. 72:39. Official results time; gun 1:12:26, chip 1:12:20, gun finish place 13,421st, chip finish place 18,376th .

David Anderson: 76:50. I enjoyed the Bridge Run. I like the competition in my age group, I'm 78. I'm glad to get over it in a decent time. Official results time; gun 1:16:46, chip 1:16:31, gun finish place 15,626th, chip finish place 20,010th.

Katherine Owens: It was fantastic. I started off a little faster than I normally do thinking I'd run out of gas, but I guess I didn't. I just did the Rome Marathon less than two weeks ago which was awesome, so all in all I'm very pleased with my time 50:45. Official results time; gun 50:47, chip 50:46, gun finish place 22,41st, chip finish place 3,137th.

Donna Lea Brown: I loved every minute of it all. 1 hour 31 minutes of it. I was glad to get over it, another one in my books. (Unable to find in results)

Pete Donnely: A lot of walkers and runners together; it was crowded. A beautiful day. I felt good, just a lot of slowing down and stopping. Time? Don't know. (Unable to find in results)

Danielle Girard: It was the 4th year I've done it. I did really well this year, about 58 minutes chip time. It didn't seem as congested this year. On the clock probably 1 hour and 6 minutes. I don't care what people say: Just watching all the people going up the bridge is fantastic. Official results time; gun 1:00:06, chip 58:51, gun finish place 6,538th, chip finish place 9,077th.

William Bolter: I had a great day. I was shooting for an hour and I did it 57:24 or so. I'm 75 and I won my age group. Official results time; gun 57:38, chip 57:32, gun finish place 5,185th, chip finish place 7,036th.

Ferris Stewart: It was my 12th in a row and I ran it and felt good the whole way. I turned and had to sprint at the end. My time was a little slow; it's got to be about an hour 14. Here's my daughter, she's 9. Official results time: gun 1:21:44, chip 1:14:08, gun finish place 17,803rd, chip 19,130th.

Gaby Stewart: It was my 1st Bridge Run. It was very hard and long. It was hard to pump it out and in the end it felt really good to finish it. About 2 hours I guess. Official results time: gun 1:58:55, chip 1:51:53, gun finish place 26,396th, chip finish place 27,712th

Huey Inman: Hey man. It was great today. It got kind of tight going up, but it wasn't bad coming down. 38:10. Official results time; gun and chip 38:12, gun finish place 153rd, chip finish place 155th.

Clyde Mizzell: Perfect day, felt good, thank God no wind, felt extremely good the whole race. I usually lose steam on Meeting Street. My time was better than last year. 55:14. Official results time: gun and chip 55:14, gun finish place 4,039th, chip finish place 6,007th.

David Quick: All right, the quest to break 35 is still on. I don't know if I can do it at the bridge. I wanted to be at least in the 35s. I was disappointed. 36:09. Official results time; gun and chip 36:09, gun finish place 91st, chip finish place 92nd.

A Bridge Run diary

By Cedric Jaggers. First appeared online: SCRunners.Com May 2009-

When John Olsen asked me to write this for SCRunners.Com, he probably didn't know that this Cooper River Bridge Run would be my 31st in a row. Wish I could say it was my 32nd since that is how many Bridge Runs there have been, but I missed the first one due to a leg that got broken playing city league soccer in Charleston. At the expo I was talking to somebody (honestly can't remember who) and they asked me how many times I'd run the Bridge Run. I said "All but the first one." They asked why I didn't run it and I told them about the broken leg. They said (jokingly I think) "What kind of lame excuse is that?" They didn't know how much I regret not having gotten to run that first one. In fact there are only four runners left who have done them all including a couple of friends of mine – Bob Schlau and Bob Walton. But I digress.

Since we live in Rock Hill now, my wife Kathy and I always drive down the Thursday before the race so we can go to the expo that day, and to the press luncheon on Friday (I cover the race for *Running Journal* magazine.) A lot of people don't know that the first day of an expo usually offers the largest selection of merchandise.

Who cares, you say? Well, if you wear an uncommon shoe size, say a 12 or 12 and a half like I do, you find out that the vendors only have a few of them and they tend to sell out of your size pretty quickly. I really like Nikes and Asics and they tend to almost always sell out of my size in both of them. I get a great deal of pleasure out of buying a pair or two or three of $100 shoes for $40 or $50 each. Of course, if you don't like saving money, don't bother to check out the expo. After all who needs half price shorts or singlets or socks or sunglasses or hats? Not to mention the free samples of food and drink and assorted other goodies. Expos are a great deal for runners, and it seems we always run into lots of old friends at the expo.

The press luncheon is always interesting. The location varies, and this year it was held at Lowndes Plantation which is on the Ashley River. All the sponsors of the race are invited as well as the elite runners. If the Kenyans and other runners stuffed down food all the time like they do at the luncheon every year, they would get so big they wouldn't be able to run fast for long. The mayors of the two cities – Mt. Pleasant where the race starts and Charleston where it ends- always read a joint proclamation. The race director, Julian Smith speaks briefly and introduces people, and *Post and Courier* reporter David Quick introduces the new inductees to the Bridge Run Hall of Fame. I always enjoy talking to them since I was inducted in the inaugural group back in 2002.

The weather forecast for the race was very good and it turned out to be accurate. Studies have shown that the ideal temperature for running is between 52 and 55 degrees and it was clear, sunny and 54 degrees at the 8 A.M. start on Saturday morning. Getting to the start on Coleman Avenue in Mt. Pleasant can be problematic. The first year after we moved to Rock Hill, Kathy and I took the shuttle buses provided by the race from downtown to the starting area. A lot of people use this option, but be in line by 6 as the buses run from 5:20 to 6:45, and after they drop you off, you get to stand around in the cold, or heat or whatever until it is time to line up. It is really nice to have a vehicle on the Mt Pleasant side where you sit and get warm, tuck your warm-ups and not have to put your stuff in a bag for the sweat shuttle (and then find it after you finish).

A lot of runners carpool or arrange for rides. Jeffrey Herndon, an old friend of ours picks us up (this year as the last few just me since Kathy can no longer run due to her multiple sclerosis – it is really a travesty since she was a state age group record holder and won Grand Masters prize money at this race the first year they offered it) at 6 a.m. by the replica of the *Hunley* submarine beside the Charleston Museum. The bridge is closed to traffic, I think at 7, so you have to get across pretty early, and you have to worry about where you will park. This year we couldn't go all the way down Coleman and park in the shopping center parking lot where we have parked a lot of years in a row.

Through a fluke of good luck, Jeffrey headed down the side road we were diverted onto by the police and then took a road cutting back to Coleman. We ended up

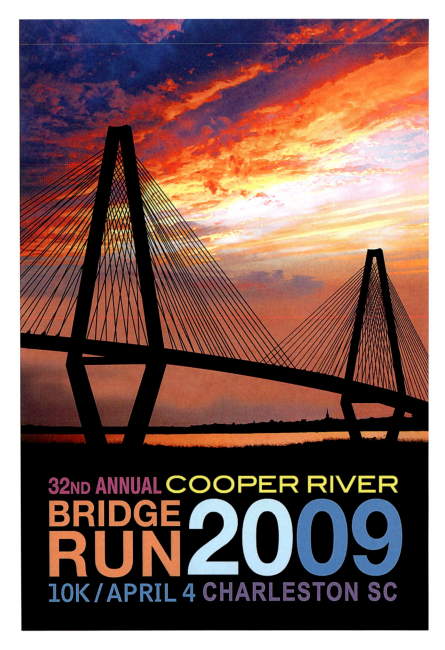

parking in a bank parking lot within sight of the starting line. We all had to head for the portable toilet line shortly after we arrived. There are hundreds, perhaps thousands of port-a-lets in groupings at various locations on both sides of the street, but with over 30,000 people waiting for a race to start, you can count on standing in line. I enjoy hearing people talk about how many times they have run the race, what kind of time they plan to run and other running and non-running topics. So there were lots of nervous runners drinking fluids and then getting back in the port-a-let line.

The Bridge Run uses a corral system to try to group runners by time. The race tries to seed runners by time. When you register you tell what you plan to run, if you are a runner, or check if you just plan to walk the race. Needless to say, the elite runners get the low numbers (as they should) and they were coded with a yellow background for easy identification. The fast, sub 40 minute, but not elite runners get blue background numbers; the under 49 minute runners get green background numbers; the 49 to 60 minute get orange, I think; the over 60 another color and the walkers yet another color.

The street is fenced off on both sides with gates guarded by volunteer monitors, who will only let you into the gate which matches the color on your number. It doesn't work perfectly unfortunately as I saw several orange numbers (mine was green since I hoped and planned to run under 50 minutes) and I also saw some walkers in front of me. I will say it is better enforced now than a few years ago when they first started using this system, and far superior to the early days when there was no seeding. It doesn't help that some people lie about their ability and what they plan to and can run.

They make announcements, have a countdown clock and have things going on from the scaffolding over the starting line. One year Bill Murray told jokes (he ran the race that year) and this year three women singers from the USO performed songs in the style of the Andrews Sisters (they had also performed at the press luncheon). At about 20 minutes before the start they called for everyone to get lined up. I was glad to see the monitor turning away people with the wrong colored number from the "green" corral. I heard her telling some of the people that runners had been standing there for over half an hour. But as I mentioned earlier there were some wrong colored high numbers already in front of and beside me.

The front edge of each corral has monitors holding an orange mesh fence type thing to keep runners from moving up into the next group. There was a gap of 10 yards or so between our group and the runners in the blue group. About 10 minutes before start time, all the monitors moved out and let us move up to the back of the blue group. Then about 5 minutes before the race they told everybody to take 10 steps backward because the elite runners didn't have room to line up on the front row. So we all shuffled backwards. I was far enough back (it took me 11 seconds to get to the starting line after the gun was fired) that I couldn't see the elite runners. It is amazing to look around and see runners from sidewalk to sidewalk stretching back for about a mile.

Finally, we got to the 10 second countdown (we could see the clock), the starting gun was fired and away we went, quite slowly at first, then it opened up a little and we could start running. The first two miles of the race in Mt Pleasant are virtually flat. In the old days (when I broke the 40 minute barrier 17 years in a row) I always started out too fast. The pundits say and experience proves that you can't run more than 10 seconds per mile faster the first mile than you are in shape to average for the race without hurting yourself. But my days of running the first mile in 5:30 or so are long gone but I was boxed in and didn't run the first mile at the pace I had planned.

Here's the plan: first mile in 7:50, second mile in 7:50, third mile (uphill) at 8:50 to 9 (I am a terrible uphill runner) then a 7:30 downhill, a couple of 7:50's to the six mile mark and then kick in. In races like they say in battle, the best laid plans get thrown out the door once you engage the enemy.

As I mentioned earlier, it took me 11 seconds to get to the starting line – I am a big believer in gun time (it is the only real time in a race since the race starts when the starting gun is fired, not when you happen to get to the starting line) so I started my watch with the gun. I had to pass a lot of overweight runners and one or two genuinely obese walkers during the first mile – wish they hadn't been in everybody's way, but they were.

The pack I was running with got to the first mile and the clock and my watch and the guy calling out the split all said 8:13, so I was already off my plan. I was also getting cotton mouthed which is never a good sign in a race. The second mile seemed to take forever and the when the clock said 17:30 I was depressed – my sub 50 minute race was out the window for sure. I didn't learn until after the race that the 2-mile mark had been misplaced and that we actually ran 1.2 miles from the first to the second mile marker. Several other people I talked to mentioned that at mile 2 they felt their race was over. I guess this just emphasizes the importance of accurate placement of mile marks to runners who consider themselves serious about the sport.

When we started the mile long climb up the bridge I felt stronger than I have in five years – rightfully so since that is how long it has been since I tried to race the race and had not had some kind of surgery within a few months of the race.

So no excuses this year, I passed a lot of people going up the span including Jeff, and Larry and Tom and I wasn't speeding up. The uphill seems to go on forever and you are actually going uphill for a solid mile. It's a lesson that holds true for all races; when people are passing you it is because you are slowing down, not because they are speeding up, except for the final kick to the finish. When we got to the 3-mile mark and my watch showed a 7:51 mile uphill I knew the 2-mile split had been off. So I had actually run the 8:51 I had planned, but the 25:33 split meant I was way off my plan.

The wind was in our face going up the bridge, but in as big a crowd as I was in, it was easy to get the wind blocked by runners who were in front of me. There have been only a couple of years in the race's 32 year history when we enjoyed a tailwind and 2009 wasn't one of them, but it was one of the lighter headwinds at between 5 to 10 miles per hour.

I always love it when we start going down the span. The downhill on the Ravenel Bridge is not steep, but if you know how, you can take advantage of it. I passed Anne Boone (an old friend who was the 3rd overall female finisher back in the day) and lots of other runners I knew and didn't know as we went down. The 4-mile mark came with a 7:43 split, but then we got off the bridge and onto the flat final miles in downtown Charleston.

The wind was behind us as soon as we got off the bridge and suddenly the temperature felt like it had shot up 20 degrees. To me it felt like an oven and my legs started telling me they had had enough and to stop trying to run. I told them to keep going but we (my legs and me) slowed to an 8:25 and got to mile 5 at 41:30. The ugly truth that I was going to finish over 50 set in. We headed down Meeting Street towards the cutover Street (John Street) and I pulled off my hat and splashed water on my head and back of my neck to try to cool off.

Kathy and I were staying at the Hampton Inn on John Street and she watched the start of the race live on television in our room (they showed eight minutes of coverage before returning to regular programming) and then came out to watch for me. As I ran by I spoke to her, tossed her my hat and told her I was suffering. Later she told me that a lot of people were suffering including Marc Embler, the 1981 race winner, and Bob Schlau who was runner-up in 1979.

As we turned left onto King Street I felt worse and worse; it seemed like thousands of runners were passing me, and when Anne caught back up with me and spoke to me, I made a serious effort to pick up the pace. Mile 6 came with an 8:12 mile and a time of 49:41. We turned the final corner and I could see the finish clock up ahead. I passed some runners, but not like in the old days when I could run the final .21 in 60 to 65 seconds. In fact it seemed to take forever and I was just glad to finish as the clock showed 51:20.

They told us to keep moving and we did as we headed up to Marion Square for refreshments: water, aide drinks, fruit, massages (if you were willing to wait in line) and other things which I hardly noticed or paid attention to or can even remember to write down now.

Since our hotel is almost adjacent to the Square I headed to our room and told Kathy about my race while grabbing a quick shower and change of clothes. Then back to the Square with notebook in hand and Press pass around my neck. I interviewed the couple of dozen Charleston Running Club members I could find for an article I do annually for the CRC newsletter called "Tell Me About Your Bridge Run".

It is always a pleasure to talk to old friends and meet new ones when I get them to tell me about how the race was for them. I could hear the awards ceremony in the distance and went over to see if my slow time was good enough to make the top 5 percent age group award in my 60-64 age group. The list showed 49:49 as the last time so I wasn't on it.

I had talked to Steve from Burns Computer the night before the race to arrange getting the results for Running Journal magazine and for my role as Cooper River Bridge Run historian. There are a number of extra files they give me every year and now instead of printing them out on paper as they used to, I get them on a stick drive, except for one printed copy of complete results and one of the awards list.

The police checked my press pass as I approached the results computer table and graciously let me by – they try to keep everyone from interrupting them while people are still finishing the race. It was about 11 a.m., three hours after the race started when I said hello to Steve and told him I wouldn't bother him, just sat and waited.

Keith Namn from the Post and Courier was there to get the results for them as they always print most of the finishers' names and times in the next day's paper. The paper used to only print the top 50 or 100 or 250 and he was itchy because they had an early deadline. Since I believe he was the one who used to decide how many names and times he typed up to get listed, I harassed him by reminding him about the old days when he would always cut off the number of finishers just before it got to me. When I finished 60th he only printed the top 50, when I finished 212th he only printed the top 200, when I finished 268th he only printed the top 250 etc.

The last walker came across the finish line well after 11, and they started breaking down the finish line setup. Steve told me he had had to reprogram the computer because the Bridge Run people told him at 10:30 the night before the race they had decided to us chip time instead of gun time. He said the software was not especially user friendly so it took a while. He printed the results for me (693 pages to print all the 31,430 finishers), put the rest of the results – I asked for real time i.e. gun time, full age group list, male and female separate lists as well and he put them all on my stick drive, and I thanked him and headed back to the hotel.

Kathy and I then went the Bridge Run post race luncheon-party at the Marina. We sat at a table with David Quick (who finished 3rd in his age group) and Bob Schlau (who finished first in his – which is also my age group), both of whom like me, were disappointed with their race. We also talked about chip time versus gun time and David felt there were arguments both ways. I don't, but didn't even know I had a horse in the race when I was talking to him. When I looked at the age group results by gun time I found out that I was the actual 25th person to cross the finish line in my age group and would have gotten a top 5 percent award if real time and place had been used (all age groups in the race award 3 deep plus the top 5% of finishers in the age group up to a maximum of 25). However since 9 people had faster chip times than mine they showed me as 34th in the age group. It makes a difference. The argument is that the people actually ran a faster 10k by chip time, and they did. But is a race from the start line to the finish line or does the race start when the starter fires the starting gun? Is it a race against other runners or a race against time – just a time trial? I think it should be a race against other runners but I wasn't asked.

At any rate it doesn't matter for most people and the experience of running such a massive race and enjoying everything that goes with it makes it worthwhile. If you have never run a mega-race such as the Cooper River Bridge Run, you are missing out on one of the great experiences for a runner.

2009 Awards

Prize money winners:

Male overall winners
1. Tilahun Regassa — Ethiopia — 28:24 — $5000
2. Mark Kiptoo — Kenya — 28:28 — $3000
3. Robert Letting — Kenya — 28:29 — $1500
4. Alene Reta — Ethiopia — 28:35 — $1000
5. Daniel Kipkoech — Kenya — 28:41 — $800
6. Linus Maiyo — Kenya — 29:01 — $600
7. Worku Beyi — Ethiopia — 29:13 — $500
8. Eric Chirchir — Kenya — 29:27 — $400
9. Peter Matelong — Kenya — 29:28 — $300
10. Tesfayi Grima — Ethiopia — 29:30 — $250
11. Kiprotich Yegon — Kenya — 29:54 — $200
12. Daniel Kanyaruhuru — Charlotte NC — 29:57 — $150
13. Daniel Muriuki — Kenya — 29:57 — $100
14. Kevin Chlimo — Kenya — 30:19 — $75
15. Japheth Ng'ojoy — Kenya — 30:31 — $50

Female overall winners
1. Amane Gobena — Ethiopia — 32:25 — $5000
2. Teyba Naser — Ethiopia — 32:38 — $3000
3. Jane Murage — Kenya — 32:59 — $1500
4. Monica Jepkoech — Kenya — 33:14 — $1000
5. Janet Cherobon — Kenya — 33:16 — $800
6. Alemitu Abera — Ethiopia — 33:42 — $600
7. Meskerem Legesse — Ethiopia — 33:59 — $500
8. Alemtsehay Misganaw — Ethiopia — 34:21 — $400
9. Everlyne Lagat — Kenya — 35:03 — $300
10. Divina Jepkogei — Kenya — 35:30 — $250
11. Caroline Rotich — Kenya — 35:33 — $200
12. Firaya Sultanova-Zhdanova — Russia — 35:37 — $150
13. Tatyana Mironova — Russia — 35:38 — $100
14. Albina Gallyamova — Russia — 35:56 — $75
15. Sopagna Eap — Johns Island, SC — 36:04 — $50

Male overall Masters
1. Elarbi Khattabi — Morocco — 31:40 — $1500
2. Paul Aufdemberge — Michigan, MI — 31:47 — $1000
3. Gideon Mutisya — Kenya — 32:05 — $750
4. Eric Ashton — Columbia, SC — 32:08 — $500
5. Alexey Korobov — Russia — 32:15 — $250

Female Overall Masters
1. Firaya Sultanova-Zhdanova — Russia — 35:37 — $1500
2. Tatyana Mironova — Russia — 35:38 — $1000
3. Albina Gallyamova — Russia — 35:56 — $750
4. Tatiana Titova — Russia — 36:45 — $500
5. Donna Anderson — Pawleys Island, SC — 36:53 — $250

Male overall Grand Masters
1. Tom Mather — Mt Pleasant, SC — 36:03 — $750
2. Peter Edge — Simpsonville, SC — 36:43 — $500
3. Trani Matthews — Tulsa, OK — 39:22 — $250

Female overall Grand Masters
1. Tatyana Pozdnyakova — Ukraine — 39:40 — $750
2. Mimi Sturgell — Kiawah Island, SC — 46:08 — $500
3. Judy Walls — Piedmont, SC — 46:13 — $250

Dr. Marcus Newberry Award
First local Tri-County area runner
Male
Brian Johnson — Mt Pleasant, SC — 32:41 — $500
Female
Sopagna Eap — Johns Island, SC — 36:04 — $500

Dewey Wise Award
Oldest runner with time under his or her age in minutes
William Boulter, 79 — Charleston, SC — 57:32

Male overall wheelchair
1. Krige Schabort — Cedartown, GA — 23:48

Female overall wheelchair
1. Shannon Franks — College Park MD — 40:30

Male overall wheelchair Masters
1. Krige Schabort — Cedartown, GA — 23:48

Female overall wheelchair Masters
1. Jacqui Kapinowski — Mt Pleasant, SC — 45:42

Age division awards
presented to top 3 in each division; Top 5% awards presented in each division up to a maximum of 25 per division

Note: In 2009 age group awards were presented for the first time by re-arranged chip time finish order rather than the actual order in which runners crossed the finish line.

Male 9 & Under (75 finishers, 4 awards)
1. Noah Spencer — Mt Pleasant SC — 47:45
2. Sage Costen — Matthews, NC — 51:13
3. Jack Walker — Mt Pleasant SC — 1:02:02
4. Robert Brewer — Charleston SC — 1:02:09

Female 9 & Under (86 finishers, 4 awards)
1. Riley Reinhard — Charlotte, NC — 58:23
2. McKenzie Roberts — Weaverville NC — 1:01:24
3. Emily Benton — Bamberg SC — 1:01:56
4. Stephanie Perdue — Murfreesboro TN — 1:02:19

Male 10-14 (468 finishers, 24 awards)
1. Michael Wegner — Columbia, MD — 37:25
2. Brent Demarest — Charleston, SC — 38:41
3. Martin Morrow — Moore, SC — 40:49
4. Jacob Spencer — Mt Pleasant SC — 42:02
5. Brandon Rhodes — Anderson, SC — 42:09
6. Liam Emery — Mt Pleasant SC — 42:42
7. Brendan Ward — Mt Pleasant SC — 43:48
8. Andrew Lyons — Matthews, NC — 44:10
9. Cooper Donoho — Mt Pleasant SC — 44:20
10. Spencer Provost — Gilbert, SC — 45:01
11. Austin Pendergist — Charleston, SC — 45:15
12. Nolan Boozer — Clinton, SC — 45:59
13. Reid Haigler — Mt Pleasant SC — 46:01
14. Logan Spencer — Mt Pleasant SC — 46:20
15. Billy Walker — Mt Pleasant SC — 46:40
16. Benjamen Carroll — Summerville SC — 46:40
17. Tyler Richardson — Columbia, SC — 46:49
18. Steven Trench — Woodruff, SC — 47:20
19. Logan Oberlin — Saint Marys, GA — 47:21
20. Brandon Cook — Summerville, SC — 47:45
21. Mitchell Cook — Summerville, SC — 47:46
22. T. J. Longshore — Irmo, SC — 47:46
23. William Glenn — Charlotte, NC — 47:59
24. Cameron Brown — Spartanburg, SC — 48:16

Female 10-14 (419 finishers, 21 awards)
1. Danielle Sams — N Charleston, SC — 41:22
2. Dani Inglesby — Greenville, SC — 44:30
3. London Cara-Lyn Miller — Greenville SC — 45:03
4. Lucy Rummler — Mt Pleasant, SC — 45:45
5. Georgia Compton — Mt Pleasant SC — 45:50
6. Brooke Grice — Columbia, SC — 45:56
7. Anna Todd — Spartanburg, SC — 46:20
8. Mace Wilklow — Greenville, SC — 47:47
9. Elizabeth Berry — Rock Hill, SC — 48:11
10. Ashley Beach — Roebuck, SC — 48:59
11. Meredith Lackey — Charleston, SC — 49:19
12. Lauren Halter — Summerville, SC — 49:45
13. Andrea Cool — Charleston, SC — 50:08
14. Emmeline Wheeler — Troy, SC — 50:25
15. Tabitha Thuber — Goose Creek, SC — 50:55
16. Hunter Odom — Landrum, SC — 51:09
17. Danae Ferguson — Greer, SC — 51:26
18. Taylor Fox — Summerville, SC — 51:35
19. Alexa Leopold — Simpsonville, SC — 51:54
20. Ashley Pendergist — Charleston, SC — 52:00
21. Taylor Fox — Summerville, SC — 53:55

Male 15-19 Division (590 finishers, 25 awards)
1. Christian Bailey — Charlotte, NC — 32:54
2. Trevor Sprague — Dunwoody, GA — 33:07
3. Brett Baggett — Chapel Hill, NC — 34:19
4. William Rudisill — North Augusta, SC — 34:44
5. Eric Robertson — Dalzal, SC — 34:56
6. David Lamberson — Stafford, VA — 34:57
7. Matt Lottes — Snellville, GA — 34:59
8. Ryan Arrowsmith — Clemson, SC — 36:14
9. Gregory Barnes — Raleigh, NC — 36:15
10. Taylor Christiansen — Jamestown, NC — 36:36
11. Tim Hawkins — Aiken, SC — 37:20
12. Jordan Plumblee — Taylors, SC — 37:23
13. Joshua Fischer — Charlotte, NC — 37:49
14. Mick Francis — Lake Wylie, SC — 38:13
15. Max Welborn — Rock Hill, SC — 38:35
16. Carter Blackwell — Moncks Corner, SC — 38:47
17. Davis Owens — Merritt Island, FL — 38:50
18. Jamie Sires — West Columbia, SC — 38:54
19. Justin Weber — Charleston, SC — 38:59
20. Thomas Briggs — Mt Pleasant, SC — 39:06
21. Andrew Felber — N Charleston, SC — 39:14
22. Hunter McGahee — Chapin, SC — 39:19
23. Brian Provost — Gilbert, SC — 39:37
24. Tim Kerley — Mt Pleasant, SC — 39:52
25. Mason Williams — N Myrtle Beach, SC — 39:53

Female 15-19 Division (753 finishers, 25 awards)
1. Caitlin Lee — Harrisonburg, VA — 39:20
2. Kelsey Armstrong — Talbott, TN — 39:50
3. Elle Brewer — Knoxville, TN — 40:17
4. Josh Koth — James Island, SC — 41:11
5. Sarah Williamson — Charlotte, NC — 41:55
6. Caroline Duer — Greenville, SC — 42:55
7. Ali Cupito — Chapel Hill, NC — 43:28
8. Jenna Williamson — Charlotte, NC — 43:34
9. Samantha Eastwood — Clemson, SC — 44:40
10. Amanda Weekes — Simpsonville, SC — 44:58
11. Kimberly Simpson — Greenville, SC — 45:06
12. Kelsey Davis — Hampstead, NC — 45:25
13. Caitlin Williams — Goose Creek, SC — 45:28
14. Nicole Maitland — Chapin, SC — 45:52
15. Leslie Semken — Charleston, SC — 46:28
16. Rebekah Henderson — Montreat, NC — 46:36
17. Logan Fry — Charlestown, IN — 46:40
18. Mariah Davis — Moncks Corner, SC — 47:09
19. Cally Howell — Greer, SC — 47:12
20. Arden Mattachini — Matthews, NC — 47:19
21. Brennan McDavid — Charleston, SC — 47:23
22. Lauren Dinicola — Charleston, SC — 47:24
23. Jen Riley — Mt Pleasant, SC — 47:28
24. Amy Williams — James Island, SC — 47:30
25. Victoria Cairco — Charleston, SC — 47:33

Male 20-24 (1,261 finishers, 25 awards)
1. Andrew King — N Charleston SC — 33:26
2. John Sell — Due West, SC — 33:53
3. Jonathan Kinsey — Myrtle Beach SC — 33:56
4. Jacob Asher Morris — Aiken, SC — 33:58
5. Tim Jeffreys — Columbia, SC — 34:37
6. Richard Andrews — Richmond, VA — 34:40
7. Alexander Leveen — Charleston, SC — 35:02
8. Drew Sayce — Clemson, SC — 35:28
9. Christopher Fallis — Awendaw, SC — 35:28
10. Stephen Sykes — Spartanburg, SC — 35:52
11. Mark Emile Pepin — Blythewood, SC — 36:26
12. Brock Phillips — Chapel Hill NC — 36:35
13. Ben Sherard — Mt Pleasant, SC — 36:36
14. Logan Beytagh — Tybee Island GA — 36:38
15. Andrew Neel — Unknown, NC — 37:11
16. David Johannesmeyer — Summerville, SC — 37:40
17. Kip Thompson — Atlanta, GA — 37:50
18. Doug Coats — Wingate, NC — 38:16
19. Richard Harris — Charlotte, NC — 38:20
20. Kendal Forrester — Ladson, SC — 38:31
21. Benjamin Joslin — St Augustine FL — 38:34
22. James Flatley — Mt Pleasant, SC — 39:12
23. Roc Disanto — Morganton, NC — 39:15
24. David Brinkley — Charlotte, NC — 39:17
25. James Burya — Columbus, OH — 39:21

Female 20-24 (2,408 finishers, 25 awards))
1. Caroline Kiptoo — Kenya — 36:56
2. Caitlin Ranson — Cambridge, MA — 39:30
3. Summer James — Charlotte, NC — 40:14
4. Brittany Owens — Merritt Island, FL — 40:18
5. Maureen Campbell — Charlotte, NC — 40:28
6. Christine Clarkpounder — Summerville, SC — 40:41
7. Anna Petrov — Columbia, SC — 41:09
8. Anna Dukes — Charleston, SC — 41:49
9. Marisol Slater — Columbia, SC — 41:53
10. Guinn Garrett — Charleston, SC — 42:07
11. Sarah Madebach — Augusta, GA — 42:28
12. Mary Whaley — Charleston, SC — 42:31
13. Michele Milner — Charleston, SC — 42:55
14. Brittany Crosby — Charleston, SC — 43:03
15. Katlyn McGrattan — Charleston, SC — 43:12
16. Heather Lasley — Charlotte, NC — 43:20
17. Christine Devasto — Charleston, SC — 43:30
18. Katherine Mills — Apex, NC — 43:47
19. Nikki Jasperson — Myrtle Beach SC — 43:58
20. Emily Murphy — Columbia, SC — 44:26
21. Erin Becker — Chapel Hill NC — 44:27
22. Kristin Cook — Chapel Hill NC — 44:47
23. Cierra Burchfield — Clemson, SC — 44:55
24. Kimi Parkhill — Charleston, SC — 45:16
25. Kemian Atkins — Felton, DE — 46:48

Male 25-29 (2,146 finishers, 25 awards)
1. Tamas Kovacs — High Point, NC — 30:42
2. Jason Lokwatom — Kenya — 31:02
3. Kevin Crosby — Chapel Hill, NC — 31:54
4. Cody Angell — Belmont, NC — 32:54
5. Timothy Scarpinato — N Charleston, SC — 33:05
6. Ryan Thompson — Charleston, SC — 33:05
7. Neville Miller — Mt Pleasant, SC — 33:17
8. Christopher Lamperski — Charlotte, NC — 33:41
9. Ethan Coffey — Goose Creek, SC — 33:43
10. Kurt Russell — Summerville, SC — 34:05

— Continued on next page

2009 Awards, continued from page 263

11	Jason Holder	Charlotte, NC	34:53
12	Brooks Keys	Anderson, SC	35:49
13	Hunter Hicklin	Charleston, SC	36:01
14	Owen Speer	Roanoke, VA	36:07
15	Eric Guth	Travelers Rest SC	36:13
16	Elliott Taylor	Greenville, SC	36:39
17	Robert Christopher	Charleston, SC	36:42
18	Todd Mayes	Cornelius, NC	36:44
19	Felipe Rubio	Miami, FL	36:45
20	Hudson Belk	Charlotte, NC	37:09
21	Lat Purser	Charlotte, SC	37:15
22	Reynaldo Soto	Goose Creek, SC	37:23
23	Justin McGuinness	Charlotte, NC	37:42
24	Tyler Cross	Charleston, SC	37:50
25	Adam Byron Mayes	Cornelius, NC	38:01

Female 25-29 (3,369 finishers, 25 awards)

1	Kelly Fillnow	Huntersville NC	37:47
2	Margie Smith	Greenville, SC	38:15
3	Rachael Butler	Phoenix, AR	39:04
4	Caitlin Schier	Union, SC	40:29
5	Emily Johnson	Mt Pleasant, SC	40:29
6	Heather Knight	Mt Pleasant, SC	41:48
7	Katherine Hertwig	Greenville, SC	41:54
8	Shannon Banks	Albuquerque NM	42:12
9	Annie Schuerger	Charleston, SC	42:31
10	Stephanie Lundeby	Ladson, SC	42:44
11	Tessa Taylor	Greenville, SC	43:18
12	Paige McDowell	Glen Allen, VA	43:21
13	Kari Burger	Morehead City NC	43:21
14	Christa Kahuda	Mt Pleasant, SC	43:56
15	Blair Turnage	Mt Pleasant, SC	44:09
16	Kimberly Denta	Charlotte, NC	44:10
17	Becky Witkop	Mt Pleasant, SC	44:16
18	Pamela Jones	Columbus, GA	44:21
19	Jill Hawley	Mt Pleasant, SC	44:49
20	Katie Blaylock	Charleston, SC	44:59
21	Jenna Giroux	Atlanta, GA	45:20
22	Lindsay Hensley	Asheville, NC	45:25
23	Tiffany Cochran	Waycross, GA	45:30
24	Kelly Lee Dahlman	Jacksonville FL	45:32
25	Molly Grabow	Carrboro, NC	45:37

Male 30 - 34 (1,882 finishers, 25 awards)

1	Richard Kessio	Kenya	30:38
2	Sammy Nyanongo	Kenya	31:45
3	Daniel Hughes	Greenville, SC	32:39
4	Brian Johnson	Mt Pleasant, SC	32:41
5	Orinthal Striggles	Columbia, SC	32:49
6	Tim Briles	Greenville, SC	32:52
7	Japeth Koech	Kenya	33:16
8	Joseph Gibson	Marietta, GA	33:56
9	Karl Walsh	Mt Pleasant, SC	34:31
10	Dwayne Brown	Philadelphia PA	34:52
11	John M Watkins	Charleston, SC	35:44
12	Joshua J Rogers	Beaufort, SC	36:28
13	Jeff Baxter	N Charleston, SC	36:49
14	Kurt Wilson	Asheville, NC	36:53
15	Connor Larose	Durham, NC	36:54
16	Mike Moran	Denver, NC	37:17
17	Andrew Saar	Sandy Springs GA	37:44
18	Aaron Schaffner	Frankfort, KS	37:46
19	James Loging	Laurens, SC	37:50
20	Bobby Wilder	Myrtle Beach, SC	37:54
21	Thomas Walls	Ft Mill, SC	38:04
22	Paul Wuerslin	Waxhaw, NC	38:11
23	Emilio Castro	Charleston, SC	38:14
24	Brad Fowler	Winston-Salem NC	38:38
25	Michael Heafner	Belmont, NC	38:58

Female 30 - 34 (2,570 finishers, 25 awards)

1	Madeline Adams	Chapel Hill, NC	37:27
2	Anne Wyman Cipolla	Charleston, SC	37:52
3	Megan Duerring	Easton, PA	38:02
4	Marie Domin	Mt Pleasant, SC	40:42
5	Alice Rogers	Charlotte, NC	41:12
6	Elizabeth Weaver	Charlotte, NC	41:25
7	Margaret Florence	Hoboken, NJ	42:33
8	Colleen Angstadt	Charlotte, NC	42:38
9	Jennifer West	Richmond Hill, GA	42:50
10	Carter Monroe	Sullivans Island SC	43:25
11	Lee Walker	Columbia, SC	43:26
12	Rebecca Mayernick	Fletcher, NC	43:44
13	Truitt Pressly	Mt Pleasant, SC	44:01
14	Leah Grace	Charlotte, NC	44:05
15	Stacey Albenberg	Charleston, SC	44:13
16	Lisa Darby	Simpsonville, SC	44:18
17	Jessica Copland	Greensboro, NC	44:28
18	April Walsh	Lenoir, NC	44:37
19	Sarah Blackwell	Columbia, SC	44:39
20	Amy McDonaugh	Irmo, SC	44:58
21	Katie Minton	Augusta, GA	45:03
22	Brandy Englert	Charleston, SC	45:07
23	Erin Melton	Cary, NC	45:09
24	Andrea Pietras	Charleston, SC	45:21
25	Nikki McCollum	Sunset, SC	45:28

Male 35-39 (1,766 finishers, 25 awards)

1	Kevin Mosteller	Greenville, SC	34:16
2	Jeffrey Zickus	Minneapolis MN	35:36
3	Gerald Griffitts	Hartsville, SC	36:12
4	Doug Long	Charlotte, NC	36:32
5	Brad Schneider	Bowling Green KY	36:33
6	Matt Pryor	Greenville, SC	36:59
7	Chris Cummins	Charlotte, NC	37:16
8	Mark Harrell	Raleigh, NC	37:35
9	Brian Thill	Summerville, SC	37:41
10	Jason Philbin	Charlotte, NC	37:48
11	Mason Ferratt	N Charleston, SC	38:01
12	David Barnes	Myrtle Beach, SC	38:09
13	Brent Shealy	Lexington, SC	38:34
14	John Lovett	Newport News VA	38:38
15	Coates Kennerly	Brevard, NC	38:43
16	Emery Lloyd	Monks Corner, SC	38:46
17	Michael Cipolla	Charleston, SC	38:55
18	Hal Crosswell	Greenville, SC	38:56
19	Nicholas Mayernick	Fletcher, NC	39:16
20	Scott Putnam	Playa Del Rey CA	39:33
21	Rutherford Bryson	Charlotte, NC	39:33
22	Greg Sisson	Myrtle Beach, SC	39:42
23	Garrett Dieck	Mt Pleasant, SC	39:46
24	Alan Smith	Greenville, SC	39:51
25	Michael Domin	Mt Pleasant, SC	39:56

Female 35-39 (2,335 finishers, 25 awards)

1	Michelle LaFleur	Savannah, GA	36:22
2	Lara Shaw	Greenville, SC	39:13
3	Carol Brunson	Spartanburg, SC	39:51
4	Julie Seymour	Greenwood, SC	40:42
5	Rebecca Thomason	Charlotte, NC	40:53
6	Dana Martin	Mt Pleasant, SC	41:26
7	Molly Cherry	Mt Pleasant, SC	41:34
8	Amy Doyle	Greenville, SC	42:13
9	Ellen Parker	Chapel Hill, NC	43:49
10	Stacey Griffith	Forest City, NC	44:00
11	Michelle Kopczynski	Waxhaw, NC	44:16
12	Julie Walker	Beaufort, SC	44:33
13	Natalie Taylor	Raleigh, NC	44:50
14	Shannon Treasurer	Asheville, NC	44:59
15	Cameron Wannamaker	Mt Pleasant, SC	45:12
16	Jennifer Sabin	Houston, TX	45:18
17	Claire Veber	Charlottesville VA	45:42
18	Mandi Herring	Charleston, SC	45:57
19	Tracy D Jones	Murrells Inlet, SC	46:18
20	April Sellers	High Point, NC	46:22
21	Jennifer Bolhuis	Hudsonville, MI	46:36
22	Lynn Cecil	Rock Hill, SC	46:41
23	Karen Mateo	New York, NY	47:00
24	Stephanie Lasek	Mt Pleasant, SC	47:05
25	Kimberly Ward	Charlotte, NC	47:07

Male 40-44 (1,386 finishers, 25 awards)

1	Paul Mwangi	Kenya	32:44
2	Sergey Kaledin	Russia	32:50
3	Bruce Raymar	Canada	33:04
4	Matthew Whitis	Columbus, OH	33:20
5	John Bartlett	Alpharetta GA	33:23
6	David Honea	Boone, NC	33:32
7	Gary Curran	Asheville NC	35:39
8	Eric Vandervort	Clinton, TN	36:00
9	Chaz Hinkle	Charlotte NC	36:47
10	Todd Walter	Landrum, SC	38:35
11	Harry Carl Efird	Troutman, NC	38:57
12	Brendan Silver	Mt Pleasant SC	39:01
13	Todd Siczek	Charlotte NC	39:16
14	Karl Johnson	Spartanburg SC	39:24
15	Stephen Hudzik	Charlotte NC	39:25
16	Jody McAuley	Mt Pleasant SC	39:40
17	Todd Kerschbaumer	Charlotte NC	39:46
18	Mark Remick	Asheville NC	39:50
19	Mike Pryor	Spartanburg SC	39:53
20	Anthony Iuey	Tabor City NC	39:53
21	Clay Griffin	Charleston, SC	39:54
22	Alan Brown	Charleston, SC	39:57
23	Alan Pogroszewski	Hilton, NY	39:57
24	Billy Estes	Mt Pleasant SC	39:58
25	Randall Hrechko	Columbia, SC	39:59

Female 40-44 (1,657 finishers, 25 awards)

1	Sheila Wakeman	Cornelius, NC	41:24
2	Michelle Beaulieu	Summerville, SC	42:22
3	Camelia Marculescu	Charleston, SC	42:35
4	Molly Achille	Greenville, SC	42:58
5	Julie Jacobs	Moore, SC	43:24
6	Karen L Killeen	Richmond, VA	43:48
7	Sharryn Whitmore	Mt Pleasant, SC	44:08
8	Kari Lee Marvin	Chapel Hill, NC	44:13
9	Melanie Ann Stuart	Goose Creek, SC	44:22
10	Jana F Seppala	Travelers Rest SC	44:37
11	Anita M Freres	Reston, VA	44:45
12	Amanda S Masters	Fort Mill, SC	45:06
13	Donna Durante Cameron	Hartsville, SC	45:41
14	Beth Webster Wease	Kings Mountain NC	45:46
15	Amy Kassis	Charleston, SC	46:22
16	Betsy S Jessup	Mt Pleasant, SC	47:04
17	Sissy Renwick	Waxhaw, NC	47:10
18	Lois Jones Newberry	Charleston, SC	47:28
19	Melissa D Coleman	Mt Pleasant, SC	47:30
20	Cynthia D Bohr	Mt Pleasant, SC	47:34
21	Sheldon Y Fowler	Mt Pleasant, SC	47:47
22	Denise Burkard	Charlotte, NC	47:59
23	Caroline Price	Columbia, SC	48:24
24	Angela Greenlee	Albemarle, NC	48:27
25	Teresa Barthold	Goose Creek, SC	48:35

Male 45-49 (1,116 finishers, 25 awards)

1	Oleg Strizhakov	Russia	32:18
2	Joe Hammond	Travelers Rest, SC	36:02
3	David Quick	Mt Pleasant, SC	36:09
4	Ed Hughes	Greenville, SC	36:30
5	Jim Bertrand	Charlotte, NC	37:29
6	Lance Leopold	Simpsonville, SC	38:03
7	Huey Inman	Mt Pleasant, SC	38:12
8	Michael Seekings	Charleston, SC	38:25
9	Tim Unger	Tallahassee, FL	38:28
10	Paul Holyko	Port Orange, FL	38:30
11	John N Anderson	Moore, SC	38:40
12	George Williams	Santa Barbara, CA	38:46
13	Mark Wormuth	Wittenberg, WI	39:57
14	Jim Hanson	Ancaster, Ontario CA	40:17
15	Kenneth Clyburn	Beaufort, SC	40:20
16	James Long	Dayton OH	40:54
17	Paul Baczewski	Summerville, SC	41:44
18	Andrew Krueger	Summerfield, NC	41:52
19	Jay Hammond	Lexington, SC	42:02
20	Donald Goodman	McKees Rocks, PA	42:09
21	Chris Handal	Charleston, SC	42:12
22	Ben Howell	Greer, SC	42:15
23	Brian Ratte	Davidson, NC	42:24
24	Bryan Young	Greenville, SC	42:37
25	Tom Combes	Atlanta GA	42:46

Female 45-49 (1,384 finishers, 25 awards)

1	Laura Knapp	Wyoming, MI	40:35
2	Pamela Lovett	Newport News, VA	40:56
3	Mary Dore	Charlotte, NC	42:22
4	Geriann Bell	Greer, SC	45:14
5	Jane Godwin	Greenville, SC	45:23
6	Cheryl Quinn	Greenville, SC	45:52
7	Vicky Kosakowski	East Lyme, CT	47:37
8	Leslie Knapp	Hickory, NC	48:16
9	Elizabeth Riley	Columbia, SC	48:17
10	Germaine Ward	Mt Pleasant, SC	48:25
11	Barbara Neale	Meggett, SC	48:52
12	Virginia Evans	Knightdale, NC	49:26
13	Deborah Roszell	Peachtree City, GA	49:29
14	Heather Lord	Goose Creek, SC	50:10
15	Jennifer Brown	Anderson, SC	50:33
16	Katherine Owens	Summerville, SC	50:46
17	Betsy Steel	Charleston, SC	50:59
18	Lucia Bishop	Abbeville, SC	51:00
19	Robin Tarpinian	Greer, SC	51:01
20	Leanne Johnston	Charlotte, NC	51:05
21	Julia Engel	Charlotte, NC	51:19
22	Kathy Murray	Charlotte, NC	51:31
23	Ulricke Mersch	Mt Pleasant, SC	51:54
24	Amy Van Gurp	Waxhaw, NC	51:57
25	Jean Glick	St Augustine, FL	52:00

Male 50-54 (1,003 finishers, 25 awards)

1	Randall Rogan	Winston-Salem, NC	39:15
2	Robert Whitaker	Owens Crossroads, AL	39:19
3	Billy Tisdale	Sumter, SC	39:32
4	Eric Paul	Hillsborough, NC	39:33
5	Tim Welch	Westlake, OH	39:36

6	Jim Jordan	Lavale, MD.	39:40
7	Martin Williams.	Columbia, SC.	39:41
8	Jeffrey Armstrong	Talbott TN	39:58
9	Michael Anderson.	Tucker, GA	40:26
10	George Adickes	Cornelius, NC	40:27
11	Marc Embler.	Folly Beach, SC	40:42
12	Keith Hertling	Lexington, SC	40:47
13	George Sykes	Spartanburg, SC.	41:02
14	Edwin Holler.	Morganton, NC.	41:24
15	Robert Turner.	Charleston, SC	41:25
16	David Renneisen	Goose Creek, SC	41:27
17	Dan Bradley	Winston-Salem, NC.	41:34
18	Eric Smith	Greenwood, SC.	41:36
19	Gerald Favret	Johns Island, SC	42:43
20	F L Fleming	Mt Pleasant, SC	43:11
21	L R Hart	Jacksonville Bch FL	43:16
22	William O Young	Greensboro, NC	43:20
23	Joe Dipiro	Mt Pleasant, SC	43:53
24	Neal James-Crook	Andover	44:07
25	Robbie McLendon	Bishopville, SC	44:26

Female 50-54 (1,190 finishers, awards)

1	Becky Droginske	Wheeling, WV	45:33
2	Ann Elish	Mt Pleasant, SC	46:06
3	Helen Hiser	Mt Pleasant, SC	47:09
4	Tami Dennis	Isle of Palms SC.	47:26
5	Dell Toomer	Summerville, SC.	47:37
6	Danny Daniels	Florence, SC.	48:15
7	Kathleen Step	Ann Arbor, MI	48:28
8	Lori Pope	Charleston, SC	49:00
9	Janet Gossett	Spartanburg, SC.	49:22
10	Anne Geddes	Aiken, SC	49:36
11	Beth Rudolph	Charlotte, NC	49:38
12	Trudy Gale	Salisbury, NC.	49:41
13	Kathy Abernethy	Matthews, NC	49:42
14	Shirley Smith	Easley, SC.	49:57
15	Rachel Caldwell	Lexington, SC	50:25
16	Leslie Buller	Richmond, VA.	50:46
17	Nan Mabe Copeland	Charlotte, NC	50:46
18	Nancy Farley-Mon.	Mt Pleasant, SC	51:25
19	Sarah Ball	Charleston, SC	51:25
20	Barbara Whitmire	Lake Toxaway, NC	51:38
21	Beverly Grant	Asheville, NC.	51:45
22	Sally Rentiers	Charleston, SC	51:45
23	Debby Lea Moore	Simpsonville, SC.	52:37
24	Vickye Hinshelwood	Florence, SC.	52:45
25	Pam Berden	Dalton, GA.	52:51

Male 55-59 (817 finishers, 25 finishers)

1	Jack Todd	Spartanburg, SC.	41:37
2	Daniel Clapper	N Charleston, SC.	43:03
3	Stan Wheeler	Charleston, SC	43:20
4	Paul Myers	Charlotte, NC	43:24
5	Will Jones	Atlanta, GA	43:33
6	Samuel Jenkins	N Charleston, SC.	43:43
7	Raymond Willard	Summerville, SC.	43:52
8	Barry Schneiderman	Mt Pleasant, SC	44:06
9	Reagan Rice	Gainesville, FL	44:11
10	Michael Drose	Mt Pleasant, SC	44:16
11	King Grant-Davis	Charleston, SC	45:09
12	Milton Kelly	Wilmington, NC	45:13
13	Glenn Johnson	Exeter, NH	45:43
17	Gary Ricker	Charleston, SC	46:16
15	Bayne Selby	Sullivans Isl, SC.	46:18
16	Robert Underwood	Carolina Beach, NC	46:23
17	Emory Sanders	Woodstock, GA.	46:28
18	Rick Swenson	Gainesville, SC	46:35
19	Bob Mayer	Columbia, SC.	46:35
20	Stephen Judy	Mt Pleasant, SC	46:38
21	Joe Marshall	Greenwood, SC.	47:15
22	Tim Cunningham	Florence, SC.	47:21
23	Stephen Griffin	Charleston, SC	47:28
24	Thomas Young	Greenville, SC	47:33
25	Larry Milner	Aiken, SC	47:37

Female 55-59 (872 finishers, 25 awards)

1	Sharon Allen	Charlotte, NC	47:23
2	Catherine Lempesis	Irmo, SC	47:52
3	Toni Cruz	Concord, NC.	48:07
4	Debbie Howard	Mt Pleasant, SC	48:10
5	Jennifer Walton	Charleston, SC	49:45
6	Diane Chapman	Florence, SC.	50:01
7	Sallie Driggers	Hanahan, SC	50:09
8	Becky Sox-Morgan	Chapin, SC	50:14
9	Jude Millerplatko	Saint Augustine FL	51:13
10	Norma Lundy	Lexington, KY.	51:13
11	Michelle Withers	Charlotte, NC	51:23
12	Patty Toussaint	Clinton, SC.	51:47
13	Patricia King	Garden City, SC.	51:53
14	Kathy Maschka	Saint Helena Island SC	52:48
15	Fay Hoggard	Greensboro, NC	52:59
16	Christine Wilkins	Jonesville, NC.	53:03
17	Libby Wallace	Greenville, SC	53:18
18	Janice Wilkins	Greenville, SC	53:37
19	Lin Stewart	Concord, NC.	53:42
22	Kathy Rowe	Lewisburg, PA.	53:46
21	Patrice Katsanevakis	Mt Pleasant, SC	53:53
22	Sherri Jung	Charlotte, NC	54:20
23	Patricia Kotila	Johns Island, SC	54:39
24	Patti Enloe	Charleston, SC	54:44
25	Martha S White	Columbia, SC.	55:47

Male 60-64 (609 finishers, 25 awards)

1	Bob Schlau	Charleston, SC	41:24
2	Fred Reinhard	Sullivans Island, SC	42:15
3	Daniel Brown	Ruffin, NC	44:50
4	James Rich	Asheboro, NC	45:02
5	Thomas P Jones	Sumter, SC.	45:08
6	Linny Moore	Greer, SC	45:27
7	David Ott	Daniel Island SC	45:44
8	Jerry Sofley	Gastonia, NC.	46:05
9	Scott Willard	Weston, CT	46:28
10	Bill Dickerson	Gray TN.	46:40
11	Ed Vinson	Chapin, SC	47:06
12	Tom Korn	Homewood, IL	47:32
13	Bob Lee	Charleston, SC	47:39
14	Alan Brown	Mt Pleasant, SC	47:42
15	John Johnson	Greenville, SC	47:46
16	Eric Nicholls	Farragut, TN	47:58
17	Elbert Howard	Jamestown, SC.	48:02
18	Joseph Siever	Bradenton, FL.	48:32
19	William Anderson	Wadmalaw Isl, SC	48:45
20	David Anderson	Summerville, SC.	48:46
21	Mike Tucker	Statesville, NC	49:01
22	Tom Blankenship	Anoka, MN.	49:15
23	William Buchanan	Atlanta, GA	49:31
24	Fred Judkins	Goose Creek, SC	49:49
25	Gary Butts	Statesville, NC	49:49

Female 60-64 (490 finishers, 25 awards)

1	Myra Mayer	Charleston, SC	49:53
2	Jane Serues	N Myrtle Beach, SC	50:38
3	Anne Boone	Hollywood, SC	51:23
4	Nancy Curry	Mt Pleasant, SC	51:47
5	Kathy Seavers	Charlotte, NC	52:06
6	Lyn Hammond	Charleston, SC	53:33
7	Joan Mulvihill	Charleston, SC	54:16
8	Nancy Stinson	North Canton, OH	54:23
9	Emmy Mitchell	Goldsboro, NC.	54:32
10	Jean Sims	Charleston, SC	54:43
11	Claudia Cohen	Charleston, SC	55:14
12	Nancy Burleson	Spruce Pine, NC	56:52
13	Dorothy Anderson	Kiawah Island, SC.	57:51
14	Sheri Flower	Mooresville, NC	57:51
15	Dixie Dunbar	Sullivans Island, SC	58:13
16	Alice Faron	Champaign, IL	58:33
17	Lorena Murphy	Greenville, SC	58:35
18	Lucy Hinson	Greenville, SC	58:59
19	Jeannie Hillock	Kiawah Island, SC.	59:29
20	Vickie Sessions	Charleston, SC	59:32
21	Judith Anderson	Summerville, SC.	59:43
22	Mimi Hammock	Winston-Salem, NC.	59:48
23	Randall Prue	Inverary, Ont , CA	1:00:05
24	Connie Vogt	Knoxville, TN.	1:00:24
25	Kari Sprecher	Leesburg, VA.	1:00:39

Male 65-69 (255 finishers, 13 awards)

1	Harry Ong	Mt Pleasant, SC	46:55
2	Sonny Barber	Falls Church ,VA	48:00
3	Stephen Comer	Charleston, SC	48:18
4	James Adams	North Augusta, SC	48:56
5	Larry Crosby	Anderson, SC	49:41
6	Eric Elbel	Marietta, GA	50:51
7	Charles Sanders	Monroe, GA	51:26
8	Jim Morissey	Wilmington, NC	51:57
9	Thomas Dority	Charleston, SC	52:16
10	Joe Taylor	Greenville, SC	52:26
11	L.A. Gardner	Hilda, SC.	52:27
12	Robert Tamasy	Seabrook Isl, SC	52:53
13	George Geils	Charleston, SC	53:06

Female 65-69 (191 finishers, 10 awards)

1	Jerry Howland	North Augusta, SC	50:15
2	Pat Keller	Taylors, SC	51:32
3	Joyce Ploeger	Virginia Beach, VA	55:45
4	Barbara Lindeman	Oregon, OH	58:54
5	Joyce Rasberry	Isle of Palms, SC	59:47
6	Sooja Sung	Mt Pleasant, SC	1:00:02
7	Cecilia Keane	Stuart, FL.	1:02:43
8	Connie Comer	Charleston, SC	1:03:33
9	Sally Kaiser	Myrtle Beach, SC	1:03:45
10	Karen T. Yossef	Mt Pleasant, SC	1:06:20

Male 70-74 (103 finishers, 6 awards)

1	George Hilton	Dewees Island, SC	53:11
2	Clyde Mizzell	Charleston, SC	55:14
3	Ronald Madden	Southport, NC.	57:33
4	William Thomas	Charlotte, NC	58:23
5	George Evinski	Northfield, NJ.	58:26
6	Wendell Holland	Asheboro, NC	59:46

Female 70-74 (62 finishers, 3 awards)

1	Diana Phillips	Mt Pleasant, SC	57:09
2	Faye Davis	Mt Pleasant ,SC	1:07:11
3	Judy Kirchoffer	Waukesha, WI.	1:07:29

Male 75-79 (29 finishers, 3 awards)

1	William Boulter	Charleston, SC	57:32
2	Jim Lamarre	Hilton Head, SC.	1:00:28
3	Ken Walls	Mt Pleasant, SC	1:01:08

Female 75-79 (20 finishers, 3 awards)

1	Ethel Fortenberry	Sullivan's Island, SC.	1:31:19
2	Marilyn Lecomte	Murrells Inlet, SC	1:38:18
3	Elizabeth Rebl	Summerville, SC.	1:39:26

Male 80 & Over (12 finishers, 3 awards)

1	James Tysinger	Lexington, NC.	1:21:39
2	David Allard	Evans, GA.	1:22:18
3	Lou Nenninger	Waretown, NJ	1:24:15

Female 80 & Over (3 finishers, 3 awards)

1	Dorothy Flott	Mt Pleasant,SC	2:05:59
2	Claire Willet	Charleston, SC	2:07:28
3	Alene Parker	Camden, SC.	2:18:19

Compiled by Cedric Jaggers from complete results provided by Burns Computer Services on April 4, 2009

Eventual winner Simon Ndirangu has temporary leader Tilahun Regassa glancing back at him as they crest the Ravenel Bridge.
Post and Courier photo by Wade Spees

Chapter 33

2010

Near Perfect Conditions And Timing Chips In The Race Bibs Please Second Largest Crowd Ever

The 33rd Cooper River Bridge Run, March 27, 2010, arrived with a cool, overcast, 53-degree morning for the 8 a.m. start. Runners were aided by a 14 mile per hour tailwind as they went over the bridge, setting up a lot of fast times. The second largest number of runners in race history registered (38,413) and finished (33,057), as 19,356 women and 13,701 men completed the race, according to online results.

For the first time, the Bridge Run used the relatively new chip timing built into the race bib and announced that it was the first major race to do so.

It was a good year for first time bridge runners as Simon Ndirangu of Kenya used a strong finishing kick to win in 27:49, just 9 seconds off the course record and 2 seconds ahead of Ridouane Harroufi of Morocco in 27:51, and 3 seconds ahead of defending champion Tilahun Regassa of Ethiopia in 27:52. This was the first time that any runners had been under 28 minutes since the 2000 race. The top eight finishers were all under 29 minutes. Regassa took the early lead with a 4:08 first mile and only he and Ndirangu were together at the 3-mile mark, passing in 14:13.

"It was a very good field, some very good runners, and it was a great day to race," Ndirangu told the *Post and Courier*. "Almost perfect conditions; excellent for fast times. We had a slight wind at our backs most of the race, and it was very cool. I knew it was going to take a good time to win."

About Regassa he said, "I knew he was trying to break away from the pack and that's good tactics. I thought if I stayed close enough to him he would eventually fall back to the pack. He tried several times to break away from me. Coming down the bridge he got tired. I knew he couldn't keep up that pace for the whole race."

In fact, the pack caught up with the two leaders at the bottom of the bridge, but the two pulled away again, along with Harroufi of Morocco, before Ndirangu won the three-man sprint to the finish.

It was also the first Bridge Run for women's overall winner Meskerem Assefa of Ethiopia, who won in 32:31. The top three finished within 6 seconds of each other as Teyba Nasser of Ethiopia was second for the second year in a row, in 32:34, with Jane Kibii of Kenya third in 32:37. "It was a good race, it was close, but there was no problem," Assefa told the newspaper. "It was cool up there (on the bridge) but it was OK. The wind was good. It helped me."

Nikolay Kerimov of Russia had also never been to Charleston. Master's winner in 30:55, he said he enjoyed the city's history. Eric Ashton of Columbia, S.C., was second in 31:06 with Sean Wade of Houston, Texas, third in 31:20.

Female Masters winner was Anzhelika Averkova of Ukraine in 33:38. Second place went to Kathleen Jobes of Bethlehem, Pa., in 35:26. Trina Painter of Flagstaff, Ariz., took third place in 35:27.

Grand Masters winner was Joe Flores of Bethlehem, Pa., in 34:23. Hometown favorite Tom Mather of Charleston was second in 34:46. Paul Glannobile from Minnetonka, Minn., took third in 35:04.

Susi Smith of Greenville, S.C., ran 39:55 to win the female Grand Masters division. Second and third places also went to South Carolinians: Ruth Marie Milliman from Folly Beach in 41:06; and Dian Ford from Piedmont in 41:10.

The Bridge Run added a new prize money division for the first three male and female U.S. finishers. Simon Sawe of Albuquerque, N.M., was male winner in 30:23, followed by Wallace Campbell of Central, S.C., in 30:25, and Eric Ashton from Columbia, S.C., in 31:06. The female winner was Allison Grace of Blowing Rock, N.C., in 33:56. She was followed by Kathleen Jobes of Bethlehem, Pa., in 35:26, and Trina Painter of Flagstaff, Ariz., in 35:27.

The award for the first finisher from the Tri-county is named for race founder Dr. Marcus Newberry. Neville Miller lives in Charleston and is well known in the area since he is a local TV weatherman. He also runs well as he proved again by taking this award in 31:29, placing 24th overall. He said he learned from running the race the previous year that pushing too hard early can cause problems and paced himself this year. Rives Poe of Charleston ran a personal best time of 37:04 and also placed as the 18th female finisher. She has run a personal best in the Bridge Run four times and has won the Newberry Award the last three times she ran the race. The Dewey Wise Award was won for the second year in a row by William Boulter, 80, of Charleston, who had a chip time 57:57 and an actual finish place gun time of 59:13.

For the sixth time, the race had a wheelchair division. This year the winner was Chad Johnson of Charleston in 25:56. There were no female entrants.

For the second year in a row, the race presented age group awards by chip time rather than by USATF recognized gun time. The race used new USATF Certified Course #SC10020BS. It is very similar to the course used the previous four years. The race began in Mount Pleasant near Moultrie Middle School. The first mile is virtually flat and then the course begins climbing and goes over the Ravenel Bridge. Runners left the bridge via the Meeting Street ramp and headed towards downtown to Woolfe Street (which a number of runners found rough as it was badly in need of repaving). A right turn took them to King Street where they turned left. The next turn was at Wentworth Street, shortly after which runners reached the 6-mile mark, then made another left to Meeting Street where the final left turn was made. The finish line was just south of George Street.

For the second year in a row, a 30-minute recorded program covering the Bridge Run was shown on the evening of the race and several other times on Comcast Channel 2 for those who had cable television coverage. Channel 5 broadcast six live breaking news segments of the race on race morning. One of the segments included a brief interview with the race winner.

A total of 14 runners, all men, broke the 30-minute barrier with five of them under the 29-minute barrier. In the 2010 race, using actual finish place by gun time, a total of 291 runners broke the 40-minute barrier, surprisingly only the 11th highest number in race history: 255 males and 36 females. An additional 29 runners ran under the 40-minute barrier when the results were re-arranged by chip time finish order. Using actual time and finish place order rather than computer reordered chip time, there were 2,303 runners across the finish line under 50 minutes, the fourth highest number for the race. Using the same time criteria, a total of 6,517 runners crossed the finish line in less than 60 minutes, which was also the fourth highest number ever.

Charleston's *Post and Courier* listed the top five finishers in each age division, once again erroneously included the excluded prize money winners as age division award recipients. The paper also published the names and times of the top 10,390 male and top 9,926 female finishers in the Sunday, March 28, edition. Complete race results, sorted by age group using re-arranged chip time finish order, were mailed to all finishers as an insert included in the June 5, 2010 Post and Courier.

The race entry fee remained at $30 for early race registration and $40 after March 22 (late entry). Julian Smith was again the race director.

The 2010 Hall of Fame was made up of three inductees: Ken Bible, runner, race volunteer and former Executive Committee member; James Tomsic, race volunteer; and Liz Sheridan, race volunteer and coordinator for the CRBR Kid's Run.

For the ninth year in a row there were runners from all 50 states, the District of Columbia and a large number of foreign countries.

Other Voices
Tell Me About Your Bridge Run 2010

By Cedric Jaggers. Originally appeared in the May-June South Carolina Runner's Gazette

Listed in the order each person was interviewed in Marion Square after the race. I've added the chip and gun times and places at the end of each interview. Conditions were nearly ideal with cool weather and a rare tailwind as runners went over the bridge. This year was a little different, but a lot the same. I asked each runner one question only and tried to write down exactly what they said. I tried to ask finish time if the person did not tell me. I was slow getting to the finish after my disappointing and painful run so I did not get to talk to as many people as I had hoped. I did not limit the interviewees to Charleston Running Club members as I had in the past.

Dan Clapper: I told the newsman all my stories when he filmed me for television and I don't have anything left for you. My 27th time and I haven't gone full circle: My first time over the Bridge was still my slowest. I've been faster than the first time every time. My gun time this year was still faster than the first time I ran it. My finish time? 44:27. Official results time: chip 44:08, gun actual time 44:27, chip finish place 903rd. gun actual finish place 761st.

Dian Ford: It was a great day to run. I ran 41:05. Official results time; chip 41:10, gun actual time 41:15, chip finish place 427th, gun actual finish place 384th, 3rd place Grand Masters award.

Sunday Ford Davis: It was my first time to run it, I've always had meets in the past that conflicted. I had a 38 something. A PR? No my PR is 37 something on the track. Official results time; chip 38:39, gun actual time 38:42, chip finish place 216th, gun actual finish place 202nd , 2nd place 20-24 award.

Judy Gilman: I'm injured. Want to see my injury? I just jogged and kept to my 11 and a half minute pace. It was good. I live in McClellanville. I woke up at 7:05 and didn't know if I'd make it here. I ran 1 hour 8 minutes. Official results time: chip 1:08:51, gun actual time 1:22:45, chip finish place 17,281st, gun actual finish place 19,012th.

Anne Wyman Cipolla: It was a fast day for everyone. Not a P.R. but the wind was helpful. I ran 38:18 or 19. I haven't been training so I'm very happy with what I did. Official results time: chip 38:24, gun actual time 38:24, chip finish place 200th, gun actual finish place 189th, top 5% 35-39 age group award.

George Dunleavy: It was great. It was a beautiful day, the wind was at our back and I ran 42:08. I wanted to break 45. Official results time: chip 42:13, gun actual time 42:17, chip finish place 557th, gun actual finish place 475th, top 5% 50-54 age group award.

Emily Johnson: It couldn't have been a better day. I ran 40:40, happy for that. I'm happy with it. Official results time: chip 40:43, gun actual time 40:43, chip finish place 392nd, gun actual finish place 339th, top 5% 30-34 age group award.

Rives Poe: I'm really happy. I haven't been able to run a 10k in 2 years and I P.R.ed today. I'm happy to be running again. I had a good run. 37:05. Official results time: chip 37:04, gun actual time 37:04, chip finish place 140th, gun actual finish place 133rd, Marcus Newberry first local female $500 award.

Note- Rives Poe took the notepad out of my hands for the second year in a row, and said she was going to make me tell about my bridge run so here's what she wrote down:

Cedric Jaggers: It was a survival run. I hurt my leg last Sunday, saw the doctor on Monday; he said rest, ice, and gave me Biofreeze and I haven't run this week. It hurt the entire way – like a railroad spike through the back of the knee every step. Like a fool, I ran the first 2 miles in 15:47 since I wanted an 8 minute pace for the race. The last miles hurt like the lower regions of Dante's Inferno. I ran 53:45. Official results time: chip 53:36, gun actual time 53:51, chip finish place 5,269, gun actual finish place 3,744th.

Anne Boone: I ran about 50:30. I'm happy with it. I'd hoped to break 50, but I guess if it didn't happen today it isn't going to happen. It was cold, a tailwind; it was wonderful, I was happy. I've been doing more triathlon training than running. I've been biking and swimming. Official results time: chip 50:22, gun actual time 50:30, chip finish place 3,388th, gun actual finish place 2,481st. 2nd place 60-64 age group award.

Monica Kimbler: I P.R.ed. for the Bridge. Every year since I've been running it, I think this is my fourth time, I've P.R.ed. It was great. This year the wind was at our back – 51:59 and I beat my husband and my best friend and that was my goal. Official results time: chip 52:14, gun actual time 54:46, chip finish place 4,389th, gun actual finish place 4,095th.

Denise Brown: I might have run 49:26 only because of the wind. It was good. I ran a Personal Record, much faster than I thought. I should have run faster, if I'd had my mind set to it. Official results time: chip 49:33, gun actual time 50:03, chip finish place 2,936th, gun actual finish place 2,326th.

Karl Walsh: Pretty pleased. About 32:24. I felt strong from the beginning and just went with it. Once I got downtown I maintained and I'm happy. Official results time: chip 32:24, gun actual time 32:24, chip finish place 36th, gun actual finish place 36th, top 5% 30-34 age group award.

Brian Johnson: I was happy with it. A P.R. I was second for the fourth time for the Marcus Newberry award. Overall, I'm happy with my race. 31:56. Official results time: chip 31:56, gun actual time 31:57, chip finish place 36th, gun actual finish place 36th, top 5% 30-34 age group award.

Tom Mather: It was great. I ran what I wanted to run: 34:40, 90 seconds faster than last year. Maybe I was second grand masters. It was a great run. Official results time: chip 34:46, gun actual time 34:46, chip finish place 71st, gun actual finish place 71st. Grand Masters 2nd place $500 award.

Dee Dasburg: I had an awesome run. I'm 49, I ran with my dream who is 28. Two weeks ago I married her. Ran this race four times before; this is my fifth time. First time to run the whole thing. Did it in I think about 1:11. Not bad for running for two weeks on a back injury. Unable to find name in results.

Lennie Moore: Well, considering last year, I went eight months without running a bit due to an injury so I'm happy with my run. Today I ran 39:20 something. Official results time: chip 39:25, gun actual time 39:27, chip finish place 264th, gun actual finish place 241st, top 5%. 50-54 age group award.

Dave Andrews: It was good for me. I shot for under an hour and I did that. It was fun. Official results time: chip 1:07:11, gun actual time 1:13:19, chip finish place 16,111th, gun actual finish place 13,899th.

Scott Bates: My legs were burning the whole time except when they were about to fall out from under me. Just moved back from Louisiana and haven't run the Bridge Run since the 80s. Official results time: chip 51:29, gun actual time 52:12, chip finish place 4,193rd, gun actual finish place 3,140th.

Danny Brown: It was good. A little chilly and then breezy. My 14th time. 47:50. Official results time: chip 47:57, gun actual time 48:08, chip finish place 2,156th, gun actual finish place 1,669th.

Marc Embler: Better than last year; 36:48. I've been running very poorly so I'll take that. I ran comfortably the first half, then tried to go after that. The wind was awesome. I'm trying to chase those young guys. Official results time: chip 36:49, gun actual time 36:50, chip finish place 133rd, gun actual finish place 128th. 3rd place 50-54 age group award.

Marie Milliman: It was great. I ran faster than I thought. I was going to run under 41, maybe 40:59. It was good. I felt good the whole time. Official results time: chip 41:05, gun actual time 41:06, chip finish place 418th, gun actual finish place 371st. 2nd place Grand Masters $500 award winner.

Bob Schlau: It was actually a very good Bridge Run. I felt good the entire way. I enjoyed it. Only problem is, I'm older. Ran 40:06 or something; I was trying to break 40. Like I told you, I was on pace until we got off the bridge, somewhere in the last mile I backed off and lost it. Other than that I felt good, felt strong the whole way. Official results time: chip 40:17, gun actual time 40:17, chip finish place 347th, gun actual finish place 309th, 1st place 60-64 age group award.

Tom Dority: I trained on the bridge about six weeks. Had a good run – same speed all the way. I ran about 52:14, 14th in age group, can't complain. It was a good race. Official results time: chip 52:16, gun actual time 52:23, chip finish place 4,406th, gun actual finish place 3,204th, top 5% 65-69 age group award.

Nina Parks-Taylor: Well I just missed the money but I made it here. Remember last year my flight was delayed and I missed the race. I felt strong and I ran well and I saw all my good old friends. I even ran with Dan Clapper part of the way. Ran right over 44 minutes. Official results time: chip 44:07, gun actual time 44:11, chip finish place 892nd, gun actual finish place 714th, 1st place 50-54 age group award.

Keith Ambrose: My 20th one. It was better than last year, but I wasn't close enough to the line to start the race. 51:32. Official results time: chip 51:42, gun actual time 52:13, 4,099th, chip finish place 4,099th, gun actual finish place 3,146th, top 5% 65-69 age group.

Robert Aydelotte: (Note: incorrectly listed as Aydelotte Robert in female age group 60-64 in searchable results). It was not a stellar performance. I got tired, it was windy. I could have tried harder. I didn't feel fast. I wasn't willing to suffer. I don't have any lingering strain. 51:03. Official results time: chip 51:06, gun actual time 51:10, chip finish place 3,754th, gun actual finish place 3,146th.

Kathy Owens: I was very happy, my real P.R. I just did a marathon two weeks ago and I've been making myself run faster. That is the key. 47:37, unable to find name in results.

Susi Smith: Great race. My race was great. The tailwind was helpful – nice breeze, is not as bad as cold, but my real time was under 40. 39:55, first 50 year old. Official results time: chip 39:55, gun actual time 39:55, chip finish place 320th, gun actual finish place 284th, 1st Grand Master $750 award.

Eric Ashton: The race weather today was a great day to run fast with the tailwind pushing it was so much easier. Early on I identified all the Masters Division runners. The Russian made an aggressive move and I let him go. I said to myself I'll wait till the bridge and get him then. I couldn't close on him up or down the bridge. I tried to stick with the pack. On King Street the Russian started faltering. I closed on him but couldn't get him, cut 20 second gap down to 10. I ran a little over 31. It's always exciting when you see 30 minutes and 50 something and you are coming up on the finish line. I'm proud to represent South Carolina. Official results time: chip 31:06, gun actual time 31:06, chip finish place 21st, gun actual finish place 21st, 2nd place $1,000 Masters award, 3rd place $1,000 U.S.A finisher award.

Kathryn Ashton: I kind of had an off day today. One of those days when you don't have it. I ran 39:40, I didn't have a great day. Official results time: chip 39:44, gun actual time 39:45, chip finish place 296th, gun actual finish place 264th, top 5% 25-29 age group award.

Ed Brinkley: I'm 69 now. I've had injuries for three years. I took 90 seconds off my Summerville Flowertown 10k time. I thought it was a smooth run. (illegible writing my fault) ... in the 3rd mile, 5th mile fast, got to 6th ran my fastest mile there and that was the reason I'll come back next year and win my age group. 45:24. Official results time: chip 45:15, gun actual time 45:22, chip finish place 1,189th, gun actual finish place 940th, 2nd place 65-69 age group award.

Chris Hicks: It was great. It surprised me, I felt strong the second half of the race – ran my fastest 10k in 22 years, about 34:35. Hadn't been under 35 since 1988. Official results time: chip 34:37, gun actual time 34:38, chip finish place 67th, gun actual finish place 64th, top 5% 40-44 age group award.

Thousands of colorful runners and walkers line up at the start. Post and Courier photo by Leroy Burnell

Billy Tisdale: Little bit faster than last year; about 39:24. Shooting to be under 39, didn't quite do it. My legs got kind of rubbery coming down the last street. Good day, kind of cool, good to make it out and still run. Official results time: chip 39:24, gun actual time 39:25, chip finish place 262nd, gun actual finish place 240th, top 5% 50-54 age group award.

Michelle LaFleur: I'm really happy about it, faster than I've been lately. 36:28. Ran strong, highly competitive, I think 11th overall female 4th American. Didn't win any money, but that's okay. No, it's not, but I'd rather run faster than slower. I hadn't been in the 36's in a while. I felt good. I think the weather helped. It's always windy but there's always somebody to hide behind. Official results time: chip 36:30, gun actual time 36:30, chip finish place 124th, gun actual finish place 117th, 2nd place 35-39 age group award.

Gene Kizer: Best Bridge Run I've had in the past 3 years. I'm 57 and felt pretty good at first, then I came off the bridge and thought I might have to walk but didn't. The race is like a sacred tradition for me and my kids. Official results time: chip 1:04:00, gun actual time 1:05:37, chip finish place 13,852nd, gun actual finish place 9,629th.

The Ravenel Bridge. Post and Courier photo by Leroy Burnell

Bridge Run tradition
By Gene Kizer

The Bridge Run is a sacred tradition for my two kids and me. I wanted new traditions after their mother and I divorced 14 years ago, and the Bridge Run became it. This is my 15th in a row, my 21st overall, and the 14th of the last 15 with my kids.

I started my youngest son, Travis, when he was two-years-old, registered as a runner and on my shoulders the whole way. He is now 17 and has run every one except for one when he had a school function. He's a junior at Dutch Fork High School in Columbia, SC.

My oldest son, Trey, has run 14 of the past 15. He missed just one, too. He is 21-years-old with two Assoc. Degrees under his belt and is on active duty with the South Carolina Air National Guard, in air traffic control, and will soon be in ROTC at the University of South Carolina. We got written up in Bridge Run Magazine five years ago for our 10th in a row.

My best time was 41:12. Back in my prime, one of my running friends, Dennis, and I had a HELLACIOUS rivalry. It was always a bitter fight. In a Bridge Run long past, we were each determined, not just to beat the other, but humiliate the other if at all possible.

The race started. I lost Dennis then spotted him on the old "old bridge," 100 feet ahead. We were on the down span almost to Charleston. My strategy was to pass Dennis hard and hopefully break him, so that's what I did. I spoke in as calm a way as I could as I went past him.

Pushed myself hard the rest of the way, knowing that if I kept pushing, I'd beat him. I passed the four mile mark, pushing, pushing, then five, then six, running through the pain, trying desperately to increase my speed which would guarantee victory.

Finally, I could see the finish chute when out of the corner of my right eye there was Dennis coming up on me. He was trying to catch me at the finish line. I kicked in the afterburners and took off like a bat out of hell as hard as I could to the finish and whipped Dennis by three or four seconds. What a great win. I have a good kick and had several great wins like that.

One year my oldest son, Trey, and I, beat a Kenyan. We were on the first span of the old "new bridge" going up when we spotted him, and that Kenyan became the goal. We ran hard and decided to pass him strong on the right, which we did, not looking back until we were sure we had a good lead. Poor fellow had passed out in the heat and EMTs were giving him an IV, but we sure as hell whipped that Kenyan that day!

2010 Awards

Prize money division

Male overall

1	Simon Ndirangu	Kenya	27:49	$10,000
2	Ridouane Harroufi	Morocco	27:51	$3,000
3	Tilahun Regassa	Ethiopia	27:52	$1,500
4	Robert Letting	Kenya	28:15	$1,000
5	Julius Kiptoo	Kenya	28:35	$800
6	Enock Mitei	Kenya	28:43	$600
7	Simon Cheprot	Kenya	28:45	$500
8	Tesfaye Bekele	Ethiopia	28:47	$400
9	Richard Kandie	Kenya	29:00	$300
10	Richard Bett	Kenya	29:05	$250

Female overall

1	Mesekerem Assefa	Ethiopia	32:31	$10,000
2	Teyba Nasser	Ethiopia	32:34	$3,000
3	Jane Kibii	Kenya	32:37	$1,500
4	Janet Cherobon	Kenya	32:37	$1,000
5	Anzhelika Averkova	Ukraine	33:38	$800
6	Allison Grace	Blowing Rock, NC	33:56	$600
7	Caroline Rotich	Kenya	35:07	$500
8	Liliya Yadxhak	Russia	35:22	$400
9	Kathleen Jobes	Bethlehem PA	35:26	$300
10	Trina Painter	Arizona, AZ	35:27	$250

Male Masters winners

1	Nikolay Kerimov	Russia	30:55	$1,500
2	Eric Ashton	Columbia, SC	31:06	$1,000
3	Sean Wade	Houston, TX	31:20	$750
4	Joseph Ekuom	Kenya	31:41	$500
5	Maxim Zobov	Russia	31:52	$250

Female Masters winners

1	Anzhelika Averkova	Ukraine	33:38	$1,500
2	Kathleen Jobes	Bethlehem, PA	35:26	$1,000
3	Trina Painter	Flagstaff, AZ	35:27	$750
4	Ramilia Burangulova	Russia	35:43	$500
5	Tatiana Mirovova	Russia	36:55	$250

Male Grand Masters

1	Joe Flores	Bethlehem, PA	34:23	$750
2	Tom Mather	Charleston, SC	34:46	$500
3	Paul Glannobile	Minnetonka, MN	35:04	$250

Female Grand Masters

1	Susi Smith	Greenville, SC	39:55	$750
2	Ruth Marie Milliman	Folly Beach, SC	41:06	$500
3	Dian Ford	Piedmont, SC	41:10	$250

Top U.S.A. Finisher Award

Male

1	Simon Sawe	Albuquerque, NM	30:23	$3,000
2	Wallace Campbell	Central, SC	30:25	$2,000
3	Eric Ashton	Columbia, SC	31:06	$1,000

Female

1	Allison Grace	Blowing Rock, NC	33:56	$3,000
2	Kathleen Jobes	Bethlehem, PA	35:26	$2,000
3	Trina Painter	Flagstaff, AZ	35:27	$1,000

Marcus Newberry Award

Top area finisher Female

Male

Neville Miller ... Charleston, SC ... 31:29 ... $500

Female

Rives Poe ... Charleston, SC ... 37:04 ... $500

Dewey Wise Award

Oldest runner with time Under his or her age in minutes

William Boulter, 80 ... Charleston, SC ... 57:57

Wheelchair Division

Male overall winner (No female participants)

1 Chad Johnson ... Charleston, SC ... 25:56

Male Masters winner (No female participants)

1 Grant Berthiaume ... Tucson, AZ ... 26:51

Age group awards

Awards presented to top 3 in each division; Top 5% awards presented in each division up to a maximum of 25 per division

Note: In 2010, for the second year in a row, age group awards were presented by re-arranged chip time finish order rather than the USATF recognized gun time actual order in which runners crossed the finish line.

Male 5-9 (70 finishers, 4 awards)

1	Noah Luke Spencer	Mt Pleasant, SC	40:39
2	Patrick Spychalski	Mt Pleasant, SC	43:24
3	John Holliday	Columbia, SC	54:40
4	Cooper Gore	Mt Pleasant, SC	57:29

Female 5-9 (65 finishers, 4 awards)

1	Marianna Lonon	Columbia, SC	1:00:33
2	Aisha Elise Mann	N Charleston, SC	1:02:56
3	Danielle Winston	Mt Pleasant, SC	1:04:16
4	Kate Stribling	Mt Pleasant, SC	1:04:24

Male 10-14 (437 finishers, 22 awards)

1	Martin Murrow	Moore, SC	36:36
2	Brent Demarest	Charleston, SC	37:51
3	Brandon Rhodes	Anderson, SC	38:43
4	Bolton Sanford	Sullivans Isl, SC	38:50
5	Jacob Spencer	Mt Pleasant, SC	39:50
6	Logan Spencer	Mt Pleasant, SC	40:15
7	Liam Emery	Mt Pleasant, SC	40:22
8	Dalton Cox	Sanford, SC	40:35
9	Andrew Gawryluk	Mt Pleasant, SC	40:56
10	Logan Murray	Aiken, SC	42:12
11	Cooper Donoho	Mt Pleasant, SC	42:14
12	Matthew Brafford	Charleston, WV	42:44
13	Logan George	Greenville, SC	43:32
14	Sam Wingate	Mt Pleasant, SC	44:22
15	Brian Davis	Huntersville, NC	44:30
16	Billy Walker	Mt Pleasant, SC	44:35
17	Caleb Wishon	Charlotte, NC	44:55
18	Austin Nobles	Cross Hill, SC	45:25
19	Logan Ward	Mt Pleasant, SC	45:46
20	Cole Purvis	Mt Pleasant, SC	45:55
21	Geoffrey Oyler	Apex, NC	45:57
22	Andrew Wetzel	Simpsonville, SC	46:00

Female 10-14 (431 finishers, 22 awards)

1	Melissa Fairey	Mt Pleasant, SC	40:58
2	Brooke Grice	Columbia, SC	43:36
3	Logan Morris	Inman, SC	43:56
4	Sydney Ellen	Columbia, SC	44:27
5	Morgan Lee	Daniel Island, SC	47:23
6	Anna Stockman	Mt Pleasant, SC	48:37
7	Renee Bourgeois	Summerville, SC	48:45
8	Sarah Carlton	John's Island, SC	48:53
9	Sara Stansell	Charleston, SC	49:49
10	Maggie O'Hara	Raleigh, NC	50:13
11	Danielle Dixon	Greensboro, NC	51:34
12	Bland Ashby	Mt Pleasant, SC	52:03
13	Ida Williams	Durham, NC	52:09
14	Katie Alexander	Blowing Rock, NC	52:26
15	Madison Harman	Blowing Rock, NC	52:59
16	Kaitlyn Harman	Blowing Rock, NC	53:01
17	Riley Dobbins	Flat Rock, NC	53:17
18	Arden Hudson	Unionville Brief, NC	53:35
19	Kaitlin Sojourner	Johns Island, SC	53:36
20	Sarah Honbarger	Matthews, NC	53:42
21	Amelia Macloskie	Sumter, SC	53:58
22	Avery Haimbach	Moore, SC	54:13

Male 15-19 (566 finishers, 25 awards)

1	Greg Barnes	Cary, NC	31:41
2	Brady Lawrence	Greensboro, NC	33:11
3	William Rudisill	N Augusta, SC	33:43
4	Tom Ford	Piedmont, SC	34:18
5	Tim Hawkins	Clemson, SC	34:39
6	Matt Jordan	Matthews, NC	35:09
7	Ben Shippey	Rome, GA	36:01
8	Michael Marshburn	Mooresville, NC	36:03
9	Sean Griffin	Anderson, SC	36:07
10	Matthew Menard	Spartanburg, SC	36:15
11	Taylor Christiansen	Jamestown, NC	36:31
12	Hunter McGahee	Chapin, SC	36:53
13	Chris Elliott	Clemson, SC	37:32
14	Benjamin Stoner	Clemson, SC	37:57
15	John Fredrickson	Anderson, SC	38:05
16	Cameron Cook	Waxhaw, NC	38:27
17	Mason Williams	Nashville, NC	38:42
18	Alex Haulbrook	Lexington, SC	39:03
19	Brian Provost	Gilbert, SC	39:07
20	Eric Bohac	N Charleston, SC	39:10
21	Robert Daniell	Greenville, SC	39:26
22	Jordan Phillips	Cornelius, NC	39:30
23	Alex D'Antoni	Mt Pleasant, SC	39:31
24	Matthew Holliday	Charleston, SC	39:35
25	Sam Littlejohn	Blowing Rock, NC	39:42

Female 15-19 (730 finishers, 25 awards)

1	Alexandra Cross	Bristol, TN	40:36
2	Ganna Bowen	Greensboro, NC	41:42
3	Caroline Duer	Greenville, SC	42:30
4	Anna Todd	Spartanburg, SC	42:50
5	Briana Jackowski	Greensboro, NC	42:55
6	Leland Rayner	Spartanburg, SC	43:11
7	Gracie Herlong	Sullivans Isl, SC	43:50
8	Mary Miles Fewell	Greenville, SC	44:26
9	Maglin Beth Keaveny	Charleston, SC	44:58
10	Kelley Strong	Union, SC	45:09
11	Donna Lynn Fewell	Greenville, SC	45:25
12	Emily Morris	Raleigh, NC	45:42
13	Victoria Cairco	Charleston, SC	45:50
14	Tara Morgan	Martinez, GA	45:57
15	Dani Inglesby	Greenville, SC	46:03
16	Erica Hauser	Mt Pleasant, SC	46:22
17	Hannah Parnell	Thomasville, NC	46:28
18	Mace Wilklow	Greenville, SC	46:36
19	Julia Martens	Glenmont, NY	46:47
20	Britta Widenhouse	Lake Wylie, SC	46:50
21	Kelsey Davis	Hampstead, NC	46:55
22	Anastasia Kolesnitchenko	Inman, SC	47:00
23	Hannah Burkholder	Boiling Springs, SC	47:00
24	Savannah Mozingo	Mt Pleasant, SC	47:07
25	Rachel Miller	Waxhaw, NC	47:29

Male 20-24 (1,130 finishers, 25 awards)

1	Worku Beyi	Ethiopia	29:32
2	Bado Merdessa	Ethiopia	30:03
3	Wallace Campbell	Central, SC	30:25
4	Timothy Jeffreys	Cayce, SC	32:54
5	Matthew Lottes	Athens, GA	33:44
6	Will Huff	Augusta, GA	34:01
7	Stephen Sykes	Spartanburg, SC	34:33
8	Keith Gruchacz	Greensboro, NC	34:35
9	Ryan Arrowsmith	Clemson, SC	34:45
10	Andrew Sayce	Greer, SC	34:57
11	Sean Kelley	Athens, OH	35:01
12	Vincent Arey	Concord, NC	35:15
13	Nicholas Baer	Easley, SC	35:41
14	Ross Kimball	Smithfield, NC	35:43
15	Rafael Corona	Hanahan, SC	35:44
16	Havird Usry	Augusta, GA	35:50
17	Thomas Willauer	Winston-Salem, NC	35:55
18	Jeffrey Ford	Clemson, SC	36:37
19	Steven Fulmer	Raleigh, NC	36:42
20	David Brinkley	Charlotte, NC	36:44
21	Kip Thompson	Atlanta, GA	36:55
22	Jordan Short	N Charleston, SC	36:56
23	Jonathan Warner	Athens, GA	37:06
24	Drew Lattier	Columbia, SC	37:10
25	Taylor Johnson	Charleston, SC	37:27

Female 20-24 (2,241 finishers, 25 awards)

1	Ashley Spencer	Rock Hill, SC	38:30
2	Sunday Davis	Piedmont, SC	38:39
3	Caitlin Ranson	Pickens, SC	38:42
4	Guinn Garrett	Charleston, SC	39:31
5	Rebecca Neuren	Alexandria, VA	40:00
6	Margaret Brinson	Charleston, SC	40:41
7	Ashley Graybill	Wilmington, NC	41:26
8	Heather Cooper	Washington, DC	42:01
9	Ali Cupito	Greensboro, NC	42:02
10	Elizabeth Appleby	Simpsonville, SC	42:20
11	Lauren Clark	Durham, NC	42:29
12	Erin O'Brien	Charleston, SC	42:46
13	Anna Dukes	Tampa, FL	42:56
14	Marisol Slater	Columbia, SC	43:05
15	Casey McInerny	Charleston, SC	43:12
16	Brittany Crosby	Charleston, SC	43:17
17	Jeanne-Clai White	Boone, NC	43:25
18	Jenafer Forward	Augusta, GA	43:30
19	Carolyn Mullen	Southern Pines, NC	43:34
20	Kelsey Bristol	Charleston, SC	43:37
21	Mary Rutz	Cary, NC	43:53
22	Jani Linde	Columbia, SC	43:54
23	Caitlyn Lynch	Conway, SC	44:01
24	Brooke Carpenter	Charleston, SC	44:04
25	Kimberly Youngblood	Charleston, SC	44:10

Male 25-29 (2,071 finishers, 25 awards)

1	Shadrack Songok	Kenya	29:23
2	Jason Lokwatom	Kenya	29:26
3	Bernard Langat	Kenya	29:31
4	Zeru Gbremedhin	Ethiopia, ET	30:58
5	Neville Miller	Charleston, SC	31:29
6	Jon Stoehr	Greer, SC	32:15
7	Robert Brit Killian	Longmont, CO	32:17
8	Carlos Renjifo	Columbia, MD	32:19
9	Christopher Lamperski	Charlotte, NC	32:54
10	Jonathan Eggert	Charleston, SC	33:26
11	Hudson Belk	Charlotte, NC	33:55
12	C. Tyler Wichmann	Charlotte, NC	34:13
13	Jason Dimery	Lexington, SC	34:20
14	Billy Shue	Charlotte, NC	34:32
15	Jonathan Kinsey	Myrtle Beach, SC	34:58
16	John Leeds	Jacksonville, FL	35:13
17	Adam Jones	Goose Creek, SC	35:20

– Continued on next page

2010 Awards, continued from page 273

18	Elliott Taylor	Greenville, SC	35:27
19	Eric Guth	Travelers Rest, SC	35:30
20	Ian Blake	Charleston, SC	35:31
21	Todd Mayes	Cornelius, NC	35:35
22	Tyler Cross	James Island, SC	35:41
23	Ryan Plexico	Columbia, SC	35:43
24	Reynaldo Soto	Goose Creek, SC	35:55
25	Andrew Burness	Goose Creek, SC	36:07

Female 25-29 (3,534 finishers, 25 awards)

1	Bridget Campbell	Bluffton, SC	37:53
2	Maggie Grabow	Madison, WI	38:01
3	Anne Clinton	Charleston, SC	38:03
4	Alexa Hinton	Nashville, TN	38:55
5	Megan Schuerger	Charleston, WV	39:32
6	Jess Laurent	Centreville, VA	39:35
7	Mary Paulsen	Columbia, SC	39:39
8	Kathryn Ashton	Columbia, SC	39:44
9	Michele Milner	Charleston, SC	40:18
10	Margie Smith	Greenville, SC	40:31
11	Annie Schuerger	Charleston, SC	40:31
12	Leigh-Ann Beverley	Charleston, SC	40:51
13	Logan Gibson	Mooresville, NC	41:15
14	Savannah Fuentes	Bluffton, SC	41:36
15	Rebecca Dick	Pittsburgh, PA	42:04
16	Sara Walkington	Woodstock, IL	42:08
17	Lisa Ottens	Charlotte, NC	42:15
18	Blair Turnage	Mt Pleasant, SC	42:17
19	Ashley Anderson	Boiling Springs SC	42:52
20	Anna Louise Pigman	Asheville, NC	43:17
21	Karina Horeyseck	Winston Salem NC	43:19
22	Stephanie Lundeby	Ladson, SC	43:26
23	Bobbi Smith	Johns Island, SC	43:47
24	Katie Blaylock	Charleston, SC	43:54
25	Melissa McGehee	Cary, NC	44:04

Male 30-34 (1,970 finishers, 25 awards)

1	Sammy Nyamongo	Kenya	31:05
2	David Cheromei	Kenya	31:23
3	Tim Briles	Greenville, SC	31:45
4	Brian Johnson	Mt Pleasant, SC	31:56
5	Karl Walsh	Ireland	32:24
6	Daniel Hughes	Elgin, SC	32:30
7	Jay Upchurch	James Island, SC	32:37
8	Mike Burns	Greenville, SC	33:16
9	Jeremy Becraft	Columbia, SC	33:41
10	Stephen Cowie	Greensboro, NC	34:39
11	Jeffrey Gibbs	Greenville, SC	34:52
12	Chris Jones	Davidson, NC	34:53
13	Jeremy Gardner	Brooktondale, NY	34:58
14	Mike Moran	Denver, CO	35:08
15	Jason Putnam	Simpsonville, SC	35:20
16	Jeffrey Baxter	N Charleston, SC	35:26
17	Connor Larose	Durham, NC	35:47
18	William Isenhour	Charlotte, NC	36:02
19	Kurt Wilson	Candler, NC	36:31
20	Timothy Limbert	Mt Pleasant, SC	37:30
21	Bobby Wilder	Myrtle Beach, SC	37:40
22	David Jirousek	Beaufort, SC	37:40
23	Matthew Tooman	Mt Pleasant, SC	37:55
24	Markus Tischler	Greer, SC	38:14
25	Rhodes Roberts	Folly Beach, SC	38:32

Female 30-34 (2,924 finishers, 25 awards)

1	Denisa Costescu	Romania, RO	35:30
2	Rives Poe	Charleston, SC	37:04
3	Alice Rogers	Charlotte, NC	37:25
4	Jessica Kennedy	Leesburg, FL	38:09
5	Suzanne Hutchins	Gastonia, NC	39:28
6	Kelly Morrow	Columbia, SC	39:39
7	Amy McDonaugh	Irmo, SC	40:04
8	Marion Minaudo	Charleston, SC	40:34
9	Emily Johnson	Mt Pleasant, SC	40:43
10	Katherine Hertwig	Greenville, SC	41:58
11	Kristel Maes	Savannah, GA	42:04
12	Laura Brock	Charleston, SC	42:07
13	Stephanie Whitis	Columbia, SC	42:09
14	Elizabeth Karpiel	Huntington Beach, CA	42:32
15	Truitt Pressly	Charleston, SC	42:46
16	Diana Jacumin	Mt Pleasant, SC	42:58
17	Shana Ryberg	Tallahassee, FL	43:18
18	Sarah Hallenbeck	Chapel Hill, SC	43:19
19	Mary Mayeux	Charlotte, NC	43:57
20	Sarah Bacik	Durham, NC	44:15
21	Molly Diamond	Carrboro, NC	44:17
22	Jessica Copland	Greensboro, NC	44:25
23	Kristin Tripoli	Lakeland, FL	44:34
24	Sylvia Darby	Charleston, SC	44:44
25	Sandy O'Keefe	Summerville, SC	44:50

Male 35-39 (1,829 finishers, 25 awards)

1	Simon Sawe	Albuquerque, NM	30:23
2	Richard Allen	UK, UK	32:09
3	Kevin Mosteller	Greenville, SC	33:14
4	Jeffrey Zickus	Atlanta, SC	34:47
5	Jason Annan	Mt Pleasant, SC	35:25
6	Matt Pryor	Greer, SC	35:44
7	Brad Schneider	Bowling Green, KY	36:17
8	Mark Harrell	Raleigh, NC	36:45
9	Larry Lewis	Morehead City, NC	36:52
10	Rob Dee	Charleston, SC	37:07
11	Brian Lee	Baton Rouge, LA	37:10
12	Steven Johnson	Columbia, SC	37:25
13	Thomas Walls	Ft Mill, SC	37:36
14	Ronald Matthews	North Augusta, SC	37:45
15	Brent Shealy	Lexington, SC	38:07
16	Daniel White	Boiling Springs, SC	38:15
17	Nicholas Mayernick	Fletcher, NC	38:17
18	Bobby Fancher	Mt Pleasant, SC	38:20
19	Mike Mott	Deland, FL	38:37
20	Michael Varlas	Mt Pleasant, SC	38:48
21	Michael Graham	Myrtle Beach, SC	39:02
22	Daniel Ott	Wrightsville Bh, NC	39:02
23	Mackay Salley	Spartanburg, SC	39:04
24	Bob Mathews	Columbia, SC	39:16
25	Sean Galbally	Mt Pleasant, SC	39:25

Female 35-39 (2,681 finishers, 25 awards)

1	Shannon Carter	Honea Path, SC	35:50
2	Michelle LaFleur	Savannah, GA	36:30
3	Carol Brunson	Spartanburg, SC	37:54
4	Anne Wyman Cipolla	Charleston, SC	38:24
5	Lara Shaw	Greenville, SC	40:02
6	Stephanie Gee	Valdosta, GA	40:31
7	Molly Cherry	Mt Pleasant, SC	40:54
8	Tracy McKee	Charleston, SC	42:23
9	Angela Pilkington	Harrisburg, NC	42:28
10	Beth Smith	Charlotte, NC	43:27
11	Kristen Carmouche	Chapel Hill, NC	44:10
12	Michelle Kopczynski	Waxhaw, NC	44:13
13	Cameron Wannamaker	Mt Pleasant, SC	44:19
14	Jennifer Badik	Orlando, FL	44:22
15	Ellen Smith	Charleston, SC	44:29
16	Betsy Wallace	Mt Pleasant, SC	44:48
17	Jennifer Pryor	Greer, SC	44:52
18	Susan Quinlivan	Mt Pleasant, SC	44:54
19	Jodi Henninger	Charlotte, NC	45:02
20	Deanna Cromer	Charleston, SC	45:05
21	Megan Pritchett	Johns Island, SC	45:13
22	Angie Mays	Bristol, TN	45:16
23	Jana Dobbins	Flat Rock, NC	45:27
24	Mandi Herring	Charleston, SC	45:29
25	Ellen Seagle	Hendersonville, NC	45:37

Male 40-44 (1,502 finishers, 25 awards)

1	Gideon Mutisya	Kenya	32:01
2	Sergey Kaledin	Russia	32:11
3	Dean Whitis	Columbia, SC	32:50
4	Gregg Cromer	Summerville, SC	34:25
5	Yevgeniy Sirotin	Ukraine	34:28
6	Chris Hicks	Florence, SC	34:37
7	Mark Jobes	Bethlehem, PA	34:54
8	Brian Fancher	Charleston, SC	34:55
9	Jon Williams	Miami, FL	35:11
10	Greg Brown	Greer, SC	36:29
11	Daniel McDowell	Oakhill, WV	37:23
12	Darby Marshall	Fort Payne, AL	37:27
13	Mason Ferratt	N Charleston, SC	37:29
14	Harry Efird	Troutman, NC	37:36
15	Brendan Silver	Mt Pleasant, SC	37:36
16	Karl Johnson	Spartanburg, SC	37:45
17	Emery Lloyd	Moncks Corner, SC	38:05
18	Cory Fleming	Beaufort, SC	38:07
19	Jim Daniel	Mt Pleasant, SC	38:15
20	Mike Hedgecock	Columbia, SC	38:20
21	Brian Berrigan	Mt Pleasant, SC	38:20
22	Michael Cipolla	Charleston, SC	38:24
23	Mike Anton DeSantis	Charleston, SC	39:26
24	Dewayne Bollen	Fayetteville, GA	39:30
25	Jody McAuley	Mt Pleasant, SC	39:31

Female 40-44 (2,015 finishers, 25 awards)

1	Kristine Clay	Albemarle, NC	36:55
2	Lisa Tolley	Seneca, SC	38:02
3	Sheldon Fowler	Mt Pleasant, SC	39:44
4	Amy Ryberg-Doyle	Greenville, SC	41:31
5	Camelia Marculescu	Charleston, SC	41:47
6	Terri-Marie Mahoney	Okatie, SC	42:48
7	Catherine Hollister	Mt Pleasant, SC	43:48
8	Andrea Haschker	Charleston, SC	43:48
9	Cyndy Dail	Mt Pleasant, SC	44:08
10	Sharryn Whitmore	Mt Pleasant, SC	44:15
11	Miko Reid	Moncks Crner SC	44:17
12	Julie Jacobs	Moore, SC	44:42
13	Kim Ward	Charlotte, NC	44:59
14	Angela Gerber	Asheville, NC	45:04
15	Bonnie Darrenkamp	Huntersville NC	45:07
16	Shannon Treasurer	Summerville, SC	45:10
17	Lillian Pittroff	Charlotte, NC	46:04
18	Mary Tapia	Roswell, GA	46:04
19	Betsy Jessup	Mt Pleasant, SC	46:16
20	Lana Torkildsen	Matthews, NC	46:18
21	Lois Newberry	Charleston, SC	46:33
22	Beth Wease	Kings Mtn, SC	46:37
23	Cynthia Bohr	Mt Pleasant, SC	46:43
24	Linda Krehnbrink	Denver, NC	46:52
25	Heidi Prado	Savannah, GA	47:16

Male 45-49 (1,164 finishers, 25 awards)

1	Chris Giordanelli	Simpsonville, SC	34:27
2	David Quick	Charleston, SC	35:57
3	John Anderson	Moore, SC	36:26
4	Huey Inman	Mt Pleasant, SC	37:22
5	Lance Leopold	Simpsonville, SC	37:22
6	Peter Browne	Mooresville, NC	37:51
7	Tim Rhodes	Charlotte, NC	38:30
8	Bratton Fennell	Mt Pleasant, SC	38:31
9	David Ariola	Fairview, NC	39:05
10	Paul Baczewski	Summerville, SC	39:36
11	Kenneth Clyburn	Beaufort, SC	40:24
12	Kevin Barry	Shelter Isl, NY	40:39
13	Carl Dunkin	Statesville, NC	41:09
14	James McDaid	Charlotte, NC	41:28
15	Norman Martin	Ladson, SC	41:28
16	Dawson Cherry	Mt Pleasant, SC	41:55
17	Harold Jennings	Pauline, SC	41:55
18	David Dorans	Charlotte, NC	41:59
19	Rick Rummler	Mt Pleasant, SC	42:10
20	Gervais Hollowell	Spartanburg, SC	42:10
21	Armando Aguilar	Woodruff, SC	42:10
22	Philip Iuliano	Matthews, NC	42:11
23	Bryan Young	Greenville, SC	42:13
24	Dale Waters	Leland, NC	42:40
25	John Dunning	High Point, NC	42:44

Female 45-49 (1,620 finishers, 25 awards)

1	Firaya Sultanova-Zhdanova	Russia	38:11
2	Michelle Baulieu	Summerville, SC	41:19
3	Sheila Wakeman	Cornelius, NC	41:43
4	Claire Zimmer	Charleston, SC	42:53
5	Mary Dore	Charlotte, NC	43:41
6	Ashley Reynolds	Greenville, SC	44:12
7	Vicki Lynn Graham	Spartanburg, SC	44:29
8	Patt Loggins	Charleston, SC	45:17
9	Cheryl Lynn Quinn	Greenville, SC	45:23
10	Pamela Daubert	Hendersonville, NC	45:37
11	Jane Few	Greenville, SC	45:49
12	Kerrie Sijon	Greer, SC	45:51
13	Suzanne Blackwell	Denver, NC	46:00
14	Amy Keaveney	N Charleston, SC	46:05
15	Lisa Powell	Columbia, SC	46:22
16	Catherine Klein	Binghamton, NY	46:30
17	Tina Stutt	North Augusta, SC	46:36
18	Danna Brown	Greenville, SC	46:37
19	Deborah Baumgarten	Decatur, GA	47:30
20	Jill Hillman	Davidson, NC	47:34
21	Katherine Owens	Summerville, SC	47:37
22	Catherine Lee	Daniel Island, SC	47:40
23	Kathy Bunting	Mt Pleasant, SC	47:44
24	Susan Searle	Fort Mill, SC	47:45
25	Lisa Hanson	Covington, GA	47:48

Male 50-54 (1,058 finishers, 25 awards)

1	Tom Mather	Charleston, SC	34:46
2	Paul Glannobile	Minnetonka, MN	35:02
3	Marc Embler	Folly Beach, SC	36:49
4	David Bourgeois	Summerville, SC	37:31
5	Peter Edge	Simpsonville, SC	37:46
6	Michael Seekings	Charleston, SC	37:47
7	Trani Matthews	Tulsa, OK	38:48
8	Philip Brannigan	Wellesley, MA	39:16
9	Billy Tisdale	Sumter, SC	39:24

10	Lennie Moore	Mt Pleasant, SC	39:25
11	Kirk Flatow	San Jose, CA	39:35
12	Andrew Tedesco	Mt Pleasant, SC	39:38
13	Jim Wilhelm	Louisville, OH	40:46
14	Mark Schwarztraub	Mt Pleasant, SC	40:54
15	Dennis Getsinger	Williamston, SC	40:56
16	Michael Patrick	Marion, VA	41:14
17	William Rowell	Peoria, AZ	41:31
18	Drew Walker	Greenwood, SC	41:37
19	Eric Smith	Greenwood, SC	41:48
20	Edwin Holler	Morganton, NC	41:50
21	Dan Bradley	Winston-Salem, NC	42:01
22	Henry Martin	Irmo, SC	42:07
23	George Sykes	Spartanburg, SC	42:11
24	George Dunleavy	Mt Pleasant, SC	42:13
25	Jim Sandknop	Summerfield, NC	42:39

Female 50-54 (1,300 finishers, 25 awards)

1	Nina Parks-Taylor	New York, NY	44:07
2	Becky Droginske	Wheeling, WV	44:21
3	Mary Dixon	Travelers Rest, SC	45:33
4	Pam Drafts	Beaufort, SC	45:40
5	Trudy Carol Gale	Salisbury, NC	45:41
6	Ann Elish	Mt Pleasant, SC	46:04
7	Clara Schommer	Charlotte, NC	46:10
8	Lee Patterson	Summerville, SC	46:38
9	Caroline Geiken	St Simons Isl, GA	46:41
10	Cherry Kent	Belton, SC	46:48
11	Adele Mecionis	West Columbia, SC	47:32
12	Betty Floyd	Marion, SC	47:42
13	Ann Hynes	Quantico, MD	47:56
14	Kathy Abernethy	Matthews, NC	48:09
15	Paula Fernandez	Cowpens, SC	48:31
16	Lori Pope	Charleston, SC	48:34
17	Tami Dennis	Isle of Palms, SC	48:38
18	Kathryn King	Kittanning, PA	49:09
19	Karen Wilson	Kare Beach, NC	49:12
20	Shirley Smith	Easley, SC	50:02
21	Dottie Pollock	Indiana, PA	50:20
22	Maureen Strange	Travelers Rest, SC	50:23
23	Tina McDaniel	Greenwood, SC	50:50
24	Kerry Melson	Pawleys Island, SC	51:37
25	Ginger Van Connett	Greenville, SC	51:47

Male 55-59 (838 finishers, 25 awards)

1	Louis Anderson	Charlotte, NC	39:45
2	Harold Fallis	Awendaw, SC	41:52
3	Richard Knight	Inman, SC	41:54
4	Rob Kriegshaber	Columbia, SC	41:59
5	Anthony Glaser	Summerville, SC	42:26
6	Leslie Hart	Jacksonville Bch, FL	42:27
7	Bill Edwards	Florence, SC	42:29
8	Jack Todd	Spartanburg, SC	42:48
9	Mitch Johnson	Vero Beach, FL	43:20
10	Daniel Clapper	N Charleston, SC	44:08
11	King Grant-Davis	Charleston, SC	44:12
12	Samuel Jenkins	Charleston, SC	44:12
13	Will Jones	Atlanta, GA	44:35
14	Milton Kelly	Wilmington, NC	44:43
15	Tony Byers	Isle of Palms, SC	44:44
16	Victor Rosado	Salisbury, NC	44:48
17	John Deschenes	Charlotte, NC	44:55
18	Reuben Harris	Spartanburg, SC	45:13
19	Frank Armstrong	Denver, NC	45:19
20	Robert Underwood	Carolina Beach, NC	45:19
21	Bayne Selby	Sullivans Island, SC	45:38
22	Stephan Bagwell	Liberty, SC	45:45
23	Denis Sweeney	Boston, MA	45:47
24	David Miller	Charleston, SC	45:48
25	Bill Maddux	Mt Pleasant, SC	45:51

Female 55-59 (517 finishers, 25 awards)

1	Catherine Lempesis	Irmo, SC	47:36
2	Karen Carnes	Greenville, SC	48:08
3	Debbie Howard	Mt Pleasant, SC	48:35
4	Sue Cunningham	Concord, NC	49:01
5	Sue Strout	Merritt Isl, FL	50:07
6	Brenda Nicholson	Rock Hill, SC	50:11
7	Helen Burns Mims	Edgefield, SC	50:25
8	Nancy Porteous	Atlanta, GA	50:35
9	Libby Wallace	Greenville, SC	51:46
10	Kay Harrison	Athens, GA	51:48
11	Sallie Driggers	Hanahan, SC	51:55
12	Nitsa Andrews	N Charleston, SC	52:24
13	Pat Joyner	Sumter, SC	52:46
14	Therese Killeen	Isle of Palms, SC	52:56
15	Cynthia Brown	Sullivans Isl, SC	53:09
16	Sally McNeill	Salisbury, NC	53:26
17	Kristy McCarter	Charlotte, NC	53:40
18	Sharon Allen	Charlotte, NC	53:44
19	Janice Wilkins	Greenville, SC	54:16
20	Trisha Griffin	Summerville, SC	54:33
21	Kathy Maschka	Saint Helena, SC	54:43
22	Martha White	Columbia, SC	55:14
23	Patricia Kotila	Johns Island, SC	55:20
24	Myrna Gorman	Charleston, SC	55:21
25	Barb Watters	Shorewood, MN	55:32

Male 60-64 (497 finishers, 25 awards)

1	Bob Schlau	Kiawah Island, SC	40:17
2	Steven Annan	Mt Pleasant, SC	44:02
3	Paul Gordon	Concord, NC	44:45
4	Raymond Willard	Summerville, SC	45:05
5	Jerry Sofley	Gastonia, NC	45:22
6	Gary Richardson	Greensboro, NC	46:59
7	Linny Moore	Greer, SC	47:06
8	Scott Willard	Weston, CT	47:17
9	John Johnson	Greenville, SC	47:31
10	Bob Lee	Daniel Island, SC	47:39
11	Alan Brown	Mt Pleasant, SC	47:59
12	David Robinson	Beverley,	48:24
13	Francis Burriss	Chapin, SC	48:26
14	Joseph Siever	Bradenton, FL	48:36
15	William Anderson	Wadmalaw Isl, SC	48:39
16	Michael Cassidy	Oakton, VA	48:42
17	Daniel Brown	Ruffin, NC	48:43
18	Steve Eberhardt	Charleston, SC	48:44
19	Mike Julian	Mooresville, NC	48:48
20	Frederick Hancock	Wading River, NY	48:51
21	Charles Whetstone	St Matthews, SC	49:00
22	Bill Allen	Charlotte, NC	49:32
23	Valentine Przezdecki	Gibsonia, PA	49:43
24	Alan Struble	Hanahan, SC	49:44
25	Ripon Eadie	Summerville, SC	49:48

Female 60-64 (517 finishers, 25 awards)

1	Linda Clarkson	Johns Island, SC	50:18
2	Anne Boone	Hollywood, SC	50:22
3	Nancy Curry	Mt Pleasant, SC	50:33
4	Lyn Hammond	Charleston, SC	53:11
5	Patricia King	Garden City, SC	55:07
6	Linda Pellerine	Surfside Beach, SC	55:08
7	Sheri Flower	Mooresville, NC	57:40
8	Vickie Sessions	Charleston, SC	57:47
9	Lucy Hinson	Simpsonville, SC	58:02
10	Dorothy Anderson	Kiawah Island, SC	58:32
11	Dixie Carol Dunbar	Sullivan's Isl SC	59:13
12	Jeannie Hillock	Kiawah Island, SC	59:28
13	Ronna Resnick	Asheville, NC	59:39
14	Kari Sprecher	Fairfax, VA	59:43
15	Iris Hill	Goose Creek, SC	1:00:14
16	Marcella Farino	Lancaster, SC	1:00:26
17	Pat O'Brien-Dorner	Yorktown, VA	1:01:07
18	Tatiana Pashkevich	Mt Pleasant, SC	1:01:17
19	Toni Muse	Greer, SC	1:01:33
20	Hiddy Morgan	Cullowhee, NC	1:03:03
21	Carla Devaughn	Colorado Sp, CO	1:03:10
22	Carol Cobb	Monticello, GA	1:03:13
23	Vivi Wood	Mt Pleasant, SC	1:03:31
24	Merry Hartrick	Monroe, NC	1:03:37
25	Pamela Gartin	Charleston, SC	1:03:43

Male 65-69 (293 finishers, 15 awards)

1	Fred Reinhard	Sullivans Island, SC	43:41
2	Ed Brinkley	Charleston, SC	45:15
3	Marshall Wakat	Charleston, SC	45:58
4	Michael Kush	Burke, VA	47:15
5	Steve Comer	Charleston, SC	48:04
6	Bill O'Brien	Islamorada, FL	48:39
7	Eitan Rosen	West Palm Beach, SC	48:42
8	Elbert Howard	Jamestown, SC	48:46
9	John Toole	Tampa, FL	50:24
10	Eric Elbel	Marietta, GA	50:36
11	Tom Shuey	Charlotte, NC	51:21
12	Kenneth Decko	Kiawah Island, SC	51:32
13	Keith Ambrose	Isle of Palms, SC	51:42
14	Thomas Dority	Charleston, SC	52:16
15	Joe Taylor	Greenville, SC	52:59

Female 65-69 (193 finishers, 10 awards)

1	Jean Sims	Charleston, SC	53:54
2	Joan Mulvihill	Charleston, SC	54:00
3	Joyce Ploeger	Virginia Beach, VA	57:16
4	Joyce Rasberry	Isle Of Palms, SC	1:00:33
5	Sooja Sung	Mt Pleasant, SC	1:05:02
6	Hazel Farish	N Charleston, SC	1:07:51
7	Nada Clarke	Hidden Valley, PA	1:08:54
8	Judy Blakely	Mt Pleasant, SC	1:09:05
9	Robin Johnson	Travelers Rest, SC	1:09:27
10	Nancy Rosenberg	Kathleen, GA	1:09:49

Male 70-74 (98 finishers, 5 awards)

1	Harry Ong	Mt Pleasant, SC	47:46
2	James Adams	North Augusta, SC	47:46
3	Jim Benson	Oil City, SC	49:41
4	George Hilton	Dewees Island, SC	53:12
5	Dick Westerlund	Rochester, MN	56:14

Female 70-74 (74 finishers, 4 awards)

1	Caroline Luttrull	Fort Collins, CO	58:10
2	Faye Davis	Mt Pleasant, SC	1:05:42
3	Margie McMillan	Summerville, SC	1:05:53
4	Elfriede Tolley-Beeson	Sumter, SC	1:17:07

Male 75-79 (35 finishers, 3 awards)

1	Jerry Lardinois	Port Orange, FL	57:32
2	Michael Cotsonas	Mt Pleasant, SC	58:08
3	Ken Walls	Charleston, SC	1:01:31

Female 75-79 (19 finishers, 3 awards)

1	Jeanine Wehrmayer	Metropolis, IL	1:18:59
2	Von Chaplin	Charleston, SC	1:19:06
3	Maureen Kennedy	Anderson, SC	1:36:07

Male 80 & over (19 finishers, 3 awards)

1	William Boulter	Charleston, SC	57:57
2	Joseph Rutkowski	Dundalk, MD	1:04:34
3	Lonnie Collins	Gilbert, SC	1:11:53

Female 80 & over (8 finishers, 3 awards)

1	Garthedon Embler	Isle Of Palms, SC	1:46:14
2	Shirley Bissett	Johns Island, SC	1:51:31
3	Dorothy Flott	Mt Pleasant, SC	2:00:01

Compiled by Cedric Jaggers from complete results provided by Burns Computer Services immediately after the race on March 27, 2010, with corrections made on April 3, 2010.

Appendix A
Cooper River Bridge Run 10K Winners List (Run in March or April)
Compiled by Cedric Jaggers

USATF Certified Courses listed: SC85012WN, SC86008WN, SC94030BS, SC96010BS, SC00003BS, SC03012BS, SC05039BS, SC10020BS Website: www.BridgeRun.Com

Note: Records are listed in bold type in each category

Year	Div.	Male	Time	Female	Time	#
2010	overall	Simon Ndirangu	27:49	Mesekerem Assefa	32:31	33057 finishers
	USA div	Simon Sawe	30:23	Allison Grace	33:56	38314 entrants
	masters	Nikolay Kerimov	30:55	Anzhelika Averkova	33:38	
	gr mst	Joe Flores	34:28	Susi Smith	39:55	
	local	Neville Miller	31:29	Rives Poe	37:04	
2009	overall	Tilahun Regassa	28:24	Amane Gobena	32:25	31430 finishers
	Masters	Elarbi Khattabi	31:40	F.Sultanova-Zhdanova	35:37	37617 entrants
	gr mst	Tom Mather	36:03	Tatyana Pozdnyakova	39:40	
	local	Brian Johnson	32:41	Sopagna Eap	36:04	
2008	overall	Robert Letting	28:47	Leah Malot	33:23	29247 finishers
	masters	Sean Wade	31:13	F.Sultanova-Zhdanova	35:43	36838 entrants
	gr mst	Jerry Clark	34:48	Tatyana Pozdnyakova	38:18	
	local	Kurt Russell	33:32	Rives Poe	37:16	
2007	overall	Richard Kiplagat	28:35	Rehima Kadir	32:05	28953 finishers
	masters	Sean Wade	31:12	**Sylvia Mosqueda**	**33:30**	37161 entrants
	gr mst	Jerry Clark	34:04	Tatyana Pozdnyakova	36:48	
	local	Neil McDonagh	32:06	Rives Poe	37:33	
2006	overall	Abraham Chebii	28:16	Sally Barsosio	33:35	**33678** finishers
	masters	Albert Okemwa	31:20	Tatyana Pozdnyakova	35:16	**45497** entrants
	gr mst	**Gary Romesser**	**32:30**	T. Pozdnyakova	35:16	
	local	Neil McDonagh	31:38	Anne Wyman Cipolla	39:02	
2005	overall	Linus Mayo	29:30	Olga Romonova	34:04	18480 finishers
	masters	Paul Aufdemberg	31:32	Tatyana Pozdnyakova	35:34	24663 entrants
	gr mst	Gary Romesser	36:02	Tatyana Pozdnyakova	35:34	
	local	Tom Mather	32:53	Carre Joyce	37:22	
2004	overall	Luke Kipkosgei	28:13	Sallie Barsosio	32:28	15184 finishers
	masters	Dennis Simonaitis	31:44	Tatyana Pozdnyakova	34:55	17311 entrants
	gr mst	Gary Romesser	33:45	Terry Mahr	40:24	
	local	Irv Batten	32:37	Sarah Reed	39:29	
2003	overall	Tom Nyariki	28:57	Edna Kiplagat	33:41	14628 finishers
	masters	Andrew Masai	30:49	Lyubov Kremleva	33:58	17071 entrants
	gr mst	Gary Romesser	33:36	Terry Mahr	40:42	
	local	Nicholas Iauco	32:24	Lizl Kotz	41:22	
2002	overall	John Itati	28:06	Catherine Ndereba	31:53	14338 finishers
	masters	Eddy Hellebuyck	29:23	Lyubov Kremleva	34:04	16802 entrants
	gr mst	Gary Romesser	33:20	Debra Wagner	37:14	
	local	Sean Dollman	31:45	Laurie Sturgell	36:41	
2001	overall	James Koskei	28:45	Catherine Ndereba	32:33	13993 finishers
	masters	**Simon Karori**	**29:21**	Viazova Elena	34:48	16432 entrants
	gr mst	Gary Romesser	33:18	Terry Mahr	39:10	
	local	Irving Batten	33:13	Amy Clements	36:10	
2000	overall	**James Koskei**	**27:40**	Catherine Ndereba	31:41	14144 finishers
	masters	Simon Karori	29:13	Marie Boyd	35:25	16893 entrants
	gr mst	Bob Schlau	34:25	Terry Mahr	38:49	
	local	Mike Aiken	31:57	Kerry Robinson	38:00	
1999	overall	Laz. Nyakeraka	28:40	Eunice Sagero	33:18	12536 finishers
	masters	John Tuttle	30:27	Tatyana Pozdnyakova	33:49	15349 entrants
	gr mst	Bob Schlau	34:48	Terry Mahr	39:24	
	local	**Eric Ashton**	**30:32**	Sue Tandy	38:44	
1998	overall	Tom Nyariki	29:58	Elana Meyer	32:46	12919 finishers
	masters	Keith Anderson	31:04	Tatyana Pozdnyakova	35:09	18007 entrants
	gr mst	Bob Schlau	37:37	Betty Ryberg	42:44	
	local	Tom Mather	32:53	Clarice Marana	36:44	
1997	Overall	Paul Koech	27:57	**Elana Meyer**	**31:19**	12583 finishers
	Masters	Antoni Niemczak	31:11	Maureen de St Croix	37:31	15216 entrants
	local	Tom Mather	31:42	Clarice Marana	36:33	
1996	Overall	Joseph Kamau	28:32	Liz McColgan	31:41	11444 finishers
	Masters	Antoni Niemczak	30:14	Maureen de St Croix	35:13	14030 entrants
	Local	Mark Friedrich	31:59	Clarice Marana	37:18	
1995	Overall	Joseph Kimani	27:49	Laura Lamen-Coll	33:58	10290 finishers
	Masters	Wilson Waigwa	30:33	Irina Bondarchouck	35:13	12406 entrants
	Local	Tom Mather	31:14	Lynn MacDougall	37:59	
1994	Overall	Simon Kirori	28:35	Elaine Van Blunk	34:01	7355 finishers
	Masters	Nick Rose	30:04	R. Stockdale-Wooley	36:32	8670 entrants
	Local	Tom Mather	30:54	**Kathy Kanes**	**34:43**	
1993	Overall	Paul Bitok	28:31	Sabrina Dornhoeffer	33:53	6192 finishers
	Masters	Nick Rose	30:21	Carol McLatchie	35:50	7544 entrants
	Local	Tom Mather	31:42	Suzanne Lynch	39:56	
1992	Overall	Dominic Kirui	28:24	Jill Hunter	32:34	6403 finishers
	Masters	Nick Rose	29:52	Nancy Grayson	35:50	7602 entrants
	Local	Tom Mather	32:11	Patti Previte Clark	38:58	
1991	Overall	Jeff Cannada	29:38	Kim Bird	34:49	5503 finishers
	Masters	John Campbell	30:33	Nancy Grayson	35:39	6527 entrants
	Local	Mark Friedrich	32:18	Micky Kawohl (Reger)	35:48	
1990	Overall	Sam Obwacha	29:20	Shelly Steely	32:57	5866 finishers
	Masters	Earl Owens	31:26	Judy Greer	37:45	7820 entrants
	Local	Michael Brown	32:04	Alison Roxburgh	36:33	
1989	Overall	Ashley Johnson	29:48	Grete Waitz	33:29	5885 finishers
	Masters	Bob Schlau	32:20	Judy Greer	37:38	7510 entrants
	Local	Tom Mather	32:02	Megan Othersen	36:06	
1988	Overall	Ashley Johnson	29:56	Carla Borovicka	34:38	5465 finishers
	Masters	Mike Hurd	31:32	Gail Bailey	39:12	6904 entrants
	Local	Bob Schlau	32:19	Benita Schlau	38:11	
1987	Overall	Paul Cummings	30:19	Mary Ellen McGowan	34:31	6976* including
	Masters	Richard Weeks	34:43	Gail Bailey	38:42	unregistered
	Local	Tom Mather	32:04	Megan Othersen	37:19	6997 entrants
1986	Overall	Hans Koeleman	29:29	Leslie Welch	33:37	5318 finishers
	Masters	Tom Dooley	33:19	Gail Bailey	39:12	6684 entrants
	Local	Bob Schlau	31:26	Benita Brooks (Schlau)	38:36	

Note: Dr. Marcus Newberry award for first Local area finisher originated 1986

Year	Div.	Male	Time	Female	Time	#
1985	Overall	Mike O'Reilly	29:28	Christina Boxer	34:08	4482 finishers
	Masters	Don Coffman	32:27	Peggy Ledford	44:51	5440 entrants
1984	Overall	David Branch	29:25	Brenda Webb	34:09	3784 finishers
	Masters	Bill Voight	35:48	Cindy Dalrymple	36:57	4459 entrants
1983	Overall	David Branch	29:28	Mary Copeland	38:09	2585 entrants
	Masters	Ed Ledford	36:43	Peggy Ledford	41:44	3115 entrants
1982	Overall	Mark Donahue	30:28	Sallie Driggers	37:21	1734 finishers
	Masters	Ed Ledford	36:06	Peggy Ledford	44:49	2100 entrants
1981	Overall	Marc Embler	30:54	Kiki Sweigart	35:10	1338 finishers
	Masters	Ed Ledford	36:36	Suzanne Foster	44:49	1650 entrants
1980	Overall	Kim Burke (Tie)	31:26	Michelle Moore	41:29	1330 finishers
		Steve Littleton	31:26			1500 entrants
	Masters	Ed Ledford	37:08	Pat Rhode	49:53	
1979	Overall	Avery Goode	32:55	Marty Long	40:10	1015 finishers
	Masters	Jones	38:35	Glassman	52:04	1350 entrants
1978	Overall	Benji Durden	30:22	Lisa Lorrain	39:39	766 finishers
	Masters	Bill Wooley	36:44	A. Lipowski	46:12	1040 entrants

Appendix B
Cooper River Bridge Run Dewey Wise Award Winners:
Award began in 1980

Dewey Wise Trophy awarded to the oldest finisher who ran a time in minutes lower than his or her age:

Year	Name	Hometown	Age	Time
1980	Tom Baskett	Charleston, SC	66	47:18
1981	Carl Jenkins	N Charleston, SC	65	44:15
1982	Edward Lancaster	Lumber City, GA	70	53:05
1983	Rudy Nimmons	Seneca, SC	62	38:50
1984	Caldwell Nixon	Denver, NC	75	60:22
1985	Caldwell Nixon	LincoInton, NC	76	60:50
1986	Clayton Brelsford	Wilmington, NC	71	54:37
1987	Clayton Brelsford	Wilmington, NC	72	51:38
1988	Clayton Brelsford	Wilmington, NC	73	55:20
1989	James Sullivan	Mt Pleasant, SC	82	79:36
1990	James Sullivan	Mt Pleasant, SC	83	76:39*
1991	James Sullivan	Mt Pleasant, SC	85	76:09
1992	Cadwallader Jones	Charleston, SC	70	69:13
1993	Ed Shaffer	Walterboro, SC	74	54:23
1994	Bill Forwood	Greenville, SC	82	80:31
1995	Thomas King	Tucker, GA	75	45:54
1996	Arnold Hecht	Greensboro, NC	75	63:38
1997	Arnold Hecht	Greensboro, NC	76	67:37
1998	Ed Shaffer	Walterboro, SC	79	67:14
1999	Arnold Hecht	Greensboro, NC	78	75:42
2000	Ed Shaffer	Walterboro, SC	81	73:47
2001	Ed Shaffer	Walterboro, SC	82	77:50
2002	David Mellard	N Charleston, SC	79	63:23
2003	David Mellard	N Charleston, SC	80	64:06
2004	David Mellard	N Charleston, SC	81	65:18
2005	John Noble	Charleston, SC	75	69:52
2006	David Mellard	N Charleston, SC	83	80:50
2007	William Fulton	Greenville, SC	79	76:19
2008	James Lamarre	Charleston, SC	75	63:02
2009	William Boulter	Charleston, SC	79	57:38
2010	William Boulter	Charleston, SC	80	59:13

*1990 is last year this award was listed in the awards booklet, all years after that were reconstructed by Cedric Jaggers using complete race results to determine the runner's age and time.

Appendix C
Cooper River Bridge Run Hall of Fame

2002 inaugural inductees:
SALLIE DRIGGERS, runner and Local resident female Overall race winner (1982)

CEDRIC JAGGERS, runner, journalist and race historian

ED LEDFORD, runner, 4-time Masters Division winner

MARCUS NEWBERRY, race founder

BOB SCHLAU, runner, Overall race runner-up (1979), 2-time Marcus Newberry award winner for first Local area Tri-County finisher, 1 time Masters winner, 3-time Grand Masters winner

MARGARET WRIGHT, runner, oldest female finisher of the inaugural race and again at age 80 in 2002 when she set a state age group record

2003 Hall of Fame inductees:
KEITH HAMILTON, race director of the inaugural race

TERRY HAMLIN, runner, and measurer of the inaugural course

CHUCK MAGERA, runner and former finish line director

BRIAN SMITH, runner and former race director

GARY WILSON, race volunteer and lead bicyclist for the inaugural race

2004 Hall of Fame inductees:
BETTY BELL, race volunteer

GIL BRADHAM, race volunteer

MIKE CHODNICKI, runner and race volunteer

EMELYN COMMINS, race volunteer

2005 Hall of Fame inductees:
TOM MATHER, runner, 9-time winner of the race's Marcus Newberry award for first Local area Tri-County finisher

TOM O'ROURKE, race volunteer

THOMAS DEWEY WISE, former state senator who pushed through legislation allowing use of the bridge for the race.

2006 Hall of Fame inductees:
MARC EMBLER, the only local Overall winner of the race (1981)

HARRY HALLMAN, Mt. Pleasant mayor, helped support and sponsor the race

CADWALLADER "QUADDY" JONES, longtime endurance athlete and fitness advocate

LUCY JONES, longtime endurance athlete and fitness advocate

JOE RILEY, Charleston mayor, helped support and sponsor the race

JOHN SMYTH former Bridge Run Chairman, and also the former director of the U.S. Olympic Training Centers

CHERYLL WOODS-FLOWERS, Mt. Pleasant former mayor, helped support and sponsor the race

2007 Hall of Fame inductees:
ANNE (REED) BOONE, runner, 3rd place Overall female (1980)

RICHARD GODSEN, race volunteer handled the finish line for the inaugural race, later wrote a computer program to help handle the growing number of race finishers

JIMMY SEIGNIOUS, race volunteer, former Mt Pleasant Recreation Director, former member of the Bridge Run Executive Committee

2008 Hall of Fame inductees:
ROY HILLS, former Race Director, Bridge Run Committee Member

MARGARET KONECKY, composer of the Bridge Run theme music

LEE NEWTON, Bridge Run water station organizer and director

BRYCE MYERS and JENNY MYERS, Ham Radio Club members who have broadcast splits for every Bridge Run

2009 Hall of Fame inductees:
KARL GUELDNER, former Race Director, who was the first paid director

AL HAWKINS, race medical director for the past 18 years

2010 Hall of Fame inductee:
KEN BIBLE, runner, race volunteer, former Executive Committee member

JAMES TOMSIC, race volunteer

LIZ SHERIDAN, race volunteer, coordinator for the CRBR Kid's Run

Appendix D
Cooper River Bridge Run Facts and Figures   Compiled by Cedric Jaggers

Complete official results have been compiled and mailed to all pre-registered Cooper River Bridge Run finishers every year except for 1987 when available results were published in the Low Country Runner, newsletter of the Charleston Running Club. In 1995 complete results were mailed as part of an issue of Carolina Action Sports magazine. In 1996 complete results were mailed to all finishers in a special Bridge Run Results edition of the Low Country Runner. Complete results were compiled using the ChampionChip computer timing technology beginning 1997 and results have been mailed as a special insert section of the Post Courier newspaper since that year. The 2006 results included all walkers for the first time at which timed female participation passed male participation. This chart shows the estimated start time temperature in Mt Pleasant and the official Charleston temperature from the Southeast Regional Climate Center.

Year	Official Finishers	Number Entered	Temp est./off.	% Who Finished	No. of Males	% of Males	No. of Females	% of Females
2010	33,057	38,413	53 49	86.0%	13,701	41.5%	19,356	58.5%
2009	31,460	37,617	54 56	83.6%	13,578	43.2%	17,882	56.8%
2008	29,247	36,838	66 72	79.3%	12,828	43.9%	16,419	56.1%
2007	28,953	37,161	58 56	77.9%	12,960	45.3%	15,520	54.2%
2006	33,678	45,663	65 67	74.0%	15,461	46.0%	18,135	54.0%
2005	18,480	24,663	63 63	74.9%	10,187	55.1%	8,256	44.6%
2004	15,184	17,311	48 50	87.7%	8,299	54.5%	6,912	45.5%
2003	14,623	17,071	66 69	85.6%	8,039	54.9%	6,584	45.1%
2002	14,338	16,779	51 51	85.4%	8,079	56.3%	6,259	43.6%
2001	13,993	16,432	65 67	85.1%	7,932	56.7%	6,061	43.3%
2000	14,144	16,893	61 61	83.7%	8,201	58.0%	5,943	42.0%
1999	12,536	15,349	45 45	81.6%	7,524	60.0%	5,012	40.0%
1998	12,919	18,007	64 61	71.7%	7,916	61.3%	5,003	38.7%
1997	12,583	15,216	68 67	82.6%	7,839	62.3%	4,744	37.7%
1996	11,444	14,030	50 53	81.5%	7,362	64.3%	4,082	35.7%
1995	10,290	12,406	59 55	82.9%	6,841	66.5%	3,449	33.5%
1994	7,355	8,670	60 55	84.8%	5,063	68.8%	2,292	31.2%
1993	6,192	7,544	50 46	82.1%	4,405	71.1%	1,787	28.9%
1992	6,403	7,602	48 46	84.2%	4,675	73.1%	1,728	26.9%
1991	5,503	6,527	64 60	84.3%	4,172	75.8%	1,331	24.2%
1990	5,866	7,820	50 50	75.0%	4,432	75.5%	1,434	24.5%
1989	5,885	7,510	55 49	78.3%	4,433	75.3%	1,499	24.7%
1988	5,465	6,904	65 59	79.1%	4,105	75.1%	1,360	24.9%
1987	6,976*	6,997	39 39	Unknown	5,588	80.1%	1,388	19.9%
1986	5,318	6,684	72 62	79.5%	4,116	77.4%	1,202	22.6%
1985	4,482	5,440	70 67	82.3%	3,483	77.7%	999	22.3%
1984	3,784	4,459	50 50	84.8%	2,977	78.4%	807	21.3%
1983	2,585	3,115	50 44	82.9%	2,052	79.4%	533	20.6%
1982	1,734	2,100	45 44	82.5%	1,348	77.7%	386	22.3%
1981	1,338	1,650	60 59	81.8%	1,046	78.2%	292	21.8%
1980	1,330	1,500	59 56	88.6%	1,063	79.9%	267	20.1%
1979	1,015	1,350	60 67	75.1%	778	76.7%	237	23.3%
1978	766	1,040	82 76	73.6%	653	85.2%	113	14.8%

Appendix E
Cooper River Bridge Run Speed Chart
Under 60/50/40/30/29/28 minutes Compiled by Cedric Jaggers

How fast were the winners; and how many Bridge Runners broke certain speed barriers? Is the speed trending upward or downward? The addition of timed walkers beginning 2006, lowered the percentage of fast times, but not the actual number. The record in each category is shown by * . All numbers are from actual 'gun' times, not 'chip' times.

Year	Male win time	Female win time	Total no. finish	No. under 60 min/%	No. under 50 min/%	No. under 40 min	No. under 30 min	No. under 29/28 min
2010	27:49	32:31	33055	6517/20%	2303/07%	291	14	8/3
2009	28:21	32:24	31430	6480/21%	1984/06%	249	13	5/0
2008	28:47	33:23	29247	5410/18%	1564/05%	200	9	6/0
2007	28:35	32:05	28953	6122/21%	2063/07%	278	8	5/0
2006	28:16	33:35	33678*	6767/20%	1884/06%	262	7	3/0
2005	29:30	34:04	18480	5775/31%	1889/10%	199	5	0/0
2004	28:13	32:28	15184	5366/35%	1653/11%	214	8	7/0
2003	28:57	33:41	14628	4526/31%	1383/09%	155	4	2/0
2002	28:06	31:53	14338	6007/42%	1955/14%	286	14	7/0
2001	28:45	32:33	13993	5375/38%	1604/11%	229	11	3/0
2000	27:40*	31:41	14144	5856/41%	1860/13%	297	21*	12*/4*
1999	28:40	33:18	12536	5860/47%	2008/16%	280	10	2/0
1998	29:58	32:46	12919	5959/46%	2036/16%	211	1	0/0
1997	27:57	31:19 *	12583	7111*/56%	2398/19%	330	13	7/1
1996	28:32	31:41	11444	7002/61%	2329/20%	357	6	3/0
1995	27:49	33:58	10290	6736/65%	2692*/26%	379	12	5/1
1994	28:35	34:01	7355	5044/68%	2005/27%	327	4	3/0
1993	28:31	33:53	6192	4566/74%	1995/32%	307	4	3/0
1992	28:24	32:34	6403	4915/77%	2157/34%	332	8	3/0
1991	29:38	34:49	5503	4386/78%	1963/36%	283	4	0/0
1990	29:20	32:57	5866	4744/81%	2264/39%	360	7	0/0
1989	29:48	33:29	5885	4631/79%	2150/37%	393*	4	0/0
1988	29:56	34:38	5465	3451/65%	1768/32%	284	1	0/0
1987	30:19	34:31	6976	NA	2054/29%	322	0	0/0
1986	29:29	33:37	5318	3182/60%	1872/35%	268	5	0/0
1985	29:28	34:08	4482	3022/67%	1624/36%	299	6	0/0
1984	29:25	34:09	3784	2746/72%	1699/45%	339	4	0/0
1983	29:28	38:09	2585	2216/86%	1313/51%	234	2	0/0
1982	30:28	37:21	1734	1525/88%	1007/58%*	146	0	0/0
1981	30:54	35:10	1338	1211/90%*	763/57%	138	0	0/0
1980	31:26	41:29	1330	1185/89%	750/56%	115	0	0/0
1979	32:55	40:10	1015	821/81%	423/42%	47	0	0/0
1978	30:22	39:39	766	638/83%	425/55%	66	0	0/0